Teach Yourself
BORLAND
C++BUILDER 3
in 21 Days

Kent Reisdorph

PUBLISHING

A Division of Macmillan Computer Publishing
201 West 103rd Street
Indianapolis, Indiana 46290

This book is dedicated to my wife Jennifer. Without her love and support this book would not exist. Thanks, Jen, for everything.

Copyright © 1998 by Sams Publishing

International Standard Book Number: 0-672-31266-2

Library of Congress Catalog Card Number: 98-84151

01   00   99   98   4   3   2   1

Interpretation of the printing code: the rightmost double-digit number is the year of the book's printing; the rightmost single-digit, the number of the book's printing. For example, a printing code of 98-1 shows that the first printing of the book occurred in 1998.

Composed in AGaramond and MCPdigital by Macmillan Computer Publishing

Printed in the United States of America

Trademarks

Publisher   Joseph B. Wikert
Executive Editor   Steve Sayre
Managing Editor   Jodi Jensen

Acquisitions Editor
Renee Wilmeth

Development Editor
Sean Dixon

Project Editor
Susan Ross Moore

Copy Editors
Kate Talbot, Kate Givens,
Tonya Simpson

Technical Reviewers
Terri Bartos, Celeste Crocker,
Janet DeLu, Ellie Peters

Software Development Specialist
Dan Scherf

Indexer
Bruce Clingaman

Cover Designer
Ron Foster

Book Designer
Gary Adair

Copy Writer
David Reichwein

Production Team Supervisor
Brad Chinn

Production
Carol Bowers
Mona Brown
Ayanna Lacey
Gene Redding

Overview

Contents

About the Author

Kent Reisdorph is a senior software engineer at TurboPower Software Co. He also has his own consulting business. Kent is a contributing editor for The Cobb Group's *C++Builder Developer's Journal*. He is also a member of TeamB, Borland's online volunteer support group. As a member of TeamB, Kent puts in many hours each week on the Borland newsgroups, answering questions on C++Builder and Windows programming in general. Kent lives in Colorado Springs, Colorado, with his wife Jennifer and their six children, James, Mason, Mallory, Jenna, Marshall, and Joshua.

Acknowledgments

Naturally, a book like this is not written in a vacuum. There were a lot of people involved, both at Macmillan and at Borland. I want to thank Steve Sayre, Angie Allen, Renee Wilmeth, and Sean Dixon of Macmillan Computer Publishing for their help. Things got interesting a time or two as this project progressed, but the folks at Macmillan never wavered.

People at Borland whom I want to thank include Richard Army, Celeste Crocker, and Nan Borreson. I know that Nan probably spent some time wringing her hands over this project, and I hope that she is none the worse for it. Terri Bartos was also a big help when I had questions that I needed answered right away. Terri was almost certainly swamped with work on C++Builder, but she always took time to answer my questions (and even did some tech editing). Another person at Borland who deserves special mention is Ellie Peters (okay, and Jeff, too!). Ellie did a lot of technical editing on the book, but more importantly she was my inside contact at Borland. If I needed an answer to a question, I would call or email Ellie and she was always there to help. Jeff and Ellie are also friends, and I'm glad they could help me out with the book.

I want to thank the people at TurboPower Software for putting up with me during the time it took to write this book. Thanks to Bob DelRossi and Lee Inman for moral support. Thanks to Ralph Trickey and Terry Hughes for doing some tech editing on the database chapters.

Last but certainly not least, I want to thank my wife Jennifer. When I started this project, I knew that I would be immersed in work and that it would fall on her to keep everything going until I finally surfaced again. She took care of things exactly as I knew she would—masterfully and without a hint of complaint. I couldn't have done it without her.

Technical Support

If you have questions or need assistance with the information in this book, please contact our Technical Support Department at 317-581-3833 or email us at support@mcp.com.

Tell Us What You Think!

As part of our continuing effort to produce books of the highest possible quality, we would like to hear your comments. As a reader, you are the most important critic and commentator of our books. We value your opinion and want to know what we're doing right, what we could have done better, what areas you'd like to see us publish in, and any other words of wisdom you're willing to pass our way.

Please send your comments to the following:

programming@mcp.com

or

Macmillan Computer Publishing
Programming Group
201 W. 103rd Street
Indianapolis, IN 46290

Introduction: You Are Here

Isn't it helpful when the arrow on the map points to exactly where you are? So you are here. But why are you here? Maybe you're here because you've been a C++ programmer for years and you are attracted to C++Builder's promise of rapid application development (RAD). Maybe you are here because you have been using Borland's Delphi and you want to leverage that knowledge in a C++ programming environment. Maybe you are here because your boss told you to be here. Or maybe you are here as a complete beginner who would like to explore the wonderful world of Windows programming.

Regardless of why you are here, welcome! I can assure you that the trip will be an interesting one. You will no doubt find it enjoyable, too. It will involve some work, but there will be some fun thrown in from time to time. There's nothing quite like taking a passing thought and turning it into a working Windows program.

I encourage you to experiment as you read this book. Putting the book down and playing around for a while can prove more valuable than the best teacher. I also want to encourage you to explore the various online resources at your disposal. In particular, be sure to check out the Borland newsgroups at `forums.borland.com`. There you will find members of Borland's TeamB (a volunteer group) and fellow Borland users answering questions for beginning and experienced users alike. Also, be sure to check Borland's Web site at `www.borland.com`, where you will find additional information on C++Builder as well as available updates. You can download the source code for the book, as well as two bonus appendixes, by going to `www.mcp.com/info`.

So regardless of why you're here, I hope you enjoy your experience. Relax, put your feet up, and have fun learning how to use C++Builder. I know I did.

At a Glance

In Week 1 you begin to learn how to write Windows programs in C++. The C++ language is not an easy language to learn. It is, however, the standard programming language of many corporations and governments around the world. Learning C++ might not be the easiest task you could attempt, but it will be very rewarding, both intellectually and, eventually, monetarily.

You spend your first four days this week learning the basics of the C++ language. As you work through the first four chapters, you will write simple test programs to solidify your understanding of particular features of the C++ language. I warn you, though, that these programs are probably not the type that you purchased C++Builder to write. The test programs for the first four days are console applications; they work just like DOS programs. They lack any flash or glitter. You probably won't be terribly impressed. These programs, however, help you grasp the C++ basics.

Starting on Day 5, you begin to learn some of the things that make the visual programming aspect of C++Builder the great tool that it is. I will talk about frameworks and what a framework means to you as a Windows programmer. On Day 5 you build a simple test program, using C++Builder's visual programming tools. After that you spend a couple days going over the C++Builder IDE so that you can become familiar with how the entire C++Builder IDE works together to make your programming tasks easier. This is when things become more interesting. You have an opportunity to write some working Windows programs in the last part of this first week. So, with that in mind, let's get to it.

Day 1

Getting Started with C++Builder

Congratulations—you've chosen one of today's hottest new programming tools! Before you get started using all that C++Builder has to offer, though, you first need to learn a little about C++. In this chapter you will find

- ☐ A quick tour of C++Builder
- ☐ Information about how to write a Win32 console-mode application
- ☐ An introduction to the C++ language
- ☐ Facts about C++ variables and data types
- ☐ Information about functions in C++, including the `main()` function
- ☐ A discussion of arrays

What Is C++Builder?

By now you know that C++Builder is Borland's hot, new rapid application development (RAD) product for writing C++ applications. With C++Builder you can write C++ Windows programs more quickly and more easily than was ever possible before. You can create Win32 console applications or Win32 GUI (graphical user interface) programs. When creating Win32 GUI applications with C++Builder, you have all the power of C++ wrapped up in a RAD environment. What this means is that you can create the user interface to a program (the *user interface* means the menus, dialog boxes, main window, and so on) using drag-and-drop techniques for true rapid application development. You can also drop OCX controls on forms to create specialized programs such as web browsers in a matter of minutes. C++Builder gives you all this, but you don't sacrifice program execution speed because you still have the power that the C++ language offers you.

I can hear you saying, "This is going to be so great!" And guess what? You're right! But before you get too excited, I need to point out that the C++ language is not an easy one to master. I don't want you to think that you can buy a program like C++Builder and be a master Windows programmer overnight. It takes a great deal of work to be a good Windows programmer. C++Builder does a good job of hiding some of the low-level details that make up the guts of a Windows program, but it cannot write programs for you. In the end, you must still be a programmer, and that means you have to learn programming. That can be a long, uphill journey some days. The good news is that C++Builder can make your trek fairly painless and even fun. Yes, you can work and have fun doing it!

So roll up your sleeves and get on your hiking shoes. C++Builder *is* a great product, so have fun.

A Quick Look at the C++Builder IDE

This section contains a quick look at the C++Builder IDE (integrated development environment). I'll give the IDE a once-over now, examining it in more detail on Day 6, "The C++Builder IDE Explored." Because you are tackling Windows programming, I'll assume you are advanced enough to have figured out how to start C++Builder. When you first start the program, you are presented with both a blank form and the IDE, as shown in Figure 1.1.

The C++Builder IDE is divided into three parts. The top window can be considered the main window. It contains the toolbar on the left and the Component palette on the right. The toolbar gives you one-click access to tasks such as opening, saving, and compiling projects. The Component palette contains a wide array of components that you can drop onto your forms. (Components are text labels, edit controls, list boxes, buttons, and the like.) For convenience, the components are divided into groups. Did you notice the tabs along the top of the Component palette? Go ahead and click on the tabs to explore the different components available to you. To place a component on your form, you simply click the component's button in the Component palette and then click on your form where you want

the component to appear. Don't worry that you don't yet know how to use components. You'll get to that in due time. When you are done exploring, click on the tab labeled Standard, because you'll need it in a moment.

Figure 1.1.

The C++Builder IDE and the initial blank form.

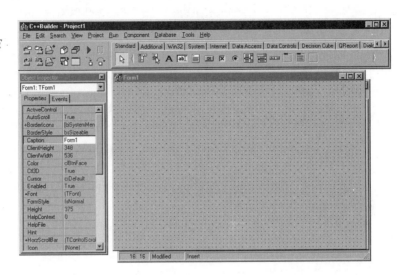

NEW TERM   A *component* is a self-contained binary piece of software that performs some specific predefined function, such as a text label, an edit control, or a list box.

Below the toolbar and Component palette and on the left side of the screen is the Object Inspector. It is through the Object Inspector that you modify a component's properties and events. You will use the Object Inspector constantly as you work with C++Builder. The Object Inspector has one or two tabs, depending on the component currently selected. It always has a Properties tab. A component's *properties* control how the component operates. For example, changing the Color property of a component changes the background color of that component. The list of properties available varies from component to component, although components usually have several common elements (Width and Height properties, for instance).

NEW TERM   A *property* determines the operation of a component.

Usually the Object Inspector has an Events tab in addition to the Properties tab. Events occur as the user interacts with a component. For example, when a component is clicked, an event is generated that tells you that the component was clicked. You can write code that responds to these events, performing specific actions when an event occurs. As with properties, the events that you can respond to vary from component to component.

An *event* is something that occurs as a result of a component's interaction with the user or with Windows.

 An *event handler* is a method that is invoked in your application in response to an event.

To the right of the Object Inspector is the C++Builder workspace. The workspace initially displays the Form Designer. It should come as no surprise that the Form Designer enables you to create forms. In C++Builder, a form represents a window in your program. The form might be the program's main window, a dialog box, or any other type of window. You use the Form Designer to place, move, and size components as part of the form creation process.

Hiding behind the Form Designer is the Code Editor. The Code Editor is where you type code when writing your programs. The Object Inspector, Form Designer, Code Editor, and Component palette work interactively as you build applications.

Now that you've had a look at what makes up the C++Builder IDE, let's actually do something.

Hello World

It's tradition. Almost all programming books start you off by having you create a program that displays Hello World on the screen. I'm tempted to do something else, but tradition is not a force to be reckoned with, so Hello World it is. You've got some work ahead of you in the next few chapters, so I thought I'd give you a taste of C++Builder's goodies before putting you to work learning the seemingly less glamorous basics of C++. You'll have a little fun first. C++Builder (and its cousin, Delphi) gives you possibly the quickest route to Hello World of any Windows programming environment to date.

Right now you should have C++Builder running, and you should be looking at a blank form. By default, the form is named Form1. (The form name is significant in C++Builder, but I'll address that a little later.) To the left of the form, the Object Inspector shows the properties for the form. Click on the title bar of the Object Inspector. The Caption property is highlighted, and the cursor is sitting there waiting for you to do something. (If the Caption property is not in view, you might have to scroll the Object Inspector window to locate it. Properties are listed in alphabetical order.) Type Hello World! to change the form's caption.

 NOTE

As you modify properties, C++Builder immediately displays the results of the property change when appropriate. As you type the new caption, notice that the window caption of the form is changing to reflect the text you are typing.

Now click the Run button on the toolbar (the one with the blue arrow). (You can also press F9 or choose Run | Run from the main menu.) C++Builder begins to build the program. The compiler status dialog box, shown in Figure 1.2, is displayed, and you can watch as C++Builder races through the files necessary to build your program. After a brief wait, the compiler status box disappears, the form is displayed, and the caption shows Hello World!. In this case, the running program looks almost identical to the blank form. You might scarcely have noticed when the program was displayed because it is displayed in the exact location of the form in the Form Designer. (There is a difference, though, because the Form Designer displays an alignment grid and the running program does not.) Congratulations—you've just written your first C++ Windows program with C++Builder. Wow, that was easy!

Figure 1.2.

The compiler status dialog box.

"But what is it?" you ask. It's not a lot, I agree, but it is a true Windows program. It can be moved by dragging the title bar, it can be sized, it can be minimized, it can be maximized, and it can be closed by clicking the Close button. You can even locate the program in Windows Explorer (it will probably be in your \CBuilder\Projects directory as Project1.exe) and double-click on it to run it.

Okay, so maybe displaying Hello World! just in the caption was cheating a little. Let's spruce it up a bit. If you still have the Hello World program running, close it by clicking the Close button in the upper-right corner of the window. The Form Designer is displayed again, and you are ready to modify the form (and, as a result, the program).

To make the program more viable, you're going to add text to the center of the window itself. To do this, you'll add a text label to the form. First, click on the Standard tab of the Component palette. The third component button on the palette has an *A* on it. If you put your mouse cursor over that button, the ToolTip will display Label. Click the label button and then click anywhere on the form. A Label component is placed on the form with a default caption of Label1. Now turn your attention to the Object Inspector. It now displays the properties for Label1 (remember that previously it was showing the properties for Form1). Again the Caption property is highlighted. Click on the title bar of the Object Inspector or on the Caption property and type Hello World!. Now the label on the form shows Hello World!. As long as you're at it, change the size of the label's text as well. Double-click on the Font property. The property will expand to show the additional font attributes below it. Locate the Size property under Font and change the font size to 24 (it is currently set to 8). As soon as you press Enter or click on the form, the label instantly changes to the new size.

Because the label is probably not centered on the form, you might want to move it. To move a component, simply click on it and drag it to the position you want it to occupy. When you have the label where you want it, you're ready to recompile and run the program. Click the Run button again. C++Builder compiles the program again and, after a moment (shorter this time), the program runs. Now you see Hello World! displayed in the center of the form as well as in the caption. Figure 1.3 shows the Hello World! program running.

Figure 1.3.
The Hello World!
program running.

With this little taste of C++Builder, you can see that writing C++ Windows programs with C++Builder is going to be a great deal more interesting than it was in the good ol' days. To prepare for what you are going to do next, you need to close the current project in the C++Builder IDE. Choose File | Close All from the main menu. Click on No when prompted to save changes to Project1, or save the project as HelloWorld if you are fond of your new creation.

Hello World, Part II—A Win32 Console Application

In the next couple of days you are going to learn the basics of the C++ language. Along the way you will write some simple test programs. These test programs work best as console applications. For all intents and purposes, these programs look like DOS programs when they run. There are some major differences between a Win32 console app and a DOS program, but you need not be concerned about that right now. So, without further ado, let's create Hello World as a Win32 console program with C++Builder.

NEW TERM A Win32 *console application* is a 32-bit program that runs in a DOS box under Windows 95 or Windows NT.

From the main menu, choose File | New. C++Builder displays the Object Repository. Curiously enough, the Object Repository's title bar says New Items, but don't be thrown by that. The Object Repository contains predefined projects, forms, dialog boxes, and other objects you can add to your applications or use to begin a new project. I will discuss the Object Repository in detail on Day 9, "Creating Applications in C++Builder." For now, click on the New tab in the Object Repository and double-click the Console Wizard icon. When the Console Application Wizard dialog comes up, just click the Finish button to create a standard console application. C++Builder creates the project and displays the Code Editor so that you can enter code for the program. Figure 1.4 shows the Code Editor as it appears when starting a new console-mode application.

Figure 1.4.

The C++Builder Code Editor window.

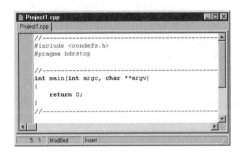

You will notice a couple of differences between the C++Builder IDE now and how it looked earlier when you created a GUI application. First, there is no Form Designer. That's because a console application, being a text-mode application, can't display forms (well, that's not completely true, but it's accurate enough for this discussion). Also notice that the Object Inspector is blank. You can only place components on a form, so the Object Inspector is useless in a console application.

> **TIP**
>
> When writing console applications, you can close the Object Inspector to make more room for the Code Editor window. Close the Object Inspector by clicking the Close button on the Object Inspector's title bar. To bring back the Object Inspector, press F11 or choose View | Object Inspector from the main menu.

When you examine the Code Editor, you will see the following text displayed in the editor window:

```
//--------------------------------
#include <condefs.h>
#pragma hdrstop
```

```
//-----------------------------------
int main(int argc, char **argv)
{
   return 0;
}
//-----------------------------------
```

> **NOTE**
>
> Don't be concerned if the console application code generated for you by C++Builder doesn't look exactly like the preceding code snippet or like that of Figure 1.4. Products like C++Builder have been known to change late in the development cycle. That can sometimes make authors look foolish and can leave readers scratching their heads in wonder.

ANALYSIS   This is a do-nothing C++ program but a valid C++ program nonetheless. You'll modify the code in just a moment to make this program actually do something, but first I want you to notice the lines that begin with //. These are comment lines that, in this program, serve no purpose other than to divide the program's code visually. (You will normally use comment lines to document your code.) C++Builder adds these comment lines automatically when a new console application is first created. (In future code listings I will not include the comment lines, to save space.) Notice also that the single statement in this code ends in a semicolon. (I know it doesn't make sense right now, but the fact is that there is only one actual executable statement in this program.) The semicolon is used at the end of each statement in a C++ program.

Very early in the process of learning the C and C++ languages, the budding programmer must learn the difference between an expression and a statement. The official definition of a *statement* is an expression that is followed by a semicolon. The semicolon closes an expression and makes it a kind of single-line block of code. I'll get into the code block soon, but for now you should realize that an *expression* is a unit of code that evaluates to some quantity. A statement is an expression that is closed. For example, consider the following statement:

```
c = a + b;
```

In this example, the portion to the right of the equal sign, a + b, is an expression. The entire line is a statement. I know this might be a bit confusing at the moment, but it will become clearer as you go along. I'll try to be very careful when I use these two terms. For now, though, just remember that a statement is followed by a semicolon and is a closed expression.

Also notice the opening and closing braces in the program. In C++ a block of code begins with the opening brace ({) and ends with the closing brace (}). The braces are used to delineate the beginning and end of code blocks associated with loops, functions, and if statements, and in other cases as well. In this program there is only one set of braces because it is a simple program.

To display Hello World! on the screen, you need to make use of a C++ class called iostream, so a quick tutorial on that class is needed. (You don't know about classes yet, but don't worry about that right now.) The iostream class uses *streams* to perform basic input and output, such as printing text on the screen or getting input from the user. The cout stream is used to send data to the standard output stream. In a console application, the standard output stream means the console or the screen. The cin stream is used to get data from the console, such as user input. iostream implements two special operators to place information on a stream or to extract information from a stream. The *insertion operator* (<<) is used to insert data into an output stream, and the *extraction operator* (>>) is used to extract b6òa from an input stream. To output information to the console, you would use

```
cout << "Do something!";
```

This tells the program to insert the text Do something! into the standard output stream. When this line in the program executes, the text will be displayed on the screen.

NOTE

> cout is for use in console-mode applications only. A Windows GUI application does not have a standard output stream (everything in a GUI app is graphics based), so the output from cout goes nowhere in a Windows GUI program. Standard Windows programs use DrawText() or TextOut() to display text on the screen. C++Builder GUI programs can also use DrawText() and TextOut(), but the easiest way to display text is by using a Label component, as you saw earlier.

Before you can use cout, you need to tell the compiler where to find the description (called the *declaration*) of the iostream class. The declaration for iostream is located in a file called IOSTREAM.H. This file is called a header file.

 A *header file* (or just *header* for short) contains the class declaration of one or more classes.

To tell the compiler to look in IOSTREAM.H for the class declaration of iostream, use the #include directive as follows:

```
#include <iostream.h>
```

 A *declaration* is a section of code that describes a function or class. The *definition* is the actual code for the function or class. In C and C++, the distinction between these two separate states is very important. In general, a declaration is stored in a header file, and a definition is contained in a source code file.

Now the compiler will be able to find the declaration for the iostream class and will understand what to do when it encounters the cout statement.

TIP

> If you forget to include the header file for a class or a function your program references, you will get a compiler error. The compiler error will say something to the effect of Undefined symbol 'cout'. If you see this error message, you should immediately check to be sure that you have included all the headers your program needs. To find out what header file a class or function's declaration is in, click on the function or class name and press F1. Windows Help will run, and the help topic for the item under the cursor will be displayed. Toward the top of the help topic, you will see a reference to the header file in which the function or class is declared.

There's one more thing I'll mention before you write the console version of Hello World. The iostream class contains special *manipulators* that can be used to control how streams are handled. The only one you are concerned with right now is the endl (end line) manipulator, which is used to insert a new line in the output stream. You'll use endl to insert a new line after you output text to the screen. Note that the final character in endl is an *L* and not a 1.

Now that you have some understanding of the iostream class, you can proceed to write Hello World as a console application. Edit the program until it looks like Listing 1.1. Each of the lines has a number that I've put there for identification. C++ doesn't use line numbers, so be sure to skip the line numbers when you type in the lines.

Listing 1.1. HELLO.CPP.

```
1: #include <condefs.h>
2: #include <iostream.h>              // add this line
3: #pragma hdrstop
4:
5: int main(int argc, char **argv)
6: {
7:   cout << "Hello World!" << endl;  // add this line
8:   return 0;
9: }
```

NOTE

In C++, whitespace is ignored. For the most part, it doesn't matter where you put spaces or new lines. Obviously, you cannot insert spaces in the middle of keywords or variable names, but other than that just about anything goes. For example, the following lines of code are equivalent:

```
int main(int argc, char **argv)
{
cout << "Hello World!";
return 0;
}
```

is the same as

```
int main(int argc,char** argv){cout<<"Hello World!";return 0;}
```

Obviously, the first form is more readable and is much more preferable. Although coding styles vary, if you adopt the coding conventions you see in this book, you will be okay when it comes to programming in the real world.

ANALYSIS Now click the Run button on the toolbar. The program compiles and runs. When the program runs, you will see a DOS box pop up and the words `Hello World!`...whoops! What happened? You probably saw the application for a split second and then watched as it disappeared. The reason for this is that at the end of the `main()` function, the program terminates and the console window immediately closes. To remedy this, you need to add a couple of lines to your program to prevent the console window from closing until you're done with it. The standard C library includes a function called `getch()` that is used to get a keystroke from the keyboard. You'll use that as a means of preventing the console window from closing. Again, edit the program in the editor window until it looks like Listing 1.2. You don't need to add the comment lines if you don't want to. Remember to skip the line numbers.

Listing 1.2. HELLO.CPP (revised).

```
1: #include <condefs.h>
2: #include <iostream.h>
3: #include <conio.h>          // add this line
4: #pragma hdrstop
5:
6: int main(int argc, char **argv)
7: {
8:   cout << "Hello World!" << endl;
9:   // add the following two lines
```

continues

Listing 1.2. continued

```
10:   cout << endl << "Press any key to continue...";
11:   getch();
12:   return 0;
13: }
```

 This time the application runs, Hello World! is displayed, and the console window stays visible. To end the program and close the console window, you can press any key on the keyboard.

 I want you to be aware of how C++Builder saves console applications in case you decide to save the program in Listing 1.1. When you save the project, C++Builder creates two files. The project file has a .BPR extension and contains the information C++Builder needs to build the project. The source file has a .CPP extension and contains the actual program code. For example, if you saved the project with a name of HELLO, your hard disk will have two files; HELLO.BPR and HELLO.CPP. To reopen the project, you open HELLO.BPR, but the Code Editor window will show HELLO.CPP. It's sort of confusing at first, but after the first couple of times you will understand what is happening. Projects are discussed in more detail on Day 6 and again on Day 10, "More on Projects."

You can also find the programs listed in the text at http://www.mcp.com/sams/codecenter.html. The examples need to be installed on your hard drive before they can be compiled. Although it's good practice early on to enter short programs by hand, you might want to load the longer sample programs from your hard drive to avoid inevitable typing errors and the compiler errors that are sure to follow.

That's all there is to it. Hello World, Part II, isn't too exciting, but you'll make good use of console-mode applications as you explore the C++ language in the following pages. That's why it is necessary for you to understand how to create and run a console-mode application. Now let's move on to the basics of the C++ language.

C++ Language Overview

C++ is a powerful language. It enables you to do things that are not possible in other languages. As is true in most of life, that kind of power does not come without responsibility. Early on you will probably get into trouble once in a while using C++. This usually comes in the form of memory overruns and access violations that cause crashes in your programs.

I will do my best to describe C++ in the short space allotted. Entire books have been written on the C++ language (and big ones at that!), so don't expect that I can cover it all in a few chapters. I strongly suggest that after reading this book and experimenting with C++Builder for a period of time, you buy a book that explains C++ in greater detail.

C++ enables you to take advantage of object-oriented programming (OOP) to its fullest. OOP is not just a buzzword. It has real benefits because it enables you to create objects that can be used in your current program and reused in future programs.

 An *object*, like components described earlier, is a binary piece of software that performs a specific programming task. (Components are objects, but not all objects are components. I'll explain that later.)

An object reveals to the user (the programmer using the object) only as much of itself as is needed to simplify its use. All internal mechanisms that the user doesn't need to know about are hidden from sight. All this is included in the concept of object-oriented programming. OOP enables you to take a modular approach to programming, thus keeping you from constantly re-inventing the wheel. C++Builder programs are OOP oriented because of C++Builder's heavy use of components. After a component is created (either one of your own or one of the built-in C++Builder components), it can be reused in any C++Builder program. A component can also be extended by inheritance to create a new component with additional features. Best of all, components hide their internal details and let the programmer concentrate on getting the most out of the component. Objects and C++ classes are discussed in detail on Day 4, "C++ Classes and Object-Oriented Programming."

Humble Beginnings

In the beginning there was C...as far as C++ is concerned, anyway. C++ is built on the C programming language. It has been described as "C with classes." This foundation in C is still very prevalent in C++ programs written today. It's not as if C++ were written to replace C, but rather to augment it. The rest of this chapter and much of the next chapter focus primarily on the part of the C++ language that has its roots in C. Actually, you will be dealing with the C language here and moving to C++ later, in Day 2, "C++ Fundamentals." You don't have to be concerned with recognizing what information is from C and what is from C++ because it's all part of the language called C++.

It would be nice if presenting the C++ language could be handled sequentially. That's not the case, though, because all the features we will be discussing are intertwined. I'll take the individual puzzle pieces one at a time and start fitting them together. Toward the end of Day 3, "Advanced C++," you'll have a complete picture of the C++ language. Don't be concerned if you don't instantly grasp every concept presented. Some of what is required to fully understand C++ can come only with real-world experience.

Variables

Well, we have to start somewhere, so let's take a look at variables. A *variable* is essentially a name assigned to a memory location. After you have declared a variable, you can then use it to manipulate data in memory. That probably doesn't make much sense to you, so let me give you a few examples. The following code snippet uses two variables. At the end of each line of code is a comment that describes what is happening when that line executes:

```
int x;          // variable declared as an integer variable
x = 100;        // 'x' now contains the value 100
x += 50;        // 'x' now contains the value 150
int y = 150;    // 'y' declared and initialized to 150
x += y;         // 'x' now contains the value 300
x++;            // 'x' now contains the value 301
```

NEW TERM   A *variable* is a location set aside in computer memory to contain some value.

Notice that the value of x changes as the variable is manipulated. A little later I'll discuss the C++ operators used to manipulate variables.

WARNING

> Variables that are declared but are not initialized contain random values. Because the memory to which the variable points has not been initialized, there is no telling what that memory location contains. For instance, look at the following code:
>
> ```
> int x;
> int y;
> x = y + 10;  // oops!
> ```
>
> In this example the variable x could contain any value because y was not initialized prior to use.
>
> The exception to this rule is that global variables and variables declared with the static modifier are initialized to 0. All other variables contain random data until initialized or assigned a value.

Variable names can mix uppercase and lowercase letters and can include numbers and the underscore (_), but they cannot contain spaces or other special characters. The variable name must start with a character or the underscore. Generally speaking, it's not a good idea to begin a variable name with an underscore because compilers often start special variable and function names with the underscore or a double underscore. The maximum allowable length of a variable name varies from compiler to compiler. If you keep your variable names to 31 characters or less, you'll be safe. In reality, anything more than about 20 characters is too long to be useful anyway. The following are examples of valid variable names:

```
int aVeryLongVariableName;   // a long variable name
int my_variable;             // a variable with an underscore
int _x;                      // OK, but not advised
int X;                       // uppercase variable name
int Label2;                  // a variable name containing a number
int GetItemsInContainer();   // thanks Pete!
```

NOTE

> Variable names in C++ are case sensitive. The following are two distinct variables:
>
> ```
> int xPos;
> int xpos;
> ```
>
> If you are coming from a language where case doesn't matter (Pascal, for instance), the case-sensitive nature of C++ might cause you some trouble until you get used to it.

C++ Data Types

NEW TERM   In C++ a *data type* defines the way the compiler stores information in memory.

In some programming languages, you can get by with assigning any type of value to a variable. For example, look at the following examples of BASIC code:

```
x = -1;
x = 1000;
x = 3.14
x = 457000;
```

In BASIC, the interpreter takes care of allocating enough storage to fit any size or type of number. In C++, however, you must declare a variable's type before you can use the variable:

```
int x1 = -1;
int x = 1000;
float y = 3.14;
long z = 457000;
```

This enables the compiler to do type-checking and to make sure that things are kept straight when the program runs. Improper use of a data type will result in a compiler error or warning that can be analyzed and corrected so that you can head off a problem before it starts. Some data types can have both signed and unsigned versions. A *signed* data type can contain both negative and positive numbers, whereas an *unsigned* data type can contain only positive numbers. Table 1.1 shows the basic data types in C++, the amount of memory they require, and the range of values possible for each data type.

Table 1.1. Data types used in C++ (32-bit programs).

Data Type	Size in Bytes	Possible Range of Values
char	1	-128 to 126
unsigned char	1	0 to 255
short	2	-32,768 to 32,767
unsigned short	2	0 to 65,535
long	4	-2,147,483,648 to 2,147,483,648
unsigned long	4	0 to 4,294,967,295
int	4	Same as long
unsigned int	4	Same as unsigned long
float	4	1.2E-38 to 3.4E381
double	8	2.2E-308 to 1.8E3082
bool	1	true or false

Examining the preceding table, you might notice that an int is the same as a long. So why does C++ have two different named date types that are exactly the same? Essentially, it's a holdover from days gone by. In a 16-bit programming environment, an int requires 2 bytes of storage and a long requires 4 bytes of storage. In a 32-bit programming environment, however, both require 4 bytes of storage and have the same range of values. C++Builder produces only 32-bit programs, so an int and a long are identical.

NOTE

In C++Builder (as well as in Borland C++ 5.0), bool is a true data type. Some C++ compilers have a BOOL keyword, but bool is not a data type in those compilers. In those cases BOOL is a typedef that makes BOOL equivalent to an int. A typedef in effect sets up an alias so that the compiler can equate one symbol with another. A typedef looks like this:

```
typedef int BOOL;
```

This tells the compiler, "BOOL is another word for int."

NOTE

Only the double and float data types use floating-point numbers (numbers with decimal places). The other data types deal only with integer values. Although it's legal to assign a value containing a decimal fraction to an integer data type, the fractional amount will be discarded, and only the whole-number portion will be assigned to the integer variable.

```
int x = 3.75;
```

will result in x containing a value of 3. Note that the resulting integer value is not rounded to the nearest whole number; rather, the decimal fraction is discarded altogether. By the way, you'd be surprised how few times you need floating-point numbers in most Windows programs.

C++ performs conversion between different data types when possible. Take the following code snippet for an example:

```
short result;
long num1 = 200;
long num2 = 200;
result = num1 * num2;
```

In this case I am trying to assign the result of multiplying two long integers to a short integer. Even though this formula mixes two data types, C++ is able to perform a conversion. Would you like to take a guess at the result of this calculation? You might be surprised to find out that the result is -25,536. This is because of *wrapping*. If you look at Table 1.1, you'll see that a short can have a maximum value of 32,767. What happens if you take a short with a value of 32,767 and add 1 to it? You will get a value of -32,768. This is essentially the same as the odometer on a car turning over from 99,999 to 00,000 when you drive that last mile. To illustrate, type in and run the program contained in Listing 1.3.

NOTE

Some of the listings you will see over the next several days don't have this statement:

```
#include <condefs.h>
```

This statement is automatically added when C++Builder creates a new console application. It is not strictly necessary for the programs you will be working on, so I have eliminated it from the code listings. Your application will run the same, regardless of whether this statement is included.

Listing 1.3. WRAPME.CPP.

```
 1: #include <iostream.h>
 2: #include <conio.h>
 3: #pragma hdrstop
 4:
 5: int main(int argc, char **argv)
 6: {
 7:   short x = 32767;
 8:   cout << "x = " << x << endl;
 9:   x++;
10:   cout << "x = " << x << endl;
11:   getch();
12:   return 0;
13: }
```

 ANALYSIS   The output will be

```
x = 32767
x = -32768
```

You won't go too far wrong if you use the int data type as your data type of choice. You are unlikely to run into the problem of wrapping because the int data type gives you a range of -2 billion to +2 billion, plus change. Your programs will be slightly larger, however, because an int requires 4 bytes of storage and a short requires only 2 bytes of storage. The difference is insignificant for most applications you will write.

Okay, where was I? Oh, yes, I was talking about automatic type conversion. In some cases, C++ cannot perform a conversion. If that is the case, you will get one of several possible compiler errors that say Cannot convert from X to Y. You might also get a compiler warning that says Conversion might lose significant digits.

> **TIP**   Learn to treat compiler warnings as errors because the compiler is trying to tell you that something is not quite right. Ultimately, you should strive for warning-free compiles. In some cases a warning cannot be avoided, but be sure to examine all warnings closely. Do your best to understand the reason for the warning and correct it if possible.

C++ Operators

Operators are used to manipulate data. Operators perform calculations, check for equality, make assignments, manipulate variables, and perform other, more esoteric duties most programmers never do. There are a lot of operators in C++. Rather than present them all here, I will list only those most commonly used. Table 1.2 contains a list of those operators.

Table 1.2. Commonly used C++ operators.

Operator	Description	Example
	Mathematical Operators	
+	Addition	`x = y + z;`
-	Subtraction	`x = y - z;`
*	Multiplication	`x = y * z;`
/	Division	`x = y / z;`
	Assignment Operators	
=	Assignment	`x = 10;`
+=	Assign and sum	`x += 10;` (same as `x = x + 10;`)
-=	Assign and subtract	`x -= 10;`
*=	Assign and multiply	`x *= 10;`
\=	Assign and divide	`x \= 10;`
&=	Assign bitwise AND	`x &= 0x02;`
¦=	Assign bitwise OR	`x ¦= 0x02;`
	Logical Operators	
&&	Logical AND	`if (x && 0xFF) {...}`
¦¦	Logical OR	`if (x ¦¦ 0xFF) {...}`
	Equality Operators	
==	Equal to	`if (x == 10) {...}`
!=	Not equal to	`if (x != 10) {...}`
<	Less than	`if (x < 10) {...}`
>	Greater than	`if (x > 10) {...}`
<=	Less than or equal to	`if (x <= 10) {...}`
>=	Greater than or equal to	`if (x >= 10) {...}`
	Unary Operators	
*	Indirection operator	`int x = *y;`
&	Address of operator	`int* x = &y;`
~	Bitwise NOT	`x &= ~0x02;`
!	Logical NOT	`if (!valid) {...}`

continues

Table 1.2. continued

Operator	Description	Example
	Unary Operators	
++	Increment operator	`x++; (same as x = x + 1;)`
--	Decrement operator	`x--;`
	Class and Structure Operators	
::	Scope resolution	`MyClass::SomeFunction();`
->	Indirect membership	`myClass->SomeFunction();`
.	Direct membership	`myClass.SomeFunction();`

As you can see, the list of operators is a bit overwhelming, so don't worry about trying to memorize each one. As you work with C++, you will gradually learn how to use all the operators.

It should be noted that the increment operator can be used as either pre-increment (++x) or post-increment (x++). A *pre-increment* operator tells the compiler, "Increment the variable's value and then use the variable." A *post-increment* operator tells the compiler, "Use the variable first and then increment its value." For example, this code:

```
int x = 10;
cout << "x = " << x++ << endl;
cout << "x = " << x << endl;
cout << "x = " << ++x << endl;
cout << "x = " x << endl;
```

results in the following output:

```
x = 10
x = 11
x = 12
x = 12
```

The same is true of the decrement operator (--). A lot of this won't make sense until you've worked with C++ for a while, but be patient and it will eventually come to you. As Pontius said to Augustus, "Relax, Augie. Rome wasn't built in a day, ya know."

1

NOTE

> In C++, operators can be *overloaded*. This is a technique by which a programmer can take one of the standard operators and make it perform in a specific manner for a specific class. For example, you can overload the ++ operator for one of your classes and have it increment the value of a variable by 10 rather than by 1. Operator overloading is an advanced C++ technique and is not covered in any detail in this book.

You will notice that some of the operators use the same symbol. The meaning of the symbol is different, depending on the context. For instance, the asterisk (*) can be used to perform multiplication, declare a pointer, or dereference a pointer. This can be confusing at first, and to be honest, it can be confusing at times no matter how long you've been programming in C++. Just keep working away and eventually you will begin to learn it.

You will see many examples of these operators as you go through this book. Rather than try to memorize the function of each operator, try instead to learn through careful study of the sample programs and code snippets.

Functions in C++

Functions are sections of code separate from the main program. These code sections are called (executed) when needed to perform specific actions in a program. For example, you might have a function that takes two values, performs a complex mathematical calculation on those two values, and returns the result. You might need a function that takes a string, parses it, and returns a portion of the parsed string.

Functions are sections of code, separate from the main program, that perform a single, well-defined service.

Functions are an important part of any programming language, and C++ is no exception. The simplest type of function takes no parameters and returns void (meaning it returns nothing at all). Other functions might take one or more *parameters* and might return a value. Rules for naming functions are the same as those discussed earlier for variables. Figure 1.5 shows the anatomy of a function.

A *parameter* is a value passed to a function that is used to alter its operation or indicate the extent of its operation.

Figure 1.5.
Anatomy of a function.

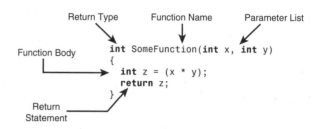

Before a function can be used, it must have first been declared. The *function declaration* or *prototype* tells the compiler how many parameters the function takes, the data type of each parameter, and the data type of the return value for the function. Listing 1.4 illustrates this concept.

NEW TERM   A *prototype* is a declaration of a function's appearance or a foreshadowing of its definition.

Listing 1.4. MULTIPLY.CPP.

```
 1: #include <iostream.h>
 2: #include <conio.h>
 3: #pragma hdrstop
 4:
 5: int multiply(int, int);
 6: void showResult(int);
 7:
 8: int main(int argc, char **argv)
 9: {
10:    int x, y, result;
11:    cout << endl << "Enter the first value: ";
12:    cin >> x;
13:    cout << "Enter the second value: ";
14:    cin >> y;
15:    result = multiply(x, y);
16:    showResult(result);
17:    cout << endl << endl << "Press any key to continue...";
18:    getch();
19:    return 0;
20: }
21:
22: int multiply(int x, int y)
23: {
24:    return x * y;
25: }
26:
27: void showResult(int res)
28: {
29:    cout << "The result is: " << res << endl;
30: }
```

1

This program asks for two numbers from the user (using the standard input stream, `cin`) in lines 11 through 14, calls the `multiply()` function to multiply the two numbers together (line 15), and then calls the `showResult()` function to display the result (line 16). Notice the function prototypes for the `multiply()` and `showResult()` functions on lines 5 and 6, just above the main program. The prototypes list only the return type, the function name, and the data type of the function's parameters. That is the minimum requirement for a function declaration.

If desired, the function prototype can contain variable names that can be used to document what the function does. For example, the function declaration for the `multiply()` function could have been written like this:

```
int multiply(int firstNumber, int secondNumber);
```

In this case, it's fairly obvious what the `multiply()` function does, but it can't hurt to document your code both through comments and through the code itself.

Look again at Listing 1.4. Notice that the function definition for the `multiply()` function (lines 22 through 25) is outside the block of code defining the main function (lines 8 through 20). The function definition contains the actual body of the function. In this case, the body of the function is minimal because the function simply multiplies the two function parameters together and returns the result.

The `multiply()` function in Listing 1.4 can be called in one of several ways. You can pass variables, literal values, or even the results of other function calls:

```
result = multiply(2, 5);      // passing literal values
result = multiply(x, y);      // passing variables
showResult(multiply(x,y));    // return value used as a
                              // parameter for another function
multiply(x, y);               // return value ignored
```

Notice in the last example that the return value is not used. In this case, it doesn't make much sense to call the `multiply()` function and ignore the return value, but ignoring the return value is something that is done frequently in C++ programming. There are many functions that perform a specific action and then return a value indicating the status of the function call. In some cases the return value is not relevant to your program, so you can just ignore it. If you don't do anything with the return value, it is simply discarded and no harm is done. For example, we have been ignoring the return value of the `getch()` function (which returns the ASCII value of the key that was pressed) in our sample programs.

Functions can (and frequently do) call other functions. Functions can even call themselves. This is called *recursion* and is one way to get into trouble in C++ programming. Recursion is best left alone until you've put in some time with the C++ language.

NEW TERM   *Recursion* is the process by which a function calls itself.

The material on functions presented in this section deals with standalone functions in a C or C++ program (they are *standalone* in that they are not members of a class). Standalone functions can be used in C++ exactly as they are used in C. However, C++ takes functions a bit farther. I'll leave that discussion for now and pick it up again later when we look deeper into C++.

House Rules for Functions

☐ A function can take any number of parameters or no parameters at all.

☐ A function can be written to return a value, but it is not mandatory that a function return a value.

☐ If a function has a return type of void, it cannot return a value. If you attempt to return a value from a function with a return type of void, a compiler error is issued. A function that returns void need not contain a return statement at all, but it can, if you want. Either way is acceptable. If no return statement is provided, the function returns automatically when it gets to the end of the function block (the closing brace).

☐ If the function prototype indicates that the function returns a value, the function body should contain a return statement that returns a value. If the function does not return a value, a compiler warning is issued.

☐ Functions can take any number of parameters but can return only one value.

☐ Variables can be passed to functions by value, by pointer, or by reference. (I'll discuss this a little later.)

SYNTAX

The function statement, in declaration (prototype) format:

```
ret_type function_name(argtype_1 arg_1, argtype_2 arg_2, ..., argtype_n arg_n);
```

The function declaration identifies a function that will be included in the code. It shows the return data type (`ret_type`) of the function and the name of the function (`function_name`) and identifies the order (`arg_1`, `arg_2`, ..., `arg_n`) and types (`argtype_1`, `argtype_2`, ..., `argtype_n`) of data arguments the function will expect.

The function statement, in definition format:

```
ret_type function_name(argtype_1 arg_1, argtype_2 arg_2, ..., argtype_n arg_n)
{
statements;
return ret_type;
}
```

 The function definition identifies the code block (*statements*) that makes up the function and shows the return data type (*ret_type*) of the function. *function_name* identifies the function. The parameters supplied to the function (*arg_1*, *arg_2*, ..., *arg_n*) and their types (*argtype_1*, *argtype_2*, ..., *argtype_n*) are included.

The `main()` Function

A C++ program must have a `main()` function. This function serves as the entry point to the program. You have seen this in each of the sample programs thus far. Not all C++ programs have a traditional `main()` function, however. Windows programs written in C and C++ have an entry-point function called `WinMain()` rather than the traditional `main()` function.

NOTE

> A C++Builder GUI application has a `WinMain()`, but it is hidden from you. C++Builder frees you from having to worry about the low-level details of a Windows program and enables you to concentrate on creating the user interface and the remainder of the program.

`main()` is a function like any other function. That is, it has the same basic anatomy. You already saw that for 32-bit console applications, C++Builder creates a default `main()` function with the following prototype:

```
int main(int argc, char** argv);
```

This form of `main()` takes two parameters and returns an integer value. As you learned earlier, you pass values to a function when you call the function. In the case of `main()`, though, you never call the function directly—it's automatically executed when the program runs. So how does the `main()` function get its parameters? The answer: from the command line. Let me illustrate.

Let's assume that you have a Win32 console application that you execute from a DOS prompt with the following command line:

```
grep WM_KILLFOCUS -d -i
```

In this case you are starting a program called `grep` with command-line arguments of `WM_KILLFOCUS`, `-d`, and `-i`. Given that example, let me show you how that translates to `argc` and `argv` inside the `main()` function. First, the integer variable `argc` will contain the number of parameters passed in the command line. This will always be at least 1 because the program name counts as a parameter. The variable `argv` is an array of pointers to strings. This array will contain each string passed in the command line. For this code example, the following are true:

```
argc      Contains 4
argv[0]   Contains c:\cbuilder\bin\grep.exe
argv[1]   Contains WM_KILLFOCUS
argv[2]   Contains -d
argv[3]   Contains -i
```

Let's prove that this works with a little sample program. Create a new console application in C++Builder and enter the program shown in Listing 1.5.

Listing 1.5. ARGSTEST.CPP.

```
 1: #include <iostream.h>
 2: #include <conio.h>
 3: #pragma hdrstop
 4:
 5: int main(int argc, char **argv)
 6: {
 7:   cout << "argc = " << argc << endl;
 8:   for (int i=0;i<argc;i++)
 9:     cout << "Parameter " << i << ": " << argv[i] << endl;
10:   cout << endl << "Press any key to continue...";
11:   getch();
12:   return 0;
13: }
```

Save the project as ARGSTEST. Rather than click the Run button, choose Project | Build All from the main menu. This will build the project but won't execute the program. When the project has finished building, choose Run | Parameters from the main menu. Type the following in the Run parameters field of the Run Parameters dialog box:

```
one two three "four five" six
```

Now click the Run button, and the program will run using the command-line parameters you specified. An alternative is to run the program from an MS-DOS prompt by using the following command line:

```
argstest one two three "four five" six
```

When the program runs, it will display the number of arguments passed and then list each of the arguments. The output will match that of Figure 1.6. Run the program several times, providing different command-line arguments each time, and observe the output.

In most programs, the value returned from main() is irrelevant because the return value is not typically used. In fact, you don't need your main() function to return a value at all. There is more than one form of main(). The following all represent valid declarations:

```
main();
int main();// same as above
int main(void); // same as above
int main(int argc, char** argv);
void main();
void main(int argc, char** argv);
```

Figure 1.6.

Sample output from
ARGSTEST.EXE.

Believe it or not, there are even more possibilities than those listed here. If you are not going to be using the command-line arguments, you can use the first form of main() listed here. This form returns an int (the default return value if none is specified) and takes no parameters (signified by the empty parentheses). Put another way, the most basic form of the main() function takes no parameters and returns an int.

Arrays

You can place any of the intrinsic C++ data types into an array. An *array* is simply a collection of values. For example, let's say you want to keep an array of ints that holds five integer values. You would declare the array as follows:

```
int myArray[5];
```

In this case the compiler allocates memory for the array, as illustrated in Figure 1.7. Because each int requires 4 bytes of storage, the entire array will take up 20 bytes in memory.

Figure 1.7.

Memory allocation for an array of five ints.

mArray[0]	mArray[1]	mArray[2]	mArray[3]	mArray[4]
baseAddr	baseAddr + 4	baseAddr + 8	baseAddr + 12	baseAddr + 16

Now that you have the array declared, you can fill it with values, using the *subscript operator* ([]) as follows:

```
myArray[0] = -200;
myArray[1] = -100;
myArray[2] = 0;
myArray[3] = 100;
myArray[4] = 200;
```

As you can see from this code, arrays in C++ are 0-based. Later in your program, you can access the individual elements of the array again by using the subscript operator:

```
int result = myArray[3] + myArray[4];   // result will be 300
```

There is a shortcut method for declaring and filling an array all at one time. It looks like this:

```
int myArray[5] = { -200, -100, 0, 100, 200 };
```

To take this one step farther, if you know exactly how many elements your array will have, and if you fill the array when you declare it, you can even leave out the array size when you declare the array. In that case you would use the following:

```
int myArray[] = { -200, -100, 0, 100, 200 };
```

This works because the compiler can figure out from the list of values being assigned how many elements are in the array and how much memory to allocate for the array.

Arrays can be multidimensional. To create a two-dimensional array of integers, you would use code like this:

```
int mdArray[3][5];
```

This allocates storage for 15 ints (a total of 60 bytes, if you're keeping score). You access elements of the array like you do with a simple array, with the obvious difference that you must supply two subscript operators:

```
int x = mdArray[1][1] + mdArray[2][1];
```

Figure 1.8 illustrates how a two-dimensional array might look in memory.

Figure 1.8.

A two-dimensional array in memory.

	mdArray[][0]	mdArray[][1]	mdArray[][2]	mdArray[][3]	mdArray[][4]
mdArray[0][]	baseAddr	baseAddr + 4	baseAddr + 8	baseAddr + 12	baseAddr + 16
mdArray[1][]	baseAddr + 20	baseAddr + 24	baseAddr + 28	baseAddr + 32	baseAddr + 36
mdArray[2][]	baseAddr + 40	baseAddr + 44	baseAddr + 48	baseAddr + 52	baseAddr + 56

WARNING

You must be careful not to overwrite the end of an array. One powerful feature of C++ is direct access to memory. Because of this feature, C++ will not prevent you from writing to a particular memory location, even if that location is memory your program isn't supposed to have access to. The following code is legal but will result in a crash in your program (or in Windows):

```
int array[5];
array[5] = 10;
```

This is a common error to make because of the fact that arrays are 0-based. You might think the last element of this array is 5 when it is really 4. If you overwrite the end of an array, you have no idea what memory you are overwriting. The results will be unpredictable at best. At worst, you will crash your program and maybe even crash Windows, too. This type of problem can be difficult to diagnose because often the affected memory is not accessed until much later, and the crash occurs at that time (leaving you wondering what happened). Be careful when writing to an array.

House Rules for Arrays

☐ Arrays are 0-based. The first element in the array is 0, the second element is 1, the third element is 2, and so on.

☐ Array sizes must be compile-time constants. The compiler must know at compile time how much space to allocate for the array. You cannot use a variable to assign an array size, so the following is not legal and will result in a compiler error:

```
int x = 10;
int myArray[x];   // compiler error here
```

☐ Be careful not to overwrite the end of an array.

☐ Allocate large arrays from the heap rather than from the stack. (You'll learn more on this later.)

☐ Arrays allocated from the heap *can* use a variable to assign the array size:

```
int x = 10;
int* myArray = new int[x];  // this is OK
```

Character Arrays

Odd as it might seem, there is no support in C++ for a *string* variable (a variable that holds text). Instead, strings in C++ programs are represented by arrays of the char data type. For instance, you could assign a string to a char array as follows:

```
char text[] = "This is a string.";
```

This allocates 18 bytes of storage in memory and stores the string in that memory location. Depending on how quick you are, you might have noticed that there are only 17 characters in this string. The reason that 18 bytes are allocated is that at the end of the string is a terminating null, and C++ accounts for the terminating null when allocating storage.

NEW TERM The *terminating null* is a special character that is represented with \0, which equates to a numerical 0.

When the program encounters a 0 in the character array, it interprets that location as the end of the string. To see how this is done, enter and run Listing 1.6 as a console application.

Listing 1.6. NULLTEST.CPP.

```
 1: #include <iostream.h>
 2: #include <conio.h>
 3: #pragma hdrstop
 4:
 5: int main(int argc, char **argv)
 6: {
 7:    char str[] = "This is a string.";
 8:    cout << str << endl;
 9:    str[7] = '\0';
10:    cout << str << endl;
11:    cout << endl << "Press any key to continue...";
12:    getch();
13:    return 0;
14: }
```

Figure 1.9 shows the output from the program in Listing 1.6.

Figure 1.9.

The output from
NULLTEST.EXE.

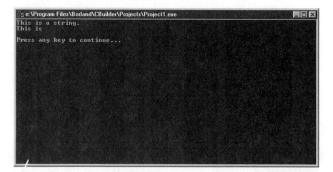

ANALYSIS Initially, the character array contains the characters This is a string. followed by the terminating null. That string is sent to the screen via cout. The next line assigns the seventh element of the array to \0, which is, of course, the terminating null. The string is again sent to the screen, but this time only This is is displayed. The reason for this is that

as far as the computer is concerned, the string ends at element 7 in the array. The rest of the characters are still in storage but can't be displayed because of the terminating null. Figure 1.10 illustrates how the character array looks before and after the line that changes element 7 to the terminating null.

Figure 1.10.

The contents of a character array.

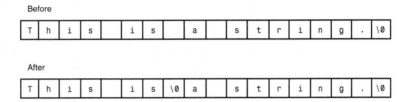

I could have simply assigned a **0** in place of '**\0**' in Listing 1.6. Either is acceptable because a numerical 0 and the char data type version, '**\0**', are equivalent. For example, the following two lines of code are equivalent:

```
str[7] = '\0';
str[7] = 0;
```

NOTE

> There is a difference between single and double quotes in a C++ program. When assigning the terminal null (or any other character value) to an element of an array, you must use single quotes. The single quotes effectively turn the character within the quotes into an integer value (the ASCII value of the character). This value is then stored in the memory location. When assigning strings to character arrays, you must use double quotes. If you get it wrong in either case, the compiler will let you know by issuing a compiler error.

String-Manipulation Functions

If you are coming from a programming language that has a string data type, all this might seem a pain. The truth is, it takes very little time to get used to. You're not completely on your own, by the way. To aid in string operations, the standard C library has several functions for string manipulation. Table 1.3 lists the most frequently used string-manipulation functions and a description of each. For a complete description of each of these functions and examples of their use, see the C++Builder online help.

Table 1.3. String-manipulation functions.

Function	Description
strcat()	*Concatenates* (adds) a string to the end of the target string
strcmp()	Compares two strings for equality
strcmpi()	Compares two strings for equality without case sensitivity
strcpy()	Copies the contents of one string to the target string
strstr()	Scans a string for the first occurrence of a substring
strlen()	Returns the length of the string
strupr()	Converts all characters in a string to uppercase
sprintf()	Builds a string based on a variable number of parameters

NOTE The string operations discussed here are how strings are handled in C. Most C++ compilers provide a cstring class that simplifies the difficulties inherent in the C way of handling strings. (C++Builder's Visual Component Library contains a class called AnsiString that handles string operations. Check the C++Builder online help for more information on AnsiString.) Although the C way of handling strings is a little quirky, it is by no means obsolete. C++ programmers use C-style string operations on a daily basis as well as string classes like cstring and AnsiString.

I won't go into examples of all the string-manipulation functions listed in the table, but I'll hit on a couple of the more widely used ones. The strcpy() function is used to copy one string to another. The source string can be a variable or a string literal. Take the following code, for example:

```
// set up a string to hold 29 characters
char buff[30];
// copy a string literal to the buffer
strcpy(buff, "This is a test.");
// display it
cout << buff << endl;
// initialize a second string buffer
char buff2[] = "A second string.";
// copy the contents of this string to the first buffer
strcpy(buff, buff2);
cout << buff << endl;
```

Accidentally overwriting the end of a character array is even easier to do than with the numeric arrays discussed earlier. For instance, imagine you had done the following:

```
char buff[10] = "A string";
// later....
strcpy(buff, "This is a test.");   // oops!
```

Here we set up a character array to hold 10 characters and initially assigned a string that requires 9 bytes (don't forget about the terminating null). Later on, possibly forgetting how large the array was, we copied a string to the buffer that requires 16 bytes, overwriting the array by 6 bytes. Six bytes of some memory location somewhere were just erased by our little mistake. Be careful when copying data to character arrays.

Another frequently used string function is sprintf(). This function enables you to build a formatted string by mixing text and numbers together. Here is an example that adds two numbers and then uses sprintf() to build a string to report the result:

```
char buff[20];
int x = 10 * 20;
sprintf(buff, "The result is: %d", x);
cout << buff;
```

When this section of code executes, the program will display this:

```
The result is: 200
```

In this example, the %d tells the sprintf() function, "An integer value will go here." At the end of the format string the variable x is inserted to tell sprintf() what value to put at that location in the string (the contents of the variable x). sprintf() is a unique function in that it can take a variable number of arguments. You must supply the destination buffer and the format string, but the number of arguments that come after the format string is variable. Here is an example of sprintf() that uses three additional arguments:

```
int x = 20;
int y = 5;
sprintf(buff, "%d + %d = %d", x, y, x + y);
cout << buff;
```

When this piece of code executes, the result displayed on the screen will be this:

```
20 + 5 = 25
```

NOTE

The single slash is used in strings to indicate special characters in C++ strings. For example '\n' is for a new line, and '\t' represents a tab character. To put an actual backslash character into a string, you must use a double backslash:

```
strcpy(fileName, "c:\\windows\\system\\win.ini");
```

> Forgetting this simple fact has caused many programmers sleepless nights trying to find a bug in their program. This is a very common mistake to make. Don't say I didn't tell you!

`sprintf()` has a cousin called `wsprintf()` that is a Windows version of `sprintf()`. You might see either of these two functions used in Windows programs. `wsprintf()` is functionally the same as `sprintf()`, with one major difference: It does not enable you to put floating-point numbers in the formatted string. You can use either function in your C++Builder programs, but `sprintf()` is preferred because it has full floating-point support (and it's one less character to type!). To get a real appreciation of what `sprintf()` can do for you, consult the C++Builder online help.

Arrays of Strings

Not only can you have character arrays, but also you can have an array of character arrays (effectively, an array of strings). That might sound complicated, but you have already seen this type of array in the ARGSTEST program earlier. You can allocate this kind of array as follows:

```
char strings[][20] = {
  "This is string 1",
  "This is string 2",
  "This is string 3",
  "This is string 4"
};
```

This code creates an array of four strings, each of which can contain up to 19 characters. Although you can use this type of string array, there are easier ways to handle arrays of strings in C++Builder. (I'll save that discussion for later, after you've had a chance to learn more about C++Builder.)

NOTE

If you are going to use arrays of strings extensively, you should look into the Standard Template Library (STL). STL provides C++ classes that enable you to store and manipulate arrays of strings much more easily than is possible using C-style character arrays. STL also includes a `string` class.

Summary

You've covered a lot of ground today. First you got to tinker with the C++Builder IDE by creating a GUI Hello World program. Following that, you were introduced to console-mode

applications, where you created `Hello World`, II. After the initial playing around, you were put to work learning the basics of C as a foundation for learning C++. You have learned about the following C and C++ features:

- [ ] Variables
- [ ] Operators
- [ ] Data types
- [ ] Functions
- [ ] The `main()` function
- [ ] Arrays
- [ ] How strings are handled in C and C++

There is a lot of material to absorb in this chapter. Don't feel bad if you can't remember it all. Go back and review if you are unclear about anything presented today.

Workshop

The Workshop contains quiz questions to help you solidify your understanding of the material covered and exercises to provide you with experience in using what you have learned. You can find answers to the quiz questions in Appendix A, "Answers to Quiz Questions."

Q&A

Q What's the difference between a Win32 GUI application and a Win32 console-mode application?

A A GUI application is a traditional Windows program. It usually has a title bar, menu, and window area. A console-mode application is a 32-bit application that runs in an MS-DOS box in Windows. The console application looks like a DOS program.

Q Do my functions have to take parameters and return values?

A Functions you write can take parameters and can return a value, but they are not required to do either. After a function has been written to return a value, you must provide a return statement that returns a value, or the compiler will issue a warning.

Q Can I assign a number containing decimal places to an integer data type variable?

A Yes, but the decimal fraction will be dropped (not rounded), and only the whole number portion will be assigned to the integer variable.

Q Will C++ make sure I don't overwrite memory somewhere if I accidentally write past the end of an array?

A No. One of the strengths of C++ is that it gives you the power to access memory directly. With that power comes responsibility. It's up to you, the programmer, to be sure that the memory you are accessing is memory that your program owns. If you accidentally overwrite memory that you are not supposed to have access to, Windows will issue an access-violation error. The access violation might come immediately, or it might not come until later when the overwritten memory is used by another part of your program, by another program, or by Windows itself.

Quiz

1. What is wrong with this program?

```
#include <iostream.h>
#include <conio.h>
#pragma hdrstop

void displayText();
displayText()
{
cout << "Hello Bubba!" << endl;
}
```

2. How many return values can a function return?

3. What does the strcpy() function do?

4. What value does a variable have when it is initially declared?

5. How many functions can a program have?

6. Can a function call another function?

7. What is wrong with this program?

```
#include <iostream.h>
#include <conio.h>
#pragma hdrstop

int main(int argc, char** argv)
{
doSomething();
return 0;
}

void doSomething()
{
cout << "I'm doing something now" << endl;
}
```

8. How many functions called main() can a program have?

9. Look at this line of code:

```
char buff[20];
```

How many characters can this string hold?

10. What is the index number of the first element of an array, 0 or 1?

Exercises

1. Write a Windows GUI program that displays the words Welcome to C++Builder! on the window when the program runs.

2. Rewrite the program you wrote in Exercise 1 and change the displayed text to Hello There!. (Hint: You only have to change the Caption property of the Label component.)

3. Write a Windows console-mode application that outputs This is a test to the screen.

4. Write a Windows console-mode application. In the program, declare two variables and assign values to those variables. Multiply the two numbers together and display the result on the screen.

5. Write a console-mode application that calls a function to display Function entered, sir!! on the screen.

6. Write a console-mode application that takes an integer as a parameter, multiplies it by itself, and returns the result.

7. Enter and compile the following program. What does the program do?

```
#include <iostream.h>
#include <conio.h>
#include <math.h>
#include <stdio.h>
#pragma hdrstop

void getSqrRoot(char* buff, int x);

int main(int argc, char** argv)
{
  int x;
  char buff[30];
  cout << "Enter a number: ";
  cin >> x;
  getSqrRoot(buff, x);
  cout << buff;
  getch();
}

void getSqrRoot(char* buff, int x)
{
  sprintf(buff, "The square root is: %f", sqrt(x));
}
```

Day 2

C++ Fundamentals

You now have a good start on learning C++. In this chapter, you will continue to learn about the C++ language by examining more of the fundamentals of C++ that have their roots in C. Today you will learn about

☐ The `if` and `else` keywords

☐ Loops: `for`, `do`, and `do-while`

☐ The `switch` statement

☐ Scope

☐ Structures

If...

There are some aspects of programming that are common to all programming languages. One such item that C++ has in common with other programming languages is the `if` statement. The `if` statement is used to test for a condition and then execute sections of code based on whether that condition is `true` or `false`. Here's an example:

```
int x;
cout << "Enter a number: ";
cin >> x;
if (x > 10)
  cout << "You entered a number greater than 10." << endl;
```

This code asks for input from the user. If the user enters a number greater than 10, the expression x > 10 evaluates to `true` and the message is displayed; otherwise, nothing is displayed. Note that when the conditional expression evaluates to `true`, the statement immediately following the `if` expression is executed.

 New Term The `if` statement is used to test for a condition and execute one or more lines of code when that condition evaluates to `true`.

Note

Be sure not to follow the `if` expression with a semicolon. A semicolon by itself represents a blank statement in code. If you accidentally follow your `if` expression with a semicolon, the compiler will interpret the blank statement as the statement to execute when the expression evaluates to `true`.

```
if (x == 10);          // Warning! Extra semi-colon!
  DoSomething(x);
```

In this case, the `DoSomething()` function will always be executed because the compiler does not see it as being the first statement following the `if` expression. Because this code is perfectly legal (albeit useless), the compiler will not warn you that anything is amiss.

Let's say you have multiple lines of code that should be executed when the conditional expression is `true`. In that case you would need braces to block those lines:

```
if (x > 10) {
  cout << "The number is greater than 10" << endl;
  DoSomethingWithNumber(x);
}
```

When the conditional expression evaluates to `false`, the code block associated with the `if` expression is ignored, and program execution continues with the first statement following the code block.

C++ contains a lot of shortcuts. One of those shortcuts involves using just the variable name to test for true. Look at this code:

```
if (fileGood) ReadData();
```

This method is shortcut for the longer form, which is illustrated with this line:

```
if (fileGood == true) ReadData();
```

This example uses a bool variable, but any data type will do. The expression evaluates to true as long as the variable contains any non-zero value. You can test for false by applying the logical NOT (!) operator to a variable name:

```
bool fileGood = OpenSomeFile();
if (!fileGood) ReportError();
```

Learning the C++ shortcuts helps you write code that contains a degree of elegance. Knowing the shortcuts will also help you understand C++ code that you read in examples and sample listings.

In some cases, you want to perform an action when the conditional expression evaluates to true and perform some other action when the conditional expression evaluates to false. In this case you can implement the else statement:

```
if (x == 20) {
  DoSomething(x);
}
else {
  DoADifferentThing(x);
}
```

NEW TERM The else statement is used in conjunction with the if statement and identifies sections of code that are executed when the if statement fails (that is, evaluates to false).

In this example, one of the two functions will be called based on the value of x, but not both.

WARNING Note that the equality operator is the double equal sign (==) and that the assignment operator is the single equal sign (=). A common coding mistake is to use the assignment operator where you meant to use the equality operator. For instance, if the previous example were inadvertently written like this:

```
if (x = 20) {
   DoSomething(x);
}
```

x would be assigned the value of 20. Because this operation would be successful, the expression would evaluate to true. A bug like this, although seemingly obvious, can be hard to spot. Fortunately, the compiler will issue a warning that says Possibly incorrect assignment to alert you to the potential problem.

You can nest if statements when needed. *Nesting* is nothing more than following an if statement with one or more additional if statements.

```
if (x > 10)
   if (x < 20)
      cout << "X is between 10 and 20" << endl;
```

Keep in mind that these are simplified examples. In the real world you can get lost in the maze of braces that separate one function block from the next. Take a look at this code snippet, for instance:

```
if (x > 100) {
   y = 20;
   if (x > 200) {
      y = 40;
      if (x > 400) {
         y = 60;
         DoSomething(y);
      }
   }
}
else if (x < -100) {
   y = -20;
   if (x < -200) {
      y = -40;
      if (x < -400) {
         y = -60;
         DoSomething(y);
      }
   }
}
```

Even this is a fairly simple example, but you get the idea.

TIP   If you are using the IDE Default keymapping, the C++Builder Code Editor has a handy function to help you find matching braces. Position the cursor on the brace for which you want to find the corresponding brace. Press either the Alt+[or the Alt+] key combination, and the cursor will be positioned at the brace you are looking for. It doesn't matter whether you start on the opening brace or the closing brace. In either case the matching brace will be located.

 TIP   When a section of code contains more than two or three consecutive if statements testing for different values of the same variable, it might be a candidate for a switch statement. The switch statement is discussed later in this chapter in the section "The switch Statement."

Earlier I mentioned C++ shortcuts. There is a shortcut for the if/else combination. Look at the following code:

```
if (direction == EAST) lost = true;
else (lost = false);
```

These two lines can be condensed into a single line:

```
direction == EAST ? lost = true : lost = false;
```

Although this shortcut notation might look a little odd at first, you will quickly learn to recognize it when you see it. I tend not to use this particular syntax because it is somewhat cryptic and reduces readability of the code.

The if statement is heavily used in C++. It's straightforward, so you won't have any trouble with it. The main thing is keeping all the braces straight.

The if statement, Form 1:

SYNTAX

```
if (cond_expr) {
    true_statements;
    }
else {
    false_statements;
    }
```

If the conditional expression, cond_expr, is true (non-zero), the block of code represented by true_statements is executed. If the optional else clause is specified, the block of code represented by false_statements is executed when the conditional expression, cond_expr, is

 false.

The if statement, Form 2:

```
if (cond_expr_1) {
    true_statements_1;
    }
else if (cond_expr_2) {
    true_statements_2;
    }
else {
    false_statements;
    }
```

If the conditional expression *cond_expr_1* is true (non-zero), the block of code represented by *true_statements_1* is executed. If it is false and the conditional expression *cond_expr_2* is true, the block of code represented by *true_statements_2* is executed. If both *cond_expr_1* and *cond_expr_2* are false, the block of code represented by *false_statements* is executed.

Using Loops

The loop is a common element in all programming languages. A loop can be used to iterate through an array, to perform an action a specific number of times, to read a file from disk...the possibilities are endless. In this section I will discuss the for loop, the while loop, and the do-while loop. For the most part they work in very similar ways. All loops have these common elements:

- ☐ A starting point
- ☐ A body, usually enclosed in braces, that contains the statements to execute on each pass
- ☐ An ending point
- ☐ A test for a condition that determines when the loop should end
- ☐ Optional use of the break and continue statements

NEW TERM   A *loop* is an element in a programming language that is used to perform an action repeatedly until a specific condition is met.

The starting point for the loop is one of the C++ loop statements (for, while, or do) followed by an opening brace. The body contains the statements that will execute each time through the loop. The body can contain any valid C++ code. The ending point for the loop is the closing brace. (When the body of a loop is a single line of code, the opening and closing braces are not required.)

Most loops work something like this: The loop is entered and the test condition is evaluated. If the test condition evaluates to false, the body of the loop is executed. When program execution reaches the bottom of the loop (usually the closing brace), it jumps back to the top of the loop where the test condition is again evaluated. If the test condition is still `false`, the whole process is repeated. If the test condition is `true`, program execution jumps to the line of code immediately following the loop code block. The exception to this description is the `do-while` loop, which tests for the condition at the bottom of the loop rather than at the top.

The test condition tells the loop when to stop executing. In effect the test condition says, for example, "Keep doing this until x is equal to 10," or "Keep reading the file until the end-of-file is reached." After the loop starts, it continues to execute the body of the loop until the test condition evaluates to `true`.

WARNING

It's easy to accidentally write a loop so that the test condition never evaluates to `true`. This will result in a program that is locked up or hung. Your only recourse at that point is to press Ctrl+Alt+Del and kill the task. The Windows Close Program box (or the Windows NT Task Manager) will come up and will display the name of your program with `(Not Responding)` next to it. You'll have to select your program from the list and click End Task to terminate the runaway program.

TIP

In C++Builder you typically run a program by using the Run button on the toolbar or by pressing F9. If you need to kill a runaway program that was run from the IDE, you can choose Run | Program Reset from the main menu or press Ctrl+F2 on the keyboard.

Given that general overview, let's take a look at each type of loop individually.

The `for` Loop

The `for` loop is probably the most commonly used type of loop. It takes three parameters: the starting number, the test condition that determines when the loop stops, and the increment expression.

The `for` loop statement:

SYNTAX

```
for (initial; cond_expr; adjust) {
    statements;
    }
```

The `for` loop repeatedly executes the block of code indicated by `statements` as long as the conditional expression, `cond_expr`, is true (non-zero). The state of the loop is initialized by the statement `initial`. After the execution of `statements`, the state is modified using the statement indicated by `adjust`.

That won't make much sense until you see some examples. First take a look at a typical `for` loop:

```
for (int i=0;i<10;i++) {
  cout << "This is iteration " << i << endl;
}
```

This code will result in the statement inside the braces being executed 10 times. The first parameter, `int i=0`, tells the `for` loop that it is starting with an initial value of `0`. (In this case I am declaring and assigning a variable, `i`, inside the `for` statement. This is perfectly legal and is common in `for` loops.) The second parameter, `i<10`, tells the loop to keep running as long as the variable `i` is less than `10`. Because I'm starting with `0`, I need to stop *before* `i` is equal to `10` in order to end up with 10 iterations. The last parameter, `i++`, increments the variable `i` by one each time through the loop.

NOTE The use of the variable name `i` has its roots in the FORTRAN language and is traditional in `for` loops. Naturally, any variable name can be used, but you will often see `i` used in `for` loops.

Let's look at a variation of this code. The following code snippet will achieve exactly the opposite effect as the first example:

```
for (int i=10;i>0;i--) {
  cout << "This is iteration " << i << endl;
}
```

This time I'm starting with `10`, stopping after `i` is equal to `1`, and decrementing `i` by one on each pass. This is an example of a loop that counts backward.

NOTE In the previous examples, the opening and closing braces are not strictly required. If no opening and closing braces are supplied, the statement immediately following the `for` statement is considered the body of the loop. It's not a bad idea to include the braces for clarity and readability even when they aren't strictly required.

Let's write a little program that illustrates the use of the `for` loop. You can enter, compile, and run the program found in Listing 2.1. The output from `FORLOOP.CPP` is shown in Figure 2.1.

Figure 2.1.

The output from
FORLOOP.EXE.

Listing 2.1. FORLOOP.CPP.

```
 1: #include <iostream.h>
 2: #include <conio.h>
 3: #pragma hdrstop
 4:
 5: int main(int argv, char** argc)
 6: {
 7:   cout << endl << "Starting program..." << endl << endl;
 8:   int i;
 9:   for (i=0;i<10;i++) {
10:     cout << "Iteration number " << i << endl;
11:   }
12:   cout << endl;
13:   for (i=10;i>0;i--) {
14:     cout << "Iteration number " << i << endl;
15:   }
16:   getch();
17:   return 0;
18: }
```

By now you know that the loop starting number can be any value you like (assuming it fits the range of the data type selected, of course). The test condition can be any C++ expression that eventually evaluates to true. The test value can be a numeric constant, as used in the examples here, a variable, or the return value of a function call. The following are examples of valid test conditions:

```
for (int i=0;i < 100;i++) {...}
for (int i=1;i == numberOfElements;i++) {...}
for (int i=0;i <= GetNumberOfElements();i+=2) {...}
```

Take a closer look at the last example. Notice the last parameter of the for statement. In this case I am incrementing the counter by 2 each time through the loop. The increment parameter can increment by any amount you want. For instance, this loop counts by tens:

```
for (int i=0;i<100;i+=10) {...}
```

Now that you've seen the `for` loop in action, it won't be too difficult to apply the same concepts to the `while` and `do-while` loops. Let's take a look at those now.

The `while` Loop

The `while` loop differs from the `for` loop in that it contains only a test condition that is checked at the start of each iteration. As long as the test condition is `true`, the loop keeps running.

```
int x;
while (x < 1000) {
  x = DoSomeCalculation();
}
```

In this example, I am calling a function that I assume will eventually return a value of greater than or equal to 1,000. As long as the return value from this function is less than 1,000, the `while` loop continues to run. When the variable x contains a value greater than or equal to 1,000, the test condition yields `false`, and program execution jumps to the first line following the `while` loop's ending brace. A common implementation of a `while` loop uses a `bool` as a test variable. The state of the test variable can be set somewhere within the body of the loop:

```
bool done = false;
while (!done) {
  // some code here
  done = SomeFunctionReturningABool();
  // more code
}
```

At some point, it is expected that the variable `done` will be `true` and the loop will terminate. The program in Listing 2.2 illustrates the use of the `while` loop.

Listing 2.2. WHILETST.CPP.

```
 1: #include <iostream.h>
 2: #include <conio.h>
 3: #pragma hdrstop
 4: int main(int argv, char** argc)
 5: {
 6:   cout << endl << "Starting program..." << endl << endl;
 7:   int i = 6;
 8:   while (i-- > 0) {
 9:     cout << endl << "Today I have " << i;
10:     cout << " problems to worry about.";
11:   }
12:   cout << "\b!\nYipee!";
13:   cout << endl << endl << "Press any key to continue...";
14:   getch();
15:   return 0;
16: }
```

2

SYNTAX

The while loop statement:

```
while (cond_expr) {
    statements;
    }
```

The while loop repeatedly executes the block of code indicated by *statements* as long as the conditional expression, *cond_expr*, is true (non-zero). The state of the loop must be initialized prior to the while statement, and modification of the state must be explicit in the block of code. When the conditional expression, *cond_expr*, evaluates to false, the loop terminates.

2

NOTE

> Due to the way the do-while loop works, the code in the body of the loop will be executed at least once, regardless of the value of the test condition (since the condition is evaluated at the bottom of the loop). In the case of the while loop, the test condition is evaluated at the top of the loop so the body of the loop might never be executed.

The do-while **Loop**

The do-while loop is nearly identical to the while loop. The distinction between the two is important, though. As you can see from Listing 2.2, the while loop checks the conditional expression at the top of the loop. In the case of the do-while loop, the conditional expression is checked at the bottom of the loop:

```
bool done = false;
do {
  // some code
  done = SomeFunctionReturningABool();
  // more code
} while (!done);
```

Whether you use a while or a do-while loop depends on what the loop itself does.

SYNTAX

The do-while loop statement:

```
do {
    statements;
    } while (cond_expr);
```

The do loop repeatedly executes the block of code indicated by *statements* as long as the conditional expression, *cond_expr*, is true (non-zero). The state of the loop must be initialized prior to the do statement, and modification of the state must be explicit in the block of code. When the conditional expression, *cond_expr*, evaluates to false, the loop terminates.

goto

I'll mention goto just so you know it exists. The goto statement enables you to jump program execution to a label that you have previously declared by using a term followed by a colon. The following code snippet illustrates this:

```
bool done = false;
startPoint:
// do some stuff
if (!done) goto(startPoint);
// loop over, moving on...
```

It is not necessary to use braces here because all lines of code between the goto statement and the label will be executed.

NOTE

> The goto statement is considered bad form in a C++ program. Just about anything you can accomplish with goto you can accomplish with a while or do-while loop. Very few self-respecting C++ programmers have goto in their code. If you are moving to C++ from another language that uses goto statements, you will find that the basic structure of C++ makes the goto statement unnecessary.

The goto statement:

```
goto label
    .
    .
    .
label:
```

The goto statement unconditionally transfers the program execution sequence to the label represented by label.

continue **and** break

Before we leave this discussion of loops, you need to know about two keywords that help control program execution in a loop. The continue statement is used to force program execution to the bottom of the loop, skipping any statements that come after the continue statement. For example, you might have part of a loop that you don't want to execute if a particular test returns true. In that case you would use continue to avoid execution of any code below the continue statement:

```
bool done = false;
while (!done) {
  // some code
  bool error = SomeFunction();
```

```
  if (error) continue;  // jumps to the top of the loop
  // other code that will execute only if no error occurred
}
```

The break statement is used to halt execution of a loop prior to the loop's normal test condition being met. For example, you might be searching an array of ints for a particular number. By breaking execution of your search loop when the number is found, you can obtain the array index where the number was located:

```
int index = -1;
int searchNumber = 50;
for (int i=0;i<numElements;i++) {
  if (myArray[i] == searchNumber) {
    index = i;
    break;
  }
}
if (index != -1)
  cout << "Number found at index " << index << endl;
else
  cout << "Number not found in array." << endl;
```

There are many situations in which the continue and break statements are useful. As with most of what I've been talking about, it will take some experience programming in C++ before you discover all the possible uses for continue and break.

The switch Statement

The switch statement could be considered a glorified if statement. It enables you to execute one of several code blocks based on the result of an expression. The expression might be a variable, the result of a function call, or any valid C++ expression that evaluates to an expression. Here is an example of a switch statement:

```
switch(amountOverSpeedLimit) {
  case 0  : {
    fine = 0;
    break;
  }
  case 10 : {
    fine = 20;
    break;
  }
  case 15 : {
    fine = 50;
    break;
  }
  case 20 :
  case 25 :
  case 30 : {
    fine = amountOverSpeedLimit * 10;
```

```
      break;
  }
  default : {
    fine = GoToCourt();
    jailTime = GetSentence();
  }
}
```

There are several parts that make up a switch statement. First, you can see that there is the expression, which in this example is the variable amountOverSpeedLimit (remember, I warned you about long variable names!). Next, the case statements test the expression for equality. If amountOverSpeedLimit equals 0 (case 0 :), the value 0 is assigned to the variable fine. If amountOverSpeedLimit is equal to 10, a value of 20 is assigned to fine, and so on. In each of the first three cases, you see a break statement. The break statement is used to jump out of the switch block—it means that a case matching the expression has been found and the rest of the switch statement can be ignored. Finally, you see the default statement. The code block following the default statement will be executed if no matching cases are found.

Notice that cases 20 and 25 have no statements following them. If the expression amountOverSpeedLimit evaluates to 20 or 25, those cases fall through and the next code block encountered will be executed. In this situation, values of 20, 25, or 30 will all result in the same code being executed.

WARNING

Don't forget your break statements! Without break statements the switch will continue on even after finding a match and might execute code you didn't intend to be executed. Sometimes that is how you want your switch to perform, but most of the time it is not.

Inclusion of the default statement is not mandatory. You could write a switch without a default statement:

```
switch (x) {
  case 10 : DoSomething(); break;
  case 20 : DoAnotherThing(); break;
  case 30 : TakeABreak();
}
```

Note that there is no break statement following the last case statement. Because this is the last line of the switch, there is no point in including the break statement for this line.

As I said earlier, you might want to use a switch if you find that you have several if statements back to back. The switch is a bit clearer to others reading your program.

2

NOTE

> You can only use the numeric C++ data types in the expression portion
> of a switch statement. The following, for example, is not allowed:
>
> ```
> switch (someStringVariable) {
>   case "One" : // code
>   case "Two" : // code
> }
> ```

2

SYNTAX

The switch statement:

```
switch (expr) {
    case value_1:
        statements_1;
        break;
    case value_2:
        statements_2;
        break;

        .
        .
        .

    case value_n:
        statements_n;
        break;
    default:
        dflt_statements;
}
```

The switch statement offers a way to execute different blocks of code, depending on various
values of an expression (*expr*). The block of code represented by *statements_1* is executed
when *expr* is equal to *value_1*, the block of code represented by *statements_2* when *expr* is
equal to *value_2*, and so on through the block of code represented by *statements_n* when
expr is equal to *value_n*. When *expr* is not equal to any of the *value_1* through *value_n*, the
block of code at *dflt_statements* is executed. The break statements are optional.

Scope

 NEW TERM
The term *scope* refers to the visibility of variables within different parts of
your program. Most variables have *local scope*. This means that the variable is visible
only within the code block in which it is declared. Take a look at the program in
Listing 2.3.

Listing 2.3. SCOPE.CPP.

```
 1: #include <iostream.h>
 2: #include <conio.h>
 3: #pragma hdrstop
 4: int x = 20;
 5: void CountLoops(int);
 6: int main(int, char**)
 7: {
 8:   int x = 40;
 9:   int i = 0;
10:   cout << "In main program x = " << x << endl;
11:   bool done = false;
12:   while (!done) {
13:     int x;
14:     cout << endl << "Enter a number (-1 to exit): ";
15:     cin >> x;
16:     if (x != -1) {
17:       cout << endl << "In while loop x = " << x;
18:       CountLoops(++i);
19:     }
20:     else
21:       done = true;
22:   }
23:   cout << "Global x = " << ::x << endl;
24:   cout << endl << "Press any key to continue...";
25:   getch();
26:   return 0;
27: }
28: void CountLoops(int x)
29: {
30:   cout << ", While loop has executed "
31:     << x << " times" << endl;
32: }
```

The first thing you might notice (if you're still awake by this time) is that the variable x is declared four times. It is declared on line 4 outside the main() function, on line 8 inside the main() function, on line 13 inside the while loop, and in the CountLoops() function on line 28. If you accidentally declare a variable more than once, the compiler spits out an error that says Multiple declaration for 'x', and the compile stops. Yet this program compiles and runs just fine. Why? Because each of the x variables in Listing 2.3 is in a different scope.

Take a closer look at Listing 2.3. The declaration for x on line 13 is inside the body of the while loop and is local to that block of code. Effectively, it does not exist outside that block. This variable has local scope. Likewise, the declaration for x on line 28 is local to the CountLoops() function and does not exist outside the function. In this case, the declaration for x is less obvious because it's part of the function's parameter list, but it's a variable declaration nonetheless.

2

Now look at the variables x and i declared inside the main() function. These variables are local to the code block in which they are declared, *plus* they are available (in scope) in any code blocks within the code block in which they are declared. In other words, the x and i variables are in scope both in the main() function *and* inside the while loop. That's easy enough to figure out in the case of i because there is only one variable named i. But what about x? Once inside the while loop, there are two variables named x (the one declared in main() and the one declared in the while loop), and both are in scope. Which one is being used? The answer: the one within the while loop, because it has the most immediate scope.

NOTE

A recent ANSI C++ draft rule change affects the visibility of a variable that is declared inside a statement like a for statement. (The C++ draft is a document that the C++ standards committee issues. It defines the rules for the C++ language.) For example, the following code generates a compiler error:

```
for (int i=0;i<10;i++) {
   if (array[i] == 40) break;
}
index = i;
```

This code generates a compiler error because the variable i is visible only inside the for loop code block. To get this code to compile, you would have to declare i outside the for statement:

```
int i;
for (i=0;i<10;i++) {
   if (array[i] == 40) break;
}
index = i;
```

Although this change won't affect you if you are just learning C++, it confused many long-time C++ programmers when it was first implemented. In the end, it doesn't really matter which form is the standard as long as we as programmers know what the rules are.

Finally, we get to the declaration of the x that falls outside the main() function (line 4). Because this variable is declared outside any function, it is called a *global variable* and is said to have *global scope.* What this means is that the global variable x is available anywhere in the program: inside the main() function, inside the while block, and inside the CountLoops() function.

As mentioned earlier, a local variable has precedence over a global variable. But what if you want to access the global variable x from inside the `main()` function? You use the *scope-resolution operator*, `::`. Line 23 of Listing 2.3 contains this line:

```
cout << "Global x = " << ::x << endl;
```

The scope-resolution operator tells the compiler, "Give me the global variable x and not the local variable x." (The scope-resolution operator is also used with classes, but I'll get to that when I talk about classes later.)

`extern` **Variables**

A real-world application usually has several source files containing the program's code. (The terms *module*, *source file*, and *unit* can be used interchangeably. I'll talk about programs using multiple source files in just a bit.) A global variable declared in one source file is global to that file but is not visible in any other modules. (It could be argued that this is not a global variable but rather a variable with *file scope*. Although that might be technically correct, the term *global* is widely used in the former manner, and I'll use it this way as well.) There are times, however, when you need to make a variable visible to all modules in your program. Doing this is a two-step process. First, declare the variable in one source file as you would any global variable. Then, in any other source file that needs to access the global variable, you declare the variable again, this time with the `extern` keyword:

```
extern int countChickens;
```

The `extern` keyword tells the compiler, "This source file uses a variable that you will find declared in another source file." The compiler sorts it all out at compile time and makes sure you get access to the correct variable.

Although global variables are convenient, they aren't particularly OOP-friendly. Usually there are better solutions (that you will learn about when I discuss classes on Day 4, "C++ Classes and Object-Oriented Programming"). In addition, global variables consume memory for the life of the program. Local variables only use memory while they are in scope. Use local variables whenever possible, and keep the use of global variables to a minimum.

Structures

A *structure* is a collection of related data rolled up into a single storage unit. For instance, let's say you want to keep a mailing list. It would be convenient to use a single data variable to hold all the fields needed in a typical mailing list. A structure enables you to do that. You first declare the structure and then later create an instance of that structure when you want to use the structure. A structure is declared with the `struct` keyword:

```
struct mailingListRecord {
  char firstName[20];
  char lastName[20];
  char address[50];
  char city[20];
  char state[4];
  int zip;
  bool aFriend;
  bool aFoe;
};
```

Each of the elements in a structure is called a *data member.* Notice that each of the data members must be declared just as if it were a variable in a code block. This example has five char arrays, one int, and two bool data members. (My apologies to my friends around the world if this looks like a U.S.-slanted mailing-list record.) Finally, make note of the semicolon following the closing brace of the structure declaration. This is a requirement for structure and class declarations.

NEW TERM   A *structure* is a collection of related data identified as a single storage unit. After a structure is declared, an instance of that structure can be created for use. Each of the elements in a structure is called a *data member.*

NOTE   You can create instances of a structure when you declare the structure. At the end of the structure declaration, insert a variable name (one or more) between the closing brace and the semicolon that follows the structure declaration—for example,

```
struct point {
  int x;
  int y;
} upperLeft, lowerRight;
```

This code declares the structure and creates two instances of the structure with variable names of upperLeft and lowerRight.

Now that the structure is declared, it can be put to use. I first need to create an instance of the structure. Here's how that looks:

```
mailingListReocrd record;
```

This statement allocates memory for the structure (120 bytes, give or take) and assigns that memory to a variable named record. Now that I have an instance of the structure set up, I can assign values to the data members:

```
strcpy(record.firstName, "Bruce");
strcpy(record.lastName, "Reisdorph");
strcpy(record.address, "123 Inspiration Pt.");
```

```
strcpy(record.city, "Merced");
strcpy(record.state, "CA");
record.zip = 95031;
record.aFriend = true;
record.aFoe = false;
```

This code snippet contains some syntax you haven't seen yet. To access the data members of a structure, you need to employ the *structure member operator*, which is a period placed between the variable name and the data member. (If you forget to add the structure member operator, you will probably have the compiler whining about undefined symbols.) The structure member operator enables you to access a particular member of the structure—either to read the value of the data member or to change the value of the data member.

If you want to, you can instantiate an object and supply its members all at once:

```
mailingListRecord record = {
    "Bruce",
    "Reisdorph",
    "123 Inspiration Pt.",
    "Merced",
    "CA",
    95031,
    true,
    false
};
```

This saves you some typing over the first method I showed you but is not always practical in real-world situations. In a real-world application, a structure would likely be filled out as a result of user input or possibly with data read from a file. Assigning data to the structure as you see here is not practical in those situations.

The struct statement:

```
struct name {
    data_member_1;
    data_member_2;
        .
        .
        .
    data_member_n;
    } instance;
```

The struct statement declares a grouping of data members (*data_member_1*, *data_member_2*, ..., *data_member_n*) and provides a name for this grouping (*name*). The optional *instance* statement creates an occurrence of this grouping.

Arrays of Structures

Just as you can have arrays of ints, chars, or longs, you can also have arrays of structures. Declaring and using an array of structures is not terribly complicated:

```
mailingListRecord listArray[5];
strcpy(listArray[0].firstName, "Chuck");
listArray[4].aFriend = false;   // grrrrr!!
// etc.
```

This is only slightly more complicated than using an array of one of the integral data types. You will notice that the subscript operator and the structure member operator are used together.

Headers and Source Files

The *source file* is an ASCII text file that contains the program's source code. The compiler takes the source code file, parses it, and produces machine language that the computer can execute.

One of the problems with books on programming is that they use simple examples to communicate concepts and ideas. You will undoubtedly find that in the real world things are never that simple. So far, we have been dealing with very short programs contained in a single source file. In practice, a program of any consequence has several source files. A program's code is divided up into different source files for a number of reasons. One of the primary reasons is that of organization. By keeping related chunks of code together, you can more easily find a certain section of code when needed.

So how do all the source files get tied together? First, the compiler compiles each source file (.cpp) into an object file (.obj). After each module has been compiled, the linker links all the object files together to make a single executable file (the .exe). The linker also can link in other needed files such as resource files (.res) and library files (.lib).

NEW TERM The declarations for classes and structures are often kept in a separate file called a *header file*. Headers have a filename extension of .h or .hpp. (I touched on headers briefly when I discussed the iostream class in Day 1, "Getting Started with C++Builder.") A header file should contain only class, structure, and function declarations. You should never put any code statements in a header.

NOTE
There is an exception to the rule that no code should be placed in headers. You can put *inline functions* in headers. An inline function is a special function in terms of the way the compiler generates code for the function. You'll learn more about inline functions on Day 4 when I discuss classes.

Use the Object Repository to create a header file from scratch. First, choose File | New from the main menu. When the Object Repository comes up, double-click on the Text icon.

C++Builder will create a new text file and display it in the Code Editor. Enter the code for your header and then save the file with an `.h` extension.

After you have created a header file for a class or structure, you can include that header in any source code module that needs to see the class or structure declaration. To do that, you use the `#include` directive:

```
#include "structur.h"
```

When you use the `#include` directive, it is as if the contents of the file being included are pasted into the source file at that point. Listing 2.4, in the next section, contains a program that uses the `#include` directive. The header file used in Listing 2.4 is contained in Listing 2.5.

TIP

Header files typically implement a *sentry* to ensure that the header is only included once for a program. A sentry essentially tells the compiler, "I've already been included once, so don't include me again." A sentry looks like this:

```
#ifndef _MYCLASS_H
#define _MYCLASS_H
class MyClass {
   // class declared here
};
#endif
```

C++Builder automatically adds sentries to units that are generated when you create a new form or component. For headers you create from scratch, you need to add the sentry code yourself.

A header file can contain more than one class or structure declaration. Using a separate header for each class or structure helps keep your project organized and makes it easier to reuse classes and structures in other programs. Sometimes you will group related classes together in one header. For instance, you can have a class that implements a helper class to carry out its duties. In that case, both the main class and the helper class would be declared in the same header. Ultimately, it's up to you how you organize your headers.

Don't be too concerned if this is a little confusing right now. It will probably take some experience writing real programs for all this to come together for you.

An Example Using Structures

Listing 2.4 contains a program that has the user input three names and addresses and stores those records in an array of structures. After the names are input, they are displayed on the screen. The user is then asked to choose one of the records. When the user chooses one of the records, it is displayed on the screen. Listing 2.5 contains the header file for the mailingListRecord structure used in the MAILLIST program shown in Listing 2.4.

Listing 2.4. MAILLIST.CPP.

```
1: #include <iostream.h>
2: #include <conio.h>
3: #include <stdlib.h>
4: #pragma hdrstop
5: #include "structur.h"
6: void displayRecord(int, mailingListRecord mlRec);
7: int main(int, char**)
8: {
9:    //
10:   // create an array of mailingListRecord structures
11:   //
12:   mailingListRecord listArray[3];
13:   cout << endl;
14:   int index = 0;
15:   // get three records
16:   //
17:   do {
18:     cout << "First Name: ";
19:     cin.getline(listArray[index].firstName,
20:       sizeof(listArray[index].firstName) - 1);
21:     cout << "Last Name: ";
22:     cin.getline(listArray[index].lastName,
23:       sizeof(listArray[index].lastName) - 1);
24:     cout << "Address: ";
25:     cin.getline(listArray[index].address,
26:       sizeof(listArray[index].address) - 1);
27:     cout << "City: ";
28:     cin.getline(listArray[index].city,
29:       sizeof(listArray[index].city) - 1);
30:     cout << "State: ";
31:     cin.getline(listArray[index].state,
32:       sizeof(listArray[index].state) - 1);
33:     char buff[10];
34:     cout << "Zip: ";
35:     cin.getline(buff, sizeof(buff) - 1);
36:     listArray[index].zip = atoi(buff);
37:     index++;
38:     cout << endl;
39:   }
40:   while (index < 3);
41:   //
42:   // clear the screen
43:   //
44:   clrscr();
45:   //
46:   // display the three records
```

continues

Listing 2.4. continued

```
47:   //
48:   for (int i=0;i<3;i++) {
49:     displayRecord(i, listArray[i]);
50:   }
51:   //
52:   // ask the user to choose a record
53:   //
54:   cout << "Choose a record: ";
55:   int rec;
56:   //
57:   // be sure only 1, 2, or 3 was selected
58:   //
59:   do {
60:     rec = getch();
61:     rec -= 49;
62:   } while (rec < 0 || rec > 2);
63:   //
64:   // assign the selected record to a temporary variable
65:   //
66:   mailingListRecord temp = listArray[rec];
67:   clrscr();
68:   cout << endl;
69:   //
70:   // display the selected recrord
71:   //
72:   displayRecord(rec, temp);
73:   getch();
74:   return 0;
75: }
76: void displayRecord(int num, mailingListRecord mlRec)
77: {
78:   cout << "Record " << (num + 1) << ":" << endl;
79:   cout << "Name:      " << mlRec.firstName << " ";
80:   cout << mlRec.lastName;
81:   cout << endl;
82:   cout << "Address:  " << mlRec.address;
83:   cout << endl << "              ";
84:   cout << mlRec.city << ", ";
85:   cout << mlRec.state << "   ";
86:   cout << mlRec.zip;
87:   cout << endl << endl;
88: }
```

Listing 2.5. STRUCTUR.H.

```
1: #ifndef _STRUCTUR_H
2: #define _STRUCTUR.H
3: struct mailingListRecord {
4:   char firstName[20];
```

```
 5:    char lastName[20];
 6:    char address[50];
 7:    char city[20];
 8:    char state[5];
 9:    int zip;
10: };
11: #endif
```

There are a couple of new things presented in this program and some variations on material we've already covered.

First, this program uses the getline() function of the cin class to get input from the user (on line 19, for instance). I did this because the cin extraction operator, >>, is not very friendly when it comes to whitespace. The second parameter of getline() is used to limit the number of characters that will be placed into the buffer (in this case the buffer is a data member of the mailingListRecord structure). I supply a value here because I don't want to overwrite the end of the arrays in the structure. The sizeof() operator is used to determine the size of the destination buffer so we know how many characters we can safely store in the buffer.

The atoi() function on line 36 is also new to you. This function takes a character string and converts it to an integer value. This is necessary to convert the text in the zip code field (which I got from the user as a string) to an integer value that can be stored in the zip data member of the mailingListRecord structure.

The displayRecord() function, which begins on line 76, takes two parameters. The first parameter, num, is an int that contains the index number of the record to display. This variable is only used to display the record number. On line 78, I add 1 to num when I display it because users are accustomed to lists beginning with 1 rather than with 0. (I aim to please!) The second parameter of the displayRecord() function is an instance of the mailingListRecord structure. Inside the displayRecord() function, I use the local instance of the structure passed in (which represents a copy of the structure) to display the contents of the structure.

NOTE

In this case, I am passing the mailingListRecord structure *by value.* What this means is that a copy of the structure is created each time the displayRecord() function is called. This is not very efficient because of the overhead required to pass a structure by value. The overhead comes in the form of the extra time and memory required to make a copy of the structure each time the function is called. It would be better to pass the structure by reference, but I haven't talked about that yet so the structure is passed by value in this program. You will learn about passing by reference tomorrow when we discuss functions in C++.

Note that the `displayRecord()` function is called from both the `for` loop when all the records are displayed (line 49) and again from the main body of the program to display the actual record chosen (line 72). That's precisely why the code to display a record has been placed in a function. By putting it in a function, I only have to write the code once and can avoid duplicating the code unnecessarily.

TIP

> Any time you find yourself repeating code more than a couple times in your programs, think about moving that code to a function. Then you can call the function when you need that code executed.

There is another segment of this program that deserves mention. Look at this `do-while` loop, which begins on line 59:

```
do {
  rec = getch();
  rec -= 49;
} while (rec < 0 ¦¦ rec > 2);
```

This code first gets a character from the keyboard using the `getch()` function. As you have seen, I have been using `getch()` at the end of the sample programs to keep the program from closing prematurely but have been ignoring the return value. The `getch()` function returns the ASCII value of the key pressed. Because the ASCII value of the 1 key is 49, I want to subtract 49 from the value of the key pressed to obtain the equivalent index number for that record in the `records` array. If the user presses 1, an ASCII 49 is returned, and 49–49 is 0, which is the first index of the array. If the user presses 2, the calculation yields 1 (50–49), and so on. The `do-while` loop ensures that the user presses a key between 1 and 3. If a key other than 1, 2, or 3 is pressed, the loop continues to fetch keystrokes until a valid key is pressed.

Finally, look at line 66 of Listing 2.4:

```
mailingListRecord temp = listArray[rec];
```

This code is not necessary in this program, but I included it to illustrate a point. This code creates an instance of the `mailingListRecord` structure and assigns to it the contents of one of the structures in the array. A simple assignment is possible here because the compiler knows how to copy one structure to another. It does a simple member-to-member copy and copies the values of all structure members to the newly created instance of the structure.

NOTE

> Our discussion of structures up to this point describes how a structure works in C. In C++ a structure operates as it does in C, but C++ extends structures to enable them to contain functions as well as data members. In fact, a structure in C++ is essentially a class where all data members and functions have public access. That won't make sense until later on, when I discuss classes on Day 4, but you can file this tidbit away for future reference.

Now you know about structures. Chances are you won't use a lot of structures in your programs. This section is important, though, because it serves as sort of a primer for discussing classes in Day 3, "Advanced C++."

Summary

This chapter contains essential information on some of C++'s basic operations. You need to understand what is presented here in order to program in C++Builder. First you learned about the different types of loops in C++; then you learned about the switch statement and how to use it. I talked a little about scope and what that means to your variables. Then you found out about structures and how they can be used in your programs. Tomorrow we'll tackle some of the big stuff.

Workshop

The Workshop contains quiz questions to help you solidify your understanding of the material covered and exercises to provide you with experience in using what you have learned. You can find answers to the quiz questions in Appendix A, "Answers to Quiz Questions."

Q&A

Q How many levels deep can I nest if statements?

A There's no limit. There is, however, a practical limit. If you have too many nested if statements, it gets very hard to keep all those brackets straight!

Q Will loops automatically terminate if something goes wrong?

A No. If you accidentally write an endless loop, that loop will continue to run until you do something to stop it. You can stop a program stuck in an endless loop by bringing up the Windows Task Manager (or the Close Program box) and ending the errant task. If you executed the program via the C++Builder IDE, you can choose Run | Program Reset from the main menu to kill the program.

Q Does a `switch` statement have to include a `default` section?

A No. The default section is optional.

Q Can I have more than one variable with the same name?

A Yes, provided they are in different scopes. You cannot have two variables named x that are both declared within a code block. You can, however, have a global variable named x and a local variable with the same name.

Q Can I use a structure by itself, without an object?

A No. Before you can use a structure, you have to create an instance of the structure and access the structure through the instance variable.

Quiz

1. What statements are executed in the event an `if` expression evaluates to `true`?
2. What do the three parameters of a `for` statement represent?
3. Besides syntax, what is the difference between a `while` loop and a `do-while` loop?
4. What do the `break` and `continue` statements do?
5. What is a global variable?
6. Can a structure contain a mixture of data types (`char`, `int`, `long`, and so on)?
7. How do you access the members of a structure?
8. Is it legal to have arrays of structures?

Exercises

1. Write a program that counts from 200 to 300 by 5s and displays the results.
2. Write a program that asks the user to input the day of the week and then displays the name of the day, using a `switch` statement.
3. See whether you can figure out what the \b and \n do in this line from Listing 2.2:

```
cout << "\b!\nYipee!";
```

Hint: Check the C++Builder online help for information on escape sequences.

4. Write a structure containing data members representing employee information. Include first name, last name, address, hire date, and a data member indicating whether the employee is in the company's insurance plan.

2

Day 3

Advanced C++

"Don't worry, I've got you." Do you remember hearing those words when you were learning to ride a bike? The C++ language is often unforgiving. With the information in this chapter, you will be navigating the concepts of C++ that most people trip over. Although I can't promise to be there to pick you up when you fall, I can at least point out some bumps in the road you might encounter. Today you will learn about

- ☐ Pointers
- ☐ References
- ☐ The `new` and `delete` operators
- ☐ Functions in C++

Pointers

Pointers are one of the most confusing aspects of the C++ language. They are also one of the most powerful features of C++. My goal in this section is not to teach you the textbook definition of pointers, but rather to teach you pointers in the context of how you will use them in your C++Builder programs. So what is a pointer? It's a variable that holds the address of another variable. There, that wasn't so bad, was it? I wish it were that simple! Because a pointer holds the address of another variable, it is said to "point to" the second variable. This is called indirection because the pointer does not have a direct association with the actual data, but rather an indirect association.

 A *pointer* is a variable that holds the address of another variable. Because the pointer does not have a direct association with the actual data, *indirection* is the term used when referring to this indirect association.

Let's look at an example. Earlier we talked about arrays. Let's say that you had an array of ints. You could access the individual elements of the array using the subscript operator, as I talked about on Day 1, "Getting Started with C++Builder."

```
int array[] = { 5, 10, 15, 20, 25 };
int someVariable = array[3];   // the value 20
```

You could also use a pointer to accomplish the same thing:

```
int array[] = { 5, 10, 15, 20, 25 };
int* ptr = array;
int someVariable = ptr[3];
```

In this example, the memory location of the beginning of the array is assigned to the pointer named ptr. Note that the pointer is a pointer of the data type int and that the indirection operator (the * symbol) is used when you declare a pointer. You can declare a pointer to any integral data types (int, char, long, short, and so on), as well as to objects (structures or classes). After the assignment, the pointer contains the memory address of the start of the array and, as such, points to the array.

 NOTE

> The name of an array variable, when used without the subscript operator, returns the memory address of the first element of the array. Put another way, the variable name of an array is a pointer to the start of the array. That makes it possible to assign an array to a pointer, as in the preceding example.

In this case you can now use the pointer, ptr, just as you would the array name itself. I can hear you wondering, though, "But why would you want to?" The truth is that in this example there is no real benefit to using a pointer. The real benefit of pointers is when you want to create objects dynamically in memory. A pointer is necessary to access the object. I really can't go on with this discussion, though, until I digress a moment and talk about the two ways you can create variables and objects.

Local Versus Dynamic Memory Usage

All the sample programs you have seen thus far use local allocation of objects. That is, the memory required for a variable or object is obtained from the program's stack.

New Term *Local allocation* means that the memory required for a variable or object is obtained from the program's stack.

New Term The *stack* is an area of working memory set aside by the program when the program starts.

Any memory the program needs for things like local variables, function calls, and so on is taken from the stack. This memory is allocated as needed and then freed when no longer needed. Usually this happens when the program enters a function or other local code block. Memory for any local variables the function uses is allocated when the function is entered. When the function returns, all the memory allocated for the function's use is freed. It all happens for you automatically; you don't have to give any thought to how or whether the memory is freed.

Local allocation has its good points and its bad points. On the plus side, memory can be allocated from the stack very quickly. The downside is that the stack is a fixed size and cannot be changed as the program runs. If your program runs out of stack space, weird things start to happen. Your program might just crash, it might start behaving oddly, or it might seem to perform normally but crash when the program terminates. This is less of a problem in the 32-bit world than in 16-bit programming, but it's still a consideration.

For things like variables of the built-in data types and small arrays, there is no point in doing anything other than local allocation. But if you are going to be using large arrays, structures, or classes, you will probably want to use dynamic allocation from the heap. The heap amounts to your computer's free physical RAM plus all your free hard disk space. In other words, you could easily have 100MB of heap memory available on a typical Windows system. The good news here is that you have virtually unlimited memory available for your programs. The bad news is that memory allocated dynamically requires some additional overhead and, as such, is just a smidgen slower than memory allocated from the stack. In most programs, the extra overhead is not noticed in the least. An additional drawback of dynamic allocation is that it requires more from the programmer. Not a lot more, mind you, but a little.

New Term *Dynamic allocation* means that memory required for an object is allocated from the heap.

New Term The *heap* in a Windows program refers to all of your computer's virtual memory.

Dynamic Allocation and Pointers

 In a C++ program, memory is allocated dynamically by using the new operator.

I'm going to talk about new a little later in the chapter, but you need a little sampler as I continue the discussion about pointers. Earlier I talked about structures and used the mailingListRecord structure as an example. Allocating a structure from the stack looks like this:

```
mailingListRecord listArray;
strcpy(listArray.firstName, "John");
strcpy(listArray.lastName, "Leier");
// etc.
```

That's what I did earlier when I talked about structures. Now I'll create the array dynamically rather than locally:

```
mailingListRecord* listArray;
listArray = new mailingListRecord;
strcpy(listArray->firstName, "John");
strcpy(listArray->lastName, "Leier");
// etc.
```

The first line declares a pointer to a mailingListRecord structure. The next line initializes the pointer by creating a new instance of a mailingListRecord structure dynamically. This is the process by which you dynamically create and access objects in C++.

And Now Back to Our Program

Now you can begin to see where pointers fit into the scheme of things. When you create an object dynamically, the new operator returns a pointer to the object in memory. You need that pointer to be able to do anything with the object. Figure 3.1 illustrates how the pointer points to the object in memory. Note that although the memory for the dynamically created object is allocated from heap memory, the actual pointer is a local variable and is allocated from the stack (a pointer requires 4 bytes of storage).

Let's go back to a code snippet you saw earlier:

```
mailingListRecord* listArray;
listArray = new mailingListRecord;
strcpy(listArray->firstName, "John");
strcpy(listArray->lastName, "Leier");
// etc.
```

On the third line you see that the firstName data member of the structure is accessed using the indirect member operator (->) rather than the structure member operator. (We discussed the structure member operator yesterday in the section entitled "Structures." The term *direct member operator* is also used and is more representative than *structure member operator*, so I will use *direct member operator* from now on.) When you create an object dynamically, you must access the object's data members and functions using this operator.

Figure 3.1.

*A pointer to an object
in memory.*

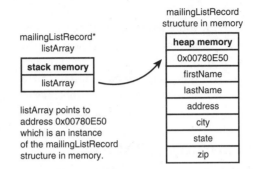

listArray points to
address 0x00780E50
which is an instance
of the mailingListRecord
structure in memory.

Creating an array of structures dynamically requires a bit more work. Again, here's the stack-based version:

```
mailingListRecord listArray[3];
listArray[0].zip = 57441;
```

and the dynamic version:

```
mailingListRecord* listArray[3];
for (int i=0;i<3;i++)
  listArray[i] = new mailingListRecord;
listArray[0]->zip = 57441;
```

Note that I have to create a new instance of the structure for each element of the array. Notice also that to access a data member of the array, I use the indirect member operator combined with the subscript operator.

WARNING

Uninitialized pointers contain random values just like any other uninitialized variable. Attempting to use an uninitialized pointer can wreak havoc on a program. In many cases, a pointer is declared and immediately initialized:

```
MyArray* array = new MyArray;
```

Sometimes, however, you will declare a pointer and then not initialize it until sometime later in the program. If you attempt to use the pointer before initializing it, the pointer will point to some random memory location, and modifying that memory could cause all sorts of nasty problems. Often the problems caused by modifying unknown memory don't show up immediately, making the bug appear to be random. To be safe, you should initialize a pointer to 0 when you declare it:

```
MyArray* array = 0;
```

> If you attempt to use a NULL pointer (any pointer set to NULL or 0), you
> will immediately get an access violation from Windows. Although this
> might not sound like a good thing, it is certainly the lesser of two evils.
> It is far better to have an immediate error at the point of the infraction
> than to have a random problem show up farther down the road.

Dereferencing a Pointer

Frequently you will need to dereference a pointer to retrieve the contents of the memory
location (the object) that a pointer points to. Take the following example:

```
int x = 20;
int* ptrx = &x;
// later...
int z = *ptrx;
```

I can just imagine your frustration right now. What a mess! Don't worry, it's not quite as bad
as it might appear. The first line in this example declares an int variable called x and assigns
it a value of 20. The next line declares a pointer to an int and assigns to the pointer the address
of the variable x. This is done by using the address-of operator (&). In this example, the
address-of operator tells the compiler, "Give me the memory address of the variable x, not
the value of x itself." After the assignment, ptrx contains the memory address of x. Later on
in the program you might need to get the value of the object pointed to by ptrx. You might
think of trying this:

```
int z = ptrx;    // wrong!
```

This won't work, however, because you are trying to assign a memory address to a regular
variable. When you try to compile this line, the compiler will spit back an error stating Cannot
convert int* to int. That makes sense because you are dealing with two different types of
variables. So you need to dereference the pointer using the indirection operator:

```
int z = *ptrx;
```

This could be considered the opposite of the address-of operator. Here you don't want the
actual value of ptrx because the actual value is a memory address. Instead, you want the value
of the object pointed to by that memory address. So in this case, the indirection operator tells
the compiler, "Give me the value of the object that ptrx points to, not the actual value
of ptrx."

NEW TERM   *Dereferencing* a pointer means to retrieve the contents of the memory location (the
object) that a pointer points to.

NOTE

> As you can see, the indirection operator is used to declare a pointer (int* x;) and also to dereference a pointer (int z = *x;). The compiler can tell from the context in which the indirection operator is used what to do in each case. You don't have to worry that the compiler won't know what you intend.

NOTE

> C++ syntax is largely a personal choice. I prefer to use the indirection operator next to the data type when declaring a pointer, and next to the pointer when dereferencing a pointer:
>
> ```
> int* x;
> SomeClass* aClass = new SomeClass;
> char* s = new char[256];
> int z = *x;
> SomeClass temp = *aClass;
> ```
>
> Others prefer to place the indirection operator next to the variable name:
>
> ```
> int *x;
> // or even...
> int * x;
> ```
>
> I happen to think that the syntax I use makes the most sense, but others could probably argue that their way is best, too. In the end, settle on the method you like best and then stay with it.

3

Putting It Together

Let's try to tie together what you have learned in the previous section. I'll take the MAILLIST program from Day 2, "C++ Fundamentals," and modify it so that it uses dynamic memory allocation. This will require a few changes. First, take a look at the modified program and then I'll explain the changes. Listing 3.1 contains the modified MAILLIST program.

Listing 3.1. POINTER.CPP.

```
1: #include <iostream.h>
2: #include <conio.h>
3: #include <stdlib.h>
4: #pragma hdrstop
5: #include "structur.h"
6: void displayRecord(int, mailingListRecord mlRec);
```

continues

Listing 3.1. continued

```
 7: int main(int, char**)
 8: {
 9:   //
10:   // create an array of pointers to
11:   // the mailingListRecord structure
12:   //
13:   mailingListRecord* listArray[3];
14:   //
15:   // create an object for each element of the array
16:   //
17:   for (int i=0;i<3;i++)
18:     listArray[i] = new mailingListRecord;
19:   cout << endl;
20:   int index = 0;
21:   //
22:   // get three records
23:   //
24:   do {
25:     cout << "First Name: ";
26:     cin.getline(listArray[index]->firstName,
27:       sizeof(listArray[index]->firstName) - 1);
28:     cout << "Last Name: ";
29:     cin.getline(listArray[index]->lastName,
30:       sizeof(listArray[index]->lastName) - 1);
31:     cout << "Address: ";
32:     cin.getline(listArray[index]->address,
33:       sizeof(listArray[index]->address) - 1);
34:     cout << "City: ";
35:     cin.getline(listArray[index]->city,
36:       sizeof(listArray[index]->city) - 1);
37:     cout << "State: ";
38:     cin.getline(listArray[index]->state,
39:       sizeof(listArray[index]->state) - 1);
40:     char buff[10];
41:     cout << "Zip: ";
42:     cin.getline(buff, sizeof(buff) - 1);
43:     listArray[index]->zip = atoi(buff);
44:     index++;
45:     cout << endl;
46:   }
47:   while (index < 3);
48:   //
49:   // display the three records
50:   //
51:   clrscr();
52:   //
53:   // must dereference the pointer to pass an object
54:   // to the displayRecord function.
55:   //
56:   for (int i=0;i<3;i++) {
57:     displayRecord(i, *listArray[i]);
58:   }
```

```
59:    //
60:    // ask the user to choose a record
61:    //
62:    cout << "Choose a record: ";
63:    int rec;
64:    do {
65:      rec = getch();
66:      rec -= 49;
67:    } while (rec < 0 || rec > 2);
68:    //
69:    // assign the selected record to a temporary variable
70:    // must dereference here, too
71:    //
72:    mailingListRecord temp = *listArray[rec];
73:    clrscr();
74:    cout << endl;
75:    //
76:    // display the selected recrord
77:    //
78:    displayRecord(rec, temp);
79:    getch();
80:    return 0;
81: }
82: void displayRecord(int num, mailingListRecord mlRec)
83: {
84:    cout << "Record " << (num + 1) << ":" << endl;
85:    cout << "Name:      " << mlRec.firstName << " ";
86:    cout << mlRec.lastName;
87:    cout << endl;
88:    cout << "Address:  " << mlRec.address;
89:    cout << endl << "          ";
90:    cout << mlRec.city << ", ";
91:    cout << mlRec.state << "   ";
92:    cout << mlRec.zip;
93:    cout << endl << endl;
94: }
```

ANALYSIS First, on line 13 I declared the listArray array as an array of pointers. Following that, I created objects for each element of the array. This takes place in the for loop on lines 17 and 18. After that, I changed the direct member operators (.) to indirect member operators (->). I also had to dereference the pointers on line 57 and again on line 72. This is necessary because an object is expected, and we cannot use a pointer in place of an object. Notice that the displayRecord function (starting on line 82) doesn't change. I haven't changed the fact that the mailingListRecord structure is passed to the function by value, so the code in the function doesn't need to be modified.

If you've had previous experience with C++, you might have noticed that this program has a bug in it. I'll let you in on the secret before the end of the chapter.

References

 A *reference* is a special type of pointer that enables you to treat a pointer like a regular object.

References, like pointers, can be confusing. A reference is declared using the reference operator. The symbol for the reference operator is the ampersand (&), which is the same symbol used for the address-of operator (don't worry, the compiler knows how to keep it all straight). As I said, a reference enables you to treat a pointer like an object. Here's an example:

```
MyStruct* pStruct = new MyStruct;
MyStruct& ref = *pStruct;
ref.X = 100;
```

Notice that you use the direct member operator with references rather than the indirect member operator, as you do with pointers. Now you can get rid of all those pesky -> operators! Although you won't use references a lot, they can be very handy when you need them. By the way, this code snippet could be condensed a little. Here's how I would write it in a real program:

```
MyStruct& ref = *new MyStruct;
ref.X = 100;
```

Although this might appear odd, it does exactly the same thing as the first example. Combining statements like this is common and avoids unnecessary overhead.

Let's go once more to the MAILLIST example. This time I'll modify it by implementing a reference in the do-while loop. Actually, I'll be modifying the POINTER example found in Listing 3.1. The new program, found in Listing 3.2, illustrates this change.

Listing 3.2. REFERENC.CPP.

```
 1: #include <iostream.h>
 2: #include <conio.h>
 3: #include <stdlib.h>
 4: #pragma hdrstop
 5: #include "structur.h"
 6: void displayRecord(int, mailingListRecord mlRec);
 7: int main(int, char**)
 8: {
 9:   cout << endl;
10:   //
11:   // create an array of mailingListRecord structures
12:   //
13:   mailingListRecord* listArray[3];
14:   //
15:   // create objects for each record
16:   //
17:   for (int i=0;i<3;i++)
18:     listArray[i] = new mailingListRecord;
```

```
19:    int index = 0;
20:    //
21:    // get three records
22:    //
23:    do {
24:       // create a reference to the current record
25:       mailingListRecord& rec = *listArray[index];
26:       cout << "First Name: ";
27:       cin.getline(rec.firstName, sizeof(rec.firstName) - 1);
28:       cout << "Last Name: ";
29:       cin.getline(rec.lastName, sizeof(rec.lastName) - 1);
30:       cout << "Address: ";
31:       cin.getline(rec.address, sizeof(rec.address) - 1);
32:       cout << "City: ";
33:       cin.getline(rec.city, sizeof(rec.city) - 1);
34:       cout << "State: ";
35:       cin.getline(rec.state, sizeof(rec.state) - 1);
36:       char buff[10];
37:       cout << "Zip: ";
38:       cin.getline(buff, sizeof(buff) - 1);
39:       rec.zip = atoi(buff);
40:       index++;
41:       cout << endl;
42:    }
43:    while (index < 3);
44:    //
45:    // display the three records
46:    //
47:    clrscr();
48:    //
49:    // must dereference the pointer to pass an object
50:    // to the displayRecord function.
51:    //
52:    for (int i=0;i<3;i++) {
53:       displayRecord(i, *listArray[i]);
54:    }
55:    //
56:    // ask the user to choose a record
57:    //
58:    cout << "Choose a record: ";
59:    int rec;
60:    do {
61:       rec = getch();
62:       rec -= 49;
63:    } while (rec < 0 || rec > 2);
64:    //
65:    // assign the selected record to a temporary variable
66:    // must dereference here, too
67:    //
68:    mailingListRecord temp = *listArray[rec];
69:    clrscr();
70:    cout << endl;
71:    //
72:    // display the selected recrord
73:    //
74:    displayRecord(rec, temp);
```

continues

Listing 3.2. continued

```
75:     getch();
76:     return 0;
77: }
78: void displayRecord(int num, mailingListRecord mlRec)
79: {
80:     cout << "Record " << (num + 1) << ":" << endl;
81:     cout << "Name:     " << mlRec.firstName << " ";
82:     cout << mlRec.lastName;
83:     cout << endl;
84:     cout << "Address:  " << mlRec.address;
85:     cout << endl << "          ";
86:     cout << mlRec.city << ", ";
87:     cout << mlRec.state << "   ";
88:     cout << mlRec.zip;
89:     cout << endl << endl;
90: }
```

ANALYSIS The only real change is in the do-while loop in lines 23 through 41. Notice that a reference to a mailingListRecord structure is declared. Each time through the loop, the reference is assigned a different object (the next element in the array). Notice that I got rid of the indirect member operators and replaced them with the direct member operators. As I said earlier, a reference enables you to treat a pointer as an object. What that does for us in this case is clean up the code a little and make it easier to read. Oh, for those of you keeping score, this program has the same bug in it as the POINTER example has. I'll remedy that at the end of the chapter.

Although it might seem that references are preferred over pointers, that is not always the case. References have some peculiarities that make them unsuitable in many cases. For one thing, references cannot be declared and then later assigned a value. They must be initialized when declared. For instance, the following code snippet will result in a compiler error:

```
MyStruct* pStruct = new MyStruct;
MyStruct& ref;
ref = *pStruct;
ref.X = 100;
```

Another problem with references is that they cannot be set to 0 or NULL as pointers can. That means you have to take special care to ensure that a reference is not deleted twice. References and pointers can often serve the same purpose, but neither is perfect in every programming situation.

Passing Function Parameters by Reference and by Pointer

Earlier I talked about passing objects to functions by value. I said that in the case of structures and classes, it is usually better to pass those objects by reference rather than by value. Any object can be passed by reference. This includes the primitive data types such as int and long, as well as instances of a structure or class. To review, when you pass function parameters by value, a copy of the object is made and the function works with the copy. When you pass by reference, a pointer to the object is passed and not the object itself. This has two primary implications. First, it means that objects passed by reference can be modified by the function. Second, passing by reference eliminates the overhead of creating a copy of the object.

The fact that an object can be modified by the function is the most important aspect of passing by reference. Take this code, for instance:

```
void IncrementPosition(int& xPos, int& yPos)
{
  xPos++;
  yPos++;
}
int x = 20;
int y = 40;
IncrementPosition(x, y);
// x now equals 21 and y equals 41
```

Notice that when the function returns, both the parameters passed have been incremented by one. This is because the function is modifying the actual object via the pointer (remember that a reference is a type of pointer).

TIP

Remember that a function can return only one value. By passing parameters by reference, you can achieve the effect of a function returning more than one value. The function still returns only one value, but the objects passed by reference are updated, so the function effectively returns multiple values.

As I said, the other reason to pass parameters by reference is to eliminate the overhead of making a copy of the object each time the function is called. When dealing with primitive data types, there is no real overhead involved in making a copy. When dealing with structures and classes, however, the overhead is something to be considered. You should pass structures of any consequence by reference, as the following code demonstrates:

```
// structure passed by reference
void someFunction(MyStructure& s)
{
```

```
    // do some stuff with 's'
    return;
}
MyStructure myStruct;
// do some stuff, then later...
someFunction(myStruct);
```

Notice that the function call looks exactly the same, whether the object is being passed by reference or by value.

Do you see a potential problem with passing by reference? If you pass by reference, you avoid the overhead of making a copy of the object, but now the object can be modified by the function. Sometimes you don't want the object to be modified by the function. So what if you want to pass by reference but make sure the object is not modified? Read on and I'll tell you.

The const Keyword

 The const keyword enables you to declare a variable as constant.

After a variable is declared with const, it cannot be changed. The solution, then, is to pass by reference *and* make the object const:

```
void someFunction(const MyStruct& s)
{
    // do some stuff with 's'
    return;
}
MyStructure myStruct;
// later
someFunction(myStruct);
```

Now you are free to pass by reference and not worry that your object might be modified by the function. Note that the function call itself stays the same and that only the function definition (and declaration) is modified with the const keyword.

NOTE

> If you attempt to modify a const object, you will get a compiler error stating Cannot modify a const object. The following code generates that error message:
>
> ```
> void someFunction(const MyStruct& s)
> {
>     s.dataMember = 100;    // cannot modify a const object
>     return;
> }
> ```
>
> After you declare an object as const, the compiler will make sure you don't modify the object.

3

Note that the object is const only within the function. The object can be modified both before and after the function returns (provided it was not initially declared as const).

Passing by pointer is essentially the same as passing by reference. Passing by pointer has a couple of syntactical headaches that make it less desirable than passing by reference. Let's take IncrementPosition() function from the first example in this section and modify it to pass by pointer rather than by reference:

```
void IncrementPosition(int* xPos, int* yPos)
{
  *xPos++;    // dereference, then increment
  *yPos++;
}
```

Note that the pointer has to be dereferenced before it can be incremented. Most of the time your needs will be best served by passing by reference, but you can pass by pointer if a situation dictates the need. When passing char arrays, you will usually pass by pointer rather than by reference because you can use a pointer to a char array and the name of the array interchangeably. When passing character arrays, it is better to pass by pointer.

The new **and** delete **Operators**

Up to this point I have talked primarily about aspects of the C++ language that come from C. From this point on we'll be looking at features that are specific to the C++ language. The new and delete operators are two important C++ language features.

As mentioned in the preceding section, memory in a C++ program is allocated dynamically using the new operator. You free memory using the delete operator. Unless you have previously programmed in C, you might not appreciate the simplicity of new and delete. In C programs you use malloc(), calloc(), realloc(), and free() to dynamically allocate memory. Windows really complicates things by offering a whole raft of local and global memory-allocation functions. Although this is not exactly difficult, it can be confusing, to say the least. C++ removes those headaches through the use of new and delete.

new

You've already seen new in action, so let's review. As discussed earlier, you can allocate memory locally (from the stack) or dynamically (from the heap). The following code snippet shows examples of allocating two character arrays. One is allocated from the stack (local allocation), and the other is allocated from the heap (dynamic allocation):

```
char buff[80];
char* bigBuff = new char[4096];
```

In the first case the buffer size is insignificant, so it doesn't really matter whether the stack or the heap is used. In the second case a large char array is needed, so it makes sense to allocate it from the heap rather than the stack. This preserves stack space. In the case of arrays (remember, a string is just an array of type char), the dynamic and local flavors can be used interchangeably. That is, they use the same syntax:

```
strcpy(buff, "Ricky Rat");
strcpy(bigBuff, "A very long string that goes on and on...");
// later on...
strcpy(bigBuff, buff);
```

Remember that the name of an array when used by itself points to the first memory location of the array. A pointer also points to the first memory location of the array, so that is why the two forms can be used interchangeably.

NOTE

> If the new operator fails to allocate the requested memory, it returns NULL. In theory, you should check the pointer after calling new to ensure that it contains a non-zero value:
>
> ```
> char* buff = new char[1024];
> if (buff) strcpy(buff, "Nothing special");
> else ReportError();  // something went wrong
> ```
>
> In reality, if the new operator fails in a 32-bit Windows program, the entire system is in trouble, and neither your program nor any other will be running for long.
>
> If you are attempting to allocate very large chunks of memory (several megabytes in size) or are trying to allocate memory at critical points in your program, you should check the pointer for validity before continuing. For routine memory-allocation chores, you can probably get by without checking to ensure that the new operator succeeded.

delete

All memory allocated must be deallocated (released or freed) after you are done with it. With local objects this happens for you automatically and you don't have to worry about it. The memory manager allocates the memory your object needs from the stack and then frees that memory when the object goes out of scope (usually when a function returns or when the code block in which the object was declared ends). When using dynamic memory allocation, the programmer must take the responsibility of freeing any memory allocated with the new operator.

NEW TERM Freeing memory allocated with new is accomplished with the delete operator.

All calls to new need to have a matching delete. If you don't free all memory allocated with the new operator, your program will leak memory. You need to be diligent in matching new/delete pairs.

Using the delete operator is extremely easy:

```
SomeObject* myObject = new SomeObject;
// do a bunch of stuff with myObject
delete myObject;     // so long!
```

That's all there is to it! There isn't a lot to the delete operator, but there are a couple of things about pointers and delete that you should be aware of. The first is that you must not delete a pointer that has already been deleted, or you will get access violations and all sorts of other problems. Second, it is okay to delete a pointer that has been set to 0. So what does that mean in the real world? Let me explain.

Sometimes you declare a pointer just in case it might be used, but you don't know for sure whether it will be used in a given instance of your program. For example, let's say you have an object that is created if the user chooses a certain menu item. If the user never chooses that menu item, the object never gets created. So far, so good. The problem is that you need to delete the pointer if the object is created but not delete the pointer if the object isn't created. Deleting an uninitialized pointer is asking for trouble because you have no idea what memory the pointer points to. There are two ways to work around this.

I said earlier that it is a good idea to initialize pointers to 0 if you don't use them right away. This is a good idea for two reasons. The first reason I explained earlier—uninitialized pointers contain random values, which is undesirable. The second reason is because it's okay to delete a NULL pointer—you can call delete for that pointer and not worry about whether it was ever used:

```
Monster* swampThing = 0;
// later when it's time to exit the program...
delete swampThing;  // so long, sucker!
```

In this case you don't really care whether memory for the object was ever allocated because the call to delete is safe whether the pointer points to an object or is NULL.

TIP

> You might run into situations where `delete` can be called more than once for an object. For instance, you can create an object in one part of your program and delete it in another part of the program. A situation might exist where the section of code that deletes the object might never be executed. In that case you will also want to delete the object when the program closes (for insurance). To avoid the possibility of a pointer getting deleted twice, form a habit of setting the pointer to `NULL` or `0` after deleting it:
>
> ```
> Monster* borg = new Monster;
> // later....
> delete borg;
> borg = 0;
> ```
>
> Now if `delete` is called twice for the object, it won't matter because it's okay to delete a `NULL` pointer.

Another way around the double-delete problem is to check the pointer for a non-zero value before calling `delete`:

```
if (swampThing) delete swampThing;
```

This assumes that you have been diligent in setting deleted pointers to `0` in other parts of the program. It doesn't matter which method you use, but be sure to use one of them in any case where a pointer can accidentally be deleted twice.

NOTE

> If you use a reference when dynamically creating an object, the syntax for `delete` requires a twist. Here's an example that illustrates this point:
>
> ```
> MyStruct& ref = *new MyStruct;
> ref.X = 100;
> // later...
> delete &ref;
> ```
>
> Note that you need the address-of operator to delete the pointer in the case of a reference. Remember that a reference cannot be set to `0`, so you must be careful not to delete a reference twice.

Another Mystery Solved

Have you figured it out yet? "Huh?" you say? The bug in the `POINTER` and `REFERENC` programs...have you figured out what it is? You got it! The program leaks memory. I created an array of structures allocated from the heap but never freed the memory. So what I need is a couple of lines to clean up things just before the program ends:

```
getch();  // existing line
for (int i=0;i<3;i++)
  delete listArray[i];
```

There! Now I have a properly behaving program. I just ran through the array of pointers and deleted each one. Nothing to it.

new[] and delete[]

When you call new to create an array, you are actually using the new[] version of operator new. It's not important that you know the details of how that works, but you do need to know how to properly delete arrays that are dynamically allocated. Earlier I gave you an example of dynamically creating a character array. Here is the same code snippet, except with the delete[] statement added:

```
char buff[80];
char* bigBuff = new char[4096];
strcpy(buff, "Ricky Rat");
strcpy(bigBuff, "Some very long string.");
// later on...
delete[] bigBuff;
```

Notice that the statement calls delete[] and not just plain delete. I won't go into a technical description of what happens here, but this ensures that all elements in the array get properly deleted. Be sure that if you dynamically allocate an array, you call the delete[] operator to free the memory.

House Rules: Pointers and Dynamic Memory Allocation

☐ Be sure to initialize pointers to 0 if they are not used right away.

☐ Be sure not to delete a pointer twice.

☐ It is okay to delete pointers set to NULL or 0.

☐ Set pointers to NULL or 0 after deleting them.

☐ Dereference pointers to obtain the object the pointer points to.

Functions in C++

A function in C++ can do everything that a function can do in C. In addition, C++ functions can do things that functions in C cannot. Specifically, this section looks at the following:

☐   Function overloading

☐   Default parameters

☐   Class member functions

☐   Inline functions

Function Overloading

C++ enables you to work with functions that have the same name but take different parameters.

 Function overloading is having two or more functions with the same name but with different parameter lists.

Functions that share a common name are called *overloaded functions.*

On Day 1, I showed you a sample program that contained a function called `multiply()`. Not surprisingly, this function multiplied two values together. The function took two integers, multiplied them, and returned the result. What if you wanted to have the function multiply two floating-point numbers? In C you would need two functions:

```
// declarations for a program written in c
int multiplyInt(int num1, int num2);
float multiplyFloat(float num1, float num2);
short multiplyShort(short num1, short num2);
```

Wouldn't it be a lot easier if you could just have a function called `multiply()` that would be smart enough to know whether you wanted to multiply `short`s, `int`s, or `long`s? In C++ you can create such a scenario, thanks to function overloading. Here's how the declarations for an overloaded function look:

```
// declarations in C++
int multiply(int num1, int num2);
float multiply(float num1, float num2);
short multiply(short num1, short num2);
```

You still have to write separate functions for each of these declarations, but at least you can use the same function name. The compiler takes care of calling the correct function, based on the parameters you pass the function.

```
float x = 1.5;
float y = 10.5;
float result = multiply(x, y);
```

The compiler sees that two `float`s are passed to the function and calls the version of the `multiply()` function that takes two floating-point values for parameters. Likewise, if two `int`s are passed, the compiler calls the version of `multiply()` that takes two integers.

NOTE

It is the parameter list that makes overloaded functions work. You can vary either the type or the number of parameters a function takes (or both), but you cannot create an overloaded function by changing just the return value. For example, the following does not constitute an overloaded function:

```
int  DoSomething();
void DoSomething();
```

If you try to compile a program containing these lines, you will get a compiler error that says `Type mismatch in redeclaration of 'DoSomething()'`. The two functions need to vary by more than just the return value to qualify as overloaded functions.

NOTE

Compilers keep track of overloaded functions internally through a process called *name mangling*. Name mangling means that behind the scenes the compiler creates a function name that takes into account the parameter list of the function. Internally, the compiler refers to the mangled name rather than the plain text name you would recognize. For example, for the `multiply` function taking two float values, the mangled name might be `multiply$qff`.

Let's take a quick detour and talk about something you will need to use on occasion when dealing with overloaded functions.

Meet the Cast

Using overloaded functions works fine as long as you use the proper data types when calling an overloaded function. What if you mix and match? In this case, you need to cast a variable or literal value.

NEW TERM A *cast* tells the compiler to temporarily treat one data type as if it were another.

A cast looks like this:

```
float x = (float)10 * 5.5;
```

In this case the cast tells the compiler, "Make the number 10 a float." (The second number is automatically interpreted as a float because it contains a decimal place.) Take a look at the following code snippet:

```
int anInt = 5;
float aFloat = 10.5;
float result = multiply(anInt, aFloat);
```

You will get a compiler error because there is an ambiguity between the parameters passed and the function declarations. The compiler error, in effect, says, "I can't figure out from the parameters passed which version of multiply() to call." The same error will be produced if you use code like this:

```
int result = multiply(10, 10);
// is 10 a float, int or short?
```

Here the compiler cannot figure out whether the numeric constants are to be interpreted as floats, ints, or shorts. When this occurs, you have two choices. First, you can simply avoid using literal values in the function call. If you want to multiply two ints, you can declare two int variables and pass those to the function:

```
int x = 10;
int y = 10;
int result = multiply(x, y);
```

Now there is no ambiguity because x and y are both obviously ints. That's probably overkill for simple situations, though. The other thing you can do is to cast the numeric constants to tell the compiler what type to expect:

```
int result = multiply((int)10, (int)10);
```

Now the compiler knows to treat the literal values as ints. A cast is also used to temporarily force the compiler to treat one data type as if it were something else. Let's go back to the first example in this section and this time cast one of the variables to remove the ambiguity:

```
int x = 5;
float y = 10.5;
float result = multiply((float)x, y);
```

In this case x is an int, but you are casting it to a float, thereby telling the compiler to treat it as a float. The compiler happily calls the float version of multiply() and goes on its way.

Ultimately, you want to write overloaded functions so that ambiguities don't exist and casting is not necessary. In some cases that is not possible, and in those cases casting will be required.

Default Parameters for Functions

NEW TERM   A function in C++ can have *default parameters* that, as the name implies, supply a default value for a function if no value is specified when the function is called.

A function implementing a default parameter might look like this:

```
// declaration, parameter 'eraseFirst' will be false by default
void Redraw(bool eraseFirst = false);
// definition
void Redraw(bool eraseFirst)
{
  if (eraseFirst) {
    // erase code
  }
  // drawing code
}
```

You can call this function with or without a parameter. If the parameter is supplied at the time the function is called, the function behaves as a regular function would. If the parameter is not supplied when the function is called, the default parameter is used automatically. Given this example, the following two lines of code are identical:

```
Redraw();
Redraw(false);
```

Note that when a parameter has a default value, it can be omitted from the function call altogether. You can mix default and non-default parameters in the same function:

```
int PlaySound(char* name, bool loop = false, int loops = 10);
// call function
int res;
res = PlaySound("chime.wav");          // does not loop sound
res = PlaySound("ding.wav", true);     // plays sound 10 times
res = PlaySound("bell.wave", true, 5); // plays sound 5 times
```

Default parameters are helpful for many reasons. For one thing, they make your life easier. You might have a function that you call with the same parameters 99 percent of the time. By giving it default parameters, you shorten the amount of typing required each time you make a call to the function. Whenever you want to supply parameters other than the defaults, all you have to do is plug in values for the default parameters.

NOTE

> Any default parameters must come at the end of the function's parameter list. The following is not a valid function declaration:
>
> ```
> int MyFunction(int x, int y = 10, int t = 5, int z);
> ```
>
> In order for this function declaration to compile, the default parameters must be moved to the end of the function list:
>
> ```
> int MyFunction(int x, int z, int y = 10, int t = 5);
> ```
>
> If you don't put the default parameters at the end of the parameter list, the compiler will generate an error message.

Class Member Functions

 As you will find out in this section, classes can contain their own functions. Such functions are called *member functions* because they are members of a class.

Class member functions follow the same rules as regular functions: They can be overloaded, they can have default parameters, they can take any number of parameters, and so on.

Class member functions can be called only through an object of the class to which the function belongs. To call a class member function, you use the direct member operator (in the case of local objects) or the indirect member operator (for dynamically created objects), just as you did when accessing data members of a structure on Day 2, "C++ Fundamentals." For example, let's say you had a class called `Airplane` that was used to track an airplane for aircraft-control software. That class would probably have the capability to retrieve the current speed of a given aircraft via a function called `GetSpeed()`. The following example illustrates how you would call the `GetSpeed()` function of an `Airplane` object:

```
Airplane plane;   // create a class instance
int speed = plane.GetSpeed();
cout << "The airplane's current speed is " << speed << endl;
```

This code uses the direct member operator to call the `GetSpeed()` function. Class member functions are defined like regular functions except that the class name and scope-resolution operator precede the function name. For example, the definition of the `GetSpeed()` function might look like this in the source file:

```
int Airplane::GetSpeed()
{
  return speed;  // speed is a class member variable
}
```

Here the scope-resolution operator tells the compiler that the `GetSpeed()` function is a member of the `Airplane` class. I'll talk more about class member functions when I discuss classes tomorrow.

NOTE

> Tradition has it that class member function names begin with upper-case letters. There is no definite rule about this, but you will find that most C++ programs follow this tradition. As a further note, I am not a fan of the underscore character in function names. For example, I much prefer the function name `GetVideoRect()` over the name `get_video_rect()`. Regardless of what naming convention you use for your functions, be consistent and use the same naming convention throughout your programs.

Inline Functions

Normally the machine code for a function appears only once in the compiled executable file. Each section of code that uses the function calls the function. This means that program execution jumps from the point of the function call to the point in the program where the function resides. The statements in the function are executed and then the function returns. When the function returns, program execution jumps back to the statement following the function call.

 An *inline function*, as its name implies, is placed inline in the compiled code wherever a call to that function occurs.

Inline functions are declared like regular functions but are defined with the `inline` keyword. Each time the compiler encounters a call to an inline function in the source code, it places a separate copy of the function's code in the executable program at that point. Inline functions execute quickly because no actual function call takes place (the code is already inlined in the program).

NOTE

Inline functions should be reserved for functions that are very small or need to be executed very quickly. Large functions or those that are called from many places in your program should not be inlined because your executable file will be larger as a result.

Inline functions are usually class member functions. Often the inline function definition (the function itself) is placed in the header file following the class declaration. (This is the one time that you can place code in your header files.) Because the `GetSpeed()` function mentioned previously is so small, it can be inlined easily. Here's how it would look:

```
inline int Airplane::GetSpeed() {
  return speed;  // speed is a class member variable
}
```

An inline function can also be defined within a class declaration. Because I haven't talked about classes yet, though, I'll hold that discussion for tomorrow.

Summary

That's a lot to learn! Because you are reading this, you must still be standing. That's good news. Today we did the difficult work and took on pointers and references. When you get a handle on pointers, you are well on your way to understanding C++. As part of the discussion on pointers, you learned about local versus dynamic memory allocation, which led to a discussion about the `new` and `delete` operators. Today ended with an explanation of how C++ extends the use of functions beyond what the C language provides.

Workshop

The Workshop contains quiz questions to help you solidify your understanding of the material covered and exercises to provide you with experience in using what you have learned. You can find answers to the quiz questions in Appendix A, "Answers to Quiz Questions."

Q&A

Q Pointers and references confuse me. Am I alone?

A Absolutely not! Pointers and references are complicated and take some time to fully understand. You will probably have to work with C++ a while before you get a handle on pointers and references.

Q Do I always have to delete an object that I created dynamically with the `new` operator?

A Yes and no. All objects created with `new` must have a corresponding `delete` or the program will leak memory. Some objects, however, have parent objects that take the responsibility for deleting them. So the question is not whether an object created with `new` should be deleted, but rather who should delete it. You will always want to call `delete` for classes you write. Later, when you learn about the VCL (on Day 5, "C++ Class Frameworks and the Visual Component Model"), you will see that VCL parent objects take the responsibility for deleting their children.

Q Should I create my objects on the stack or on the heap?

A That depends on the object. Large objects should be created on the heap to preserve stack space. Small objects and primitive data types should be created on the stack for simplicity and speed of execution.

Q Why have overloaded functions?

A Overloaded functions provide a means by which you can have several functions that perform the same basic operation and use the same function name but take different parameters. For example, you might have an overloaded function called `DrawObject()`. One version might take a `Circle` class as a parameter, another might take a `Square` class as a parameter, and a third might take a class called `Polygon` as a parameter. By having three functions with the same name, you avoid the need to have three different function names.

Q Should I use a lot of inline functions?

A That depends on the function, of course. In general, though, the answer is no. Inline functions should be reserved for functions that are very small or seldom used, or when execution speed is critical.

Quiz

1. What is a pointer?
2. What does it mean to dereference a pointer?
3. What is the return value of operator new?
4. Should instances of classes and structures be passed to functions by reference or by value?
5. What does the const keyword do?
6. Does the following qualify as an overloaded function?

```
void MyFunction(int x);
long MyFunction(int x);
```

Why or why not?

7. Which is better to use, a reference or a pointer?
8. What is a class member function?
9. How does the compiler treat an inline function as opposed to a regular function?
10. What, if anything, is wrong with the following code snippet?

```
char* buff = new char[200];
// later...
delete buff;
```

Exercises

1. Write a program that declares a structure, dynamically creates an instance of the structure, and fills the structure with data. (Hint: Don't forget to delete the pointer.)
2. Modify the program from Exercise 1 to use a reference rather than a pointer.
3. Rewrite the REFERENC program in Listing 3.2 so that the mailingListRecord structure is passed to the displayRecord() function by reference rather than by value.
4. What is wrong with the following function declaration?

```
void SomeFunction(int param1, int param2 = 0, int param3);
```

5. Explain to a five-year-old the difference between pointers and references.

Day 4

C++ Classes and Object-Oriented Programming

Today you get to the good stuff. In this chapter you will learn about classes. Classes are the heart of C++ and a major part of object-oriented programming. Classes are also the heart of the Visual Component Library (VCL), which you will use when you start writing Windows GUI applications. (The VCL is discussed in detail on Day 5, "C++ Class Frameworks and the Visual Component Model.") First you will find out what a class is and how it's expected to be used. Along the way you will learn the meaning of C++ buzzwords like *inheritance*, *object*, and *data abstraction*. At the end of the chapter you will get an introduction to file input and output in C++.

What's a Class?

A *class*, like a structure, is a collection of data members and functions that work together to accomplish a specific programming task. In this way a class is said to *encapsulate* the task. Classes have the following features:

- ☐ The capability to control access
- ☐ Constructors
- ☐ Destructors
- ☐ Data members
- ☐ Member functions
- ☐ A hidden, special pointer called this

Before diving into an explanation of these features, let me give you a quick example of how a class can work. Let's use a typical Windows control as an example—a check box, for instance. A class that represents a check box could have data members for the caption of the check box and for the state (checked or unchecked). This class could also have functions that would enable you to set and query both the check box caption and the check state. These functions might be named GetCheck(), SetCheck(), GetCaption(), and SetCaption(). After the class has been written, you can create an instance of the class to control a check box in Windows. (It's not quite that simple, but this is just an example after all.) If you have three check boxes, you could have three instances of the CheckBox class that could then be used to control each check box individually.

```
MyCheckBox check1(ID_CHECK1);
MyCheckBox check2(ID_CHECK2);
MyCheckBox check3(ID_CHECK3);
check1.SetCaption("Thingamabob Option");
check1.SetCheck(true);
check2.SetCaption("Doohickey Options");
check2.SetCheck(false);
check3.SetCaption("Whodyacallum Options");
check3.SetCheck(true);
if (check1.GetCheck()) DoThingamabobTask();
if (check2.GetCheck()) DoDoohickeyTask();
// etc.
```

In this example, each instance of the class is a separate object. Each instance has its own data members, and the objects operate independently of one another. They are all objects of the same type but are separate instances in memory. With that brief introduction, let's roll up our sleeves once more and go to work on understanding classes.

4

Anatomy of a Class

A class, like a structure, has a declaration. The class declaration is usually contained in a header file. In simple cases, both the class declaration and the definition can be contained in a single source file, but you typically won't do that for real applications. Usually you create a class source file with a filename closely matching the class name and with a .cpp extension. Because Windows 95 and Windows NT both support long filenames, you can use filenames that exactly match your class name if you want. The header file for the class usually has the same name as the source file but with an extension of .h. For example, if you had a class called MyClass, you would have a source file named MYCLASS.CPP and a header named MYCLASS.H.

Class Access Levels

 Classes can have three levels of access: *private*, *public*, or *protected*. Each of these access levels is defined in this section.

Class access levels control how a class can be used. As a sole programmer, you might be not only the class's creator but also a user of the class. In team programming environments one programmer might be the creator of the class and other programmers the users of the class.

NOTE
> Let me clarify a couple of comments I made on Day 2, "C++ Fundamentals." I said that a structure is a class in which all data members and functions are public by default. In fact, in C++ this is the only thing that distinguishes a structure from a class. A structure can have functions as well as data members and can have private, protected, and public sections. I also said that you probably won't use structures very much in your C++ programs. Because a class and a structure are nearly the same, you will probably prefer to use classes instead of structures.

To understand the role that levels of access play in class operation, you first need to understand how classes are used. In any class there is the *public* part of the class, which the outside world has access to, and there is the private part of a class. The *private* part of a class is the internal implementation of the class—the inner workings, so to speak.

Part of a well-designed class includes hiding anything from public view that the user of the class doesn't need to know.

 Data abstraction is the hiding of internal implementations within the class from outside views.

Data abstraction prevents the user from knowing more than he or she needs to know about the class and also prevents the user from messing with things that shouldn't be messed with.

For instance, when you get in your car and turn the key to start it, do you want to know every detail about how the car operates? Of course not. You only want to know as much as you need to know to operate the car safely. So in this analogy the steering wheel, pedals, gear shift lever, speedometer, and so on represent the public interface between the car and the driver. The driver knows which of those components to manipulate to make the car perform the way he or she wants.

Conversely, the engine, drive train, and electrical system of the car are hidden from public view. The engine is tucked neatly away where you never have to look at it if you don't want to. It's a detail that you don't need to know about, so it is hidden from you—kept private, if you prefer. Imagine how much trouble driving would be if you had to know everything the car was doing at all times: Is the carburetor getting enough gas? Does the differential have enough grease? Is the alternator producing adequate voltage for both the ignition and the radio to operate? Are the intake valves opening properly? Who needs it! In the same way, a class keeps its internal implementation private so the user of the class doesn't have to worry about what's going on under the hood. The internal workings of the class are kept private, and the user interface is public.

The *protected* access level is a little harder to explain. Protected class members, like private class members, cannot be accessed by users of the class. They can, however, be accessed by classes that are derived from this class. Continuing with the car analogy, let's say you wanted to extend the car (literally) by making it a stretch limousine. To do this, you would need to know something about the underlying structure of the car. You would need to know how to modify the drive shaft and frame of the car at the very minimum. In this case you would need to get your hands dirty and, as a limousine designer, get at the parts of the car that were previously unimportant to you (the protected parts). The internal workings of the engine are still kept private because you don't need to know how the engine works to extend the frame of the car. Similarly, most of the public parts of the car remain the same, but you might add some new public elements, such as the controls for the intercom system. I've strayed a little here and given you a peek into what is called *inheritance*, but I won't go into further details right now. I will talk more about protected access a little later in the section "Member Functions," and about inheritance in the section "Inheritance."

The C++ language has three keywords that pertain to class access. The keywords are (not surprisingly) `public`, `private`, and `protected`. You specify a class member's access level when you declare the class. A class is declared with the `class` keyword. A class declaration looks like a structure declaration with the access modifiers added:

```
class Vehicle {
  public:
    bool haveKey;
    bool Start();
    void SetGear(int gear);
    void Accelerate(int acceleration);
```

```
    void Break(int factor);
    void Turn(int direction);
    void ShutDown();
  protected:
    void StartupProcedure();
  private:
    void StartElectricalSystem();
    void StartEngine();
    int currentGear;
    bool started;
    int speed;
};
```

Notice how you break the class organization down into the three access levels. You might not use all three levels of access in a given class. You are not required to use any of the access levels if you don't want, but typically you will have a public and a private section at the least.

NOTE

Class-member access defaults to private. If you don't add any access keywords, all data and functions in the class will be private. A class where all data members and functions are private is not very useful in most cases.

Constructors

Classes in C++ have a special function called the constructor.

NEW TERM

The *constructor* is a function that is automatically called when an instance of a class is created.

The constructor is used to initialize any class member variables, allocate memory the class will need, or do any other startup tasks. The Vehicle example you just saw does not have a constructor. If you don't provide a constructor, the C++Builder compiler will create a default constructor for you. Whereas this is fine for simple classes, you will almost always provide a constructor for classes of any significance. The constructor must have the same name as the class. This is what distinguishes it as a constructor. Given that, let's add a constructor declaration to the Vehicle class:

```
class Vehicle {
  public:
    Vehicle();        // constructor
    bool haveKey;
    bool Start();
    void SetGear(int gear);
    void Accelerate(int acceleration);
    void Break(int factor);
    void Turn(int direction);
    void ShutDown();
```

```
  protected:
    void StartupProcedure();
  private:
    void StartElectricalSystem();
    void StartEngine();
    int currentGear;
    bool started;
    int speed;
};
```

Notice that the constructor does not have a return type. A constructor cannot return a value, so no return type is specified. If you try to add a return type to the constructor declaration, you will get a compiler error.

A class can have more than one constructor. This is possible through function overloading, which I discussed on Day 3, "Advanced C++." For instance, a class can have a constructor that takes no parameters (a default constructor) and a constructor that takes one or more parameters to initialize data members to certain values. For example, let's say you have a class called Rect that encapsulates a rectangle (rectangles are frequently used in Windows programming). This class could have several constructors. It could have a default constructor that sets all the data members to 0, and another constructor that enables you to set the class's data members through the constructor. First, let's take a look at how the class declaration might look:

```
class Rect {
  public:
    Rect();
    Rect(int _left, int _top, int _right, int _bottom);
    int GetWidth();
    int GetHeight();
    void SetRect(int _left, int _top, int _right, int _bottom);
  private:
    int left;
    int top;
    int right;
    int bottom;
};
```

The definitions for the constructors would look something like this:

```
Rect::Rect()
{
  left = 0;
  top = 0;
  right = 0;
  bottom = 0;
}
Rect::Rect(int _left, int _top, int _right, int _bottom)
{
  left = _left;
  top = _top;
  right = _right;
  bottom = _bottom;
}
```

The first constructor is a default constructor by virtue of the fact that it takes no parameters. It simply initializes each data member to 0. The second constructor takes the parameters passed and assigns them to the corresponding class data members. The variable names in the parameter list are local to the constructor, so each of the variable names begins with an underscore to differentiate between the local variables and the class data members. Here is one case in which using a leading underscore in a variable name is harmless.

> **TIP**
>
> Remember that an uninitialized variable will contain random data. This is true for class data members as well as other variables. To be safe, you should set class member variables to some initial value.

 NEW TERM *Instantiation* is the creation of an object, called an instance, of a class.

It's important to understand that you can't call a constructor directly. So how do you use one of these constructors instead of the other? You do that when you create or *instantiate* an instance of a class. The following code snippet creates two instances of the Rect class. The first uses the default constructor, and the second uses the second form of the constructor:

```
Rect rect1;      // object created using default constructor
Rect rect2(0, 0, 100, 100);  // created using 2nd constructor
```

You can have as many constructors as you like, but be sure that your constructors don't have ambiguous parameter lists (as per the rules on function overloading).

Initializer Lists

NEW TERM C++ provides a means by which you can initialize class data members in what is called an *initializer list*.

The following is the proper way to initialize data members of a class. Rather than try to explain how to use an initializer list, let me show you an example. Let's take the two constructors for the Rect class and initialize the data members in an initializer list rather than in the body of the function as I did before. It looks like this:

```
Rect::Rect() :
  left(0),
  top(0),
  right(0),
  bottom(0)
{
}

Rect::Rect(int _left, int _top, int _right , int _bottom) :
  left(_left),
  top(_top),
```

```
    right(_right),
    bottom(_bottom)
{
}
```

Notice two things in this code snippet. First, notice that the initializer list is preceded by a colon. (The colon is at the end of the function header, so you might not have noticed it.) Notice also that each variable in the initializer list is followed by a comma—except the last variable. Forgetting either of these two things will cause compiler errors.

NOTE

On Day 3, I talked about references. You can have a class data member that is a reference, but the reference can only be initialized in the initializer list of the class and nowhere else.

```
class MyClass {
  public:
    MyClass();
    // other public stuff
  private:
    OtherClass& other;     // reference to another class
    // other private stuff
};
MyClass::MyClass() :
    other(*new OtherClass)  // must do this here!
{
}
```

Attempts to initialize the reference anywhere else will result in compiler errors.

In most cases it doesn't matter whether you initialize your data members in the body of the constructor or the initializer list. I have done it both ways but prefer the initializer list.

Destructors

NEW TERM The *destructor* is a special function that is automatically called just before the object is destroyed.

The destructor could be considered the opposite of the constructor. It is usually used to free any memory allocated by the class or do any other cleanup chores. A class is not required to have a destructor, but if it does, it can have only one. A destructor has no return value and takes no parameters. The destructor's name must be the name of the class preceded by a tilde (~).

As mentioned, the destructor is called just before the class is destroyed. The class might be destroyed because it was allocated from the stack and is going out of scope, or it might be destroyed as a result of delete being called for the class (if the class was created dynamically). In either case, the destructor will be called just before the class breathes its last breath.

The following shows the updated code for the Rect class:

```
class Rect {
  public:
    Rect();
    Rect(int _left, int _top, int _right, int _bottom);
    ~Rect();          // destructor added
    int GetWidth();
    int GetHeight();
    void SetRect(int _left, int _top, int _right, int _bottom);
  private:
    int left;
    int top;
    int right;
    int bottom;
char* text;       // new class member added
};
Rect::Rect() :
  left(0),
  top(0),
  right(0),
  bottom(0)
{
    text = new char[256];
    strcpy(text, "Any Colour You Like");
}
// code omitted
Rect::~Rect()
{
  delete[] text;
}
```

The modified version of the Rect class allocates storage for a char array named text in its constructor and frees that storage in the destructor. (I can't think of a good reason for a class that handles rectangles to have a text data member, but you never know!) Again, use the destructor for any cleanup tasks that need to be done before the instance of the class is destroyed.

Data Members

Data members of a class are simply variables that are declared in the class declaration. They could be considered as variables that have class scope. Data members in classes are essentially the same as data members in structures except that their access can be controlled by declaring them as private, public, or protected. Regardless of a data member's access, it is available for use in all functions of the class. Depending on the data member's access level, it can be visible outside the class as well. Private and protected data members, for instance, are private to the class and cannot be seen outside the class. Public data members, however, can be accessed from outside the class but only through an object. Take the Rect class declared previously, for example. It has no public data members. You could try the following, but you'll get a compiler error:

```
Rect rect(10, 10, 200, 200);
int x = rect.left;  // compiler error!
```

The compiler error will say `Rect::left is not accessible`. The compiler is telling you that `left` is a private data member and you can't get to it. If `left` were in the `public` section of the class declaration, this code would compile.

You can use *getters* and *setters* to change private data members: getters are functions that get the value of a private data member, and setters are functions that set the value of a private data member. Both getters and setters are public member functions that act on private data members.

To illustrate, let's say that for the `Rect` class you had the following getters and setters for the `left` data member:

```
int Rect::GetLeft()
{
  return left;
}
void Rect::SetLeft(int newLeft)
{
  left = newLeft;
}
```

Now when you want to obtain the value of the `left` member of the `Rect` class, you can use:

```
Rect rect;
int x = rect.GetLeft();
```

In some cases this is overkill. Setters have one main advantage, though—they enable you to validate input. By validating input, you can control the values your data members contain.

NOTE

> Some OOP extremists say that data members should never be public. They would advise you to use getters and setters to access all data members. On the other end of the spectrum is the group that recommends making all your data members public. The truth lies somewhere in between. Some data members are noncritical and can be left public if it is more convenient. Other data members are critical to the way the class operates and should not be made public. If you are going to err, it is better to err on the side of making data members private.

Each instance of your class gets its own copy of the class's data members in memory. The exception to this is that if any class data members are declared with the `static` storage modifier, all instances of the class will share the same copy of that data member in memory. In that case only one copy of that data member will exist in memory. If any one instance of the class changes a static data member, it changes in all the classes. Use of static data members in classes is not common, so don't worry about it if this doesn't make sense right now.

House Rules: Class Data Members

☐ Use as many data members as you need for vital class operations, but use local variables where possible.

☐ Don't make all data members public.

☐ Use getters and setters for data members that you want to remain private but need to be able to access.

☐ Validate data in your setters to ensure that improper values are not being input.

☐ Initialize all data members in either the initializer list or in the body of your constructor.

☐ Don't forget to delete any data members that dynamically allocate memory.

Member Functions

Class member functions are functions that belong to your class. They are local to the class and don't exist outside the class. Class member functions can only be called from within the class itself or through an instance of the class. They have access to all public, protected, and private data members of the class. Member functions can be declared in the private, protected, or public sections of your class. Good class design requires that you think about which of these sections your member functions should go into.

Public member functions represent the user interface to the class. It is through the public member functions that users of the class access the class to gain whatever functionality the class provides. For example, let's say you have a class that plays and records wave audio. Public member functions might include functions like Open(), Play(), Record(), Save(), Rewind(), and so on.

Private member functions are functions that the class uses internally to do its thing. These functions are not intended to be called by users of the class; they are private in order to hide them from the outside world. Frequently a class has startup chores to perform when the class is created. (For example, you have already seen that the constructor is called when a class is created.) In some classes the startup processing might be significant, requiring many lines of code. To remove clutter from the constructor, a class might have an Init() function that is called from the constructor to perform those startup tasks. This function would never be called directly by a user of the class. In fact, more than likely bad things would happen if this function were to be called by a user at the wrong time, so the function is private in order to protect both the integrity of the class and the user.

Protected member functions are functions that cannot be accessed by the outside world but can be accessed by classes derived from this class. I haven't talked yet about classes being derived from other classes; I'll save that discussion for a little later when it will make more sense. I discuss deriving classes in the section "Inheritance."

On Day 3 we talked briefly about inline functions in the section, "Inline Functions." Then I said that an inline function is different because the code for the function is placed in the compiled executable each time a call to the inline function appears in the application's code. This differs from regular functions where only one copy of the function exists in the compiled executable regardless of how many times it is called. Inline functions can be declared in one of two ways. Here is the syntax for the first form:

The `inline` function, Form 1:

```
class ClassName {
  public:
    ReturnType FunctionName();
};

inline ReturnType ClassName::FunctionName() {
  statements
}
```

The function *FunctionName* is declared within the body of the class *ClassName*. The function definition (the function itself) is defined outside of the class declaration using the `inline` keyword. *FunctionName* must be proceeded by *ClassName* and the scope resolution operator.

The function can be defined within the class declaration to which the function belongs:

```
class MyClass {
  public:
    // other stuff
    int GetSomething()
    {
      return Something;
    }
  private:
    int Something;
};
```

Here the function is automatically an inline function by virtue of the fact that the entire function is contained within the class declaration.

The other way to declare a function is to declare it with the `inline` keyword.

SYNTAX

The `inline` function, Form 2:

```
class ClassName {
  public:
    ReturnType FunctionName()
    {
      statements
    }
};
```

The function *FunctionName* is declared and defined entirely within the *ClassName* declaration. The function is an inline function by virtue of the fact that it is contained within the *ClassName* declaration. The `inline` keyword is not required.

The following example illustrates how this form of the inline function would be used in a header file:

```
class MyClass {
  public:
    // other stuff
    int GetSomething();
  private:
    int Something;
};

inline int MyClass::GetSomething()
{
  return Something;
}
```

Using this syntax, the function is declared, as usual, in the class declaration; but in the function definition, the `inline` keyword is used to specify that the function should be an inline function. Normally you shouldn't place any executable code in the header, but inline functions are a special case. They can be, and often are, placed in the header, usually just after the class declaration. Many class libraries use this method of declaring and defining inline functions.

As with data members, member functions can be declared with the `static` modifier. A static member function operates more like a regular function than a member function. Specifically, a static member function cannot access data members of the class. (In just a bit I'll tell you why this restriction exists.) Most of the time you will not use static member functions, but sometimes you will be required to. For instance, some Windows API functions use callbacks to perform repeated tasks. If you use this kind of function in your class, the callback function has to be declared as static.

4

House Rules: Class Member Functions

☐ Make public only those functions that users need in order to properly utilize the class.

☐ Make private any functions that users don't need to know about.

☐ Make protected any functions that derived classes might need access to but that users don't need to know about.

☐ Use static member functions only under special circumstances.

☐ Declare any class member functions that have to be executed quickly as inline functions. Remember to keep inline functions short.

☐ Place any code duplicated more than twice in a function.

What's this?

 All classes have a hidden data member called this. this is a pointer to the instance of the class in memory. (A discussion on the this pointer quickly starts to sound like a "Who's on First?" comedy sketch, but I'll try anyway.)

Obviously this (pun intended) will require some explanation. First, let's take a look at how the Rect class would look if this were not a hidden data member:

```
class Rect {
  public:
    Rect();
    Rect(int _left, int _top, int _bottom, int _right);
    ~Rect();
    int GetWidth();
    int GetHeight();
    void SetRect(int _left, int _top, int _bottom, int _right);
  private:
    Rect* this;          // if 'this' were not invisible
    int left;
    int top;
    int bottom;
    int right;
    char* text;
};
```

This is effectively what the Rect class looks like to the compiler. When a class object is created, the this pointer automatically gets initialized to the address of the class in memory:

```
Rect* rect = new Rect(20, 20, 100, 100);
// now 'rect' and 'rect->this' have the same value
// because both point to the same object in memory
```

"But," you ask, "what does this mean?" Remember that each class instance gets its own copy of the class's data members. But all class instances share the same set of functions for the class (there's no point in duplicating that code for each instance of the class). How does the compiler figure out which instance goes with which function call? Class member functions all have a hidden this parameter that goes with them. To illustrate, let's say you have a function for the Rect class called GetWidth(). It would look like this (no pun intended):

```
int Rect::GetWidth()
{
  return (right - left);
}
```

That's how the function looks to you and me. To the compiler, though, it looks something like this:

```
int Rect::GetWidth(Rect* this)
{
  return (this->right - this->left);
}
```

That's not exactly accurate from a technical perspective, but it's close enough for this discussion. From this code you can see that this is working behind the scenes to keep everything straight for you. You don't have to worry about how that happens, but you need to know that it does happen.

WARNING

Never modify the this pointer. You can use it to pass a pointer to your class to other functions or as a parameter in constructing other classes, but don't change its value. Learn to treat this as a read-only variable.

Although this works behind the scenes, it is still a variable that you can access from within the class. As an illustration, let's take a quick peek into VCL. Most of the time you will create components in VCL by dropping them on the form at design time. When you do that, C++Builder creates a pointer to the component and does all sorts of housekeeping chores on your behalf, saving you from concerning yourself with the technical end of things. Sometimes, however, you will create a component at runtime. VCL insists (as all good frameworks do) on wanting to keep track of which child objects belong to which parent. For instance, let's say you wanted to create a button on a form when another button is clicked. You need to tell VCL what the parent of the new button is. The code would look like this:

```
void __fastcall TMyForm::Button1Click(TObject *Sender)
{
  TButton* button = new TButton(this);
  button->Parent = this;
  button->Caption = "New Button";
  button->Left = 100;
```

```
  button->Top = 100;
  button->Show();
  // more code
}
```

In this code you can see that `this` is used in the constructor (this sets the `Owner` property of the button, but I'll get into that on Day 8, "VCL Components") and also that it is assigned to the `Parent` property of the newly created button. This is how you will use the `this` pointer the vast majority of the time in your C++Builder applications.

NOTE

> Earlier I said that static member functions can't access class data members. The reason this is true is because static member functions don't have a hidden `this` parameter; regular class member functions do. Without `this`, a function cannot access class members.

Don't worry too much about this...er, `this` (whatever!). When you begin to use VCL, it will quickly become clear when you are required to use `this` in your C++Builder applications.

An Example

Right now it would be nice if you had an example that uses classes. The following listings contain a program that implements classes. This program enables you to play air traffic controller by issuing commands to three aircraft. Listing 4.1 is the header for the `Airplane` class, Listing 4.2 is the source code for the `Airplane` class, and Listing 4.3 is the main program.

Listing 4.1. AIRPLANE.H.

```
 1: //--------------------------------------------------------
 2: #ifndef airplaneH
 3: #define airplaneH
 4: #define AIRLINER      0
 5: #define  COMMUTER     1
 6: #define  PRIVATE      2
 7: #define  TAKINGOFF    0
 8: #define  CRUISING     1
 9: #define LANDING       2
10: #define ONRAMP        3
11: #define  MSG_CHANGE   0
12: #define  MSG_TAKEOFF  1
13: #define  MSG_LAND     2
14: #define  MSG_REPORT   3
15: class Airplane {
16:   public:
17:     Airplane(const char* _name, int _type = AIRLINER);
18:     ~Airplane();
```

4

```
19:      virtual int GetStatus(char* statusString);
20:      int GetStatus()
21:      {
22:      return status;
23:      }
24:       int Speed()
25:      {
26:        return speed;
27:      }
28:      int Heading()
29:      {
30:        return heading;
31:      }
32:      int Altitude()
33:      {
34:        return altitude;
35:      }
36:      void ReportStatus();
37:      bool SendMessage(int msg, char* response,
38:        int spd = -1, int dir = -1, int alt = -1);
39:      char* name;
40:   protected:
41:      virtual void TakeOff(int dir);
42:      virtual void Land();
43:   private:
44:      int speed;
45:      int altitude;
46:      int heading;
47:      int status;
48:      int type;
49:      int ceiling;
50: };
51: #endif
```

Listing 4.2. AIRPLANE.CPP.

```
1: #include <stdio.h>
2: #include <iostream.h>
3: #include "airplane.h"
4: //
5: // Constructor performs initialization
6: //
7: Airplane::Airplane(const char* _name, int _type) :
8:    type(_type),
9:    status(ONRAMP),
10:   speed(0),
11:   altitude(0),
12:   heading(0)
13: {
14:    switch (type) {
15:      case AIRLINER : ceiling = 35000; break;
16:      case COMMUTER : ceiling = 20000; break;
```

continues

Listing 4.2. continued

```
17:      case PRIVATE  : ceiling = 8000;
18:    }
19:    name = new char[50];
20:    strcpy(name, _name);
21: }
22: //
23: // Destructor performs cleanup.
24: //
25: Airplane::~Airplane()
26: {
27:    delete[] name;
28: }
29: //
30: // Gets a message from the user.
31: //
32: bool
33: Airplane::SendMessage(int msg, char* response,
34:    int spd, int dir, int alt)
35: {
36:    //
37:    // Check for bad commands.
38:    //
39:    if (spd > 500) {
40:      strcpy(response, "Speed cannot be more than 500.");
41:      return false;
42:    }
43:    if (dir > 360) {
44:      strcpy(response, "Heading cannot be over 360 degrees.");
45:      return false;
46:    }
47:    if (alt < 100 && alt != -1) {
48:      strcpy(response, "I'd crash, bonehead!");
49:      return false;
50:    }
51:    if (alt > ceiling) {
52:      strcpy(response, "I can't go that high.");
53:      return false;
54:    }
55:    //
56:    // Do something based on which command was sent.
57:    //
58:    switch (msg) {
59:      case MSG_TAKEOFF : {
60:        // Can't take off if already in the air!
61:        if (status != ONRAMP) {
62:          strcpy(response, "I'm already in the air!");
63:          return false;
64:        }
65:        TakeOff(dir);
66:        break;
67:      }
68:      case MSG_CHANGE : {
69:        // Can't change anything if on the ground.
70:        if (status == ONRAMP) {
```

```
71:        strcpy(response, "I'm on the ground.");
72:        return false;
73:      }
74:       // Only change if a non-negative value was passed.
75:      if (spd != -1) speed = spd;
76:      if (dir != -1) heading = dir;
77:      if (alt != -1) altitude = alt;
78:      status = CRUISING;
79:      break;
80:    }
81:    case MSG_LAND : {
82:      if (status == ONRAMP) {
83:        strcpy(response, "I'm already on the ground.");
84:        return false;
85:      }
86:      Land();
87:      break;
88:    }
89:    case MSG_REPORT : ReportStatus();
90:   }
91:   //
92:   // Standard reponse if all went well.
93:   //
94:   strcpy(response, "Roger.");
95:   return true;
96: }
97: //
98: // Perform takeoff.
99: //
100: void
101: Airplane::TakeOff(int dir)
102: {
103:   heading = dir;
104:   status = TAKINGOFF;
105: }
106: //
107: // Perform landing.
108: //
109: void
110: Airplane::Land()
111: {
112:   speed = heading = altitude = 0;
113:   status = ONRAMP;
114: }
115: //
116: // Build a string to report the airplane's status.
117: //
118: int
119: Airplane::GetStatus(char* statusString)
120: {
121:   sprintf(statusString, "%s, Altitude: %d, Heading: %d, "
122:     "Speed: %d\n", name, altitude, heading, speed);
123:   return status;
124: }
125: //
```

4

continues

Listing 4.2. continued

```
126: // Get the status string and output it to the screen.
127: //
128: void
129: Airplane::ReportStatus()
130: {
131:    char buff[100];
132:    GetStatus(buff);
133:    cout << endl << buff << endl;
134: }
```

Listing 4.3. AIRPORT.CPP.

```
 1: //------------------------------------------------------
 2: #include <condefs.h>
 3: #include <iostream.h>
 4: #include <conio.h>
 5: #pragma hdrstop
 6:
 7: USEUNIT("airplane.cpp");
 8: #include "airplane.h"
 9: int getInput(int max);
10: void getItems(int& speed, int& dir, int& alt);
11: int main(int argc, char **argv)
12: {
13:    char returnMsg[100];
14:    //
15:    // Set up an array of  Airplanes and create
16:    // three Airplane objects.
17:    //
18:    Airplane* planes[3];
19:    planes[0] = new Airplane("TWA 1040");
20:    planes[1] = new Airplane("United Express 749", COMMUTER);
21:    planes[2] = new Airplane("Cessna 3238T", PRIVATE);
22:    //
23:    // Start the loop.
24:    //
25:    do {
26:      int plane, message, speed, altitude, direction;
27:      speed = altitude = direction = -1;
28:      //
29:      // Get a plane to whom a message will be sent.
30:      // List all the planes and let the user pick one.
31:      //
32:      cout << endl << "Who do you want to send a message to?";
33:      cout << endl << endl << "0. Quit" <<  endl;
34:      for (int i=0;i<3;i++)
35:        cout << (i + 1) << ". " << planes[i]->name << endl;
36:      //
37:      // Call the getInput() function to get the plane number.
38:      //
```

```
39:     plane = getInput(4);
40:     //
41:     // If the user chose item 0, then break out of the loop.
42:     //
43:     if (plane == -1) break;
44:     //
45:     // The plane acknowledges.
46:     //
47:     cout << endl << planes[plane]->name << ", roger.";
48:     cout << endl << endl;
49:     //
50:     // Allow the user to choose a message to send.
51:     //
52:     cout << "What message do you want to send?" << endl;
53:     cout << endl << "0. Quit" << endl;
54:     cout << "1. State Change" << endl;
55:     cout << "2. Take Off" << endl;
56:     cout << "3. Land" << endl;
57:     cout << "4. Report Status" << endl;
58:     message = getInput(5);
59:     //
60:     // Break out of the loop if the user chose 0.
61:     //
62:     if (message == -1) break;
63:     //
64:     // If the user chose item 1, then we need to get input
65:     // for the new speed, direction, and altitude. Call
66:     // the getItems() function to do that.
67:     //
68:     if (message == 0)
69:       getItems(speed, direction, altitude);
70:     //
71:     // Send the plane the message.
72:     //
73:     bool goodMsg = planes[plane]->SendMessage(
74:       message, returnMsg, speed, direction, altitude);
75:     //
76:     // Something was wrong with the message
77:     //
78:     if (!goodMsg) cout << endl << "Unable to comply.";
79:     //
80:     // Display the plane's response.
81:     //
82:     cout << endl << returnMsg << endl;
83:   } while (1);
84:   //
85:   // Delete the Airplane objects.
86:   //
87:   for (int i=0;i<3;i++) delete planes[i];
88: }
89: int getInput(int max)
90: {
91:   int choice;
92:   do {
93:     choice = getch();
94:     choice -= 49;
```

continues

Listing 4.3. continued

```
 95:    } while (choice < -1 || choice > max);
 96:    return choice;
 97: }
 98: void getItems(int& speed, int& dir, int& alt)
 99: {
100:    cout << endl << "Enter new speed: ";
101:    cin >> speed;
102:    cout << "Enter new heading: ";
103:    cin >> dir;
104:    cout << "Enter new altitude: ";
105:    cin >> alt;
106:    cout << endl;
107: }
```

 Let's look first at the header file in Listing 4.1. First, notice all the lines that begin with #define. What I am doing here is associating one text string with another. At compile time the compiler just does a search-and-replace and replaces all occurrences of the first string with the second. #defines are used because it's much easier to remember a text string than a number. Which of the following do you prefer?

```
if (type == AIRLINER) ...
// or
if (type == 0) ...
```

Tradition has it that names for #defines be in uppercase, but you can use any mixture of uppercase and lowercase letters. I like all uppercase because it tells me at a glance that this is a defined constant and not a variable.

> **NOTE**
>
> Another way of declaring constants is to declare a variable using the const modifier.
>
> `const int airliner = 0;`
>
> Using a const variable is probably the more modern method of defining constants.

The next thing to note in the header is that the class includes some inline functions. These functions are so small that it makes sense to inline them. You will also notice that the Airplane class has one overloaded function called GetStatus(). When called with a character array parameter, it will return a status string as well as the status data member. When called without a parameter, it just returns status. Note that there is only one public data member. The rest of the data members are kept private. The only way to access the private data members is via the public functions. For instance, you can change the speed, altitude, and heading of an airplane only by sending it a message. To use an analogy, consider that an air traffic controller cannot physically change an aircraft's heading. The best he can do is send a message to the pilot and tell him to change to a new heading.

Now turn your attention to Listing 4.2. This is the definition of the Airplane class. The constructor performs initialization, including dynamically allocating storage for the char array that holds the name of the airplane. That memory is freed in the destructor. The SendMessage() function does most of the work. A switch statement determines which message was sent and takes the appropriate action. Notice that the TakeOff() and Land() functions cannot be called directly (they are protected) but rather are called through the SendMessage() function. Again, you can't make an aircraft take off or land; you can only send it a message telling it what you want it to do. The ReportStatus() function calls GetStatus() to get a status string, which it outputs.

The main program is shown in Listing 4.3. The program first sets up an array of Airplane pointers and creates three instances of the Airplane class. Then a loop starts. You can send messages to any airplane by calling the object's SendMessage() function. When you send a message, you get a response back from the airplane. The do-while loop cheats a little in this program. Notice that the test condition is simply 1. This means that the loop will keep running indefinitely. In this case it's not a problem because I am using the break statement to break out of the loop rather than relying on the test condition. Run the program and play with it to get a feel for how it works.

Inheritance

One of the most powerful features of classes in C++ is that they can be extended through inheritance.

 Inheritance means taking an existing class and adding functionality by deriving a new class from it.

 The class you start with is called the *base class*, and the new class you create is called the *derived class*.

Let's take the Airplane class as an example. The civilian and military worlds are quite different, as you know. To represent a military aircraft, I can derive a class from Airplane and add functionality to it:

```
class MilitaryPlane : public Airplane {
  public:
    MilitaryPlane(char* name, int _type);
    virtual int GetStatus(char* statusString);
  protected:
    virtual void TakeOff();
    virtual void Land()
    virtual void Attack();
```

```
    virtual void SetMission();
private:
    Mission theMission;
};
```

A `MilitaryPlane` has everything an `Airplane` has, plus a few more goodies. Note the first line of the class definition. The colon after the class name is used to tell the compiler that I am inheriting from another class. The class name following the colon is the base class from which I am deriving. The `public` keyword, when used here, means that I am claiming access to all the public functions and data members of the base class.

NOTE

> When you derive a class from another class, the new class gets all the functionality of the base class plus whatever new features you add. You can add data members and functions to the new class, but you cannot remove anything from what the base class offers.

You'll notice that in the `private` section there is a line that declares a variable of the `Mission` class. The `Mission` class could encapsulate everything that deals with the mission of a military aircraft: the target, navigation waypoints, ingress and egress altitudes and headings, and so on. This illustrates the use of a data member that is an instance of another class. In fact, you'll see that a lot when programming in C++Builder.

There's something else here that I haven't discussed yet. Note the `virtual` keyword. This specifies that the function is a virtual function.

NEW TERM A *virtual function* is a function that is automatically called if a function of that name exists in the derived class.

For example, note that the `TakeOff()` function is a virtual function in the `Airplane` class. Refer back to Listing 4.2. Notice that `TakeOff()` is called by `SendMessage()` in response to the `MSG_TAKEOFF` message. If the `MilitaryPlane` class did not provide its own `TakeOff()` function, the base class's `TakeOff()` function would be called. Because the `MilitaryPlane` class does provide a `TakeOff()` function, that function will be called rather than the function in the base class.

NEW TERM Replacing a base class function in a derived class is called *overriding* the function.

In order for overriding to work, the function signature must exactly match that of the function in the base class. In other words, the return type, function name, and parameter list must all be the same as the base class function.

You can override a function with the intention of replacing the base class function, or you can override a function to enhance the base class function. Take the TakeOff() function, for example. If you wanted to completely replace what the TakeOff() function of Airplane does, you would override it and supply whatever code you wanted:

```
void MilitaryPlane::TakeOff(int dir)
{
  // new code goes here
}
```

But if you wanted your function to take the functionality of the base class and add to it, you would first call the base class function and then add new code:

```
void MilitaryPlane::TakeOff(int dir)
{
  Airplane::TakeOff(dir);
  // new code goes here
}
```

By calling the base class function, you get the original behavior of the function as written in the base class. You can then add code before or after the base class call to enhance the function. The scope-resolution operator is used to tell the compiler that you are calling the TakeOff() function of the Airplane class. Note that the TakeOff() function is in the protected section of the Airplane class. If it were in the private section, this would not work because even a derived class cannot access the private members of its ancestor class. By making the TakeOff() function protected, it is hidden from the outside world but still accessible to derived classes.

NOTE

The scope-resolution operator is required only when you have derived and base class functions with the same name and the same function signature. You can call a public or protected function of the base class at any time without the need for the scope-resolution operator, provided they aren't overridden. For example, if you wanted to check the status of the aircraft prior to takeoff, you could do something like this:

```
void MilitaryPlane::TakeOff(int dir)
{
  if (GetStatus() != ONRAMP) Land(); // gotta land first!
  Airplane::TakeOff(dir);
  // new code goes here
}
```

In this case, the GetStatus() function exists only in the base class, so there is no need for the scope-resolution operator. In the case of the Land() function, the MilitaryPlane version will be called because it has the most immediate scope.

4

When you derive a class from another class, you must be sure to call the base class's constructor so that all ancestor classes are properly initialized. Calling the base class constructor is done in the initializer list. Here's how the constructor for MilitaryPlane might appear:

```
MilitaryPlane:: MilitaryPlane(char* _name)
  : Airplane(_name, MILITARY)                // call base class
{
  // body of constructor
}
```

Be sure to call the base class constructor whenever you derive a class from a base class. Figure 4.1 illustrates the concept of inheritance.

Figure 4.1.

An example of inheritance.

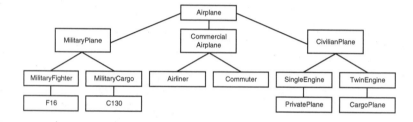

You can see from Figure 4.1 that the class called F16 is descended from the class called Fighter. Ultimately, F16 is derived from Airplane because Airplane is the base class for all classes.

Multiple Inheritance

NEW TERM   The act of deriving a class from two or more base classes is called *multiple inheritance*.

Multiple inheritance is not used frequently, but it can be very handy when needed. For an example, let's say you had a class called Armaments that kept track of the armaments for a particular aircraft. It might look like this:

```
class Armaments {
  public:
    Armaments();
    LoadArms();
  private:
    bool isArmed;
    int numSidewinders;
    int numSparrows;
    // etc.
};
```

Now let's say that you were to create a class to represent a military fighter. You could inherit from both MilitaryPlane and Armaments:

```
class Fighter : public MilitaryPlane, public Armaments {
  public:
    Fighter(char* name);
  private:
    // other stuff
};
```

Now you have a class that contains all the public elements of `MilitaryPlane` and all the public elements of `Armaments`. This would enable you to do the following:

```
Fighter fighter("F16");
fighter.LoadArms();
fighter.SendMessage(...);
// etc.
```

The two base classes are blended to form a single class.

NOTE

> You should call the base class constructor for all base classes. The following illustrates:
>
> ```
> F16::F16(char* _name)
>   : MilitaryPlane(_name, F16), Armaments()
> {
>   // body of constructor
> }
> ```
>
> If a class has a default constructor, it is not strictly necessary to call the base class constructor for that class. In most situations, though, you will call the base class constructor for all ancestor classes.

Let me give you one other example. In the United States, the Military Air Command (MAC) is responsible for moving military personnel from place to place. MAC is sort of like the U.S. military's own personal airline. Because personnel are ultimately cargo, this requires a military cargo plane. But because people are special cargo, you can't just throw them in the back of a plane designed to haul freight (not usually, anyway). So what is needed is a military cargo plane with all the amenities of a commercial airliner. Look back to Figure 4.1. It would appear that to get what we want, we can derive from both `MilitaryCargo` and `Airliner`—and we can. Figure 4.2 illustrates.

Although you might not use multiple inheritance often, it is a very handy feature to have available when you need it.

4

Figure 4.2.
*An example of
multiple inheritance.*

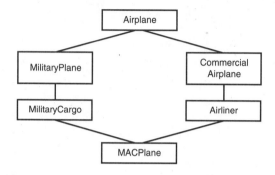

NOTE

Because Object Pascal does not have multiple inheritance, you cannot use multiple inheritance in classes derived from VCL classes. You can still use multiple inheritance in any C++ classes you write outside the VCL framework.

Basic File I/O

It won't be long before you are going to need the ability to read and write files in your applications. I saved this discussion for now because you needed an understanding of classes in order to understand how file input and output is handled in C++.

If you are going to be doing heavy database operations with C++Builder, you will be relieved to know that you don't have to worry about dealing with reading and writing database files directly. That is all handled for you behind the scenes through C++Builder's VCL database components. VCL also provides support for reading and writing the contents of edit controls, list boxes, and other basic Windows controls. The Windows API provides functions for reading configuration files (.INI files). Many OCX and ActiveX controls know how to save and load files specific to the type of action the control performs.

As you can see, many of the objects you will use in C++Builder handle file I/O for you. Still, there will be times when you have to read and write your own files, and you'll need a basic understanding of file I/O to do that.

Basic file I/O is accomplished via three C++ classes:

☐ The ofstream class, which handles file output

☐ The ifstream class, which handles file input

☐ The fstream class, which handles both file input and output

Sometimes the labyrinth of the streaming classes can be pretty confusing. What I am going to do here is give you a cursory glance at file I/O, but then we'll have to move on. You'll be relieved to know that basic file I/O is not complicated. To do sophisticated file operations, you'll need to dig into the Rouge Wave Standard C++ Library 2.0 online documentation or get a good book on the Standard Library that deals with file I/O in detail.

Basic File Input

Reading a text file in C++ is a painless task. Listing 4.4 contains a program that reads its own source file and displays each line as it reads it from disk. First, enter the program as it appears in the listing (remember, don't type the line numbers). Then save the project with the name READFILE. If you don't save the program with this name, the program will not run properly. Compile and run the program. Because the program reads its own source file, the output from the program will be the contents of Listing 4.4.

Listing 4.4. READFILE.CPP.

```
1: #include <condefs.h>
2: #include <fstream.h>
3: #include <conio.h>
4: #pragma hdrstop
5:
6: int main(int argc, char **argv)
7: {
8:   char buff[80];
9:   ifstream infile;
10:   infile.open("readfile.cpp");
11:   if (!infile) return 0;
12:   while (!infile.eof()) {
13:     infile.getline(buff, sizeof(buff));
14:     cout << buff << endl;
15:   }
16:   infile.close();
17:   cout << endl << "Press any key to continue...";
18:   getch();
19:   return 0;
20: }
```

ANALYSIS The code on line 9 creates an instance of the `ifstream` class called `infile`. Line 10 opens the file READFILE.CPP for input. Line 11 checks to see whether the file was opened successfully. If not, the program terminates. Line 12 starts a loop. Notice that the loop expression is a call to the `eof()` function of the `istream` class. This function returns `true` when the file encounters the end of the file. On line 13, one line of text is read from the file using the `getline()` function. The line of text is placed in the character array called `buff`. After that, the contents of the character array are sent to the screen. Finally, line 16 closes the file. Notice that on line 2 I `#include` the FSTREAM.H header file so the compiler can see the declaration for the `ifstream` class. As you can see from this example, reading a text file does not require a lot of programming, thanks to C++ and the `ifstream` class.

One of the `ifstream` constructors takes a `char*` as a parameter so that you can provide a filename when you instantiate the class. Using this constructor, lines 9 and 10 can be condensed into a single line:

```
ifstream infile("readfile.cpp");
```

If you create the object this way, the call to `open()` is unnecessary because the file will automatically be opened from the constructor.

TIP

> Don't forget about the double backslashes in constant strings! For example, if you want to open the `WIN.INI` file in the Windows directory, you have to use this:
>
> ```
> ifstream infile("c:\\windows\\win.ini");
> ```
>
> I know I've mentioned this before, but I'll guarantee you that at some point you'll forget the double backslashes. When you do, it'll cause you all sorts of grief, so I want to keep reminding you of this while I have the opportunity.

The call to `close()` on line 16 of Listing 4.4 is not strictly needed. The `ifstream` destructor checks to see whether the file was left open. If it was, the destructor calls `close()` to ensure that the file is closed before the instance of the class is destroyed. In my programs I almost always call `close()` even though it is not strictly required. Explicitly calling `close()` has the added benefit of documenting that the file is no longer needed.

NOTE

> The program in Listing 4.4 contains a minor bug. Because of the way the end-of-file is determined, the program will print one blank line before the loop terminates. To avoid the extra line, the loop should be written like this:
>
> ```
> while (!infile.getline(buff, sizeof(buff)).eof()) {
>   cout << buff << endl;
> }
> ```
>
> Chaining functions like this is perfectly legal, but it's confusing to new C++ programmers. To make the code easier to understand, I allowed the bug to live rather than squash it.

Because the file-handling classes are derived from iostream, you can use the insertion and extraction operators just as you do when writing to the console using cout and reading from the console using cin. The reason getline() is used in Listing 4.4 is because the extraction operator (>>) stops at the first whitespace it encounters. (*Whitespace* includes blank spaces, tabs, and so on.) The getline() function, on the other hand, reads from the file until an EOL (end-of-line) character is detected, which is what you want when reading lines of text. When reading single values without whitespace, the extraction operator is very useful. The following code snippet reads a file containing numbers and outputs the numbers to the screen:

```
ifstream infile("somefil.dat");
while (!infile.eof()) {
  int x;
  infile >> x;    // read number from file and assign it to x
  cout << x << endl;
}
```

Note that the file being read is still a text file and not a binary file. The extraction operator knows how to read text from the file and convert it into an integer.

Basic File Output

In some ways, file output is easier than file input. The insertion operator (<<) makes it easy. The procedure is nearly identical to what is done when reading a file. Instead of creating an instance of the ifstream class, you create an instance of the ofstream class and start throwing things at it. Listing 4.5 contains a program that creates a new file, writes 10 lines of text to it, and closes it. Following that, the file is reopened in read mode, and the contents are read and displayed.

Listing 4.5. WRITEFIL.CPP.

```
 1: #include <condefs.h>
 2: #include <fstream.h>
 3: #include <conio.h>
 4:
 5: #pragma hdrstop
 6:
 7: int main(int argc, char **argv)
 8: {
 9:   char buff[81];
10:   cout << "Creating File..." << endl;
11:   ofstream outfile("test.dat");
12:   if (!outfile) return 0;
13:   cout << "Writing File..." << endl;
14:   for (int i=0;i<10;i++) {
15:     outfile << "This is line #" << (i + 1) << endl;
16:   }
17:   outfile.close();
18:   cout << "Opening File for Input..." << endl;
```

continues

Listing 4.5. continued

```
19:    ifstream infile("test.dat");
20:    if (!infile) return 0;
21:    cout << "Reading File..." << endl << endl;
22:    while (!infile.eof()) {
23:      infile.getline(buff, sizeof(buff));
24:      cout << buff << endl;
25:    }
26:    infile.close();
27:    cout << endl << "Press any key to continue...";
28:    getch();
29:    return 0;
30: }
```

ANALYSIS Line 11 creates an instance of the `ofstream` class and creates a file called `TEST.DAT`. After the file has been created, a loop writes 10 lines of text to the file. Line 15 illustrates the use of the insertion operator to write to the file. Notice that a text string is written followed by an integer value (`i + 1`). The integer is converted to a string and inserted in the output stream. Last but not least, the `endl` manipulator is inserted to terminate the string. This is repeated for each iteration of the loop. Line 17 closes the file after the loop ends. In this case it is necessary to close the file because we are going to reopen it to read the file. If we don't close the file, it cannot be opened for reading. In lines 22–25 I use code similar to that used in the `READFILE.CPP` example to display the contents of the file. When the program in Listing 4.5 runs, the output will look like this:

OUTPUT
```
Creating File...
Writing File...
Opening File for Input...
Reading File...

This is line #1
This is line #2
This is line #3
This is line #4
This is line #5
This is line #6
This is line #7
This is line #8
This is line #9
This is line #10

Press any key to continue...
```

Specifying File Modes

Files can be opened in several different modes. For example, sometimes you want to append data to the end of an existing file rather than create a new file. In that case you can append data to the end of a file by opening the file in append mode. To specify append mode, you must use one of the ios class's open_mode specifiers in the ofstream constructor when you create the object:

```
ofstream outfile("test.dat", ios::app);   // open in append mode
```

This file will be opened in append mode, and any new data written to the file will be written to the end of the file. Notice that the app flag is preceded by the scope resolution operator for the ios class. Because the open_mode enumeration is a member of the ios class, you must use the scope resolution operator when referencing any of the open_mode members. There are several specifiers you can use when opening files. Table 4.1 lists the open_mode enumeration's values and their descriptions.

Table 4.1. ios **class** open_mode **specifiers.**

Specifier	Description
app	Opens the file, and any new data is appended to the end of the file.
ate	Seeks to the end of the file when the file is opened.
in	Opens the file for input (reading). This is the default for the ifstream class.
out	Opens the file for output (writing). This is the default for the ofstream class.
binary	Opens the file in binary mode. The default is to open the file in text mode. In text mode, when the file is read, carriage-return/linefeed (CR/LF) pairs are converted to a single linefeed character (LF). When the file is written, linefeed characters are converted to CR/LF pairs before being written to the file. In binary mode no conversion of CR/LR pairs takes place.
trunc	Opens the file and clears the contents. If neither app nor ate are specified, trunc is the default.

You can or together two or more of the values listed in Table 4.1, if needed. For example, let's say you want to open a file in binary mode and to append data to the end of the file. In that case the constructor would look like this:

```
ofstream outfile("test.dat", ios::app ¦ ios::binary);
```

This will open the file in binary mode and move the file pointer to the end of the file. Any new data will be written to the end of the file.

Dealing with Binary Data

Dealing with binary data is somewhat different than dealing with text data. For one thing, the data must be written in some logical arrangement and then read in again in exactly the same way. A data structure enables you to do that easily. Take this structure, for example:

```
struct NameData {
  char Name[20];
  char Phone[20];
  int  Age;
  int  ID;
};
```

This is a logical, albeit simple, arrangement of data. Writing this structure to disk using the `ofstream` class is as simple as the following:

```
NameData MyData = {"Bill DesCamps", "none", 41, 1};
ofstream outfile("names.dat", ios::binary);
outfile.write((char*)&MyData, sizeof(NameData));
```

The `write()` method of the `ofstream` class expects a `char*` rather than a `void*`, so it is necessary to take the address of the structure and cast it to a `char*`. This code writes the exact number of bytes contained in a `NameData` structure by implementing the `sizeof` operator. This means that the same number of bytes is written regardless of the actual data in the structure. This writes the file in block format with each block occupying the same number of bytes. (Later on we can use this arrangement to read a particular block in the file.) Notice that I used the `ios::binary` flag when the file is opened for writing. If you write a file in binary mode, you also need to specify the `ios::binary` flag when you open the file for reading.

Speaking of reading a file, reading the binary data is just as easy:

```
ifstream infile("names.dat", ios::binary);
if (!infile) return;
NameData MyData;
infile.read((char*)&MyData, sizeof(NameData));
```

Here the structure is filled in with the bytes read from the file. You can then do whatever you want with the data in the structure.

A Word About File Position

Perhaps one of the most important aspects of the C++ file stream classes is the concept of the file position. The *file position* is a numerical value that indicates where the next bits of data will be read from (in the case of `ifstream`) or written to (in the case of `ofstream`). When you initially open a file, the file position is 0. If you read 10 bytes of data, the file position advances to 10. If you then read an additional 20 bytes of data, the file position advances by 20 to contain a value of 30. Something similar happens when you write to a file. The file position is automatically updated as you read and write data.

Although the file position is automatically updated, there are functions that you can use to get or set the file position. In the case of the `ifstream` class, the `seekg()` function positions the file position marker to a specific location in a file, and the `tellg()` function returns the current file position. Using these two functions you can control where data is read from a file. In the case of the `ofstream` class, the functions that perform the identical tasks are called `seekp()` and `tellp()`. Changing the current file position to read or write to a specific part of the file is called *random file access*. We'll soon look at that in more detail in the section entitled "Random File Access."

Raw binary data can be read from a file a byte at a time using the `get()` function and written to a file using the `put()` function. For example, a file copy operation might look like this:

```
ifstream infile("names.dat", ios::binary);
ofstream outfile("temp.fil", ios::binary);
infile.seekg(0, ifstream::end);
int numBytes = infile.tellg();
infile.seekg(0);
for (int i=0;i<numBytes;i++) {
  char c;
  infile.get(c);
  outfile.put(c);
}
```

Notice the use of the `seekg()` and `tellg()` functions in the preceding code. The `seekg()` function moves the file position indicator to the end of the file (the `ifstream::end` flag tells `ifstream` to seek to the end of the file). Next, the `tellg()` function asks for the file position. The returned value will be the size of the file, in bytes. When the file size is known, the input file is read a byte at a time. As each byte is read, it is written to the output file.

Random File Access

Imagine you have a file in which 1000 records are stored. Let's further say you want to read record number 999. You could loop through the file, reading records until you finally get to record 999, but obviously this isn't very efficient. A better way would be to set the file stream pointer to the exact location of record 999 in the file and then read just that record. Random file access only works effectively when a file is filled with records of a known size or if you know the exact layout of a file. In this case you know the record size, so getting the correct file position is a matter of a simple calculation. Going back to our `NameData` structure example, it would look like this:

```
int pos = 998 * sizeof(NameData);
```

Note that because the first record is at file position `0`, the 999th record is at `998` multiplied by the size of a record. Now you can open the file, seek to record number 999, and read the record at that position:

```
ifstream infile("names.dat", ios::binary);
infile.seekg(pos);
```

```
NameData MyData;
infile.read((char*)&MyData, sizeof(NameData));
```

You can do something similar to replace or update a record in a file. To do that, open the file in update mode:

```
ofstream outfile("names.dat", ios::binary ¦ ios::ate);
int pos = 998 * sizeof(NameData);
outfile.seekp(pos);
outfile.write((char*)&MyData, sizeof(NameData));
```

Here I used the `ios::ate` flag in addition to the `ios::binary` flag. I could have used `ios::app` (append mode) and achieved the same results. If I had not specified `ios::ate`, the previous file would have been overwritten when the file was opened. The rest is straightforward—just seek to the appropriate place in the file and write the new information to the file.

Finally, I want to point out that you could open the file for simultaneous reading and writing by using the `fstream` class rather than using `ofstream` to write a file and `ifstream` to read the file. Because `fstream` is derived from both `ostream` and `istream` (the ancestor classes of `ofstream` and `ifstream`, respectively), all the previously mentioned functions are available for use in `fstream`. The following example shows how you could use `fstream` to swap the first and the 10th records in a file:

```
NameData record1;
NameData record2;
// open the file in read and write mode
fstream iofile("temp3.dat", ios::binary ¦ ios::in ¦ ios::out);
// seek to the 10th record and read the record
iofile.seekg(9 * sizeof(NameData));
iofile.read((char*)&record1, sizeof(NameData));
// seek to the first record and read it
iofile.seekg(0);
iofile.read((char*)&record2, sizeof(NameData));
// seek to the first record again and write
// the data read from the 10th record
iofile.seekg(0);
iofile.write((char*)&record1, sizeof(NameData));
// go back to record #10 and write the data
// read from record #0
iofile.seekg(9 * sizeof(NameData));
iofile.write((char*)&record2, sizeof(NameData));
iofile.close();
```

Notice that I set the `ios::in` and `ios::out` flags in the constructor. This is necessary in order to tell `iostream` that we will be doing both read and write operations on the file. Aside from that, the preceding code snippet contains nothing new other than the fact that the `read()` and `write()` functions are used together.

Basic file I/O is easy, really. But as I said earlier, if you need to do complicated file I/O, you are going to have to tie into the online help or get a hold of a good book on file I/O using Rouge Wave's Standard C++ Library 2.0.

NOTE

> VCL's TFileStream class enables you to perform file I/O in much the same ways as the fstream class does. Although TFileStream is not quite as capable as the C++ file stream classes, it is good enough in most cases. TFileStream also has the added benefit of being much more straightforward to use.

Summary

Today you have learned about classes in C++. A well-designed class is easy to use and saves many programming hours. I'd even go so far as to say a well-designed class is a joy to use—especially when it's your own creation. Early in the chapter you learned about some of the features of functions that are specific to C++. You learned about function overloading, virtual functions, inline functions, and default parameters in functions. All these are heavily used in designing classes in C++. Finally, the day ended with an introduction to basic file I/O operations.

The lessons of these first four days are important to understand as you progress through this book. If they don't make complete sense to you yet, don't despair. As we continue through the next days, you will see these concepts repeated and put to use in programs that have more practical application than the console applications we've been working with thus far.

WARNING

> Learning C++ can and will lead to brain overload! It's natural and you shouldn't worry about it. You might put down this book for the evening, turn out the lights, and think, "I'll never get it." Trust me, you will.
>
> Sometimes it's necessary to take a couple days off and let it all soak in. In fact, if I thought I could get by with it, I'd make Day 5 a blank chapter called "A Day of Rest." Take it a little at a time, and one of these days you'll be just like Archimedes—you'll be running around your office or your house shouting "Eureka!" because the light just came on in your head. But keep track of your clothes, will you? The neighbors could be watching.

4

Workshop

The Workshop contains quiz questions to help you solidify your understanding of the material covered and exercises to provide you with experience in using what you have learned. You can find the answers to the quiz questions in Appendix A, "Answers to Quiz Questions."

Q&A

Q How can I keep a class member function private to the outside world but enable derived classes to call it?

A Make it protected. A protected function is not accessible to users of your class but is accessible to derived classes.

Q What does *data abstraction* mean?

A Data abstraction means hiding the details of the class that the users of the class don't need to see. A class might have dozens of data members and functions, but only a few that the user can see. Only make visible (public) the functions that a user needs to know about to use the class.

Q What is an object?

A Effectively, an object is any block of code that can be treated as a separate entity in your programs. An object in C++ generally means a class. In C++Builder that definition is expanded to include VCL components. ActiveX controls are also objects.

Q Can my class have more than one constructor?

A Yes. Your class can have as many constructors as needed, provided you follow the rules of function overloading.

Q Do I have to understand every aspect of file I/O in order to program in C++Builder?

A No. C++Builder has plenty of built-in file I/O through its use of components. A basic understanding of file I/O is a good idea in any case. As always, it depends on what your program does.

Q Can I open a file in such a way that I can read from and write to the file as needed?

A Yes. Both the C++ library fstream class and the VCL TFileStream class enable you to read from a file, write to a file, and reposition a file pointer as needed.

Quiz

1. How do classes and structures differ in C++?
2. What is the purpose of having private data members and functions?

3. How can you keep data members private and yet enable users to read and set their values?

4. How and when is a class's destructor called?

5. What does it mean to override a function of the base class?

6. How can you override a base class function and still get the benefit of the operation the base class function performs?

7. What does an initializer list do?

8. Can a class contain other class instances as data members?

9. How can you get the functionality of two separate classes all rolled up into a single class?

10. What does the seekg() function of the iostream class do?

Exercises

1. Write a class that takes a person's height in inches and returns the height in feet.

2. Derive a class from the class in Exercise 1 that also returns the height in meters, centimeters, or millimeters. (Hint: There are 26.3 millimeters in an inch.)

3. Write a program that takes user input and writes it to a data file.

4. Modify the program in Exercise 3 so that it reads the data file and displays the output after the file is written.

5. Take a day off. You've earned it!

4

Day 5

C++ Class Frameworks and the Visual Component Model

Today I am going to talk about class frameworks. I will tell you what a framework is and what your options are for writing Windows programs in today's fast-paced software industry. In doing so, we will look at the following:

☐ Borland's Object Windows Library (OWL)

☐ Microsoft's Microsoft Foundation Class Library (MFC)

☐ Borland's Visual Component Library (VCL)

Frameworks Fundamentals

"In the beginning there was C..." If you recall from Day 1, "Getting Started with C++Builder," I began my discussion of the C++ programming language with that statement. The same is true of Windows programming. In the beginning, the vast majority of Windows programs were written in C. In fact, the Windows Application Programming Interface (API) is just a huge collection of C functions—hundreds of them. There are still undoubtedly thousands of programmers out there writing Windows programs in C.

Somewhere along the line, folks at Borland decided, "There has got to be an easier way." (Actually, the framework revolution might have started on several different fronts, but Borland was certainly a leader.) It was apparent that Windows programming was very well suited to the C++ language, and vice versa. By creating classes that encapsulate common Windows programming tasks, a programmer could be much more productive. After a class was created to encapsulate a window's various duties, for instance, that class could be used over and over again. The framework revolution began.

But I haven't yet told you what a framework is.

 A *framework* is a collection of classes that simplifies programming in Windows by encapsulating often-used programming techniques. Frameworks are also called *class libraries*.

Popular frameworks have classes that encapsulate windows, edit controls, list boxes, graphics operations, bitmaps, scrollbars, dialog boxes, and on and on.

So Why Should I Care?

That's a good question. The bottom line is that frameworks make Windows programming much easier than it would be in straight C. Let me give you an example. Listing 5.1 contains a portion of a Windows program written in C. This section of code loads a bitmap file from disk and displays the bitmap in the center of the screen. None of this will make sense to you right now, but be patient.

Listing 5.1. C code to load and display a bitmap.

```
1: HPALETTE hPal;
2: BITMAPFILEHEADER bfh;
3: BITMAPINFOHEADER bih;
4: LPBITMAPINFO lpbi = 0;
5: HFILE hFile;
6: DWORD nClrUsed, nSize;
7: HDC hDC;
8: HBITMAP hBitmap;
9: void _huge *bits;
10: do
```

```
11: {
12:   if ((hFile = _lopen(data.FileName, OF_READ)) == HFILE_ERROR) break;
13:   if (_hread(hFile, &bfh, sizeof(bfh)) != sizeof(bfh)) break;
14:   if (bfh.bfType != 'BM') break;
15:   if (_hread(hFile, &bih, sizeof(bih)) != sizeof(bih)) break;
16:   nClrUsed =
17:     (bih.biClrUsed) ? bih.biClrUsed : 1 << bih.biBitCount;
18:   nSize =
19:     sizeof(BITMAPINFOHEADER) + nClrUsed * sizeof(RGBQUAD);
20:   lpbi = (LPBITMAPINFO) GlobalAllocPtr(GHND, nSize);
21:   if (!lpbi) break;
22:   hmemcpy(lpbi, &bih, sizeof(bih));
23:   nSize = nClrUsed * sizeof(RGBQUAD);
24:   if (_hread(hFile, &lpbi->bmiColors, nSize) != nSize) break;
25:   if (_llseek(hFile, bfh.bfOffBits, 0) == HFILE_ERROR) break;
26:   nSize = bfh.bfSize-bfh.bfOffBits;
27:   if ((bits = GlobalAllocPtr(GHND, nSize)) == NULL) break;
28:   if (_hread(hFile, bits, nSize) != nSize) break;
29:   hDC = GetDC(hWnd);
30:   hBitmap = CreateDIBitmap(hDC, &(lpbi->bmiHeader), CBM_INIT,
31:                            bits, lpbi, DIB_RGB_COLORS);
32:   if (hBitmap) {
33:     LPLOGPALETTE lppal;
34:     DWORD nsize = sizeof(LOGPALETTE)
35:       + (nClrUsed-1) * sizeof(PALETTEENTRY);
36:     lppal = (LPLOGPALETTE) GlobalAllocPtr(GHND, nSize);
37:     if (lppal) {
38:       lppal->palVersion = 0x0300;
39:       lppal->palNumEntries = (WORD) nClrUsed;
40:       hmemcpy(lppal->palPalEntry, lpbi->bmiColors,
41:         nClrUsed * sizeof(PALETTEENTRY));
42:       hPal = CreatePalette(lppal);
43:       (void) GlobalFreePtr(lppal);
44:     }
45:   }
46: } while(FALSE);
47: if (hFile != HFILE_ERROR) _lclose(hFile);
48: HPALETTE oldPal = SelectPalette(hDC, hPal, FALSE);
49: RealizePalette(hDC);
50: HDC hMemDC = CreateCompatibleDC(hDC);
51: HBITMAP oldBitmap =(HBITMAP)SelectObject(hMemDC, hBitmap);
52: BitBlt(hDC, 0, 0, (WORD)bih.biWidth, (WORD)bih.biHeight,
53:   hMemDC, 0, 0, SRCCOPY);
54: SelectObject(hMemDC, oldBitmap);
55: DeleteDC(hMemDC);
56: SelectPalette(hDC, oldPal, FALSE);
57: ReleaseDC(hWnd, hDC);
58: if (bits) (void) GlobalFreePtr(bits);
59: if (lpbi) (void) GlobalFreePtr(lpbi);
```

5

That looks just a little intimidating, doesn't it? The fact is, even I had to get some help from my friends on the BCPPLIB forum of CompuServe (thanks, Paul!). Now look at the equivalent using Borland's Object Windows Library, shown in Listing 5.2.

Listing 5.2. OWL code to load and display a bitmap.

```
1: TDib dib("test.bmp");
2: TPalette pal(dib);
3: TBitmap bitmap(dib, &pal);
4: TClientDC dc(*this);
5: dc.SelectObject(pal);
6: dc.RealizePalette();
7: TMemoryDC memdc(dc);
8: memdc.SelectObject(bitmap);
9: dc.BitBlt(0, 0, bitmap.Width(), bitmap.Height(), memdc, 0, 0);
```

So which would you rather use? You don't even have to know what these code snippets do to make that decision. It's easy to see that the OWL version is shorter and more readable. (VCL makes the task even easier by providing a bitmap component that you drop on a form. I don't want to get ahead of myself, though, so I'll save that discussion for a little later.)

These examples sum up what frameworks are all about. Frameworks hide details from you that you don't need to know. Everything that is contained in Listing 5.1 is performed behind the scenes in the OWL code in Listing 5.2. You don't need to know every detail about what goes on behind the scenes when OWL does its job, and you probably don't want to know. All you want is to take the objects that make up a framework and put them to use in your programs.

A good framework takes full advantage of OOP. Some do that better than others. Borland's Object Windows Library and Visual Component Library are excellent examples of object-oriented programming. They provide the proper abstraction needed for you to rise above the clutter and get down to the serious business of programming.

So What's the Catch?

A little skeptical, are you? Good. You're bright enough to figure out that if you have all that ease of use, you must be giving up something. Truth is, you are right. You might think that a program written with a framework would be larger and slower than its counterpart written in C. That's partially correct. Applications written with frameworks don't necessarily have to be slower than programs written in C, though. There is some additional overhead inherent in the C++ language, certainly, but for the most part it is not noticeable in a typical Windows program.

The primary trade-off is that Windows programs written in C++ tend to be larger than programs written in straight C. For example, let's say you had a simple Windows program written in C that was 75KB. The equivalent program written with one of the framework libraries might be 200KB. That's a significant difference, but this example demonstrates the worst-case scenario. The difference in final program size between a C application and a C++ application written with a framework is most noticeable in very small programs. As your programs increase in size and sophistication, the size difference is much less noticeable.

One distinction is simply the difference between C and C++. C++ carries additional overhead for features such as exception handling, runtime type information (RTTI), and other C++ goodies. In my opinion, the difference in code size is an acceptable trade-off for the features that C++ provides. Now, before you label me as a code-bloat proponent, let me say that I am as conscientious as the next person when it comes to code bloat. I believe that we should all write the tightest code we can, given the tools we use. I am also a realist, and I understand that time-to-market is a driving force in the software industry today. I am willing to trade some code size for the power that C++ and an application framework give me.

Frameworks Teach Object-Oriented Programming and Design

If you end up getting serious about this crazy game we call Windows programming, you will eventually end up peeking into the source code of your favorite framework. Sooner or later you'll want to know how the pros do things. The OWL or VCL source code is a great place to go for that kind of information.

NOTE

> The MFC source code is not the best place to find good object-oriented design in action. MFC lacks the elegance, abstraction, and overall design that makes a top-notch framework. In addition, it tends to break OOP rules from time to time. MFC might well be the most popular framework, but that doesn't mean it is the best framework from an OOP standpoint.

Some weekend when the leaves are raked, the house trim is painted, the laundry is done, the kids are at grandma's, and you think you have a good handle on C++, you should spend some time browsing your favorite framework's source code. It can be intimidating at first, but after a while you'll see what the designers were doing. Don't strain yourself. Attempt to understand the things that bump up against the limits of your knowledge regarding C++. Leave the complicated stuff for next month. But notice how the framework designers use private, protected, and public access in classes. Notice how and when they implement inline functions. Notice how things that should be kept hidden from the user aren't in public view. Studying a good C++ class library can teach you a great deal about C++ and object-oriented design.

The C++ Framework Wars

The frameworks need to be separated into two categories: C++ frameworks and VCL. First, I'll discuss the C++ frameworks, and then I'll move on to VCL. There are really only two viable C++ frameworks, and they are Borland's OWL and Microsoft's MFC.

5

Borland's Object Windows Library

Borland took the lead role in the framework race with OWL a few years back. First, there was OWL 1. OWL's first version was a separate product sold by Borland for use with its Borland C++ 3 compiler. (The very first OWL was written for Turbo Pascal and was later converted to C++.) OWL 1 was a good framework, but because of some proprietary syntax and other issues, it wasn't the design that Borland stayed with. OWL 1 did, however, do the entire Windows programming community a service—it brought attention to frameworks. Although OWL 1 was not the first framework ever written, it certainly was the first to gain mass market appeal.

After OWL 1 came OWL 2. OWL 2 was a masterpiece. It implemented many of the latest C++ language features—not because they were new, but because they made sense. Best of all, OWL 2 was included as part of the Borland C++ 4 compiler. From that point on, Borland included OWL as part of its Borland C++ package. Borland C++ compilers have always been the first to implement new C++ features, and OWL 2 put those features to good use. OWL 2 also did away with the proprietary syntax that plagued OWL 1. OWL 2 was standard C++ that could be compiled with any C++ compiler—at least in theory. As it was, there were few C++ compilers implementing the latest and greatest C++ features, so OWL 2 was typically used only with Borland compilers.

Borland released a revision of OWL 2 called OWL 2.5. For the most part, the changes were minor in the sense that they didn't add a lot to OWL 2 itself—a few bug fixes here and there and a few new classes. But in one way OWL 2.5 was a major release—it added OLE (object linking and embedding) support in a new set of classes called the Object Components Framework (OCF). OCF is not technically part of OWL. It works very well with OWL, but it can be used independently of OWL.

The latest and greatest OWL is 5. OWL 5 represents significant enhancements to OWL 2.5. The primary changes come in new OWL classes that encapsulate the new Win32 custom controls. OCF was also updated in the OWL 5 release.

OWL's strengths are considerable. First, it is an architectural wonder. It is obvious that OWL was very well thought out from the beginning. I can't say enough about my admiration for OWL designers Carl Quinn and Bruneau Babet and the other OWL team members. OWL is very OOP-friendly and follows all the OOP rules. Its level of abstraction strikes a good balance between ease of use and power. OWL has one major advantage over its competitors: It can be used in both 16-bit and 32-bit programs. Borland has even emulated some of the 32-bit custom controls for use in 16-bit programs. Although these emulations are not perfect in all cases, they are usable and give you a method of creating the 32-bit look and feel in 16-bit programs.

Ironically, one of OWL's strengths leads, in some people's minds, to one of its weaknesses: OWL has done a great job of encapsulating the Windows environment, which makes OWL complex and sometimes difficult in the beginning. It takes time to master, no question about it. But when you master OWL, you will be very efficient in writing Windows programs.

The Microsoft Foundation Class Library

Sometime between OWL 1 and OWL 2, the Microsoft Foundation Class Library (MFC) was born. MFC is included as part of Microsoft's Visual C++ compiler package. Actually, versions of MFC ship with compilers by Symantec, Watcom, and, believe it or not, Borland (there might be others as well). Microsoft has not licensed the most current version of MFC to other compiler vendors (Symantec and Watcom), but Borland C++ 5.01 included MFC version 4.1, which at the time was the latest version of MFC (a newer version, 4.2, came out shortly thereafter).

It could be said that MFC is a different type of class library than OWL. MFC is less abstract and lies closer to the Windows API. MFC's strengths come in three primary areas. First, it is relatively easy to learn (now, understand that no C++ framework dealing with Windows programming is going to be easy to learn, but MFC is a little easier to pick up than the competition), primarily because it is less abstract in some areas. If you are new to Windows programming, you will probably find OWL and MFC about equal when it comes to learning the framework. If you are coming from a C programming background and already know the Windows API, MFC is almost certainly going to be easier to learn.

Another strength of MFC, according to some, is that it is a thin wrapper around the Windows API. Again, for Windows programmers who are moving from programming in C to programming in C++ with MFC, this is an advantage. They can begin to use MFC and feel somewhat at home.

Finally, MFC has the distinct advantage of belonging to Microsoft. When new Windows features and technologies emerge, MFC can be the first to implement them. Microsoft releases a new technology, and MFC can already have support for that technology when it is announced. That certainly doesn't hurt.

MFC has its weaknesses, too. First and foremost, it is a thin wrapper around the Windows API. "Wait a minute!" you say. "I thought you said that was one of MFC's strengths." Yes, I did. It's also one of its weaknesses. Some folks consider MFC's close tie to the API a strength. I consider it a weakness. The whole idea behind a class library is to shield the user from things he or she doesn't need to know. MFC fails to do that in many cases. Folks who are coming from Windows programming in C consider that a strength. You can form your own opinion. Along those same lines, MFC is not OOP-friendly. Sometimes it seems to be a hastily implemented collection of classes that don't work and play well together, rather than something planned and designed from the ground up to work as a unit.

Another potential problem with MFC is that the versions that ship with Visual C++ 4 and later are 32-bit only. Although you can still write 16-bit programs using Microsoft's Visual C++ 1.5 (which comes with later versions of Visual C++), you will likely find a disappointing development environment.

So Who's Winning?

Without question, MFC is more widely used than OWL. Part of the reason is that both MFC and the Visual C++ compiler bear the Microsoft name. It's no secret that Microsoft is king of the PC software industry. It is also no secret that Microsoft has marketing power that other companies can only dream about. In addition, there is a prevailing attitude of (to modify a coined phrase) "No one ever got fired for buying Microsoft."

I firmly believe that OWL is the better framework. Few who have extensively used both OWL and MFC will argue that point. But MFC is undoubtedly the C++ framework of choice today. There are many reasons, some of which I've alluded to already. Other reasons include a perceived lack of direction on Borland's part in recent years. Some managers prefer to play it safe and buy a product produced by "the big M" regardless of technical merit. I hope that attitude won't eventually lead us to a software industry with a gross lack of competition. This industry desperately needs companies that will push the envelope like Borland.

So what is the future of C++ frameworks? It's nearly impossible to guess at this point. It could be that both MFC and OWL are losing to the new kid on the block—components. Let's take a look at the Visual Component Library now.

The Visual Component Library

In 1995, Borland introduced a revolutionary new product called Delphi. It was an instant hit. Delphi offered rapid application development (RAD) using something called *components*. Components are objects that can be dropped on a form and manipulated via properties, methods, and events. It's visual programming, if you will.

The concept of form-based programming was first popularized by Microsoft's Visual Basic. Unlike Visual Basic, though, Delphi used a derivative of Pascal as its programming language. This new language, called Object Pascal, introduced OOP to the Pascal language. In a sense, Object Pascal is to Pascal what C++ is to C. Delphi and Object Pascal represented the marriage of object-oriented programming and form-based programming. In addition, Delphi could produce standalone executables. Real programs. Programs that did not require a runtime DLL to run; programs that were compiled, not interpreted; programs that ran tens of times faster than Visual Basic programs. The programming world was impressed.

Delphi didn't just throw Object Pascal at you and let you flounder. It also introduced the Visual Component Library (VCL). VCL is an application framework for Windows programming in Object Pascal. But VCL is not really comparable to OWL and MFC. Yes, it is a framework, but the core is very different, primarily because it was designed around the concept of properties, methods, and events.

You might be wondering why I'm talking about Delphi. The reason is simple—because the very same VCL that is the heart of Delphi is also the heart of C++Builder. That might come as a shock to you. If you come from a C++ background, you are scratching your head right now, wondering how that works. If you are coming from a Pascal background, you're probably grinning from ear to ear. If you are coming to C++Builder from any other type of background, you probably don't care either way. In the end, it doesn't really matter, because it works. Let's look a little deeper into VCL.

Components

As I talked about on Day 1, VCL components are objects that perform a specific programming task. VCL components are wrapped up in Object Pascal classes. From now on in this book, we will be encountering components on a daily basis. I won't spend a lot of time explaining every detail of components right now because you will see by example how they work throughout the rest of the book. Tomorrow I'll explain components in more detail.

Properties, Methods, and Events

On Day 1, I gave you a brief introduction to the properties, methods, and events model. These three ingredients make up the public interface of components in VCL (the part of the component the user will see). Let's take a look at these elements one at a time.

Properties

Properties are elements of a component that control how the component operates. Many components have common properties. All visual components, for example, have a Top and a Left property. These two properties control where the component will be positioned on a form, both at design time and at runtime. All components have an Owner property, which VCL uses to keep track of the child components a particular parent form or component owns.

A picture is always worth a thousand words, so let's start up C++Builder again and see properties in action. When you start C++Builder, you are greeted with a blank form and the Object Inspector.

NOTE   If you have the C++Builder options configured to save the desktop when you close C++Builder, you might see the last project you were working on when you start C++Builder. If that's the case, choose File | New Application from the main menu to get a blank form.

The Object Inspector will look something like Figure 5.1. (When C++Builder starts, it sizes the Object Inspector based on your current screen resolution, so your Object Inspector might be taller or shorter than the one shown in Figure 5.1.) If necessary, click on the Properties tab of the Object Inspector window so that the form's properties are displayed. The component's properties are arranged in alphabetical order. If more properties exist than can be displayed at one time, the Object Inspector has a scrollbar so that you can view additional properties. The Object Inspector window can be moved and sized. I like my Object Inspector as tall as my screen permits so that I can see the maximum number of properties at one time. Scroll through the properties until you locate the Left property and then click on it. Change the value for the Left property (any number between 0 and 600 will do) and press Enter on the keyboard. Notice how the form moves as you change the value.

Figure 5.1.

The Object Inspector.

This illustrates an important aspect of properties—they are more than simple data members of a class. Each property has an underlying data member associated with it, but the property itself is not a class data member. Changing a property often leads to code executed behind the scenes.

 Properties are often tied to *access methods* that execute when the property is modified.

 NOTE

> Things start to get confusing at this point. As I said, VCL is written in Pascal. Pascal uses the term *method,* whereas C++ uses the term *function.* To further muddy the waters, Pascal uses the term *function* to refer to a method that returns a value, and the term *procedure* to refer to a method that doesn't return a value. I would be happy enough to call all of them functions (being the old C++ hacker that I am), but when discussing VCL I will use the Pascal parlance. For the most part I will use the generic term *method.*

Properties can be changed at *design time* (when you are designing your form) and at *runtime* (when the program is running through code you write). In either case, if the property has an access method, that access method will be called and executed when the property is modified. You already saw an example of changing a property at design time when you changed the Left property and watched the form move on the screen. That is one of the strengths of VCL and how it is used in C++Builder: You can instantly see on the screen the result of your design change. Not all properties show a visible change on the form at design time, however, so this doesn't happen in every case. Still, when possible, the results of the new property value are immediately displayed on the form.

To change a property at runtime, you simply make an assignment to the property. When you make an assignment, VCL works behind the scenes to call the access method for that property. To change the Left property at runtime, you use code like this:

```
MainForm->Left = 200;
```

In the case of the Left property (as well as the Top property), VCL moves and repaints the form. (For you Windows API programmers, you can figure out that this eventually translates into calls to the Windows API functions SetWindowPos() and InvalidateRect().)

NOTE

> Notice that the previous code line uses the indirect member operator (->) to set the property. All VCL components are allocated from the heap. The indirection operator is always used to access a component's properties and methods. Classes you write for use in your C++Builder applications can be allocated from either the heap or the stack, but all VCL component classes, and all classes derived from them, must be allocated from the heap.

 NEW TERM Properties have two *access specifiers*, which are used when properties are read or modified. There is a *read specifier* and a *write specifier*.

Suffice it to say that access specifiers associate read and write methods (functions) with the property. When the property is read or written to, the functions associated with the property are automatically called. When you make an assignment as in the previous example, you are accessing the write specifier. In effect, VCL checks to see whether an access method exists for the write specifier. If so, the access method is called. If no access method exists, VCL assigns the new value to the data member associated with the property.

When you reference a property (use the property as the right side of an equation), you are accessing the read specifier:

```
int x = MainForm->Left;
```

In this case, VCL calls the read specifier to read the value of the Left property. In many cases, the read specifier does very little more than return a property's current value.

5

The properties of the property (sorry, I couldn't resist) are determined by the writer of the component. A property can be read-only. A read-only property can be read—its value can be retrieved—but not written to. In other words, you can fetch the property's value, but you can't change it. In rare cases, a property can be made write-only (a property that can be written to but not read isn't very useful in most cases). This is obviously the opposite of a read-only property.

Finally, some properties can be specified runtime-only. A runtime-only property can be accessed only at runtime, not design time. Because a runtime-only property doesn't apply at design time, it is not displayed in the Object Inspector. A runtime-only property can be declared as read-only, too, which means that it can be accessed only at runtime and can only be read (not written to).

Some properties use an array as the underlying data member. To illustrate, let's put a memo component on our blank form. Go to the C++Builder Component palette, choose the Standard tab, and click the Memo button. (The ToolTip will tell when you are over the Memo button.) Now move to the form and click on it where you want the memo's top-left corner to appear. As soon as you place the memo component on the form, the Object Inspector switches to show you the properties of the component just placed on the form, in this case a TMemo. Locate the Lines property and click on it. Notice that the property value contains the text (TStrings) and that there is a little button with an ellipsis (...) to the right of the property value.

NOTE

> The ellipsis button tells you that this property can be edited by using a property editor. For an array of strings, for instance, a dialog box will be displayed in which you can type the strings. In the case of the Font property, clicking the ellipsis button will invoke the Choose Font dialog box. The exact type of the property editor is property specific, although certain properties can share a common editor. You can bring up the property editor by clicking the ellipsis button or by double-clicking the property value.

The Lines property for a memo component is an array of strings. When you double-click the Value column, the string editor is displayed and you can then type the strings you want displayed in the memo component when the application runs. If you don't want any strings displayed in the memo component, you need to clear the property editor of any strings.

Properties can be instances of other VCL classes. The Font property is an obvious example. A *font* includes things like the typeface, the color, the font size, and so on. Locate the Font property in the Object Inspector. (It doesn't matter whether you have selected the memo component or the form.) Notice that there is a plus sign before the word *Font*. This tells you that there are individual properties within this property that can be set. If you double-click on the property name, you will see that the Object Inspector expands the property to reveal its individual elements. You can now individually edit the Font property's elements. In the case of the Font property, these same settings can be edited by invoking the Property Editor. You can use either method with the same results.

NEW TERM A *set* is a collection of possible values for a property.

Some properties are sets. The Style property within the Font object is a good example of a set. Notice that Style has a plus sign in front of it. If you double-click on the Style property, you will see that the Style node expands to reveal the set's contents. In this case the set consists of the various styles available for fonts: bold, italic, underline, and strikeout. By double-clicking a style, you can turn that style on or off. A set can be empty or can contain one or more of the allowed values. We'll talk more about sets in the section entitled "Sets."

NEW TERM Some properties can be *enumerations*, a list of possible choices.

An *enumeration* is a list of possible choices for a property. When you click on an enumeration property, a drop-down arrow button appears to the right of the value. To see the choices in the enumeration, click the drop-down button to display the list of choices. Alternatively, you can double-click the Value column for the property. As you double-click on the property's value, the Object Inspector will cycle through (or enumerate) the choices. The Cursor property gives a good example of an enumerated property. Locate the Cursor property and click the arrow button to expose the list of possible cursors to choose from. Enumerations and sets differ in that with an enumeration property only one of the presented choices can be selected (only one cursor can be in effect at any time). The set can contain none or any number of the choices (a font style can contain bold, underline, italic, or none of these).

As long as you have C++Builder running and a blank form displayed, you might as well spend some time examining the various components and their properties. Go ahead, I'll wait.

5

House Rules: Properties

☐ Properties appear to be class data members and are accessed like class data members.

☐ Properties are *not* class data members. They are a special category of class member.

☐ Properties often invoke an access method when they are written to (assigned a value), but not always. It depends on how the particular component is written.

- [ ] Properties usually have default values. The default value is the value that initially shows up in the Object Inspector when a component is first utilized and is the value that will be used if no specific value is assigned.
- [ ] Properties can be designed as read-only, write-only, or runtime-only.
- [ ] Runtime-only properties don't show up in the Object Inspector and can be modified only at runtime.
- [ ] Properties can include
  - [ ] Simple data types
  - [ ] Arrays
  - [ ] Sets
  - [ ] Enumerations
  - [ ] VCL class objects

Methods

Methods in VCL components are functions (ahem...*procedures* and functions) that can be called to make the component perform certain actions. For example, all visual components have a method called Show(), which displays the component, and a method called Hide(), which hides the component. Calling these methods is exactly the same as calling class member functions as we did on Day 3, "Advanced C++."

```
MyWindow->Show();
// do some stuff, then later...
MyWindow->Hide();
```

In C++ parlance, methods are member functions of a component class. Methods in VCL can be declared as public, protected, or private just as functions in C++ can be public, protected, or private. These keywords mean the same thing in Object Pascal classes as they do in C++ classes. Public methods can be accessed by the component's users. In this example, both the Show() and Hide() methods are public. Protected methods cannot be accessed by the component users but can be accessed by classes (components) derived from a component. Of course, private methods can be accessed only within a class itself.

Just like C++ functions, some methods take parameters and return values, and others don't. It depends entirely on how the method was written by the component writer. For example, the GetTextBuf() method retrieves the text of a TEdit component. This method can be used to get the text from an edit control as follows:

```
char buff[256];
int numChars = EditControl->GetTextBuf(buff, sizeof(buff));
```

As you can see, this particular method takes two parameters and returns an integer. When this method is called, the edit control contents are placed in buff, and the return value is the number of characters retrieved from the edit control.

For now, that's all you need to know in order to use methods. I'll go into more detail later when I talk about writing components.

> ## House Rules: Methods
>
> ☐ Methods can be private, protected, or public.
>
> ☐ Methods are called by using the indirect member operator.
>
> ☐ Methods can take parameters and can return values.
>
> ☐ Some methods take no parameters and return no values.
>
> ☐ Only public methods can be called by component users.

Events

NEW TERM Windows is said to be an *event-driven* environment. Event-driven means that a program is driven by events that occur within the Windows environment. Events include mouse movements, mouse clicks, and keypresses.

Programmers moving from DOS or mainframe programming environments might have some difficulty with the concept of something being event-driven. A Windows program continually polls Windows for events. Events in Windows include a menu being activated, a button being clicked, a window being moved, a window needing repainting, a window being activated, and so forth. Windows notifies a program of an event by sending a Windows message. There are somewhere in the neighborhood of 175 possible messages that Windows can send to an application. That's a lot of messages. Fortunately, you don't have to know about each and every one of them to program in C++Builder; there are only a couple dozen that are used frequently.

In VCL, an event is anything that occurs in the component that the user might need to know about. Each component is designed to respond to certain events. Usually this means a Windows event, but it can mean other things as well. For example, a button component is designed to respond to a mouse click, as you would expect. But a nonvisual control such as a database component can respond to non-Windows events such as the user reaching the end of the table.

NEW TERM When you respond to a component event, you are said to *handle* the event. Events are handled through functions called *event handlers*.

A typical Windows program spends most of its time idle, waiting for some event to occur. VCL makes it incredibly easy to handle events. The events that a component has been designed to handle are listed under the Events tab in the Object Inspector window. Event names are descriptive of the event to which they respond. For instance, the event to handle a mouse click is called OnClick.

> You don't have to handle every event that a component defines. In fact, you rarely do. If you don't respond to a particular event, the event message is either discarded or handled in a default manner, as described by either VCL or the component itself. You can handle any events you have an interest in and ignore the rest.

This will make more sense if you put it into practice. To begin, let's start a new application. Choose File | New Application from the main menu. If you are prompted to save the current project, click No. Now you will again have a blank form. First, let's set up the main form:

1. Change the Name property to PMEForm (PME for properties, methods, and events).
2. Change the Caption property to PME Test Program.

Next, we need to add a memo component to the form:

1. Choose the Standard tab on the Component palette and click the Memo button.
2. Click on the form to place a memo component on the form.
3. Change the Name property to Memo. Be sure the memo component is selected so you don't accidentally change the form's name instead of the memo component.
4. Double-click on the Lines property in the Value column. The String list editor will be displayed.
5. Delete the word Memo and type A test program using properties, methods, and events. Click OK to close the String list editor.
6. Resize the memo component so that it occupies most of the form. Leave room for a button at the bottom.

Your form will now look like the form shown in Figure 5.2.

Figure 5.2.

The form with a memo component added.

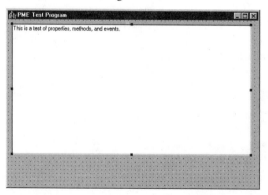

Now let's place a button on the form:

1. Choose the Standard tab on the Component palette and click the Button component button.
2. Click on the form below the memo component to place the button on the form.
3. Change the Name property for the button to Button.
4. Change the Caption property to Show/Hide.
5. Center the button horizontally on the form.

TIP

> You can center components visually, but for a more exact method, use the Alignment palette. Choose View | Alignment Palette from the main menu and then click the Center horizontally in window button on the Alignment palette to center a component horizontally on the form.

We will use this button to alternately show and hide the memo component. Now we need to write some code so that the button does something when clicked. Be sure that the button component is selected, and then click on the Events tab in the Object Inspector. A list of the events that a button component is designed to handle is presented. The top event should be the OnClick event. Double-click on the Value column of the OnClick event. What happens next is one of the great things about visual programming. The Code Editor comes to the top and displays the OnClick function ready for you to type code. Figure 5.3 shows the Code Editor with the OnClick handler displayed.

Figure 5.3.
The C++Builder Code Editor with the OnClick *handler displayed.*

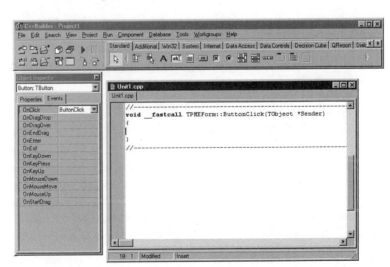

NOTE

This function looks like the class member functions I discussed on Day 3 and, in fact, that's exactly what it is. The only difference is that C++Builder functions use the `__fastcall` keyword (note that two underscores proceed the `fastcall` keyword). It's not important that you understand what `__fastcall` does but that every C++Builder function uses this calling convention.

Before we go on, let's save the project. Choose File | Save All from the main menu. The first thing you are prompted for is the name of the unit (source file). Type `PMEMain` and click OK. Next, you are prompted for a filename for the project. Type `PMETest` and press Enter or click Okay. Now on to the good stuff...

Notice that the function is already set up for you, and all you have to do is type the code. If you take a good look at the function, you will see that the function is called `ButtonClick`, that it is a member function of the `TPMEForm` class, that it returns `void`, and that it takes a pointer to a `TObject` called `Sender` as a parameter. (I'll talk about the `Sender` parameter in just a bit.) All that is left to do now is type code that shows and hides the button each time the button is clicked. We'll borrow a little code from our earlier discussion of methods. Edit the `ButtonClick` function until it looks like this:

```
void __fastcall TPMEForm::ButtonClick(TObject *Sender)
{
  static bool isVisible;
  isVisible = !isVisible;
  if (isVisible) Memo->Hide();
  else Memo->Show();
}
```

This code sets up a static variable named `isVisible`.

NEW TERM A *static* variable is one that retains its value between function calls.

Static variables are the exception to the rule regarding uninitialized variables—static variables are initially set to `0`. In this case, `isVisible` is a `bool` variable, so it is initially set to `false`.

The second line of code in this function flips the `bool` variable between `true` and `false` by applying a logical `NOT` to the variable's present value. It works like this: Initially the static variable is set to `false`. The first time the function executes, the variable is assigned `NOT false`, which is, of course, `true`. The next time the function executes, the variable is assigned `NOT true`, and so on. Each time the function executes, `isVisible` contains the opposite value it had on the previous function call. After that, the `if`/`else` pair calls either `Show()` or `Hide()`, depending on the value of `isVisible`.

NOTE

> As soon as you drop a component on a form, C++Builder goes to work behind the scenes. Remember when you dropped a memo component on the form? As soon as you did that, C++Builder created a `TMemo*` variable in the form's class declaration. At runtime VCL will create a dynamic instance of the `TMemo` class and assign it to the variable named `Memo`. That is why the `Show()` and `Hide()` functions are accessed using the indirect member operator.

That's all there is to it. But does it work? Let's find out. Click the Run button on the toolbar. After being compiled, the program runs and is displayed. It's the moment of truth. Click the button, and the memo component is hidden. Click the button again, and the memo component is again displayed. It works! After playing with that for a minute, close the program (use the Close Program button in the upper-left corner of the title bar) and you are back to the Code Editor.

All that work with the static `bool` variable is a bit cumbersome. Think back to the discussion about properties. Wouldn't it be nice if the memo component had a property that could tell us whether the component was currently visible? Is there such a beast? Of course there is. It's called, predictably, `Visible`. Let's make use of it. Again, edit the function until it looks like this:

```
void __fastcall TPMEForm::ButtonClick(TObject *Sender)
{
  if (Memo->Visible) Memo->Hide();
  else Memo->Show();
}
```

Again click the Run button. The program is displayed and, lo and behold, the button does what it's supposed to. How about that? We managed to use properties, methods, and events in the same example.

Are you getting the fever yet? Hold on, because there's much more to come. Oh, and wipe that silly grin off your face…your boss thinks you're working!

As you can see, the `ButtonClick()` function takes a pointer to a `TObject` called `Sender`. Every event-handling function will have at least a `Sender` parameter. Depending on the event being handled, the function might have one or more additional parameters. For instance, the `OnMouseDown` event handler looks like this:

```
void __fastcall TPMEForm::ButtonMouseDown(TObject *Sender,
  TMouseButton Button, TShiftState Shift, Integer X, Integer Y)
{
}
```

5

Here you are getting information on the button that was pressed, which keyboard keys were pressed at the time the mouse was clicked, and the X, Y coordinates of the cursor when the mouse button was clicked. The event-handling function contains all the information you need to deal with the particular event the event handler is designed to handle.

So what exactly is Sender? Sender is a pointer to the component that is sending the message to the message handler. In this example, the Sender parameter is extra baggage because we know that the Show/Hide button is the sender. Sender exists to enable you to have more than one component use the same event handler. To illustrate, let's create a new button and make one of our buttons the Show button and the other the Hide button.

1. If the Code Editor is on top, press F12 to switch back to the Form Editor.

2. Click on the Show/Hide button to select it. Change both the Name and Caption properties to Show.

3. Add a new button to the form to the right of the Show button. Arrange the buttons if you want to give an even look to the form.

4. Change the Name property for the new button to Hide. The Caption property will also change to Hide (you'll have to press Enter before the Caption property will change).

5. Click the Show button and then click on the Events tab in the Object Inspector. Notice that the OnClick event now says ShowClick. Edit it to say ButtonClick again. (The initial event-handler name is a default name. You can change it to any name you want.)

6. Click the Hide button and find the OnClick event in the Object Inspector (it will be selected already). Next to the value is a drop-down arrow button. Click the arrow button and then choose ButtonClick from the list that drops down (there will be only one function name in the list at this point).

7. Double-click on the value ButtonClick. You are presented with the Code Editor with the cursor in the ButtonClick() function. Modify the code so that it reads like this:

```
void __fastcall TPMEForm::ButtonClick(TObject *Sender)
{
  if (Sender == Hide) Memo->Hide();
  else Memo->Show();
}
```

8. Bake at 425 degrees for one hour or until golden brown. (Just checking.)

Your form will look similar to Figure 5.4. Compile and run the program. Click each button to be sure that it functions as advertised.

5

Figure 5.4.

The form with all components added.

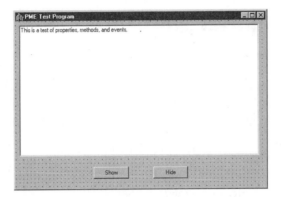

What we have done here is create a single event-handling function that handles the OnClick event of both buttons. We use the Sender parameter to determine which button sent the OnClick event and then either hide or show the memo component as needed. We could have created a separate OnClick handler for each button, but with this method the code is more compact. Besides, it's a good illustration of how Sender can be used.

Step 6 in the previous exercise illustrates an important point: After you create an OnClick event handler for a particular component, you can attach that same handler to the OnClick event of any component on the form. This enables you to use the same event handler for multiple components. I'll discuss events in more detail as we progress through the book.

House Rules: Events

- [ ] You can respond to any of a component's events as needed.
- [ ] You are not required to respond to all events a component defines.
- [ ] Events are handled by event-handling functions called event handlers.
- [ ] Several components can share a common event handler.
- [ ] Event-handler names produced by C++Builder are default names and can be changed by the programmer.
- [ ] Be sure to change an event handler's name only in the Object Inspector.
- [ ] An event handler's Sender parameter can be used to determine which component generated the event.
- [ ] Double-clicking the event handler's name in the Object Inspector displays the Code Editor and takes you to the section of code containing the event handler.
- [ ] Each event handler contains the function parameters needed to properly handle that event.

5

C++Builder and VCL

As I have said, VCL is a library written in Object Pascal. VCL is written in Object Pascal because it was written for Delphi. It made perfect sense for the people at Borland to take an already existing class library and adapt it for use in C++Builder. There was no point in starting from scratch to build C++Builder when they could hit the ground running by implementing Delphi's VCL. An added benefit is that Delphi users can easily move to C++Builder, and vice versa. Because both use the same VCL, you don't have to learn a new framework when moving around in the Delphi/C++Builder family.

C++Builder is a C++ compiler, and VCL is a library written in Object Pascal. How does that work exactly? Truthfully, you shouldn't be concerned about how it works at the compiler level but rather how it affects the way you program in C++Builder. Trust me, the fact that the VCL is written in Object Pascal is virtually invisible. Take the following code snippet, for instance:

```
int screenW = GetSystemMetrics(SM_CXSCREEN);
int screenH = GetSystemMetrics(SM_CYSCREEN);
int h = MainForm->Height;
int w = MainForm->Width;
MainForm->Top = (screenH / 2) - (h / 2);
MainForm->Left = (screenW / 2) - (w / 2);
TPoint cPt;
GetCursorPos(cPt);
h -= 150;
w -= 150;
MainForm->Height = h;
MainForm->Width = w;
for (int i=0;i<150;i+=6) {
  MainForm->Height = h + i;
  MainForm->Width = w + i;
  SetCursorPos(
    MainForm->Left + MainForm->Width,
    MainForm->Top + MainForm->Height);
}
SetCursorPos(cPt.x, cPt.y);
```

Now, in this code, which is Object Pascal and which is C++? The fact is, as far as you are concerned, it's all C++. VCL and C++ work together seamlessly to give you rapid application development using C++. VCL gives you RAD through components, and the rest of your code can be written in C++.

VCL for C++ Programmers

This section is for current C++ programmers moving to C++Builder but will also interest new C++ programmers. Although the following is not advanced, it is aimed at C++ programmers, so if you get lost, please muddle your way through and meet us on the other side.

There are a couple of things that C++ programmers might find odd when moving to C++Builder. First, don't forget that VCL is Object Pascal and not C++. The system works very well as long as you understand that and work within those parameters. Don't try to make it C++. All the code you write will be C++, but remember that VCL itself is not C++. With that in mind, let me give you a couple things to consider when using VCL.

All VCL Objects Must Be Allocated Dynamically

When you drop components on a form, C++Builder automatically writes code that dynamically creates the components, so you don't have to think about it. However, you might need to create and use VCL classes at runtime. For instance, let's say you need to display a File Open dialog box and you don't have a TFileOpen component on your form. No problem—you can just create the object on the fly. The code would look something like this:

```
TOpenDialog* dlg = new TOpenDialog(this);
dlg->Title = "Open a New File";
dlg->Execute();
```

Note that the object must be created using the new operator. If you attempt to use local allocation, you will get a compiler error that says VCL style classes must be constructed using operator new.

NOTE

> Most VCL components can be created at runtime as well as design time. It's easier to create the components at design time because it is much easier to set the properties using the Object Inspector rather than through code. Still, there are times when you need to create components at runtime, and C++Builder enables you to do that.

5

There is a seeming contradiction to this rule. Take the following code, for example:

```
TRect rect;
rect.top = 0;
rect.top = 0;
rect.right = 100;
rect.bottom = 100;
```

Hmmmm…I thought all VCL classes had to be created dynamically. The difference is that TRect is not a class. TRect is a structure that wraps the Windows RECT structure. Put another way, in VCL TRect is just another name for a Windows RECT structure. This is true of TPoint, TSize, TLogFont, TDrawItemStruct, or any of a host of other Windows structures available for use in VCL.

VCL Doesn't Have Default Parameters for Functions

To illustrate, let's examine the Windows API function `MessageBox()`. This function takes four parameters: the window handle of the window displaying the message box, the message box text, the message box title, and a `Flags` parameter controlling which buttons and icons are displayed on the message box. In MFC or OWL, you can call a message box by just specifying the message box text:

```
MessageBox("This is a message.");
```

This is possible because the OWL and MFC versions of `MessageBox()` have default parameters for the message box title and style flags. You can specify the additional parameters, but if you don't, the default values will be used. This is convenient for creating message boxes with a minimum of fuss. Here is the VCL equivalent to the previous line:

```
Application->MessageBox("This is a message", "Message", MB_OK);
```

Because VCL doesn't have default parameters, you have to specify all the parameters. Not convenient, but not the end of the world, either. Note that in all three cases (MFC, OWL, and VCL), the framework takes care of supplying the window handle parameter.

VCL Classes Don't Support Multiple Inheritance

This means that you cannot create a new component derived from two existing VCL components. I don't see this as a serious restriction because multiple inheritance is not widely used. I would prefer to use multiple inheritance any time I want. In reality, though, I have rarely missed multiple inheritance in my C++Builder applications. It is important to understand that this restriction applies only to classes derived from the VCL classes. Regular C++ classes that you write for use in your C++Builder applications can use multiple inheritance.

NOTE

In Delphi, all classes you create are automatically derived from `TObject`. This is not the case with C++Builder. Your C++Builder classes will not be derived from `TObject` unless you specifically create them that way.

VCL String Classes

On Day 1, in the section "Character Arrays," I talked about how the C language handles strings. As a language, C++ handles strings the same way that C does. It must be apparent to you by now, though, that the C++ language enables you to create a class to perform just about any programming task you can think of. It stands to reason, then, that someone would have created a class that addresses some of C's limitations in dealing with strings. Well, I have good

5

news and bad news. The good news is that there does, indeed, exist a class that makes dealing with strings much easier. The bad news is that there are several such classes for you to choose from. In this section I will address the types of string classes available and recommend the string class to use in your VCL applications.

Who Needs a String Class?

You might be thinking, "What's so important about a string class? Can't you do anything you want with C characters arrays?" Yes, you can, but a class that simplifies C-style character arrays is just plain easier to use. Let me give you an example. First, let's look at the C way of doing things:

```
char buff[20];    // will 20 characters be enough space?
strcpy(buff, "Hello There!");
if (!strcmp(buff, "Hello There!"))
  strcat(buff, " What's up?");
```

Now let's look at how the preceding might be accomplished with a C++ string class:

```
String S = "Hello There!"; // direct assignment
if (S == "Hello There!")   // test for equality
  S = S + " What's up?";   // concatentation using + operator
```

I don't know about you, but I find the second piece of code more intuitive and much easier to understand. Notice in particular that with a string class you can use syntax that makes sense. You can assign a string using the = operator, you can test for equality using the == operator, and you can add strings together using the + operator. It just makes sense. C++ string classes also have methods. These methods enable you to get the length of a string, search a string for a particular sub-string, delete portions of the string, convert the string to uppercase, and do much more. The bottom line is that string classes give you more flexibility in dealing with strings in C++.

As I said earlier, you have several choices of string classes. Let me first rule out a couple that you won't likely use in your C++Builder VCL applications. (I say "C++Builder VCL applications" to distinguish this type of application from others such as console applications, OWL applications, or MFC applications. I am assuming you bought C++Builder to take advantage of all its power, and that means using VCL.) One string class that you probably won't use is part of the C++ class library and is called, simply, string. Another is the STL class called basic_string. Both are good string classes, but you just won't need them much in your VCL applications.

NOTE

My statements advising you against using string, particularly STL's basic_string class, will almost certainly be met with some opposition. Certainly there are reasons to use these classes, but for the most part there are more compelling reasons not to.

This probably leads you to wonder, "So, if not these string classes, then what string class should I use?" Before I answer that, let me introduce you to the two string classes that VCL provides. You will have your answer before long.

The SmallString Template

The C++Builder SmallString class emulates the Pascal short string data type. (I'm not going to try to teach Pascal in addition to C++, but suffice it to say that Pascal has two string types: the short string and the long string.) The SmallString class is implemented as a template. (A *template* is a special kind of C++ class.) This class is provided for Pascal compatibility reasons, and I don't see any reason to use the SmallString class when writing new code in C++Builder. If you were to use this class, the syntax would look like this:

```
SmallString<30> s;
s = "Hello World";
```

There is only one reason I can think of to use this class in your C++Builder applications: Some components originally written for Delphi require it. I won't go into further detail, but rest assured that you won't run into this scenario very often and you certainly won't run into it with any of VCL's built-in components.

The AnsiString Class

Before we go into the specifics of the AnsiString class, some background would be helpful. VCL makes heavy use of the Pascal long string data type—nearly all text-based VCL properties are based on the Pascal long string. For example, the Text, Name, and Caption properties are all Pascal long string properties. VCL also uses this data type in many component methods and event-handling functions.

There are two things to understand about this data type. First, in Pascal the long string is an actual language data type and not just a character array, as in C and C++. Second, C++ has no built-in equivalent for the Pascal long string. Because long string is used so heavily in VCL and because C++Builder uses the Pascal VCL, Borland created a C++ class to approximate the Pascal long string. This class, AnsiString, can be used wherever a Pascal long string is required.

Let's face it, the name AnsiString is not particularly appealing. Somewhere in SYSDEFS.H you will find the following line:

```
typedef AnsiString String;
```

This enables you to use the name String (uppercase *S*) when declaring an instance of the AnsiString class rather than use the official class name of AnsiString:

```
String s = "This is a test";
```

5

Because String is the recommended alias for the AnsiString class, there is no reason to use the name AnsiString itself in your C++Builder programs (although you certainly can, if you prefer). For clarity I'll probably refer to the class as AnsiString in the text, but I'll use the short form, String, in code examples.

AnsiString is a very capable string class. The AnsiString class constructors enable you to create an AnsiString object from a char, a char*, an int, or a double. These constructors make it easy to assign a literal string to an AnsiString and convert an integer or floating-point number to a string. All the following examples use the AnsiString constructors, either explicitly or implicitly:

```
String FloatString = 127.123;
String AnotherFloatString(0.999);
String IntString = 49;
String CharString = 'A';
Label1->Caption = "This is a test";
double d = 3.14 * 20;
Edit1->Text = d;
```

You are probably not too interested in the intimate details, but in the cases where a direct assignment is made, the C++ compiler is working behind the scenes to apply the appropriate AnsiString constructor. Take this line, for example:

```
String S = 127.123;  // create an AnsiString from a double
```

Internally the compiler generates something like this:

```
String S = String((double)127.123);
```

So it's the AnsiString constructor that performs the conversion when a direct assignment is made. Another reason the previous code example works is that the AnsiString class has overridden the assignment operator (=). Other operators are overloaded to simplify things like concatenation (using the + operator) and testing for equality (using the == operator).

The AnsiString class, like the other C++ classes, has many methods that make string manipulation easier. Table 5.1 lists a few of the most commonly used AnsiString methods. This is by no means a complete list. Consult the C++Builder online help for a list of all the AnsiString methods.

Table 5.1. Commonly used AnsiString methods

Method	Description
c_str	Returns a pointer (char*) to the string's data.
Delete	Deletes part of a string.
Insert	Inserts text into an existing string at the specified location.

continues

Table 5.1. continued

Method	Description
Length	Returns the length of the string. This doesn't include a terminating NULL.
LowerCase	Converts the string to lowercase.
Pos	Returns the position of a search string within a string.
SubString	Returns a sub-string within the string, starting at a given position within the string and of the given length.
ToDouble	Converts the string to a floating-point number. If the string cannot be converted into a floating-point value, an exception is thrown.
ToInt	Converts the string to an integer. If the string cannot be converted, an exception is thrown.
ToIntDef	Converts the string to an integer and supplies a default value in case the string cannot be converted. No exception is thrown if the string cannot be converted.
Trim	Trims leading and trailing blank space from a string.
UpperCase	Converts a string to uppercase.

A few of these methods deserve special mention. One is the c_str() method. This oddly named method is necessary when you want to get a pointer to the character buffer of an AnsiString. Why would you want to do that? Some Windows API functions require a char* as a parameter. Remember that AnsiString is a class. You can't just pass an AnsiString to a function that is expecting a pointer to a character array. For example, if you were to use the Windows API function DrawText(), you would have to do something like this:

```
RECT R;
Rect(0, 0, 100, 20);
// first, the C way
char buff[] = "This is a test";
DrawText(Canvas->Handle,  buff, -1, &R, DT_SINGLELINE);
// now the VCL way
String S = "This is a test";
DrawText(Canvas->Handle,  S.c_str(), -1, &R, DT_SINGLELINE);
```

The second parameter of the DrawText() function requires a pointer to a character buffer, and the c_str() provides exactly that. This might not make much sense at the moment, but file it away in your mind for future reference.

5

NOTE

Don't worry too much about understanding the DrawText() function right now. This example does illustrate a point, however. Although VCL insulates you from the Windows API, you can still use the Windows API. As you delve deeper into Windows programming, you will want to use the API occasionally. It's there any time you need it.

Another AnsiString method is ToInt(). This method will convert a text string to an integer value. Let's say you have an edit component on a form that will be used to retrieve an integer value from the user. Because an edit component only holds text, you need to convert that text to an integer. You can do it like this:

```
int value = Edit1->Text.ToInt();
```

The ToDouble() method works in exactly the same way. Note that both these methods will throw an exception if the conversion cannot be made. If, for example, the user enters S123, an exception would be thrown because the letter S cannot be converted to an integer. I haven't talked about exceptions yet, so I won't go into detail at this time.

NOTE

Several AnsiString methods don't operate on the string itself but instead return a new string. Take the UpperCase() method, for example. You might think that the following code would convert the string to all uppercase:

```
String FileName = "c:\\mystuff\\mydata.dat";
FileName.UpperCase();
```

This won't work, however, because the UpperCase() function returns a new string and doesn't work on the existing string. The proper way to call this function is

```
FileName = FileName.UpperCase();
```

Before using the AnsiString methods, consult the online help to be sure how the method operates. Oh, and lest I forget...don't forget the double backslashes!

I'll mention one other AnsiString method simply because I dislike it. The Format() method enables you to build a string using variables just as the sprintf() function does. sprintf() was discussed on Day 1 in the section entitled "String Manipulation Functions." Here's the example of sprintf() from Day 1:

```
char buff[20];
int x = 10 * 20;
sprintf(buff, "The result is: %d", x);
```

This code will build a string with the contents The result is: 200. This same thing can be accomplished with the Format() method of AnsiString, as follows:

```
String S;
int x = 10 * 20;
S = S.Format("The result is: %d", OPENARRAY(TVarRec, (x)));
```

That's ugly. There are reasons this function is written this way, but I won't explain them right now. Let me just say that I never use the Format() method. For one thing, I can never remember that weird syntax. For another, the sprintf() function works fine and is less convoluted. Here's what I would do to format an AnsiString:

```
int x = 10 * 20;
char buff[20];
sprintf(buff, "The result is: %d", x);
String S = buff;
```

Sure, there is a degree of inelegance here, but I'll take this over the inelegance offered by Format() any day. In the end, you can try both techniques and choose for yourself.

There is at least one oddity of the AnsiString class that I'll mention before we move on. The index operator ([]) can be used to reference a particular element of the string:

```
String S = "Hello World!";
Label1->Caption = S[7];
```

This code assigns the character W to the Caption property of a label component. The important thing to note here is that the string's first element is at array index 1 and not array index 0 as with other C++ arrays. The 1-based index is required for technical reasons, primarily for compatibility with Delphi. Although it's necessary, I suspect that this feature will cause grief for some experienced C++ programmers at first. For example, the following code will fail silently:

```
String S = "c:\\myprog\\myprog.exe";
int index = S.LastDelimiter("\\");
S.Delete(0, index);
```

This code will fail because 0 is not a valid index number for a string. The correct code is

```
S.Delete(1, index);
```

Remembering that the string is 1-based rather than 0-based will save you a lot of trouble when writing C++Builder applications.

There are a lot of options available to you when dealing with strings in your C++Builder applications. For me the choice is easy—I'll use AnsiString for my day-to-day string needs. I rarely need anything else. AnsiString is fast, it has the features I need, and it is designed to integrate seamlessly with VCL.

Sets

There are certain features of Pascal that are not found in C++, and vice versa. One feature that Pascal has, but C++ doesn't, is the set. Sets are used frequently throughout VCL, so you need to know what sets are and how they work.

NEW TERM A *set* is a collection of like objects.

That description doesn't say too much, does it? An example that comes to mind is the TFont class' Style property. This property can include one or more of the following values: fsBold, fsItalic, fsUnderline, and fsStrikeout. Keep that in mind, and we'll get back to it in just a bit.

As I said earlier, there is no built-in support for sets in the C++ language. C++ programmers use bitfields where Pascal programmers use sets. I won't try to explain bitfields right now, but understand that bitfields are a way of specifying a group of possible options using just one variable (usually an int or a long). This mechanism works perfectly well; it's just that it doesn't fit with the way VCL does things. Plus, the concept of a set is easier to understand for beginning C++ programmers than the concept of bitfields. Obviously, a way of approximating sets in C++ was needed. Because VCL makes heavy use of sets and C++ lacks native support for sets, Borland had to come up with some way to emulate sets in C++Builder.

Fortunately, the C++ language is powerful enough to enable you to do whatever needs to be done. Although there are several ways to solve this particular problem, the folks at Borland decided to implement sets in the form of a template class called, predictably, Set. The good news is that the Set template is very easy to use when you understand it.

So how do you use a set? Let's get back to the font style example from earlier in this section. Typically, you turn the individual Style values for the font on or off at design time. Sometimes, however, you need to set the font's Style property at runtime. For example, let's say that you want to add the bold and italic attributes to the font style. One way is to declare a variable of type TFontStyles and then add the fsBold and fsItalic styles to the set. Here's how it looks:

```
TFontStyles Styles;
Styles << fsBold << fsItalic;
```

Notice the use of the << operator. This operator is overloaded in the Set class to enable you to add elements to a set. Note that this code doesn't actually change a font's style; it just creates a set and adds two elements to it. To change a font's style, you have to assign this newly created set to the Font->Style property of some component:

```
Memo->Font->Style = Styles;
```

5

Now, let's say that you wanted the font to be bold but not italic. In that case, you would have to remove the italic style from the set. To remove an element from a set, you use the >> operator:

```
Styles >> fsItalic;
Memo->Font->Style = Styles;
```

Often you want to know whether a particular item is in a set. Let's say we want to know whether the font is currently set to bold. You can find out whether the fsBold style is in the set by using the Contains() method:

```
bool hasBold = Memo->Font->Style.Contains(fsBold);
if (hasBold) DoSomething();
```

Sometimes you need to make sure you are starting with an empty set. You can clear a set of its contents using the Clear() method—for example:

```
// start with an empty set
Memo->Font->Style.Clear();
// now add the bold and italic styles
Memo->Font->Style = Memo->Font->Style << fsBold << fsItalic;
```

Here the font style is cleared of all contents, and then the bold and italic styles are added. If you want, you can create a temporary set and add elements to it all at one time. The previous code snippet could also have been written like this:

```
Memo->Font->Style = TFontStyles() << fsBold << fsItalic;
```

This code creates a temporary TFontStyles set, adds the fsBold and fsItalic styles, and then assigns the temporary set to the Style property. Although this looks odd, it is perfectly valid and is a handy way of creating a temporary set on the fly.

NOTE

> Because of an oddity in the way the Set class works, you should always make an assignment when changing a property that is a set. Take the following code, for example:
>
> ```
> Memo->Font->Style << fsBold << fsItalic;
> ```
>
> This code will compile, but it won't actually change the font style because the write method for the Style property won't be called. To be sure that the Style property is properly updated, use an explicit assignment instead:
>
> ```
> Memo->Font->Style = Memo->Font->Style << fsBold << fsItalic;
> ```
>
> This ensures that the write method for the Style property is called and that the font's style is updated.

Sets are a way of life in VCL and in C++Builder programming. Sets are easy after you get the hang of them. The Set template in C++Builder is your route to VCL sets. The extraction and insertion operators, although odd looking at first, are a simple way of adding and removing elements from a set.

VCL Explored

The Visual Component Library is a well-designed framework. As with most good frameworks, VCL makes maximum use of inheritance. The bulk of the VCL framework is composed of classes that represent components. Other VCL classes are not related to components. These classes perform housekeeping chores, act as helper classes, and provide some utility services.

The VCL class hierarchy dealing with components is complex. Fortunately, you don't have to know every detail of VCL to begin programming in C++Builder. At the top of the VCL chain you will find TObject. Figure 5.5 shows some of the main base classes and classes derived from them.

Figure 5.5.

The VCL class hierarchy.

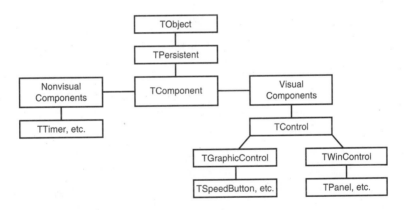

TObject is the granddaddy of all VCL component classes. Below TObject you see TPersistent. This class deals with a component's capability to save itself to files and to memory, as well as other messy details we don't need to know about. I'm thankful (and you should be, too) that we don't need to know much about TPersistent to program most applications in C++Builder.

The TComponent class serves as a more direct base class for components. This class provides all the functionality that a basic component requires. Nonvisual components are derived from TComponent itself. Visual components are derived from TControl, which, as you can see from Figure 5.5, is derived from TComponent. TControl provides additional functionality that visual components require. The individual components, then, are derived from either TGraphicControl or TWinControl.

When you drop a component on a form, C++Builder creates a pointer to that component in the form's class declaration so that you can access the component in your code. C++Builder uses the component's Name property for the pointer variable's name. When we created the sample application earlier, we placed a memo component on the form. At that point C++Builder created a TMemo* variable and gave it the name Memo. Similarly, when we created a button on the form, C++Builder created TButton* to represent the button. Before any of that took place, C++Builder had already derived a new class from TForm and, of course, created an instance of that class to represent the form.

Some understanding of the VCL classes is obviously necessary before working with VCL. Although I cannot review each and every VCL class, I can hit the high points. Let's take a look at some of the classes that you will use most frequently.

Form and Application Classes

Form and application classes represent forms and the Application object in VCL. These classes are derived from TComponent and indeed are components themselves. They are listed separately to distinguish them from the controls you drop on a form.

TApplication

The TApplication class encapsulates the basic operations of a Windows program. TApplication takes care of things like managing the application's icon, providing context help, and doing basic message handling. Every C++Builder application has a pointer to the TApplication object called Application. You use the TApplication class primarily to execute message boxes, manage context help, and set hint text for buttons and status bars. TApplication is a bit of an oddity in VCL in that some of its properties (Icon, HelpFile, and Title) can be set via the Application page of the Project Options dialog box.

TForm

The TForm class encapsulates forms in VCL. Forms are used for main windows, dialog boxes, secondary windows, and just about any other window type you can imagine. TForm is a workhorse class in VCL. It can respond to nearly 60 properties, 45 methods, and 20 events. I am going to discuss forms in detail tomorrow, so I won't continue now.

Component Classes

This group encompasses a wide range of classes and can be further divided into separate categories, which I've done in the following sections.

Standard Component Classes

The standard components are those that encapsulate the most common Windows controls. The standard component classes include TButton, TEdit, TListBox, TMemo, TMainMenu, TPopupMenu, TCheckBox, TRadioButton, TRadioGroup, TGroupBox, and TPanel.

Most of these classes encapsulate a Windows control, so I won't discuss all of them right now. The TMainMenu class encapsulates an application's main menu. At design time, double-clicking the MainMenu component's icon brings up the Menu Designer. TMainMenu has properties that control whether the menu item is grayed out, whether it is checked, the help context ID, the item's hint text, and others. Each menu item has a single event, OnClick, so that you can attach a function to a menu item being selected. I'll discuss menus and the Menu Designer in more detail on Day 7, "Working with the Form Designer and the Menu Designer."

Another standard component of interest is TPanel.

NEW TERM A *panel* represents a rectangular region on a form, usually with its own components, that can be treated as a single unit.

For instance, if you want to build a toolbar for an application, you start with a panel and then place speed buttons on the panel. If you move the panel, the speed buttons move with it. Panels can be used for a wide variety of tasks in C++Builder. You can use a panel to build a status bar, for example. Panels have properties that control what type of edge the panel should have; whether the panel is raised, sunken, or flat; and the width of the border. Combinations of these properties can be used to create a variety of 3D panels.

C++Builder has another group of components that I'll throw in with the standard controls. These controls can be found under the Additional tab on the Component palette. The classes representing these components include TBitBtn, TSpeedButton, TMaskEdit, TStringGrid, TDrawGrid, TImage, TShape, TBevel, and TScrollBox. The TBitBtn class represents a button that has an image on it. TSpeedButton is also a button with an image, but this component is designed to be used as a speed button on a control bar. A TSpeedButton is not a true button but rather a graphical depiction of a button. This enables you to have a large number of speed buttons and not consume Windows resources for each button. The TImage component enables you to place an image on a form that can then be selected from a file on disk. You can use the TBevel component to create boxes and lines that are raised (bumps) or lowered (dips). Bevels can be used to divide a form into visual regions and to provide an aesthetically pleasing form. The TStringGrid and TDrawGrid classes give you a means to present information in a tabular format.

Win32 Custom Control Classes

VCL has component classes that encapsulate many of the Windows 32-bit custom controls. These classes include TListView, TTreeView, TProgressBar, TTabControl, TPageControl, TRichEdit, TImageList, TStatusBar, TAnimate, TToolBar, TCoolBar, and a few others. Some of these controls are, by nature, complicated, and the VCL classes that represent them are complicated as well. Trust me when I say that VCL does much to ease the burden of working with these common controls. You have to spend some time with these classes before you fully understand them.

Database Component Classes

VCL has a host of database components that include both visual and nonvisual classes. Nonvisual database components include TDataSource, TDatabase, TTable, and TQuery. These classes encapsulate behind-the-scenes database operations.

Visual database component classes are the part of the VCL database operations that users see and interact with. For instance, a TDBGrid component is used to give users access to a database table that can be represented as a TTable component. In this way, the TDBGrid acts as the interface between the user and the TTable. Through the TDBGrid, the user can view and edit the database table on disk.

The TDBNavigator component provides buttons that enable the user to move through a database table. This class includes buttons for next record, previous record, first record, last record, cancel edit, accept edit, and undo edit.

Other data-aware component classes hook standard Windows controls to database fields. These classes include TDBText, TDBEdit, TDBListBox, and TDBImage, among others.

Common Dialog Classes

As you are no doubt aware, Windows has common dialog boxes for things like opening files, saving files, choosing fonts, and choosing colors. VCL encapsulates these common dialog boxes in classes representing each type. The classes are TOpenDialog, TSaveDialog, TOpenPictureDialog, TSavePictureDialog, TFontDialog, TColorDialog, TPrintDialog, and TPrinterSetupDialog. VCL also adds the TFindDialog and TReplaceDialog classes to this component group. All the components in this group are nonvisual in that they don't have a design-time visual interface. The dialog boxes are visible when displayed at runtime, of course.

System Component Classes

The System tab on the Component palette contains a mixture of visual and nonvisual components. The TTimer class is used to represent a Windows system timer. Its single event is OnTimer, which is called each time the timer fires. The timer interval is set through the Interval property. TTimer is a nonvisual component.

Tucked into this group of classes is the TMediaPlayer class. This class enables you to play media files like wave audio, AVI video, and MIDI audio. The media can be played, stopped, paused, or positioned at a particular point in the file, as well as many other operations. This class has many properties and events that greatly simplify the complex world of the Windows Media Control Interface (MCI).

The TPaintBox component gives you an empty canvas on which you can draw anything you want. This component has many potential uses. The System group includes OLE and dynamic data exchange (DDE) classes as well.

5

The Win 3.1 Group

Don't make the mistake of automatically discarding this component group just because of the name of the tab on which they reside. This group contains some great components. (The Win 3.1 tab has its roots in Delphi.) In particular I like the TTabSet and TNotebook components. This group also includes several component classes that enable you to build your own custom File Open or File Save dialog box. The classes are TFileListBox, TDirectoryListBox, TDriveComboBox, and TFilterComboBox.

GDI Classes

The GDI (graphics device interface) classes get a lot of work in Windows GUI applications. These classes encapsulate the use of bitmaps, fonts, device contexts (DCs), brushes, and pens. It is through these GDI objects that graphics and text are displayed on a window. The GDI classes are not associated with a specific component, but many components have instances of these classes as properties. For example, an edit control has a property called Font that is an instance of the TFont class.

The term *device context* is well known by Windows programmers, whether they program in C or with one of the C++ frameworks. In VCL, though, the term is not widely used. This is because VCL encapsulates Windows DCs in the TCanvas class. VCL uses the term *canvas* to refer to a Windows device context. A canvas provides a surface that you can draw on, using methods like MoveTo(), LineTo(), and TextOut(). Bitmaps can be displayed on the canvas using the Draw() or StretchDraw() methods. The concept of a canvas that you draw on makes more sense than the archaic term *device context*, don't you think?

The TCanvas class contains instances of the other GDI classes. For example, when you do a MoveTo()/LineTo() sequence, a line is drawn with the current pen color. The Pen property is used to determine the current pen color and is an instance of the TPen class. TPen has properties that determine what type of line to draw: the line width, the line style (solid, dashed, dotted, and so on), and the mode with which to draw the line.

The TBrush class represents a brush used as the fill pattern for canvas operations like FillRect(), Polygon(), and Ellipse(). TBrush properties include Color, Style, and Bitmap. The Style property enables you to set a hatch pattern for the brush. The Bitmap property enables you to specify a bitmap for the fill pattern.

TBitmap encapsulates bitmap operations in VCL. Properties include Palette, Height, Width, and TransparentColor. Methods include LoadFromFile(), LoadFromResourceID(), and SaveToFile(). TBitmap is used by other component classes such as TImage, TBitBtn, and TSpeedButton in addition to TCanvas. An instance of the TBitmap class can also be used as an offscreen bitmap. Offscreen bitmaps are commonly used in graphics-intensive applications to reduce flicker and improve graphics performance.

The TFont class handles font operations. Properties include Color, Height, and Style (bold, italic, normal, and so on). The TFont class is used by all component classes that display text.

5

In addition to the GDI classes listed here, there are others that either work as helper classes or extend a base class to provide extra functionality. As you work with C++Builder, you will learn more about these classes and how to use them. Figure 5.6 shows the hierarchy of the VCL classes that encapsulate GDI operations.

Figure 5.6.

VCL GDI class hierarchy.

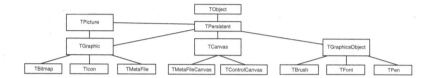

Utility Classes

So far I have discussed component classes. VCL also contains utility classes you can use in your applications. A *utility class* simplifies some task in Windows programming. For instance, the TIniFile class eases the use of writing and reading Windows configuration files (.INI files). Conventional wisdom has it that the use of .INI files is out and the Registry is in. To aid in Registry operations, VCL has the TRegistry and TRegkeyInfo classes.

The TStringList class allows for arrays of strings. TStringList is used by many of the component classes to store strings. For instance, the TMemo class uses a TStringList object for its Lines property. TStringList has the capability to save its list of strings to file or load strings from a file using the LoadFromFile() and SaveToFile() methods.

Another useful VCL utility class is the TList class. This class enables you to create arrays of any type of object you want. The TList class simply stores a list of pointers. The main advantage of the TList class is that it provides you with an array that will dynamically grow or shrink as new objects are added or removed.

VCL also includes a set of classes to enable reading and writing of streams. The TStream, TFileStream, TMemoryStream, and TResourceStream classes all enable you to read or write data to streams. These classes are for more advanced uses but are invaluable when you need the particular functionality they provide.

And That's Not All...

By no means did I cover all the VCL classes here. I did, however, touch on those classes that you are most likely to use in your applications.

Flip back a few pages and take another look at Listing 5.1 and the OWL example that performs the equivalent code in Listing 5.2. If you recall, I said that placing a bitmap image on a window is even easier in C++Builder. Let me show you what I mean. First, begin a new application in C++Builder. You will be looking at a blank form. Perform the following steps:

1. Change the Caption property of the form to Bitmap Test Program.
2. Click on the Additional tab on the Component palette, choose the Image component, and place the component on the form.

3. Locate the `Align` property and change it to `alClient`. The picture component fills the client area of the form.

4. Locate the `Stretch` property and change it to `true`.

5. Locate the `Picture` property and double-click the Value column.

6. The Picture Editor dialog box is displayed. Click the Load button. The File Open dialog box is displayed.

7. Navigate to the `\Program Files\Common Files\Borland Shared Files\Images\ Splash\256Color` directory and choose an image from those presented (I like `HANDSHAKE.BMP`). Click OK.

8. You are now back to the Picture Editor dialog box, and the bitmap you chose is displayed in the preview window. Click OK. (If you want to choose a different bitmap, click the Load button again.) The bitmap now fills the client area of the form.

9. Click the Run button. When the application runs, you can size the window, and the bitmap will always fill the client area of the window.

See how easy it is? It would have been even easier if we hadn't bothered to make the image fill the form's client area. Figure 5.7 shows the bitmap test program running.

Figure 5.7.

The bitmap test program running.

Summary

Today you learned about frameworks. I first discussed OWL and MFC and the role they have had in shaping Windows programming today. After that I moved to a discussion of VCL and how it differs from the C++ frameworks. I discussed properties, methods, and events and gave you some hands-on experience in the process. We finished today with an overview of the VCL classes that you are likely to encounter when programming in C++Builder. I didn't cover them all, but I gave you a brief look at the most commonly used classes.

So where is this industry going? The wave of the future appears to be components, but it is apparent that there will be a need for class libraries like MFC and OWL for quite some time to come. Some of you who are now using MFC or OWL will abandon them in favor of programming environments like C++Builder and Delphi. Others of you will use both your old tool and the new RAD tools. Still others will stick with what you know best. In any event, it is important to realize that each of these frameworks is a tool. My advice is simple: Use the most appropriate tool for the current job.

If you have never used OWL or MFC, you needn't worry about what you are missing. C++Builder and VCL enable you to build robust applications in much less time than you could with either OWL or MFC. This is particularly true when you take into account the learning curve of VCL compared to MFC or OWL. Programming in C++Builder is much easier to learn, and you can write programs faster, too.

Workshop

The Workshop contains quiz questions to help you solidify your understanding of the material covered and exercises to provide you with experience in using what you have learned. The answers to the quiz questions are in Appendix A.

Q&A

Q What is a framework?

A A framework, also called a class library, is a set of classes that simplifies Windows programming. A good framework implements object-oriented design and object-oriented programming to apply an object-oriented approach to writing Windows applications.

Q Is VCL a C++ framework?

A No. VCL is a framework that works with C++ in C++Builder, but it is written in Object Pascal rather than C++. VCL is written in Object Pascal because it was initially created for Borland's Delphi.

Q Am I supposed to know how to program in Pascal and C++ in order to write Windows programs with C++Builder?

A No. The fact that VCL is written in Pascal is virtually invisible to you. As far as you are concerned, you are just programming in C++. Advanced C++ users might notice some situations where VCL limits their choices, but most users of C++Builder will not.

Q It seems as though the component way of doing things is the best approach. Is that true?

A It is true for many applications but certainly not for all. In some cases, a framework such as OWL or MFC is better suited to the task. For applications that use a lot of dialog boxes and windows and for database applications, VCL is probably a very good choice. Overall, C++Builder is much easier to learn and use than the C++ class libraries.

Q Are properties just class data members?

A No. Properties are special creatures. Some properties simply set a data member in the class. Other properties, when modified, invoke a method that performs special operations with that property. In these cases, a property does more than just set a data member.

Q Do I have to respond to each and every event a component defines?

A No. You can respond to as many events as appropriate for your application or not respond to any events at all.

Q There sure are a lot of VCL classes. I thought programming with C++Builder was going to be easy.

A Programming with C++Builder is much easier than programming Windows in C and easier than programming with a C++ framework like OWL or MFC. Windows programming, no matter how good the programming tool, requires a lot of experience and knowledge to master. You will master it if you keep at it.

Q Can I use C++Builder forms in my OWL and MFC programs?

A Yes. Later in the book I'll show you how you can do that.

Quiz

1. Are all components visible at design time?
2. Which is better: OWL, MFC, or VCL?
3. Can VCL objects be allocated locally (from the stack) as well as dynamically?
4. Are methods in VCL components equivalent to functions in C++?
5. Are all VCL classes ultimately derived from TObject?
6. Name one nonvisual VCL component.
7. Do all components share certain common properties?
8. Name two common properties that all visual components share.
9. Can two or more components share the same event-handling function?
10. What is the VCL terminology for a Windows device context? What is the name of the VCL class that encapsulates device contexts?

5

Exercises

1. Write a paragraph describing how properties and class data members differ.
2. Create a C++Builder application that displays a bitmap on the main form when a button is clicked.
3. Create a C++Builder application that displays a message box saying `Hello, Bubba!` when the main form is clicked.

4. Create a C++Builder application that displays the text I've been resized! in red letters when the application is resized.

5. Extra credit: Modify the program in Exercise 4 so that the text disappears again after five seconds.

5

Day 6

The C++Builder IDE Explored

One of the most difficult aspects of learning how to use a new programming environment is finding your way around: getting to know the basic menu structure, what all the options do, and how the environment works as a whole. If you are new to programming or new to C++, this task is complicated by the fact that you have to learn a new program (the C++Builder IDE) *and* learn a new language at the same time. It can be overwhelming at times. I'll do my best to make learning the C++Builder IDE a painless experience. For the most part you will learn by example, which is more interesting (not to mention more effective). So, without further ado, and referring to Figure 6.1, let's get on with it. Oh, by the way, if you are coming to C++Builder from Delphi, you might find this chapter and the one that follows elementary. If that is the case, you might want to at least skim the chapters lightly to catch any tidbits that you did not previously know.

Figure 6.1.

The C++Builder IDE.

Main menu

Toolbar

Component palette

Form Designer

Object Inspector

Code Editor

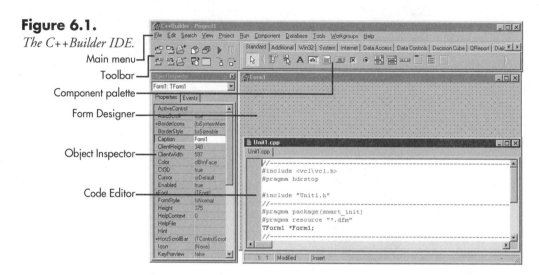

The C++Builder IDE consists of these main parts:

☐ The main menu and toolbar

☐ The Component palette

☐ The Form Designer

☐ The Code Editor

☐ The Object Inspector

☐ The Project Manager

I can't cover all these in a single chapter, so over the next several chapters I will show you around the C++Builder IDE and examine each of these features in detail. I'll start today by discussing projects and how they are used in writing C++Builder applications. After that we'll look at the C++Builder toolbar and the Component palette. Then I'll move to discussing forms in greater detail than I have up to this point. Along the way we'll create some sample programs to illustrate various aspects of C++Builder. We'll close the day by looking at the Object Inspector. This will be a warm-up for tomorrow, when you will learn all about the C++Builder Form Designer.

For starters, let's look at the way C++Builder views applications and how it has simplified the process of creating programs.

Projects in C++Builder

As you know by now, a lot goes on behind the scenes as you write a C++Builder application. In fact, more goes on than I have told you about up to this point. It's not vital that you know every detail about what happens behind the scenes as you write a C++Builder application, but it is a good idea to have a general overview.

 A *project* is a collection of files that work together to create a standalone executable file or DLL.

 In addition to a single project, C++Builder allows you to create what is known as a project group. A *project group* is a collection of C++Builder projects.

A project group is used to manage a group of C++Builder projects that work together to form a complete software product. I'll talk about project groups in more detail on Day 10, "More on Projects." For now, you only need to understand that C++Builder creates a new, unnamed project group for you each time you start C++Builder. Any new projects you create will go into that project group. You can save the project group if you like, or you can treat the default project group as temporary.

Files Used in C++Builder Projects

C++Builder manages a project through the use of several support files. To illustrate, let's create a simple application to get a look at some of what goes on when C++Builder builds an executable file for your program. Do the following:

1. Before you begin, create a fresh directory on your hard drive.
2. First choose File|Close All from the main menu so you are starting from scratch. Now choose File|New Application from the main menu. A blank form is displayed.
3. Before you do anything else, choose File|Save All from the main menu.
4. First, you will be prompted for the name of the unit file. Be sure to switch to the empty directory you just created.
5. Next, type in the name MyUnit for the unit filename and click the Save Button.
6. Now you are prompted for the project name. Type Test in the File name field and click Save.
7. Now choose Project|Build Test from the main menu. C++Builder displays the compile status box and goes to work compiling the program.
8. After a while the compile status box reports that it is done compiling, and the OK button is enabled. Click OK to close the compile status dialog box.
9. Now choose File|Close All from the main menu. (Yes, this exercise does have a purpose.)
10. Now run Windows Explorer and locate the directory where you saved the project. You will see a number of files.

Wow! All that to create just one little program that does nothing? Yes, it's true. First, let me tell you what happens when C++Builder builds an application; then I'll explain what each of these files is for.

6

NOTE

Files with extensions that begin with a tilde (~) are backup files. C++Builder might create several backup files, depending on the number of source files in the project and the project options you have set. Project options are discussed on Day 10.

When you first create a project, C++Builder creates a minimum of six files (assuming a typical C++Builder GUI application):

- [ ] The project source file
- [ ] The main form source file
- [ ] The main form header file
- [ ] The main form resource file
- [ ] The project resource file
- [ ] The project makefile

The *project source file* is the file that contains the WinMain() function and other C++Builder startup code. You can view the project source file by choosing View | Project Source from the main menu. The *main form source file* and *main form header file* are files that contain the class declaration and definition for the main form's class. C++Builder will create an additional source file and header for each new form you create. The *main form resource file* and *project resource file* are binary files that describe the main form and the application's icon. I'll explain that in more detail later in the section titled "Dialog Boxes in Traditional Windows Programs."

Somewhere in this process, C++Builder creates the *project makefile*. The makefile is a text file that contains information about the compiler options you have set, the names of the source files and forms that make up the project, and what library files have to be included.

NOTE

There are two types of library files. A *static library* contains common code that an application needs in order to run. An *import library* is needed when your application references functions in a DLL, such as the Windows API functions. The number and exact filenames of the library files required depend on the features your application uses. Fortunately, you don't have to worry about managing the library files because C++Builder takes care of that detail for you. Library files have an .LIB extension and are tucked away in your C++Builder \lib directory.

6

There are a few more odds and ends, but that's the bulk of what is contained in the makefile. When you tell C++Builder to compile the project, it hands the makefile to the compiler. (Technically, the makefile is read by the Make utility, but why quibble over details?) The compiler reads the makefile and begins compiling all the source files that make up the project.

NOTE

> A C++Builder makefile is a specialized makefile. You cannot use makefiles from other programming environments such as Borland C++ or Visual C++ with C++Builder.

Several things happen during this process. First, the C++ compiler compiles the C++ source files into binary object files. Then the resource compiler compiles any resources, such as the program's icon and form files, into binary resource files. Next, the linker takes over. The linker takes the binary files the compilers created, adds any library files the project needs, and binds them all together to produce the final executable file. Along the way it produces more files that perform some special operations (I'll get to that in a minute). When it's all over, you have a standalone program that can be run in the usual ways.

Okay, but what are all those files for? Table 6.1 lists the file extensions C++Builder uses with a description of the role that each file type plays.

Table 6.1. Types of files used in C++Builder.

Extension	Description
.CPP	The C++ source files. There will usually be one for each unit, one for the main project file, as well as any other source files that you add to the project.
.DFM	The form file. This file is actually a binary resource file (.RES) in disguise. It is a description of the form and all its components. Each form has its own .DFM file.
.DSK	The desktop file. This file keeps track of the way the desktop appeared when you last saved (or closed) the project. All the open windows' sizes and positions are saved so that when you reopen the project it looks the same as you left it. This file is only created if you turn on the option to save your desktop (Environment Options dialog box).
.EXE	The final executable program.
.H	C++ header files that contain class declarations. These could be C++Builder-generated files or your own class headers.

continues

Table 6.1. continued

Extension	Description
.HPP	Also C++ headers files. Headers with an .HPP extension are created by C++Builder when you install components. The VCL header files (located in the \CBuilder\Include\VCL directory) also have an extension of .HPP to distinguish them from the .H files that C++Builder generates for each unit.
.IL?	The four files whose extensions begin with .IL are files created by the incremental linker. The incremental linker saves you time by linking only the parts of the program that have changed since the last build.
.OBJ	The compiled binary object files. These are the files that the compiler produces when it compiles your C++ source files.
.BPR	The project makefile. This is a text file that contains a description of which files C++Builder needs to compile and link. It also contains special flags that tell the compiler and linker which options to apply when building the project.
.RES	A compiled binary resource file produced by the resource compiler.
.TDS	The debugger symbol table. This file is used by the debugger during debugging sessions.

 NOTE

C++Builder has other associated file extensions as well. For example, the .BPG extension is used to denote a project group, the .BPK extension is used to designate a C++Builder package makefile, and the .BPL extension represents a compiled package. Both project groups and packages will be discussed in detail on Day 10.

The files that C++Builder produces can be broken down into two categories: files C++Builder relies on to build the project and files that it will create when it compiles and links a project. If you were to move your source files to another computer, for instance, you wouldn't have to move all the files, just the files C++Builder needs to build the application. Conveniently, the source files happen to be the smallest files in the project. It does not take a lot of disk space to back up just the project source files.

The minimum set of files consists of the .CPP, .H, DFM, and .BPR files. All other files are files that C++Builder will re-create when you compile the program. The desktop file (.DSK) is one that you may want to hang on to because it keeps track of the state your project was in when you last worked on it.

NOTE

In addition to the source files I've mentioned, some applications use a *resource script file*. Resource scripts have an .RC extension. Resource scripts are text files that are used to define resources like bitmaps, icons, or cursors. If you use a resource script, be sure to keep it with the project if you move the project to another location.

Figure 6.2 illustrates how C++Builder takes source files and compiles and links them to form the final executable file.

Figure 6.2.

The C++Builder compile/link process.

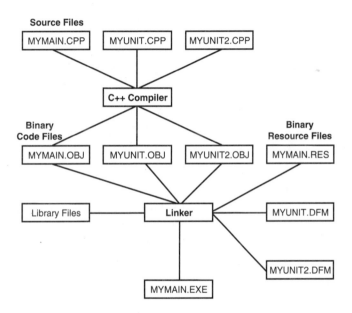

TIP

If you find yourself running low on hard disk space, you can delete some of the C++Builder files from projects you are not currently working on. It is safe to delete the files with the .OBJ, .RES, and .TDS extensions, as well as any files with extensions beginning with .IL. Some of these files can grow quite large, and there is no use in keeping them for non-current projects.

6

WARNING

Do not delete any files from the C++Builder directories other than the Examples directory. If in doubt, *don't delete*!

Source Code Units

Earlier I mentioned that most applications of any size have several source files, which are called *units*. The use of the term *unit* in C++Builder is a holdover from Delphi. C++Builder has its roots in the Delphi IDE, and *unit* is used throughout both VCL and the C++Builder IDE itself. C++ programmers would typically refer to a file containing a program's source as a *module*. Whereas using the term *module* would have been more C++ friendly (and less Pascal-like), replacing the word *unit* with *module* would have required major changes to the C++Builder infrastructure, so the term *unit* was left in. If you are coming from a C++ programming background, it might seem odd to refer to modules as units, but you will get used to it soon enough. In the end, there's no point in getting hung up over terminology.

 New Term C++Builder uses the term *unit* to refer to source files.

Each time you create a new form, C++Builder does the following:

- ☐ Creates a form file (.DFM)
- ☐ Derives a class from TForm
- ☐ Creates a header (.H file) containing the class declaration
- ☐ Creates a unit (.CPP file) for the class definition
- ☐ Adds the new form information to the project makefile

Initially C++Builder assigns a default name of Form1 to the form, Unit1.cpp for the associated unit, and Unit1.h for the header. The second form created for the project would have a default name of Form2, and so on. Each time you create a new form C++Builder creates a new unit (.CPP) and header file (.H) for that form.

 Note

> As soon as you create a new project, you should save it with a meaningful name. Likewise, every time you create a new form, you should save it with a descriptive name. This makes it easier to locate forms and units when you need to make modifications.

Note

> When writing a technical book, a nasty situation often arises. I want to use meaningful examples to reinforce the presentation of information. In order to write those examples, I have to use techniques or methods that I haven't talked about yet. But I can't talk about those methods until I've given you some good, meaningful examples. But I can't... well, you see my dilemma. So I'm going to digress a little here and talk about the main menu, toolbar, and Component palette. As you read the next section, remember that we're off on a tangent.

The C++Builder Main Menu and Toolbar

The C++Builder main menu has all the choices necessary to make C++Builder work. Because programming in C++Builder is a highly visual operation, you may not use the main menu as much as you might with other programming environments. Still, just about anything you need is available from the main menu if you prefer to work that way. I'm not going to go over every item on the main menu here because you will encounter each item as you work through the next several chapters.

The C++Builder toolbar is a convenient way of accomplishing often-repeated tasks. A button is easier to locate than a menu item, not to mention that it requires less mouse movement. The C++Builder toolbar's default configuration is illustrated in Figure 6.3.

Figure 6.3.

The C++Builder toolbar.

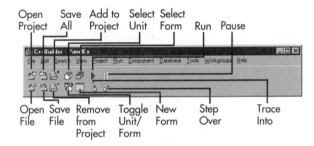

If you are like me, you often forget to use the toolbar. But I'm telling you: Don't forget to learn and use the toolbar. As the old saying goes, "Do as I say, not as I do." If you take the time to learn the toolbar it will save you time and make you more efficient in the long run. One of the reasons you bought C++Builder was to produce Windows applications quickly, so you might as well make the most of it.

The C++Builder toolbar is fully customizable. As you saw back in Figure 6.1, between the toolbar and the Component palette is a vertical line that acts as a sizing bar. When you place the mouse cursor over the sizing bar, you will see the sizing cursor (a double-headed black arrow). Once you have the sizing cursor, you can drag the sizing bar right or left to make the toolbar take more or less room on the C++Builder main window.

Customizing the toolbar is remarkably easy. C++Builder allows you to add buttons to the toolbar, remove buttons, and rearrange buttons however you see fit. To configure the toolbar, you must use the context menu. Point to the toolbar and right-click to display the context menu choices listed in Table 6.2.

Table 6.2. Items on the toolbar's context menu.

Menu Item	Description
Show Hints	Controls whether the hints (ToolTips) are displayed for the toolbar buttons.
Hide	Hides the toolbar.
Help	Invokes C++Builder help with the toolbar page displayed.
Properties	Displays the Toolbar Editor dialog box, which allows you to customize the toolbar.

NOTE

When you have hidden the toolbar, you will have to choose View | Toolbar from the main menu to display the toolbar again.

To customize the toolbar, right-click and choose Properties. When you choose this menu item, the Toolbar Editor dialog box is displayed. This dialog box contains all the possible toolbar buttons. To add a button to the toolbar, just locate it in the Toolbar Editor and drag it to the place you want it to occupy on the toolbar. To remove a button, grab it and drag it off the toolbar. It's as simple as that. If you really make a mess of things, just click the Reset button in the Toolbar Editor dialog box (see Figure 6.4) and the toolbar will revert to its default settings.

Figure 6.4.

Customizing the toolbar.

If you want to make room for more buttons, drag the sizing bar to the right to make the toolbar wider. Now just drag any buttons you want from the Toolbar Editor to the toolbar.

The toolbar has an invisible grid that aids you when dropping new buttons; just get the buttons close to where you want them and they will snap into place. I happen to like the Make, Compile Unit, and Build buttons on the toolbar, so I have customized my toolbar to include those buttons. Figure 6.4 illustrates the process of dragging a button to the toolbar.

Feel free to customize the C++Builder IDE any way you like. It's your development environment, so make it work for you.

Using the Component Palette

The C++Builder Component palette is used to select a component or other control (such as an ActiveX control) in order to place that control on a form. The Component palette is a multipage window. Tabs are provided to allow you to navigate between pages. Clicking on a tab will display the available components or controls on that page.

Placing a component on a form is a two-step process. First, go to the Component palette and select the button representing the component you want to use. Then click on the form to place the component on the form. The component appears with its upper-left corner placed where you clicked with the mouse.

You have already seen the Component palette's basic operations, but it has a couple of other features that you haven't seen yet. The following sections explain these features.

Placing Multiple Copies of a Component

So far you have only placed one component at a time on a form. You can easily place multiple components of the same type without selecting the component from the Component palette each time. To place multiple components on the form, press and hold the Shift key when selecting the component from the Component palette. After you select the component you can release the Shift key. The component's button on the Component palette will appear pressed and will be highlighted with a blue border. Click on the form to place the first component. Notice that the button stays pressed in the Component palette. You can click as many times as you like; a new component will be placed each time you click the form. To stop placing components, click the selector button on the Component palette (the arrow button). The component button pops up to indicate that you are done placing components.

Seeing is believing, so follow these steps:

1. Create a new project.
2. Press and hold the Shift key on the keyboard and click the Label component button in the Component palette.
3. Click three times on the form, moving the cursor each time to indicate where you want the new component placed.

6

4. Click the arrow button on the Component palette to end the process and return to form design mode.

TIP

It's fastest to place all components of a particular type on your form at one time using this technique. Components can always be rearranged and resized at a later time.

NOTE

When placing multiple copies of a particular component, it's easy to forget to click the arrow button when you're done. If you accidentally place more components than you intended, you can simply delete any extras.

Placing and Centering a Component on the Form

C++Builder provides a shortcut method of placing a component on a form. Simply double-click the component's button in the Component palette, and the component will be placed on the form. The component will be centered on the form both horizontally and vertically. Components placed with this method can be moved to another location on the form just like components placed in the usual method.

NOTE

Each time you double-click a button on the Component palette, a component will be placed on the center of the form in the component's default size. If you repeatedly double-click the component button, multiple copies of the component will be placed on the form. Each component will be placed in the center of the form and will be stacked on top of the previous one. It will appear as if you have a single component, so you may not realize that you have several components occupying the same space. If you accidentally place multiple components, just click the extra components and delete them from the form.

The Component Palette Context Menu

When you place the mouse cursor over the Component palette and right-click, you will see a menu specific to the Component palette (see Figure 6.5).

Figure 6.5.

*The Component
palette context menu.*

The Show Hints item toggles the ToolTips on and off for the component buttons. Unless you really dislike ToolTips, this should be left on. The Hide item on the context menu hides the Component palette. In order to show the Component palette again, you will have to choose View | Component Palette from the main menu. The Help item on the context menu brings up C++Builder help with the Component Palette page displayed. The Properties item brings up the Palette page of the Environment Options dialog box, where you can customize the Component palette. Here you can add and remove pages of the Component palette. You can also add, remove, or rearrange the order of components on the individual pages. I'll discuss this in more detail on Day 10 when we look at setting the environment options.

Navigating the Component Palette

As mentioned earlier, you can drag the sizing bar, located between the toolbar and the Component palette, to make the Component palette occupy more or less room on the C++Builder main window. If the Component palette is sized small enough so that it cannot display all its tabs, you will see scroll buttons in the upper-right corner of the Component palette. Click these scroll buttons to display tabs not currently in view. Likewise, if a particular page of the Component palette contains more buttons than will fit the width of the display window, scroll buttons will be enabled to allow you to scroll through the available buttons. Figure 6.6 shows the Component palette with both types of scroll buttons enabled.

Figure 6.6.

*The Component
palette scroll buttons.*

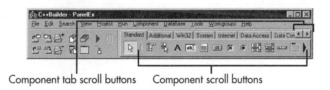

Component tab scroll buttons   Component scroll buttons

The Component palette is not terribly complicated, but a basic understanding of its use is vital for programming with C++Builder. Now that we've finished with these little tasks, we can return to the main topic again.

A Multiple-Form Application

To illustrate how C++Builder uses units, let's create an application with multiple forms. We'll create a simple application that displays a second form when you click a button:

1. Create a new project by choosing File | New Application from the main menu.

2. Change the Name property to MainForm and the Caption property to Multiple Forms Test Program.

3. Save the project. Save the unit as Main and the project as Multiple.

4. Now place a button on the form. Make the button's Name property ShowForm2 and the Caption property Show Form 2.

5. Choose File | New Form from the main menu (or click the New Form button on the toolbar) to create a new form.

   At this point, the new form has a name of Form1 and is placed exactly over the main form. We want the new form to be smaller than the main form and more or less centered on the main form.

6. Size and position the new form so that it is about 50 percent of the size of the main form and centered on the main form. Use the title bar to move the new form. Size the form by dragging the lower-right corner.

7. Change the new form's Name property to SecondForm and the form's Caption property to A Second Form.

8. Choose File | Save from the main menu (or click the Save File button on the toolbar) and save the new form with the name Second.

9. Choose a Label component and drop it on the new form. Change the label's Caption property to This is the second form. Change the label's size and color as desired. Center the label on the form. Your form should now look roughly similar to the one in Figure 6.7.

Figure 6.7.

The form up to this point.

10. Click on the main form. Notice that the second form is covered by the main form. Double-click the Show Form 2 button. The Code Editor is displayed, and the cursor is placed just where you need it to begin typing code (double-clicking a button is a shortcut way of generating an OnClick event handler).

11. Type in code so that the function looks like this (you only have to type one line of code):

```
void __fastcall TMainForm::ShowForm2Click(TObject *Sender)
{
  SecondForm->ShowModal();
}
```

12. Run the program.

At this point you will get a compiler error that says Undefined symbol 'SecondForm'. Hmmm...SecondForm should be a valid symbol because that's the name of the second form we created...I wonder...Aha! Remember, we have two source files with a header for each source file. The problem is that the MainForm unit can't see the declaration for the SecondForm variable (which is a pointer to the TSecondForm class). We have to tell it where to find the class declaration. (Recall back to Day 2, "C++ Fundamentals," that we have to #include the header for SecondForm in MainForm's source file.) Switch to the Code Editor and click the Main.cpp tab to display the unit for the main form. Scroll up to the top of the file. The first few lines look like this:

```
//-------------------------------
#include <vcl.h>
#pragma hdrstop

#include "Main.h"
//-------------------------------
```

You can see the #include for Main.h, but there isn't one for Second.h. That's because we haven't yet told C++Builder to add it. Let's do that now:

1. Choose File | Include Unit Hdr from the main menu. The Include Unit dialog box is displayed (see Figure 6.8).

Figure 6.8.

The Include Unit dialog box.

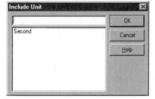

2. You will see a list of available units. In this case, the only unit in the list is Second. Click Second and then click OK to close the dialog box (you could have double-clicked the name of the unit instead).

NOTE

The Include Unit dialog box will show only those units that exist in the project *and* have not yet been included in this unit. Units that have already been included do not show in the list of available units.

6

If you blinked, you missed it, but C++Builder added the #include for Second.h when you clicked OK. Now the first few lines of the file show this:

```
//-------------------------------
#include <vcl.h>
#pragma hdrstop
#include "Main.h"
#include "Second.h"
//-------------------------------
```

Now the Main unit can see the class declaration for the Second unit. Click the Run button to run the program. This time the compile goes off without a hitch, and the program runs. When you click the Show Form 2 button on the main form, the second form is displayed. You can close the second form by clicking the system close box on the form's title bar.

As you can see, C++Builder does a good job of managing units for you. You have to be sure that you use the Include Unit Hdr option so that one unit can see the class declarations of other units, but for the most part C++Builder frees you from having to worry about your source files. Later, when your programming needs are more sophisticated, you'll have to do a little more source file management, but at this stage of the game C++Builder does most of the work for you.

Now let's take a moment to look at the different compiling options available to you when writing programs in C++Builder.

Compiling, Building, and Linking

Each time you click the Run button, C++Builder compiles and links your program. But it doesn't necessarily compile every unit in the project. It only compiles any units that have changed since the last compile. This feature saves you time because you don't have to wait for the compiler to compile files that haven't changed. C++Builder keeps track of which files have changed and which haven't, so you don't need to do anything special to use this feature—it's automatic.

Most of the time you want to see in action the results of any changes you have made. In those cases you click the Run button and the program is compiled, linked, and executed. Sometimes, however, you don't want to run the program. For instance, you might just want to compile the program to see if there are any errors. C++Builder has three menu items in addition to Run that allow you to control the compile/link process. If you choose the Project menu item on the main menu, you will see three menu items called Compile Unit, Make, and Build. The Make and Build menu item's text changes to reflect the name of the active project. For example, when you first start C++Builder these menu items will say Make Project1 and Build Project1. (There are also menu items called Compile All Projects and Build All Projects but we'll save that discussion for Day 10 when we discuss project groups.) Let's take these in order of simplest to most complex (from the compiler's perspective).

6

The Compile Unit option is one I really like. This feature causes C++Builder to compile the current unit in the Code Editor and report any errors and warnings. This is the fastest way to check for errors in your code. C++Builder only compiles the unit—it does not perform a link. The purpose of the Compile Unit option is to check your code for syntax errors as quickly as possible. Because the link phase takes extra time, the Compile Unit option skips that step.

The Make option compiles any units that have changed since the last compile just as the Compile Unit options does, but it also links the entire project. Naturally, this takes slightly longer than the Compile Unit option. Use the Make option when you want to be sure the program will compile and link but you don't want to run the program.

NOTE   The first time you make or run a project always takes longer than subsequent makes. This is because the incremental linker is building all the files it needs to do its thing. Subsequent links are much faster, usually only taking a second or two.

TIP   The keyboard shortcut for Make is Ctrl+F9.

The Build option takes the longest to perform. This option compiles every unit in the project regardless of whether it has changed since the last build. After compiling all units, C++Builder links the entire project. So far we have been letting C++Builder add units to our projects. Further on down the road you may have to do some hand-editing of your source files to add headers and other needed directives. You may even end up editing the makefile. From time to time, you know, things can get goofed up (we all make mistakes). Performing a Build will bring everything up to date so you can better sort out any problems you might be running into. Sometimes a Build will resolve compiler and linker errors without the need for you to do anything further. Another thing to remember is that a Build rebuilds all the incremental linker files which results in the build taking longer to complete.

6

TIP   Any time you get unexpected (out of the ordinary) compiler or linker errors, first try a Build. It could just be that something is out of sync, and a Build may cure it. If performing a Build doesn't fix the problem, you'll have to go to work figuring out where the problem lies.

Regardless of the method chosen to compile the project, if errors are detected the compile
status dialog box will report There are errors. and will list the number of errors that were
detected as well as any warnings. Figure 6.9 shows the compile status dialog box after
detecting errors.

Figure 6.9.

*The Compile Status
dialog box showing
warnings and errors.*

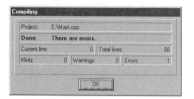

 NOTE

> The compile status dialog box can be turned off if you don't want to
> view the compiler progress. You can turn the compile status dialog off
> through the Environment Options dialog box (Preferences page).

After you click OK to dismiss the compile status dialog box, the Code Editor will come to
the top with the first error line highlighted. The message window at the bottom of the Code
Editor is displayed, and the errors and warnings are listed there. After a successful Compile
Unit, Make, or Build you can immediately run the program via the Run button if you choose.

Compiling and Building Other C++ Programs

C++Builder's strength is in its visual programming environment. That environment is tied
directly to VCL and cannot be separated from it. To get the most out of C++Builder, you
will most likely be writing applications based on VCL. There are times, however, where you
may want to write other types of applications. C++Builder is a standard C++ compiler, so you
can compile any type of 32-bit C++ program with C++Builder.

 NEW TERM   A *dynamic link library* (DLL) is an external file which contains code that can be
executed from a program or from another DLL.

Probably the most obvious type of "other" program you may want to build is a DLL. DLLs
might seem a bit like black magic, but they are really not very complicated; they are simply
bits of compiled code that you can call from your application. Once you have the DLL created
and your main program's source file has the needed header, calling a function contained in
a DLL is no different than calling a function contained in your main program.

Another type of application you might write with C++Builder is a *console application.* Earlier
we built several Win32 console applications when you were learning about the C++ language.

Console applications are useful for teaching situations and for quick test programs. They can also be very useful for small utility programs, servers such as Web servers or mail servers, and a whole host of other possibilities. Basically, any application that does not require a graphical interface is a good candidate for a console application.

You can also compile programs written in either MFC or OWL. This allows you to use a single compiler for all your development regardless of what framework you are using. Although you probably won't develop full-scale MFC or OWL applications with C++Builder, there is certainly no reason why you could not do so if you chose to. Of course, you would have to have the OWL or MFC library files and headers in order to build an OWL or MFC application.

You can also write Windows programs using just the API if you prefer. Listing 6.1 contains a Windows API version of the Hello World program. To build this program do the following:

1. From the C++Builder main menu choose File | New Application to create a new application.
2. Select Project | Remove from Project and remove the main form (Form1) from the project.
3. Select View | Project Source from the main menu.
4. Replace all the code in the project source file with the code in Listing 6.1
5. Compile and run the program and you have a Windows API program created with C++Builder.

Listing 6.1. WINHELLO.CPP.

```
 1: #define STRICT
 2: #include <windows.h>
 3: #pragma hdrstop
 4:
 5: LRESULT FAR PASCAL _export WndProc(HWND, UINT, WPARAM, LPARAM);
 6:
 7: int PASCAL WinMain(HINSTANCE hInstance,
 8:   HINSTANCE hPrevInstance, LPSTR lpszCmd, int nCmdShow)
 9: {
10:    static char AppName[] = "HelloWorld";
11:    HWND        hwnd;
12:    MSG         msg;
13:    WNDCLASS    wndclass;
14:    if (!hPrevInstance)
15:    {
16:      wndclass.style        = CS_HREDRAW | CS_VREDRAW;
17:      wndclass.lpfnWndProc  = (WNDPROC)WndProc;
18:      wndclass.cbClsExtra   = 0;
19:      wndclass.cbWndExtra   = 0;
20:      wndclass.hInstance    = hInstance;
21:      wndclass.hIcon        = LoadIcon(NULL, IDI_APPLICATION);
```

continues

Listing 6.1. continued

```
22:     wndclass.hCursor       = LoadCursor(NULL, IDC_ARROW);
23:     wndclass.hbrBackground = (HBRUSH)GetStockObject(WHITE_BRUSH);
24:     wndclass.lpszMenuName  = 0;
25:     wndclass.lpszClassName = AppName;
26:
27:     RegisterClass(&wndclass);
28:   }
29:
30:   hwnd = CreateWindow(AppName,
31:     "Hello World",
32:     WS_OVERLAPPEDWINDOW,
33:     CW_USEDEFAULT,
34:     CW_USEDEFAULT,
35:     CW_USEDEFAULT,
36:     CW_USEDEFAULT,
37:     NULL,
38:     NULL,
39:     hInstance,
40:     NULL);
41:
42:   ShowWindow(hwnd, SW_NORMAL);
43:
44:   while (GetMessage(&msg, NULL, 0, 0))
45:   {
46:     TranslateMessage(&msg);
47:     DispatchMessage(&msg);
48:   }
49:   return msg.wParam;
50: }
51:
52: LRESULT FAR PASCAL _export
53: WndProc(HWND hwnd, UINT message, WPARAM wParam, LPARAM lParam)
54: {
55:   switch(message)
56:   {
57:     case WM_PAINT :
58:     {
59:       char text[] = "Hello World!!";
60:       PAINTSTRUCT ps;
61:       BeginPaint(hwnd, &ps);
62:       TextOut(ps.hdc, 20, 20, text, 13);
63:       EndPaint(hwnd, &ps);
64:       break;
65:     }
66:     case WM_DESTROY : {
67:       PostQuitMessage(0);
68:       return 0;
69:     }
70:     default:
71:       return DefWindowProc(hwnd, message, wParam, lParam);
72:   }
73:   return 0;
74: }
```

6

More About C++Builder Forms

Before I continue with the discussion about the C++Builder IDE, I need to spend some time explaining forms. You have seen several forms in action as you have worked through this book, and tomorrow you are going to learn all about the Form Designer. Before we get there, you need some more background information on forms, so I'll cover that now.

Main Window Forms

Forms are the main building block of a C++Builder application. Every GUI application has at least one form that serves as the main window. The main window form might be just a blank window, it might have controls on it, or it might have a bitmap displayed on it. In a typical Windows program, your main window would have a menu. It might also have decorations such as a toolbar or a status bar. Just about anything goes when creating the main window of your application. Each application is unique, and each has different requirements.

Dialog Box Forms

Forms are also used where traditional Windows programs use dialog boxes. In fact, to the user there is no difference between a C++Builder form acting as a dialog box and a true dialog box. Dialog boxes usually have several traits that distinguish them from ordinary windows:

- Dialog boxes are not usually sizable. They usually perform a specific function, and sizing of the dialog box is neither useful nor desirable.

- Dialog boxes almost always have an OK button. Some dialog boxes have a button labeled Close that accomplishes the same thing. Simple dialog boxes like an About dialog box typically have only the OK button.

- Dialog boxes may also have a Cancel button and a Help button.

- Dialog boxes typically have only the system close button on the title bar. They do not usually have minimize and maximize buttons.

- Some dialog boxes are *tabbed dialog boxes* that display several tabs from which the user can choose. When a tab is clicked on, a different page of the dialog box is displayed.

- The Tab key can be used to move from one control to the next in most dialog boxes.

There are certainly exceptions to every rule. Most dialog boxes have the usual characteristics, but some dialog boxes perform specialty tasks and as such depart from the norm in one way or another.

Dialog boxes in C++Builder are slightly different than in other programming environments. First, let's take a look at how other programming environments handle dialog boxes; then we'll look at how they are implemented in C++Builder.

6

Dialog Boxes in Traditional Windows Programs

In a traditional Windows program (one written in C, or with one of the C++ frameworks), a dialog box is created with a dialog box editor. In most cases, the dialog box editor is a visual tool that works somewhat like the C++Builder Form Designer. When the user is done designing the dialog box, the visual representation of the dialog box is converted into a dialog box definition in a resource script file. (A *resource script* is a text file that is later compiled into a binary resource file by the resource compiler.) To illustrate, take a look at the dialog box in Figure 6.10.

Figure 6.10.

A typical About dialog box.

Figure 6.10 represents a typical About dialog box. It contains the program name, the copyright information, and the application's icon. The resource script definition for the dialog box is shown in Listing 6.2.

Listing 6.2. A dialog box resource definition.

```
 1: IDD_ABOUT DIALOG 58, 53, 194, 119
 2: STYLE DS_MODALFRAME ¦ WS_POPUP ¦
 3:   WS_VISIBLE ¦ WS_CAPTION ¦ WS_SYSMENU
 4: CAPTION "About TMMPlayer Example Program"
 5: FONT 8, "MS Sans Serif"
 6: {
 7:  DEFPUSHBUTTON "OK", IDOK, 72, 96, 50, 14
 8:  CTEXT "TMMPlayer Example Program", -1, 48, 22, 128, 8
 9:  CTEXT "Copyright © 1996, by Kent Reisdorph", -1, 32, 47, 136, 8
10:  CTEXT "March 15, 1996", -1, 24, 59, 146, 8
11:  CONTROL "", 99, "button", BS_GROUPBOX ¦
12:    WS_CHILD ¦ WS_VISIBLE ¦ WS_GROUP, 12, 4, 176, 70
13:  CONTROL 1, 1, "static", SS_ICON ¦
14:    SS_SUNKEN ¦ WS_CHILD ¦ WS_VISIBLE, 24, 17, 20, 20
15: }
```

The resource script contains information that Windows uses to build the dialog box at runtime. This information includes the number and type of controls on the dialog box, their size, position, text, options, and so on. Of course, the resource script also includes the same type of information for the dialog box itself.

Some Windows programmers don't use a dialog box editor at all, but prefer to write the dialog box definition from scratch with a text editor. While I can't fault those programmers for creating dialog boxes in that manner, I can say that for most programmers to take that approach would be, er, less than 100 percent efficient. It would take many times longer to create a dialog box in that manner as opposed to the visual approach.

Usually all the application's dialog box definitions are contained in a single resource script file that has a filename extension of .RC. At some point in the program-creation process, the resource script is compiled into an .RES file (the binary resource file), which then gets linked to the .EXE by the resource linker. At runtime the dialog box is displayed either modally or modelessly depending on the dialog box's intended purpose. When the dialog box is executed, Windows loads the dialog box resource from the executable file, builds the dialog box, and displays it.

NOTE

A *modal* dialog box is one that must be dismissed before the user can continue using the application. The main window of an application is disabled while this type of dialog box is open. Most dialog boxes are modal. The compile status dialog box in C++Builder is an example of a modal dialog box.

A *modeless* dialog box is one that allows the user to continue to work with the application while the dialog box is displayed. The Find dialog box in some word-processing programs is an example of a modeless dialog box.

Now, with that background information on how dialog boxes are handled in a traditional Windows program, let's take a look at how C++Builder handles dialog boxes.

Dialog Boxes in C++Builder

In C++Builder, dialog boxes are simply another form. You create a dialog box just like you do a main window form or any other form. To prevent the dialog box from being sized, you can change the BorderStyle property to bsDialog or bsSingle. If you use bsDialog, your dialog box will have only the close box button on the title bar, which is traditional for dialog boxes. Other than that, you don't have to do anything special to get a form to behave like a dialog box. All C++Builder forms have tabbing support built in. You can set the tab order by altering the TabOrder property of the individual controls on the dialog box.

A C++Builder dialog box (any C++Builder form, actually) is modal or modeless depending on how it is displayed. To execute a modal dialog box, you call the ShowModal() method of TForm. To create a modeless dialog box, you call the Show() method.

Let's add an About box to the multiple-forms project we created earlier. If you don't have that project open, choose File | Open from the main menu or click the Open Project button on the toolbar and locate the file (you should have saved it with the project name of Multiple).

6

TIP

C++Builder keeps a list of the files and projects you have used most recently. Chose File | Reopen to view the MRU (most recently used) list. The MRU list is divided into two parts. The top part shows the projects you have used most recently, and the bottom part shows the individual files that you have used most recently. Just click on one of the items to reopen that project or file.

First we'll add a button to the form that will display the About dialog box:

1. Bring the main form into view. Choose the button component from the Component palette and drop a button on the form.
2. Arrange the two buttons that are now on the form to balance the look of the form.
3. Change the Name property of the new button to AboutButton and the Caption property to About....
4. Double-click the AboutButton you just created on the form. The Code Editor is displayed with the cursor placed in the event-handler function. Add this line of code at the cursor:

```
AboutBox->ShowModal();
```

We haven't actually created the About box yet, but when we do we'll name it AboutBox so we know enough to type the code that will display the About box.

Now we'll create the dialog box itself:

1. Create a new form (click the New Form button on the toolbar). Size the form to the size of a typical About box (roughly the same size as the form named SecondForm that we created earlier).
2. Change the Name property to AboutBox and change the Caption property to About This Program.
3. Locate the BorderStyle property (it's just above Caption) and change it to bsDialog.
4. Now add three text labels to the box. Edit the labels so that the About box resembles the one in Figure 6.11. (You can type any text you want, of course.) You can leave the default names C++Builder generates for the text labels' Name properties. We aren't actually going to do anything with the Name property, so we don't need a descriptive name.

6

Figure 6.11.

The About box with text labels added.

 TIP

The copyright symbol (©) has an ASCII value of 169 in most type-faces. To create the copyright symbol, press and hold the Alt key and type the numbers 0169 on the numeric keypad (be sure Num Lock is on). When you let go of the Alt key, the copyright symbol appears. You can insert the ASCII value of any character this way. You must type all four numbers, though. For example, the ASCII value of a capital A is 65. To insert an A, you would have to hold down Alt and type 0065 on the numeric keypad.

Next, we'll add an icon to the About box:

1. Click the Additional tab on the Component palette and choose the Image component. Place the component to the left of the text on the form.

2. Locate the AutoSize property for the Image component and change it to true.

3. Locate the Picture property and double-click the Value column. The Picture Editor dialog box is displayed.

4. Click the Load button. In the File Open dialog box, navigate to the \Borland Shared Files\Images\Icons directory and choose an icon from the icon files listed. Click Open. The icon you selected is displayed in the Picture Editor window. Click OK to close the Picture Editor. The icon is displayed on the form. Note that the Image component has sized itself to the size of the icon.

5. Position the icon as desired.

At this point we need an OK button on the form. Let's branch out a little and take a look at a new component:

1. If you're not already there, click the Additional tab on the Component palette. Select the BitBtn component and place a BitBtn on the form near the bottom and centered horizontally.

2. Locate the Kind property and change it to bkOK. Notice that a green check mark has appeared on the button, and the Caption property has changed to OK. That's all we have to do with the button. The BitBtn component already includes code to close the form when the OK button is clicked.

Let's add one final touch to the About box:

1. Locate the Bevel button (on the Additional tab in the Component palette) and click it.

2. Move to the form, but rather than clicking on the form drag a box around the three text labels. The Bevel component appears when you stop dragging. If you didn't get it quite right, you can resize or reposition the component.

3. Locate the Shape property and change it to bsFrame. You now have a 3D frame around the static text.

Your form should now look something like the one shown in Figure 6.12. Save the unit (File | Save) and give it the name About.

Figure 6.12.

The finished About box.

Are we ready to compile and run the program? Not yet. We need to tell the main form to #include the About unit:

1. Switch to the Code Editor (press F12) and select the Main.cpp tab.

2. Choose File | Include Unit Hdr from the main menu.

3. Choose the About unit from the Include Unit dialog box and click OK.

Now you're ready to run the program. Click the Run button. When the program runs, click the About button, and the About dialog box is displayed. Note that the dialog box is modal (you can't go back to the main window while the dialog box is displayed) and that it cannot be sized. The About form behaves in every way like a regular Windows dialog box.

NOTE

The common dialog box classes (TOpenDialog, TSaveDialog, TFontDialog, and so on) do not represent dialog boxes created as C++Builder forms. Windows provides these dialog boxes as a set of common dialog boxes that all Windows applications can use (the actual dialog boxes are contained in a file called COMDLG32.DLL). The VCL dialog box classes encapsulate the common dialog boxes to make using them easier.

NOTE

C++Builder includes several prebuilt forms that you can choose from to help you build dialog boxes as quickly as possible. I'll discuss those on Day 9, "Creating Applications in C++Builder."

Secondary Windows Versus Dialog Boxes

A *secondary window* is a form that you display from your main window. So when is a form a secondary window and when it is a dialog box? When it really comes down to it, there is no difference between a secondary window and a dialog box in C++Builder. You might have windows that resemble dialog boxes, and you might have other windows that resemble a traditional window. In the grand scheme of things, they all are forms and it doesn't make much sense to differentiate between the terms *dialog box* and *secondary form*. It's all the same in the end. In traditional programming environments, you have to specifically create a dialog box or specifically create a secondary window in an application. C++Builder frees you from that restriction and allows you to treat both dialog boxes and windows exactly the same.

The Multiple Document Interface Model

So far we have built only *single document interface* (SDI) applications. An SDI application has a single main window and typically displays dialog boxes as needed, but does not otherwise display child windows.

Some programs follow the *multiple document interface* (MDI) model. MDI applications consist of a main window (the MDI parent) and child windows (the MDI children). Examples of programs that use the MDI model are Windows System Configuration Editor (SYSEDIT) and the Windows 3.1 Program Manager. One of the most obvious characteristics of the MDI model is that the MDI child windows are confined to the parent. You can drag the child windows within the parent window, but you cannot drag them outside the parent. MDI applications almost always have a Window item on their main menu. This menu usually contains items named Cascade and Tile, which allow you to display the MDI child windows in either a cascaded or tiled arrangement. When an MDI child is minimized, its icon is contained within the MDI parent's frame. When a regular (non-MDI) child window is minimized, its icon is placed on the Windows desktop.

6

To create an MDI application in C++Builder, you must set the main form's FormStyle property to fsMDIForm. Each of the MDI child windows must have the FormStyle property set to fsMDIChild. Aside from that restriction, there is very little to creating an MDI application in C++Builder. You simply create the main window form and one or more forms to be used as child windows, and you're off and running.

Key Properties for Forms

The TForm class has a lot of properties. Some of these properties are obscure and rarely used; others are widely used. I'll touch on the most widely used properties here. I won't include obvious properties like Color, Left, Top, Width, and Height unless they have a particular feature you should be aware of.

Runtime and Design-Time Properties

The properties outlined in this section can be set at design time and also at runtime. Almost all these properties can be read at runtime as well.

ActiveControl

The ActiveControl property is used to set the control that will have focus when the form is activated. For instance, you may want a particular edit control to have focus when a dialog box form is displayed. At design time the Value column for the ActiveControl property contains a list of components on the form. You can choose one of the components from this list to make that component the active control when the form is first displayed.

AutoScroll, HorzScrollBar, and VertScrollBar

Together, the AutoScroll, HorzScrollBar, and VertScrollBar properties control the scrollbars for a form. If AutoScroll is set to true (the default), scrollbars automatically appear when the form is too small to display all its components. The HorzScrollBar and VertScrollBar properties each have several properties of their own that control the scrollbar operations.

BorderStyle

The BorderStyle property indicates what type of border the form will have. The default value is bsSizeable, which creates a window that can be sized. Non-sizable styles include bsDialog and bsNone.

ClientWidth and ClientHeight

You can specify the client area width and height rather than the full form's width and height by using the ClientWidth and ClientHeight properties. (The *client area* of the form is the area inside of the borders and below the title bar and menu bar.) Use these properties when you want the client area to be a specific size and the rest of the window to adjust as necessary. Setting the ClientWidth and ClientHeight properties makes automatic changes to the Width and Height properties.

Font

The Font property specifies the font that the form uses. The important thing to understand here is that the form's font is inherited by any components placed on the form. This also means that you can change the font used by all components at one time by changing just the form's font. If an individual control's font had been manually changed, that control's font will not be changed when the main form's font changes.

FormStyle

This property is usually set to fsNormal. If you want a form to always be on top, use the fsStayOnTop style. MDI forms should use the fsMDIForm style and MDI child forms should use the fsMDIChild style. MDI forms and MDI child windows are discussed earlier in this chapter, in the section "The Multiple Document Interface Model."

HelpContext

The HelpContext property is used to set the help context ID for a form. If context help is enabled for a form, the Windows Help system will activate when the F1 key is pressed. The context ID is used to tell the Help system which page in the help file to display.

Icon

The Icon property sets the icon that is used on the title bar for the form when the form is displayed at runtime, and also when the form is minimized. In some cases, setting this property has no effect. For instance, when the FormStyle is set to fsDialog, the Icon property is ignored.

Position

The Position property determines the size and position of the form when the form is initially displayed. The three basic choices are poDesigned, poDefault, and poScreenCenter. poDesigned causes the form to be displayed in the exact position it was in when it was designed. poDefault allows Windows to set the size and position according to the usual Windows Z-ordering algorithm. (Z-ordering is what Windows uses to decide where it displays a new window on the screen. If the new window does not have specific placement information, it will be displayed just below and to the right of the last window displayed on the screen.) The poScreenCenter option causes the form to be displayed in the center of the screen each time it is shown.

Visible

The Visible property controls whether the form is initially visible. This property is not particularly useful at design time, but at runtime it can be read to determine whether the form is currently visible. It can also be used to hide or display the form.

WindowState

The WindowState property can be read to determine the form's current state (maximized, minimized, or normal). It can also be used to indicate how the form should initially be displayed. Choices are wsMinimized, wsMaximized, and wsNormal.

Runtime-Only Properties

Some properties can be accessed only at runtime through code. The following are the most commonly used runtime properties.

ActiveMDIChild

When read, the ActiveMDIChild property returns a pointer to the currently active MDI child window. This property is read-only. If no MDI child is currently active or if the application is not an MDI application, ActiveMDIChild returns NULL.

Canvas

The form's canvas represents the drawing surface of the form. The Canvas property gives you access to the form's canvas. By using the Canvas property you can draw bitmaps, lines, shapes, or text on the form at runtime. Most of the time you will use a Label component to draw text on a form, an Image component to display graphics, and a Shape component to draw shapes. However, there are times when you need to draw on the canvas at runtime and the Canvas property allows you to do that. The Canvas property can also be used to save an image of the form to disk.

ClientRect

The ClientRect property contains the top, left, right, and bottom coordinates of the client area of the form. This is useful in a variety of programming situations. For instance, you may need to know the client area's width and height in order to place a bitmap on the center of the form.

Handle

The Handle property returns the window handle (HWND) of the form. Use this property when you need the window handle to pass to a Windows API function.

ModalResult

The ModalResult property is used to indicate how a modal form was closed. If you have a dialog box that has OK and Cancel buttons, you can set ModalResult to mrOK when the user clicks the OK button, and to mrCancel when the user clicks the Cancel button. The calling form can then read ModalResult to see which button was clicked to close the form. Other possibilities include mrYes, mrNo, and mrAbort.

Owner

The Owner property is a pointer to the owner of the form. The owner of the form is the object that is responsible for deleting the form when the form is no longer needed. The parent of a component, on the other hand, is the window (a form or another component) which acts as the container for the component. In the case of a main form, the application object is both the owner of the form and the parent of the form. In the case of components, the owner would be the form, but the parent could be another component, such as a panel.

6

Parent

The `Parent` property is a pointer to the parent of the form. See the previous section about `Owner` for an explanation of `Owner` versus `Parent`.

Form Methods

Forms are components, too. As such, forms have many methods in common with components. Common methods include `Show()`, `ShowModal()`, and `Invalidate()`, to name just a few. There are some methods, however, that are specific to forms. As before, I'll only discuss the most commonly used methods.

BringToFront()

The `BringToFront()` method causes the form to be brought to the top of all other forms in the application.

Close() and CloseQuery()

The `Close()` method closes a form after first calling `CloseQuery()` to ensure that it's okay to close the form. The `CloseQuery()` function in turn calls the `OnCloseQuery` event handler. If the `bool` variable passed to the `OnCloseQuery` handler is set to `false`, the form is not closed. If it is set to `true`, the form closes normally. You can use the `OnCloseQuery` event handler to prompt the user to save a file that needs saving and to control whether a form can close.

Print()

The `Print()` method prints the contents of the form. Only the client area of the form is printed, not the caption, title bar, or borders. `Print()` is handy for quick screen dumps of a form.

ScrollInView()

The `ScrollInView()` method scrolls the form so that the specified component is visible on the form.

SetFocus()

The `SetFocus()` method activates the form and brings it to the top. If the form has components, the component specified in the `ActiveControl` property will receive input focus (see the `ActiveControl` property in the section "Runtime and Design-Time Properties").

Show() and ShowModal()

The `Show()` and `ShowModal()` methods display the form. The `Show()` method displays the form as modeless, so other forms can be activated while the form is visible. The `ShowModal()` method executes the form modally. A modal form must be dismissed before the user can continue to use the application.

6

MDI Methods

Several form methods deal specifically with MDI operations. The `ArrangeIcons()` method arranges the icons of any minimized MDI children in an MDI parent window. The `Cascade()` method cascades all non-minimized MDI child windows. The `Tile()` method tiles all open MDI child windows. The `Next()` method activates (brings to the top) the next MDI child in the child list, and the `Previous()` method activates the previous MDI child in the child list. The MDI methods apply only to MDI parent windows.

Form Events

Forms can respond to a wide variety of events. Some of the most commonly used are listed in the following sections.

OnActivate

The `OnActivate` event occurs when the form is initially activated. The form might be activated as a result of its initial creation or when the user switches from one form to another. The `Application` object also has an `OnActivate` event which is generated when the user switches from another application to your application.

OnClose and OnCloseQuery

When an application is closed, the `OnClose` event is sent. `OnClose` calls the `OnCloseQuery` event to see if it is okay to close the form. If the `OnCloseQuery` event returns `false`, the form is not closed.

OnCreate

The `OnCreate` event occurs when the form is initially created. Only one `OnCreate` event will occur for any instance of a particular form. Use the `OnCreate` handler to perform any startup tasks that the form needs in order to operate.

OnDestroy

The `OnDestroy` event is the opposite of `OnCreate`. Use this event to clean up any memory a form allocates dynamically or to do other cleanup chores.

OnDragDrop

The `OnDragDrop` event occurs when an object is dropped on the form. Respond to this event if your form supports drag-and-drop.

OnMouseDown, OnMouseMove, and OnMouseUp

Respond to the `OnMouseDown`, `OnMouseMove`, and `OnMouseUp` events in order to respond to mouse clicks and mouse movements on a form.

OnPaint

The `OnPaint` event occurs whenever the form needs repainting, which could happen for a variety of reasons. Respond to this event to do any painting that your application needs to display at all times. In most cases, individual components will take care of painting themselves, but in some cases you may need to draw on the form itself.

OnResize

The OnResize event is sent every time the form is resized. You may need to respond to this event to adjust components on the form or to repaint the form.

OnShow

The OnShow event occurs just before the form becomes visible. You could use this event to perform any processing that your form needs to do just before it is shown.

NOTE

> When a form is created, many different events are generated. Likewise, when a form is destroyed, several different events are generated. But in what order are these events generated? When a form is created, the following events occur in this order (the constructor is listed in addition to the events):
>
> ```
> the form's constructor
> OnCreate
> OnShow
> OnActivate
> ```
>
> When a form is destroyed, the following events are generated in this order:
>
> ```
> OnCloseQuery
> OnClose
> OnDestroy
> the form's destructor (if any)
> ```
>
> Keeping the order straight generally is not important in most cases, but in some cases it can be critical. Knowing the order the event handlers, the constructor, and the destructor are called can save you some frustration when you really need to know.

6

The Object Inspector

An integral part of the C++Builder IDE is the Object Inspector. This window works in conjunction with the Form Designer to aid in the creation of components. I'm going to discuss the Form Designer tomorrow, but before I do I want to talk a little about the Object Inspector.

The Object Inspector is where you set the design-time properties that affect how the component acts at runtime. The Object Inspector has three main areas:

☐ The Component Selector
☐ The Properties page
☐ The Events page

You have been using the Object Inspector quite a bit up to this point, so I'll review what you already know and show you a few things you don't know.

The Component Selector

The Component Selector is a drop-down combo box that is located at the top of the Object Inspector window. The Component Selector allows you to choose a component to view or modify.

 NOTE

> Usually the quickest way to select a component is by clicking the component on the form. Choosing the component from the Component Selector is convenient if the component you are looking for is hidden beneath another component or is off the visible area of the form.

The Component Selector displays the name of the component and the class from which it is derived. For example, a memo component named Memo would appear in the Component Selector as

```
Memo: TMemo
```

The class name does not show up in the drop-down list of components, but only in the top portion of the Component Selector. To select a component, click the drop-down button to reveal the list of components and then click the one you want to select.

 NOTE

> The Component Selector shows only the components available on the current form and the name of the form itself. Other forms and their components will not be displayed until made active in the Form Designer.

After you select a component in the Component Selector, the component is selected on the form as well. The Properties and Events tabs change to display the properties and events for the selected component. (Remember that a form is a component, too.) Figure 6.13 shows the Object Inspector with the Component Selector list displayed.

Figure 6.13.

*The Component
Selector list.*

The Properties Page

The Properties page of the Object Inspector displays all the design-time properties for the currently selected control. The Properties page has two columns. The Property column is on the left side of the Properties page and shows the property name. The Value column is on the right side of the Properties page and is where you type or select the value for the property.

If the component selected has more properties than will fit in the Object Inspector, a scrollbar will be provided so you can scroll up or down to locate other properties.

NOTE

> If you have multiple components selected on the form, the Object Inspector shows all the properties that those components have in common. You can use this feature to modify the properties of several components at one time. For example, to change the width of several components at one time, you can select all the components and then modify the Width property in the Object Inspector. When you press Enter or move to another property, all the components you selected will have their Width property modified.

Figure 6.14 shows the Object Inspector when a Memo component is selected.

On Day 5, "C++ Class Frameworks and the Visual Component Model," I discussed how properties can be integer values, enumerations, sets, other objects, strings, and other types. The Object Inspector deals with each type of property according to the data type of the property. C++Builder has several built-in property editors to handle data input for the property. For example, the Top property accepts an integer value. Because an int is a basic data type, no special handling is required, so the property editor is fairly basic. The property editor for this type of property allows you to type a value directly in the Value column for integer properties such as Top, Left, Width, and Height.

6

Figure 6.14.

The Object Inspector showing Memo *component properties.*

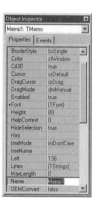

 NOTE

In most cases, the property editor does parameter checking for any properties in which you can enter an integer value. The Width property, for instance, cannot be a negative number. If you attempt to enter a negative number for the Width of a control, C++Builder will force the width to the minimum allowed for that control (usually 0). If you enter a string value for a property that expects an integer value, C++Builder will display an error message. It is the job of the property editor to do parameter checking.

In many cases, the property editor for the property contains a list of items from which you can choose. Properties that have an enumeration or boolean value as their base data type fall into this category. When you click the Value column with this type of property editor, you will see a drop-down button on the right side of the Value column. Clicking this button will display the list of possible values.

 TIP

If you double-click the Value column for this type of property, the property editor will cycle through the possible choices. To quickly change a bool property, for instance, simply double-click its value. Because the only choices are true and false, double-clicking the value has the effect of toggling the property's value.

If you look closely at the Object Inspector, you will see that some properties have a plus sign preceding the property name. Properties that are sets and properties that are objects both have the plus sign in front of their name. The plus sign indicates that the property node can be expanded to show the set or, in the case of properties that are objects, the properties of that object. To expand a node, double-click on the Property column for that property (on the property name) or choose Expand from the Object Inspector context menu. To collapse the node, double-click it again or choose Collapse from the Object Inspector context menu.

To see an example of a set, choose a form and then double-click the BorderIcons property. The node expands and you see four members of the set. You can turn on or off any of the four members as needed.

In the case of properties that are objects (instances of a VCL class), you have two choices in editing the property. First, you can click the Value column for the property and then click the button to the right side of the value. This button is indicated by an ellipsis (...) on its face. Clicking this button will invoke the property editor for that particular control. For example, click the Font property and then click the ellipsis button. The Choose Font dialog box is displayed so that you can select the font. The second way you can edit this type of property is by expanding the property node. The property's properties (yes, it's true) will be displayed, and you can edit them just like any other property. Again, locate the Font property and double-click it. The TFont properties will be displayed. You can now modify the font's Height, Color, Name or other properties.

Some properties have only the ellipsis button as a means of editing the property. Earlier you used the Image component to select an icon for the Multiple program's About box. As you found out then, the Image component's Picture property can be changed only by invoking that property's property editor. In that case, the property editor is the C++Builder Picture Editor.

Rest assured that each property knows what it needs to do to present you with the correct property editor. You will see different types of property editors as you are introduced to new components and new properties.

The Events Page

The Events page lists all the events that the component is designed to handle. Using the Events page is pretty basic. In order to create an event handler for an event, you simply double-click in the Value column next to the event you want to handle. When you do, C++Builder creates an event-handling function for you with all the parameters needed to handle that event. The Code Editor is displayed, and the cursor is placed in the event handler. All you have to do is start typing code. The name of the function is generated based on the Name property of the component and the event being handled. If, for instance, you had a button named OKBtn and were handling the OnClick event, the function name generated would be OKBtnClick().

You can let C++Builder generate the name of the event-handling function for you or you can provide the function name for C++Builder to use. To provide the function name yourself, type the name in the Value column next to the event and press Enter. The Code Editor is displayed, and so is the event-handling function, complete with the name you supplied.

6

NOTE

> C++Builder will remove any empty event handlers when you run, compile, or save a unit. For example, let's say you created an event handler for the OnCreate event but didn't type any code. The next time you run, compile, or save the unit, C++Builder will remove the event handler you just created because it doesn't contain any code. This is the way C++Builder is designed and makes perfect sense but can be a bit puzzling if you aren't aware of what is going on. If you don't want C++Builder to remove the event handler, either type code right away or type a comment line so that the event handler won't be removed.

After you have created an event-handling function for a component, you can use that event handler for any component that handles the same event. Sometimes it's convenient to have several buttons use the same OnClick event, for instance. To take it a step farther, you might have a main menu item, a pop-up menu item, and a toolbar button all use the same OnClick handler. You will learn to appreciate this kind of code reuse as you gain experience with C++Builder. Even though you are dealing with three different components, they can still share a common OnClick handler. The Value column of the Events page contains a drop-down button that can be used to display a list of all event handlers compatible with the current event. All you have to do is choose an event from the list.

An MDI Example Program

To help solidify today's discussion of projects and forms, let's create an MDI application. This application will allow you to open and save graphics files like bitmaps, icons, and metafiles. In order to complete our task, we'll have to have a master plan. Here's what we need to do:

1. Create the main window form (an MDI parent), including a menu.
2. Write code for the File | Open and File | Save menu selections.
3. Write code for the Cascade, Tile, and Arrange All items on the Window menu.
4. Create the MDI child forms.
5. Create an About box.
6. Stand back and admire our work.

There's no point in dawdling (time is money!), so let's get right to it.

Step 1: Create the Main Window Form

First we'll create the main window form. The main window for an MDI application must have the FormStyle property set to fsMDIForm. We will also need to add a menu to the application, as well as File Open and File Save dialog boxes.

1. Start C++Builder and choose File | New Application from the main menu.

2. For the main form, change the Name property to MainForm.

3. Change the Caption property to Picture Viewer.

4. Change the Height to 450 and the Width to 575 (or other suitable values for your display resolution).

5. Change the FormStyle to fsMDIForm.

Okay, now we've got the main part of the form done. Next we'll add a menu to the form. Because I haven't discussed the Menu Designer yet, we'll take the easy route to creating a menu. To do that, we'll take advantage of a C++Builder feature that allows us to import a predefined menu.

1. Click the Standard tab of the Component palette and click the MainMenu button.

2. Drop a MainMenu component on the form. It doesn't matter where you drop it because the icon representing the menu is just a placeholder and won't show on the form at runtime. This is how non-visual components appear on a form.

3. Change the Name property to MainMenu.

4. Double-click the MainMenu component. The Menu Designer is displayed. (We'll look at the Menu Designer in more detail tomorrow.)

5. Place your cursor over the Menu Designer and click your right mouse button. Choose Insert from Template from the context menu. The Insert Template dialog box appears. Figure 6.15 shows the Insert Template dialog box with the Menu Designer behind it.

Figure 6.15.

The Menu Designer with the Insert Template dialog box open.

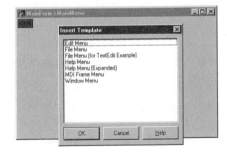

6. Choose MDI Frame Menu and click OK. The menu is displayed in the Menu Designer.

7. Click the system close box on the Menu Designer to close it.

Now you should be back to the main form. Notice that you have a menu on the form. You can click on the top-level items to see the full menu. Don't click on any menu subitems at this point—we'll do that in a minute. Notice that there are a lot of menu items. We won't need them all, but for now we'll just leave the extra items where they are.

Now we need to prepare the File Open and File Save dialog boxes:

1. Click the Dialogs tab on the Component palette. Choose an OpenDialog component and place it on the form. The OpenDialog component's icon can be placed anywhere on the form.

2. Change the Name property of the Open dialog box to OpenDialog.

3. Change the Title property to Open a Picture for Viewing.

4. Add a SaveDialog component.

5. Change the Name property of the component to SaveDialog and the Title property to Save a Picture.

Your form should now look like the one in Figure 6.16.

Figure 6.16.

The form up to this point.

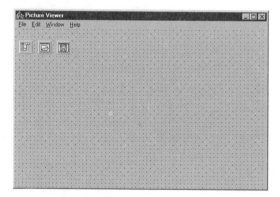

Step 2: Write Code for the File Open and File Save As Menu Items

Now let's write the code to implement the File|Open and File|Save As menu items. C++Builder provides a slick way of writing menu handlers with a minimum amount of fuss. We haven't created the MDI child form yet, but we know enough about it to write the code for the menu handlers. Keep in mind that the application won't compile until you get through Step 4. Here we go:

1. On the main form, choose File|Open from the menu. An event handler is created for that menu item, and the Code Editor is displayed.

2. Type code so that the event handler looks like this:

```
void __fastcall TMainForm::Open1Click(TObject *Sender)
{
```

```
if (OpenDialog->Execute())
{
  TChild* child = new TChild(this);
  child->Image->Picture->LoadFromFile(OpenDialog->FileName);
  child->ClientWidth = child->Image->Picture->Width;
  child->ClientHeight = child->Image->Picture->Height;
  child->Caption = ExtractFileName(OpenDialog->FileName);
  child->Show();
}
}
```

This code first executes the File Open dialog box and gets a filename. If the Cancel button on the File Open dialog box is clicked, the function returns without doing anything further. If the OK button on the File Open dialog box is clicked, a new TChild object is created (TChild will be the name of the MDI child class we're going to create later). The image file is loaded into the Image component on the child form; then the MDI child's client area is sized to match the size of the image. Finally, the Caption property is set to the filename selected and the child window is displayed.

NOTE In Step 2, the ExtractFileName() function is used to extract just the filename from the path and filename contained in the FileName property of the OpenDialog component. Related functions include ExtractFilePath(), ExtractFileDir(), ExtractFileDrive(), and ExtractFileExt().

NOTE Remember our earlier discussion about calling delete for all objects created with new? Notice that I appear to be violating that rule in the preceding code. In reality I am not, because VCL will take the responsibility of freeing the memory allocated for the MDI child windows. Notice that the single parameter in the TChild constructor is this. That tells VCL that the Owner of the MDI child is the MDI form window. When the MDI form is destroyed (when the application closes), it will be sure to delete all its MDI child objects.

3. Press F12 to switch back to the form. Now choose File | Save As from the menu. The File | Save As event handler is displayed.

4. Type code so that the File | Save As event handler looks like this:

6

```
void __fastcall TMainForm::SaveAs1Click(TObject *Sender)
{
  TChild* child = dynamic_cast<TChild*>(ActiveMDIChild);
  if (!child) return;
  if (SaveDialog->Execute())
  {
    child->Image->Picture->SaveToFile(SaveDialog->FileName);
  }
}
```

The code for the File | Save As menu item is simple. The first two lines check to see whether an MDI child window is active. If so, the File Save dialog box is displayed. If the user clicks OK, the image is saved to disk using the TPicture class's SaveToFile() method.

NOTE

In the preceding code you see a special C++ operator called dynamic_cast. dynamic_cast is used to cast a pointer of a base class to a pointer of a derived class. The ActiveMDIChild property returns a pointer to a TForm object. What we actually need in this case is a pointer to a TChild object (our MDI child class, derived from TForm) so that we can access the Image property of the MDI child form.

If dynamic_cast is unable to perform the cast, it returns NULL. Attempting to use a NULL pointer will result in an access violation, but the debugger will conveniently point out the offending line so you know exactly where the problem lies. This is much better than the alternative of attempting to use the old-style cast, where a bad cast could result in some random memory location being overwritten.

Before we go on, it would be a good idea to save the project. Choose File | Save All from the main menu. Save Unit1 (the default name C++Builder assigns to a new unit) as ViewMain and the project as ViewPict.

Step 3: Write Code for the Window Menu

Now we'll add code to the Window menu. This part is simple:

1. Switch back to the form by pressing F12. Choose Window | Tile from the form's menu.

2. You only need to enter a single line of code for the event handler. The finished event handler will look like this:

```
void __fastcall TMainForm::Tile1Click(TObject *Sender)
{
  Tile();
}
```

3. Switch back to the form and repeat the process for Window | Cascade. The finished function looks like this:

```
void __fastcall TMainForm::Cascade1Click(TObject *Sender)
{
  Cascade();
}
```

4. Repeat the steps for the Window | Arrange All menu item. The single line of code to add for the function body is

```
ArrangeIcons();
```

Okay, now we're done with the main form. We can now move on to creating the MDI child form.

Step 4: Create the MDI Child Form

The MDI child form is surprisingly simple. In fact, we don't have to write any code at all.

1. Create a new form using the New Form button on the toolbar or by choosing File | New Form from the main menu.

2. Change the Name property to Child. The Caption property can be ignored because we will be setting the dialog box's caption at runtime.

3. Change the FormStyle property to fsMDIChild. This is necessary for the form to be treated as an MDI child window.

That's it for the form itself. Now let's put an Image component on the form. The Image component will display the graphics file selected by the user.

1. Click the Additional tab on the Component palette. Click the Image button and place an Image component anywhere on the form.

2. Change the Name property to Image.

3. Change the Stretch property to true.

4. Change the Align property to alClient. The Image component expands to fill the client area of the form.

5. Choose File | Save and save the form's unit as MDIChild.

6. Switch to the Code Editor (press F12 to toggle between the Form Designer and the Code Editor). Click the ViewMain.cpp tab. Now choose File | Include Unit Hdr from the main menu, select the MDIChild unit, and click OK. This is so the compiler is happy when we reference the TChild object.

The form is fairly unimpressive at this point, but it should look similar to Figure 6.17.

6

Figure 6.17.
*The MDI child form
with an* Image
component.

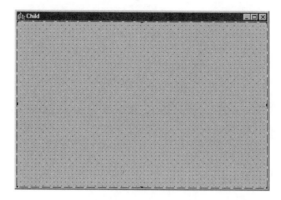

We still have to create the About box, but right now you're probably eager to try the program out. Go ahead and click the Run button. After a while, the program is displayed. You can choose File | Open and open any graphics file (any file with a `.BMP`, a `.WMF`, or an `.ICO` extension, that is). Notice that the MDI child window sizes itself to the graphic it contains. Open several files and then try out the Cascade and Tile options under the Window menu. If you want, you can save a file with a different name using the File | Save As menu item.

Step 5: Create the About Box

By now you should know enough about C++Builder to create the About box on your own. Create the About box so that it looks something like Figure 6.18. If you get stuck, you can jump back a few pages and review the steps you took to create the About box earlier in the chapter. Feel free to make your About box as personalized as you like.

Figure 6.18.
*The About box for the
application.*

After you have the box created you can take these steps to call the box from the menu:

1. Change the Name property to AboutBox.
2. Save the unit as PVAbout.

NOTE

C++Builder has full support for long filenames. I use the 8.3 file-naming convention in this book for reasons related to electronic publishing. For applications you write, you can take advantage of long filenames.

3. Switch to the `ViewMain.cpp` tab in the Code Editor (press F12). Choose File | Include Unit Hdr from the main menu and include the `PVAbout` header.

4. Press F12 to switch back to the main form. Choose Help | About from the menu. You are taken to the Code Editor with the `OnClick` handler for the menu item displayed.

5. Add this line to the event handler:

```
AboutBox->ShowModal();
```

That should do it for now. Click the Run button and try out the About item on the Help menu. Figure 6.19 shows the Picture Viewer program running with several child windows open.

Figure 6.19.

The Picture Viewer program running.

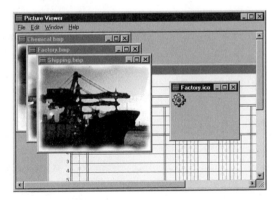

At this point the program is functional, but it isn't polished by any means. Still, for a 30-minute programming job it's not too bad! There are a few problems with the program as it stands right now. If you try to open a file that is not a graphic, you will find that the program will throw an exception. We'll deal with that later. Also, we have a lot of extra menu items that we need to get rid of. We'll show you how to do that tomorrow as we work more with the Menu Designer.

There are two problems that I think we should deal with because they are easy to fix. First, did you notice that a blank MDI child window was displayed when the application started? That's because a C++Builder application automatically creates all forms when the application runs. In the case of an MDI child, that means the window is displayed when the application becomes visible. We are creating each MDI child form as needed, so we don't need to have C++Builder auto-create the form for us.

Fortunately, removing the MDI child window form from the auto-create list is easy. Choose Project|Options from the main menu. The Project Options dialog box is displayed. If necessary, click the Forms tab. The list of forms to auto-create is displayed. Click the child form and then click the > button. This removes the child form from the auto-create list and puts it in the Available forms list. Figure 6.20 shows the Project Options dialog box after moving the child form to the Available forms list.

Figure 6.20.

The Project Options dialog box.

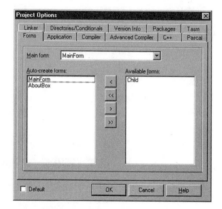

Now run the program again. This time the blank MDI child is not displayed.

WARNING

> If you remove a form from the auto-create list, you must be sure to specifically create the form prior to using it. If you do not create the form, the pointer to the form is uninitialized (remember the pointer is automatically created by C++Builder). Attempting to use the pointer will result in an access violation or erratic program behavior. Once you remove a form from the auto-create list, it is your responsibility to make sure the form has been created before using it.

Our application has one other problem we need to address. When you click the close button on one of the MDI windows you will find that the window minimizes instead of closing. Believe it or not this is the standard behavior as prescribed by Microsoft. Standard behavior or not, it's weird, so we'll fix things so that clicking the close box actually closes the window (as any rational person would expect). Bring up the child window form in the Form Designer.

Be sure the form itself is selected and not the Image component on the form (choose the `Child` from the Component Selector at the top of the Object Inspector, if necessary). Double-click the Value column next to the `OnClose` event in the Object Inspector. Add a line of code to the event handler so that it looks like this:

```
void __fastcall
TForm1::FormClose(TObject *Sender, TCloseAction &Action)
{
  Action = caFree;
}
```

Setting the close action to `caFree` tells VCL to close the child window and to free the memory associated with the window. Now the child window will behave as it should when the close box is clicked. Again run the program to prove that the program behaves as advertised.

Summary

The C++Builder IDE can be intimidating until you get familiar with it. If you learn it a little at a time, it's not nearly so daunting. Today you learned more about the various pieces that make up the C++Builder IDE. Then you learned about how projects are used to create an executable file. You also learned more about forms. You found out how C++Builder deals with dialog boxes and other child windows. After that, you got to create a program that actually does something interesting. Tomorrow we'll find out about the Form Designer and the Menu Designer.

Workshop

The Workshop contains quiz questions to help you solidify your understanding of the material covered and exercises to provide you with experience in using what you have learned. Answers to the quiz questions are in Appendix A, "Answers to Quiz Questions."

Q&A

Q **The C++Builder toolbar doesn't have buttons for the features I use most often. Can I change the toolbar?**

A Absolutely. The toolbar is fully customizable. You can add or remove buttons as you see fit.

Q **I placed multiple `Label` components on a form and then attempted to select them all by dragging. Instead I just got another big `Label` component. What have I done wrong?**

A You forgot to turn off the multiple placement option. After placing multiple components on the form, you need to click the arrow button on the Component palette to turn off the multiple placement option.

6

Q I have several components on a panel. I'm trying to select the components by dragging, but I keep moving the panel instead. What must I do to select a group of components on a panel?

A Either use Shift+click to select each component or hold down the Ctrl key and drag a bounding rectangle around the components.

Q Can I write, compile, and run a simple C++ program in the IDE without a project?

A No. In order to create an executable file from the IDE, you need a project. The project makes sure that all needed library routines are linked to the final executable. You *can* compile and link a program from the command line using the command line tools, but you probably won't do this unless you are already an experienced user of the command line tools.

Q What are library files for?

A There is a common set of routines used in C++ programs. The string-manipulation functions I discussed on Day 1, "Getting Started with C++Builder," are examples of such routines. If your program calls a C++ function, that function must be included in the executable file for your program. These functions are contained in a library file (.LIB). The linker makes a copy of the function found in the library file and places it in your executable. Any VCL methods your program calls are handled in the same way.

Q Why does C++Builder use the term *unit* to refer to a source file?

A C++Builder uses the term *unit* because C++Builder was created from Borland's Delphi. Delphi is based on Pascal, and *unit* is a Pascal term for a source file.

Q What do I need to do in order for my application to be an MDI application?

A Just be sure that the main form has a FormStyle of fsMDIForm and that any MDI child forms have a FormStyle of fsMDIChild.

Q What's the difference between a dialog box and a child window in C++Builder?

A There is no real difference. A dialog box form might have certain traits such as a dialog box border rather than a sizing border; OK, Cancel, and Help buttons; and no minimize or maximize buttons. But a dialog box is still just a form like any other. A form might have the appearance of a dialog box or of a child window, but a form is just a form.

Q Can I check the unit I'm working on for errors without running the program?

A Yes. Just choose Project | Compile Unit from the main menu. C++Builder will compile any units that have changed since the last compile and will report any errors encountered.

Q Can I build OWL or MFC applications with C++Builder?

A Yes. Certainly C++Builder's main strengths lie in its RAD capabilities. However, you can easily build OWL or MFC applications with C++Builder.

Quiz

1. How do you invoke the Toolbar Editor dialog box?
2. When you have the Toolbar Editor dialog box, how do you add buttons to the toolbar?
3. How do you remove buttons from the toolbar?
4. What's the easiest way to place multiple components of the same type on a form?
5. What's the easiest way to place a component in the center of the form?
6. List the file types needed to build an application in C++Builder.
7. What VCL method do you use to display a form modelessly?
8. What VCL method do you use to display a form modally?
9. How can you attach an event to an event handler that has been previously defined?
10. When using the Object Inspector, how can you enumerate the choices for a particular property?

Exercises

1. Remove the Pause, Step Over, and Trace Into buttons from the C++Builder toolbar. Add Cut, Copy, and Paste buttons to the toolbar.
2. Reset the toolbar to its default settings.
3. Spend some time looking over the components on each page of the Component palette. Place any components you are curious about on a form and experiment with them.
4. Create a new directory on your hard drive. Create a new application in C++Builder. Add three new forms to the project (they can be blank if you want). Save the project to the new directory you created and run the program. Close the program. Now examine the directory where the project was saved. Compare the files you see there with the file types listed in Table 6.1.
5. Run the Picture Viewer program you created earlier. Open several graphics files. Drag the MDI child windows around in the parent window. Attempt to move a child window outside the parent. What happens?
6. With the Picture Viewer program still running, minimize all windows. Drag the minimized windows to random locations on the screen and then choose Window|Arrange All from the menu.

6

7. Start a new application. Place several components on the form. Click on each component and observe the properties for each component in the Object Inspector.

8. Create a blank form. Double-click in the Value column next to the `Color` property to invoke the Color dialog box. Choose a color and click OK.

9. Get some rest. Tomorrow is going to be a big day.

Day 7

Working with the Form Designer and the Menu Designer

As you know by now, C++Builder is heavily form based, a model that takes maximum advantage of the visual programming environment. In this chapter you will explore

☐ The Form Designer

☐ The Menu Designer

To illustrate the use of the Form Designer, we will build an application that approximates the Windows Notepad program. Along the way you will gain valuable experience working with the Form Designer. Later in the chapter, you'll explore the Menu Designer in detail.

This chapter might seem elementary if you have used Delphi extensively. Even so, be sure to take a quick look, to discover things previously unknown or to rediscover things you've forgotten. I'm willing to bet there is at least one thing in this chapter that will be new to you.

Working with the Form Designer

The C++Builder Form Designer is a powerful visual programming tool. It enables you to place, select, move, resize, and align components, and much more. The Form Designer also enables you to size and position the form itself, add menus, and create specialized dialog boxes—everything you need to create the user interface to a typical Windows program.

We'll examine each Form Designer feature in the following sections. As you read, I encourage you to stop and experiment any time you are curious about how something works. Sometimes a few minutes playing around can teach you a technique that you will carry with you for a long time to come.

The Form Designer's Context Menu

When you first start C++Builder or when you create a new project, you are presented with a blank form in the Form Designer. The Form Designer, like most C++Builder windows, has a context menu associated with it. Table 7.1 lists and describes each item on the Form Designer context menu.

Table 7.1. The Form Designer's context menu items.

Item	Description
Align to Grid	Aligns selected components to the Form Designer grid.
Bring to Front	Brings selected components to the front of all other components.
Send to Back	Sends selected components behind all other components.
Revert to Inherited	Causes the selected control to revert back to its original state when you are working with a form you have inherited from the Object Repository. (Inheriting forms from the Object Repository is covered on Day 9, "Creating Applications in C++Builder.")
Align	Displays the Alignment dialog box.
Size	Displays the Size dialog box.
Scale	Displays the Scale dialog box.
Tab Order	Displays the Edit Tab Order dialog box.
Creation Order	Displays the Creation Order dialog box.
Add to Repository	Adds this form to the Object Repository. Custom forms can be saved to be used later. (The Object Repository is discussed on Day 9.)
View as Text	Shows the form description as text in the Code Editor. You can edit the form's text version if you like. Choose View as Form from the Code Editor context menu to go back to the form. You can also use Alt+F12 to switch from the View as Text and View as Form options.

C++Builder creates a form file (DFM) for every form you create and places it in your project's directory. The form file is a binary resource file that can't be read by mere humans. When you choose the View as Text context menu item, C++Builder converts the binary resource to a readable form. When you switch back to the View as Form option, C++Builder recompiles the form file to implement any changes you have made.

Most of the context menu options are discussed in the following sections. Others are discussed in later chapters when we examine the particular aspect of C++Builder to which they pertain.

Placing Components

Placing a component on a form is a trivial act. You simply select the component you want from the Component palette and click on the form to place the component. When you click on the form, the component's upper-left corner is placed at the location you clicked. Notice that when you click a button on the Component palette, the button appears as pressed. When you click on the form to place the component, the button on the Component palette pops up again to indicate that the action is completed.

TIP

As you learned on Day 6, "The C++Builder IDE Explored," to place a component on a form multiple times, press and hold Shift when you first select the component's button on the Component palette. Each time you click on the form, a new component will be added. Click the Arrow button on the Component palette to stop placing components.

Most components can be sized. You can place a component on a form and then size it, or you can size the component at the same time you place it on the form. To size while placing the component, click on the form where you want the top-left corner to be placed and then drag with the mouse until the component is the desired size. When you release the mouse, the component will be placed at the size you specified.

NOTE

Not all components can be sized in this manner. Nonvisual components, for instance, are represented on the form by an icon. Although you can click and drag to place a nonvisual component, the drag size will be ignored. Another example is a single-line edit component. The edit component can be placed by dragging, but only the drag width will be used. The drag height will be ignored because the height of a single-line edit component defaults to the height of a single-line edit control.

 TIP

If you change your mind while placing the control via the dragging method, you can press the Esc key on the keyboard before you release the mouse button to cancel the operation. The component's button will still be pressed on the Component palette, however, so you might need to click the Arrow button to return to component-selection mode.

Placing components is simple enough that we don't need to spend much time on the subject. You had some experience with placing components yesterday, so let's move on to other things.

The Form Designer Grid

The Form Designer has a built-in grid that aids in designing forms. By default, C++Builder shows the grid. The grid size is initially set to 8 pixels horizontally and 8 pixels vertically. When the Form Designer is set to display the grid, a dot is placed at the intersection of each grid point. Components placed on a form will snap to the nearest grid point. By *snap to*, I mean that the component's top-left corner will automatically jump to the nearest grid point. This is an advantage because you frequently want a group of controls to be aligned either on their left, right, top, or bottom edge. When the Snap to Grid option is on, you merely get close enough to the correct location and the Form Designer will automatically place your component at the nearest grid point. This saves you time by sparing you from tweaking the individual component's size or position on the form.

The grid settings can be modified via the Preferences page of the Environment Options dialog box. (I'll discuss the Environment Options in detail on Day 10, "More on Projects.") Here you can change the grid size or turn off the Snap to Grid feature. You can also turn the grid display on or off. When the grid display is off, the grid is still active (assuming Snap to Grid is on), but the dots marking grid points are not drawn on the form.

Selecting Components

After you place a component on a form, you often have to select the component in order to modify it in some way. You might have to select a component to perform one of the following actions:

☐ Move the component.

☐ Change the component's properties.

☐ Align the component.

☐ Size the component.

☐ Cut or copy the component.

☐ Order the component (bring to front or send to back).

☐ Delete the component.

Selecting Individual Components

To select a single component, just click on it. When you select the component, eight black sizing handles appear around the component to indicate that it is selected. (I'll discuss the sizing handles in a moment.) Figure 7.1 shows a form with a button component selected.

Figure 7.1.

A form with a button component selected.

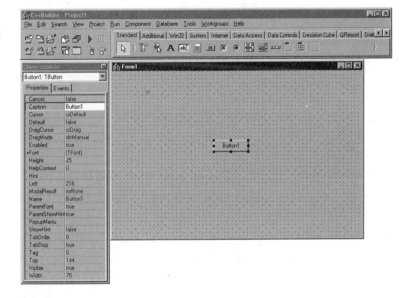

As soon as you select a component, the Object Inspector changes to show the properties and events for the control selected. To deselect a control, click on the form's background or Shift+click on the control. (Shift+click is described in the next section.)

 TIP

Each component has a default event handler associated with it. When you double-click a component on a form, the Code Editor displays the default event handler for that component, ready for you to type code.

> In most cases, the default event handler is the OnClick handler. Exactly what happens when the component is double-clicked depends on how the component is designed. For example, in the case of the Image component, double-clicking will display the Picture Editor dialog box.

Group Selection

You can also select multiple components so that you can act on them as a group. This is accomplished in one of three ways:

☐ Shift+click with the keyboard and mouse.

☐ Drag with the mouse.

☐ Choose Edit | Select All from the main menu.

To select all components on the form, choose Edit | Select All from the main menu.

Selecting Components with Shift+Click

To use the Shift+click sequence, first select one control. Then press and hold the Shift key on the keyboard and click on any other controls you want to include in the selection. Each control you click is bounded by four gray boxes to indicate that it is part of the selection.

You can remove a control from the selection by continuing to hold the Shift key and again clicking on the component. In other words, the Shift+click sequence toggles a component's inclusion in the selection.

To illustrate, first start with a blank form and then perform the following steps:

1. Place three button components anywhere on the form. They will automatically be labeled Button1, Button2, and Button3.
2. Click Button1. The black sizing rectangles appear around the component.
3. Press and hold the Shift key on the keyboard. Click Button2. It is added to the selection. Gray boxes now appear at the corners of both Button1 and Button2.
4. Shift+click on Button3. Now all three buttons are part of the selection.
5. Shift+click again on Button2. Button2 is removed from the selection (the gray boxes disappear), but Button1 and Button3 are still in the selection.
6. Shift+click on Button1. Now Button3 is the only component in the selection. The gray boxes are replaced with the black sizing rectangles.
7. Shift+click on Button1 and Button2. All three buttons are now part of the selection again.

Figure 7.2 shows the form as it will look at the end of this sequence. Keep in mind that your buttons could have been placed anywhere on the form.

Figure 7.2.

A form with three buttons selected.

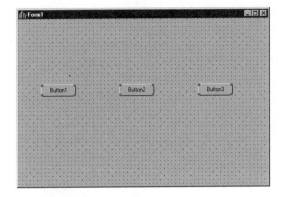

Keep the form handy because you'll use it again in the next exercise.

NOTE

If you click on a component that is part of a selection, nothing will happen. To select a single control that is currently part of a group selection, you need to first click on the form's background or press the Esc key to remove the group selection. Then you can click on the individual control you want to select.

Multiple Selection by Dragging

You can select multiple controls by dragging a bounding rectangle around the controls to be selected. The *bounding rectangle* is a broken-line rectangle that changes size as you drag. In fact, you don't have to drag the bounding rectangle completely around the components. You only have to touch a component with the bounding rectangle in order for it to be included in the selection.

Be sure that you start by placing the mouse cursor over the form's background and not on a component. Hold the primary mouse button down and begin dragging. You will see the bounding rectangle as you drag. Surround or touch the components you want selected and release the mouse button. Any components that were inside the bounding rectangle (or touching it) are included in the selection.

When you have selected a group of controls, you can use the Shift+click technique explained in the previous section to add other controls from the selection or to remove controls from the selection. For example, you might want to select all controls in one area of your form except for one. Surround the controls and then deselect the control you want to exclude from the selection.

7

Go back to the form with the three buttons created earlier (if you've already discarded that form, create a new one and place three buttons on it). Start at the top-left corner and drag down and to the right to surround the buttons. Let go of the mouse button and the controls will be selected. Figure 7.3 shows the form and the bounding rectangle being dragged.

Figure 7.3.

Controls being selected by dragging.

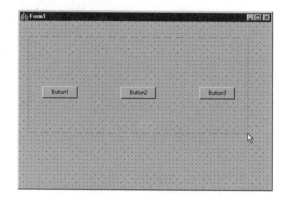

 TIP   You can use Shift+drag to select non-adjacent groups of controls. If, for instance, you had two separate groups of controls in different areas on your form, you could drag around the first set and then hold the Shift key down and drag around the second set. Both groups would be selected.

 NOTE   You don't have to drag down and to the right. You can drag in any direction to select components.

Selecting Multiple Items: Components Within Components

Frequently you will have components placed within other components. The `Panel` component is often used as a container for other components. Toolbars are built this way, for example. To select a group of components on a panel, you have to hold down the Ctrl key on the keyboard while you drag to select the components. (Try it without holding down the Ctrl key and see what happens!) In case you're wondering, yes, you can use a combination of Ctrl+Shift+drag. (I suppose the Borland designers could have figured out some way of working the Alt key in there, too.)

To illustrate, first start with a blank form. Then do the following:

1. Select a `Panel` component from the Component palette and place it on the form using the drag method. Drag it so that it occupies most of the form.

2. Now select a `Button` component and place six buttons on the form. Your form will look something like Figure 7.4.

Figure 7.4.

*The form with a
panel and six buttons.*

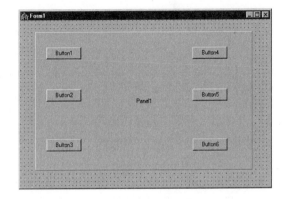

3. Drag a bounding rectangle around Button1, Button2, and Button3. Notice that you moved the panel, which is not what you expected (and not what you wanted). Move the panel back to where it was.

4. Hold down the Ctrl key and drag a rectangle around Button1, Button2, and Button3. The buttons are selected.

5. Now hold down both the Ctrl and Shift keys and drag the bounding rectangle around Button5 and Button6. Now all buttons are selected except Button4.

Using the Ctrl+drag sequence is the only way to select a group of components contained within another component if you are using the drag method. You can use the Shift+click method to select components contained within another component just as you do when selecting components on a form.

Moving Components

Moving components is a common and simple task. To move an individual component, place the mouse cursor over the component and drag. As you drag, a rectangle that represents the component moves with the mouse cursor. When you have the rectangle where you want it, let go of the mouse button, and the component will be moved to that location.

NOTE

When you move a control via drag and drop, the control's `Left` and `Top` properties are automatically updated.

NOTE

It's easiest to move a component by drag and drop. If you need finer control, you can modify the component's Left and Top properties. You can also use various alignment options, which I'll discuss later in this chapter in the section "Aligning Components."

If you have the Snap to Grid option on, the dragging rectangle will snap to the nearest grid point as you drag.

TIP

If you change your mind while dragging, you can press the Esc key on the keyboard before you release the mouse button to cancel the drag operation. The component will return to its original position.

Dragging a group of controls works the same way. After you have a group of components selected, place the mouse cursor over any one of the controls and begin dragging. The dragging rectangle will be displayed for each control in the group. This enables you to visualize where the group will be placed when you release the mouse button.

NOTE

You cannot move a group of components if components in the group have different parent controls. For instance, let's say you select both a Button component on the main form and a SpeedButton on a panel. Because these two components have different parent controls, you cannot move them as a group.

TIP

When you have selected a control, you can nudge it by holding down the Ctrl key while using the arrow keys on the keyboard. This enables you to move the control one pixel at a time. This technique works for both groups of controls and individual controls. The Snap to Grid feature is overridden when using this technique.

After you have moved a component using this method, the component is no longer on a grid point—it is offset by some amount. If you now drag the component, it will maintain its offset from the grid point as you drag.

7

TIP If you have moved a control by using the Ctrl+arrow method and want to align it again to the grid, choose Edit | Align to Grid from the main menu. The control's top-left corner will snap to the nearest grid point.

A control cannot be dragged outside its parent. If you drag a component off the form's left or top edge, you will see that the component is clipped at the form's edge. If, however, you drag the component off the right or bottom of the form and drop it, scrollbars will appear on the form so that you can scroll to see the rest of the form. The form's Width and Height properties are not altered. If you drag the component back onto the visible part of the form, the scrollbars disappear again. This is the default behavior and will occur unless you change the form's AutoScroll property to false. Figure 7.5 shows a Memo component that has been dragged partially off the form's right edge. Notice the scrollbar that appears at the bottom of the form.

Figure 7.5.
A form with
AutoScroll *in*
action.

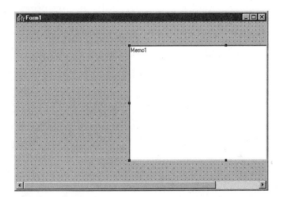

Preventing Components from Being Moved or Sized

Components can be locked into place so that they cannot be moved. Locking components is useful if you know that a form's design is final and you don't want to worry about accidentally moving controls. To lock a form's controls, choose Edit | Lock Controls from the main menu. Locked controls cannot be moved or sized. When controls are locked, their sizing handles are gray with a black border. To unlock the controls again, choose Edit | Lock Controls again. The controls can now be moved as before.

Ordering, Cutting, Copying, and Pasting Components

You will place some components on top of one another to achieve a visual effect. For example, a shadowed box can be created by placing a white box over a black box (both would be Shape components). Obviously you can't have the shadow on top of the box, so you have to have some way of ordering the controls to tell C++Builder which controls go on top and which go on the bottom. Let's do a simple exercise that illustrates this. Along the way you will also see how you can use Copy and Paste with components. First, start with a blank form (you know the drill by now). Now do this:

1. Click on the Additional tab on the Component palette and choose the Shape component. Click on the form to place the shape. A white square appears on the form.

2. Size the shape as desired (mine ended up being 209 pixels by 129 pixels).

3. Be sure the Shape component is selected. Choose Edit | Copy from the main menu.

4. Choose Edit | Paste from the main menu. A copy of the shape is placed below and to the right of the original shape. Conveniently, this is exactly where we want it.

NOTE

> After a Paste operation, the component just pasted will be selected.

5. Double-click the Brush property and change its Color property to clBlack. The new shape is now black, but it is on top of the original shape. Can't have that!

6. Click the secondary mouse button and choose Send to Back from the context menu (you could also choose Edit | Send to Back from the main menu). The black shape is moved behind the white shape. You now have a box with a shadow. (As an alternative, we could have clicked on the white shape and used Bring to Front to move it on top of the black shape.)

This exercise illustrates two features of the Form Designer. It shows how you can change the stacking order of controls and how you can use Copy and Paste to copy components. The original component's properties are copied exactly and pasted in as part of the pasting process. Each time you paste a component, it is placed below and to the right of the previous component pasted.

NOTE

> If a component that can serve as a container is selected when you perform Paste, the component in the Clipboard will be pasted as the container component's child. For instance, you might want to move a button from the main form to a panel. You could select the button and then choose Edit | Cut from the main menu to remove the button from the form and place it in the Clipboard. Then you could select the panel and choose Edit | Paste from the main menu to paste the button onto the panel.

I don't need to go into much detail on the Cut operation. When you cut a component, the component disappears from the form and is placed in the Clipboard. Later you can paste the component onto the form or onto another component, such as a `Panel` component.

TIP

You can also copy a component and paste it into your source code. The results will be something like this:

```
object Edit1: TEdit
  Left = 24
  Top = 16
  Width = 457
  Height = 21
  TabOrder = 0
  Text = 'Edit1'
end
```

This is not code that will compile, but this technique will give you a component's size and position as it appears on the form. This comes in handy when creating components on the fly at runtime rather than at design time. You can place a dummy component visually on the form, get its size and position using Copy and Paste, and then delete the component. Then you can write code to create the component at runtime and know that it will be properly sized and positioned.

Sizing Components

With some components, you drop them on a form and accept the default size. Buttons are a good example. A standard button has a height of 25 pixels and a width of 75 pixels. For many situations, the default button size is exactly what you want. With some components, however, the default size is rarely exactly what you need. A `Memo` component, for example, nearly always has to be sized to fit the specific form on which you are working.

Sizing by Dragging

When you select a control, eight black sizing handles appear around the control. When you place the mouse cursor over one of the sizing handles, the cursor changes to a double-headed arrow known as the *sizing cursor*. When you see the sizing cursor, you can begin dragging to size the control. How the component is sized depends on which sizing handles you grab.

The sizing handles centered at the top and bottom of the component size it vertically (taller or shorter). Likewise, the right and left sizing handles size the component horizontally (wider or narrower). If you grab one of the sizing handles in the component's corners, you can size both horizontally and vertically at the same time. As with moving a component, a sizing rectangle appears as you drag. When you have the sizing rectangle at the desired size, let go of the mouse button and the component will be resized. Figure 7.6 illustrates a `Memo` component being sized by dragging; Figure 7.7 shows the form after the Drag operation.

7

Figure 7.6.

A Memo *component being sized.*

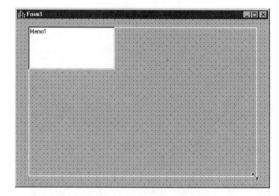

Figure 7.7.

The form after sizing the Memo *component.*

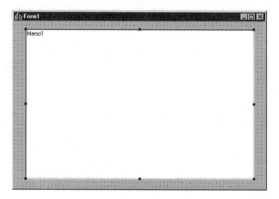

NOTE

Sizing applies to visual components only. Nonvisual components appear on the form as icons that cannot be sized. The sizing handles appear on nonvisual components, and the handles can be dragged, but the result of the dragging operation will be ignored.

Groups of controls cannot be sized by dragging. The sizing handles (black squares) are replaced by selection indicators (gray squares) when you select more than one component.

TIP

To size all the components in a group at one time, modify the Width or Height property in the Object Inspector or use the Size dialog box (the Size dialog box is discussed in the preceding section, "Sizing Components"). All components in the selection will take on the new values.

7

TIP

> To size a control or group of controls by one pixel at a time, hold down the Shift key and press any arrow key on the keyboard. The up and down arrows size the control vertically, and the right and left arrows size it horizontally. Only the component's Width and Height properties are affected. The Top and Left properties are not modified.

Sizing with the Size Dialog Box

Another sizing option is the Size dialog box. You can bring up the Size dialog box by choosing Edit | Size from the main menu. Figure 7.8 shows the Size dialog box.

Figure 7.8.

The Size dialog box.

The Size dialog box is used when you want to force a group of controls to the same width or height. For instance, let's say you had six edit components on a form, all with different widths. To make the form appear more balanced, you might want to make all the edit components the same width. You would first select the components and then invoke the Size dialog box. From there you could choose Shrink to smallest, in the Width column, to make all the components the width of the shortest edit component, or Grow to largest, to make all the components the width of the longest component in the group. You could also enter an exact width in the Width box, in which case you would leave the Height set on No change. When you click OK, the components will all be the same width.

TIP

> The Size dialog box can also be invoked from the Form Designer context menu.

Sizing with the Scale Dialog Box

Another sizing tool is the Scale dialog box, shown in Figure 7.9. This dialog box enables you to specify a scaling percentage. To make the components twice as large, enter 200 in the Scaling factor box. To reduce the components' size by half, enter 50 in the Scaling factor box. The Scale dialog box is convenient for quickly changing the size of all the form's components. You can bring up the Scale dialog box by choosing Edit | Scale from the main menu or Scale from the Form Designer context menu.

7

Figure 7.9.

The Scale dialog box.

A control can also be sized and moved by using the various Alignment options. Let's take a look at those now.

NOTE

Remember, components can always be moved by modifying their Left and Top properties and sized by modifying their Width and Height properties.

Aligning Components

Regardless of whether you have the Snap to Grid option turned on, you sometimes need to align components after placing them. Aligning components could mean aligning several components along a common edge, centering components on the form, or spacing components. There are two different ways to go about aligning components:

☐ Use the Alignment palette and Alignment dialog box.

☐ Modify a component's Align property.

The following sections explain these two methods.

NOTE

You might have noticed the Alignment property for some components. This property pertains only to the way the component's text is aligned (centered, right-justified, or left-justified) and has nothing to do with aligning components on a form.

The Alignment Palette and the Alignment Dialog Box

It is often necessary to move or size components relative to the form or relative to one another. The Alignment palette contains several buttons that aid in that task. The Alignment dialog box performs the same operations as the Alignment palette but in a different format. To display the Alignment palette, choose View | Alignment Palette from the main menu. Figure 7.10 shows the Alignment palette and describes each button.

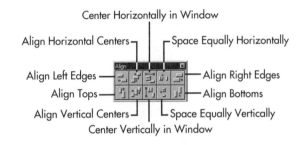

Figure 7.10.

The Alignment palette.

Center Horizontally in Window

Align Horizontal Centers

Space Equally Horizontally

Align Left Edges

Align Right Edges

Align Tops

Align Bottoms

Align Vertical Centers

Space Equally Vertically

Center Vertically in Window

TIP

The Alignment palette can save you a lot of work. Don't spend too much time trying to get controls to line up exactly. Place the components on the form and then use the Alignment palette to position them.

The Align Left Edges button is used to line up components on their left edges. Start with a blank form and then do the following:

1. Place five button components vertically on the form without regard to their left edges.

2. Select the buttons by dragging a bounding rectangle around them (or just touching them). The selection indicators show that all the buttons are selected. The form will look something like the one in Figure 7.11.

Figure 7.11.

The form with the buttons randomly placed.

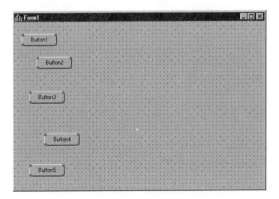

3. Choose View|Alignment Palette from the main menu. The Alignment palette is displayed. Move the Alignment palette, if necessary, so that it doesn't obscure the form.

4. Click the Align Left Edges button on the Alignment palette. The buttons are all lined up.

7

See how easy that is? As long as we have the buttons selected, let's look at another alignment option. The Space Equally Vertically alignment option can now be used to space the buttons evenly. The buttons should still be selected, so all you have to do is click the Space Equally Vertically button on the Alignment palette, and voilà! The buttons are perfectly spaced. The form will now look like Figure 7.12.

Figure 7.12.

The form with the buttons aligned and equally spaced.

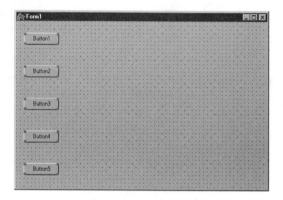

NOTE

The Space Equally Vertically alignment option spaces the components equally between the first component in the column (the top component) and the last component in the column (the bottom component). Be sure to set the first and last components where you want them before choosing the Space Equally Vertically alignment option. This is true of the Space Equally Horizontally alignment option as well.

The Center Horizontally in Window and Center Vertically in Window alignment options do exactly as their names indicate. These options are convenient for centering a single control, such as a button, on the form or for centering a group of controls. As long as you still have the group of buttons selected, click both the Center Horizontally in Window and Center Vertically in Window buttons on the Alignment palette. The buttons will be centered on the form both horizontally and vertically.

NOTE

When you select a group of controls and click one of the centering buttons, the controls will be treated *as a group.* If you choose each control individually and center it both horizontally and vertically on the form, all the controls will be stacked on top of one another in the middle of the form. By selecting the group and then centering, you will get the entire group centered as you intended.

The form will now look like the one in Figure 7.13.

Figure 7.13.

The form with the buttons centered.

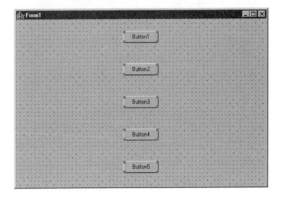

NOTE

> The Center Horizontally in Window and Center Vertically in Window alignment options can be used to align components contained within other components, such as buttons on a panel. The components will be centered horizontally or vertically on their parent component, whether the parent is a panel or a form.

The Align Tops, Align Bottoms, and Align Right Edges options work just like the Align Left Edges option we used earlier. There's not much point in going over all the possibilities that exist for their use.

TIP

> The first component selected will be the anchor point when using any edge-alignment option. Refer back to Figure 7.4. Let's say you had selected Button3 first and then used Shift+click to select the remaining buttons. When you chose Align Left Edges, Button3 would have remained where it is and all other buttons would have lined up with Button3's left edge because Button3 is the anchor component.

The Align Horizontal Centers and Align Vertical Centers options can be used to center components relative to one another. This is best illustrated with shapes. Start with a new form (or delete the buttons from the form you have been working on). Now do the following:

1. Click on the Additional tab on the Component palette and choose the Shape component. Click somewhere on the upper left of the form to add the shape.

2. Change the Shape property to stCircle.

7

3. Change the Width and Height properties to 150.

4. Double-click the Brush property and change its Color property to clBlack.

5. Place another Shape component on the form.

6. Change the second shape's Shape property to stCircle as well. Now you have two circles of different sizes on the screen—a white circle and a black circle.

7. Click on the black circle. Hold the Shift key and click on the white circle. Both shapes are selected.

8. Choose View | Alignment Palette from the main menu, if necessary (it might already be displayed). Arrange the Alignment palette so you can see the two shapes on the form. Observe the shapes as you perform the last two steps.

9. Click the Align Vertical Centers button on the Alignment palette. The vertical centers are aligned.

10. Click the Align Horizontal Centers button on the Alignment palette. The horizontal centers are aligned. Congratulations—you made a tire!

Did you see the effect as you performed the last two steps? Notice that because you selected the black circle first, it did not move (it is the anchor component), but the white circle moved as you clicked the alignment buttons. You can use these alignment options to center any number of controls on one another. These two alignment options have no effect when used on a single control.

Like the Component palette, the Alignment palette has a context menu associated with it. Place the mouse cursor over the Alignment palette and click the secondary mouse button. The context menu is displayed. Table 7.2 lists the items on the Alignment palette's context menu and explains their use.

Table 7.2. The Alignment palette's context menu items.

Menu Item	Description
Stay on Top	Forces the Alignment palette to always be on top. This is useful if you are frequently switching back and forth between the Form Designer and the Code Editor. Because the Alignment palette is a small window, it's easy to lose it.
Show Hints	Turns the hints (ToolTips) for the Alignment palette buttons on and off.
Hide	Hides the Alignment palette. (You can also use the close box on the Alignment palette to hide it.) To show the Alignment palette again, you have to choose View	Alignment Palette from the main menu.
Help	Brings up C++Builder Help with the Alignment palette page displayed.

The Alignment dialog box performs the same actions as the Alignment palette. To bring up the Alignment dialog box, choose Edit | Align from the main menu or Align from the Form Designer's context menu. Figure 7.14 shows the Alignment dialog box.

Figure 7.14.

The Alignment dialog box.

In most cases, the Alignment palette is easier to use, but you certainly can use the Alignment dialog box if you prefer.

The `Align` Property

Another type of alignment can be set using the `Align` property. This property controls how a component is aligned with its parent. The possible values for the `Align` property and a description of each are listed in Table 7.3.

Table 7.3. Possible values for the `Align` property.

Value	Description
alBottom	The component will be aligned at the bottom of the parent window. A status bar is an example of a component aligned along the bottom of a main form.
alClient	The component will expand to fill the parent window's client area. If other components occupy part of the client area, the component will fill what client area remains. Examples include `Memo` components, `Image` components, and `RichEdit` components.
alLeft	The component will be aligned along the parent window's left edge. A vertical toolbar is an example of a left-aligned component.
alNone	The component will be placed as designed, with no special relationship to the parent. This is the default for most components.
alRight	The component will be aligned along the parent's right edge.
alTop	The component will be aligned along the top of the parent's window. A toolbar is an example of this type of alignment.

7

An illustration will help explain alignment. Start with a blank form. Then perform these steps:

1. Click on the Standard tab on the Component palette and choose a `Panel` component. Place the panel anywhere on the form.

2. Locate the `Align` property in the Object Inspector (it's at the top of the list). Notice that it is set on `alNone`. Change the `Align` property to `alTop`. The panel is aligned at the top of the form, and it expands to fill the form's width.

3. Try to move the panel back to the middle of the form. The panel will snap back to the top.

4. Try to make the panel narrower. Notice that the panel retains its width.

5. Change the panel's height. Note that the panel's height can be changed (the width cannot).

6. Change the `Align` property to `alBottom`. Now the panel is glued to the bottom of the form.

7. Change the `Align` property to `alRight` and then `alLeft`. The width is now the same as the height was before. In effect, the panel is rotated. Again, attempts to move or size the panel vertically fail.

8. Change the `Align` property to `alClient`. The panel expands to fill the form's entire client area. The panel cannot be resized in any dimension.

9. Change the `Align` property to `alNone`. The panel can again be sized and moved.

As you see, changing `Align` to anything other than `alNone` effectively glues the panel to one edge of the form. In the case of `alClient`, the panel is glued to all four edges. To illustrate how different components work together, let's build a prototype of an application that resembles Windows Notepad.

 A *prototype* is an application that has the appearance of a working application but lacks full functionality.

 NOTE

C++Builder is perfect for quick prototyping of an application. You can have the main screens and dialog boxes designed and capable of being displayed in much less time than it would take with traditional C++ Windows programming tools like OWL or MFC. That is not, however, to say that C++Builder is just for prototyping. C++Builder is fully capable of handling all your 32-bit Windows programming needs.

Step 1: Start a New Application

1. Choose File | New Application from the main menu. If prompted to save the current project, click No.

2. The form is selected, so change the `Name` property to `ScratchPad`.

3. Change the `Caption` property to `ScratchPad 1.0`.

4. Choose Project|Options from the main menu. Click on the Application tab and enter `ScratchPad 1.0` for the application's title. Click OK to close the Project Options dialog box.

Step 2: The Beginnings of a Toolbar

Most Windows applications these days have a toolbar. Building a toolbar requires several steps in itself. First, we'll put a spacer at the top of the window. (You'll see the benefit of the spacer later when we add a menu to the application.) Here we go:

1. Choose a `Bevel` component from the Component palette and place it on the form (it's located on the Additional tab).

2. Change the `Height` property to `2`.

3. Change the `Align` property to `alTop`. The bevel is placed along the top of the form's client area.

Step 3: Creating the Toolbar Container

Now we can add the panel that will serve as the container for the toolbar buttons.

1. Choose a `Panel` component from the Component palette and place it anywhere on the form.

2. Change the `Name` property to `Toolbar`.

3. Change the `Height` property to `32`.

4. Change the `BevelOuter` property to `bvNone`.

5. Clear the `Caption` property.

6. Change the `Align` property to `alTop`. The panel moves to the top but just underneath the bevel we placed there earlier.

 NOTE

> The last step in this sequence illustrates a point about the `Align` property. If you make a component's `Align` property `alTop`, it will move to the top of the client area or to the bottom edge of the first component it encounters that also has its alignment property set to `alTop`. This enables you to place several components on the top of a form and have them adjust automatically as the form is sized.

Step 4: Decorating the Panel

Now all that's left to do is add a button or two to the panel:

1. Click on the Additional tab of the Component palette and choose a `SpeedButton` component.

7

2. Place a speed button on the panel (not on the main form). Don't worry about its exact placement.

3. Change the Name property to FileOpenBtn.

4. Change the Left property to 5.

5. Choose View|Alignment Palette from the main menu. Click the Center Vertically in Window button.

6. Locate the Glyph property and double-click the Value column. The Picture Editor is displayed.

7. Click the Load button on the Picture Editor. The Load Picture dialog box is displayed. Navigate to the Borland Shared Files \Images\Buttons subdirectory (by default, this is located in the \Program Files\Borland directory) and double-click the fileopen.bmp file. Click OK.

8. Repeat the first seven steps to add a File Save button (omitting Step 4). Place the new button to the right of the File Open button. Name it FileSaveBtn and use the filesave.bmp file for the Glyph.

The form will now look like Figure 7.15.

Figure 7.15.

The ScratchPad *form up to this point.*

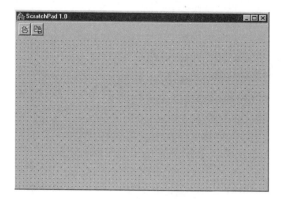

Step 5: Adding a Status Bar

Okay, so far, so good. Windows Notepad doesn't have a status bar (or a toolbar, for that matter), but we'll put one in our application:

1. Click on the Win32 tab on the Component palette and choose the StatusBar component.

2. Click anywhere on the form. The status bar is automatically placed at the bottom of the form. The status bar has a default Align value of alBottom.

3. Change the Name property to StatusBar.

Step 6: Adding the Memo Component

We need some component in which to type text, so we'll use a Memo component (believe it or not, we're almost done with our prototype):

1. Click on the Standard tab on the Component palette and choose a Memo component. Place the memo anywhere on the form's client area.

2. Change the Name property to Memo.

3. Double-click the Value column next to the Lines property. The String List Editor is displayed. Delete the word Memo and click OK.

4. Change the Scrollbar property to ssVertical. (Initially, we only want a vertical scrollbar on the memo.)

5. Change the Name property of the Font property to Fixedsys. (Because this is a Notepad copycat, we'll use the system font.)

6. Change the Align property to alClient. The memo expands to fill the client area between the toolbar and the status bar.

Stand back and admire your work. This is starting to look like a real application! If the form looks too large or too small, resize it by dragging the lower-right corner. It's your program, so make it look the way you want it to look.

TIP

> Pressing the Esc key selects the parent of the control that currently has the selection. For example, our form's client area is covered by components, making it impossible to select the form itself. To make the form the active component in the Object Inspector, select the Memo component and then press the Esc key on the keyboard. You can also choose the form from the Component Selector combo box on the Object Inspector.

Notice that all the controls automatically resize themselves to retain their relationship with the parent window—the form, in this case. That is one of the main advantages to the Align property. The form now looks like the one in Figure 7.16.

Run the Program

You can now click the Run button to run the program. You can type text in the window's client area, and you can press the toolbar buttons (although they don't do anything at this point). Keep in mind that this is a prototype and is mostly for show right now. We'll add more to the program by the end of the day.

We'd better save the project because we're going to use it later in the chapter. Choose File | Save All from the main menu. Save the main form's source unit as SPMain and the project as Scratch.

Figure 7.16.

*The completed
prototype.*

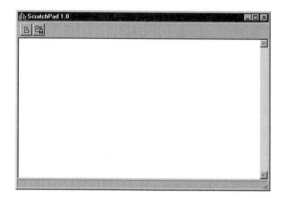

Setting the Tab Order

 The *tab order* refers to the order in which components will receive input focus
when the user presses the Tab key on the keyboard.

C++Builder forms automatically support component navigation using the Tab key. You can
move forward from component to component by using Tab and backward by using Shift+Tab.

> **NOTE**
>
> There are two types of visual components. *Windowed* components are
> components that accept focus. Windowed components include the `Edit`,
> `Memo`, `ListBox`, `ComboBox`, and `Button` components, as well as many more.
>
> *Non-windowed* components are components that don't accept keyboard
> focus. Components such as `Image`, `SpeedButton`, `Label`, `Shape`, and
> many others are non-windowed components.
>
> The tab order only applies to windowed components. Non-windowed
> components are excluded from the tab order.

The tab order is initially set based on the order the components were placed on the form when
the form was designed. You can modify the tab order by changing the `TabOrder` property for
each control in the Object Inspector. That method is tedious because you have to go to each
control individually. The Edit Tab Order dialog box provides an easier way (see Figure 7.17).

The Edit Tab Order dialog box is invoked by choosing Edit | Tab Order from the main menu.
This dialog box displays all windowed components currently on the form. Non-windowed
components are not displayed. To change the tab order, click on the name of the component
you want to move in the tab order and then click the up or down buttons as needed. You can
also drag the component to its new position in the tab order. After you get the tab order the
way you want it, click OK and the tab order will be set. You can confirm the new settings by
viewing each control's `TabOrder` property.

Figure 7.17.

The Edit Tab Order dialog box.

NOTE

The tab order starts with 0. The first component in the tab order is 0, the second is 1, and so on.

May I See a Menu, Please?

Menus are a big part of most Windows applications. Some Windows programs don't have menus, but the vast majority do. C++Builder makes creating menus easy with the Menu Designer. The Menu Designer has the following features:

- ☐ It can create both main menus and pop-up menus (context menus).
- ☐ It provides immediate access to the Code Editor to handle the OnClick events for menu items.
- ☐ It can insert menus from templates or from resource files.
- ☐ It can save custom menus as templates.

All the Menu Designer's commands are accessed via the Menu Designer context menu or by interacting with the Object Inspector. Figure 7.18 shows the Menu Designer's context menu.

Figure 7.18.

The Menu Designer's context menu.

For the most part, these menu items are self-explanatory, so I'm not going to go over each one. Rather, you can learn about them by working with them. To begin, let's add a main menu to the ScratchPad application we created earlier. After that we'll add a context menu.

Creating a Main Menu

The Menu Designer enables you to build any menu quickly. The menu structure for a main menu consists of a MainMenu component, which is represented by the VCL class TMainMenu. Each item on the menu is a MenuItem component that is encapsulated in the TMenuItem class. You don't need to be too concerned about the intricacies of how these classes work together because the Menu Designer makes creating menus easy. With that brief overview, let's add a main menu to the ScratchPad application.

Adding a Main Menu to the Form

The first thing you must do is add a MainMenu component to your form.

NOTE

> By now you have had some experience with C++Builder. From this point on I will abbreviate some steps that you need to take to perform certain actions. For example, from here on I'll say, "Place a MainMenu component on the form" rather than "Click on the Standard tab on the Component palette. Click the MainMenu button and click on the form to place the component." Don't worry, I'll still give plenty of details when new operations are introduced.

1. Open the ScratchPad project created earlier in the chapter.
2. Place a MainMenu component on the form and change its Name property to MainMenu. Notice that a MainMenu component has very few properties and no events. All the menu's work is done by the individual menu items.
3. Double-click on the MainMenu icon. The Menu Designer is displayed.

The Menu Designer looks like a blank form without grid points. The Menu Designer can be sized in any way you want. The size is just for your convenience and has no bearing on how the menu operates at runtime. At this point, the Menu Designer is waiting for you to begin building the menu. After you have created your first menu, you will find that menu creation is easy and intuitive.

Creating a Menu by Hand

Although there are easier ways to create a File menu, you will create your first menu by hand. The Menu Designer always has a blank menu item that acts as a placeholder for any new menu items you will create. When you first start the Menu Designer, the blank item is selected.

1. Change the Name property to FileMenu.
2. Click on the Caption property in the Object Inspector, type &File, and press Enter.

NOTE

The ampersand (&) is used to create the underlined character for a menu item. The underlined character is the *accelerator* the user can type, in combination with the Alt key, to navigate a menu using the keyboard. You can put ampersands anywhere in the menu item's text. For instance, the customary text string for the Exit menu item would be E&xit. All you have to do is provide the ampersands where appropriate, and Windows will take it from there.

At this point, several things happen. First, the File menu shows up in the Menu Designer. It also shows on the main form behind the Menu Designer. (Remember when we added the `Bevel` component to the `ScratchPad` main form to use as a spacer? Now you can see why. The bevel provides visual distinction between the menu and the toolbar.) The other thing that happens is that a new, blank placeholder is added below the File menu you just created (you'll have to click on the File menu in the Menu Designer to see the placeholder). In addition, a new pop-up placeholder is created to the right of the File menu. The Object Inspector is displaying a blank `MenuItem` component, waiting for you to enter the `Caption` and `Name` property values. Figure 7.19 shows the Menu Designer as it appears at this point.

Figure 7.19.

The Menu Designer and Object Inspector after creating the File menu.

Let's continue with the creation of the menu:

1. Change the `Name` property for the new item to `FileNew`.

2. Change the `Caption` property to `&New` and press Enter. Again, a blank item is created in the Menu Designer.

3. Repeat Steps 1 and 2 and create menu items for Open, Save, and Save As. If you need help on where to place the ampersand, see Figure 7.20. Don't worry that you might not get it exactly right. You can always go back later and fix any errors.

7

TIP

> Make your menus as standard as possible. Be sure that your accelerators (the underlined characters) are the same as in other Windows programs. Also, remember that an ellipsis (...) following a menu item's text is a visual cue to the user that choosing the menu item will invoke a dialog box.

At this point, we need a menu separator.

 NEW TERM A *separator* is the horizontal line on a menu that separates groups of menu items.

Adding a separator is easy with the C++Builder Menu Designer. All you have to do is put in a hyphen for the Caption property. Select the blank menu item under Save As, type a hyphen for the Caption property, and press Enter. A separator is placed in the menu. Continue adding menu items until your menu looks like the one in Figure 7.20. If you need to modify a menu item, just click on it and change properties in the Object Inspector as needed.

Figure 7.20.

The Menu Designer with the finished File menu.

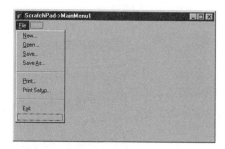

 NOTE

> The Menu Designer always provides a blank menu item at the bottom of each pop-up menu and on the menu bar's right side. You cannot delete these blank items, but there's no need to—they are used only in the Menu Designer and won't show on the menu when your program runs.

Now that the File menu is done, we need to create an Edit menu and a Help menu.

Inserting a Menu from a Template

This time we'll take the easy approach. First, click on the blank pop-up menu placeholder to the right of the File menu. Now click your secondary mouse button and choose Insert From Template from the context menu. The Insert Template dialog box is displayed, as shown in Figure 7.21.

 7

Figure 7.21.

*The Insert Template
dialog box.*

This dialog box shows a list of templates from which you can choose. You can use the predefined templates or create your own. In this case we are only interested in adding an Edit menu, so choose Edit Menu and click OK. A full Edit menu is immediately inserted into the Menu Designer. In fact, it's a little too full. We'll deal with that in a moment.

As long as we're here, let's add the Help menu, too. Click on the placeholder to the right of the Edit menu. Choose Insert From Template again, and this time insert a Help menu. (Don't choose the Expanded Help menu, though.) We'll tidy up both the Edit and Help menus in the next section. Notice that the main form has been updating to show the new menu items as they are placed.

NOTE You can insert templates to create pop-up menus as easily as when creating main menu items.

Yes, inserting from a template is really that easy. After using C++Builder for a while, you will no doubt have your own custom templates to choose from for building menus quickly and easily. You still have to update the Name properties to meaningful names, but it's much easier than creating the whole menu from nothing.

NOTE The Insert From Resource choice works the same as Insert From Template except that it expects a resource script file (a resource script file has the extension .RC) containing a valid menu definition. You won't use this option as much as Insert From Template except when converting existing C or C++ programs to C++Builder.

If you do use this feature, it is important to note that the menu resource must use the begin/end menu resource syntax and cannot use braces. For example, the following is an invalid menu resource:

7

```
MENU_1 MENU
{
 POPUP "File"
 {
  MENUITEM "Open", 100
  MENUITEM "About", 101
 }
}
```

The following menu resource, however, is legal:

```
MENU_1 MENU
BEGIN
 POPUP "File"
 BEGIN
  MENUITEM "Open", 100
  MENUITEM "About", 101
 END
END
```

This only applies to menus inserted with Insert From Resource and not to menu resources in general.

Deleting Menu Items

The process of creating a Windows application is a living, breathing thing. Rarely will you get everything exactly right the first time. Users will request new features, the boss will come up with a few of his own, and some features will even be dropped. You will often need to update your application's menus as these changes occur. For example, the Edit menu inserted earlier is a little verbose for our needs; there are several items that we just don't need. No problem—we'll just delete them:

1. Click on the Edit menu.
2. Click on the item called Repeat <command>.
3. Press Delete on the keyboard or choose Delete from the Menu Designer context menu to delete the item. The item disappears and the remaining items move up.
4. Delete the Paste Special menu item as well.

There, that was easy! We're not quite done with the Edit menu, but before we go on I want to mention a very useful feature of the Menu Designer. You are probably familiar with using Shift+click and Ctrl+click when selecting items in other Windows programs. These techniques can be used in Windows Explorer to select files, for instance. The Menu Designer supports Shift+click and Ctrl+click with one qualification—you can use these to select multiple menu items but not to deselect an item. As always, an exercise will illustrate better than I can explain.

1. The Edit menu should still be displayed. If not, click on Edit to reveal the Edit menu.
2. Click on the menu item called Goto.

3. Hold down the Shift key and click on the menu item called Object. All items between those two points are selected.

4. Press Delete on the keyboard to delete all the items at one time.

5. Move to the Help menu and delete the middle two items. Only the Contents and About items will remain.

As you can see, the Shift+click technique can be used to delete unwanted menu items quickly. Now we have the menus trimmed back to the way we want them to appear in the ScratchPad application.

Inserting Menu Items

Inserting menu items is pretty straightforward. Just click on the menu item above which you want to insert a new item and press the Insert key on the keyboard (or choose Insert from the Menu Designer's context menu). A blank menu item is inserted, and you can now modify the Name and Caption properties just as you did earlier. Let's insert an item into the Edit menu:

1. Click on Edit to display the Edit menu.

2. Click on the Find menu item.

3. Press the Insert key on the keyboard. A new menu item is provided, and all other menu items below the new item move down.

4. Change the Name property to EditSelectAll and change the Caption property to Select &All.

5. Click on the empty placeholder at the bottom of the Edit menu. Add a menu separator (remember, just enter a hyphen for the Caption property).

6. Click on the placeholder again and add a new item. Make the Name property EditWordWrap and the Caption property &Word Wrap.

Moving Menu Items

You can easily move menu items as needed. You can move them up or down within the pop-up menu they are already in, or you can move them across pop-ups. There are two ways to move a menu item. The first is by using Cut and Paste. Cut and Paste work as you would expect, so there's no need to go over that. The other way to move a menu item is just by dragging it to a new location and dropping it. Let's try it. We really want the Select All menu item just below the Undo item. No problem—just move it:

1. Click on Edit to display the Edit menu.

2. Click on the Select All item and drag it up until the separator under the Undo item is highlighted.

3. Let go of the mouse, and the menu item is moved.

Too easy, right? Yes, but that's what C++Builder is all about.

7

Batch Modifying of Properties

Sometimes you want to modify several menu items' properties at once. For example, we have a few menu items in the ScratchPad application that we are not ready to implement at this time. We aren't ready for printing support, for instance, nor are we ready to implement the Help system. We need to gray out (disable) those menu items:

1. Choose Help | Contents in the Menu Designer.
2. Change the Enabled property to false. The menu item is grayed out.
3. Click on the File menu.
4. Click on the Print menu item, hold the Shift key down, and click on the Print Setup menu item. Both items are selected.
5. In the Object Inspector, change the Enabled property to false. Both menu items are disabled.
6. Repeat Steps 4 and 5 to disable the Find and Replace items on the Edit menu.

You can modify a group of menu items at one time with this method. Simply select the items you want to modify and then change the property you want to modify. All menu items currently selected will have the new property value.

Creating Submenus

There's nothing special or tricky about creating submenus. A *submenu* is a menu item that, when clicked, expands to show more menu choices. A submenu is denoted by a right-pointing arrow next to the menu item text. You can create a submenu by choosing Create Submenu from the Menu Designer context menu or by holding down the Ctrl key and pressing the right-arrow key. When you create a submenu, a blank menu item is placed to the right of the menu item. You can add menu items to the submenu just as you did when creating the main menu. You can create a submenu by inserting a menu template as well.

Adding Shortcuts

You can easily add a keyboard shortcut to a menu item by changing its ShortCut property in the Object Inspector. The Edit menu that we inserted earlier already had keyboard shortcuts built in. For instance, the customary shortcut for Cut is Ctrl+X. If you look at the Edit menu, you will see Ctrl+X listed next to the Cut item. Click on the Cut menu item and you will see that the ShortCut property says Ctrl+X. Click on the Value column next to the ShortCut property. On the Value column's right side, you will see a drop-down button. Click the button to display the list of available shortcuts. The list you see there contains just about any keyboard shortcut you need. To set the keyboard shortcut for a menu item, simply pick a shortcut from the list.

The standard shortcut for Select All is Ctrl+A, so let's add that as a shortcut for our Select All menu item:

1. Choose Edit | Select All from your menu in the Menu Designer.

2. Click on the ShortCut property in the Object Inspector.

3. Choose Ctrl+A from the list of available shortcuts. Now the Select All menu item shows Ctrl+A next to it.

That's all you have to do; C++Builder takes care of it from there. The shortcuts function without your having to write any code.

Final Touches

Let's finish off our menu. First, we'll make the Word Wrap menu item on by default. This menu item is going to be used to turn word wrapping on or off. When word wrapping is on, the Word Wrap menu item will have a check mark next to it. When word wrapping is off, it will not have a check mark next to it. Click on the Word Wrap menu item and then change the Checked property to true. A check mark shows up to indicate that the word wrap feature is on.

Another thing we need to do is to change the Name property on all of the menu items that we inserted from a template. They were given default names, and we want to change them to more meaningful names. Click on the Edit | Undo menu item. Change the Name property from Undo1 to EditUndo. Notice that we prepend the pop-up menu name, Edit, to the front of the menu item name and remove the 1 at the end. You can use any naming convention you like, but be consistent. Repeat the process for the Cut, Copy, Paste, Find, and Replace menu items. Now move to the Help menu and modify the Name property of the Contents item to HelpContents and that of the About menu item to HelpAbout.

That about finishes our menu. Run through the menu to check it once more. If you find any errors, make the necessary changes. When you are satisfied that the menu is correct, click the close box to close the Menu Designer.

NOTE

You can access the Code Editor directly from the Menu Designer by double-clicking any menu item. When you double-click a menu item, the Code Editor will display the OnClick event for that item, and you can start typing code. In this case, we are going to go back to the main form and do our code editing there.

Writing the Code

Okay, so we have all these menu items but no code to make them work. It's going to be a lot of work implementing all these, right? Actually, it's easy. Most of the required code is already part of the TMemo class. All we have to do is call the appropriate TMemo methods in our menu handlers. We'll have to do a few other things, but most of what we will add is code you have seen before.

7

Before we write the code, we need to add the usual `OpenDialog` and `SaveDialog` components to the form:

1. Place an `OpenDialog` component on the form.
2. Change the `Name` property to `OpenDialog`.
3. Place a `SaveDialog` component on the form.
4. Change the `Name` property to `SaveDialog`.
5. Line up the `MainMenu`, `OpenDialog`, and `SaveDialog` icons on the form.

Okay, that was easy enough. Now let's get on with writing the code for the menu items. We'll start with the File Exit menu item (hey, it's the easiest!). Be sure that the Menu Designer is closed so you don't confuse the Menu Designer with the Form Designer.

1. Choose File | Exit from the main menu. The Code Editor comes to the top, and the `FileExitClick()` event handler is displayed.
2. The cursor is positioned and ready to go. Type the following at the cursor:

```
Close();
```

NOTE

> In Step 2 I had you use the `Close()` function to close the form. That works fine here because this is the application's main form. But if you want to terminate the application from anywhere in the program, you should use this:
>
> ```
> Application->Terminate();
> ```
>
> This will ensure that the application is terminated regardless of which form is currently open.

That's it. I told you it was the easiest. Let's do one more; then I'm going to turn you loose to finish the rest on your own.

1. Choose Edit | Cut from the main menu. The Code Editor comes to the top, and the `EditCutClick()` event handler is displayed.
2. Type the following at the cursor:

```
Memo->CutToClipboard();
```

And that's all there is to that particular menu item. You might not fully realize it, but VCL does a lot for you behind the scenes. The whole idea of a framework is to take the burden of the low-level details off the programmer's back. Life is good.

One of the interesting aspects of a program like C++Builder is that you rarely view your program as a whole. C++Builder conveniently takes you to the section of code you need to work on to deal with a particular event, so you usually only see your program in small chunks. Listing 7.1 contains the header for the ScratchPad program up to this point. The header is entirely C++Builder generated. The entire Scratch.cpp program is shown in Listing 7.2. Follow the examples you've just worked through to write code for each of the remaining menu items. Copy the code for each of the menu OnClick handlers from Listing 7.2. (The comment lines are there to explain to you what the code is doing. You don't have to include them when you type the code.)

NOTE

> The event handlers appear in the source file in the order in which they were created. Don't be concerned if the order of the event handlers in your source file doesn't exactly match Listing 7.2. The order in which the functions appear makes no difference to the compiler.

Listing 7.1. SPMAIN.H.

```
 1: //-----------------------------------------------------------
 2: #ifndef SPMainH
 3: #define SPMainH
 4: //-----------------------------------------------------------
 5: #include <Classes.hpp>
 6: #include <Controls.hpp>
 7: #include <StdCtrls.hpp>
 8: #include <Forms.hpp>
 9: #include <ExtCtrls.hpp>
10: #include <Buttons.hpp>
11: #include <ComCtrls.hpp>
12: #include <Menus.hpp>
13: #include <Dialogs.hpp>
14: //-----------------------------------------------------------
15: class TScratchPad : public TForm
16: {
17: __published:    // IDE-managed Components
18:     TPanel *Panel1;
19:     TBevel *Bevel1;
20:     TSpeedButton *SpeedButton1;
21:     TSpeedButton *SpeedButton2;
22:     TStatusBar *StatusBar;
23:     TMainMenu *MainMenu;
24:     TMenuItem *FileMenu;
25:     TMenuItem *FileOpen;
26:     TMenuItem *FileSave;
27:     TMenuItem *FileSaveAs;
28:     TMenuItem *N1;
29:     TMenuItem *FilePrintSetup;
30:     TMenuItem *N2;
31:     TMenuItem *FileExit;
```

continues

Listing 7.1. continued

```
32:        TMenuItem *FilePrint;
33:        TMenuItem *Edit1;
34:        TMenuItem *EditReplace;
35:        TMenuItem *EditFind;
36:        TMenuItem *N4;
37:        TMenuItem *EditPaste;
38:        TMenuItem *EditCopy;
39:        TMenuItem *EditCut;
40:        TMenuItem *N5;
41:        TMenuItem *EditUndo;
42:        TMenuItem *Help1;
43:        TMenuItem *HelpAbout;
44:        TMenuItem *HelpContents;
45:        TMenuItem *EditSelectAll;
46:        TMenuItem *N3;
47:        TMenuItem *EditWordWrap;
48:        TOpenDialog *OpenDialog;
49:        TSaveDialog *SaveDialog;
50:        TMenuItem *FileNew;
51:        TMemo *Memo;
52:        void __fastcall FileOpenClick(TObject *Sender);
53:        void __fastcall FileSaveClick(TObject *Sender);
54:        void __fastcall FileSaveAsClick(TObject *Sender);
55:        void __fastcall FileExitClick(TObject *Sender);
56:        void __fastcall EditSelectAllClick(TObject *Sender);
57:        void __fastcall EditCutClick(TObject *Sender);
58:        void __fastcall EditCopyClick(TObject *Sender);
59:        void __fastcall EditPasteClick(TObject *Sender);
60:
61:
62:        void __fastcall EditWordWrapClick(TObject *Sender);
63:        void __fastcall FileNewClick(TObject *Sender);
64: private:          // User declarations
65: public:           // User declarations
66:     virtual __fastcall TScratchPad(TComponent* Owner);
67: };
68: //------------------------------------------------------------
69: extern TScratchPad *ScratchPad;
70: //------------------------------------------------------------
71: #endif
```

Listing 7.2. SPMAIN.CPP.

```
1: //------------------------------------------------------------
2: #include <vcl.h>
3: #pragma hdrstop
4: #include "SPMain.h"
5: //------------------------------------------------------------
6: #pragma resource "*.dfm"
7: TScratchPad *ScratchPad;
8: //------------------------------------------------------------
```

```
 9: __fastcall TScratchPad::TScratchPad(TComponent* Owner)
10:   : TForm(Owner)
11: {
12: }
13: //------------------------------------------------------------
14: void __fastcall TScratchPad::FileNewClick(TObject *Sender)
15: {
16:   //
17:   // Open a file. First check to see if the current file
18:   // needs to be saved.
19:   //
20:   if (Memo->Modified) {
21:     //
22:     // Display a message box.
23:     //
24:     int result = Application->MessageBox(
25:       "The current file has changed. Save changes?",
26:       "ScratchPad Message", MB_YESNOCANCEL);
27:     //
28:     // If Yes was clicked then save the current file.
29:     //
30:      if (result == IDYES) FileSaveClick(Sender);
31:     //
32:     // If No was clicked then do nothing.
33:     //
34:      if (result == IDCANCEL) return;
35:   }
36:   //
37:   // Delete the strings in the memo, if any.
38:   //
39:   if (Memo->Lines->Count > 0) Memo->Clear();
40:   //
41:   // Set the FileName property of the Save Dialog to a
42:   // blank string. This lets us know that the file has
43:   // not yet been saved.
44:   //
45:   SaveDialog->FileName = "";
46: }
47: //------------------------------------------------------------
48: void __fastcall TScratchPad::FileOpenClick(TObject *Sender)
49: {
50:   //
51:   // Open a file. First check to see if the current file needs
52:   // to be saved. Same logic as in FileNewClick() above.
53:   //
54:   if (Memo->Modified) {
55:     int result = Application->MessageBox(
56:       "The current file has changed. Save changes?",
57:       "ScratchPad Message", MB_YESNOCANCEL);
58:      if (result == IDYES) FileSaveClick(0);
59:      if (result == IDCANCEL) return;
60:   }
61:   //
62:   // Execute the File Open dialog. If OK was pressed then
63:   // open the file using the LoadFromFile() method. First
```

7

continues

Listing 7.2. continued

```
64:    // clear the FileName property.
65:    //
66:    OpenDialog->FileName = "";
67:    if (OpenDialog->Execute())
68:    {
69:      if (Memo->Lines->Count > 0) Memo->Clear();
70:      Memo->Lines->LoadFromFile(OpenDialog->FileName);
71:      SaveDialog->FileName = OpenDialog->FileName;
72:    }
73: }
74: //-------------------------------------------------------------
75: void __fastcall TScratchPad::FileSaveClick(TObject *Sender)
76: {
77:    //
78:    // If a filename has already been provided then there is
79:    // no need to bring up the File Save dialog. Just save the
80:    // file using SaveToFile().
81:    //
82:    if (SaveDialog->FileName != "")
83:    {
84:      Memo->Lines->SaveToFile(SaveDialog->FileName);
85:      //
86:      // Set Modified to false since we've just saved.
87:      //
88:      Memo->Modified = false;
89:    }
90:    //
91:    // If no filename was set then do a SaveAs().
92:    //
93:    else FileSaveAsClick(Sender);
94: }
95: //-------------------------------------------------------------
96: void __fastcall TScratchPad::FileSaveAsClick(TObject *Sender)
97: {
98:    //
99:    // Display the File Save dialog to save the file.
100:   // Set Modified to false since we just saved.
101:   //
102:   SaveDialog->Title = "Save As";
103:   if (SaveDialog->Execute())
104:   {
105:     Memo->Lines->SaveToFile(SaveDialog->FileName);
106:     Memo->Modified = false;
107:   }
108: }
109: //------------------------------------------------------------
110: void __fastcall TScratchPad::FileExitClick(TObject *Sender)
111: {
112:    //
113:    // All done. Close the form.
114:    //
115:    Close();
116: }
117: //------------------------------------------------------------
118: void __fastcall TScratchPad::EditUndoClick(TObject *Sender)
```

```
119: {
120:    //
121:    // TMemo doesn't have an Undo method so we have to send
122:    // a Windows WM_UNDO message to the memo component.
123:    //
124:    SendMessage(Memo->Handle, WM_UNDO, 0, 0);
125: }
126: //-------------------------------------------------------------
127: void __fastcall TScratchPad::EditSelectAllClick(TObject *Sndr)
128: {
129:    //
130:    // Just call TMemo::SelectAll().
131:    //
132:    Memo->SelectAll();
133: }
134: //-------------------------------------------------------------
135: void __fastcall TScratchPad::EditCutClick(TObject *Sender)
136: {
137:    //
138:    // Call TMemo::CutToClipboard().
139:    //
140:    Memo->CutToClipboard();
141: }
142: //-------------------------------------------------------------
143: void __fastcall TScratchPad::EditCopyClick(TObject *Sender)
144: {
145:    //
146:    // Call TMemo::CopyToClipboard().
147:    //
148:    Memo->CopyToClipboard();
149: }
150: //-------------------------------------------------------------
151: void __fastcall TScratchPad::EditPasteClick(TObject *Sender)
152: {
153:    //
154:    // Call TMemo::PasteFromClipboard().
155:    //
156:    Memo->PasteFromClipboard();
157: }
158: //-------------------------------------------------------------
159: void __fastcall TScratchPad::EditWordWrapClick(TObject *Sender)
160: {
161:    //
162:    // Toggle the TMemo::WordWrap property. Set the Checked
163:    // property of the menu item to the same value as WordWrap.
164:    //
165:    Memo->WordWrap = !Memo->WordWrap;
166:    EditWordWrap->Checked = Memo->WordWrap;
167:    //
168:    // If WordWrap is on then we only need the vertical scroll
169:    // bar. If it's off, then we need both scroll bars.
170:    //
171:    if (Memo->WordWrap) Memo->ScrollBars = ssVertical;
172:    else Memo->ScrollBars = ssBoth;
173: }
174: //-------------------------------------------------------------
```

7

And Now, the Moment You've All Been Waiting For

After you have created the event handlers for the menu items, you are ready to run the program. Click the Run button and the program should compile and run. If you get compiler errors, carefully compare your source code with the code in Listing 7.2. Make any changes and click the Run button again. You might have to go through this process a few times before the program will compile and run. Eventually, though, it will run (I promise!).

When the program runs, you will find a program that, although not yet 100 percent feature-complete, acts a lot like Windows Notepad. Even though we have a few things to add before we're finished, we have a fairly good start—especially when you consider the actual time involved up to this point. Figure 7.22 shows the ScratchPad program running.

Figure 7.22.

The ScratchPad *program in action.*

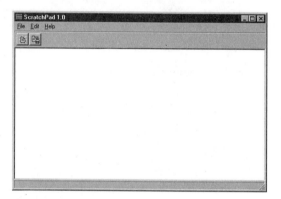

Pop-Up Menus (Context Menus)

We're not quite done with our discussion of menus. In C++Builder, you can create pop-up menus as easily as you can a main menu. A nice feature of C++Builder is that you can assign a particular pop-up menu to a component via the component's PopupMenu property. When the cursor is placed over the component and the secondary mouse button is clicked, that pop-up will automatically be displayed. Writing event handlers for pop-up menus is exactly the same as writing event handlers for main menus.

A common feature of text-editing programs is to place the Cut, Copy, and Paste operations on a context menu. We'll add that capability to ScratchPad. To create the pop-up, we'll cheat and copy part of the main menu. Here we go:

1. Choose a PopupMenu component from the Component palette and place it on the form.

2. Change the Name property to MemoPopup.

3. Double-click the PopupMenu icon to run the Menu Designer.

4. Click the secondary mouse button to bring up the Menu Designer context menu. Choose Select Menu from the context menu. A dialog box is displayed that shows the menus available for your application. Choose MainMenu and click OK.

5. Click on the Edit menu. Click on the Cut menu item, hold down the Shift key, and click on the Paste menu item. Cut, Copy, and Paste are all now highlighted.

6. To copy the selected items to the Clipboard, choose Edit | Copy from the C++Builder main menu (don't choose Edit | Copy from the menu you are creating in the Menu Designer) or press Ctrl+C.

7. Again, choose Select Menu from the Menu Designer context menu. This time, choose MemoPopup and click OK. The Menu Designer shows a blank pop-up menu.

8. Choose Edit | Paste from the main menu or type Ctrl+V on the keyboard. The Cut, Copy, and Paste menu items are inserted into the pop-up.

Okay, just a few more things and we'll be done. We need to change the Name property for the new menu items:

1. For the Cut menu item, change the Name property to PopupCut.

2. For the Copy menu item, change the Name property to PopupCopy.

3. For the Paste menu item, change the Name property to PopupPaste.

The final step is to write event handlers for the pop-up menu items. Hmmm…we have already written code for the main menu's Cut, Copy, and Paste items. It would be a shame to duplicate that effort (even if it is just a single line in each case). Could we just use the same event handlers that we created earlier? Sure we can. Just follow these steps:

1. Click on the Cut pop-up menu item.

2. Click on the Events tab in the Object Inspector.

3. Click the drop-down arrow button in the Value column next to the OnClick event (the only event in the list). A list of event handlers created so far is displayed.

4. Choose the EditCutClick event handler from the list. Now, when the Cut pop-up menu item is clicked, the Edit | Cut handler will be called. No code duplication is required.

5. Repeat Steps 1 through 4 for the Copy and Paste items on the pop-up menu. When you are done, close the Menu Designer.

6. On the main form, click on the Memo component. Change the PopupMenu property to MemoPopup (by choosing it from the list).

You can attach just about any event to any event handler by using this method. Now run the program again to test the new context menu. Of course it works!

7

TIP

You can attach a speed button OnClick event to an existing event handler just as easily as you did with the pop-up menu. Click the File Open speed button on your form. Locate the OnClick event in the Object Inspector and select the FileOpenClick event handler. Repeat this for the File Save speed button, except choose the FileSaveClick event handler.

Creating and Saving Menu Templates

C++Builder provides you with several menu templates that you can insert into your main menus and pop-ups. You can also create and save your own templates for future use in your programs. First, start the Menu Designer and create the menu.

NOTE

When creating menus to use as templates, you first must have a main menu or a pop-up menu on a form in order to start the Menu Designer. You can use a temporary, blank form if you want. Start with a blank form, place a MainMenu component on it, and double-click the Menu component's icon to start the Menu Designer. After you are done creating menu templates, discard the blank form without saving.

When you have created the menu, choose Save As Template from the Menu Designer's context menu. The Save Template dialog box is displayed. Give the menu a meaningful name and click the OK button; the menu is saved as a template. To insert the menu, choose Insert From Template from the Menu Designer's context menu just as you did earlier. Any menus you have created will show up along with C++Builder's prebuilt templates.

To remove a template that you previously added, choose Delete Templates from the Menu Designer's context menu. The Delete Templates dialog box is displayed, and you can choose the templates you want to delete. When you click the OK button, the selected menu templates will be deleted. Press Cancel to close the dialog box without deleting any templates.

Summary

Congratulations! You have just covered the bulk of the C++Builder visual programming features. I hope it was enjoyable as well as educational. The Form Designer is a powerful tool that enables you to do as much programming as possible visually. If you haven't had to place controls on a window in C or C++, you might not fully appreciate that advantage. Trust me, it's significant. The Menu Designer is also a powerful tool, particularly because of the capability to import menus, which makes menu creation easy and actually fun with C++Builder. The Menu Designer also makes updating existing menus a snap.

Workshop

The Workshop contains quiz questions to help you solidify your understanding of the material covered and exercises to provide you with experience in using what you have learned. Answers to the quiz questions are found in Appendix A, "Answers to Quiz Questions."

Q&A

Q **I'm using the Alignment palette a lot, and every time I switch from the Code Editor back to the Form Designer, the Alignment palette gets lost somewhere. Is there anything I can do about that?**

A Locate the Alignment palette (it's there somewhere!) and click your secondary mouse button to bring up the Alignment palette's context menu. Choose the Stay on Top item from the context menu. Now the Alignment palette will always be on top where you can find it.

Q **I am trying to select a group of components on a panel by dragging the selection rectangle around them, but I keep moving the panel. What's wrong?**

A You need to hold down the Ctrl key while dragging when you are selecting components contained on a panel.

Q **I've moved my components around my form several times and now the tab order is erratic. What can I do to fix that?**

A Choose Tab Order from the Form Designer's context menu. Arrange the tab order the way you want it. When you click OK, the new tab order will be implemented.

Q **The menu templates provided are nice, but they have so much stuff on them that I don't need. What can I do about that?**

A You can do two things. First, you can import a menu and then simply delete the items you don't want. Using the click/Shift+click method, you can get rid of unwanted menu items in just a few seconds. Deleting items from a menu inserted from a template has no adverse effects. The second thing you can do is to use the click/Shift+click method and then, when you have the menu just the way you want it, save it as a new template. That way you can keep the original C++Builder-supplied template and have your customized template as well.

Q **Can I save my own menus as templates?**

A Yes. First create the menu and then choose Save As Template from the Menu Designer context menu. Give the template a name, click OK, and the template is saved. Now all you have to do to reuse the menu later is insert the menu using the Insert From Template feature.

7

Quiz

1. When do you use Ctrl+drag in selecting components?
2. What significance does the first component selected have when aligning a group of components?
3. What is the quickest method to select a group of components?
4. How can you make a group of components all have the width of the group's widest component?
5. What happens when you double-click a component on a form?
6. What does the `Align` property's `alClient` option do?
7. What does the ellipsis following a menu item mean?
8. What two ways can you move a menu item?
9. How do you add menu accelerators to menu items?
10. How do you initially disable a menu item?

Exercises

1. Place five edit components on a form and arrange them so that they are stacked vertically with their left edges aligned.
2. Turn the Snap to Grid option off (choose Tools | Environment Options from the main menu). Place five controls of your choice on a form and align their right edges.
3. Place a `ListBox` component on a blank form and modify it so that it always occupies the form's entire client area.
4. Add an About box to the `ScratchPad` program. Use the Alignment palette to quickly align the text labels.
5. Add an Undo item and a menu separator to the context menu for the `ScratchPad` program.
6. Start a new application. Place six edit components on a form in random fashion. Now arrange the tab order so that tabbing proceeds from top to bottom. Run the program to test the tabbing order.
7. Add toolbar buttons for Cut, Copy, and Paste to the `ScratchPad` program, as well as any others you want to add. Assign the menu event handlers for the same functions to the speed buttons.
8. Add the Ctrl+S keyboard shortcut to the File | Save menu item in the `ScratchPad` program.
9. Open the Picture Viewer project you created on Day 6. Remove all unused menu items.

In Review

You covered a lot of ground this week. In some ways this was the toughest week. C++ is not an easy language to learn. But there is no doubt that you can learn to be a C++ programmer if you stay with it. Don't forget to take a break now and then. This book is titled *Teach Yourself Borland C++Builder 3 in 21 Days*, but that doesn't mean they have to be consecutive days! Sometimes it's good to take a few days off to let it all soak in.

If you are confused by some of the C++ syntax, don't feel you are alone. Pointers and references; * versus &; direct and indirect operators...it can all be confusing at first. Don't worry, though, because you will start to get the hang of it before long. As you work with C++Builder, little by little it begins to make sense. What you probably lack at this point is real-world experience. That is where you really learn. Knowledge gained by experience is the kind that really sticks. My advice is to take an idea and turn it into a working program. You can't necessarily do that at this point, but you can get a good start. The program doesn't have to be a Word, a Netscape Navigator, or an Excel program, mind you. It just needs to be a little something to help you tie your education in with some experience.

The first part of this week you worked on C++ language keywords and syntax. Things such as loops and if statements are easy to comprehend. Don't be concerned, though, if you have to go back and look up the syntax once in a while. There is a lot to learn, and you aren't expected to memorize every keyword and its syntax. Later on you will, but at this stage of the game it isn't expected.

Toward the middle of the week you were introduced to structures and then to C++ classes. Classes are the bulk of what C++ is about. The things we discussed on Days 1, 2, and 3 are primarily features of the C++ language that come from the C language. Classes, though, are pure C++. Sometimes it takes a while to perceive where classes can be used in your programs. For a long time you might deal only with the classes that the VCL provides and not write any classes of your own. Later on you will probably find situations where a class would fit perfectly with a particular task you have to accomplish. When that time comes, you will be ready to tackle writing your own class. After you've written one or two, you will be off and running.

On Day 5, I gave you an introduction to class libraries, also known as *frameworks*. VCL is a framework. A framework makes your life easier by encapsulating difficult Windows programming tasks into classes that you can deal with on a more rational level. Believe me, sometimes the raw Windows API seems to be anything but rational. VCL takes care of dealing with those issues for you and provides you with a higher level of programming objects that you can easily incorporate in your applications. No, VCL is not easy, but it is much easier than dealing with the API that VCL shields you from. As part of the discussion on frameworks, you were introduced to the PME (properties, methods, and events) model. You learned about properties, methods, and events, and how you use them to build Windows programs in C++Builder.

At the end of this first week, you were able to play around with the IDE a little. You learned about the IDE: how to customize it to your liking, how the Component palette works, what the Object Inspector is for, and how to use the Menu Designer. This part of the week you experienced the fun stuff. It's okay to use the word *fun*. I find all kinds of programming a great deal of fun. That's why I do it. I hope that you find it fun, too.

Finally, you ended the week by learning all about the Form Designer. The Form Designer is where the bulk of your C++Builder applications will be designed—the graphical part of the application, anyway. Working with the Form Designer can be fun, too. Using the Form Designer, you can create great-looking forms. Remember, a form represents a window in your applications. Most applications have a main window and several dialog boxes that are displayed, based on user interaction with the program. The Form Designer gives you an advantage that you can't appreciate unless you have had to design dialog boxes with more traditional programming tools. The resource editors that come with Borland C++ or Visual C++ are great, but they are no match for C++Builder when it comes to building forms. Being able to place forms and set their properties at design time gives you a big edge when it comes to beating the competition to market. C++Builder's visual programming model is both powerful and easy to use. What could be better?

On Day 7 you created a simple, but useful, program. This program, ScratchPad, gave you a start in building an application with C++Builder. We are going to use ScratchPad throughout the book. As you build your programming knowledge, we will add new features to ScratchPad to give you practice with the techniques presented. If you are developing an application of your own, I encourage you to add new features to your program as you learn about them.

I hope this week hasn't left you too worn out. If it has, take a short break and then jump right back into the game. If you found this week exhilarating and energizing, then just keep on turnin' those pages. I'm ready if you are.

WEEK

2

At a Glance

Are you ready for the fun stuff? This week you learn about Windows programming in earnest. I start with a discussion of components that goes well beyond the introduction you had during Week 1. You find out about specific components and how to use them. You will spend some time reading and, I hope, a lot of time experimenting. Reading this book is not a race. The first one done does not receive a prize. Better to be the tortoise than the hare when it comes to learning programming. Take time to experiment.

This week you learn about creating applications by using C++Builder's wizards. These wizards help you get a program up and running in minimum time. After that you learn about debugging your programs. Yes, your programs will have bugs. Don't fight it. Just learn how to find those nasty critters in your programs and squash them. Debugging is a vital application development tool, and you must learn how to debug your programs. Knowing how to use the debugger will save you hours and hours of effort in the long run.

Finally, late in the week you begin more advanced programming techniques, such as status bars, toolbars, and printing. On Day 14 you learn how to use context help and how to use the Windows Registry to store information for your program. I think you'll like what you find there. By the end of the week, you will be on a steamroller that can't be stopped.

Day 8

VCL Components

As you know by now, components are much of what gives C++Builder its power. Components are designed using the properties, methods, and events model. Using the Form Designer, you can place a component on a form and modify its design-time properties. In some cases, that's all you have to do. If needed, you can also manipulate the component at runtime by changing its properties and calling its methods. Further, each component is designed to respond to certain events. I discussed properties, methods, and events on Day 5, "C++ Class Frameworks and the Visual Component Model," so I'm not going to go over that again.

Today you will find out more about components. You will learn about often-used components and, as a result, learn about the VCL classes that represent those components. As you go through this chapter, feel free to experiment. If you read something that you want to test, by all means do so. Learning by experience is as valuable as anything you can do, so don't be afraid to experiment.

Review

Let's review some of what you already know about components. But first, I want to take a moment to explain the differences between a VCL component and a

Windows control. Windows controls include things such as edit controls, list boxes, combo boxes, static controls (labels), and buttons, not to mention all the Windows 95 controls. Windows controls, by nature, don't have properties, methods, and events. Instead, messages are used to tell the control what to do or to get information from the control. To say that dealing with controls on this level is tedious and cumbersome would be an understatement.

A VCL component is a class that encapsulates a Windows control (not all VCL components encapsulate controls, though). A VCL component in effect adds properties, methods, and events to a Windows control to make working with the control easier. You might say that VCL takes a fresh approach to working with Windows controls. It could be said that all VCL components are controls, but not all controls are components. A VCL Edit component, for instance, is a control, but a standard Windows edit control is not a VCL component. VCL components work with Windows controls to raise the job of dealing with those controls to a higher level.

Given that discussion, then, I will use the terms *control* and *component* interchangeably when referring to VCL components. (But I will never call a Windows control a component!)

Visual components include things like edit controls, buttons, list boxes, labels, and so on. Most components you will use in a C++Builder application are visual components. Visual components, as much as possible, show you at design time what the component will look like when the program runs.

NEW TERM Some components are visual components; others are nonvisual components. A *visual component*, as its name implies, is one that can be seen by the user.

NEW TERM A *nonvisual component* is one that cannot be seen by the user.

Nonvisual components work behind the scenes to perform specific programming tasks. Examples include system timers, database components, and image lists. Common dialog boxes like File Open, File Save, Font, and so on are considered nonvisual components as well. (They are nonvisual because they don't show themselves at design time. At runtime, they become visible when they are invoked.) When you place a nonvisual component on a form, C++Builder displays an icon representing the component on the form. This icon is used to access the component at design time in order to change the component's properties, but the icon does not show up when the program runs. Nonvisual components have properties, methods, and events just as visual components do.

The Name Property

The Name property serves a vital role in components. On Day 5 in the section "VCL Explored," I discussed some of what happens when you place a component on a form. As soon as you place a component on a form, C++Builder goes to work in the background while you

ponder your next move. One thing C++Builder does is create a pointer to the component and assign the `Name` property as the variable name. For example, let's say you place an `Edit` component on a form and change the `Name` property to `MyEdit`. At that point C++Builder places the following in the header file for the form:

```
TEdit* MyEdit;
```

When the application runs, C++Builder creates an instance of the `TEdit` class and assigns it to `MyEdit`. You can use this pointer to access the component at runtime. To set the text for the edit control, you would use

```
MyEdit->Text = "Jenna Lynn";
```

C++Builder also uses the `Name` property when creating event-handler names. Let's say that you want to respond to the `OnChange` event for an `Edit` component. Normally, you double-click the Value column next to the `OnChange` event to have C++Builder generate an event handler for the event. C++Builder creates a default function name based on the `Name` property of the component and the event being handled. In this case, C++Builder would generate a function called `MyEditChange()`.

You can change the `Name` property at any time, provided that you change it *only* via the Object Inspector. When you change a component's `Name` property at design time, C++Builder goes through all the code that it had previously generated and changes the name of the pointer and all event-handling functions.

NOTE

C++Builder will change all the code generated by C++Builder to reflect the new value of the component's `Name` property, but it will not modify any code you wrote. In other words, C++Builder will take care of modifying the code it wrote, but it is up to you to update and maintain the code you wrote. Generally speaking, you should change the `Name` property when you initially place the component on the form and leave it alone after that.

Continuing with this example, if you change the `Name` property of the edit control from `MyEdit` to `FirstName`, C++Builder will change the pointer name to `FirstName` and the `OnChange` handler name to `FirstNameChange()`. It's all done automatically; you don't have to do anything but change the `Name` property and trust that C++Builder will do the rest of the work.

WARNING Never change the Name property at runtime. Never manually change a component's name (the name that C++Builder assigned to the component's pointer) or event-handler names in the Code Editor. If you perform either of these actions, C++Builder loses track of components and the results are not good, to say the least. You might even lose the ability to load your form. The only safe way to change the Name property of a component is through the Object Inspector.

C++Builder assigns a default value to the Name property for all components placed on a form. If you place an Edit component, for example, C++Builder assigns Edit1 to the Name property. If you place a second Edit component on the form, C++Builder assigns Edit2 to that component's Name property, and so on. You should give your components meaningful names as soon as possible to avoid confusion and extra work later on.

NOTE You can leave the default names for components that will never be referenced in code. For example, if you have several label components that contain static (unchanging) text, you can leave the default names because you won't be accessing the components at runtime.

House Rules: The Name Property

☐ Change the Name property of a component from the default name to a meaningful name as soon as possible.

☐ Components not referenced at runtime can be left with the C++Builder-supplied name.

☐ Never change the Name property of a component in the class header or at runtime.

☐ Make your component's names meaningful but not overly long.

Important Common Properties

All components have certain properties in common. For instance, all visual components have Left and Top properties that determine where the component is placed on the form. Properties such as Left, Top, Height, and Width are self-explanatory, so I won't go over them. A few of the common properties, however, warrant a closer look.

Align

On Day 7, "Working with the Form Designer and the Menu Designer," I discussed the Align and Alignment properties, so I won't go over those again in detail. Refer back to Day 7 for complete information on Align. It should be noted here, however, that not all components expose the Align property at design time. A single-line edit control, for instance, should occupy a standard height, so the features of the Align property do not make sense for that type of component. As you gain experience with C++Builder, and depending on the type of applications you write, you will probably rely heavily on the Align property.

Color

The Color property sets the background color for the component. (The text color is set through the Font property.) Although the Color property is simple to use, there are a few aspects of component colors that should be pointed out.

The way the Color property is handled in the Object Inspector is somewhat unique. If you click the Value column, you will see the drop-down arrow button indicating that you can choose from a list of color values. That is certainly the case, but there's more to it than that. If you double-click the Value column, the Color dialog box will be displayed. This dialog box allows you to choose a color from one of the predefined colors or to create your own colors by clicking the Define Custom Colors button. Figure 8.1 shows the Color dialog box after the Define Custom Colors button has been clicked.

Figure 8.1.

The Color dialog box.

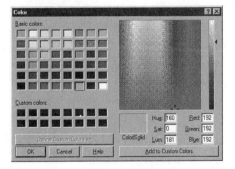

NOTE

This is the same Color dialog box that will be displayed if you implement the ColorDialog component in your application.

If you choose a color from the Color dialog box, you will see that the value of the Color property changes to a hexadecimal string. This string represents the red, green, and blue (RGB) values that make up the color. If you know the exact RGB value of a color, you can type it in (not likely!).

Most of the time you will probably choose a color from the list of color values provided. When you click the drop-down button to display the list of possible values, you will see what amounts to two groups of values. The first group of colors begins with clBlack and ends with clWhite. These are the C++Builder predefined colors; this list represents the most commonly used colors. To choose one of the listed colors, click the color in the list. If you can't find a color in the list that suits your needs, you can invoke the Color dialog box as I've discussed.

The second group of colors in the list begins with clScrollBar. This group of colors represents the Windows system colors. If you use colors from this list, your application will automatically adjust its colors when the user changes color schemes in Windows. If you want your application to follow the color scheme the user has chosen for his or her system, you should choose colors from this list rather than from the first list.

Use of color should be carefully considered. Proper use of color provides an aesthetically pleasing environment for the user. Abuse of colors makes for an obnoxious application that is annoying to use. Color is like a magnet to new programmers. It is common to want to throw lots of colors on a form because it's fun and easy, but don't get caught up in the fun at the expense of your users.

House Rules: Colors

- [ ] Use color for accent and emphasis.
- [ ] Don't use loud colors that are hard on the eyes.
- [ ] Use the system colors in your application where appropriate. If the user changes color schemes, your application will follow suit.
- [ ] Be consistent in your use of colors across your forms.

Cursors

The Cursor property controls the cursor that is displayed when the user moves the mouse cursor over the component. Windows automatically changes cursors for some components. For example, Windows changes the cursor to an I-beam when the cursor is moved over an Edit, Memo, or RichEdit component, to name just a few. To let Windows manage the cursor, leave the Cursor property set to crDefault. If you have specialized windows (components), you can specify one of the other cursors. When the mouse is moved over that component, Windows will change the cursor to the one you have specified.

Frequently you will need to change cursors at runtime. A long process, for instance, should be indicated to the user by displaying the hourglass cursor. When you reset the cursor, you need to be sure to set the cursor back to whatever it was originally. The following code snippet illustrates:

```
TCursor oldCursor = Screen->Cursor;
Screen->Cursor = crHourGlass;
// do some stuff which takes a long time
Screen->Cursor = oldCursor;
```

This ensures that the cursor that was originally set for the application is properly restored.

Another cursor property, DragCursor, is used to set the cursor that is used when the mouse cursor is over a component that supports drag and drop. As with colors, you should be prudent in your use of cursors. Use custom cursors when needed, but don't overdo it.

Enabled

Components can be enabled or disabled through the Enabled property. When a component is disabled, it cannot accept focus (clicking on it has no effect), and usually it gives some visual cue to indicate that it is disabled. In the case of buttons, for instance, the button text is grayed out, as is any bitmap on the button. Enabled is a Boolean property—set it to true to enable the component or set it to false to disable the component. Enabling and disabling windows (remember that windowed components are windows, too) is a feature of Windows itself.

NOTE   Some components show their disabled state at design time, but most don't. The BitBtn component is one that does show its disabled state at design time.

The Enabled property applies mostly to windowed components but can apply to non-windowed components as well. The SpeedButton component is an example of a non-windowed component that can be disabled.

NOTE   Modifying the Enabled property for a Panel component has additional implications. Panels are often used as containers for other controls. Therefore, a panel becomes the parent of the controls that are placed on the panel. If you disable a panel, the components on the panel will not show as disabled but will not function because their parent (the panel) is disabled.

Although components can be disabled at design time, enabling and disabling components is something that is usually done at runtime. Menu items, for instance, should be enabled or disabled according to whether they apply at a given time. The same is true of buttons. There are a variety of reasons why you might want to disable other types of controls as well.

To disable a component at runtime, just assign `false` to its `Enabled` property, and to enable a component, assign `true` to `Enabled`. The following code snippet enables or disables a menu item based on some condition:

```
if (saveEnabled) FileSave->Enabled = true;
else FileSave->Enabled = false;
```

This process is often referred to as *command enabling* and is an important part of a professional-looking Windows program.

Font

The `Font` property is a major property and therefore needs to be included here, but there is not a lot that needs to be said about it. The `Font` property is an instance of the `TFont` class and as such has its own properties. You can set the `Font` properties by double-clicking on the font name in the Object Inspector (which will expand the Font node and show the `Font` properties) or by invoking the Font dialog box. (The Font dialog box is discussed in more detail later in this chapter in the section "The Font Dialog Box.") Figure 8.2 shows the Object Inspector with the `Font` property node expanded to reveal the `TFont` properties.

Figure 8.2.

The Object Inspector showing the Font *property.*

The `Color` property sets the color of the font, and the `Name` property allows you to choose the typeface for the font.

The `Height` and `Size` properties of `TFont` deserve special mention. The `Height` property is used to specify the height of the font in pixels, whereas the `Size` property is used to specify the height of the font in points. When you change one of these properties, the other will change automatically. The `Height` is often specified as a negative number. Refer to the online help for `TFont` for an explanation of why this is the case.

The `Pitch` property is not particularly useful. I'll explain it in just a moment, but first a quick tutorial on fonts. A font can be either proportionally spaced or fixed space. Most fonts are proportionally spaced. This means that each letter only takes as much space as needed. For example, an uppercase *M* takes up much more space than a lowercase *i.* Take a look at the letters in this book and you will see what I mean. Examples of proportional fonts include

8

Times New Roman, Arial, and Bookman. With a fixed space font (typically called a fixed-pitch font), on the other hand, all characters take exactly the same amount of space. This is convenient for windows such as code editors (the C++Builder Code Editor, for instance) or any other window where a fixed-pitch font is desired. Courier New is probably the most commonly used fixed-pitch font, although Fixedsys is the Windows fixed-pitch font of choice in some Windows applications.

In theory, the Pitch property can be used to force a proportionally spaced font to fixed space and vice versa. The problem is that Windows might perform font substitutions to carry out the conversion. In other words, you really don't know what you might get. It is far better to pick exactly the font you require than to rely on the Pitch property.

Finally, the Style property of TFont can be used to toggle bold, italic, underline, or strikethrough. These styles are not mutually exclusive, so you can mix styles in any way you choose.

TIP

> Although you can use the Object Inspector to change font properties, the Font dialog box (invoked when you click the ellipsis button next to the Font property) has the added benefit of showing you a sample of what the font looks like as you choose different font options. To simply change the font's Style property or Size property, use the Object Inspector. If you are looking for just the right font, the Font dialog box is a better choice.

Hint

The Hint property is used to set hint text for a component. The hint text has two parts. The first part is sometimes called the *short hint*. This is the hint text that is displayed when the user places the cursor over the component and pauses. The pop-up window that displays the hint text is called a *ToolTip*.

The second part of the hint text is sometimes called the *long hint*. The long hint is the optional hint text that will show in the status bar when the user moves the mouse cursor over the component. The short and long hint texts are separated by a pipe (¦). For example, to specify both the short hint text and the long hint text for a File Open speed button, you would enter the following for the Hint property:

```
File Open¦Open a file for editing
```

In order for short hints to show, you must have the Application object's ShowHint property set to true (the default) as well as the component's ShowHint property. Displaying the long hint in the status bar requires a little more work, so I'll save that discussion for tomorrow.

> **NOTE**
> You can specify the short hint text, the long hint text, or both. You can use the pipe to tell C++Builder which hint text you are supplying. If you don't use the pipe, both the short hint and the long hint will use the same text.

`ParentColor`, `ParentCtl3D`, `ParentFont`, and `ParentShowHint`

The `ParentColor`, `ParentCtl3D`, `ParentFont`, and `ParentShowHint` properties work the same way, so I'll discuss them at the same time. When these properties are set to `true`, the component takes its `Color`, `Ctl3D`, `Font`, or `ShowHint` settings from its parent. For example, for most components the `ParentFont` property is set to `true` by default. This means the component will inherit the font that its parent is currently using. To illustrate, do this exercise:

1. Create a blank form. Set the `Font` property's `Size` property to 16.
2. Place a `Label` component on the form. Notice that the label automatically uses the 16 point font.
3. Place a `Button` component on the form. It also uses the 16 point font.

You can set this property to `false`, but by the time the component is placed, it is already too late and you will have to change the font manually to the font you want for the component.

Tag

The `Tag` property is nothing more than a 4 byte variable set aside for your use. You can use the `Tag` property to store any data that your component might need. The data stored might be a pointer to another class, an index value, or any number of other possibilities. Using the `Tag` property would probably be considered an advanced programming technique.

Other Common Properties

Table 8.1 lists other common properties that are frequently used. These properties don't require as much explanation, so they are listed here for your reference. Not all components have each of the properties listed.

Table 8.1. Additional component properties.

Property	Description
BorderStyle	Can be bsSingle or bsNone. Use bsNone when you want the component to blend in with the background.

Property	Description
Caption	Sets the component's caption. Many components don't have captions, so for those components the Caption property is not exposed.
Ctl3D	Indicates whether the control should be drawn with a 3D border. If BorderStyle is set to bsNone, this property has no effect.
Height	Sets the component's height.
HelpContext	Associates an index number in a help file with a particular component.
Left	Sets the x-coordinate of the component.
PopupMenu	Specifies the pop-up menu that will be displayed when the user clicks the secondary mouse button.
TabOrder	Sets this component's position in the tab order. For windowed components.
TabStop	Indicates that this component can be tabbed into. Setting this property to false removes the component from the tab order. For windowed components.
Top	Sets the y-coordinate of the component.
Visible	Indicates whether the component is currently visible when read. Either hides or shows the component when written to.
Width	Sets the width of the component.

Primary Methods of Components

There are more than 20 methods that most components have in common. Windowed components have more than 40 common methods from which to choose. Interestingly, not many of these are widely used. Much of the functionality of components is accomplished via properties. For example, to hide a component, you can call the Hide() method or you can set the Visible property to false. In addition, components typically have methods specific to their purpose, and it will likely be those methods that you use most when dealing with a particular component.

There are a few methods worthy of note, however, so I'll list them here (see Table 8.2). Note that some of these methods are not available to all controls. These are not the most often used methods common to every component, but rather the most commonly used methods of components in general. Also, this list concentrates on components representing controls (components placed on forms) rather than components as forms. Methods particular to forms were discussed on Day 6, "The C++Builder IDE Explored."

Table 8.2. Common methods of components.

Method	Description
Broadcast	Used to send a message to all windowed child components.
ClientToScreen	Converts client window coordinates into screen coordinates.
ContainsControl	Returns true if the specified component is a child of the component or form.
HandleAllocated	Returns true if the Handle property for the component has been created. Simply reading the Handle property automatically creates a handle if it hasn't already been created, so HandleAllocated() can be used to check for the existence of the handle without creating it.
Hide	Hides the component. The component is still available to be shown again later.
Invalidate	Requests that the component be redrawn. The component will be redrawn at Windows's earliest convenience.
Perform	Sends a message directly to a component rather than go through the Windows messaging system.
Refresh	Requests that a component be redrawn immediately and erases the component before repainting.
Repaint	Requests that a component be redrawn immediately. The component's background is not erased before repainting.
SetBounds	Enables you to set the Top, Left, Width, and Height properties all at one time. This saves time having to set them individually.
SetFocus	Sets the focus to a component and makes it the active component. Applies only to windowed components.
Update	Forces an immediate repaint of the control. Typically, you should use Refresh or Repaint to repaint components.

Now let's take a look at some of the events to which a component is most likely to respond.

Common Events

As with properties and methods, there are some events that will be responded to most often. Components cover a wide variety of possible Windows controls, so each component will have individual needs. Events specific to forms are not covered here because I covered that information on Day 6. The most commonly used events are listed in Table 8.3.

Table 8.3. Commonly handled component events.

Event	Description
OnChange	This event is triggered when a control changes in one way or another. Exact implementation depends on the component.
OnClick	This event is sent when the component is clicked with either mouse button.
OnDblClick	This event occurs when the user double-clicks the component.
OnEnter	This event occurs when a windowed component receives focus (is activated).
OnExit	This event occurs when a windowed component loses focus as the result of the user switching to a different control. It does not occur, however, when the user switches forms or switches to another application.
OnKeyDown	This event is triggered when the user presses a key while the control has focus. Keys include all alphanumeric keys as well as keys such as the arrow keys, Home, End, Ctrl, and so on.
OnKeyPress	This event is also triggered when the user presses a key, but only when alphanumeric keys or the Tab, Back Space, Enter, or Esc keys are pressed.
OnKeyUp	This event occurs whenever a key is released.
OnMouseDown	This event is triggered when the mouse button is pressed while over the component. The parameters passed to the event handler give you information on which mouse button was clicked, special keys that were pressed (Alt, Shift, Ctrl), and the x,y coordinate of the mouse pointer when the event occurred.
OnMouseMove	This event occurs any time the mouse is moved over the control.
OnMouseUp	This event is triggered when the mouse button is released while over a control. The mouse button must first have been clicked while on the control.
OnPaint	This event is sent any time a component needs repainting. You can respond to this event to do any custom painting a component requires.

Dealing with Mouse Events

Mouse events have a couple of peculiarities that you should be aware of. If you are responding just to a mouse click on a component, you will want to keep it simple and only respond to the OnClick event. If you must use OnMouseDown and OnMouseUp, you should be aware that the OnClick event will be sent as well as the OnMouseDown and OnMouseUp events. For example, a single click will result in these events occurring (and in this order):

```
OnMouseDown
OnClick
OnMouseUp
```

Similarly, when the user double-clicks with the mouse, it could result in the application getting more events than you might think. When a component is double-clicked, the following events occur:

```
OnMouseDown
OnClick
OnDblClick
OnMouseUp
```

The point I am trying to make is that you need to take care when responding to both double-click and single-click events for a component. Be aware that you will get four events for a double-click event.

Multiple events will occur when a key is pressed, too. A keypress in an edit control, for instance, will result in OnKeyDown, OnKeyPress, OnChange, and OnKeyUp events occurring.

In just a moment we're going to look at some of the VCL components in more detail. First, however, I want to introduce you to a class that is used by certain VCL components.

TStrings

The TStrings class is a VCL class that manages lists of strings. Several VCL components use instances of TStrings to manage their data (usually text). For example, on Day 7 you used TStrings when you built the ScratchPad application. "I don't recall using a TStrings class," you say. Well, you did, but you just weren't aware of it. Remember when we saved and loaded files? You used something like this:

```
Memo->Lines->SaveToFile(SaveDialog->FileName);
```

8

The Lines property of TMemo is an instance of the TStrings class. The SaveToFile() method of TStrings takes the strings and saves them to a file on disk. You can do the same thing to load a list box from a file on disk or save the contents of a list box to disk. In the case of the TListBox class, the property that holds the list box items is called Items. For example, do this exercise:

1. Create a new application and place a ListBox component on the form. Size the list box as desired.

2. Change the Name property of the list box to ListBox.

3. Double-click the background of the form (not on the list box). The Code Editor displays the FormCreate() function.

4. Type the following code in the FormCreate() function:
```
char winDir[256], fileName[256];
GetWindowsDirectory(winDir, sizeof(winDir));
sprintf(fileName, "%s\\win.ini", winDir);
ListBox->Items->LoadFromFile(fileName);
```

5. Click the Run button to compile and run the program.

When the program runs, the list box will contain the contents of your WIN.INI file. Using this method, it's easy to load a list box from any ASCII text data file. The ComboBox component also has an Items property, and it works in exactly the same way.

You can add, delete, insert, and move items in a list box, combo box, or memo by calling the Add(), Append(), Delete(), Insert(), and Move() methods of the TStrings class.

NOTE
> How Add() performs depends on the value of the Sorted property. If the Sorted property is set to true, Add() will insert the string where it needs to be in the list of items. If Sorted is false, the new string will be added at the end of the list.

A component can be cleared of its contents by calling the Clear() method. An individual string can be accessed by using the Strings property of TStrings and the array subscript operator. For example, to retrieve the first string in a list of strings, you would use

```
Edit->Text = ListBox->Items->Strings[0];
```

Each string in a TStrings array contains the string itself and four bytes of extra storage. This extra storage can be accessed through the Objects property. You can use the extra storage any way you like. Let's say, for example, that you were creating an owner-drawn list box that displayed bitmaps. You could store the string in the usual way, plus store a pointer to the TBitmap object in the Objects array.

TIP

There might be times when you need to manage a list of strings unrelated to a component. The TStringList class is provided for exactly that purpose. This class works just like TStrings but can be used outside components.

NOTE

In reality TStrings is what is called an *abstract base class*. An abstract base class is never used directly but only serves as a base class from which to derive other classes. The Lines property is actually an instance of the TMemoStrings class instead of the TStrings class, as I said in this section. This can be confusing because the Lines property *is* declared as a TStrings pointer but is actually an instance of TMemoStrings. Translating this into C++ might look something like this:

```
TStrings* Lines;
Lines = new TMemoStrings;
```

This is why the Lines property appears to be a TStrings but is really not. I didn't mean to lead you astray, but I thought it was best to make this distinction after the discussion on TStrings rather than confuse you with this information during that discussion.

Standard Windows Control Components

Back in the Jurassic age, there was something called Windows 3.0. Windows 3.0 gave us things like edit controls (single line and multiline), list boxes, combo boxes, buttons, check boxes, radio buttons, and static controls. These controls must have been fairly well designed because they are prevalent in Windows programs today—even considering all the new Win32 controls.

8

I'm not going to go over every Windows control and its corresponding VCL component. There are a few things, though, that you should know regarding the standard components that I will point out.

Edit Controls

C++Builder comes with four edit-control components. The `Edit`, `Memo`, and `MaskEdit` components are based on the standard Windows edit control. The `RichEdit` component is based on the Win32 rich edit control, which is not one of the standard Windows controls. Still, I will discuss `RichEdit` here because it has many things in common with the other edit controls.

The `Edit` component encapsulates the basic single-line edit control. This component has no `Align` or `Alignment` property. It has no `Alignment` property because the text in a single-line edit control can only be left-justified. The `Edit` component has no `Align` property because it cannot (or more accurately, should not) be expanded to fill the client area of a window.

TIP

If you need text in an edit component to be right-justified or centered, use a `Memo` component but make its height the height of a standard `Edit` component. Then set the `Alignment` property as needed.

NOTE

Keep your forms standard whenever possible. Although you can make an `Edit` component as tall as you like, it will confuse users if you make its height greater than a standard Windows edit control (it might appear to the user to be a multiline edit).

The `MaskEdit` component is an `Edit` component with an input filter, or mask, attached. The `MaskEdit` does not represent a Windows control per se but rather is just a VCL extension of a standard edit control. A mask is used to force input to a specific range of numbers or characters. In addition, the mask can contain special characters that are placed in the edit control by default. For example, a date is commonly formatted as follows:

10/25/97

An edit mask for a date can already have the slashes in place, so the user only has to enter the numbers. The edit mask specifies that only numbers can be entered to avoid the possibility of the user entering a nonnumeric character.

NOTE

> The DateTimePicker component (found on the Win32 tab) enables you to pick a date or a time from a specialized edit component. When the Kind property is set to dtkDate, the component displays a drop-down calendar from which the user can choose a date. When Kind property is set to dtkTime, the DateTimePicker displays a multi-field edit control that enables the user to set the hours, minutes, seconds, and AM or PM. The DateTimePicker is preferred over the MaskEdit for date and time entry.

The EditMask property controls the mask used. When you press the ellipsis button in the Value column for the EditMask property, the Input Mask Editor is displayed. This dialog box enables you to choose from one of the predefined masks or to create your own. You can choose prebuilt masks from several countries. Figure 8.3 shows the Input Mask Editor displaying the United Kingdom set of predefined input masks.

Figure 8.3.

The Input Mask Editor.

For more information on building your own masks, see the C++Builder online help.

The Memo component encapsulates a multiline edit control. The Lines property is the most significant property in a Memo component. As I mentioned earlier in the discussion on TStrings, the Lines property enables you to save the contents of the Memo component to disk or load the Memo with text from a file, as well as other things. The ScrollBars property is unique to the Memo component. This property enables you to specify whether your component has a horizontal scrollbar, a vertical scrollbar, or both. You used the ScrollBars property on Day 7 when you wrote the ScratchPad application. The Memo component is a very versatile component that you will probably find yourself using frequently.

The RichEdit component is the biggest and the best of all the edit components. It is based on the Win32 rich edit control. The RichEdit component enables you to change fonts, use indentation, set text to bold, italic, or underlined, and much more. Basically, the RichEdit component is a mini word processor in one neat package. RichEdit has, surprisingly, only a few more design-time properties than the Memo component. Key runtime properties include SelAttributes and Paragraph. The RichEdit component is complex but still easy to use, considering its complexities. See the C++Builder online help for full details on the RichEdit component.

Table 8.4 lists the properties specific to components based on edit controls.

Table 8.4. Properties for edit controls.

Item	Applies To	Description
		Properties
AutoSelect	Edit, MaskEdit	When set to true, text in the edit control is automatically selected when the user tabs to the control. Default: true
AutoSize	Edit, MaskEdit	When set to true, the edit control automatically resizes itself when the font of the edit control changes. Otherwise, the edit control does not change size when the font changes. Default: true
CharCase	Edit, MaskEdit	Determines whether the edit control displays uppercase (ecUpperCase), lowercase (ecLowerCase), or mixed text (ecNormal). Default: ecNormal
HideScrollBars	RichEdit	When set to true, the scrollbars are shown when needed but hidden otherwise. When set to false, the scrollbars are shown as determined by the value of the ScrollBars property.
HideSelection	Edit, Memo, RichEdit	When set to true, any text selected does not show as selected when the user tabs to another control. Default: false
Lines	Memo, RichEdit	The text contained in the component. Lines is an instance of the TStrings class.
MaxLength	All	Specifies the maximum number of characters that the component will hold. When set to 0, the amount of text that can be input is unlimited (limited only by system considerations). When set to any non-zero value, limits the number of characters to that value. Default: 0

continues

Table 8.4. continued

Item	Applies To	Description
		Properties
OEMConvert	Edit, Memo	Set this property to true when the text input will consist of filenames. Default: false
PasswordChar	Edit, MaskEdit	When this property is set to a value other than ASCII #0, any text entered is echoed with the character provided. The actual text in the edit control is unaffected. Most password edits use the asterisk (*) as the password character. Default: #0
PlainText	RichEdit	When set to true, RTF (rich text format) files are shown as plain text without character and paragraph formatting. When set to false, RTF files are displayed with full formatting. Default: false
ReadOnly	All	When set to true, the component displays its text, but new text cannot be entered. The user can, however, highlight text and copy it to the Clipboard. Default: false
ScrollBars	Memo, RichEdit	Determines which scrollbars to display. Choices are ssNone, ssBoth, ssHorizontal, and ssVertical. Default: ssNone
Text	Edit, MaskEdit	Contains the text in the component.
WantReturns	Memo, RichEdit	When set to true, the component keeps the return character and a new line is inserted in the edit control when the user presses Enter. When set to false, return characters go to the form and are not placed in the edit control. If you have a form with a default button and WantReturns set to false, pressing Enter causes the form to close. Default: true

Item	Applies To	Description
		Properties
WantTabs	Memo, RichEdit	When set to `true`, a tab character is placed in the edit control when the user presses the Tab key. When set to `false`, tab characters go to the form, which enables tabbing out of the edit control. Default: `false`
WordWrap	Memo, RichEdit	When set to `true`, text entered wraps to a new line when the right edge of the edit control is reached. When set to `false`, the edit control automatically scrolls as new text is entered. Default: `true`
		Runtime Properties
Modified	All	Indicates whether the contents of the edit control have changed since the last time the `Modified` property was set. After saving the contents of a `Memo` or `RichEdit` component to a file, you should set `Modified` to `false`.
SelLength	All	Contains the length of the text currently selected in the edit control.
SelStart	All	Contains the starting point of the selected text in the edit control. The first character in the edit control is 0.
SelText	All	Contains the currently selected text in an edit control.

Edit controls have many common methods; they are too numerous to list here. The `CutToClipboard()`, `CopyToClipboard()`, `PasteFromClipboard()`, and `Clear()` methods deal with Clipboard operations and text manipulation. The `GetSelTextBuff()` and `GetTextBuff()` methods retrieve the selected text in the component and the entire text in the component, respectively. See the C++Builder online help topics `TEdit`, `TMaskEdit`, `TMemo`, and `TRichEdit` for a complete list of methods associated with each edit component.

The edit component events that you are most likely to be interested in are dependent on the type of edit control you are using. In general, though, the `OnEnter`, `OnExit`, `OnChange`, `OnKeyDown` (or `OnKeyPress`), and `OnKeyUp` events will be the most widely used.

The `ListBox` and `ComboBox` Components

The `ListBox` and `ComboBox` components are also widely used. The `ListBox` component represents a standard Windows list box, which presents a list of choices that the user can choose from. If the list box contains more items than can be shown at one time, scrollbars appear, to enable access to the rest of the items in the list box.

NEW TERM Some list boxes are *owner-drawn* list boxes. In an owner-drawn list box, the programmer takes the responsibility for drawing the items in the list box.

You can do owner-drawn list boxes if needed. Owner-drawn list boxes are common, although you may not realize it. On Day 6, I talked about customizing the C++Builder toolbar. As part of that discussion, we looked at the C++Builder Toolbar Editor dialog box, which was shown in Figure 6.4. Go back and take another look at that figure. The Toolbar Editor dialog box contains two list boxes. The list box on the left is a regular list box. It lists the possible button groups you can choose from. The list box on the right is an owner-drawn list box. It shows the actual button as it will appear on the toolbar, as well as a textual description of what function the button performs.

Combo boxes are specialized list boxes. Actually, a combo box is a combination of a list box and an edit control. The user can choose from the list or type in a value in the edit portion. When the user chooses an item from the list, that item is placed in the edit control. There are three types of combo box. The combo box type is determined by the `Style` property. Table 8.5 lists the types of combo boxes and a description of each.

Table 8.5. Types of combo boxes.

Item	Description
Simple	This is nothing more than an edit control placed on top of a list box. The user can choose from the list or type text in the edit portion.
Drop-down	This is similar to the simple style, except the list box portion is not initially displayed. A drop-down button is provided so that the user can view the list and choose an item. The user can also type text in the edit portion.
Drop-down list	This is the most restrictive type of combo box. As with the drop-down style, the list is not initially exposed. The user can click the drop-down button to expose the list and choose an item from the list but cannot enter text in the edit portion. Use this style when you want the user to select only from a predetermined set of choices.

Figure 8.4 shows the test program, called ComboBox Test, running. Run the program and try out the combo boxes to get a feel for how each works.

Figure 8.4.

The ComboBox Test *program.*

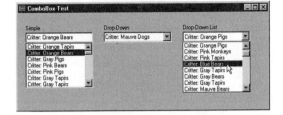

Table 8.6 lists the properties common to list boxes and combo boxes.

Table 8.6. Properties for edit controls.

Property	Applies To	Description
		Properties
Columns	ListBox	Contains the number of columns in the list box. You create multiple columns by making this property greater than 1. Default: 0
ExtendedSelection	ListBox	Determines whether extended selection is allowed. *Extended selection* enables the user to select items using Shift+click and Ctrl+click. Has no effect if MultiSelect is set to false. Default: true
IntegralHeight	ListBox	When true, resizes the list box height to be sure that no partial lines are displayed. When false, the list box might show partial lines. Default: false
ItemHeight	Both	Sets the height of the items in the control. For use with owner-drawn list boxes and combo boxes. Default: 13
Items	Both	Contains the list of items in the list box. This is a TStrings instance. (See the section on TStrings earlier in this chapter for a description of available properties and methods.)

continues

Table 8.6. continued

Property	Applies To	Description
		Properties
MaxLength	ComboBox	The maximum number of characters the user can type in the edit portion of the combo box. Same as MaxLength in edit controls. Default: 0 (no limit)
MultiSelect	ListBox	When true, the list box enables multiple items to be selected. Default: false
Sorted	Both	When set to true, the list box items are sorted in ascending order. When set to false, the items are not sorted. Default: false
Style	ComboBox	Offers style choices for the combo box: csSimple, csDropDown, csDropDownList, lbOwnderDrawFixed, and csOwnerDrawVariable. (See Table 8.5 for a description of the three basic styles.) Default: csDropDown
	ListBox	Offers style choices for the list box: lbStandard, lbOwnderDrawFixed, and csOwnerDrawVariable. Default: lbStandard
TabWidth	ListBox	Sets the tab width in pixels for tabs in list boxes. Default: 0
Text	ComboBox	Contains the text in the edit portion of the combo box.
		Runtime Properties
ItemIndex	ListBox	Contains the index of the currently selected item, with 0 being the first item in the list. Returns -1 if no item is selected. When written to, selects the specified index.
SelCount	ListBox	Contains the number of items selected in a multiple-selection list box.
Selected	ListBox	Returns true if the specified item is selected or false if it is not.
SelLength	ComboBox	Contains the length of the text currently selected in the edit control part of the combo box.

Property	Applies To	Description
Runtime Properties		
SelStart	ComboBox	Contains the starting point of the selected text in the edit control. The first character in the edit control is 0.
SelText	ComboBox	Contains the currently selected text in the edit control.
TopIndex	ListBox	Returns the list box item that is at the top of the list box. Can be used to set the top item to a certain list box item.

As with the edit components we looked at earlier, there are very few ListBox and ComboBox methods. The Clear() method will clear the control of all data. The ItemAtPos() methods will return the list box item at the specified x and y coordinates. The SelectAll() method will select the text in the edit control portion of a combo box.

Easily the most used event when dealing with combo boxes and list boxes is the OnClick event. Use this event to determine when a selection has been made in the list box.

NOTE

Clicking the edit portion of a combo box or the drop-down button does not result in an OnClick event being sent. Only when the list box portion of a combo box is clicked will the OnClick event occur.

The OnChange event can be used to detect changes to the edit portion of a combo box just as it is used with edit controls. The OnDropDown event is used to detect when the drop-down button on a combo box has been clicked. The OnMeasureItem and OnDrawItem events are used with owner-drawn list boxes and owner-drawn combo boxes.

Buttons

VCL contains several types of buttons that you can use in your applications. Although not all of them are based on the standard Windows button control, I will still address all the button types here. Before we look at the specific Button components, though, let's cover some of the basics.

NOTE

> When setting a button's Caption property, use the ampersand (&) just as you would when setting the Caption property of menu items. The character after the ampersand will be underlined and will be the accelerator for the button.

Button Properties

The Button components have only four properties of note.

ModalResult

The ModalResult property is used to provide built-in form closing for forms displayed with ShowModal(). By default, ModalResult is set to mrNone (which is 0). Use this value for buttons that are used as regular buttons on the form and that don't close the form. If you use any non-zero value for ModalResult, pressing the button will close the form and return the ModalResult value. For example, if you place a button on a form and set the ModalResult property to mrOk, pressing the button will close the form, and the return value from ShowModal() will be mrOk (1). Given that, you can do something like the following:

```
int result = MyForm->ShowModal();
if (result == mrOK) DoSomething();
if (result == mrCancel) return;
```

Table 8.7 lists the ModalResult constants that VCL defines.

Table 8.7. VCL ModalResult constants.

Constant	Value
mrNone	0
mrOk	1
mrCancel	2
mrAbort	3
mrRetry	4
mrIgnore	5
mrYes	6
mrNo	7
mrAll	8
mrNoToAll	9
mrYesToAll	10

8

NOTE

You don't have to use one of the predefined `ModalResult` constants for your buttons. You can use any value you like. Let's say, for example, you had a custom dialog box that could be closed by using a variety of buttons. You could assign a different `ModalResult` value to each button (100, 150, and 200, for example), and you would then know which button closed the dialog box. Any nonzero number is valid, up to the maximum value of an `int`.

Default

The `Default` property is another key property of buttons. Windows has a standard mechanism for dealing with dialog boxes. One feature of this mechanism is as follows: If a control other than a button has keyboard focus and the user presses the Enter key on the keyboard, the dialog box will behave as if the user had clicked the *default button*. The default button is the button that has the `BS_DEFPUSHBUTTON` style set (usually the OK button). This feature has been the bane of programmers and the curse of data-entry personnel for years. The `Default` property is used to set a button as the default button for a form. The default value for this property is `false`. To make a button the default button, set its `Default` property to `true`. If you don't specifically set any button's `Default` property to `true`, the form will not close when the user presses the Enter key.

NOTE

When the user closes the form by pressing the Enter key, the `OnClick` handler of the default button (if one exists) will be called before the form closes.

Cancel

The `Cancel` property works with the Esc key in much the same way as the `Default` property works with the Enter key. When the user presses the Esc key to close a form, the return value from `ShowModal()` will be the `ModalResult` value of the button whose `Cancel` property is set to `true`. If no button has its `Cancel` property set to `true`, `mrCancel` will be returned if the user uses the Esc key to close the form (`mrCancel` is equal to 2; see Table 8.7).

NOTE

Closing a form by clicking the system close box or by pressing Alt+F4 will result in mrCancel being returned from ShowModal(), as you would expect. Pressing the Esc key, however, will result in a return value of the ModalResult property being set to whatever button has the Cancel property set to true. The OnClick handler for the Cancel button will be called before the form closes. No OnClick handler is called if the user uses the system close box or Alt+F4 to close the form. Be sure to anticipate the different ways users might use (or abuse) your forms.

NOTE

You can have more than one button with a Default property set to true. Likewise, you can have more than one button with the Cancel property set to true. However, when the user presses Enter on the keyboard, the first button in the tab order that has its Default property set to true will be invoked. Similarly, when the user presses the Esc key to close the form, the return value from ShowModal() will be the ModalResult value of the first button in the tab order that has its Cancel property set to true.

Enabled

Earlier I discussed the Enabled property when I discussed components in general. This property is used a lot with buttons to enable or disable the button, depending on the current state of the program or of a particular form. When a button is disabled (its Enabled property is set to false), its text is grayed out and the button does not function. In the case of buttons with bitmaps on them (BitBtn and SpeedButton), the bitmap is also grayed out automatically.

Button components have only one method of interest: The Click() method, which simulates a mouse click. When you call Click() for a button, the OnClick event of the button is executed just as if the user had clicked the button. As for events, typically only the OnClick event is used.

Now let's take a look at the different button components C++Builder provides.

The Button Component

The standard Button component is sort of like actor Danny DeVito—it ain't pretty, but it sure gets a lot of work. There really isn't anything to add concerning the standard Button component. It has a default Height property value of 25 pixels and a default Width property value of 75. Typically you will place a button on a form and respond to its OnClick event, and that's about it.

The BitBtn **Component**

The BitBtn component is a perfect example of how a component can be extended to provide additional functionality. In this case the standard Button component is extended to enable a bitmap to be displayed on the face of the button.

The BitBtn component has several more properties than the Button component. All these properties work together to manage the bitmap on the button and the layout between the bitmap and the button's text. They are explained in the following sections.

Glyph

The Glyph property represents the bitmap on the button. The value of the Glyph property is a picture, or glyph.

NEW TERM   A *glyph* is a picture that is usually in the form of a Windows bitmap file (.BMP).

The glyph itself consists of one or more bitmaps that represent the four possible button states: up, down, disabled, and stay down. If you are creating your own buttons, you can probably get by with supplying just one glyph, which the BitBtn component will then modify to represent the other three possible states. The bitmap will move down and to the right when the button is clicked and will be grayed out when disabled. The glyph in the stay-down state will be the same as in the up state, although the button face will change to give a pressed look.

If you provide more than one glyph, the glyphs must all be the same height and width and must be contained in a bitmap strip. The bitmaps that ship with C++Builder provide two glyphs. Figure 8.5 shows the bitmap for the print button that comes with C++Builder (print.bmp) in both its actual size and zoomed in to show detail. Note that the two glyphs each occupy the same width in the bitmap.

Figure 8.5.

The print.bmp *bitmap.*

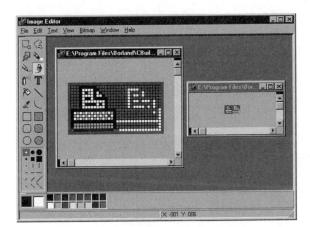

TIP

The pixel in the lower-left corner of the bitmap is the color that will be used for the transparent color. Any pixels in the bitmap having that color will be transparent when the glyph is displayed on the button. You must keep this in mind when designing your bitmaps. If you are not using transparency, you will need the pixel in the lower-left corner to be a color not present anywhere else on the bitmap.

To set the glyph for a BitBtn, double-click the Value column in the Object Inspector next to the Glyph property. The Picture Editor will be displayed, and you can choose the bitmap that will be used for the glyph.

NOTE

The standard button glyphs that come with C++Builder are 15×15 pixels in size. This size fits well with the standard button height of 25 pixels. Your glyphs can be any size you like, but the BitBtn component makes no effort to size the button according to the size of the bitmap. If you use larger glyphs, you will have to size the button accordingly.

Kind

The Kind property is a nice feature of the BitBtn component that enables you to choose from several predefined kinds of buttons. The default value for the Kind property is bkCustom, which means that you will supply the glyph and set any other properties for the button. Choosing any of the other predefined kinds will result in these five things happening:

- [ ] The Glyph property is automatically set for the kind of button chosen.
- [ ] The Cancel or Default properties are modified according to the kind of button chosen.
- [ ] The Caption property is modified for the type of button chosen.
- [ ] The ModalResult property is set according to the kind of button chosen.
- [ ] The button on the form is updated to reflect all these settings.

For instance, if you set the value of Kind to bkOK, the button will become an OK button. The glyph is set to a green check mark, the Cancel property is set to false, the Default property is set to true, the ModalResult property is set to mrOk, the Caption property is set to OK, and the results show up on the form. You can always override any of the properties modified by changing the Kind property, but it is not usually necessary to do so. Figure 8.6 shows the

Button Test program with the BitBtn Test form displayed. The form contains each of the predefined button types available plus one custom button.

Figure 8.6.

The predefined
BitBtn *types.*

Layout

The Layout property determines where the button is placed relative to the text. The default is blGlyphLeft. You can also choose to place the glyph on the face of the button to the right of the text, above the text, or below the text.

Margin

The Margin property specifies the margin between the glyph and the edge of the button. (Which edge this property affects is determined by the value of the Layout property.) The default is -1, which centers the glyph and the text in the button. Enter any positive value to set an absolute margin (in pixels).

NumGlyphs

The NumGlyphs property specifies the number of glyphs you have in your bitmap strip for a particular button. You can supply from one to four glyphs, as I've mentioned. The glyphs must appear in the bitmap strip in this order: Up, Disabled, Down, Stay Down.

Spacing

The Spacing property controls the distance, in pixels, between the glyph and the button's text. The default value is 4 pixels.

The SpeedButton Component

The SpeedButton component was designed to be used in conjunction with the Panel component to build toolbars. It is different from the Button and BitBtn components in that it is not a windowed component. This means that a speed button cannot receive input focus and cannot be tabbed to. On the other hand, the SpeedButton component has several things in common with the BitBtn component. The way in which the Glyph property is handled by the SpeedButton component is exactly the same as with the BitBtn component, so I'm not going to go over that ground again. There are a couple of major differences, though, so let's look at those.

By default, speed buttons are square and are 25×25 pixels. Your speed buttons can be any size you like and can contain text, although speed buttons don't usually contain text. There are some properties specific to speed buttons that you should be aware of, which I've broken down in the following sections.

NOTE

> The C++Builder 1.0 method of creating toolbars involved using a `Panel` component on which various components (`SpeedButtons`, primarily) were placed. C++Builder 3.0 has the `Toolbar` component, which is probably the preferred method of creating a toolbar. The `Toolbar` component has some added benefits but is slightly more complicated to use.

GroupIndex

Speed buttons can be grouped to make them behave like radio buttons (radio buttons are discussed later in the chapter in the section "Radio Buttons and Check Boxes"). When one button in the group is pressed, it stays down, and the button that was previously pressed pops up again. To group speed buttons, simply assign the same value to the `GroupIndex` property for all buttons in a group. (The default value of 0 indicates that the button is not part of any group.) To illustrate, do the following exercise:

1. Create a blank form and place five speed buttons on the form. (I won't bother adding glyphs to the buttons in this simple exercise, but you certainly can if you want.)

2. Select all the buttons and change the value of the `GroupIndex` property to 1. The `GroupIndex` for all buttons will be changed to 1.

3. Optional: Change the `Down` property of one of the buttons to `true`.

4. Click the Run button to compile and run the program.

When you run the program, click several of the buttons. You will notice that only one button can be in the down state at one time. As you can see when you assign a nonzero value to `GroupIndex`, the speed buttons change their behavior. A speed button with a `GroupIndex` of 0 pops back up when you click it, whereas a speed button that is part of a group stays down when clicked.

AllowAllUp

By default, one button in the group must be down at all times. You can change that behavior by setting the `AllowAllUp` property to `true`. Doing this for one button automatically changes the `AllowAllUp` property to `true` for all other buttons in the group. Now you can have any one button in the group selected or no buttons at all.

TIP

> Sometimes you want a speed button to act as a toggle button. A toggle button is used to turn an option on or off and is not part of a button group. To make an individual speed button a toggle button, assign a nonzero value to its GroupIndex property and set its AllowAllUp property to true. Be sure to set the GroupIndex property to a value not used by any other components on the form. When the user clicks the button, it stays down. When the button is clicked again, it pops back up.

Down

The Down property, when read, returns true if the button is currently down and false if it is not. When written to, the Down property can be used to toggle a button as pressed or not pressed. Writing to the Down property has no effect unless the speed button is part of a group.

Radio Buttons and Check Boxes

Although radio buttons and check boxes are specialized buttons, they are, in the end, still buttons. I'm not going to spend a lot of time discussing these two components because implementing them is straightforward. Both the RadioButton and CheckBox components have a property called Checked that can be used to set the check state and can be read to retrieve the current check state.

The radio button is usually used in a group of buttons. A radio button typically signifies a group of options, only one of which can be selected at one time (like a group of speed buttons, which you just learned about). Although you can use a radio button by itself, it is not recommended because it is confusing to your users. When tempted to use a radio button by itself, use a check box instead—that's what a check box is for, after all.

Any buttons placed on a form will automatically be considered part of the same group. If you have more than one group of radio buttons, and those groups need to operate independently of one another, you need to use a RadioGroup component. This component enables you to quickly set up a group of radio buttons with a 3D frame around the buttons and a caption as well. To illustrate this concept, do the following exercise:

1. Create a blank form or use the form you created in the previous exercise. Place a RadioGroup component on the form.

2. Locate the Items property and double-click the Value column.

3. The String list editor is displayed. Type the following lines in the String list editor:
   ```
   Redtailed Hawk
   Peregrine Falcon
   Gyrfalcon
   Northern Goshawk
   ```

4. Click OK to close the String list editor. The group box is populated with radio buttons containing the text you typed.

5. Change the `Caption` property of the radio group box to `Apprentice Falconers Can Legally Possess:`.

6. Click Run to compile and run the program.

When you click one of the radio buttons, the previously selected button pops up as expected. Using the `RadioGroup` component, you can put more than one group of radio buttons on a form. Like the list box and combo box components discussed earlier, the `RadioGroup` component has an `ItemIndex` property that you can read at runtime to determine which item in the group is selected. Oh, by the way—if you live in the U.S., the answer to the quiz is Redtailed Hawk (American Kestrel would also have been an acceptable answer, but it was not presented in the list).

NOTE

You can also use a `GroupBox` component to hold radio buttons. The `GroupBox` component is less convenient to use than the `RadioGroup` component, but it has more flexibility. You can place any type of control in a group box. When placed in the group box, the controls and the group box itself can be moved as a unit at design time.

The `CheckBox` component is used to enable users to turn an option on or off or to indicate to a user that an option is currently on or off. A check box can have up to three states, depending on its style: on, off, or grayed. If the check box's `AllowGrayed` property is `false`, it can only be checked or unchecked. When the `AllowGrayed` property is `true`, the check box can be any one of the three states. The grayed, or indeterminate, state is handled programmatically. In other words, it's up to you to decide what the grayed state means for your application. If the `AllowGrayed` property is `false` (the default), you can use the `Checked` property to determine whether the check box is checked or unchecked. If the `AllowGrayed` property is `true`, you must use the `State` property to determine (or set) the check box state. `State` will return either `cbChecked`, `cbUnchecked`, or `cbGrayed`.

TIP

Sometimes you might want to use a check box to indicate that some feature is on or off but not enable the user to change the state by clicking on the check box. In that case you would want the check box to be disabled but to appear normal. To make a check box read-only but not grayed out, place it on a panel and change the panel's `Enabled` property to `false`.

The `Label` **Component**

The `Label` component is used to display text on a form. Sometimes the label text is determined at design time and never changed. In other cases, the label is dynamic and is changed at runtime as the program dictates. Use the label's `Caption` property to set the label text at runtime. The `Label` component has no specialized methods or events beyond what is available with other components. Table 8.8 lists the properties specific to the `Label` component.

Table 8.8. Properties for the `Label` component.

Property	Description
AutoSize	When set to `true`, the label will size itself according to the text contained in the `Caption` property. When set to `false`, text will be clipped at the right edge of the label.
FocusControl	A label is a non-windowed component, so it cannot receive input focus and it cannot be tabbed to. Sometimes, however, a label serves as the text for a control such as an edit control. In those cases you could assign an accelerator key to the label (using the ampersand) and then change the `FocusControl` property to the name of the control you want to receive focus when the label's accelerator key is pressed.
ShowAccelChar	When set to `true`, an actual ampersand shows up in the label instead of the ampersand serving as the accelerator key.
Transparent	When this property is set to `true`, the `Color` property is ignored and anything beneath the label shows through. This is useful for placing labels on bitmap backgrounds, for instance.
WordWrap	When set to `true`, text in the label will wrap around to a new line when it reaches the right edge of the label.

The `ScrollBar` **Component**

The `ScrollBar` component represents a standalone scrollbar. It's standalone in the sense that it is not connected to an edit control, list box, form, or anything else. I have not found that the scrollbar is a control I use very frequently. Certain types of applications use scrollbars heavily, of course, but for day-in, day-out applications its use is fairly uncommon. The scrollbar's performance is set by setting the `Min`, `Max`, `LargeChange`, and `SmallChange` properties. The scrollbar's position can be set or obtained via the `Position` property. The `Kind` property enables you to specify a horizontal or vertical scrollbar.

The `Panel` Component

The `Panel` component is sort of a workhorse in C++Builder. There is almost no limit to what you can use panels for. Panels can be used to hold toolbar buttons, to display text labels such as a title for a form, display graphics, and to hold regular buttons as well. One of the advantages of a panel is that components placed on the panel become children of the panel. As such, they go with the panel wherever the panel goes. This can be a great aid at runtime and at design time.

Much of the power of the `Panel` component lies in its `Align` property. For instance, let's say you want a title to be displayed on the top of a form. Let's further assume that you want it centered no matter how the user sizes the window. By setting the `Align` property to `alTop` and the `Alignment` property to `taCenter`, your title will always be centered. It's as simple as that.

A panel can have many different appearances. The panel's appearance can be altered by changing the `BevelInner`, `BevelOuter`, `BorderStyle`, and `BorderWidth` properties, as displayed in Figure 8.7.

Figure 8.7.

*The panel styles
example showing
different styles.*

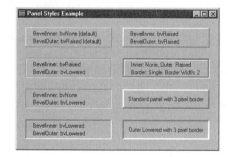

The `Panel` component is so versatile that it will take you a while to discover all its possible uses.

And That's Not All...

Unfortunately, there isn't sufficient space here to go over all the components C++Builder provides. You saw the `Image` component on Day 6, when you created the Picture Viewer program. You also had a brief glimpse at the `Bevel` component on Day 6 when you built an About dialog box, and the `Shape` component on Day 7 as part of an exercise on aligning components. These represent just a sampling of the components that are waiting for you. You need to test drive each one of them to determine their usefulness for you.

There is one other group of components that I need to discuss before we move on: the `Dialog` group.

The Common Dialog Boxes

Windows provides a set of common dialog boxes that any Windows program can use, including

☐ File Open

☐ File Save

☐ File Open Picture

☐ File Save Picture

☐ Font

☐ Color

☐ Print

☐ Printer Setup

☐ Find

☐ Replace

The common dialog boxes are found on the Dialogs tab of the Component palette. These components are considered nonvisual because they don't have a visual design-time interface. The following sections discuss each of these dialog boxes with one exception—I'll leave the discussion of the Print and Printer Setup dialog boxes for later when I discuss printing.

The Execute Method

One thing that all the common dialog boxes have in common is the Execute() method, which is used to create and display the dialog box. The dialog box is displayed modally except for the Find and Replace dialog boxes, which are displayed modelessly. Execute() returns true if the user clicked the OK button, double-clicked a filename (in the case of the file dialogs), or pressed Enter on the keyboard. Execute() returns false if the user clicked the Cancel button, pressed the Esc key, or closed the dialog box with the system close box. A common dialog box is often implemented like this:

```
if (OpenDialog->Execute()) {
  // user pressed OK so use the filename
  Memo->Lines->LoadFromFile(OpenDialog->FileName);
}
return;
```

This code displays the File Open dialog box and gets a filename from the user. If the user clicked the OK button, the code inside the if block is executed and the file is loaded in to a Memo component. If OK was not pressed, the code inside the if block is ignored and no action takes place.

> The code used in the previous snippet is another example of C++
> shortcut syntax. The first line,
>
> ```
> if (OpenDialog->Execute()) {
> ```
>
> is equivalent to
>
> ```
> if (OpenDialog->Execute() == true) {
> ```
>
> Use either method, but the first is preferred.

The File Open and File Save Dialog Boxes

The File Open and File Save dialog boxes have several properties in common. File Open is used when you want to allow the user to open a file in your application (see Figure 8.8). It is encapsulated in the OpenDialog component. The File Save dialog box is used when getting a filename from the user in order to save a file. It is also used as the Save As dialog box. The File Save dialog box is encapsulated by the SaveDialog component.

Figure 8.8.

A typical File Open dialog box.

The file dialog boxes are fairly easy to use in their most basic form. They do have a few features, however, that need to be explained in order for you to get the full benefit of using them. The following sections examine the properties that are specific to the file dialog boxes.

> The OpenDialog and SaveDialog components merely retrieve a filename
> from the user. It is up to the programmer to write code that actually
> does something with the filename.

The DefaultExt Property

Use the DefaultExt property to set the default extension that the dialog box will use. The *default extension* is the extension that will automatically be appended to the filename if the user does not supply an extension.

The FileName Property

The FileName property is the most obvious of the file dialog box properties: It holds the text of the file that the user chose. Set this property prior to calling the dialog box if you want a filename to show in the edit portion of the file dialog box when it is initially displayed. After the user clicks OK to close the dialog box, this property will contain the full path and filename of the file chosen.

The Files Property

Files, a read-only property, is a TStrings instance that contains the list of files selected when multiple file selection is enabled.

The Filter Property

The Filter property contains a list of the file types from which the user can choose. The file types are displayed in the File of type: combo box in the file dialog box. You can set Filter to reflect types of files specific to your application. For instance, a simple text-editing program could have the filter set to show files of type .TXT, .INI, and .LOG, to name just a few. The filter can easily be set at design time through the Filter Editor dialog box. To invoke the Filter Editor, double-click the Value column next to the Filter property in the Object Inspector. Figure 8.9 shows the Filter Editor for a File Open dialog box as described previously.

Figure 8.9.

The Filter Editor dialog box.

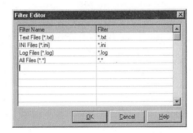

The Filter Name column contains a textual description of the file type. The Filter column is the actual file mask that will be used to display files of that type.

Although you can enter the filter string directly in the Value column of the Object Inspector, it is easiest to use the Filter Editor. If you are only using a single filter, you can type it directly into the Value column for the Filter property. Separate the description and filter with a pipe. For instance, to have a single filter for all file types, you would enter the following:

```
All Files (*.*)|*.*
```

The FilterIndex Property

The FilterIndex property is used to set the filter that will be used when the dialog box is initially displayed. The index is not 0-based as you might expect, however. The first filter in the list is 1, the second is 2, and so on. For example, refer back to Figure 8.9. If you wanted the All Files filter to be the one initially displayed, you would set the `FilterIndex` property to 4.

The `InitialDir` Property

The `InitialDir` property is used to specify the directory that will be used as the initial directory when the file dialog box is displayed. If no value is supplied for the `InitialDir` property, the current directory will be used (as determined by Windows).

> **TIP**
>
> A top-notch Windows program keeps track of the last directory the user used both when opening files and when saving them. Usually this information is stored in the Registry. Before displaying a File Open or File Save dialog box, set the `InitialDir` to the previous directory the user used. After the user selects a file, update the Registry to reflect the new directory if necessary.

The `Options` Property

The `Options` property controls the way the file dialog box is used. The list of options is too long to list here, but common items include whether you allow new files or directories to be created, whether the Help button is shown on the dialog box, whether long filenames are allowed, whether multiple file selection is allowed, and others. See the C++Builder online help for the `OpenDialog` and `SaveDialog` components for complete information.

The `Title` Property

The `Title` property is used to set or read the title of the file dialog box. If no title is specified, the common dialog box defaults of Open for the `OpenDialog` component and Save for the `SaveDialog` component will be used.

> **TIP**
>
> A Save As dialog box is nothing more than a `SaveDialog` component with the `Title` property set to `Save As`.

The file dialog boxes have no events associated with them.

TIP You can implement a File Open dialog box (or any of the common dialog boxes) at runtime without ever placing an `OpenDialog` component on your form. To accomplish this, create an instance of the `TOpenDialog` class and then call its `Execute()` method:

```
TOpenDialog* openDlg = new TOpenDialog(this);
if (openDlg->Execute()) {
  // do something here
}
delete openDlg;
```

If necessary, you can set any of the `OpenDialog` component's properties prior to calling `Execute()`.

The File Open Picture and File Save Picture Dialog Boxes

These two dialog boxes are nothing more than the regular File Open and File Save dialog boxes with an extra feature—they display a preview window that enables you to see the image that is currently selected. These dialog boxes also have the `Filter` property pre-set to the common Windows image formats. Otherwise they behave just like the File Open and File Save dialog boxes. Figure 8.10 shows a File Open Picture dialog box in action.

Figure 8.10.

The File Open Picture dialog box.

The Color Dialog Box

The Color dialog box enables the user to choose a color. When the OK button is clicked, the `Color` property will contain the color information. (Refer back to Figure 8.1 to see the Color dialog box.) The Color dialog box, like the file dialog boxes, has no events to respond to.

The Font Dialog Box

The Font dialog box enables the user to choose a font from the list of fonts available on his or her system. Through the `Device` property, you can choose whether you want screen fonts, printer fonts, or both types of fonts to be displayed. You can limit the maximum and minimum font sizes that the user can select by modifying the MaxFontSize and MinFontSize properties. As with the file dialog boxes, the Options property contains a wide variety of options you can use to control how the Font dialog box functions.

If the user clicks OK, the Font property will contain all the information needed to implement the new font. Figure 8.11 shows the Font dialog box in the default configuration.

Figure 8.11.

The Font dialog box.

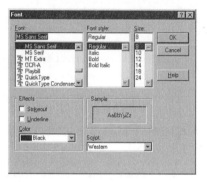

The Font dialog box has a single event, OnApply, that will occur when the user clicks the Apply button on the Find dialog box. The Apply button will not be present on the Font dialog box unless you have first created a valid (not empty) event handler for the OnApply event.

The Find and Replace Dialog Boxes

The Find and Replace dialog boxes provide users the capability to enter text to search for and text to replace the found text with, and a variety of search and replace options. The Find dialog box is encapsulated in the VCL component FindDialog, and the Replace dialog box is represented by the ReplaceDialog component. The Replace dialog box, which contains everything found on the Find dialog box plus the extra replace features, is shown in Figure 8.12.

Figure 8.12.

The Replace dialog box.

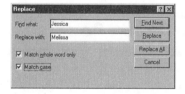

Major properties of the FindDialog and ReplaceDialog components include FindText (the text to find), ReplaceText (the text with which to replace the found text), and Options. Obviously, the FindDialog component does not have a ReplaceText property. The Options

8

property contains a wide variety of information about the various options that the user had set at the time the Find Next, Replace, or Replace All button was clicked.

The Execute() method for the FindDialog and ReplaceDialog components is a little different than it is with the other common Dialog components. First of all, the Find and Replace dialog boxes are modeless dialog boxes. As soon as the dialog box is displayed, the Execute() method returns. Because the dialog box is modeless, the return value from Execute() is meaningless (it's always true). Instead, the Find and Replace dialog boxes use the OnFind and OnReplace events along with the Options property to determine what is happening with the dialog box. The OnFind event occurs when the Find Next button is clicked. The ReplaceDialog has an OnFind event, but it also has an OnReplace event that is fired when the Replace or Replace All button is clicked. Use these events to determine when the user has requested a Find or Replace action. Your programs should read the Options property to determine how the user intended the Find or Replace operation to be carried out.

Summary

Today you have had a look at some of the basic components that C++Builder provides. You have learned about components in general, and then you learned about some of the specifics of the components that are based on Windows controls. It is important to understand the basic controls available in Windows and the C++Builder components that represent those controls. Finally, you examined some of the Windows common dialog boxes today.

Workshop

The Workshop contains quiz questions to help you solidify your understanding of the material covered and exercises to provide you with experience in using what you have learned. You can find answers to the quiz questions in Appendix A, "Answers to Quiz Questions."

Q&A

Q **If I change the Name property of a component using the Object Inspector, C++Builder will automatically change all references to that component in my code, right?**

A Yes and no. C++Builder will change all references to that component name in C++Builder-generated code, but it will not change any user-written code.

Q **The OpenDialog component is obviously a visible component. Why is it called a nonvisual component?**

A Because it is not visible at design time. It is visible only at runtime when you invoke it with the Execute() method.

Q **Why is it important to change the** Name **property only with the Object Inspector?**

A As you work with the Form Designer, C++Builder writes code based on the Name property. If you later change the Name property either by directly editing the source files or at runtime, all references to that form or component will be incorrect and will likely lead to your program refusing to compile or crashing at runtime.

Q **I seem to be using properties more than methods when dealing with my components in code. Is that wrong?**

A Not at all. In fact, that's the way VCL components are designed. A well-written component makes maximum use of properties. For this reason you cannot use a component's methods very often. Use methods when necessary, but otherwise use properties to manipulate your components at runtime.

Q **I'm responding to both the** OnDblClick **and the** OnClick **events for a component. Every time I double-click a component, both the** OnClick **and the** OnDblClick **event handlers are called. Why?**

A Because when you double-click a component, Windows will generate both single- and double-click messages. You can't prevent it, so you will have to write code to account for that fact.

Q **I want to use the features of the** TStrings **class to keep a list of strings my program needs in order to operate. The compiler won't let me use a** TStrings **object. What do I do?**

A Use a TStringList object instead. The TStringList class is provided for this purpose.

Q **I need a single-line edit control to be right-justified, but there is no** Alignment **property for the** Edit **component. Can I right-align text in a single-line edit?**

A No. What you can do, though, is use a Memo component and make it appear to be a regular Edit component. Be sure to set the Memo component's WantReturn property to false, its Height to the height of a standard edit component (21 pixels), and its Alignment property to taRightJustify. The component will give all appearances of being a single-line edit control that is right-justified.

Q **I have a form that has several buttons on it. When the user closes the form using the Esc key, I get one return value from** ShowModal() **, and when the user closes the form with the system close box, I get a different return value from** ShowModal()**. Why?**

A You have a button on the forum that has a Cancel property set to true. When the user presses the Esc key, the ModalResult value of that button is used as the return value from ShowModal(). When the user closes the form with the system close box, you will always get a return value of mrCancel. You need to be prepared to take into account both ways a form can be closed.

Quiz

1. Can you change the `Name` property of a component at runtime?

2. What property is used to enable and disable controls?

3. How can you tell at runtime that a button is disabled?

4. What is the difference between the long hint and the short hint?

5. Name three of the four methods that can be used to force a control to repaint itself.

6. How many types of combo boxes are there?

7. How is the `ModalResult` property used for button components?

8. What component is often used as a container for other components?

9. What is the return value from the `Execute()` method for an `OpenDialog` component if the user clicks OK to close the dialog box?

10. How do you make the `SaveDialog` component into a Save As dialog box?

Exercises

1. Create a program that contains two edit components. When the user types information in the first control, make it appear in the second edit control as it is entered.

2. Create a program with a list box. Write code to load the list box from a text file prior to the application being visible.

3. Add an edit component to the program in Exercise 2. When the user selects an item in the list box, have the item's text appear in the edit control.

4. Add a button to the program in Exercises 2 and 3. Write code so that when the button is clicked, any text in the edit control is added as a new item in the list box.

5. Create a program that has a `RadioGroup` with four items in the group. Add a label component whose text changes depend on which radio button is clicked.

6. Create a program that has a title on the form that is centered at the top of the form regardless of how the program's window is sized.

7. Modify the program in Exercise 6 so that the font of the title can be changed to any font available on the system by clicking a button.

8. Reopen the Picture Viewer program created on Day 5. Modify the program so that it uses File Open Picture and File Save Picture dialog boxes rather than the regular dialog boxes.

Day **9**

Creating Applications in C++Builder

C++Builder provides a variety of tools that aid you in creating forms, dialog boxes, and applications. Today you will learn about

☐ The Object Repository

☐ The Dialog Wizard

☐ The Application Wizard

☐ Adding functions and data members to your code

☐ Component templates

☐ Using resources in your C++Builder applications

☐ Packages

For starters, I'll spend some time discussing the Object Repository, which is where C++Builder stores any prebuilt forms, applications, or other objects for you to reuse. Following that discussion, you will meet the wizards. Wizards provide a series of dialog boxes that guide you step by step through the creation process. You provide the details, and C++Builder builds the form or application based on the information you provided. The wizards are a powerful tool for rapid application development. Later in the day I'll tell you how you can use resources in your C++Builder applications. Finally, we'll close the day by talking about packages in C++Builder.

Working with the Object Repository

The Object Repository dialog box is the means by which you can select predefined objects to use in your applications.

NOTE

> The Object Repository itself is actually a text file (`BCB.DRO` in the `BIN` directory, if you want to take a look) that contains the information that the Object Repository dialog box displays. For the sake of simplicity, I will refer to the Object Repository dialog box and the repository file collectively as simply the Object Repository.

The Object Repository enables you to do the following:

- ☐ Choose a predefined application, form, or dialog box to implement in your application
- ☐ Add your own forms, dialog boxes, and applications to the Object Repository
- ☐ Add other objects to your application such as ASCII text files and additional source code units
- ☐ Manage data modules
- ☐ Create new components
- ☐ Create new packages
- ☐ Create new ActiveX controls or active forms
- ☐ Invoke wizards to help you build a dialog box or an application

That's just a sampling of what the Object Repository provides. There are other objects you can create in addition to those listed here.

Object Repository Pages and Options

The Object Repository is displayed automatically whenever you choose File | New from the main menu. Figure 9.1 shows the Object Repository window as it initially appears if you choose File | New with no project open.

Figure 9.1.

The Object Repository window.

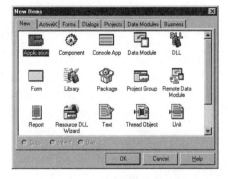

NOTE

Strange as it might seem, the Object Repository dialog box is titled New Items, and the Object Repository configuration dialog box is titled Object Repository. To say that this is confusing is a bit of an understatement.

The Object Repository has several pages, each of which contains different objects that you can incorporate into your applications. As you can see from Figure 9.1, the New tab is what is initially selected when the Object Repository is displayed. Table 9.1 lists the Repository pages and a description of the items you will find on each page.

Table 9.1. The Object Repository pages.

Page/Tab	Description
New	Enables you to create a new application, console app, form, or source code unit for use in your application. Also enables you to create advanced objects such as packages, DLLs, components, and data modules.
ActiveX	Enables you to create new ActiveX controls, type libraries, or active forms.
Forms	Enables you to create standard forms from prebuilt forms such as an About box, a dual list box, tabbed pages, or Quick Reports.
Dialogs	Presents choices of several different basic dialog box types from which you can choose. Also contains the Dialog Wizard.
Projects	Displays full projects that you can choose from to initially set up an application. Also contains the Application Wizard.
Data Modules	Enables you to choose from data modules in your application.
Business	Includes wizards for database forms, reports, and charts, and a Decision Cube example application.

NOTE

> If you invoke the Object Repository when you already have a project open, you will see an additional tab in the Object Repository. The tab will have the name of your project on it. Clicking this tab will display a page that contains all the objects currently in the project. This enables you to quickly reuse a form or other object by simply selecting it from the Object Repository.

Across the bottom of each page you see three radio buttons. These buttons, labeled Copy, Inherit, and Use, determine how the selected object is implemented.

NOTE

> Depending on the object selected, some (or all) of the radio buttons might be disabled. For example, all three radio buttons are always grayed out when the New page is displayed. This is because Copy is the only option available for objects on this page, so C++Builder grays out all choices and applies the Copy option automatically.

Copy

When you choose the Copy radio button, C++Builder creates a copy of the selected object and places it in your application. At this point you are free to modify the object in any way you choose. The original object in the Repository is not altered when you make changes to the new object in your application.

To illustrate, let's say you had an often used form (a form in the traditional sense, not in the C++Builder sense) printed on paper—a work schedule, for instance. Let's say that you wanted to fill in that form with scheduling information. You wouldn't modify the original form because it would then be unusable for future reuse. Instead, you would put the original form in the copy machine, make a copy, and then return the original to some location for safekeeping. You would then fill out the copy of the form as needed. Making a copy of an object in the Repository works in exactly the same way. You are free to modify the copy in any way you choose while the original remains safely tucked away. Making a copy is the safest method of object usage.

Inherit

The Inherit method of usage is similar to Copy, but with one important distinction: The new object is still tied to the base object. If you modify the base object, the newly created object will be updated to reflect the changes made to the base object. The inverse is not true, however. You can modify the new object without it having any effect on the base object.

To illustrate this type of object usage, consider the following scenario: Frequently, information managers will create a spreadsheet in a spreadsheet program and use the contents of that spreadsheet in a word-processing program to present a report. They will usually opt to link the data to the spreadsheet when pasting from the clipboard or importing the spreadsheet into the word processor. That way, when changes are made to the spreadsheet, the word-processing document is automatically updated to reflect the new data. In the same way, changes made to a base form will automatically be reflected in all forms inherited from the base form. Use the Inherit option when you want to have several forms based on a common form that might change at some point. Any changes in the base form will be reflected in all inherited forms.

Use

The Use option is not common. When you Use an object, you are opening that object directly for editing. Use this option when you have saved an object in the Repository and you want to make permanent changes to that object. In the section about the Inherit option, I said that changes made to a base form would be reflected in all inherited forms. If you wanted to make changes to a base form, you would open it in the Object Repository with the Use option.

Using the Object Repository

Exactly what takes place when you select an object from the Object Repository depends on several factors. The factors include the type of object selected, whether a project is currently open, and the usage type you have selected (Copy, Inherit, or Use). If you have an application open and you choose to create a new application from the Object Repository, you will be prompted to save the current project (if necessary) before the new project is displayed.

TIP

> Choosing File | New Application from the main menu is a shortcut for starting a new application. It is equivalent to choosing New from the main menu and then choosing the Application object from the Object Repository. Similarly, the New Form, New Data Module, and New Unit items on the main menu are shortcuts for their equivalents in the Object Repository.

Creating a new form from the Object Repository is treated differently based on whether a project is open at the time. If a project is open, the new form is added to the application as a form/unit pair. If no project is open, a new form and unit are created as a standalone form. A form created outside of a project must be added to a project before it can be used at runtime. Use this option when creating a new base form to add to the Object Repository.

If you choose to create a new unit or text file, the new file is simply created in the Code Editor (and, in the case of a new unit, added to the current project). You might create a new text file for several reasons. For example, let's say you wanted to implement a configuration file (an .INI file) in your application. You could create a new text file in the Object Repository to initially create the configuration file. Create a new unit any time you want to start a new source file for your application that is not associated with a form (a specialized header file, for instance).

Choosing a new DLL or console application results in a new project being created with the project set up for a DLL or console application target. Creating a new Automation, Component, or Thread object will result in a dialog box being presented that asks for more information about the object you are creating.

The Object Repository Views

The actual Object Repository window is a Win32 list view control similar to the right side of Windows Explorer (where the files are listed). As such, it has several views that you can choose from: Large Icons, Small Icons, List, and Details. By default, the view is set to Large Icons. To change the Object Repository view, right-click on the Object Repository and choose the view you want from the Object Repository context menu. Figure 9.2 shows the Object Repository with the Forms page selected and the view set to Details.

Figure 9.2.

*The Object Repository
in Details view.*

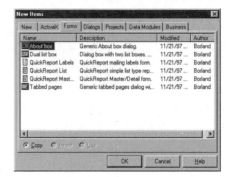

The Object Repository context menu also shows several sorting options. You can sort by object name, description, date, or author.

 TIP

> When the Object Repository is in the Details view, you can click a column header (Name, Description, Date, or Author) to instantly sort by that category.

Creating New Objects from the Object Repository

Certainly the most basic use of the Object Repository is creating a new object using an object from the Repository. To illustrate, let's create a simple application with a main form, an About dialog box, and a second form. Follow these steps:

1. Ensure that no other application is open. Choose File | New from the main menu. The Object Repository is displayed.

2. Click the Application icon and click OK to create a new application. A new application is created, and a blank form is displayed.

3. Place two buttons on the form. Change the Caption property of one of the buttons to About... and the Caption property of the other button to Display Form2. Change the Name properties if desired.

4. Choose File | New from the main menu. The Object Repository is displayed again.

5. Click the Forms tab in the Object Repository.

6. Choose the About box object. Ensure that the Copy radio button is selected, and click OK to create a new About Box form. The About box is displayed. Change any properties as needed.

7. Modify the About box as desired. (Enter your own information, change the icon, size, position, and so on.)

8. Select File | New from the main menu again. The Object Repository is displayed for the third time.

9. Click the Forms tab and choose the Dual list box object. Click OK to close the Object Repository. A dual list box form is displayed. (I had you choose this one just so you could see it.)

10. Write event handlers for the two buttons that display the About box and the second form as required.

11. Compile, run, and test the program.

No, this program doesn't do anything, but it does illustrate how you can use the Object Repository to quickly prototype an application. As time goes on, you will add your own custom objects to the Object Repository and then you can really be effective! Let's look at that next.

Adding Objects to the Object Repository

The Object Repository wouldn't be nearly as effective a tool if you couldn't add your own objects to it. But you can add your own objects and you should. Adding often used objects to the Object Repository makes you a more efficient and, therefore, a more valuable programmer. There is no point in reinventing the wheel over and over again. After you have an application, form, or other object created, save it to the Repository so that you can reuse it whenever you want. Of course, you don't want to save every form you ever created in the Object Repository, just the ones you will reuse most often.

You can set out to create an object with the express purpose of adding it to the Repository, or you can add an object to the Repository during the normal course of application development. (The term *object* is pretty broad, so I'll have to use a specific example in order for this to make sense.) Let's say that you create an About box form while creating an application. Suddenly it dawns on you that you'd like to save this About box to use in all your programs. After all, it has your company name, logo, and all the copyright information all laid out just the way you want it, so it'd be a shame to have to re-create the same About box for every application you write. No problem—just add it to the Repository. To add a form to the Object Repository, first save the form (if you don't save the form, you will be prompted to save it before continuing). Next, right-click the mouse anywhere on the form and choose Add To Repository from the Form Designer context menu. When you do, the Add To Repository dialog box is displayed as shown in Figure 9.3.

Figure 9.3.

The Add To Reposi-tory dialog box.

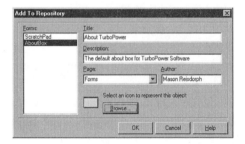

The Forms list box on the left side of this dialog box lists the current forms as well as any other objects in the application (such as data modules). First, select the form that you want to add to the Object Repository.

 NOTE

> The active form in the Form Designer will already be selected in the Forms list box in the Add To Repository dialog box.

Now enter the object's title. This is the title that will appear below the icon in the Object Repository. The Description field is used to give further information about the object. This description is displayed when the Object Repository view is set to display all object details (refer back to Figure 9.2). The Author field is where you type your name as the author of the object. You can enter your personal name, a company name, or any other identifying name.

NOTE The prebuilt objects in the Object Repository that come with C++Builder have "Borland" as the author name.

The Page field is used to select the Object Repository page where the new object will be placed. You can choose from one of the existing pages or simply type in the name of a new page in the Page field. If a page with the name you type doesn't exist, C++Builder will create a new page with that name. Near the bottom of the dialog box is a button labeled Browse that you can use to select the icon used to represent the object.

TIP You can choose icons from the Borland Shared Files\Images\Icons directory or the CBuilder\Objrepos directory. The icons in the CBuilder\Objrepos directory are the icons used by C++Builder for the items it places in the Object Repository.

After you've filled in all the fields and selected an icon, you can click OK to add the object to the Repository. The object is added to the Object Repository on the page you specified. You can now reuse that object any time you want. As you can see, adding an object to the Object Repository is nearly as easy as using an object.

WARNING When you add an object to the Object Repository, C++Builder makes an entry in the object repository file that describes the object. This information includes the pathname where the form and source file for the object are located. If you move or delete an object's form or source file, you will not be able to use the object from the Object Repository.

Adding Projects to the Object Repository

Adding projects to the Object Repository is not much different than adding individual forms. To add a project to the Object Repository, choose Project | Add To Repository from the main menu. The Add To Repository dialog box is displayed just like it is when adding objects to the Repository, except the Forms list box is not displayed. Fill in any required information (Title, Description, Author, and so on) and click OK, and the project is added to the Repository.

After you are familiar with C++Builder, you should create an application shell that has the features you use most often in your applications. Each time you start a new standard application, make a copy of the shell from the Object Repository. This way you can have your menus, speedbar, About box, and other standard dialog boxes all set up and ready to go in a matter of seconds. After the new application has been created, it can then be modified as with any project. You can add new forms, delete any unwanted forms, and so on.

Object Repository Housekeeping

You can manage the pages and objects in the Object Repository by using the Object Repository configuration dialog box.

To view the Object Repository configuration dialog box, choose Tools | Repository from the main menu or, if you have the Object Repository open, choose Properties from the Object Repository context menu. The configuration dialog box is displayed, as shown in Figure 9.4.

Figure 9.4.

The Object Repository configuration dialog box.

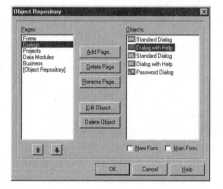

This dialog box enables you to delete objects and pages from the Object Repository, move objects from one page to another, change the order of pages in the Object Repository, and more. The list of pages in the Object Repository is displayed in the list box labeled Pages on the left side of the dialog box. When you select one of the pages in the Pages list, the list box on the right (labeled Objects) displays the objects contained on that page.

NOTE

The Pages list box has two important items of note. First, notice that the New page, which is always the first page displayed when the Object Repository is invoked, is not listed here. The New page is fixed and cannot be altered. Also notice that there is an item labeled [Object Repository]. This item is actually a list of all items on all pages of the Repository.

Managing Objects

Before you can edit, delete, or move an object you must first select it. To select an object, click the object in the Objects list box. After you have selected an object, you can edit it by clicking the Edit Object button. Editing an object enables you to change the object's name, description, and author, as well as the page on which the object is displayed.

TIP

To quickly edit an object, double-click the object in the Objects list box.

You can delete an object by selecting it and then clicking the Delete Object button. You are prompted for confirmation before the object is removed from the page and from the Repository.

NOTE

When an object is deleted from the Object Repository, it is removed from the object repository file and no longer shows up on any page in the Object Repository. However, the actual form file and source file that describe the object are not deleted from your hard drive.

Objects can be moved from one page to another by simply dragging the object from the Objects list box to the Pages list box. Drop the object on the page on which you want the object to be located, and the object is moved.

Managing Pages

The previous section deals with editing, deleting, and moving individual objects. You can also add, delete, or remove Object Repository pages through the Object Repository configuration dialog box. Before you can delete a page, you must first delete all the objects on the page. After a page is empty, you can remove the page by clicking on the page name in the Pages list box and then clicking the Delete Page button. After checking to be sure the page is empty, C++Builder deletes the page from the Object Repository.

A new page can be added by clicking the Add Page button. A dialog box pops up, asking for the name of the new page. Just supply a new page name, and when you click OK, the new page appears in the Pages list box. Renaming a page works essentially the same way. When you select a page and click the Rename Page button, a dialog box appears, prompting you for the new page name.

The order in which the pages appear in the Object Repository can be changed. To change a page's position in the page order, click the page to highlight it and then click the up or down arrow button underneath the Pages list box to move the page up or down in the list. You can also drag a page to its new location if you want.

Setting Default Forms and Projects

The Object Repository configuration dialog box enables you to set three default objects:

☐ The default form that will be used when you choose File | New Form from the main menu.

☐ The default form that will be used as the main form when you choose File | New Application from the main menu.

☐ The default project that will be used when you choose File | New Application from the main menu.

You will notice that, depending on the object you have selected, one or two check boxes appear beneath the Objects list box. If you have selected a form, the New Form and Main Form check boxes appear. If you have selected a project, the New Project check box appears. Making a form or project the default is easy. Let's say you had created a main form that you want to be the default main form when a new application is created. Select the form from the Objects list box and click the Main Form check box at the bottom of the screen. When you click OK, that form will now be the default. Similarly, if you have a project that you want to be the default project, first locate it in the Object Repository configuration dialog box, click on it, and then check the New Project check box. From that point on, when you choose File | New Application from the main menu, the project you set as the default will appear.

NOTE

If you aren't careful, you can accidentally select a form as the default form for a new application. If this happens, be sure you check each form in the Object Repository configuration dialog box. One form will have the Main Form check box checked. Clear the check box and all will be back to normal. This also applies to the default project. Check the Projects page for any items that have the New Project check box checked.

Building Forms and Applications with the Wizards

C++Builder has two built-in wizards designed to guide you through the application creation process. The Dialog Wizard aids you in creating dialog boxes, and the Application Wizard helps you create the basic layout of an application. Now let's see what the individual wizards do.

The Dialog Wizard

Truthfully, there isn't very much for a dialog box wizard to do because dialog boxes of any real value will have to be customized with the Form Designer. The Dialog Wizard is started from the Object Repository. First, choose File | New from the main menu to display the Object Repository. Next, switch to the Dialogs page and then double-click the Dialog Wizard icon. The Dialog Wizard is displayed, as shown in Figure 9.5.

Figure 9.5.

The Dialog Wizard.

You can choose to create a single-page dialog box or a tabbed (multipage) dialog box. The icon on the left side of the dialog box shows you what the dialog box will look like at each step. If you choose to create a single-page dialog box, when you click the Next button, you will see the next page of the Dialog Wizard (see Figure 9.6).

Figure 9.6.

The second page of the Dialog Wizard.

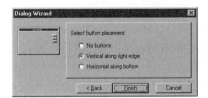

This page enables you to choose whether you want buttons on the dialog box and, if so, whether you want them on the right side or the bottom of the dialog box. As you can see from Figure 9.6 (see the Finish button?), this is the last page of the Dialog Wizard when creating a single-page dialog box. After choosing the button layout you want, click the Finish button to have C++Builder create the dialog box for you.

The new dialog box is displayed on the Form Designer complete with the features you chose through the wizard. It also has its BorderStyle property set to bsDialog, which is customary for forms used as dialog boxes. After the Dialog Wizard has created the basic dialog box, you can go to work with the Form Designer to add functionality to the dialog box.

If you choose to create a tabbed dialog box, the second page of the dialog box looks like the one in Figure 9.7.

Figure 9.7.

*The Dialog Wizard
creating a tabbed
dialog box.*

This page has a multiline edit control where you can enter the names of the individual tabs you want to see on the dialog box. Enter the text for each tab on a separate line, as illustrated in Figure 9.7. When you click the Next button, you will see the last page of the Dialog Wizard as you saw in Figure 9.6. Choose the location of the buttons, if any, and click the Finish button to have C++Builder create the tabbed dialog box.

> The Dialog Wizard is most useful when creating tabbed dialog boxes. When creating single-page dialog boxes, it is easier to choose one of the predefined dialog boxes from the Object Repository rather than going through the Dialog Wizard.

Creating Applications with the Application Wizard

The Application Wizard is a useful tool that can help you quickly set up the shell of an application. To create a new application using the Application Wizard, choose File | New from the main menu. When the Object Repository is displayed, click the Projects tab and then double-click the Application Wizard icon.

> The New Application item on the main menu creates a new application based on the current default project setting. It doesn't start the Application Wizard as you might expect.

Let's walk through the Application Wizard one page at a time.

Page One: Selecting the Menus

When you start the Application Wizard, the first page is displayed, as shown in Figure 9.8.

This page enables you to select the items you want on your application's main menu. You can choose to add a File menu, an Edit menu, a Window menu, and a Help menu. Place a check in the box for each menu item you want to appear on your menu bar.

Figure 9.8.

Page one of the Application Wizard.

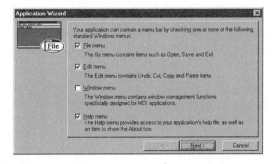

TIP

The Window menu is usually reserved for MDI applications. You probably won't put a Window menu on your SDI application's menu bar unless you have a specialty app that requires it.

NOTE

The menus added by the Application Wizard are a reasonable representation of the menu items that are most commonly used in Windows applications. Remember that the Application Wizard is intended to give you a head start in creating your application. It is up to you to take the basic structure and modify it to make a working application.

After you have chosen the menus you want for your application, click the Next button to move on to the next page.

Page Two: Setting the File Dialog Filters

If you chose to add a File menu to your application, the next page displayed will look like the one in Figure 9.9.

Figure 9.9.

Setting filters for the file dialog boxes.

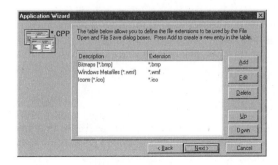

This page enables you to set the filters that your application's File Open and File Save dialog boxes will use. (Figure 9.9 shows the dialog box after the filters have been added.) Click the Add button to add a new filter. A dialog box is displayed, asking for the description and the filter. Enter the filters exactly as you do when setting the Filter property for the common file dialog box components. Enter the textual description and then the actual file mask (*.bmp, for instance). The Edit, Delete, Up, and Down buttons can be used as necessary to change, delete, or move the filter in the list.

NOTE

Pages two and three will be displayed only if you had previously selected menus on page one of the Application Wizard. More specifically, page two will be displayed only if you selected a File menu on page one.

Page Three: Setting Up the Speedbar

Page three of the Application Wizard aids you in setting up a speedbar (also called a toolbar) for your application. This is possibly the most useful feature of the Application Wizard (not that the other features aren't useful). You can quickly lay out your speedbar through this page. Figure 9.10 shows the third page of the Application Wizard after a speedbar has been created.

Figure 9.10.

Setting up the speedbar.

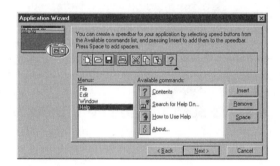

The list box on the left side of the page, labeled Menus, shows the four menus for which you can add buttons. When you choose one of the menus, the available buttons for that menu are displayed in the list box to the right of the Menus list box (labeled Available Commands). To add a speedbar button, click the button in the Available Commands list box and then click the Insert button. The button will be added to the sample speedbar at the top of the page. The Space button can be used to add a separator to the speedbar. Adding separators visually distinguishes groups of buttons. Continue to add buttons and spaces as needed until the speedbar is completed. If you decide to remove a button, just click it in the sample speedbar and then click the Remove button.

NOTE

If you elected not to add a particular menu to your application, no buttons will be shown for that menu group. For instance, if you did not add a Window menu, the Available Commands list box will be empty when you click on the Window item in the Menus list box.

The Application Wizard even takes care of setting the short hint text for the speed buttons. Do you remember creating a toolbar by hand on Day 7, "Working with the Form Designer and the Menu Designer"? Compare that process with the process of creating the speedbar through the Application Wizard. It should be apparent that using the Application Wizard is by far the easiest way to create a speedbar.

TIP

Some specialty applications have a speedbar but don't have a menu. To create a speedbar with the Application Wizard, you must first have created a menu. To work around this, tell the Application Wizard that you want a menu and then build the speedbar. After the application has been generated, you can delete the `MainMenu` component from the application to remove the menu.

Page Four: Setting the Final Options

The fourth and last page of the Application Wizard enables you to set the program name, the path where the project should be stored on disk, and a few final options. Figure 9.11 shows the last page of the Application Wizard.

Figure 9.11.

The final Application Wizard settings.

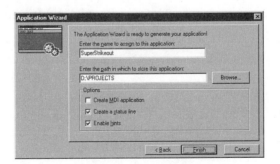

The first field on this page is where you specify the name of the application. This is not the name as it appears on the Project Options dialog box, but rather the filename that C++Builder will use to save the project. You will still need to set the application name in the Project Options dialog box. The second field is used to specify the directory where the project should be saved. If you don't know the exact path, click the Browse button to the right of this field and choose the path from the Select Directory dialog box.

TIP

> You can use the Select Directory dialog box to create a directory as well as to select a directory. Click the Browse button to display the Select Directory dialog box. Enter the path for the directory you want to create and then click OK or press Enter. C++Builder will prompt you to create the new directory if the directory you entered doesn't exist.

The bottom half of this page gives you three additional options. If you are creating an MDI application, click the check box marked Create MDI Application. (MDI applications were discussed on Day 6, "The C++Builder IDE Explored.") The remaining two check boxes enable you to implement a status bar and hint text for your components.

When you are sure you have made all the choices for your new application, click the Next button. C++Builder creates the application based on the options you specified. C++Builder writes as much code as possible for the application. This doesn't amount to a lot of code, but some of the basic code is already written for you. For example, if you chose a File menu, the `FileOpenClick()` handler has been written and looks like this:

```
void __fastcall TMainForm::FileOpen(TObject *Sender)
{
  if (OpenDialog->Execute())
  {
    //---- Add code to open OpenDialog->FileName ----
  }
}
```

The code to execute the File Open dialog box is in place; you only have to write the code that actually deals with the returned filename.

TIP

> After you create an Application Wizard project, you can choose Project | Save To Repository to save the project for later use. This will save you the trouble of going through the Application Wizard to create your basic application. You might want to add an About box before saving the project to the Repository.

Using the wizards is fast and easy. You will still need to write the program, of course, but C++Builder gives you a head start by saving you from the tedium of creating the basic application elements. As RAD-friendly as C++Builder is overall, the wizards simplify things even more. The C++Builder wizards are sort of like RAD on RAD!

NOTE

C++Builder provides wizards other than the Dialog Wizard and the Application Wizard. For example, the Database Form Wizard is used to create database forms and the Resource DLL Wizard aids in internationalization of your applications. These are specialized wizards so I didn't cover them in this chapter.

9

Adding Functions and Data Members to Code

As you know by now, C++Builder is a great tool for quickly creating the UI portion of a Windows application. It creates event handlers for you so that you can begin entering code to drive your application. It won't be long, however, before you find the need to start adding more complicated code to your applications. Part of that means adding your own data members and functions to the code that C++Builder generates. For example, a simple application might contain two dozen event handlers of various types. C++Builder creates all these event handlers for you; you simply fill in the blanks with working code. To make the application a viable, working application, however, you might have to write another two dozen functions of your own.

Adding your own functions and data members to code generated by C++Builder is not a difficult task, but you need to know the rules or you can get into trouble.

How C++Builder Manages Class Declarations

As you know, when you create a new form in the Form Designer, C++Builder creates three files for you: the form file, the source code unit, and the unit's header. When C++Builder creates the class declaration in the header, it essentially creates two sections. The first section is the part of the class declaration that C++Builder manages. The second section is the part that you manage. On Day 7 you created the ScratchPad program. If you did the exercises at the end of that chapter, you also created an About box for the program and added a few more buttons. Listing 9.1 contains the main form's header as it appears after adding these enhancements.

Listing 9.1. SPMain.h.

```
1: class TScratchPad : public TForm
2: {
3: __published:    // IDE-managed Components
4:     TPanel *Panel1;
```

continues

Listing 9.1. continued

```
5:      TBevel *Bevel1;
6:      TSpeedButton *FileOpenBtn;
7:      TSpeedButton *FileSaveBtn;
8:      TStatusBar *StatusBar;
9:      TMainMenu *MainMenu;
10:     TMenuItem *FileMenu;
11:     TMenuItem *FileOpen;
12:     TMenuItem *FileSave;
13:     TMenuItem *FileSaveAs;
14:     TMenuItem *N1;
15:     TMenuItem *FilePrintSetup;
16:     TMenuItem *N2;
17:     TMenuItem *FileExit;
18:     TMenuItem *FilePrint;
19:     TMenuItem *Edit1;
20:     TMenuItem *EditReplace;
21:     TMenuItem *EditFind;
22:     TMenuItem *N4;
23:     TMenuItem *EditPaste;
24:     TMenuItem *EditCopy;
25:     TMenuItem *EditCut;
26:     TMenuItem *N5;
27:     TMenuItem *EditUndo;
28:     TMenuItem *Help1;
29:     TMenuItem *HelpAbout;
30:     TMenuItem *HelpContents;
31:     TMenuItem *EditSelectAll;
32:     TMenuItem *N3;
33:     TMenuItem *EditWordWrap;
34:     TOpenDialog *OpenDialog;
35:     TSaveDialog *SaveDialog;
36:     TMenuItem *FileNew;
37:     TMemo *Memo;
38:     TPopupMenu *MemoPopup;
39:     TMenuItem *PopupCut;
40:     TMenuItem *PopupCopy;
41:     TMenuItem *PopupPaste;
42:     TSpeedButton *EditCutBtn;
43:     TSpeedButton *SpeedButton2;
44:     TSpeedButton *SpeedButton3;
45:     TSpeedButton *SpeedButton4;
46:     void __fastcall FileOpenClick(TObject *Sender);
47:     void __fastcall FileSaveClick(TObject *Sender);
48:     void __fastcall FileSaveAsClick(TObject *Sender);
49:     void __fastcall FileExitClick(TObject *Sender);
50:     void __fastcall EditSelectAllClick(TObject *Sender);
51:     void __fastcall EditCutClick(TObject *Sender);
52:     void __fastcall EditCopyClick(TObject *Sender);
53:     void __fastcall EditPasteClick(TObject *Sender);
54:     void __fastcall EditWordWrapClick(TObject *Sender);
55:     void __fastcall FileNewClick(TObject *Sender);
56:     void __fastcall EditUndoClick(TObject *Sender);
57:     void __fastcall HelpAboutClick(TObject *Sender);
58:     void __fastcall FormCreate(TObject *Sender);
```

```
59: private:        // User declarations
60: public:         // User declarations
61:    virtual __fastcall TScratchPad(TComponent* Owner);
62: };
```

Look at line 3 in the code. Notice the __published keyword and the comment that says IDE-managed Components. The section between the __published keyword and the private keyword (on line 59 in this case) should be considered off-limits. As they say, "Don't go there." Leave the __published section to C++Builder to manage.

WARNING

Placing any code between the __published keyword and the private keyword can cause problems with your program. In some cases, you might just get compiler or linker errors. In other cases, your program might be beyond repair (unusual but possible). Get in the habit of avoiding the __published section like the plague.

NOTE

If you're an astute student, you might be scratching your head right now. In the first four chapters we covered the basics of the C++ language. You learned about private, protected, and public class access, but not a word about the __published keyword. The reason is simple: __published is not a C++ keyword. The __published keyword is a Borland extension to C++ and doesn't exist in ANSI standard C++. This keyword was added to allow the C++ language to take advantage of the power of components.

Notice that lines 59 and 60 in Listing 9.1 have comments that say User declarations. You can safely place any of your own class data members or class member function declarations in either the private or the public section of the class declaration. You could add a protected section and place data members or functions there too, of course.

A Word About Status Bars and Hints

In a moment we're going to add support for hint text displayed in the status bar of the ScratchPad program. Before we do, though, you need a brief primer on how hint text is handled.

When the `Application` object's `ShowHint` property is set to `true` (the default), and the mouse cursor is placed over a component that also has its `ShowHint` property set to `true`, a hint event is triggered. The `Application` object has an event called `OnHint` that occurs whenever a hint event is triggered. The `Application`'s `Hint` property will contain the hint text for the control that generated the hint event. An application can use the `OnHint` event to display the hint on a status bar.

The problem is that you can't directly access the `OnHint` event of the `Application` object. What you can do, however, is reassign the value of `OnHint` to point to one of your own functions. Then, when the hint event occurs, the event gets rerouted to your own `OnHint` handler. To do that, you have to write your own event handler for the `OnHint` event. Let's do that next.

Adding a Function to Your Code

To illustrate adding a function to an application, let's implement hint text for the `ScratchPad` program you wrote earlier. First, reopen the `ScratchPad` program.

First, we need to prepare the way. We need to assign hint text to each of the speed buttons and prepare the status bar to receive the hints. Do the following:

1. Ensure that the `ScratchPad` main form is visible. Click the File Open speed button on the main form's speedbar.

2. Locate the `Hint` property in the Object Inspector and type the following for the hint text:

   `Open¦Open an Existing File`

3. Change the `ShowHint` property to `true`.

4. Repeat Steps 2 and 3 for all buttons on the speedbar, adding appropriate hint text for each type of button.

5. Click the status bar component along the bottom of the main form. Change the `SimplePanel` property to `true`. This will allow the full status bar to display a text string through the `SimpleText` property.

Okay, now we have everything ready to go, so it's time we did what you came here for. We're going to create our own `OnHint` handler and, not surprisingly, we're going to name the function `OnHint()`. Let's take this one step at a time. First, we'll add the function declaration to the class declaration. Here goes:

1. Switch to the Code Editor and click the `SPMain.cpp` tab.

2. Right-click on the Code Editor window and choose Open Source/Header File from the context menu. The `SPMain.h` tab appears next to the `SPMain.cpp` tab and

becomes the active code window.

3. Scroll down through the class declaration for the TScratchPad class until you locate the private section. Add this line of code after the private keyword:

```
void __fastcall OnHint(TObject* Sender);
```

To give you perspective, the last few lines of the class declaration should now look like this:

```
    void __fastcall FormCreate(TObject *Sender);
private:        // User declarations
    void __fastcall OnHint(TObject* Sender);
public:         // User declarations
    virtual __fastcall TScratchPad(TComponent* Owner);
};
```

Okay, so far, so good. Now you've added the function declaration for your new function. Two more steps and we'll be done. First we need to add the actual function to the source unit. After that, we need to assign our new function to the Application object's OnHint event.

1. Click the SPMain.cpp tab and scroll to the bottom of the file.

2. Enter the following code:

```
void __fastcall TScratchPad::OnHint(TObject* Sender)
{
  StatusBar->SimpleText = Application->Hint;
}
```

3. Go to the Object Inspector. Select the main form, ScratchPad, from the Object Selector.

4. Switch to the Events page in the Object Inspector and double-click in the Value column next to the OnCreate event. The Code Editor is displayed and is ready for you to type code.

5. Enter this code at the cursor:

```
Application->OnHint = OnHint;
```

The complete FormCreate() function should now look like this:

```
void __fastcall TScratchPad::FormCreate(TObject *Sender)
{
  Application->OnHint = OnHint;
}
```

6. Compile and run the program. The long hint text you entered will show in the status bar, and the short hint text will be displayed in the ToolTip over the button.

Step 2 sets the hint text (from the Hint property of the Application object) to the SimpleText property of the StatusBar class. Step 5 takes the function we created in Step 2 and assigns its address to the OnHint event of the Application class. Each time an OnHint event occurs, your OnHint() function is called and the hint text is displayed in the status bar.

NOTE

> Methods that will be used as event handlers need to be declared with the __fastcall modifier. Functions you create for general purpose use don't need the __fastcall modifier.

Adding a Class Data Member

Adding a class data member to a class generated in C++Builder works in exactly the same way. All you have to do is to ensure that you add the data member to the private or public section of the class declaration as you did earlier when adding a class member function.

Deleting C++Builder-Generated Code

There might be a time when you'll need to delete code that C++Builder generated in your application. For instance, you might have a button on a form that, due to design changes, is no longer needed. To delete the button, of course, all you have to do is select the button in the Form Designer and press the Delete button on the keyboard. No more button. C++Builder deletes the button, but the OnClick handler associated with that button is still in the code. C++Builder knows that the button associated with that OnClick handler is gone, but it still doesn't delete the event handler because it is possible that other components are using the same event handler. It's up to you to delete the event handler if you want it removed from your code.

The actual deletion of the event handler is a trivial task:

- ☐ Delete the function definition from the source unit.
- ☐ Delete the function declaration from the header.

NOTE

> This is the exception to the rule that you should never modify the __published section of your forms' class declaration.

TIP

> The fastest and easiest way to remove an event handler from your code is to delete all the code inside the event handler and save the project. C++Builder will remove any empty event handlers it finds.

Before you delete the event handler, you need to make sure that no other components are using that handler. Unfortunately, there is no simple way of determining whether another component is using a particular event handler. You need to be aware of how the components in your application interact.

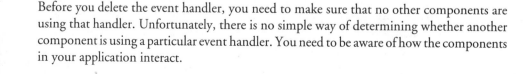

NOTE   Some might say that if you are unsure about an event handler being used by other components, just leave it in the code. That's a bad solution, in my opinion. You need to take the responsibility for knowing what is in your code and getting rid of any unused functions. Although unused code doesn't hurt anything, it leads to a larger .EXE file. In some cases, unused code can lead to performance degradation. Be diligent in paring your programs of unused or inefficient code.

Component Templates

Component templates enable you to create, save, and reuse groups of components. In fact, a component template doesn't have to be a group of components at all—it can be a single component. A quick example would probably help you see how useful component templates can be. First a quick lesson on the Windows edit control.

The standard Windows single-line edit control, like all Windows controls, has certain predefined behaviors. One of those behaviors deals with the way the Enter key is handled. If the user presses the Enter key when in an edit control, Windows looks for a default button on the window. If a default button is found, Windows essentially clicks the button. What does this mean to you? Let's say you have several edit controls on a form and a default button such as an OK button (or any button with the Default property set to true). When you press the Enter key when an edit control has focus, the form will close. If there is no default button on the form, Windows will just beep. Although this is standard Windows behavior, many users find it annoying and confusing. What many users prefer, particularly when working with a form that has several edit fields, is that the Enter key moves focus to the next control rather than closing the form.

The solution to this problem is really pretty simple. All you have to do is provide an event handler for the OnKeyPress event and add code so that it looks like this:

```
void __fastcall TForm1::Edit1KeyPress(TObject *Sender, char &Key)
{
  if (Key == VK_RETURN) {
    Key = 0;
    PostMessage(Handle, WM_NEXTDLGCTL, 0, 0);
  }
}
```

This code first checks to see whether the key pressed was the Enter key (VK_RETURN). If so, it sets the value of Key to 0. This eliminates the beep that Windows emits when the Enter key is pressed in an Edit control. The next line posts a WM_NEXTDLGCTL message. This message will set focus to the next control in the tab order. That's all there is to it.

After you have written the code for your new Edit component, you can save it as a component template. When you do, all the code is saved as well. Any code templates you create go into the Templates page of the Component palette. Let's create a component template so you can see how it works. Perform these steps:

1. Place an Edit component on a blank form. Change its Name property to EnterAsTab and clear its Text property.

2. Switch to the Events page in the Object Inspector and create an event handler for the OnKeyPress event. Enter this code in the event handler:

    ```
    if (Key == VK_RETURN) {
      Key = 0;
      PostMessage(Handle, WM_NEXTDLGCTL, 0, 0);
    }
    ```

3. Be sure the Edit component is selected and choose Component | Create Component Template from the main menu. The Component Template Information dialog box is displayed.

4. Enter TEnterAsTab in the Component name field. The Component Template Information dialog box should now look like the one in Figure 9.12.

Figure 9.12.

The Component Template Information dialog box.

5. Click OK to save the component template.

Now your Component palette will have a tab called Templates. Switch to the Templates tab (you might have to scroll the Component palette tabs to find it), select your new component, and place it on the form. You will see that the code for the OnKeyPress event handler was included when the component was placed on the form.

 TIP

If you had several of these components on a form, the code for the OnKeyPress event handler would be repeated for every EnterAsTab component on the form. Rather than duplicating code you could just place one EnterAsTab component on the form. Any other components could be standard Edit components that have their OnKeyPress events hooked up to the OnKeyPress event handler for the EnterAsTab component.

One of the biggest advantages of component templates is that the code written for each component's event handlers is saved along with the component. Component templates enable you to have a collection of customized components at your disposal: common dialog boxes with predefined filters and titles, speed buttons with glyphs already included, list boxes or combo boxes that automatically load items from a file, or any of a number of other possibilities.

Although the concept of a component template works for a single component, it makes even more sense when dealing with multiple components. If you have a group of components that you place on your forms over and over again, you can create a component template from those components. After you have created a component template, reusing a group of components is only a click away.

NOTE

There are certainly some similarities between component templates and saving forms in the Object Repository. Use component templates for groups of components that you typically use as part of a larger form. Use the Object Repository to save entire forms that you want to reuse.

Using Resource Files

 Every Windows program uses resources. *Resources* are those elements of a program that support the program but are not executable code.

A typical Windows program's resources include:

- ☐ Accelerators
- ☐ Bitmaps
- ☐ Cursors
- ☐ Dialog boxes
- ☐ Icons
- ☐ Menus
- ☐ Data tables
- ☐ String tables
- ☐ Version information
- ☐ User-defined specialty resources (sound files and AVI files, for example)

NOTE

> Version information can be easily added to your C++Builder projects through the Version Info tab of the Project Options dialog box. The Project Options dialog box is discussed in detail on Day 10, "More on Projects."

Resources are generally contained in a *resource script file* (a text file with an .RC extension), which is compiled by a resource compiler and then bound to the application's .EXE file during the link phase.

Resources are usually thought of as being bound to the executable file. Some resources, such as bitmaps, string tables, and wave files, can be placed in external files (.BMP, .TXT, and .WAV), or they can be bound to the .EXE and contained within the application file. You can opt to do it either way. Placing resources in the .EXE file has two main advantages:

☐ The resources can be accessed more quickly because it takes less time to locate a resource in the executable file than it does to load it from a disk file.

☐ The program file and resources can be contained in a single unit (the .EXE file) without the need for a lot of supporting files.

The downside to this approach is that your .EXE will be slightly larger. The program file won't be any larger than the combined external resource files plus the executable, but the extra size could result in slightly longer load times for the program.

Your exact needs will determine whether you decide to keep your resources in external files or have your resources bound to the .EXE. The important thing to remember is that you can do it either way (or even both ways in the same program).

A traditional Windows program will almost always contain at least one dialog box and an icon. A C++Builder application, however, is a little different. First of all, there are no true dialog boxes in a C++Builder application, so there are no dialog box resources per se (C++Builder forms are stored as resources, but they are RCDATA resources and not dialog box resources). A C++Builder application does have a traditional icon resource, though. C++Builder takes care of creating the resource file for the icon for you when you create the application. Similarly, when you choose bitmaps for speed buttons, Image components, or BitBtn components, C++Builder includes the bitmap file you chose as part of the form's resource. The form and all its resources are then bound to the program file when the application is built. It's all more or less handled for you automatically.

There are times, however, when you will want to implement resources aside from the normal C++Builder processes. For instance, if you want to do animation, you will have to have a series of bitmaps that can be loaded as resources for the fastest possible execution speed. In this kind of situation, you are going to need to know how to bind the resources to your C++Builder program file.

The act of binding the resource file to the executable is trivial, actually. It's much more difficult to actually create the resources. Creating basic resources such as bitmaps, icons, and cursors is not difficult with a good resource editor, but creating professional quality 3D bitmaps and icons is an art in itself. How many times have you seen a fairly decent program with really awful bitmap buttons? I've seen plenty. (Sorry, I'm getting off track here.) You can create bitmaps, icons, and cursors with the C++Builder Image Editor. If you are going to create string resources, user data resources, wave file resources, or other specialty resources, you will probably need a third-party resource editor.

NOTE

> If you have Borland C++, you can use the Resource Workshop from that product to edit specialty resources. After creating the resources, you will have an .RC file that you can either add to your C++Builder project directly, or compile into a .RES file using the Borland Resource Compiler (BRCC32.EXE). The Borland Resource Compiler comes with both Borland C++ and C++Builder. Technically, you could create the .RC file with any text editor and compile it with the Resource Compiler, but in reality it is much easier to use a resource editor.

You can add either a .RES file or a .RC file to your project via the Project Manager. To add a resource file to a project using the Project Manager, you first choose View | Project Manger from the main menu to display the Project Manager. If there is more than one project in the project group, double-click the project name of the project to which you want to add the resource file. Now click the Add File To Project button on the C++Builder toolbar or right-click the project name and choose Add from the Project Manager context menu. When the File Open dialog box appears, select the resource file you want to add to the project and click Open. The resource file shows up in the Project Manager with the rest of the application's files. I'll discuss the Project Manager in more detail tomorrow.

Listings 9.2 and 9.3 contain the header and main form unit for a program called Jumping Jack. This program shows a simple animation with sound effects. The main form contains just two buttons, an Image component and a Label component. The Jumping Jack program illustrates several aspects of using resources in a C++Builder application. Specifically, it shows how to load a bitmap stored as a resource, how to load and display a string resource, and how to play wave audio contained as a resource. Listing 9.4 is a partial listing of the resource file that is used by the Jumping Jack program. Examine the listings, and then we'll discuss what the program does.

Listing 9.2. JJMain.h.

```
 1: //--------------------------------
 2: #ifndef JJMainH
 3: #define JJMainH
 4: //--------------------------------
 5: #include <vcl\Classes.hpp>
 6: #include <vcl\Controls.hpp>
 7: #include <vcl\StdCtrls.hpp>
 8: #include <vcl\Forms.hpp>
 9: #include <vcl\ExtCtrls.hpp>
10: //-----------------------------------
11: class TMainForm : public TForm
12: {
13: __published:     // IDE-managed Components
14:     TButton *Start;
15:     TButton *Stop;
16:     TImage *Image;
17:     TLabel *Label;
18:     void __fastcall FormCreate(TObject *Sender);
19:
20:     void __fastcall StartClick(TObject *Sender);
21:     void __fastcall StopClick(TObject *Sender);
22: private:         // User declarations
23:     bool done;
24:     void DrawImage(String& name);
25: public:          // User declarations
26:     virtual __fastcall TMainForm(TComponent* Owner);
27: };
28: //--------------------------------
29: extern PACKAGE TMainForm *MainForm;
30: //--------------------------------
31: #endif
```

Listing 9.3. JJMain.cpp.

```
 1: //----------------------------------------------------------------
 2: #include <vcl\vcl.h>
 3: //
 4: // have to add this include for the PlaySound() function
 5: //
 6: #include <vcl\mmsystem.hpp>
 7: #pragma hdrstop
 8:
 9: #include "JJMain.h"
10: #pragma package(smart_init)
11: #pragma resource "*.dfm"
12: //
13: // defines for the string resources
14: //
15: #define IDS_UP    101
16: #define IDS_DOWN  102
17:
```

```
18: TMainForm *MainForm;
19: //------------------------------------------------------------
20: __fastcall TMainForm::TMainForm(TComponent* Owner)
21:    : TForm(Owner),
22:    done(false)
23: {
24: }
25: //------------------------------------------------------------
26: void __fastcall TMainForm::FormCreate(TObject *Sender)
27: {
28:    //
29:    // load and display the first bitmap
30:    //
31:    Image->Picture->Bitmap->
32:      LoadFromResourceName((int)HInstance, "ID_BITMAP1");
33: }
34: //------------------------------------------------------------
35: void __fastcall TMainForm::StartClick(TObject *Sender)
36: {
37:    //
38:    // When the Start button is clicked the animation
39:    // loop starts. The bitmap resources are named
40:    // ID_BITMAP1 through ID_BITMAP5 so we'll start with
41:    // a string called "ID_BITMAP" and append the last
42:    // digit when needed.
43:    //
44:    String s = "ID_BITMAP";
45:    //
46:    // a buffer for the string resources
47:    //
48:    char buff[10];
49:    //
50:    // a flag to let us know when we're done
51:    //
52:    done = false;
53:    //
54:    // start the loop and keep looping until the 'Stop'
55:    // button is pressed
56:    //
57:    while (!done) {
58:      //
59:      // loop through the five bitmaps starting with
60:      // 1 and ending with 5
61:      //
62:      for (int i=1;i<6;i++) {
63:        //
64:        // append the value of 'i' to the end of the string
65:        // to build a string containing the resource name
66:        //
67:        String resName = s + String(i);
68:        //
69:        // call a class member function to display the bitmap
70:        //
71:        DrawImage(resName);
72:      }
```

continues

Listing 9.3. continued

```
 73:    //
 74:    // load the "Up" string resource using the WinAPI
 75:    // function LoadString(), display the string,
 76:    // and tell Windows to repaint the Label
 77:    //
 78:    LoadString(HInstance, IDS_UP, buff, sizeof(buff));
 79:    Label->Caption = buff;
 80:    Label->Refresh();
 81:    //
 82:    // play the 'up' sound using the WinAPI function
 83:    // PlaySound(), play it asynchronously
 84:    //
 85:    PlaySound("ID_WAVEUP",
 86:      HInstance, SND_ASYNC | SND_RESOURCE);
 87:    //
 88:    // pause for a moment at the top of the jump
 89:    //
 90:    Sleep(200);
 91:    //
 92:    // repeat all of the above except in reverse
 93:    //
 94:    for (int i=5;i>0;i--) {
 95:      String resName = s + String(i);
 96:      DrawImage(resName);
 97:    }
 98:    PlaySound("ID_WAVEDOWN",
 99:      HInstance, SND_ASYNC | SND_RESOURCE);
100:    LoadString(HInstance, IDS_DOWN, buff, sizeof(buff));
101:    Label->Caption = buff;
102:    Label->Refresh();
103:    Sleep(200);
104:   }
105: }
106: //-------------------------------------------------------------
107: void __fastcall TMainForm::StopClick(TObject *Sender)
108: {
109:   //
110:   // Stop button pressed, so tell the loop to stop executing
111:   //
112:   done = true;
113: }
114: //-------------------------------------------------------------
115: //
116: // a class member function to display the bitmap
117: //
118: void
119: TMainForm::DrawImage(String& name)
120: {
121:   //
122:   // load the bitmap from a resource
123:   // using the name passed to us
124:   //
125:   Image->Picture->Bitmap->
126:     LoadFromResourceName((int)HInstance, name);
```

```
127:   //
128:   // must pump the message loop so that Windows gets
129:   // a chance to display the bitmap
130:   //
131:   Application->ProcessMessages();
132:   //
133:   // take a short nap so the animation doesn't go too fast
134:   //
135:   Sleep(20);
136: }
```

Listing 9.4. `JJRes.rc`.

```
 1: #define IDS_UP      101
 2: #define IDS_DOWN    102
 3:
 4: STRINGTABLE
 5: {
 6:   IDS_UP, "Up"
 7:   IDS_DOWN, "Down"
 8: }
 9:
10: ID_WAVEUP    WAVE "up.wav"
11: ID_WAVEDOWN WAVE "down.wav"
12:
13: ID_BITMAP1 BITMAP LOADONCALL MOVEABLE DISCARDABLE IMPURE
14: {
15:   '42 4D 76 02 00 00 00 00 00 00 76 00 00 00 28 00'
16:   '00 00 20 00 00 00 20 00 00 00 01 00 04 00 00 00'
17:   //
18:   //  remainder of bitmap resources follow
```

ANALYSIS Notice lines 23 and 24 in the header for the main form class in Listing 9.2. Line 23 declares a `bool` data member that is used to determine when to stop the animation. The class member function declared on line 24 is used to display the bitmap in the `Image` component.

In Listing 9.3 you will notice that two Windows API functions are used to load the string and wave file resources. On line 78, the `LoadString()` function loads a string resource into a text buffer based on the numerical identifier of the string (see Listing 9.4 to see how the string resources are created). The string is then assigned to the `Caption` property of the label component on the form. On line 83, the `PlaySound()` function is used to play a wave file contained as a resource. The `SND_ASYNC` flag used with the `PlaySound()` function tells Windows to play the sound and immediately return control to the program. This enables the animation to continue while the sound is being played. The `SND_RESOURCE` flag tells Windows that the sound is contained as a resource and not as a file on disk. Both the `LoadString()` and `PlaySound()` functions use the `HInstance` global variable to tell Windows to look in the executable file for the resources.

Lines 1 through 8 of Listing 9.4 illustrate how a string table looks in a resource script file. Creating string tables is very easy with any text editor. On lines 10 and 11, a WAVE resource is created for each of the two wave files, which were previously recorded and reside in the project's directory. When the resource compiler sees the WAVE declaration, it reads the individual sound files and compiles them into the binary resource file.

NOTE

> As you can see from Listing 9.4, you can create some types of resources easily with a text editor. If you have bitmaps or wave audio stored as external files, you can include them in a .RC file as illustrated in Listing 9.4 and have them compiled into the binary resource file using the resource compiler. Later, the binary resource file can be bound to your application's executable file.

Listing 9.4 is a partial listing. Bitmaps created with a traditional resource editor are often contained in the resource file as numerical data. The resource descriptions for bitmaps can get very long. The rest of the bitmap resource descriptions for the Jumping Jack bitmaps require about 200 lines of resource code, so I decided not to list them all. Figure 9.13 shows Jumping Jack in mid-stride.

Figure 9.13.

Jumping Jack in action.

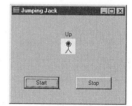

Creating additional resources for your programs is not rocket science, but it is not exactly trivial, either. It takes some time to realize how it all fits together. You might never need to add additional resources to your applications. If you do, though, it's good to have an idea where to begin. If this section left you a little dazed and confused, don't worry. Over time, it all starts to make sense.

NOTE

> Bitmaps, icons, and cursors found in other programs are usually copyrighted material. Don't use resources from any copyrighted program without permission. Further, assume all programs are copyrighted unless they are specifically said to be freeware. You are free to use the bitmaps, icons, and cursors that are provided with C++Builder (in the Common Files\Borland Shared Files\Images directory) in your applications without permission from Borland.

Packages

After your application is written you can deploy it in one of two ways. (*Deploying* means the act of distributing your application to your users.) You might be distributing your application to the general public or possibly to users within your company. Either way, you need to know what options are available to you. Essentially you have two choices: static linking or dynamic linking using packages. In this section I'll discuss those options so that you can make an informed choice on how to deploy your application. I'll start with a discussion of packages and then I'll discuss deployment options.

What's a Package?

Before I discuss the options available to you, it would be a good idea to define what a package is. When you take off the wrappings, a package is, essentially, just a DLL with an extension of .BPL rather than the traditional .DLL extension. There are two types of packages in C++Builder—runtime packages and design packages. I'll go over each of these two types next so you can get an understanding of how packages work. Because a package is just a form of DLL, I'll use the term package and DLL interchangeably.

Runtime Packages

A runtime package contains code your application needs to run. Although C++Builder provides many different packages, the primary package is called VCL30.BPL. This package contains all the base VCL code in one DLL. If you choose to use packages in your application, your application will load a package called VCL30.BPL and call routines from that package as needed. If your application is a database application, it will also load VCLDB30.BPL and call routines from that package as needed. There are other C++Builder packages in addition to the two mentioned here.

In addition to the VCL packages, your application might require other packages. This will be the case if you are using any third-party components or any components that you write yourself. You will have to check the documentation for any third-party components to find out which packages your application requires to run. I'm getting ahead of myself a little so let me tell you about design packages and then I'll get back to deploying applications that use packages.

Design Packages

To explain design packages it might be a good idea to first give you a short tutorial on component design. Most components created for C++Builder include a runtime package and a design package. The runtime package contains all the code needed for a component to operate. The design package contains the code needed for the component to operate on a form at design time. The design package has a Requires list that tells C++Builder which packages it requires to operate. The design package almost always requires code from the runtime package and probably code from one or more VCL packages as well. It's important to understand that one package (both runtime and design) can contain the code for several components. It's not necessary to have a separate package for each component.

Because design packages contain just the code needed to display components at design time they are usually much smaller than their runtime counterparts. Design packages are only used by C++Builder at design time—they are not needed for your application to operate.

Static Linking Versus Dynamic Linking

Now that you know a little about packages we can talk about static linking versus dynamic linking.

Static Linking

When an application uses static linking of the VCL and RTL, it doesn't use packages at all. Any code your application requires to run is linked directly into your application's executable file. Your application is a standalone program and doesn't require any supporting packages or DLLs.

NOTE

There are exceptions to every rule. The statement that a statically linked application doesn't require any supporting DLLs makes a couple of assumptions. The first assumption is that the application is not a database application. A C++Builder database application needs the Borland Database Engine (BDE) to operate. The BDE is primarily a collection of DLLs so a database application will require DLLs to operate, even if the application is statically linked. The second assumption is that the application doesn't use any ActiveX controls. ActiveX controls are actually a form of DLL, so if your application uses ActiveX controls, it is no longer a standalone application.

In the beginning there was C++Builder 1.0. C++Builder 1.0 only created applications that were statically linked. There were no packages in C++Builder 1.0, so dynamic linking of the VCL was not an option. (C++Builder 1.0 did have an option to use the dynamic version of the RTL but I doubt that it was widely, if ever, used.)

Although C++Builder 3.0 gives you a choice of linking options, static linking is the default. Static linking has two primary advantages over dynamic linking. The first is that you don't have to worry about shipping any additional files with your application. Your application contains all the code it needs to run and no runtime libraries are required. The second advantage is that an application that is statically linked is generally smaller in total size than an application that requires packages. I'll talk about this more in just a bit when I talk about the advantages and disadvantages of dynamic linking.

Static linking has one major drawback but it only shows up in applications that use many user-defined DLLs. The drawback is that the VCL and RTL code is duplicated in every module (the main application itself) and in every DLL. This means that code is duplicated unnecessarily. For example, let's say that every module requires a minimum of 200KB of VCL base code and RTL code. Now let's say that you have a main application and 10 supporting DLLs. That means that 2200KB of code is used (11 modules * 200KB each) when only 200KB is actually required. The application and DLLs are all statically linked and can't share the VCL and RTL code amongst themselves.

Dynamic Linking

Dynamic linking refers to a scenario where an application dynamically loads its library code at runtime. In the case of a C++Builder application, this means that any required packages and the runtime library DLL are loaded at runtime. Required packages will certainly include one or more VCL packages and might require third-party packages as well.

 NOTE

> The loading of packages by your application is automatic. You don't have to write code to load the packages or the runtime library DLL. C++Builder takes care of that for you. Choosing dynamic linking over static linking doesn't require any changes to your code. It does require changes to the way you deploy your application, which I will tell you about shortly.

Dynamic linking has one primary advantage over static linking: several modules can share code from a central location (the packages and RTL DLL). Remember earlier when I gave an example of an application and 10 supporting DLLs? Using dynamic linking, the application and all DLLs can all share code from the VCL package and the RTL DLL. Each module will be at least 200K smaller because all the base code is contained in the runtime DLLs. This is an advantage when your overall product contains several applications or many DLLs.

Dynamic linking comes with a couple of problems. The first problem is that the packages and DLLs that you need to ship with your application can be quite large. The primary VCL package, VCL30.BPL, is 1.4MB alone. The runtime library DLL, CP3240MT.DLL, is another 1.2MB or so. This means that your application will require at least 2.6MB of DLLs to run.

A second problem with dynamic linking is more subtle and more troublesome. The problem could be summed up in one word: versioning. To explain the problem let me give you a possible scenario. Let's say you create an application using C++Builder 3.02 (assuming a couple of revisions to C++Builder) and that you use dynamic linking, requiring you to ship the VCL packages and RTL DLL. Your customer installs your application on his or her machine and everything works fine. Meanwhile, I build an application using C++Builder 3.0 (I'm too cheap to pay the shipping for the upgrade) and I also use dynamic linking. Your customer buys my application and installs it. My installation program is homemade and doesn't play by the rules so I overwrite the packages and DLLs that your application installed. Suddenly your application quits working because my packages and RTL DLL are older than yours and the two are not compatible. Do you see the problem?

In reality, commercial software companies like Borland prevent this problem by naming their packages and DLLs by different names for each release of a product and by embedding version information in the packages and DLLs. (A good installation program will check the version number and only install a package if the package is newer than any existing packages on the user's system.) But packages from Borland aren't the real problem. The real problem comes when using components from companies that are less careful about how they do business. If you buy a component package from Billy Bob's Software Company, you are trusting that Billy Bob knows what he is doing when it comes to creating packages. That might or might not be a good assumption. Let's face it, with the boom of the Internet, components are available from a wide variety of sources. You don't know what you are getting in a lot of cases so be careful when purchasing inexpensive or freeware components.

So Which Is Better?

I can hear you thinking, "So should I use static linking or dynamic linking?" The answer to that question depends on the type of applications you write. In general, if you are writing a single, small- or medium-sized application, you should use static linking. If you are writing very large applications, or applications with a large number of DLLs, you should probably use dynamic linking.

A simple case study might help put this in perspective. On Day 7 you created the ScratchPad program. That program compiles to around 500KB (give or take a few KB) when static linking is used. If you link ScratchPad using packages and the dynamic version of the RTL, you can get the EXE size down to around 75KB, *but* you have to ship 2.5MB of DLLs. As you can see, dynamic linking is not a good choice in this case.

Using Runtime Packages in Your Applications

If you choose to use dynamic linking, you only need to change a couple of settings in the project options. Here's what you need to do:

1. Choose Project | Options from the main menu to bring up the Project Options dialog box.
2. Click the Linker tab and check the Use Dynamic RTL option on the Linker page.
3. Click the Packages tab and check the Build with runtime packages option near the bottom of the page (you can ignore the top of the page that deals with design packages).
4. Click OK to close the Project Options dialog box.
5. Rebuild the project.

That's all there is to it. Remember, using dynamic linking doesn't require any changes to your code.

Deploying Applications Using Packages

Deploying an application that uses dynamic linking requires you to know which packages and DLLs your application uses. If you followed the steps in the previous section, you can be assured that you need VCL30.BPL and CP3240MT.DLL at a minimum. You might need other VCL packages as well, depending on the components your application uses. To find out for sure, you will have to run a utility such as TDUMP.EXE and examine the imports that your EXE references. TDUMP can be found in your \Cbuilder\bin directory. To run TDUMP just open a command-prompt box and switch to the directory where your application resides. Then type the following at the command line (because TDUMP is on your path, you don't have to type the path to your bin directory):

```
tdump myproject.exe
```

Get ready on the Pause button because TDUMP will start displaying information right away. Somewhere along the line you will see some lines like this:

```
Imports from VCL30.bpl

    Sysconst::initialization() __fastcall

    Sysconst::Finalization() __fastcall
```

This might be repeated several times. You will have to watch for any files with a .BPL extension and make note of their filenames. When you are done, you will have a list of packages that you will have to ship with your application. Don't forget CP3240MT.DLL if you are using the dynamic RTL.

NOTE

> The output from TDUMP can be redirected to a text file for easier viewing. For example:
>
> ```
> tdump myproject.exe > dump.txt
> ```
>
> Now you can open DUMP.TXT in the C++Builder Code Editor and view the contents.
>
> You can save yourself a lot of time and trouble by getting a good installation program. Install Shield Express comes with C++Builder Professional and Client/Server versions, so you might already have an installation program that you can use. I also like Wise Install from Great Lakes Business Solutions. The better installation programs will figure out which packages your application requires and automatically include them in the installation. I don't recommend writing your own installation program under any circumstances. There are just too many things that you can fail to take into account when writing an installation program.

9

Most of the time you probably won't use runtime packages in your applications. On the other hand, sometimes packages are just what you need.

Summary

The Object Repository is a great tool for reusing previously created forms, dialog boxes, projects, and other objects. The capability to add your own objects to the Repository is a huge advantage when doing RAD. The Dialog Wizard and Application Wizard take it a step further and guide you through the creation process. The Application Wizard, in particular, is a very useful tool. In the middle of the chapter you learned how to add data members and functions to the classes that C++Builder generates. Toward the end of the chapter, I touched on the different types of resources that you might need to incorporate into your applications and how to add them to your C++Builder projects. At the end of the chapter we talked about packages. Packages give you flexibility in deciding how to deploy your applications and also make installing custom components easier.

Workshop

The Workshop contains quiz questions to help you solidify your understanding of the material covered and exercises to provide you with experience in using what you have learned. The answers appear in Appendix A, "Answers to Quiz Questions."

Q&A

Q When would I use the Use option of the Object Repository?

A When you have an object stored in the Object Repository that you want to update or make other changes to.

Q Is there a limit to the number of objects that can be stored in the Object Repository?

A Technically, you can store as many objects as you like. Remember, though, that the purpose of the Object Repository is to help you quickly locate and reuse your forms, dialog boxes, and other objects. If you put too many seldom used objects in the Object Repository, you will start to lose efficiency because it takes longer to find the specific object you are looking for. It also takes longer for the Object Repository to load and display all those objects.

Q I have a bunch of old objects in the Object Repository that I don't use any more. How can I get rid of them?

A Choose Tools | Repository from the main menu. The Object Repository configuration dialog box is displayed. To remove an object, first select the object in the Objects list box, and then click the Delete Object button. The object will be removed from the Object Repository.

Q **I had an object stored in the Object Repository. Now, when I try to use that object, I get a message box that says, "Unable to find both a form and a source file." What's the problem?**

A You have either moved or deleted the source or form file for the object. The Object Repository keeps track of the directory where the object is stored. If you move or delete the object, the Object Repository is unable to find the object and reports an error.

Q **Can I add objects to the New page of the Object Repository?**

A No. The New page of the Object Repository is fixed. It cannot be deleted or modified. You'll have to place your objects on another page.

Q **I added a function to my main form class. Now I can't compile. What's the problem?**

A You probably added the function declaration to the __published section of the class declaration accidentally. Be sure that the declaration for your function is in either the public or the private section of the class declaration (or the protected section if you have one).

Q **I have a resource editor that enables me to decompile resources contained in other programs. This lets me "borrow" bitmaps and other resources from other programs. Is this okay?**

A The short answer is, "No." You should assume all resources in other programs to be copyrighted material that cannot be freely copied. Consult a lawyer for a qualified opinion.

Q **I have a lot of bitmaps and sound files that go with my application. Can I put all those resources in a file other than the program's executable file?**

A Yes. You can have resources stored in a dynamic link library (DLL).

Quiz

1. When do you use the Inherit option when selecting an object in the Object Repository?

2. What is the procedure for saving a project to the Object Repository?

3. What happens to inherited forms when you change the base form?

4. Where in the form's class declaration do you place user function declarations?

5. Where do you place the function definition (the function itself) when you add your own functions to C++Builder code?

6. How can you determine who wrote a particular object in the Object Repository?

7. Where do you add and delete pages in the Object Repository?

8. Is it easier to create a basic application from scratch or by using the Application Wizard?

9. Which is better for small applications: static linking or dynamic linking using packages?

10. Can you create a resource script file containing a string table with a text editor?

Exercises

1. Create a new form. Add several components of your choosing to the form. Save the form to the Forms page of the Object Repository with the name BaseForm.

2. Start a new application. Choose File | New to view the Object Repository. Switch to the Forms page. Click the Inherit radio button. Choose the BaseForm object you created in Exercise 1 and add it to the application. (Be sure you used the Inherit option.) Save the project and close it.

3. Open the BaseForm object you created in Exercise 1. Delete all components on the form and save the form.

4. Reopen the project you created in Exercise 2. Display the new form you created in that exercise. Note that the components are all gone. (Remember, you inherited this object, so all changes made to the base form were also made to the inherited form.)

5. Choose Tools | Repository from the main menu. Delete the BaseForm created earlier.

6. Create a project using the Application Wizard. Use all menu options and make the application an MDI application. Create a speedbar for the application.

7. Add a multipage dialog box to the application you created in Exercise 6. Use the Dialog Wizard.

8. Use the Object Repository to add an About box to the program you created in Exercise 6.

9. Create a string table resource with a text editor and compile it with the resource compiler (BRCC32.EXE). (**Extra Credit:** Write a program to load the strings and display them on a form.)

10. Create a simple program and build it. Run Windows Explorer and examine the size of the .EXE created by C++Builder. Now change the project options to use runtime packages and the dynamic RTL. Rebuild the program. Check the size of the .EXE now. What is the difference in size?

11. Write "I will not borrow bitmaps from other programs." 100 times on the blackboard.

9

Day 10

More on Projects

On Day 6, "The C++Builder IDE Explored," you were introduced to C++Builder projects and found out a little about how projects work. Today you will find out about projects in more detail.

You will also learn more about the C++Builder Code Editor. The Code Editor has features that make working with code easier; you'll find out all about those features today.

Everyone Needs a Project

Projects are a fact of life with C++Builder. You cannot create a program without a project. The project makes sure that everything works together to create a working application. This section talks about

- ☐ The Project Manager
- ☐ Project groups
- ☐ The Project Options dialog box

Using the Project Manager

At some point, every project needs some management. Maybe you must add a new source unit to the project, or maybe you must remove a source unit. You might need to add other types of files to the project, such as a binary resource file or an import library for a DLL. You add and remove units and other project files through the Project Manager.

Project Groups

On Day 6 I said that a project is a collection of files that work together to create a standalone executable file or DLL. That's the definition of a project as far as the C++Builder IDE is concerned. In the real world you might have a different kind of project; a job that you have to complete. A large project might include one or more executable files and several DLLs. Because some projects consist of more than a single executable program, C++Builder enables you to group several C++Builder projects together and deal with them as a single unit. This unit is called a *project group*.

Why use project groups? Project groups give you the following:

- [ ] Better control over a complete software project.
- [ ] The ability to work on a DLL and a test EXE for the DLL at the same time.
- [ ] The ability to build (compile and link) a group of projects all at one time.
- [ ] The ability to have several projects open at one time and to easily switch between open projects.
- [ ] A way to organize related projects.

A project that creates a single executable file doesn't need a project group. A single project can hardly be considered a group, right? In the case of a single project the concept of a project group is out of place. But imagine for a moment a program that includes an EXE and a single supporting DLL. Both the DLL and the EXE go together. Usually, if you are working on the DLL, you will want the EXE present so you can immediately test any changes you make to the DLL. In this scenario, a project group makes perfect sense because EXE and DLL go everywhere together. You can create a project group that contains these two individual projects and save it. When you want to work on the application, you can open the project group rather than an individual project. When you open the project group, both the EXE project and the DLL project will be displayed. You can work on either the DLL or the EXE in the Code Editor and switch back and forth between them any time you want. Figure 10.1 shows the Project Manager window with this type of project group open.

10

Figure 10.1.

The Project Manager window, showing a simple project group.

Another reason to have a project group is so that you can group related projects. That probably sounds like it doesn't make much sense, so let me explain. Here at TurboPower Software we have a product called Async Professional, which is a collection of serial communications components. These components include three main categories: basic serial communications, faxing, and TAPI. We include dozens of sample programs with Async Professional, covering each of these three categories. Given that scenario, we could create a project group for all of our faxing examples, one for all of our TAPI examples, and one for all of our basic serial communications examples. Our users could then open the TAPI Examples project group and have all the TAPI examples in one neat package. The entire project group could be built at one time, thereby saving the time and aggravation of opening and building each project individually. In this case the projects don't work together like a DLL and EXE do, but the projects are related so the concept of a project group makes just as much sense.

In any project group there is always an active project. The active project is displayed in the Project Manager in bold type. In Figure 10.1, the active project is the project called `MainProgram`. The active project is the project that will be built when you choose Make or Build from the Project menu on the C++Builder main menu. These menu items are modified each time a project is made the active project. For example, if the active project is called `Project1`, then the menu items will be called `Make Project1` and `Build Project1`. If a project called `PictView` is made the active project, then these two menu items will be called `Make PictView` and `Build PictView`.

The active project also has significance when a new form or a new unit is added using the Project Manager. When you create a new form using the Project Manager, the new form will be added to the active project regardless of which node in the Project Manager is currently selected. The active project is also the project to which new forms or units will be added if you add new elements via the C++Builder main menu or the C++Builder toolbar.

You can make a project the active project in one of several ways. One way is to select any item in the project node you want to make the active project and click the Activate button on the top of the Project Manager. Another way is to simply double-click the project node itself. Finally, you can choose Activate from the project node context menu to activate a particular project.

10

The Project Manager Window

The Project Manager is the central controller for all of your projects and program groups. It enables you to add files to a project, delete files from a project, view a unit or form, add projects to the project group, change the order of projects, and more. To display the Project Manager, choose View | Project Manager from the main menu, or press Ctrl+Alt+F11.

The Project Manager window contains a tree view control that displays up to four levels. Those levels are

- [ ] The project group
- [ ] The projects within the project group
- [ ] Forms and other files within the project
- [ ] Individual form files and units under the form node

Naturally, the individual nodes can be collapsed or expanded as with any tree view control. The Project Manager nodes have icons that indicate whether the node contains a project, an individual file, a form, or a form/unit pair. Refer to Figure 10.1 to see the different icons and levels that the Project Manager displays.

The Project Manager Context Menus

Most of the Project Manager's work is done through the Manager's context menus. There are three separate context menus for the Project Manager. The first is the context menu you see when you right-click the project group node at the top of the Project Manager tree. Table 10.1 lists the Project Manager context menu items that appear on this menu.

Table 10.1. The project group context menu items.

Item	Description
Add New Project	Opens the Object Repository so you can choose a new project. Projects include applications, DLLs, forms, data modules, components, or any other object available from the Object Repository.
Add Existing Project	Opens a project file from disk and adds it to the project group or the active project.
Save Project Group	Saves the project group. Project groups have a .BPG extension.
Save Project Group As	Saves the project group with a new name.
View Project Group Source	Displays the project group source. The project group source is a special makefile that contains references to all projects within the project group.

The project context menu is displayed when you right-click a project node in the Project Manager. Table 10.2 lists the context menu items on to the project node context menu.

Table 10.2. The project context menu items.

Item	Description
Add	Opens the Add To Project dialog box so you can add a file to the project. The same as choosing Project | Add to Project from the main menu or from the C++Builder toolbar.
Remove File	Opens the Remove From Project dialog box so you can remove a file from the project. The same as choosing Project | Remove from Project from the main menu or from the C++Builder toolbar.
Save	Saves the project. The same as choosing File | Save Project As from the C++Builder main menu.
Options	Displays the Project Options dialog box for this project. The same as choosing Project | Options from the C++Builder main menu.
Activate	Makes this project the active project.
Make	Makes this project. The difference between make and build was discussed on Day 6.
Build	Builds this project.
View Source	Displays the project source file. The same as choosing View | Project Source from the C++Builder main menu.
View Project Makefile	Displays the project makefile. The same as choosing View | Project Makefile from the C++Builder main menu.
Close	Closes this project and all its files. If the project is part of a saved project group, the project node icon will be displayed as grayed out. The project is still part of the group but is not open in the IDE. If the project is part of the default project group, then the project is closed and removed from the default group.
Remove Project	Removes this project from the project group. The project is not deleted from your hard drive, just removed from the project group.

continues

Table 10.2. continued

Item	Description
Build Sooner	Moves the project up in the project tree. Projects are built from the top of the Project Manager down.
Build Later	Moves the project down in the project tree.

In addition to these two menus, a third menu is displayed when you right-click a node other than the project group node or a project node. This menu changes depending on the type of node you have selected. It will always contain an item called Open. Depending on the type of node selected, it may also have items called Save, Save As, Remove From Project, and Compile. The Open menu item displays the selected node in either the Code Editor or the Form Designer, depending on the type of the selected node. This does not apply to binary files such .RES files or .LIB files. The remaining menu items are self-explanatory.

The Project Manager Toolbar and Keyboard Commands

In addition to the Project Manager context menus, the Project Manager has a toolbar to make working with the Project Manager easier. The Project Manager toolbar contains three buttons. The New button displays the Object Repository so you can create a new object, whether it be an application, a DLL, a form, a unit, or any other object available from the Object Repository. This is essentially the same as clicking the Add New Project menu item from the Project Manager's context menu. The Remove button removes the selected project from the project group. Use this button only to remove an entire project, and not to remove a particular form or file from a project. The Activate button makes the selected project the active project.

Keyboard commands include the Delete key and the Insert key. When you press Delete, the Remove From Project dialog box is displayed just as it is if you choose Remove File from the project context menu. The Remove From Project dialog box presents a list of all forms and units in the active project, regardless of which node was selected when you pressed Delete. The Insert key behaves exactly the same as choosing Add from the project context menu.

> **TIP**
>
> The Project Manager toolbar buttons can be either large or small. By default, the Project Manager toolbar buttons are large. You can change the toolbar button size by dragging the bottom of the toolbar either up (to show the small buttons) or down (to show the large buttons).

Creating and Using Project Groups

Project groups are a great benefit for complex projects, but using a project group is not mandatory. You don't have to use project groups with every project. The Project Manager has a default project group called ProjectGroup1 that will be used if you don't specifically open or create a project group. Try this:

1. Choose File | Close All to close any open projects or project groups.

2. Choose File | New Application to create a new application.

3. Choose View | Project Manager to display the Project Manager. The Project Manager is displayed as shown in Figure 10.2.

Figure 10.2.

The Project Manager, showing the default project group.

The project group called ProjectGroup1 is a temporary project group. When you choose Save All from the File menu you are prompted to save the project, but not the project group. If you want to save the project group, you must explicitly save it using the Save Project Group or Save Project Group As menu item from one of the Project Manager context menus.

Adding Units

When you add files to your projects, you use the Add To Project dialog box. The Add To Project dialog box has file filters for the following types of files:

- ☐ C++Builder unit (.cpp)
- ☐ Pascal unit (.pas)
- ☐ C source file (.c)
- ☐ Resource script file (.rc)
- ☐ Assembler file (.asm)
- ☐ Module definition file (.def)
- ☐ Compiled resource file (.res)
- ☐ Object file (.obj)
- ☐ Library file (.lib)

If you add files of any of these types, C++Builder will know what to do with them. For example, if you add a C source file (`.c`), C++Builder will compile it as C rather than C++ (the differences are subtle, and most people don't care about the differences, but it matters to some programmers). If you add a Pascal file (`.pas`), the Pascal compiler will compile the source file before passing it to the linker. If you add a binary object file (`.obj`), C++Builder passes it to the linker at link time.

NOTE

> You cannot add a unit to a project if a form with the same name already exists in the project. For example, if you have a form called `MainForm` and try to add a unit from another project that also has a form named `MainForm`, you will get an error message from C++Builder even if the filenames are different.

You can add some file types to your project other than those listed here. For example, you might want to add a text file to your project that describes what the project does and how it is expected to be used. You might also want to add your header files to the project. The header files are already part of the project by virtue of the fact that they go with a unit. Adding a header to the project, however, gives you access to the header in the Project Manager.

Removing Units

You use the Remove File option to remove files from the project. Files removed from the project are not deleted from your hard drive but are just removed from the project compile/link process.

WARNING

> Be careful when removing units from your projects. You must be careful to not remove units that are referenced by other units in the project. If you remove units that are required by your project, a compiler or linker error will result. Before removing a unit, be sure it is used nowhere else in your project.

The Remove From Project dialog box enables multiple selection, so you can remove several units from a project at one time if you want.

Viewing Units or Forms

To view a unit, form, or other file, just double-click the node representing the form or unit you want to view. You can also choose Open from the Project Manager context menu. The form or unit will be displayed in the Form Designer or Code Editor, depending on the type of node you are viewing.

10

Building Projects or Project Groups

To make a particular project, you can do one of the following:

☐ Right-click the project node in the Project Manager and choose Make from the context menu.

☐ Choose Project | Make Project from the C++Builder main menu. The name of this menu item will change, based on the name of the active project.

☐ Press Ctrl+F9 on the keyboard to make the active project.

To build a project, choose Project | Build Project from the main menu or right-click a project node in the Project Manager and choose Build from the context menu.

To build an entire project group, choose Project | Build All Projects from the C++Builder main menu. All projects in the project group will be built, starting with the first project in the group (the project at the top of the Project Manager tree) and proceeding down through the last project in the group.

Understanding Project Options

Project options are another of those things that are easy to ignore. For one thing, the defaults are usually good enough when you are just starting out. After all, who has time to worry about all those compiler/linker options when you are just struggling to learn a new programming environment? At some point, though, you will start to become more interested in what all those options do, and it's good to have some reference when the time comes.

This section looks at the Project Options dialog box. You can invoke this dialog box by choosing Project | Options from the main menu. The Project Options dialog box is a tabbed dialog box with several pages:

☐ Forms
☐ Application
☐ Compiler
☐ Advanced Compiler
☐ C++
☐ Pascal
☐ Linker
☐ Directories/Conditionals
☐ Version Info
☐ Packages
☐ Tasm

10

I won't discuss every page of the Project Options dialog box, but you'll take a look at the most important pages so that you can understand exactly what each of these pages does. I'll start you out easy by discussing the Forms and Application pages. After that we'll move on to the more complicated pages.

> **NOTE**
>
> At the bottom of each page of the Project Options dialog box is a check box labeled Default. If you want the current settings to become the default settings for all new projects created, check the Default box. When you click OK, the current settings will become the new default settings.

The Forms Page

The Forms page of the Project Options dialog box is where you control how your application handles its forms. You saw this dialog box on Day 5, "C++ Class Frameworks and the Visual Component Model," when you created the Picture Viewer program. Figure 10.3 shows the Forms page of the Project Options dialog box for the ScratchPad program.

Figure 10.3.

The Forms page of the Project Options dialog box.

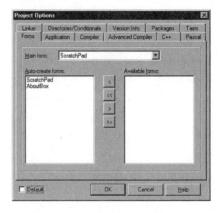

At the top of the Forms page is the Main Form combo box. This is where you tell C++Builder which form to display when the application starts. By default, the first form you create will be the main form. If you change your project around in such a way that a different form becomes the main form, you must change this setting so that the new form becomes the application's main form.

In the middle of the dialog box are two list boxes. The list box on the left is labeled Auto-Create Forms; the one on the right is labeled Available Forms. Before I talk about how to use these two list boxes, take a moment to learn about auto-creation of forms.

Each time you create a form, C++Builder places that form in the auto-create list for the application. *Auto-creation* means that C++Builder will construct the form during the application startup process. Forms that are auto-created are displayed more quickly than forms that are not auto-created. The disadvantage to auto-creation of forms is that your application will use more memory than it would if your forms were not auto-created. Another disadvantage, although probably insignificant, is that your application will take slightly longer to load if you are auto-creating a lot of forms.

NOTE

> The first form in the Auto-Create Forms list box is always the main form. If you change the main form, the new form selected will move to the top of the Auto-Create Forms list box. Another way to set the main form is to drag and drop any of the forms in the Auto-Create Forms list box to the top of the list.

10

The nice thing about auto-creation is that displaying an auto-created form is easy. All you must do is call that form's Show() or ShowModal() function:

```
AboutBox->ShowModal();
```

If you do not have your forms auto-created by C++Builder, you must take responsibility for creating the form before you use it:

```
TAboutBox* aboutBox = new TAboutBox(this);
aboutBox->ShowModal();
delete aboutBox;
```

This example does not use the C++Builder-generated pointer to the About box. It creates a local pointer, displays the form, and then deletes the pointer as soon as the form is no longer needed. As is often the case in C++ programming, there are several ways to perform this particular task. Because C++Builder always creates a pointer to the form object, you could have written the previous code like this:

```
if (!AboutBox)
  AboutBox = new TAboutBox(this);
AboutBox->ShowModal();
```

This code checks to see whether the form has already been created. If it has not, the object is created and then the ShowModal() method is called. Deciding which method of form creation you will use is up to you, but I prefer the former because it handles everything locally.

NOTE

Each time you create a form in the Form Designer, C++Builder creates a pointer to the form. If you allow C++Builder to auto-create a form, you don't have to worry about the pointer being valid. If you choose not to have a form auto-created, the pointer to the form will be NULL until you explicitly create the form and initialize the pointer. If you forget and use the pointer before it is initialized, Windows will generate an access-violation error.

Okay, now turn your attention back to the Project Options dialog box. The Auto-Create Forms list box contains a list of the forms that will be auto-created. If you do not want a form to be auto-created, drag the form from the Auto-Create Forms list box to the Available Forms list box. You can move forms from one list box to the other using drag and drop, too. To move several forms at one time, simply select the forms you want to move (both list boxes support multiple selection) and drag and drop them all at once. It's that easy.

NOTE

You can use the buttons between the two list boxes to move forms from one list box to the other, but it's usually easier to use drag and drop.

The Application Page

The Application page of the Project Options dialog box is very simple. (See Figure 10.4.)

Figure 10.4.

The Application page.

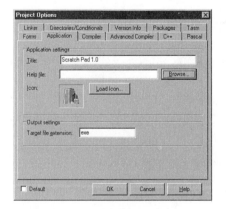

The Title field on this page is used to set the title of the application. The title is the text that will appear on the Windows taskbar when your application is minimized.

NOTE

> The application's title and the caption of the main form are two separate items. If you want your program's name to show up when you minimize your program, you must be sure that you set the title for the application in the Project Options dialog box. If you do not provide an application title, the name of the project file will be used by default.

The Help File field of the Application page is used to set the help file that your application will use. This is the help file that the program will load when you press F1 while your application is running. You can use the Browse button to locate the help file if you can't remember the name or location of the help file. If you do not supply a help file, pressing F1 in your application will have no effect.

The Icon option enables you to choose an icon for your application. This is the icon that will be displayed in the Windows taskbar when your application runs and when it is minimized. In addition, this icon will be displayed on your main form's title bar unless you have explicitly set an icon for the main form. To choose an icon, click the Load Icon button and locate the icon file (.ico) using the Application Icon dialog box.

You use the Target File Extension to specify the filename extension of the project when the project is built. For example, if you were creating a screen saver, you would change this field to scr so that your screen saver would be created with an extension of .scr rather than .exe. Control panel applets are another example. These are special programs saved with a .cpl extension. I could give you other examples, but you get the idea. This field is automatically set to exe for executable projects (console applications and GUI applications) and to .dll for DLLs, and normally you won't have to change it.

The Compiler Page

The Compiler page of the Project Options dialog box is where you set the options that the compiler uses to build your project. Figure 10.5 shows this page of the Project Options dialog box.

At the top of this page is a section called Speed settings that contains two buttons. The Full Debug button sets the default compiler options for a typical debug session. These are the settings you will be most likely to use while debugging your application. The Release button sets the compiler options for a typical release build. Use the Release settings after you have debugged your application and are ready to ship the final product. Be sure that you do a build of your project after changing compiler settings.

10

Figure 10.5.

*The Compiler page of
the Project Options
dialog box.*

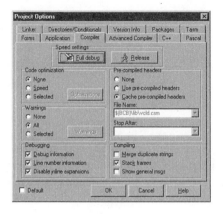

NOTE

The Full Debug and Release buttons set the compiler settings to the suggested settings for debugging or final release, respectively. You can always change individual options after choosing one of these speed buttons.

The remainder of the C++ page is broken down into five sections. Now take each section and examine it so that you can better understand the different options on this page.

Code Optimization

The compiler can be configured to perform optimizations on your code. When optimizations are turned off (the None radio button is selected), the compiler makes no attempts to optimize code in any way.

If you choose the Speed option, the compiler will generate the fastest code possible without regard to code size. When optimizations are set to Selected, the specific optimizations you select will be implemented. Click the Optimizations button to see a list of available optimization methods from which you can choose. In most cases you should leave this option on the default setting chosen when you press either the Full Debug or Release speed button.

NOTE

The result of changing optimization settings can vary widely. Each application is different. Sometimes optimizing for speed has a major impact on the final executable file size and speed; other times the difference is negligible.

Warnings

Warnings can be set to None, All, or Selected. When set to All, any compiler warnings are displayed in the Code Editor message window. When the Warnings option is set to Selected, you can click the Warnings button and view a list of warnings to turn on or off. I always leave the Warnings option set to All. Compiler warnings should not be ignored in the long term (in the short term you can ignore warnings that you know are due to temporary conditions in your code). Usually, compiler warnings can and should be resolved.

Debugging

The Debugging section of the Compiler page of the Project Options dialog box controls how the compiler generates code for debugging sessions. This section has three options, which I explain in the following sections. (I'll discuss debugging operations in detail tomorrow.)

Debug Information

When the Debug Information option is enabled, C++Builder will generate debug information for the project. The debug information is stored in a separate file in the project's directory. The filename of the file containing the debug information has a .TDS extension. For example, if you had a program with a project name of MyApp, C++Builder would generate a symbol file called MyApp.tds. This file is read by the debugger during debug sessions. If you do not generate debug information, you will not be able to stop on breakpoints and inspect variables during debugging. Put another way, you can't debug your program unless you tell C++Builder to generate debug information.

Line Number Information

The Line Number Information option tells C++Builder to generate line number information for the project. The debugger uses line number information to enable you to step through your code line by line. This option is automatically enabled when you have the Debug Information option turned on (even though the check box doesn't show it). You can, however, turn Debug Information off and then turn Line Number Information on. This will enable you to set breakpoints and step through your code, but you won't be able to inspect any variables. The benefit is that your .tds file will be smaller. In reality, it is unlikely you will opt to turn Debug Information off and Line Number Information on.

Disable Inline Expansions

The Disable Inline Expansions option controls how the compiler handles inline functions. By default, inline functions are expanded inline (placed in the code where necessary) as you would expect. If you turn on this option, thereby disabling inline expansion, inline functions will be treated as regular functions rather than as inline functions. Use of this option is rare, but you might need to use it occasionally when debugging certain inline functions.

NOTE

> If you change any of the options on the Compiler, Advanced Compiler, or C++ pages, you should do a build immediately following. This will ensure that all modules are built using the same compiler settings.

Pre-Compiled Headers

The settings in this section of the C++ page enable you to control how pre-compiled headers will be used in your application. A *pre-compiled header* is essentially an image of the project's symbol table stored on disk. The first time you build your program, C++Builder creates the pre-compiled header. On subsequent makes, C++Builder can load the pre-compiled header from disk, which is much faster than compiling the headers for each build. In addition, you can opt to cache the pre-compiled header in memory. This increases compile speed even more because the pre-compiled header can be held in memory rather than be loaded from disk when needed. You can set the pre-compiled headers option to None, Use pre-compiled headers, or Cache pre-compiled headers, depending on your needs and the hardware available on your system. Generally, you will use pre-compiled headers in one way or another. Turning off pre-compiled headers almost always results in much slower build times.

NOTE

> The option to cache pre-compiled headers will dramatically speed up compile and build times *if* you have enough system RAM. If you do not have enough system RAM, caching pre-compiled headers can actually slow down your builds. Do your own tests to determine whether caching pre-compiled headers is faster or slower on your system. In general, though, I would recommend turning caching off if you have less than 32MB of system RAM.

The File Name field enables you to set the location of the pre-compiled header file that your project uses. This is particularly important if you are using C++Builder over a network. The pre-compiled header should always be stored on a local drive and not on a network drive.

The Stop After field is used to specify the name of a header file that marks the end of the headers that should be included in the pre-compiled header. You usually should leave this blank because the `#pragma hdrstop` directive is automatically added to your source files by C++Builder and serves the same purpose.

Compiling

The Compiling group of options on the Compiler page is used to control how the C++ compiler performs certain options. For the most part, you should leave these options set at

10

the defaults until you become more familiar with C++Builder and C++ in general. You can trust the settings chosen for you when you click the Full Debug or Release speed setting.

When the Merge Duplicate Strings option is on, it tells the compiler to merge duplicate strings into one memory location. This saves overall program size but can lead to problems if one of the strings is modified.

Leave the Stack Frames option on when debugging. When you are finished debugging, you can turn off this option to have the compiler generate smaller and faster code, but compile times will be slightly longer with the Stack Frames option off. Usually the speed and size savings are not significant enough to warrant turning off this option. As always, do your own test to be sure.

When the Show General Msgs option is on, various status messages are displayed in the message window of the Code Editor. For example, when you compile the ScratchPad program with general messages turned on, the following text is output to the message window:

```
[C++] Compiling: Scratch.cpp
[C++] Compiling: SPMain.cpp
[C++] Loaded cached pre-compiled headers.
[C++] Compiling: SPAbout.cpp
[Linker] Incremental Linking: D:\Projects\Scratch\Scratch.exe
```

Turn on this option if you want to see the status messages in the message window. This option is off by default.

The Advanced Compiler Page

The Advanced Compiler page is used to set advanced compiler options. Because these are advanced options that you might never use, I won't discuss every option on this page. I will, however, discuss some of the more important options. This page is also affected by the Full Debug and Release speed settings on the Compiler page. The Advanced Compiler page is shown in Figure 10.6.

Figure 10.6.

The Advanced Compiler page of the Project Options dialog box.

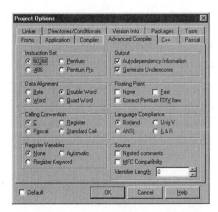

Instruction Set

The Instruction Set option tells the compiler to generate code for a specific CPU instruction set. For example, if you know that your application will only run on machines with Pentium Pro processors, you can choose the Pentium Pro option. This will result in more efficient and faster code. Be aware, though, that your application probably won't run on 386, 486, or even first-generation Pentium machines. The default setting of 80386 means that your application will run on virtually any Windows machine.

Data Alignment

Data alignment refers to the way in which the compiler stores data in memory. For VCL applications you should leave the data alignment set to Double Word. This means that the compiler aligns data on 8-byte boundaries. If you have a non-VCL application, you might be able to get by with setting the Data Alignment to one of the other settings.

Register Variables

When the Register Variables option is set to Automatic, the compiler will use register variables as it sees fit. The use of register variables allows for much faster code. Register variables can, however, be a bit of a pain while debugging. The compiler might optimize your variables during debugging, making the variable unavailable for inspection. When a variable has been optimized, the watch window will display the message Variable 'x' has been optimized and is not available when you attempt to inspect the variable.

If you set the Register Variables option to Register Keyword, you can still force the compiler to treat a particular variable as a register variable by declaring it with the register keyword. Here's an example:

```
register int x = 20;
```

When Register Variables is set to None, register variables are not used in any circumstance.

Output

The Generate Underscores option in this group is the option you probably will be most interested in. When this option is checked, any exported functions will be prepended with a leading underscore. For example, suppose you were creating a DLL that exports a function called ShowForm(). The actual function name would be exported as

```
_ShowForm
```

All types of problems can occur when this DLL is called from non-Borland applications. You should consider turning this option off when building a DLL that will be used from a wide variety of applications. Leave this option on when building DLLs that will be called from C++Builder applications.

Source

Check the MFC Compatibility option if you are going to build MFC programs. This option is necessary due to the large number of concessions Borland had to make in order to get MFC to compile with the Borland compiler. This option loosens certain compiler rules and turns certain warnings off so that MFC applications will compile.

The Nested Comments option can be turned on to allow nested comments. This option is meaningless unless you are coming from a compiler where nested comments are used frequently.

You can use the Identifier Length field to specify the maximum length of identifiers (variable names and function names). When this field is set to 0, the maximum length of 250 characters is implemented. Normally you should leave this option alone.

The C++ Page

The C++ page enables you to select specific C++ compiling options. This page contains advanced options that you will not generally be concerned with.

The Pascal Page

The Pascal page of the Project Options dialog box is used to set the Pascal compiler options. The Pascal compiler is used if you add Pascal units (.pas) to your C++Builder projects. The Pascal compiler settings are numerous and beyond the scope of this discussion so I'm not going to go over each one. See the C++Builder online help for details about the settings on this page.

The Linker Page

The Linker page of the Project Options dialog box is where you set options that specify how you want the linker to function. Until you become very familiar with C++Builder, you can leave this page alone and accept the default settings. Figure 10.7 shows the Linker page of the Project Options dialog box. The options available on this page are explained in the following sections.

Linking

The Linking section has several linker options that I will go over briefly. The In-Memory EXE option tells C++Builder to create the project's executable file in memory rather than on disk. This speeds build times because the executable file is never written to disk. This option is available only when running under Windows NT. Use this option only if you have plenty of system RAM. Exactly how much RAM is enough depends on your system. Experiment to see whether using this option enhances your build times. This option is used only during development. Eventually you will have to turn the In-Memory EXE option off in order to get an executable file on disk that you can ship.

10

Figure 10.7.

*Project Options
Linker options.*

The Include Debug Information option goes with the Debug Information on the Compiler page. This item must be checked in order for you to debug your application in the IDE. This option is set for you automatically when you choose either the Full Debug or Release speed setting on the Compiler page.

The Use Dynamic RTL option determines whether the runtime library code is linked into your application or extracted from the RTL DLL. If you are using runtime packages with your application, you will probably want to use the dynamic RTL as well. If you choose this option, you must ship the runtime library DLL (CP3240MT.DLL) with your application.

The Link Debug Version of VCL option enables you to link to the version of VCL that is built with debug information. This will enable you to step into the VCL source code while debugging your application.

NOTE

> Stepping into VCL code generally is not a fruitful endeavor. This is particularly true if you are not an experienced programmer. Any problems you are experiencing in your application are almost certainly in your code and not in the VCL code. There are times when stepping into the VCL source code is useful, but it has been my experience that those times are infrequent. Remember also that VCL is written in Object Pascal, so if the VCL source code looks like a foreign language, it is.

The Generate import library option pertains only to DLLs. When this option is on (the default for DLL projects), an import library file will automatically be created for the DLL. This is a great feature when creating DLLs because you don't have to create manually the LIB file yourself using the IMPLIB utility.

You use the Max Errors field to specify the maximum number of linker errors that can occur before a build is aborted. You should leave this field set to 0.

NOTE

C++Builder 1.0 had an option on the Linker page called Use Incremental Linker. This option is gone in C++Builder 3.0 because the incremental linker (also called ILINK) is the linker of choice. The incremental linker saves a lot of time when you are developing your applications. For example, suppose you have a project with 20 units. If you change one line of a unit, that unit must be recompiled and relinked. With the incremental linker, only the object file that has changed is relinked. Without the incremental linker, the linker would have to relink every binary file in the project regardless of whether it has changed since the last link. Linking takes a fair amount of time, so the incremental linker is a big advantage when working on a project of any significance.

The incremental linker has a few minor disadvantages. First, the initial link takes slightly longer when incremental linking is enabled. Second, the incremental linker sets up several work files to make linking as fast as possible. These files have extensions of .ilc, .ild, .ilf, and .ils. They can become very large (several megabytes) and use up a lot of disk space. You can always delete these files (and the .tds file, which also gets quite large) for any projects on which you are not currently working. The linker files will be regenerated if you must recompile a project for which you have deleted these files.

You can still use the old linker (TLINK) but only from the command line.

Map File

The Map File settings control whether a map file is generated and how much detail is included in the map file. A map file is an advanced debugging tool and is something that you will not likely use until you get further into C++Builder. For that reason I won't go into more detail on the Map File options.

Warnings

When the Warnings option is set to All, all linker warnings will show up in the Code Editor message window. When it is set to Selected, specific linker warnings can be selected from a dialog box. The default settings are usually sufficient, so you shouldn't have to change this option.

PE File Options

The PE File Options section enables you to set the minimum and maximum stack and heap sizes used by your application or DLL. You can also set the major and minor subsystem version numbers that will be used for your application or DLL's PE header. Changing these settings usually is not necessary.

The Directories/Conditionals Page

The Directories/Conditionals page of the Project Options dialog box is where you set the directories that your project uses to find library files and headers. Figure 10.8 shows the Directories/Conditionals page. The fields on this page are described in the following sections.

Figure 10.8.

*The Directories/
Conditionals page.*

Include Path

The Include Path setting is the path where C++Builder will look for the headers it needs to build your application (the .h and .hpp files). By default, this field is set to point to the various C++Builder directories where the system headers are found. You should leave this field set to the default directories unless you have a third-party library that resides in a separate directory. If you must add directories to the Include Path, you can add them to the end of the existing directories. Separate each directory with a semicolon, and be sure to include the full path.

NOTE

You will notice that the Include and Library path fields have something like the following:

`$(BCB)\include;$(BCB)\include\vcl`

The $(BCB) symbol is a macro that contains the location of the C++Builder root directory. This value is read from the Registry each time C++Builder starts. If you manually move C++Builder to a different directory, things will probably quit working unless you update the Registry by hand.

Library Path

The Library Path field contains the paths where the C++Builder library files (.lib) can be found. As with the Include Path field, you can add directories by separating each with a semicolon.

WARNING

Do not remove the list of default directories in either the Include Path or Library Path field. If you must modify these fields, add directories to the end of the directories listed, but do not delete any of the default directories. If you remove the default directories, your application will not compile.

Debug Source Path

Use this field to specify the directory where immediate output Files (such as .obj files) should be placed when C++Builder compiles the project. Using an intermediate directory eliminates clutter in your project's main directory.

Conditional Defines

You use the Conditional Defines field to specify any defines that you want to add at the project level. For example, to add support for the TRACE and WARN diagnostic macros, you would add this text to the Conditional Defines field:

`__TRACE;__WARN`

Note that each defined symbol is separated by a semicolon. Sometimes C++Builder will add symbols to this field as well.

Aliases

The Unit Aliases field associates a Pascal unit name with a specific C++ header file. Any aliases are separated by a semicolon.

The Version Info Page

The Version Info page enables you to set the version information for your applications. Version information is stored in your program's EXE file or in a DLL or ActiveX file. It is used by installation programs to determine whether a file being installed is older or newer than the file it is replacing. Version Info has other uses as well. You can view the version information for a file from Windows Explorer. Just right-click the file and choose Properties from the Explorer context menu. When the Properties dialog box comes up, click the Version tab to view the version information for the file. Figure 10.9 shows the Properties dialog box, displaying version information for the Database Desktop utility that comes with C++Builder.

Figure 10.9.

The Properties page showing version information for Dbd32.exe.

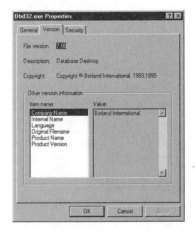

Figure 10.10 shows the Version Info page of the Project Options dialog box. At the top of the page is a check box labeled Include Version Information In Project. When this check box is checked, version information will be included in the project's executable file. When this check box is not checked, version information is not included in the project, and the rest of the page is disabled.

The remaining fields on the Version Info page are used to specify the various pieces of version information. The Major Version, Minor Version, Release, and Build fields work together to form the file version number. The version number of the file in Figure 10.10 is version 2.02, build 11. If you check the Auto-Increment Build Number option, the build number will automatically increment by one each time you perform a make or a build.

Figure 10.10.

*Version information
for your projects can
be supplied on the
Version Info page.*

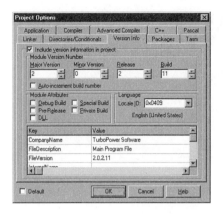

The Module Attributes section can be used to specify any special attributes you want specified for the file. The Language section enables you to select a locale identifier for the file. For more information on the possible values for the Locale ID field, see the Windows API online help under the topic "Language Identifiers and Locales."

The table at the bottom of the Version Info page can be used to set a variety of information. This information includes your company name, the file description, the internal name of the file, the legal copyright or trademark information, the product name, product version, and any comments you want to add. You can provide information for any of these fields or none at all (the FileVersion field is set based on the fields in the Module Version Number section). Adding version information to a project has never been so easy!

The Packages Page

The Packages page is where you determine the type of linking that your projects will use. The top part of the page enables you to add or remove design packages, but that really doesn't have anything to do with the current project. The only thing that pertains to the current project is the Build With Runtime Packages check box. When this option is selected, your application will use dynamic linking of the VCL and any third-party components. This means that your executable file will be smaller, but you will have to be sure to ship the correct packages with your application. When this check box is off, your application uses *static linking*. Static linking means that any VCL code and the code from any third-party components your application uses are linked directly into your executable file. Packages were discussed in detail yesterday in the section called "Packages." Figure 10.11 shows the Packages page of the Project Options dialog.

The Tasm Page

The Tasm page enables you to set the options for the Turbo Assembler. Turbo Assembler is used when your project includes inline assembly code. As you might guess, the Tasm page contains advanced options that are beyond the scope of this book.

Figure 10.11.

The Packages page.

The C++Builder Code Editor

There is no question that C++Builder is highly visual in nature—that's one of the great things about programming with it. Still, any program of any significance will have a great deal of code that must be written by hand. After you get the UI part of your application written with C++Builder's impressive visual tools, you'll likely spend a long stretch with the C++Builder Code Editor. The Code Editor has some features you'll learn to appreciate when you discover them.

In this section you will learn about

☐ Basic editor operations

☐ Specialized editor features

☐ The Code Editor context menu

☐ Changing the editor options

NOTE

The C++Builder Code Editor enables you to choose from four keyboard-mapping configurations: Default, IDE Classic, BRIEF, and Epsilon. The rest of this chapter assumes Default keyboard mapping. If you are already familiar with one of the other keyboard mapping configurations, you can ignore any references to specific keystrokes.

Basic Editor Operations

I'm going to assume that you know enough to be able to enter and delete text, highlight text with the mouse, cut, copy, and paste, and so on. I won't spend any time going over things at that level.

NOTE

If you have spent a lot of time writing code, you might be a heavy keyboard user. If that is the case, you will likely use the keyboard shortcuts for simple things like cutting, copying, and pasting. If you are not as experienced with the keyboard (or you just prefer using the mouse), you might want to customize your C++Builder toolbar to add speed buttons for operations like Cut, Copy, and Paste. Whichever method you choose, you will probably get lots of practice—if you are anything like me, you will do a lot of cutting, copying, and pasting while writing your programs.

When it comes right down to it, the C++Builder Code Editor is a typical code editor. It features syntax highlighting, which makes identifying keywords, strings, numeric constants, and comments at a glance easy. You'll look at setting the editor preferences a little later.

The Code Editor is a tabbed window. You can open as many editor windows as you like; each will be represented by a tab along the top of the editor window. The tab will display the name of the file. To switch to a source file, simply click the tab corresponding to the file you want to view. If more tabs exist than can be displayed at one time, scroll buttons will appear so that you can scroll among the tabs.

The status bar at the bottom of the Code Editor gives status information (obviously). The current line number and the cursor position on the line are reported in the left panel of the status bar. If the file has changed since it was last saved, the status bar will say Modified in the center panel of the status bar. The right panel of the status bar shows the current mode, either Insert or Overwrite. If the file has been set to read-only, this panel will say Read Only.

The editor window has a gray strip in the left margin that is called the *gutter*. The gutter is used to display icons at different stages of the development process. For example, when you set a debugger breakpoint (discussed tomorrow), a red dot is placed in the gutter. When you set a bookmark (discussed in just a bit), an icon representing the bookmark is placed in the gutter.

NOTE

If you accidentally click on the gutter when trying to select text or place the cursor, you will find that a breakpoint is set on that line. Click the gutter again to clear the breakpoint.

Opening and Saving Files

Nothing is very mysterious about opening and saving files in the Code Editor. It should be pointed out, though, that there is a difference between opening a project and opening a source file. When you choose File | Open Project from the main menu, you are prompted for the name of a project file to open. When you choose File | Open from the main menu, you can open any text file (.cpp, .rc, .h, .hpp, .pas, .txt, and so on). (You can also open a form file, but that's a different discussion.) Both the Open and Open Project menu items have corresponding toolbar buttons.

NOTE

If you open a source file (.cpp) that is the source code unit for a form, C++Builder will open the source file in the Code Editor and will also open the form in the Form Designer.

You can open multiple files at one time. To open multiple files, choose the files you want to open in the Open dialog box and click OK. Each file selected will be loaded, and a tab for each file will be placed at the top of the editor window.

TIP

You can also use drag and drop to open files. For example, you can choose a file (or a group of files) in Explorer, drag it onto the Code Editor, and drop it. The file will be opened in the Code Editor.

To save a file, choose File | Save or File | Save As from the main menu or type Ctrl+S on the keyboard. If the file has not been previously saved, the Save As dialog box will appear, and you can enter a filename at that time.

Highlighting Text

Although text highlighting is basic text-editor stuff, I thought it wouldn't hurt to remind you of a few basic highlighting techniques you can use in the C++Builder Code Editor.

To highlight a short block of text, you can use the mouse to drag across any text you want to highlight. After you've selected the text, you can cut, copy, or paste as needed. To highlight longer blocks of code, you can use the Click+Shift+Click method. First, click at the beginning of the block you want to highlight. Next, hold the Shift key on the keyboard and then click again at the end of the block. All text between the starting point and the ending point is highlighted.

Another useful feature is the capability to quickly select an individual word. To select a keyword, function name, or variable, just double-click on the word. Now you can perform any editing operations you want with the highlighted word.

TIP

To select a single line of code with the mouse, click at the beginning of the line and drag straight down to the beginning of the next line. To highlight a single line of code with the keyboard, first press the Home key to move to the beginning of the line and then use Shift+down-arrow key to highlight the line.

Dozens of keyboard combinations can be used to highlight text and do other editing chores. For a complete list of all the keyboard shortcuts available, consult the C++Builder online help.

TIP

As you program, you often add, delete, or move blocks of text. Sometimes you will need to indent an entire block of code. At other times you will need to un-indent (outdent?) an entire block of code. To indent a block of code, highlight the lines that you want to indent and then press Ctrl+Shift+I on the keyboard. The entire block will be indented. To un-indent a block of code, press Ctrl+Shift+U on the keyboard.

The Code Editor also supports drag-and-drop editing. To move a section of code, first highlight it. Next, place the mouse cursor over the highlighted text and drag. Drag until the cursor reaches the location where you want the code to be placed. Release the mouse button, and the code will be moved to the new location. To copy text rather than move it, repeat the preceding steps but hold down the Ctrl key before you drop the text.

Undo

The Code Editor has a virtually limitless number of undo levels (32,767 by default). Normally, you can only undo commands up to the last time you saved a file. By changing the editor options, you will be able to undo past commands even after saving the file. I'll talk about editor options and preferences later in the chapter in the section titled "Changing the Editor Options."

In general, it pays to remember this simple maxim: "Undo is your friend."

Find and Replace

Find and Replace are used fairly heavily in programming. You might use Find to find a specific piece of code or a specific variable in your code. You might use Replace to change a variable's name or to change the name of a function. The possibilities are endless.

The C++Builder Find Text and Replace Text dialog boxes implement more or less standard find-and-replace operations. To bring up the Find Text dialog box, choose Search|Find from the main menu or press Ctrl+F. Enter text in the Text to find field and click OK or press Enter. If the text is found, it will be highlighted.

NOTE

> Text highlighted by the Find Text dialog box is not the same as text highlighted with the mouse. You will notice that searched text is highlighted in black, whereas text selected with the mouse is highlighted in blue (assuming you haven't changed the editor defaults). Text highlighted after a search operation is not selected for editing, but is just marked so you can see it better.

To invoke the Replace Text dialog box, choose Search | Replace from the menu or press Ctrl+R. Figure 10.12 shows the C++Builder Replace Text dialog box. With a few obvious exceptions, the Find Text dialog box contains the same options.

Figure 10.12.

The Replace Text dialog box.

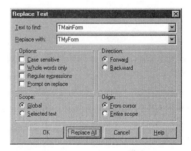

For the most part, the options on the Find Text and Replace Text dialog boxes do exactly what they indicate. If you choose the Case Sensitive option, you must type the search text exactly as it appears in the source file.

Use the Whole Words Only option when you want to be sure that text for which you are searching is not part of a longer word or variable name. For example, suppose you were converting a Delphi application to C++Builder. In that case you might search for all occurrences of the word end and replace them with a closing brace, }. In this case you would want to search for whole words only because the e-n-d sequence of characters is commonly used within words. Failing to use this option would cause this code:

```
DataSet->Append();
```

to be modified like this:

```
DataSet->App}();
```

The Regular Expressions option requires explanation as well. When this option is on, you can use special and wildcard characters when doing searches. The special characters enable you to find things such as the beginning of a line or the end of a line in your search strings. Wildcard characters work much like they do in directory operations. For a complete description of regular expressions, see the C++Builder online help under the topic "Regular Expressions."

When replacing text, it is safest to leave the Prompt On Replace option on. When you do a Replace All operation with this option on, the editor will highlight each found word and prompt you whether to replace it. It is easy to miscalculate the results of a Replace All operation, so always use Replace All with care. Even then, it still pays to remember that maxim: "Undo is your friend."

The rest of the Find and Replace options are self-explanatory and therefore don't need additional mention.

Find in Files

Find in Files is a great tool for searching for text in multiple files. This tool replaces the venerable old GREP utility. I frequently use Find in Files to search the VCL source code for particular functions, variables, or classes. This tool is useful and convenient, and you should learn how to use it. To display the Find in Files dialog box, you can choose Search | Find in Files from the main menu. Perhaps an easier way is to type Ctrl+F on the keyboard to bring up the Find Text dialog box and then click the Find in Files tab. Figure 10.13 shows the Find Text dialog box.

Figure 10.13.

The Find Text dialog box.

Find in Files uses some of the same search options as the regular Find operation (case-sensitive, whole word only, and regular expressions). In addition, you have the option to search all files in the project, all open files, or files in a particular directory, including subdirectories. When you start Find in Files, a small window with a title of Searching appears in the lower-right portion of your screen. This window shows the status of the Find in Files operation. It will show you the current file being searched and the number of matches up to this point. To cancel the search, just close the Searching window.

Any matches are reported in the Code Editor's message window. The message window shows the filename of the file in which the text was found, the line number where the text was found, and the line containing the search text, with the search text displayed in bold. To view the file that contains a match, just double-click a line in the message window. C++Builder will open the appropriate file and display the exact line containing the text for which you are searching. Figure 10.14 shows C++Builder searching a set of files.

Figure 10.14.

C++Builder searching for text.

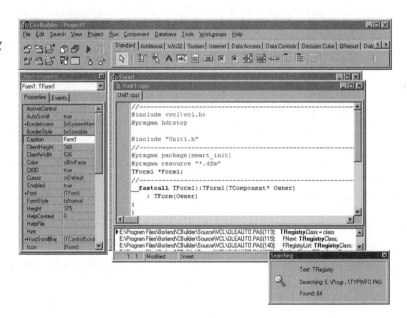

When specifying the file mask, all the usual wildcard characters apply. For example, if you wanted to search all VCL headers, you would enter the following in the File masks field:

```
c:\Program Files\Borland\CBuilder\Include\VCL\*.hpp
```

Find in Files is an indispensable tool. I find myself using it all the time. Learning to use Find in Files will save you a lot of time.

Getting Help

One of the most useful features of the Code Editor is its integration with the C++Builder help system. Just place the editor cursor over a C++ keyword, a VCL property or method, or any other C++Builder-specific text and press F1. If a help topic for the text under the cursor exists in the C++Builder help files, Windows Help will run with the appropriate page showing. If no help topic exists for the selected text, an error message will be displayed. This feature is extremely useful when you can't remember how to use a particular aspect of C++Builder, C++, or VCL. Help, as they say, is just a keystroke away.

Specialized Editor Features

The C++Builder Code Editor has a few features that are extremely useful when you are writing a lot of code. They are explained in the following sections.

Code Templates

Code templates are another nice feature of the C++Builder Code Editor. Code templates enable you to insert any predefined code (or any text, for that matter) in your source units. To use Code templates, just type Ctrl+J on the keyboard while editing in the Code Editor. When you do, a list box will pop up, giving you a list of templates from which to choose. Choose a template from the list, press Enter, and the text corresponding to that code template will be inserted into your source code. Figure 10.15 shows the code template list box as it appears when you type Ctrl+J.

Figure 10.15.

The C++Builder code template list box.

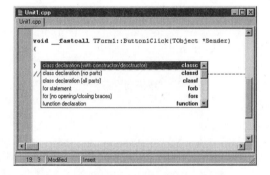

You can add new templates or edit existing templates via the Code Insight page of the Environment Options dialog box. Or if you prefer, you can open the code template file with any text editor (such as the C++Builder Code Editor) and edit the code templates there. The code template file is called BCB.DCI and is located in the CBuilder\Bin directory.

Feel free to modify the code templates in any way you see fit. For example, I have modified my code template representing the for statement to look like this:

```
for (int i=0;i<|;i++) {

}
```

Notice the pipe character (|) in the code snippet. The pipe in a code template entry is a placeholder that determines where the cursor will be placed after the text is inserted into your source code.

TIP

If you make a lot of modifications to the code template file, be sure to keep a backup of the file in a safe location. You will need a backup because the C++Builder installation program will overwrite your modified BCB.DCI file when you update or reinstall C++Builder.

You can use code templates for more than just code. Here at TurboPower Software, our source files always have a header at the top of the unit. It looks something like this:

```
{************************************************************}
{*                 Filename and version                   *}
{*           Copyright (c) TurboPower Software 1998        *}
{*                  All rights reserved.                   *}
{************************************************************}
```

Because most of this text stays constant, I have a template that quickly inserts the header in any new source units I create. Use code templates for any text that you use frequently in your day-to-day programming.

Using Bookmarks

You can set bookmarks in your code to temporarily mark your place in a source file. For example, you often must temporarily leave a block of code on which you are working to review previously written code or to copy code from another location. By dropping a bookmark at that point in your code before running off to do your other work, you can return to that section of code with a simple keystroke. You can have up to 10 bookmarks set at any one time.

To set a bookmark at a particular location, press Ctrl+Shift and the number of the bookmark to set. For example, to set bookmark 0 (the first bookmark), place the editor cursor at the location you want to mark and then press Ctrl+Shift+0 (Ctrl+K+0 will work as well). When you set a bookmark, an icon is placed in the Code Editor gutter to indicate that a bookmark exists on that line. The icon shows the number of the bookmark. Figure 10.16 shows the Code Editor with a bookmark dropped on a line.

Figure 10.16.

The Code Editor with a bookmark set.

```
SPMain.cpp
SPMain.cpp
    //-----------------------------------------------------
    void  __fastcall TScratchPad::FormCreate(TObject *Sender)
    {
        Application->OnIdle = &OnIdle;
        Application->OnHint = &OnHint;
    }
    //-----------------------------------------------------
    void  __fastcall TScratchPad::OnHint(TObject* Sender)
    {
        StatusBar->SimpleText = Application->Hint;
    }
    //-----------------------------------------------------
    void  __fastcall TScratchPad::OnIdle(TObject* Sender, boo
    {
    379: 2              Insert
```

10

To return to the bookmark, press Ctrl plus the number of the bookmark to which you want to return. Using the same example, you would type Ctrl+0 to go back to the bookmark. To clear a bookmark, place the editor cursor anywhere on the line containing the bookmark and again press Ctrl+Shift+0.

Note

> Bookmarks can be set for each file you have open in the Code Editor. For example, you can have bookmark #0 set in one source file and another bookmark #0 set in another source file. This means that bookmarks cannot be found across source files. If you set bookmark #0 in Unit1.cpp, you cannot press Ctrl+0 from Unit2.cpp and expect to be taken to the bookmark in Unit1.cpp.

To illustrate the use of bookmarks, do the following:

1. Open any source file in the Code Editor.
2. Scroll almost to the bottom of the file and click on a line of code.
3. Press Ctrl+Shift+0 to set a bookmark. The bookmark icon shows in the Code Editor gutter.
4. Press Ctrl+Home to move to the top of the source file.
5. Now press Ctrl+0 to jump back to the bookmark. The Code Editor changes to show the line of code where the bookmark was set, and the cursor is placed exactly where it was when you set the bookmark.
6. Type Ctrl+Shift+0 again to clear the bookmark. The bookmark is cleared, and the bookmark icon disappears from the Code Editor gutter.

Bookmarks are temporary. When you close the source file and reopen it, the bookmark is not preserved.

Incremental Search

You can use the incremental search option to quickly find a short series of characters. To start an incremental search, choose Search | Incremental Search from the main menu or press Ctrl+E on the keyboard. To understand how the incremental search works, it is easiest to do an exercise. Do the following:

1. Create a new text file from the Object Repository. (It doesn't matter whether you currently have a project open.)
2. Type the following text:

```
Learning to write Windows
programs a bit at a time
is not so bad. Isn't it
time you got back to work?
```

10

3. Move the cursor back to the top of the file (Ctrl+Home).

4. Press Ctrl+E to start the incremental search. You will be searching for the word back. Note that the Code Editor status bar says `Searching for:`.

5. Type a `b` on the keyboard. The letter `b` in the word `bit` is highlighted. That's not what you are looking for.

6. Now type an `a` on the keyboard. The next occurrence of `ba` is found, this time in the word `bad`. That's still not what you are looking for.

7. Type a `c` on the keyboard. The letters `bac` in the word `back` are highlighted. Now type a `k`. The Code Editor status bar now says `Searching for: back` and the word `back` is highlighted. Congratulations, you found what you were looking for!

8. Press Esc (or Enter) on the keyboard to stop the incremental search. Close the text file without saving it.

That's all there is to it. The incremental search is handy when you are searching for short amounts of text.

TIP

> If you make a mistake when typing the characters while doing an incremental search, you can use the backspace key to remove from the search string the last character typed.

Finding Matching Braces and Parentheses

As you have seen, C++ code can often become fairly convoluted when you start nesting `if` statements, `if/else` pairs, and so on. To tell the truth, getting lost is easy. The Code Editor has a feature to help you find a brace that matches the brace the cursor is currently on. To find a matching brace, place the cursor before a brace (it doesn't matter whether it's the opening or closing brace). Now press Alt+[on the keyboard. The cursor jumps to the brace that matches the brace on which you started. Press Alt+[again, and the cursor jumps back to where you started. Getting lost in the maze of braces in a long series of `if` statements is still a possibility, but at least now you know how to find your way out again. This feature also works with parentheses.

The Code Editor Context Menu

Like most of the different windows you encounter in C++Builder, the Code Editor has its own context menu. The Code Editor context menu can essentially be broken down into two parts: editor items and debugger items. I will leave the debugger items of the context menu for tomorrow, when I discuss debugging, but I'll go over the editor items on the context menu now. Table 10.2 contains a list of the context menu items that pertain to the editor, along with a description of each.

10

Table 10.2. The Code Editor context menu items.

Item	Description
Open Source/Header File	If the header file corresponding to the current source file is not opened in the Code Editor, choosing this menu item opens the header file, creates a new tab for it, and changes focus to that window. Choosing this option when both the .cpp and .h files are open switches focus back and forth between the two files.
Close Page	Closes the active page in the edit window. If the file on the page has been modified since it was last saved, you will be prompted to save the file.
Open File At Cursor	Opens the file under the cursor. This option has an effect only when the text under the cursor represents a source code file. For example, if you had a header included with #include "myclass.h", you could place the cursor over the filename and choose this menu item to open the file. The file will be placed in a new editor window, and focus will be set to the window.
New Edit Window	Opens a new copy of the Code Editor. This is convenient if you want to compare two source files side by side.
Topic Search	Displays the help topic for the item under the cursor (if it can be found). Same as pressing F1 on the keyboard.
View As Form	If the active file in the Code Editor is displaying a form's contents as text, choosing this option will again display the form in the Form Designer.
Read Only	Toggles the currently active file between read-only and read/write mode. When set to read-only, the file cannot be modified, although text can be selected and copied to the clipboard. The status bar displays Read Only to indicate the file is read only. When the file is closed and reopened, it is again in read/write mode.
Message View	Displays or hides the C++Builder message window. The message window automatically appears when there are compiler or linker errors or warnings, but can be specifically shown or hidden with this command.
Properties	Displays the Environment Options dialog box so that the editor options can be set.

10

Depending on the current state of the Code Editor and the particular type of file open, some of the items in Table 10.2 can be disabled at any given time.

Changing the Editor Options

The editor options occupy three pages of the Environment Options dialog box. To view this dialog box, choose Tools | Environment Options from the main menu.

Tip	You can also choose Properties from the Code Editor context menu to view the editor options. The difference with this method is that only the three pages pertaining to the editor options will be displayed in the Environment Options dialog box.

The three pages of the Environment Options that are specific to the Code Editor are the Editor, Display, and Colors pages. We'll examine these pages next.

The Editor Page

The Editor page of the Environment Options dialog box enables you to control how the editor works for you. As you can see from Figure 10.17, a lot of options are available on this page.

Figure 10.17.

The Editor page of the Environment Options dialog box.

At the top of the page is a combo box labeled Editor Speed Setting. You can choose Default Keymapping, IDE Classic, BRIEF emulation, or Epsilon emulation from the combo box. If you change the setting in this combo box, the Editor Options will change to reflect the defaults for the type you chose.

NOTE

If you are new to programming or if you have been using other Borland compilers using the Default keymapping, you don't have to worry about what you are missing. If you are accustomed to years of using a particular type of editor, you will be glad to know that you can still use the keyboard shortcuts and editor options you know and love simply by changing the Editor speed setting on this page and on the Display page.

Toward the bottom of the screen you will see the Block Indent and Tab Stops fields. You can use these two fields to change the amount by which code is indented when you block indent or when you tab to the next tab stop. Block indenting is discussed in the section "Highlighting Text," earlier in this chapter.

NOTE

Real programmers use tab stops of either two or three characters. (I use two-character tabs.)

The Undo limit of 32,767 is probably sufficient for most needs (I hope!), so I doubt you'll feel the need to modify that setting. The Syntax Extensions field enables you to select the types of files for which syntax highlighting will be applied. For example, you probably don't want syntax highlighting applied to regular text files (.txt) that you open in the Code Editor, so that file type is not listed by default.

In the middle of the Editor page you will find a whole gaggle of editor options from which to choose. Because so many options are available, and because determining exactly which of the available options are the most important is difficult, I'll refer you to the C++Builder online help. Simply press F1 while on this page or click the Help button and you will have explanations of each of the editor options you see on this page. As with some of the other options you looked at today, you can probably feel comfortable in accepting the C++Builder defaults.

The Display Page

The Display page of the Environment Options dialog box has additional options from which you can choose. These options pertain to the actual display of the text in the Code Editor window. (See Figure 10.18.)

In the Display and File Options section, you will find the BRIEF Cursor Shapes option. Turn on this option if you want the horizontal cursor in the editor window rather than the vertical cursor. Check the Create Backup File option if you want C++Builder to create a backup file every time you save your file or your project. Backup file extensions begin with a tilde (~). For example, the backup file for a source file called MyApp.cpp would be MyApp.~cp.

Figure 10.18.

The Display page.

NOTE I usually get fed up with all those backup files cluttering up my project directories and turn off file backups. Suit yourself.

The Zoom to full screen option controls how the Code Editor acts when maximized. If this option is on, the Code Editor will fill the entire screen when maximized. When this option is off (the default), the top of the Code Editor window will stop at the bottom of the C++Builder main window when maximized. In other words, the C++Builder main window will always be visible when the Code Editor is maximized if this option is off.

You can also choose whether your editor windows have a visible right margin. The right margin is not binding—you can still type text beyond it—but it gives you a visual cue that your lines might be getting too long. This section also enables you to determine whether you want a visible gutter and how wide the gutter should be (in pixels).

You can also change the Code Editor font and point size. A combo box is provided for you to choose these options. Only fixed-space screen fonts are listed; proportional and printer fonts are not. Choose the typeface and point size that best suit your needs. A preview window is provided so that you can see how the font you have chosen will look.

The Colors Page

The Colors page of the Environment Options dialog box enables you to fully customize the Code Editor's window and syntax highlighting options (see Figure 10.19).

At the top of the page is the Color Speed Setting combo box. This combo box gives you four predefined color schemes from which to choose. You can choose one of these color schemes or use one of them as a base for creating your own color scheme.

Figure 10.19.

The Colors page in the Environment Options dialog box.

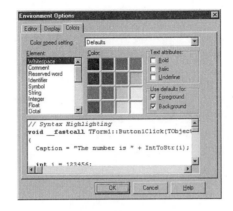

The Colors page is very easy to use. At the bottom of the page is a text window that contains sample code. If you click one of the key elements of the code, that element will be selected in the Element list box, and its current settings will be displayed on the Color grid. To change the foreground, background, and text attributes for that element, simply choose the settings you like. For example, keywords are displayed in bold text with a black foreground and a white background (assuming the default color scheme). To change the keywords to green, bold text, click the `void` keyword in the sample code window and then change the foreground color to green. The text colors in the sample window change to reflect the new color you have chosen. Continue changing colors until you have the sample window just the way you want it. When you click OK, the Code Editor will change to the new colors you have chosen.

Summary

Today was one of those days when you learned a lot about the kinds of things that often get overlooked. I hope you picked up some tips that you can use as you work with C++Builder projects and the C++Builder Code Editor. You also got an explanation of what some of the project and editor options are for. Even if it didn't make much sense to you now, this chapter is something you can refer back to at a later date.

Workshop

The Workshop contains quiz questions to help you solidify your understanding of the material covered and exercises to provide you with experience in using what you have learned. You can find answers to the quiz questions in Appendix A, "Answers to Quiz Questions."

Q&A

Q Must I use a project group even if I have just one project?

A No. You don't need a project group for a single project. You can use the default project group instead.

Q When I start my application, one of my dialog boxes is displayed instead of my main form. What gives?

A You have accidentally set the main form for the application to be the dialog form. Go to the Project Options dialog box, click the Forms tab, and select your main form from the Main Form combo box on the top of the page. Run your program again, and the main form will be displayed as you would expect.

Q All those project compiler and linker options confuse me. Do I need to know about each of those options to write programs with C++Builder?

A No. The default project options work well for almost all C++Builder applications. At some point you might get further into the mysteries of the compiler and linker, and at that time you can learn more about the project options. Until then, don't worry about it.

Q When my application is minimized, the icon and caption do not match what I set up in my application's main form. Why not?

A Setting the icon and caption of the main form does not affect how your application is displayed when minimized. To set the caption and icon for the application, go to the Project Options dialog box, choose the Application page, and supply the application name and icon.

Q Can I open several source files at one time in the Code Editor?

A Yes. You can also select multiple files in Windows Explorer and drop them onto the Code Editor.

Q Can I find and replace a variable name across all my source files?

A No. You will have to open each source file and execute the Replace dialog box in each source file. You can, however, use the F3 key to repeat the last find or replace command. Remember not to change any C++Builder-generated variable names.

Q I find that 32,767 undo levels is not enough for my needs. What do you suggest?

A Don't quit your day job.

Quiz

1. How can you quickly switch between a unit's form and source code when working with C++Builder?

10

2. If you remove a file from your project via the Project Manager, does the file get removed from your hard drive?

3. How do you set the main form for an application?

4. What does it mean if you do not have C++Builder auto-create forms?

5. What's the minimum amount of memory your computer should have before you turn on the option to cache pre-compiled headers?

6. What is the significance of generating debug information for your application?

7. What is the Find in Files option used for?

8. What is the keyboard shortcut for saving a file in the Code Editor?

9. How do you set a bookmark in an editor window? How many bookmarks are available?

10. How do you set a file to read-only in the Code Editor?

Exercises

1. Create a new application. Display the Project Manager. Click the Add Unit button to add a new unit to the project. Navigate to the \CBuilder\Examples\Apps\Canvas directory and choose the file called Canmain.cpp. Click OK to add the file to the project.

2. Remove the Canmain.cpp unit from the project in Exercise 1.

3. Open the ScratchPad project. Change the main form to the AboutBox form. Close the Project Options dialog box and run the program. The About box will be displayed when the program starts. Close the About box to end the program and change the main form back to the ScratchPad form.

4. Create a new application. Save the project and the project group. Now add a new project to the project group.

5. Open any source file in the Code Editor. Set four bookmarks at random locations in the source file. Jump from bookmark to bookmark and observe the effects in the Code Editor. When you are finished, clear all the bookmarks.

6. Open the ScratchPad project (or any other project) and switch to the Code Editor. View the project's main form source file. Choose Search | Find from the main menu. Type Click in the Text To Find box and click OK to find the first occurrence of the word Click.

7. Press F3 several times to repeat the search until the entire file has been searched.

8. Continuing with the same project, press Ctrl+Home to go to the top of the file. Press Ctrl+R to display the Replace Text dialog box. Type Click in the Text To Find box and Test in the Replace With box. Turn off the Prompt On Replace

option and then click the Replace All button. Scroll through the file to view the results. **IMPORTANT:** Select Edit | Undo to undo the replace operation. Close the project without saving (just to be safe).

9. Open a file in the Code Editor. Choose Properties from the Code Editor context menu. Change the syntax highlighting for strings, integers, and floats to dark gray. Click OK to view the results in the Code Editor.

10. Change the colors back to the default color scheme.

10

Day 11

Using the Debugger

A major feature of the C++Builder IDE is the integrated debugger. The debugger enables you to easily set breakpoints, watch variables, inspect objects, and do much more. Using the debugger, you can quickly find out what is happening (or not happening) with your program as it runs. A good debugger is vital to efficient program development.

Debugging is easy to overlook. Don't tell anyone, but when I first started Windows programming (not with C++Builder, of course), I ignored the debugger for a long time because I had my hands full just learning how to do Windows programming. When I found out how valuable a good debugger is, I felt a little silly for cheating myself out of the use of that tool for so long. Oh well, live and learn. You have the luxury of learning from my mistakes. Today you will learn about what the debugger can do for you.

The IDE debugger provides several features and tools to help you in your debugging chores. The following are discussed today:

- ☐ Debugger menu items
- ☐ Using breakpoints
- ☐ Inspecting variables with the Watch List
- ☐ Inspecting objects with the Debug Inspector
- ☐ Other debugging tools
- ☐ Stepping through code
- ☐ Debugging techniques

Why Use the Debugger?

The quick answer is that the debugger helps you find bugs in your program. But the debugging process isn't just for finding and fixing bugs—it is a development tool as well. As important as debugging is, many programmers don't take the time to learn how to use all the features of the IDE debugger. As a result, they cost themselves time and money, not to mention the frustration caused by a bug that is difficult to find.

You begin a debugging session by starting up the program under the debugger. You automatically use the debugger when you click the Run button on the toolbar. You can also choose Run | Run from the main menu or press F9 on the keyboard.

The Debugging Menu Items

Before we get into the details of the debugger, let's review the menu items that pertain to the debugger. Some of these menu items are on the main menu under Run, and others are on the Code Editor context menu. Table 11.1 lists the Code Editor context menu items specific to the debugger along with their descriptions.

Table 11.1. Code Editor context menu debugging items.

Item	Shortcut	Description
Toggle Breakpoint	F5	Toggles a breakpoint on or off for the current line in the Code Editor.
Run to Cursor	F4	Starts the program (if necessary) and runs it until the line in the editor window containing the cursor is reached.
Inspect	Alt+F5	Opens the Debug Inspect window for the object under the cursor.

Item	Shortcut	Description
Goto Address	None	Enables you to specify an address in the program at which program execution will resume.
Evaluate/Modify	None	Enables you to view and/or modify a variable at runtime.
Add Watch at Cursor	Ctrl+F5	Adds the variable under the cursor to the Watch List.
View CPU	None	Displays the CPU window.

The Run item on the main menu has several selections that pertain to running programs under the debugger. The Run menu items enable you to start a program under the debugger, to terminate a program running under the debugger, and to specify command-line parameters for your program, to name just a few functions. Some items found here are duplicated on the Code Editor context menu. Table 11.2 shows the Run menu items that control debugging operations.

Table 11.2. The Run menu's debugging items.

Item	Shortcut	Description
Run	F9	Compiles the program (if needed) and then runs the program under the control of the IDE debugger. Same as the Run toolbar button.
Parameters	None	Enables you to enter command-line parameters for your program and to assign a host application when debugging a DLL.
Step Over	F8	Executes the source code line at the execution point and pauses at the next source code line.
Trace Into	F7	Traces into the function at the execution point.
Trace to Next Source Line	Shift+F7	Causes the execution point to move to the next line in the program's source code.

continues

Table 11.2. continued

Item	Shortcut	Description
Run to Cursor	F4	Runs the program and pauses when program execution reaches the current line in the source code.
Show Execution Point	None	Displays the program execution point in the Code Editor. Scrolls the source code window if necessary. Only works when program execution is paused.
Program Pause	None	Pauses program execution as soon as the execution point enters the program's source code.
Program Reset	Ctrl+F2	Closes down the program and returns to the C++Builder IDE.
Inspect	None	Displays the Inspect dialog box so that you can enter the name of an object to inspect.
Inspect Local Variables	None	Displays the Debug Inspect window with all variables local to the current function displayed.
Add Watch	Ctrl+F5	Displays the Watch Properties dialog box.
Add Breakpoint	None	Displays the Edit Source Breakpoint dialog box to enable you to add a breakpoint.
Evaluate/Modify	Ctrl+F7	Displays the Evaluate/Modify dialog box.

You will use these menu items a lot when you are debugging your programs. You should also become familiar with the various keyboard shortcuts for the debugging operations.

Now let's take a look at breakpoints and how to use them in your program.

Breakpoints

When you run your program from the C++Builder IDE, it runs at full speed, stopping only where you have set breakpoints.

 A *breakpoint* is a marker that tells the debugger to pause program execution when that place in the program is reached.

Setting and Clearing Breakpoints

To set a breakpoint, click in the editor window's gutter to the left of the line on which you want to pause program execution (the gutter is the gray margin along the Code Editor window's left edge). The breakpoint icon (a red circle) appears in the gutter, and the entire line is highlighted in red. To clear the breakpoint, click on the breakpoint icon and the breakpoint is removed. You can also press F5 or choose Toggle Breakpoint from the Code Editor context menu to toggle a breakpoint on or off.

 NOTE

> A breakpoint can be set only on a line that generates actual code. Breakpoints are not valid if set on blank lines, comment lines, or declaration lines. You are not prevented from setting a breakpoint on these types of lines, but the debugger warns you if you do. Attempting to set a breakpoint on any of the following lines will produce an invalid breakpoint warning:
>
> ```
> // this is a comment followed by a blank line
>
> int x;  // a declaration
> ```
>
> Breakpoints *can* be set on return statements or on the right brace of a function.

If you set a breakpoint on an invalid line, the Code Editor will display the breakpoint in green (assuming the default color scheme) and the breakpoint icon in the gutter will be grayed out.

When the program is run under the debugger, it behaves as it normally would—until a breakpoint is hit, that is. When a breakpoint is hit, the IDE is brought to the top and the breakpoint line is highlighted in the source code. If you are using the default colors, the line where the program has stopped is highlighted in red because red indicates a line containing a breakpoint.

NEW TERM   The *execution point* indicates the line that will be executed next in your source code.

As you step through the program, the execution point is highlighted in blue, and the editor window gutter displays a green arrow glyph. Understand that the line highlighted in blue has not yet been executed but will be when program execution resumes.

NOTE

> The current execution point is highlighted in blue unless the line containing the execution point contains a breakpoint. In that case the line is highlighted in red. The green arrow glyph in the gutter is the most accurate indication of the execution point because it is present regardless of the line's highlighting color.

When you stop at a breakpoint, you can view variables, view the call stack, browse symbols, or step through your code. After you have inspected any variables and objects, you can resume normal program execution by clicking the Run button. Your application will again run normally until the next breakpoint is encountered.

NOTE

> It's common to detect coding errors in your program after you have stopped at a breakpoint. If you change your source code in the middle of a debugging session and then choose Run to resume program execution, the IDE will prompt you with a message box asking whether you want to rebuild the source code. If you choose Yes, the current process will be terminated, the source code will be recompiled, and the program will be restarted.
>
> The problem with this approach is that your program doesn't get a chance to close normally, and any resources currently in use might not be freed properly, which could result in memory leaks. Although Windows 95 and Windows NT handle resource leaks better than 16-bit Windows, it is still advisable to terminate the program normally and then recompile.

The Breakpoint List Window

The C++Builder IDE keeps track of the breakpoints you have set in the Breakpoint List window. To view the breakpoint list, choose View | Breakpoints from the main menu. The Breakpoint List window will be displayed, as shown in Figure 11.1.

Figure 11.1.

The Breakpoint List window.

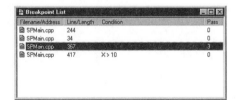

The Breakpoint List window has four columns. The first column, Filename/Address, shows the filename of the source code unit in which the breakpoint is set. The second column, labeled Line/Length, shows the line number on which the breakpoint is set. The Condition column shows any conditions that have been set for the breakpoint, and the Pass column shows the pass count condition that has been set for the breakpoint. (Breakpoint conditions and pass count conditions are discussed later, in the section "Conditional Breakpoints.") The columns can be sized by dragging the dividing line between two columns in the column header.

NOTE

> The Pass column doesn't show the number of times the breakpoint has been hit; it only shows the pass condition that you have set for the breakpoint.

The Breakpoint List window has two context menus. Table 11.3 lists the context menu items you will see when you click the right mouse button over any breakpoint. I will refer to this as the window's *primary context menu.*

11

Table 11.3. The primary Breakpoint List context menu.

Item	Description
Enable	Enables or disables the breakpoint. When a breakpoint is disabled, its glyph is grayed out in the Breakpoint List window. In the source window the breakpoint glyph is also grayed, and the breakpoint line is highlighted in green to indicate that the breakpoint is disabled.
Delete	Removes the breakpoint.
View Source	Scrolls the source file in the Code Editor to display the source line containing the breakpoint. (The breakpoint list retains focus.)
Edit Source	Places the edit cursor on the line in the source file where the breakpoint is set and switches focus to the Code Editor.
Properties	Displays the Edit Source Breakpoint dialog box.

TIP

> To quickly edit the source code line on which a breakpoint is set, double-click on the breakpoint in the Filename column of the Breakpoint List window. This is the same as choosing Edit Source from the Breakpoint List context menu.

The secondary context menu is displayed by clicking the right mouse button while the cursor is over any part of the Breakpoint List window that doesn't contain a breakpoint. This context menu has items called Add, Delete All, Disable All, and Enable All. These items are self-explanatory, so I won't bother to comment on them.

> **NOTE**
>
> In my opinion, the Add context menu item isn't very useful. It is much easier to set a breakpoint in the Code Editor than to add a breakpoint via the Add command in the Breakpoint List window.

Breakpoints can be enabled or disabled any time you like. You disable a breakpoint if you want to run the program normally for a while; you can enable the breakpoint later without having to re-create it. The debugger ignores breakpoints that are disabled.

If you want to modify a breakpoint, you choose Properties from the primary Breakpoint List context menu. When you do, the Edit Source Breakpoint dialog box is displayed (see Figure 11.2).

Figure 11.2.

The Edit Source Breakpoint dialog box.

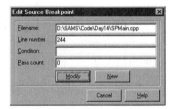

The primary reason for modifying a breakpoint is to add conditions to it. (Conditional breakpoints are discussed in the next section.) The New button in the Edit Source Breakpoint dialog box creates a new breakpoint item on the same line as the selected breakpoint. This is useful if you want two or more breakpoints on the same line, but with different conditions. The Modify button is used when you have made changes to the breakpoint and want to apply those changes.

To remove a breakpoint, you select the breakpoint in the Breakpoint List windows and then press the Delete key on the keyboard. To delete all breakpoints, right-click and then choose Delete All.

Now let's take a look at the two breakpoint types: simple and conditional.

Simple Breakpoints

A *simple breakpoint* causes program execution to be suspended whenever the breakpoint is hit. When you initially set a breakpoint, it is by default a simple breakpoint. Simple breakpoints don't require much explanation. When the breakpoint is encountered, program execution pauses, and the debugger awaits your bidding.

Conditional Breakpoints

In the case of a *conditional breakpoint*, program execution is paused only when predefined conditions are met. To create a conditional breakpoint, first set the breakpoint in the Code Editor. Then choose View|Breakpoints from the main menu to display the Breakpoint List window. Right-click on the breakpoint for which you want to set conditions and choose Properties. When the Edit Source Breakpoint dialog box is displayed, set the conditions for the breakpoint.

Conditional breakpoints come in two flavors. The first type is a *conditional expression breakpoint*. Enter the conditional expression in the Condition field of the Edit Source Breakpoint dialog box (refer back to Figure 11.2). When the program runs, the conditional expression is evaluated each time the breakpoint is encountered. When the conditional expression evaluates to true, program execution is halted. If the condition doesn't evaluate to true, the breakpoint is ignored. For example, look back at the last breakpoint in the Breakpoint List window, shown in Figure 11.1. This breakpoint has a conditional expression of X > 10. If at some point in the execution of the program, X is greater than 10, the program will stop at the breakpoint. If X is never greater than 10, program execution will not stop at the breakpoint.

The other type of conditional breakpoint is the *pass count breakpoint*. With a pass count breakpoint, program execution is paused only after the breakpoint is encountered a specified number of times. To specify a pass count breakpoint, edit the breakpoint and specify a value for the Pass Count field in the Edit Source Breakpoint dialog box. Figure 11.1 shows a breakpoint that has the pass count set to 3. Program execution will stop at this breakpoint the third time the breakpoint is encountered.

NOTE

The pass count is 1-based, not 0-based. As indicated in the preceding example, a pass count of 3 means that the breakpoint will be valid the third time the breakpoint is encountered by the program.

Use pass count breakpoints when you need your program to execute through a breakpoint a certain number of times before you break to inspect variables, step through code, or perform other debugging tasks.

NOTE

> Conditional breakpoints slow down the normal execution of the program because the conditions need to be evaluated each time a conditional breakpoint is encountered. If your program is acting sluggish during debugging, check your breakpoint list to see whether you have conditional breakpoints that you have forgotten about.

TIP

> The fact that conditional breakpoints slow down program execution can work in your favor at times. If you have a process that you want to view in slow motion, set one or more conditional breakpoints in that section of code. Set the conditions so that they will never be met, and your program will slow down but not stop.

The `Run to Cursor` **Command**

There is another debugging command that deserves mention here. The `Run to Cursor` command (found under the Run menu on the main menu and on the Code Editor context menu) runs the program until the source line containing the editing cursor is reached. At that point the program stops as if a breakpoint were placed on that line.

`Run to Cursor` acts as a temporary breakpoint. You can use this command rather than set a breakpoint on a line that you want to immediately inspect. Just place the cursor on the line you want to break on and choose Run to Cursor (or press F4). The debugger behaves exactly as if you had placed a breakpoint on that line. The benefit is that you don't have to clear the breakpoint after you are done debugging that section of code.

Watching Variables

So what do you do when you stop at a breakpoint? Usually you stop at a breakpoint to inspect the value of one or more variables. You might want to ensure that a particular variable has the value you think it should, or you might not have any idea what a variable's value is and simply want to find out.

The function of the Watch List is basic: It enables you to inspect the values of variables. Programmers often overlook this simple but essential feature because they don't take the time to learn how to fully use the debugger. You can add as many variables to the Watch List as you like. Figure 11.3 shows the Watch List during a debugging session.

11

Figure 11.3.

*The Watch List
in action.*

The variable name is displayed in the Watch List followed by its value. How the variable value is displayed is determined by the variable's data type and the current display settings for that watch item.

ToolTip Expression Evaluation

The debugger and Code Editor have a nice feature that makes checking the value of a variable easy. This feature, the ToolTip expression evaluator, is on by default, so you don't have to do anything special to use it. If you want, you can turn off the ToolTip evaluator via the Code Insight page of the Environment Options dialog box (the Environment Options dialog box is discussed in detail on Day 16, "C++Builder Database Architecture").

So what is ToolTip expression evaluation (besides hard to say)? It works like this: After you have stopped at a breakpoint, you place the editing cursor over a variable, and a ToolTip window pops up, showing the variable's current value. This makes it easy to quickly inspect variables. Just place your cursor over a variable and wait a half second or so.

The ToolTip evaluator has different displays for different variable types. For regular data members (int, char, long, and so on), the actual value of the variable is displayed. For dynamically created objects (an instance of a class, for example), the ToolTip evaluator shows the memory location of the object. In the case of AnsiString variables, the ToolTip evaluator is smart enough to show the contents of the string. For structures the ToolTip evaluator shows all the structure elements. Figure 11.4 shows the ToolTip expression evaluator inspecting a structure's contents.

Figure 11.4.

*ToolTips are a great
debugger feature.*

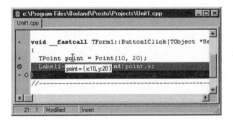

NOTE

> Sometimes the ToolTip evaluator acts as if it's not working properly. If, for example, you place the editing cursor over a variable that is out of scope, no ToolTip appears. The ToolTip evaluator has nothing to show for that particular variable, so it doesn't display anything.
>
> Be aware, also, that variables optimized by the compiler might not show correct values. Optimization was discussed yesterday and is also discussed later in this chapter.

The ToolTip expression evaluator is a great feature, so don't forget to use it.

The Watch List Context Menu

As with every other C++Builder window discussed so far, the Watch List has its own context menu. (You'd be disappointed if it didn't, right?) Table 11.4 lists the Watch List context menu items and their descriptions.

Table 11.4. The Watch List context menu.

Item	Description
Edit Watch	Enables you to edit the watch item with the Watch Properties dialog box.
Add Watch	Adds a new item to the Watch List.
Enable Watch	Enables the watch item.
Disable Watch	Disables the watch item.
Delete Watch	Removes the watch item from the Watch List.
Enable All Watches	Enables all items in the Watch List.
Disable All Watches	Disables all items in the Watch List.
Delete All Watches	Deletes all items in the Watch List.
Stay on Top	Forces the Watch List to the top of all other windows in the IDE.
Break When Changed	When the variable in the watch window changes, the debugger will break. The watch variable is displayed in red to indicate that Break When Changed is in effect.

Both the Edit Watch and Add Watch context menu items invoke the Watch Properties dialog box, so let's look at that next.

Using the Watch Properties Dialog Box

You use the Watch Properties dialog box when you add or edit a watch. Figure 11.5 shows the Watch Properties dialog box as it looks when editing a variable called buff.

Figure 11.5.

The Watch Properties dialog box.

The Expression field at the top of the Watch Properties dialog box is where you enter a variable name to edit or add to the watch list. This field is a combo box that can be used to select previously used watch items.

You use the Repeat Count field when you are inspecting arrays. For example, let's say you have an array of 20 integers. To inspect the first 10 integers in the array, you would enter the first element of the array in the Expression field (array[0], for example) and then enter 10 in the Repeat Count field. The first 10 elements of the array would then be displayed in the Watch List.

NOTE

If you add just the array name to the Watch List, all elements in the array will be displayed. Use the Repeat Count field when you want to view only a specific number of array elements.

The Digits field is used only when inspecting floating-point numbers. Enter the number of significant digits you want to see when your floating-point number is displayed in the Watch List. The displayed digits are rounded, not truncated. Another field in this dialog box, the Enabled field, determines whether the watch item is currently enabled.

The remainder of the Watch Properties dialog box is composed of various display options. Each data type has a default display type, which is used if you choose the Default viewing option. The Default viewing option is the default. (Sorry, there's just no other way to say it.) Select the other viewing options to view the data in other ways. Figure 11.6 shows the Watch List window with two variables added and with various viewing options applied. The buff variable is a character array, and the i variable is an integer.

Figure 11.6.

The Watch List with various viewing options.

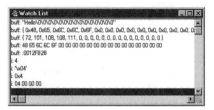

To modify a watch item, click the item in the Watch List and choose Edit Watch from the Watch List context menu. You can also double-click a watch item to edit it. The Watch Properties dialog box is displayed, and you can edit the watch item as needed.

 TIP

> The fastest way to edit a watch item is to double-click its name in the Watch List.

Enabling and Disabling Watch Items

As with breakpoints, individual items in the Watch List can be enabled or disabled. When a watch item is disabled, it is grayed and its value shows `<disabled>`.

To disable a watch item, click the item's name in the Watch List and choose Disable Watch from the Watch List context menu. To enable the watch item again, choose Enable Watch from the context menu.

 NOTE

> You might want to disable watch items that you don't currently want to watch but will need later. Having a number of enabled items in the Watch List slows down program execution during the debugging process because all the Watch List variables must be updated each time a code line executes. It doesn't take many items to slow things down, so don't forget to delete or disable any unused items in the Watch List.

Adding Variables to the Watch List

You can add variables to the Watch List in several ways. The quickest is to click the variable name in the editor window and then select Add Watch at Cursor from the Code Editor context menu or press Ctrl+F5. The watch item will be immediately added to the Watch List. You can then edit the watch item to change the display properties, if needed.

To add a variable to the watch without first locating it in the source file, choose Run | Add Watch from the main menu. When the Watch Properties dialog box comes up, enter the name of the variable you want to add to the Watch List and click OK.

NOTE   Although you can add a class instance variable to the Watch List, the displayed value will not likely be useful. In the case of pointers to objects, this is useful for determining whether the pointer is valid, but often you want to view the details of the class. For viewing all the class data members, you should use the Debug Inspector, which I'll discuss in a minute.

Using the Watch List

When a breakpoint is hit, the Watch List displays the current value of any variables that have been added to the Watch List. If the Watch List isn't currently open, you can choose View | Watches from the main menu to display it.

Under certain circumstances, a message will be displayed next to the variable instead of the variable's value. If, for instance, a variable is out of scope or not found, the Watch List displays `Undefined symbol 'x'` next to the variable name. If the program isn't running or isn't stopped at a breakpoint, the Watch List will display `[process not accessible]` for all watch items. A disabled watch item will have `<disabled>` next to it. Other messages can be displayed depending on the current state of the application or the current state of a particular variable.

As I said yesterday, you might on occasion see `Variable 'x' has been optimized and is not available` in the Watch List. This is one of the minor disadvantages to having an optimizing compiler. If you need to inspect variables that are subject to optimization, either declare the variable with the `volatile` keyword or turn off the Register Variables option on the Advanced Compiler page of the Project Options dialog box (the Register Variables option is off by default, so you shouldn't have to worry about it). Declaring a variable with the `volatile` keyword looks like this:

```
volatile int x = 20;
```

The `volatile` keyword tells the compiler not to use CPU registers for storing the variable's data. This prevents the variable from being optimized. However, you should be aware that allowing the compiler to use register variables results in faster code execution, so you should remove the `volatile` modifier after debugging a particular section of code.

> The Watch List can be used as a quickie decimal/hexadecimal converter. To convert a hex number to decimal, choose Run | Add Watch from the main menu. Type the hexadecimal number in the `Expression` field and click OK. Both the hexadecimal number and the decimal equivalent will be displayed in the Watch List. To convert a decimal number to hex, perform the same procedure, except click the Hexadecimal option button to change the display type to hexadecimal. Because the `Expression` field will accept a mathematical expression, you can also use the Watch List as a hex calculator. You can even mix hexadecimal and decimal values in the same expression.

The Watch List is a simple but vital tool in debugging applications. To illustrate the use of the Watch List, perform this exercise:

1. Create a new application and place a button on the form. Change the button's `Name` property to `WatchBtn` and its `Caption` to `Watch Test`. Change the form's `Name` property to `DebugMain` and the `Caption` property to whatever you like.

2. Double-click the button to display its `OnClick` handler in the Code Editor. Enter the following code at the cursor:

```
String s;
int x = Width;
s = String(x);
int y = Height;
x *= y;
s = String(x);
x /= y;
s = String(x);
Width = x;
Height = y;
```

3. Save the project. Name the unit `DbgMain` and the project `DebugTst`.

4. Set a breakpoint on the second code line from Step 2. Run the program.

5. Click the Watch Test button. The debugger will stop at the breakpoint.

6. Add watches for the variables s, x, and y. (Initially the variables x and y will contain random values, but don't worry about that.)

7. Arrange the Watch List and Code Editor so that you can see both.

8. Switch focus to the Code Editor and press F8 to execute the next line of code. That line is executed, and the execution point moves to the next line. The variable x now shows a value.

9. Continue to step through the program by pressing F8. Watch the results of the variables in the Watch List.

10. When the execution point gets to the last line in the function, click the Run button on the toolbar to continue running the program.

11. Click the Watch Test button as many times as you want to get a feel for how the Watch List works. Experiment with different watch settings each time through.

NOTE

The code in this example obtains the values for the form's Width and Height properties, performs some calculations, and then sets the Width and Height back to where they were when you started. In the end nothing changes, but there is a good reason for assigning values to the Width and Height properties at the end of the function.

If you don't actually do something with the variables x and y, you can't inspect them because the compiler will optimize them and they won't be available to watch. Essentially, the compiler can look ahead, see that the variables are never used, and just discard them. Putting the variables to use at the end of the function avoids having them optimized away by the compiler.

I've brought this up several times now, but I want to make sure you have a basic understanding of how an optimizing compiler works. When you start debugging your applications, this knowledge will help avoid some frustration when you start getting those Variable 'x' has been optimized and is not available messages in the Watch List.

The Debug Inspector

Simply stated, the Debug Inspector enables you to view data objects such as classes and components (components are really just classes, anyway). You can also inspect simple data types such as integers, character arrays, and so on, but those are best viewed with the Watch List. The Debug Inspector is most useful in examining classes and structures.

NOTE

You can use the Debug Inspector only when program execution is paused under the debugger.

To inspect an object, click the object's name in a source file and choose Inspect from the Code Editor context menu (or press Alt+F5). You can also choose Run | Inspect from the main menu.

NOTE

> When you use Inspect from the context menu or use Alt+F5, the Debug Inspector automatically displays the object under the cursor. If you choose Run | Inspect from the main menu, you first see a dialog box that asks you to input the object to inspect. Enter a variable name and click OK. The Debug Inspector will be shown with the requested object displayed.

The Debug Inspector window contains details of the object displayed. If the object is a simple data type, the Debug Inspector window shows the current value (in both decimal and hex for numeric data types) and the status line at the bottom displays the data type. For example, if you inspect an integer variable, the value will be shown and the status bar will say int. At the top of the Debug Inspector is a combo box that initially contains a description of the object being inspected.

If you are inspecting a class, the Debug Inspector will look like Figure 11.7.

Figure 11.7.

The Debug Inspector inspecting a form class.

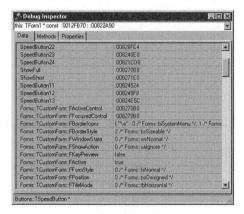

To better understand the Debug Inspector, do the following:

1. Load the DebugTst program you created earlier (if it's not already loaded).
2. Set a breakpoint somewhere in the WatchBtnClick() function.
3. Run the program and click the Watch button. The debugger stops at the breakpoint you have set.
4. From the main menu, choose Run | Inspect. The Inspect dialog box is displayed.
5. Type this in the Expression field and click OK.
6. The Debug Inspector is displayed.

11

NOTE

You can only inspect this from within a class member function. If you happen to set a breakpoint in a regular function and then attempt to inspect this, you will get an error message stating that this is an invalid symbol. In the previous example this refers to the application's main form.

When inspecting classes, the Debug Inspector window contains three pages, as you can see. The Data page shows all the class data members in a hierarchical list. The first items listed are the data items that belong to the immediate class. Next are the data members of that class's immediate ancestor class—in this case, TForm. If you scroll through the Debug Inspector list, you will see that following the TForm data members are the data members for the TScrollingWinControl class (TForm's immediate ancestor) and on and on.

By using the arrow keys to move up and down the data members list, you can tell at a glance what each data member's type is (look at the status bar on the Debug Inspector window). To further inspect a data member, double-click the Value column on the line showing the data member. A second Debug Inspector window is opened with the selected data member displayed. You can have multiple Debug Inspector windows open simultaneously.

NOTE

The Debug Inspector has a lot of information to display, so scrolling the list of items can be slow on some systems.

The Methods page of the Debug Inspector displays the class's methods. Like the data members list, the methods list is hierarchical. The first methods are those in the immediate class, followed by the methods in the ancestor classes. In some cases the Methods tab isn't displayed (when inspecting simple data types, for instance).

The Properties page of the Debug Inspector shows the properties for the class being inspected. Inspecting properties through the Debug Inspector is very slow if you are inspecting a VCL inherited class. Most of the time you can accomplish the same thing by inspecting the data member associated with a particular property on the Data page. Inspecting the data member is much faster than inspecting properties.

NOTE

The Methods page and the Properties page of the Debug Inspector are available only when you're inspecting a class. When you're inspecting simple data types, the Data page alone is displayed.

> **TIP**
>
> If you want your Debug Inspector windows always on top of the Code Editor, go to the Debugger page of the Environment Options dialog box and check the Inspectors stay on top check box.

The Debug Inspector context menu has several items that enable you to work with the Debug Inspector and the individual variables. For example, rather than open a new Debug Inspector window for each object, you can right-click and choose Descend to replace the current object in the Debug Inspector window with the object under the cursor. This method has an added advantage: The IDE keeps a history list of the objects you inspect. To go back to an object you have already inspected, just choose the object from the combo box at the top of the Debug Inspector window. Choosing one of the objects in the history list will again show that object in the Debug Inspector window.

The Change item on the Debug Inspector context menu enables you to change a variable's value. Change any variables with care. Changing the wrong data member or specifying a value that is invalid for that data member might lead to your program crashing. The Inspect item on the context menu enables you to open a second Debug Inspector window with the item under the cursor displayed. The New Expression context menu item enables you to enter a new expression to inspect in the Debug Inspector.

The Show Inherited item on the Debug Inspector context menu is a toggle that determines how much information the Debug Inspector should display. When the Show Inherited option is on, the Debug Inspector shows all data members, methods, and properties of the class being inspected as well as the data members, methods, and properties of all ancestor classes. When the Show Inherited option is off, only the data members, methods, and properties of the class itself are shown. Turning off this option can greatly speed up the Debug Inspector because it doesn't have as much information to display.

> **TIP**
>
> If you have a class data member and you don't remember its type, you can click on it when stopped at a breakpoint and press Alt+F5 to display the Debug Inspector. The status bar at the bottom of the Debug Inspector window will tell you the variable's data type. This also works for Windows and system-defined constants such as HINSTANCE, HWND, DWORD, and so on.

Inspecting Local Variables

Often you want to inspect all the variables pertinent to the function you are currently debugging. One way is to add each variable to the Watch List. This takes time, though, especially if you have more than a few variables to watch. A better way is to choose Run | Inspect Local Variables from the main menu. When you do, a Debug Inspector window will appear, and all the variables local to the function you are in will be displayed. In the section "Using the Watch List," you performed an exercise. Figure 11.8 shows how the C++Builder Code Editor and Debug Inspector appear when inspecting local variables during that exercise.

Figure 11.8.

The Debug Inspector showing local variables.

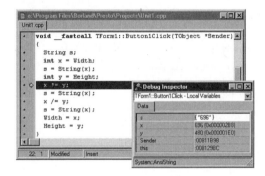

The Inspect Local Variables option is a quick and easy way to inspect local variables with minimum effort.

Other Debugging Tools

C++Builder has some additional debugging tools to aid you in tracking down bugs. Some of these tools are, by nature, advanced debugging tools. Although the advanced debugging tools are not as commonly used as the other tools, they are very powerful in the hands of an experienced programmer.

Evaluate/Modify

The Evaluate/Modify dialog box enables you to inspect a variable's current value and to modify the value if you want. Using this dialog box, you can test for different outcomes by modifying a particular variable. This enables you to play a what-if game with your program as it runs. Figure 11.9 shows the Evaluate/Modify dialog box inspecting a variable.

Figure 11.9.

The Evaluate/Modify
dialog box.

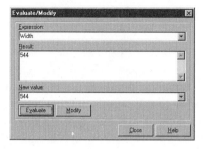

The Evaluate/Modify dialog box works similarly to the Watch List or the Debug Inspector. If you click a variable in the source code and choose Evaluate/Modify from the Code Editor context menu, the variable will be evaluated. If you want to enter a value not currently showing in the source code, you can choose Run | Evaluate/Modify from the main menu and then type a variable name to evaluate.

The Evaluate field is used to enter the variable name or expression you want to evaluate. When you click the Evaluate button (or press Enter), the expression will be evaluated and the result displayed in the Result field.

TIP
The Evaluate/Modify dialog box can be used as a quickie calculator. You can enter hex or decimal numbers (or a combination) in a mathematical formula and have the result evaluated. For instance, if you type

```
0x400 - 256
```

in the Evaluate field and press Enter, the result, 768, will be displayed in the Result field.

You can also enter logical expressions in the Evaluate field and have the result shown in the Result field. For instance, if you entered

```
20 * 20 == 400
```

the Result field would show true. The only problem with this scenario is that the program must be stopped at a breakpoint for the Evaluate/Modify dialog box to function.

If you want to change a variable's value, enter a new value for the variable in the New Value field and click the Modify button. The variable's value will be changed to the new value entered. When you click the Run button to restart the program (or continue stepping), the new value will be used.

NOTE

> The Evaluate/Modify dialog box doesn't update automatically when you step through your code, as do the Watch List and Debug Inspector. If your code modifies the variable in the Evaluate/Modify dialog box, you must click the Evaluate button again to see the results. A typical interaction with this dialog box would be to evaluate a variable or expression and then immediately close the Evaluate/Modify dialog box.

View Call Stack

While your program is running, you can view the call stack to inspect any functions your program called. From the main menu, choose View | Call Stack to display the Call Stack window. This window displays a list of the functions called by your program and the order in which they were called. The most recently called function is at the top of the window. The functions listed are a combination of your program functions, VCL methods, and functions contained in Windows DLLs. Figure 11.10 shows the call stack as it appears after clicking a button in a simple test program.

Figure 11.10.

The Call Stack window.

In this case the first function on the list is `TForm1::Button1Click()`. Following that, you see calls to some VCL functions and a couple calls to functions (unnamed) in the Windows `USER32.DLL`. Remember that the functions are listed in reverse order—the function executed last shows up first in the call stack list.

Double-clicking a function name in the Call Stack window takes you to the source code line for that function if the function is in your program. In case of functions in Windows DLLs, the Call Stack window contains just an address and the name of the DLL. Double-clicking a listed function contained in a DLL will display the CPU View window (the CPU View is discussed in the next section).

11

NOTE

> If you have linked to the debug version of VCL, double-clicking a VCL method in the Call Stack window will display the VCL source code for that method. If you have not linked to the debug version of VCL, double-clicking a VCL method in the Call Stack window will display the CPU View. You can set the option to link to the VCL debug version on the Linker page of the Project Options dialog box.

Viewing the call stack is most helpful after a Windows Access Violation error. By viewing the call stack, you can see where your program was just before the error occurred. Knowing where your program was just before it crashed is often the first step in determining what went wrong.

TIP

> If the call stack list contains seemingly nonsensical information, it could be that the call stack was corrupted. A corrupted call stack is usually an indicator of a stack problem. This isn't as likely to occur in a 32-bit program as in a 16-bit program, but it still can happen.

CPU View

The CPU View enables you to view your program at the assembly level. Obviously this is an advanced debugging feature. Using this view you can step into or over instructions one assembly instruction at a time. You can also run the program to a certain assembly instruction just as you can run the program to a certain source line with the regular debugger. The CPU view window has five panes: the disassembly pane, the register pane, the flags pane, the raw stack pane, and the dump pane. Each pane has a context menu associated with it. The context menus provide all the functions necessary to use that pane. To be used effectively, the CPU view requires a knowledge of assembly language. To display the CPU View, choose View | CPU from the main menu.

The Go to Address Command

The Go to Address command is also an advanced debugging tool. When your program crashes, Windows displays an error message showing the address of the violation. You can use the Go to Address command to attempt to find out where in your program the crash occurred. When you get an Access Violation error message from Windows, you will see a dialog box similar to the one in Figure 11.11.

Figure 11.11.
A Windows message box reporting an access violation.

When you see this error message, write down the address at which the violation occurred and then choose Search | Go to Address from the main menu to display the Goto Address dialog box. Enter the address you just wrote down in the Address field of the Goto Address dialog box. When you click OK, the debugger will attempt to find the source code line where the error occurred. If the error occurred in your code, the cursor will be placed on the line that generated the error. If the error occurred somewhere outside your code, you will get a message box saying that the address could not be found. As I said, this is an advanced debugging tool that you might never use.

Stepping Through Your Code

Stepping through code is one of the most basic debugging operations, yet it still needs to be mentioned here. Sometimes we fail to see the forest for the trees. (Just as sometimes authors of programming books fail to include the obvious!) Reviewing the basics from time to time can reveal something you were not previously aware of.

Before we begin this section, I'll say a few words about the symbols that appear in the Code Editor gutter during a debugging session. In the section "Setting and Clearing Breakpoints," I told you that a red circle appears in the gutter when you set a breakpoint on a code line. I also said that a green arrow glyph indicates the execution point when you are stepping through code. One thing I didn't mention, though, is the little blue dots that appear in the gutter next to certain code lines. These dots indicate lines in your source code that actually generate assembly code. Figure 11.12 shows the Code Editor with the debugger stopped at a breakpoint. It shows the small dots that indicate generated code, the arrow glyph indicating the execution point, and the breakpoint glyph as well. The check mark on the breakpoint glyph indicates that the breakpoint was checked and was determined to be a valid breakpoint.

Figure 11.12.
The Code Editor showing gutter symbols.

Take a closer look at Figure 11.12. Notice that the small dots only appear next to certain code lines. Lines without the dots don't generate any code. Take these lines, for instance:

```
int x;
x = 20;
```

Why don't these lines generate code? Here's that word again: *optimization.* The compiler looks ahead and sees that the variable x is never used, so it completely ignores all references to that variable.

Okay, back to stepping through code. When you stop at a breakpoint, you can do many things to determine what is going on with your code. You can set up variables to watch in the Watch List, inspect objects with the Debug Inspector, or view the call stack. You can also step through your code to watch what happens to your variables and objects as each code line is executed. As you continue to step through your code, you will see that the line in your source code to be executed next is highlighted in blue. If you have the Watch List and Debug Inspector windows open, they will be updated as each code line is executed. Any changes to variables or objects will be immediately visible in the watch or inspector window.

NOTE

Seemingly odd things happen when the Optimize for Speed compiler option is turned on. (Optimization options were discussed yesterday, Day 10, "More on Projects.") When the compiler optimizes code, it rearranges your source code using mysterious means about which mere mortals can only speculate. Your source code isn't rearranged per se, but the resulting assembly code might not exactly match the source code in your source file. The end result is a program that runs faster, and that, of course, is a good thing.

This benefit does come at a cost, however. Earlier I discussed the fact that variables can be optimized by the compiler making them unavailable for inspection, and this is one of the disadvantages of using optimizations.

An interesting side effect of having your code rearranged is that when you step through your code, the execution point might not proceed sequentially from line to line as you expect. Rather, the execution point might appear to jump around in your source and even land on a single line of code multiple times.

This is all perfectly normal, but it can be disconcerting when you are learning to use the debugger. If you prefer to see the execution point proceed sequentially through your code, turn off optimizations while debugging. Turn optimizations back on again for your final builds. Remember that when you change optimization settings, you need to do a Build All for all modules to be rebuilt using the new settings.

11

The IDE debugger has two primary stepping commands to aid in your debugging operations: Step Over and Trace Into. Step Over means to execute the next line in the source code and pause on the line immediately following. Step Over is sort of a misnomer. The name indicates that you can step over a source line and the line won't be executed. That isn't the case, however. Step Over means that the current line will be executed and any functions which that source line calls will be run at full speed. For instance, let's say you have set a breakpoint at a line that calls another function in your program. When you tell the debugger to step over the function, the debugger will execute the function and stop on the next line. (Contrast this with how Trace Into works, which you'll learn about in a minute, and it will make more sense.) To use Step Over to step through your program, you can either press F8 or choose Run | Step Over from the main menu.

NOTE
As you step through various source code units in your program, the Code Editor will automatically load and display the needed source units if they are not already open.

The Trace Into command enables you to trace into any functions that are encountered as you step through your code. Rather than execute the function and return to the next line as Step Over does, Trace Into places the execution point on the first source code line in the function being called. You can then step line by line through that function using Step Over or Trace Into as necessary. The keyboard shortcut for Trace Into is F7.

After you have inspected variables and done whatever debugging you need to do, you can again run the program at full speed by clicking the Run button. The program will function normally until the next breakpoint is encountered.

TIP
If you have enabled the Link Debug Version of VCL linker option, then when you encounter a VCL method, Trace Into will take you into the VCL source code for that method. You can inspect whatever variables you need to see. If you turn on this option, you must do a Build All for it to take effect. As I said earlier, stepping into the VCL source is of doubtful benefit to most programmers. Experienced programmers, though, will find it useful.

Another, less frequently used, debugging command is Trace To Next Source Line (Shift+F7 on the keyboard). You will not likely use this command a lot, particularly not until you get more familiar with debugging and Windows programming in general. Some Windows API functions use what is termed a *callback function*. This means that the Windows function calls one of your own functions to perform some action. If the execution point is on a Windows API function that uses a callback function, using Trace To Next Source Line will jump the execution point to the first line in the callback function. The effect is similar to Trace Into, but the specific situation in which Trace To Next Source Line is used is altogether different. If that doesn't make sense to you, don't worry about it. It's not important for what you need to learn today.

NOTE

When you are stepping through a function, the execution point will eventually get to the right brace. If the function you are stepping through returns control to Windows when it finishes, pressing F8 when on the right brace will exit the function and return control to the program being debugged. There is no obvious indication that the program is no longer paused because the IDE still has focus. This behavior can be confusing the first few times you encounter it unless you are aware of what has happened. To switch back to your program, just activate it as you would any other program (click its glyph on the Windows taskbar or use Alt+Tab).

As I said, stepping through your code is a basic debugging technique, but it is one that you will use constantly while debugging. Of all the keyboard shortcuts available to you in C++Builder, F7 (Trace Into), F8 (Step Over), and F9 (Run) should definitely be in your arsenal.

TIP

On some systems the debugger might take a long time between steps when single-stepping through code. To help alleviate this problem, make sure that you don't have any more than the minimum number of variables in the Watch List. Be sure, also, that you close any Debug Inspector windows that you aren't currently using.

A big factor in debugger speed is the amount of system RAM. RAM is cheap, so you might consider adding more memory to your system if the debugger is too slow for you and if the preceding suggestions don't increase speed.

Debugging a DLL

For the most part, debugging a DLL is the same as debugging an executable file. You place breakpoints in the DLL's code and when a breakpoint is hit, the debugger will pause just as it does when debugging an EXE. Normally you test a DLL by creating a test application and running the test application under the debugger. Sometimes, however, you need to test a DLL for use with executable files built with other development environments. For example, let's say you are building a DLL that will be called from a Visual Basic application. You certainly can't start a VB application running under the C++Builder debugger. What you can do, though, is tell the C++Builder debugger to start the VB application as a host application. (Naturally, the host application has to contain code that loads the DLL.) You tell C++Builder to start an external host application through the Run Parameters dialog box. To display the Run Parameters dialog box, choose Run | Parameters from the main menu. Type an EXE name in the Host Application field, click the Load button, and the host application will run. Figure 11.13 shows the Run Parameters dialog box as it appears just before debugging a DLL.

Figure 11.13.

Specifying a host application with the Run Parameters dialog box.

After the host application has started, you test your DLL just as you do when using a C++Builder test application: You place breakpoints in the DLL and begin debugging.

The Event Log

The Event Log is a special C++Builder file that shows diagnostic messages—messages generated by C++Builder, by your own applications, and sometimes by Windows itself. For example, the Event Log tells you that modules were loaded (mostly DLLs), whether they include debug info, when your application was started, when it was stopped, when a breakpoint was encountered, and more. To view the Event Log, choose View | Event Log from the C++Builder main menu. Figure 11.14 shows the Event Log while debugging an application.

Figure 11.14.

The Event Log.

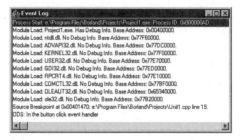

The Event Log has a context menu that enables you to clear the Log, save it to a text file, or add comments to the Event Log. Saving the Event Log to a text file enables you to browse the messages list more thoroughly or search for specific text you want to see. The Event Log context menu also has an Options menu item that enables you to further customize the Event Log. When you choose this menu item, a dialog box is displayed that enables you to change Event Log options. This dialog box is the same as the Debugger page in the Environment Options dialog box (shown in Figure 11.16, in the section "Debugging Options").

You can send your own messages to the Event Log using the Windows API function `OutputDebugString()`. `OutputDebugString()` is discussed later in the section "`OutputDebugString()`."

The Module View

The Module view shows you the modules currently loaded, source files attached to those modules, and symbols (functions and variables) exported from that module. You can invoke the Module view by choosing View | Modules from the main menu. The Module view is primarily an advanced debugging tool, so I won't go into a detailed discussion of its features here. You should take some time to experiment with the Module view to see how it works. Figure 11.15 shows the Module view in action.

Figure 11.15.

The Module view.

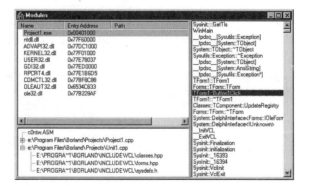

Debugging Techniques

I have already touched on a few debugging techniques as we examined the various aspects of the IDE debugger in this chapter. I will mention a few more techniques that make your debugging tasks easier.

OutputDebugString()

Sometimes it is helpful to track your program's execution as your program runs. Or maybe you want to see a variable's value without stopping program execution at a breakpoint. The OutputDebugString() function enables you to do exactly that. This function is a convenient debugging tool that many programmers overlook, primarily because of a general lack of discussion on the subject. Look at the last entry in the Event Log shown in Figure 11.14. That entry was generated using this code:

```
OutputDebugString("In the button click event handler");
```

That's all you have to do. Because C++Builder is installed as the system debugger, any strings sent using OutputDebugString() will show up in the Event Log. You can place calls to OutputDebugString() anywhere you want in your code.

NOTE Because of the way Windows works, any messages sent using OutputDebugString() won't show up in the Event Log until your program exits or stops at a breakpoint.

TIP To view the Event Log without setting a breakpoint, choose Run | Program Pause from the main menu. Program execution will pause and the Event Log will be updated. Click the Run button to resume program execution after viewing the Event Log.

To view the value of a variable, you have to format a string and send that string to OutputDebugString()—for example,

```
char buff[20];
wsprintf(buff, "x = %d", x);
OutputDebugString(buff);
```

Using OutputDebugString() you can see what is going on with your program even in time-critical sections of code.

11

Tracking Down Access Violations

When a program attempts to write to memory that it doesn't own, Windows issues an Access Violation error message. All Windows programmers encounter access violations while developing their applications.

NOTE

> The term GPF (General Protection Fault) was used in 16-bit Windows. Its use is still prevalent in the 32-bit Windows programming world even though 32-bit Windows actually generates Access Violation errors instead of General Protection Faults.

Access violations can be difficult to track down for beginning and experienced Windows programmers alike. Often, as programmers gain experience in writing Windows programs, they develop a sixth sense for locating the cause of access violations. Here are some things to look for when trying to track down the elusive access violation. These are not the only situations that cause a program to crash, but they are some of the most common.

Uninitialized Pointers

An *uninitialized pointer* is a pointer that has been declared but not set to point to anything meaningful in your program. An uninitialized pointer contains random data. In the best case it points to some harmless spot in memory. In the worst case the uninitialized pointer points to a random memory location somewhere in your program. This can lead to erratic program behavior because the pointer might point to a different memory location each time the program is run. Always set a pointer to NULL both before it's used for the first time and after the object it points to is deleted. If you try to access a NULL pointer, your program will stop with an access violation, but the offending line in the source code will be highlighted by the debugger, and you can immediately identify the problem pointer.

Deleting Previously Deleted Pointers

Deleting a pointer that has already been deleted results in an access violation. The advice given for working with uninitialized pointers applies here as well: Set deleted pointers to NULL or 0. In C++ it is perfectly safe to delete a NULL pointer. By setting your deleted pointer to NULL, you ensure that no ill effects will occur if you accidentally delete the pointer a second time.

Array Overwrites

Overwriting the end of an array can cause an access violation. In some cases the overwritten memory might not be critical, and the problem might not show up right away, but later the program will crash. When that happens, you will likely look for a bug at the point the program crashed, but the actual problem occurred in a completely different part of the program. In other cases the memory that is overwritten is critical, and the program will immediately stop.

In extreme cases you might even crash Windows. Check each array to ensure you are not overwriting the end of the array.

Access Violation on Program Termination

When a program halts with an access violation on normal shutdown, it usually indicates that the stack size is set too small. Although this isn't likely in a 32-bit program, it could happen under extreme circumstances. An access violation on program termination can also be caused by deleting an already deleted pointer, as already discussed.

Debug Quick Tips

In addition to the many tips offered on the preceding pages, you might want to implement these:

☐ Change the form's Caption property to display a variable without using breakpoints. Because placing a Label component on a form is so easy, you can use a label, too. Change the text in the label to show the variable's value or any other information you want to display.

☐ Enable a conditional breakpoint or a data watch breakpoint to temporarily slow down your program (possibly to view program effects in slow motion). These breakpoints slow down program execution while they check the breakpoint's condition.

☐ Use the Evaluate/Modify dialog box to temporarily change a variable's value at runtime. This enables you to view the effects that different values have on your program without recompiling your code each time.

☐ Turn on the Disable inline expansions option on the C++ page of the Project Options dialog box to trace into inline functions. Turn off the option again before your final build. Ordinarily you cannot use Trace Into with inline functions.

☐ Choose Run | Inspect from the main menu and enter this in the Expression field to inspect the class where the debugger is currently stopped.

☐ Use MessageBeep(-1) as an audible indicator that a certain point in your program has been reached. This Windows API function beeps the PC speaker when called with a parameter of -1.

☐ Choose Run | Program Reset from the main menu or press Ctrl+F2 to stop an errant debugee.

☐ Use temporary variables to break down long equations or chained function calls so that you can examine the results in more manageable pieces.

☐ Use the MessageBox() function to display program tracing information.

WARNING

If you are running C++Builder on Windows 95, use the Program Reset option sparingly. In some cases using Program Reset to kill an application can crash Windows 95. Not all Windows 95 systems behave the same way, so you might not experience this problem. Windows NT doesn't suffer from this problem, so you can use Program Reset more liberally under Windows NT. Personally, I only use Program Reset if the application I am debugging locks up.

Debugging Options

Debugging options can be set on two levels: the project level and the environment level. Project debugging options were discussed on Day 10, in the sections "The Compiler Page" and "The Advanced Compiler Page." The debugging options you set at the global level can be found on the Debugging page of the Environment Options dialog box. Figure 11.16 shows the Debugger page of the Environment Options dialog box.

Figure 11.16.

The Environment Options dialog box Debugger page.

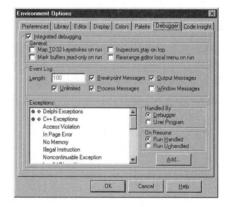

Integrated Debugging

This option controls whether the IDE debugger is used for debugging. If the Integrated debugging check box is checked, the IDE debugger is used. If this option is unchecked, the IDE debugger isn't used. This means that when you click the Run button, the program will execute, but the debugger is disabled, so no breakpoints will function.

General

The Map TD32 keystrokes on run option in this section tells the Code Editor to use the keystroke mapping used in Borland's standalone debugger, Turbo Debugger. This is a nice feature if you have spent a lot of time using Turbo Debugger and are familiar with that program's key mappings.

The Mark buffers read-only on run option sets the Code Editor buffers to read-only when the program is run under the debugger. After you start the program under the debugger, you cannot edit your source code until the program is terminated. I leave this option off because I frequently make changes to my source code while debugging.

The Inspectors stay on top check box controls whether the Debug Inspector windows are always on top of the Code Editor. This is a nice feature because most of the time you want the Debug Inspector windows to stay on top when stepping through your code.

The Rearrange editor local menu on run option changes the appearance of the Code Editor context menu when a program is running under the debugger. When this option is on, the Code Editor context menu items specific to debugging are moved to the top of the context menu, so they are easier to find.

Event Log

This section enables you to set the options for the Event Log. You can choose a maximum number of messages that can appear in the Event Log at any one time or leave the number unlimited. You can also select the types of messages you want to see in the Event Log.

Exceptions

This section controls which exceptions are handled by the debugger and which are handled by the user program. When the Handled By option is set to User Program, the debugger pauses program execution when an exception is thrown. When this option is set to Debugger, the VCL exception is handled in the usual way—with a message box informing the user of what went wrong in the program.

NOTE

When the Handled By option is set to Debugger, the debugger breaks on exceptions *even if the exception is handled in your program.* If you don't want the debugger to break on every exception, set this option to User Program. This option replaces the Break on exception option found in C++Builder 1.0.

The On Resume option determines how the exception will be treated when program execution is resumed following an exception.

The Exceptions list box contains a list of possible exception types. To set the options for a particular type, click on the exception in the Exceptions list box and then set the Handled

By or On Resume option as desired. Glyphs next to the exception name indicate which options are set for a particular exception.

Summary

Debugging is a never-ending task. Debugging means more than just tracking down a bug in your program. Savvy programmers learn to use the debugger from the outset of a new project. The debugger is a development tool as well as a bug-finding tool. After today, you should have at least a basic understanding of how to use the debugger. You will still have to spend a lot of time actually using the debugger before you are proficient at it, but you now have a place to start.

Workshop

The Workshop contains quiz questions to help you solidify your understanding of the material covered and exercises to provide you with experience in using what you have learned. You can find the answers to the quiz questions in Appendix A, "Answers to Quiz Questions."

Q&A

Q **My program used to run at regular speed when I ran it from the IDE. Now it's as slow as molasses in January. Why is that?**

A More than likely you have either a large number of breakpoints that you disabled and forgot about or one or more conditional breakpoints in your code. Go to the Breakpoint List and delete any breakpoints you are not currently using. Also, be sure you don't have a lot of variables listed in the Watch List.

Q **I have a variable that I want to view in both decimal and hexadecimal format. Can I do that with the Watch List?**

A Yes. First, add the variable to the Watch List. Next double-click on the variable in the Watch List. When the Watch Properties dialog box comes up, choose the Decimal viewing option. Now add the variable to the Watch List again, but this time choose the Hexadecimal viewing option. Both items will be listed in the Watch List, one in decimal format and the other in hex format.

Q **I want to stop at a breakpoint when a variable reaches a certain value *and* after the breakpoint has been hit a certain number of times. Can I do that?**

A Sure. Enter a conditional expression in the Condition field of the Edit Source Breakpoint dialog box and a value in the Pass Count field. When the condition is met for the number of times indicated by the pass count, the program will pause at the breakpoint.

Q **I'm stepping through my code and I get to a function in my program that I want to debug. When I press F8, the execution point jumps right over the function. How do I get into that function?**

A When the execution point is on the line where the function is called, press F7 (`Trace Into`) instead of F8. Now you can step through the function a line at a time.

Q **When I step through my code, the execution point jumps all over the place rather than proceed through my code a line at a time. What causes that?**

A In a word: optimization. If you want to debug your program one source code line at a time, sequentially, turn off all optimizations and do a Build All to rebuild the project.

Q **I step through a function line by line. Sometimes when I get to the function's right brace, I press F8 one more time and nothing happens. Why?**

A Because when that particular function returns, your program has nothing more to do, so it goes back into its idle state. Essentially, there is no more code to step through at that point, so the debugger returns control to the program being debugged.

Q **How do I use the CPU View when debugging?**

A Just choose View | CPU from the main menu to display the CPU View. Knowing what to do with the CPU View, however, is another matter entirely!

Quiz

1. How do you set a breakpoint on a particular code line?
2. What is an invalid breakpoint?
3. How do you set a conditional breakpoint?
4. How can you change the properties of an item in the Watch List?
5. What's the quickest way to add a variable to the Watch List?
6. What tool do you use to view the data members and methods of a class?
7. How do you trace into a function call when stepping with the debugger?
8. How can you change the value of a variable at runtime?
9. How can you send your own messages to the Event Log?
10. What is the easiest way to view the local variables while stepping through a function?

Exercises

1. Load the `ScratchPad` program that you created on Day 7, "Working with the Form Designer and the Menu Designer." Place breakpoints in the `FileOpenClick()` and

FileSaveClick() functions. Run the program. When program execution pauses, inspect the OpenDialog and SaveDialog classes, respectively.

2. Continuing with Exercise 1, step through the program when you stop at a breakpoint and examine the program's operation as you step through the functions.

3. Load the DebugTst program you created earlier in this chapter. Place a breakpoint in the WatchBtnClick() function. Add the s and x variables to the Watch List. Add each variable to the Watch List four times. Edit each of the watches and change the display options. Run the program and step through the function to see the effects in the Watch List.

4. Add a conditional breakpoint to the function in Exercise 3. Place it on the line immediately after the line that reads int x = Width. Make the condition x == 0 and run the program. What happens?

5. Continuing with Exercise 4, edit the breakpoint and change the condition to x > 400. Run the program. Change the window's size and click the Watch Test button. Repeat this process several times, changing the window's size each time. What happens?

6. Load any program and switch to the Code Editor. Place the cursor on any code line and choose the Run to Cursor item from the Code Editor context menu. Experiment with the program until the breakpoint is hit.

7. Again load the DebugTst program you created earlier. Place a breakpoint in the WatchBtnClick() function and run the program. When the breakpoint is hit, use the Debug Inspector to inspect the WatchBtn.

11

Day 12

C++Builder Tools and Options

C++Builder comes with several tools to aid in your application development. Some are standard Windows GUI applications and others are Win32 console applications. Today you will learn specifically about

- [ ] The Image Editor
- [ ] Messages and the Windows messaging system
- [ ] WinSight
- [ ] Command-line tools
- [ ] Configuring the Tools menu

First, we will take a look at these tools. Then you will learn how to add your own tools to the C++Builder Tools menu. The day will end with a look at the C++Builder Environment Options dialog box.

In addition to the tools listed here, C++Builder also comes with a host of database tools such as Database Desktop, BDE Administrator, SQL Builder, and SQL Explorer. A discussion of those tools would be too lengthy for today's purposes.

The Image Editor

The C++Builder Image Editor is a tool that enables you to create and edit bitmaps (.bmp), icons (.ico), and cursors (.cur). You also can create a resource project containing multiple bitmaps, icons, and cursors in a single resource file (.res). The resource file can then be added to your C++Builder project, and you can use the resources as needed. Figure 12.1 shows the Image Editor editing a bitmap.

Figure 12.1.

The Image Editor.

NOTE

All Windows images are bitmaps, whether they are actual Windows bitmap files (.bmp) or are icons or cursors. In this chapter I will refer to all images collectively as *bitmaps*.

NOTE

Image Editor only deals with Windows bitmap files. Other file formats such as PCX, TIFF, JPEG, and GIF are not supported.

You can start the Image Editor by either double-clicking on the Image Editor icon in the C++Builder folder or choosing Tools|Image Editor from the C++Builder main menu. The Image Editor is a standalone program and doesn't have to be run from the C++Builder IDE.

Foreground and Background Colors

The Image Editor enables you to create 2-color, 16-color, and in the case of bitmap files, 256-color images. You can choose any available colors when drawing on a bitmap. In the bottom-left corner of the Image Editor are two boxes containing the current foreground and background colors. (The foreground color is represented by the far left box.)

When using a drawing tool, you can draw with either the foreground color or the background color. To draw with the foreground color, use the left mouse button. For example, if you choose the filled rectangle tool and draw a rectangle on the bitmap, the rectangle will be filled with the foreground color. To draw a filled rectangle with the background color, use the right mouse button to drag the rectangle. The same is true for most of the other drawing tools.

NOTE

> The Text tool uses only the foreground color. You cannot place text with the background color. If you want to use the background color, you have to change the foreground color and then place your text.

To change the foreground color, click a color on the color palette with the left mouse button. (The color palette is located along the bottom of the Image Editor window.) When you choose a new foreground color, the square that represents the foreground color changes to show the new color selected. To change the background color, click a color in the color palette with your right mouse button.

NOTE

> If you are editing a 256-color image, the color palette will have scroll buttons on either side so that you can scroll through the available colors.

The colors that appear in the color palette are determined by the bitmap itself if you are loading a bitmap that already exists. If you are starting a new 256-color image, the default 256-color palette is used.

You also can set the foreground or background colors with the Eyedropper tool. The Eyedropper enables you to set the foreground or background color by picking up a color that is already used on the image. To set the foreground color with the Eyedropper, choose the Eyedropper tool from the Tools palette, place the tip of the Eyedropper over a portion of the

12

image that has the color you want to use, and then click the left mouse button. The foreground color changes to the color under the Eyedropper. To set the background color, click with your right mouse button instead of the left mouse button. The Eyedropper tool is invaluable when you want to exactly match a color previously used on your bitmap.

NOTE | The foreground and background colors might work differently in the Image Editor than in other bitmap editors you have used. For example, in some bitmap editors the outline of a filled rectangle is drawn with the foreground color and filled with the background color. With the Image Editor, filled objects have no discernible border. A filled rectangle is in either the foreground or the background color.

Transparent and Inverted Colors

In the case of icons and cursors, you can also choose the transparent color (the word *color* being relative here). When you use the transparent color, the background beneath the icon shows through wherever the transparent color is used. That could mean the Windows background in the case of a shortcut, or it could mean the title bar of your application. Whether you use the transparent color depends on your personal tastes and the particular icon you are creating. In the case of cursors, you will almost always use the transparent color as the background for the icon. Rarely do you have a cursor that appears as a solid block.

Choosing the inverted color causes the background underneath the icon to be inverted (like reverse video). Use of the inverted color isn't common, but it is there if and when you need it.

Both the transparent and inverted colors are shown next to the color palette when editing icons and cursors. They are represented by color squares with a curved line running through them.

NOTE | By default, new icon and new cursor resources have the background filled with the transparent color.

Image Editor Drawing Tools

The Image Editor drawing tools are similar to most paint programs. Because these are common drawing tools, I'm not going to go over each and every one. Fifteen minutes of experimentation with the Image Editor will be more beneficial than anything I can tell you. Fire up the Image Editor and experiment with it for a while. I'll wait.

At the top of the Image Editor Tools palette, you find the Marquee and Lasso tools. These work in essentially the same way, so I'll cover them together. Both tools enable you to select a region on the current image. The Marquee tool is used to define a rectangular region. Choose the Marquee tool and then drag a bounding rectangle on the image. When you stop dragging, a marquee is drawn around the region to mark it. The Lasso tool works in much the same way but enables you to drag a freehand region. A Lasso region is filled with a hatch pattern to identify it.

TIP

> When using the Lasso tool, you don't have to close the region. When you release the mouse button, the Image Editor will automatically close the region by drawing a connection line between the start point and the end point.

When a region is defined, you can cut or copy the image within the region and paste it somewhere else on the image or to another image you are working on (you can have multiple bitmaps open at one time). When you choose Edit | Paste from the main menu, the image within the marquee is placed in the upper-left corner of the bitmap with a marquee around it. The pasted image can now be dragged into position. When you place your mouse cursor within the marquee, the cursor changes to a hand. When you see the hand cursor, you can drag the bitmap within the marquee to another location and drop it. You can continue to move the bitmap until you have it positioned exactly where you want it. After you have the bitmap where you want it, click again on the image outside the marquee, and the bitmap within the marquee will be merged into the existing image.

TIP

> The Image Editor has a shortcut method of cut and paste. Create a Marquee or Lasso region, place your mouse cursor inside the region, and drag. The image within the region will move as you drag.

When you cut a region or move it by dragging, the current background color will fill the area that the image originally occupied. The background shows through the hole created by the cut operation.

12

You can copy portions of one bitmap to another by using cut and paste. First, open both images in the Image Editor. Place a marquee around the portion of the original image you want to copy and then choose Edit | Copy from the main menu. Switch to the other image and choose Edit | Paste from the main menu. Move the pasted image as needed.

NOTE   If you have a marquee selected when you paste, the pasted image will shrink or stretch to fit the size of the marquee.

The Eraser tool works just the opposite of the other tools in regard to the left and right mouse buttons. With the Eraser, the left mouse button draws with the background color and the right mouse button draws with the foreground color.

The Text tool enables you to place text on the image. The text is drawn using the current text settings. The text settings can be changed by clicking the Text item on the main menu. Here you can set the text alignment (left, right, or centered) or the font (typeface). To change the typeface, choose Text | Font from the main menu. Now you can choose a new typeface or make the font bold, italic, underlined, and so on.

The other drawing tools are self-explanatory. As I said earlier, a little time behind the wheel of the Image Editor will teach you just about everything you need to know about those tools.

TIP   When drawing rectangles, you can press and hold the Shift key to force a rectangle to a square. Likewise, you can draw a perfect circle by choosing the Ellipse or Filled Ellipse tool and holding the Shift key as you drag. Using the Shift key with the Line tool enables you to draw straight lines (vertical, horizontal, or 45-degree angles).

Zooming

The Image Editor enables you to zoom in so that you can work on your bitmaps up close and personal. You can zoom either by using the Zoom tool or via the View menu. To zoom in on a particular part of your image using the Zoom tool, first select the Zoom tool from the Tools palette and then drag a bounding rectangle around the portion of the image you want to see up close. The magnification will change depending on the size of the rectangle you created when you dragged. You can now see well enough to change fine details in your bitmap.

To zoom using the menu, choose View|Zoom In or press Ctrl+I. When you choose Zoom In from the menu, the image is magnified by a predetermined amount. To zoom out again using the menu, choose View|Zoom Out (Ctrl+U) or View|Actual Size.

When you are creating a cursor or an icon, the Image Editor will set you up with a split view. Figure 12.2 shows an Image Editor window while creating an icon.

Figure 12.2.

Editing an icon.

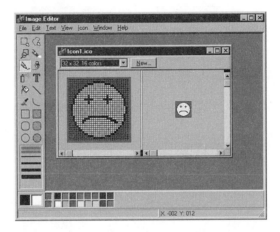

Although you can zoom either side of the split window, you will usually work with a zoomed-in copy on the left side and an actual-size image on the right, as shown in the figure.

The Line Width Palette

The Line Width palette is displayed directly below the Tools palette. Depending on the currently selected tool, the Line Width palette might show line widths or brush shapes that you can choose. To pick a line width, click one of the five widths displayed. Subsequent drawing operations will use the new line width until you change it. Similarly, to change a brush shape, just click the brush shape you want to use. If you refer back to Figure 12.1, you will see the Line Width palette showing brush shapes.

Working with Bitmap Files

You can create a bitmap from scratch or load an existing bitmap and modify it. To open an existing bitmap file, choose File|Open from the main menu. To create a new bitmap file, choose File|New from the main menu and then choose Bitmap File from the pop-up menu. The Bitmap Properties dialog box will be displayed, as shown in Figure 12.3.

Here you can set the initial size of the bitmap (in pixels) as well as the color depth. You can create a 2-color, 16-color, or 256-color bitmap.

12

Figure 12.3.

The Bitmap Proper-
ties dialog box.

 NOTE

> The Image Editor does not support bitmaps of more than 256 colors.

Select the size and color depth you want and click OK. A blank bitmap is displayed in an editor window. Do any drawing you want on the bitmap. When you are finished editing, choose File | Save or File | Save As to save the bitmap file to disk.

Any time you are working with a bitmap file, the Image Editor main menu has a menu item called Bitmap. This menu has a single item under it called Image Properties. Choosing Bitmap | Image Properties will display the Bitmap Properties dialog box just as when you create a new bitmap file. The Bitmap Properties dialog box enables you to change the size and color depth of the bitmap. Select a new width, height, or color depth and click OK.

 NOTE

> There is one difference in the Bitmap Properties dialog box when it is displayed for an existing bitmap as opposed to when you're creating a new bitmap. When displayed for an existing bitmap, the Bitmap Properties dialog box has a check box labeled Stretch. This is used by the Image Editor when changing the bitmap size. If the Stretch option is off, the bitmap will not be stretched (either larger or smaller) when the bitmap size is changed. If the Stretch option is on, the bitmap will be stretched to fill the new bitmap size. Stretching a bitmap is an inexact science, so sometimes the results of stretching are less than perfect.

All in all, there isn't much to working with bitmap files. Although the Image Editor is fine for simple bitmaps, you will probably not find it adequate for sophisticated graphics. If you need high-quality bitmaps, you might consider purchasing a full-featured image-editing package or hiring a computer artist to create your bitmaps.

12

TIP

Don't forget to check online sources for computer-graphic artists. These people know their craft far better than all but the most gifted programmers and are often very reasonable in their pricing. Repeat this 10 times: "I am a programmer, not an artist." (Okay, maybe some of you are doubly blessed.)

Working with Icons

Creating icons is also an art form, but icons are not quite as demanding as full-color bitmaps. Most of the time you can create your own icons, but great-looking icons still require skill. If you flip back to Figure 12.2, you will see an icon as it is displayed in the Image Editor while editing.

TIP

Load icon files from any source you can find and zoom in on them to get tips on how the best-looking icons are created. Creating 3D icons takes practice (and is something I never get quite right).

An icon in 32-bit Windows is actually two icons in one. The large icon is 32×32 pixels. The large icon can be placed on a dialog box such as an About box. It is also the icon that Windows uses when creating a shortcut to your application. In addition, the large icon is used by Windows Explorer when the file list view is set to display large icons.

The small icon is 16×16 pixels and is the icon used by Windows on the title bar of your application, on the Windows taskbar, in the File Open dialog box, and in Windows Explorer when the view is set to small icons. Both the large and the small icons are stored in the same icon file (.ico).

NOTE

You don't have to supply both a large icon and a small icon. If you supply only the large icon, Windows will shrink the large icon when it needs to display a small icon. Sometimes, however, the results are not quite what you expect and might not be good enough quality for your tastes. In those cases you also can create the small icon so that you are in control of how your application looks, rather than rely on Windows to do the right thing.

12

To create a new icon resource, choose File | New from the main menu and then choose Icon from the pop-up menu. When you create a new icon in the Image Editor, you will see the Icon Properties dialog box, as shown in Figure 12.4.

Figure 12.4.

*The Icon Properties
dialog box.*

This dialog box enables you to choose the icon you are creating (either the large or the small icon) and the number of colors to use for the icon. The default is to create the standard icon (the large icon) and to use 16 colors. (In reality, 2-color icons are rarely used. When was the last time you saw one?)

 NOTE

> Even if you are creating both the large icon and the small icon, you must choose one or the other to start with. For example, if you are creating a new icon, you should start with the large icon. After creating the large icon, you can then create the small icon.

When you are editing an icon, the Image Editor menu bar has an item called Icon. The Icon menu has items called New, Delete, and Test. The New menu item enables you to create a new large or small icon. For instance, if you had already created the large icon, you could choose Icon | New from the main menu to create the small icon.

 TIP

> The icon editor window has a button called New that does the same thing and is faster than using the main menu. (Refer to Figure 12.2.)

When you choose New to create a second icon, the Icon Properties dialog box is displayed just as before. If you already have created the large icon, the small icon will be selected by default, and all you have to do is click OK. The editor window will change to display the new, blank icon. The Image Editor will not let you create an icon that already exists in the icon file.

12

NOTE

> When both icons are present, you can switch between them by using the combo box at the top of the icon editor window.

The Delete item on the Icon menu enables you to delete either the large or the small icon from the icon resource. You cannot delete the last icon in the icon resource.

The Test item on the Icon menu displays the Icon Tester dialog box, which shows you what the icon will look like when displayed. Figure 12.5 shows the Icon Tester dialog box in action.

Figure 12.5.

The Icon Tester dialog box.

The Icon Tester enables you to change the background color so that you can view the effect that different backgrounds have on the appearance of your icon. If you are currently editing the large icon, the large icon appears in the Icon Tester. If you are currently editing the small icon, the Icon Tester dialog box displays the small icon.

Working with Cursors

Working with cursors is not much different than working with icons. A cursor has only two colors: white and black. (Multicolor and animated cursors are not supported by the Image Editor.) Draw the cursor as you want it to appear.

NOTE

> A peculiarity of the cursor editor is that the transparent color is set to the color of your system's background color instead of the dark green color used for the icon editor. If you have your Windows background color set to a very light color, it can be difficult to see what is transparent and what is white. If you are having difficulty distinguishing the background color from white, set your Windows background color to a different value (such as dark green).

As when editing bitmap files and icons, the Image Editor menu displays a menu item called Cursor when you are editing a cursor. This menu item has two items: Set Hot Spot and Test.

The Set Hot Spot item enables you to specify the cursor's hot spot. The *hot spot* is the specific pixel of the cursor that Windows uses to report the mouse coordinates when your cursor is being used. To set the hot spot, choose Cursor | Set Hot Spot from the main menu. The Set Cursor Hot Spot dialog box appears, where you can enter the x and y coordinates of the hot spot.

TIP

You must enter the exact x and y coordinates for the hot spot. To make this easier, before setting the hot spot, place the editing cursor over the point on the cursor where the hot spot will be placed. The Image Editor status bar will display the x and y coordinates of the point under the cursor. Make note of the x and y coordinates; then choose Cursor | Set Hot Spot from the main menu and enter the x and y coordinates.

The Test item on the Cursor menu gives you the opportunity to try out your new cursor. Choose Cursor | Test from the main menu, and the Cursor Tester dialog box will be displayed, as shown in Figure 12.6.

Figure 12.6.

Testing the cursor.

Hold down either mouse button to draw on the Cursor Tester window. If you haven't yet set the hot spot, you will probably notice that the hot spot is set to the upper-left corner of the cursor by default. You should always set the hot spot to a point on your cursor that will be logical to users of your application.

Image Editor Context Menus

The Image Editor has context menus for each editing mode (Bitmap, Cursor, and Icon). You might recall that the right mouse button is used for drawing, so you can't bring up the context menus by clicking the mouse button while over the image. To display the Image Editor context menus, right-click when the mouse cursor is within the editor window but outside the image itself. The context menus contain the same items found on the individual menus, as discussed in the previous sections.

Creating Resource Projects

The Image Editor also enables you to create a resource project file for storing all your bitmaps, icons, and cursors. To create a resource project, choose File | New from the main menu and then choose Resource File from the pop-up menu. A project window will be displayed. The project window is a tree view control that shows the bitmaps, icons, and cursors in the project. Figure 12.7 shows the project window for a sample project.

Figure 12.7.

The Image Editor project window.

The project window has a context menu that can be used to create new resources, edit resources, rename resources, and delete resources. The items on the context menu are also duplicated on the main menu under the Resource menu item.

When you save the resource project, the Image Editor will compile it into a binary resource file (.res). You can then add the binary resource file to your C++Builder project.

Creating New Resources

To create a new resource for your project, choose New from the project window context menu or Resource | New from the main menu. You then can choose to create a new bitmap, icon, or cursor, as you did before when creating an individual resource file. A resource editor window will be displayed, where you can create the resource using the drawing tools as needed.

Editing Resources

When you have a resource created, you may need to edit it in order to make changes to the resource. To edit a resource in a resource project, locate the resource in the project window tree and double-click the resource name. A resource editor window will appear, where you can edit the resource as needed.

Renaming Resources

Renaming resources can be accomplished using in-place editing on the tree view. To select the item you want to rename, just click it and then click on it again to begin editing the item. You can also choose Rename from the context menu to begin the in-place editing. After you have typed a new name for the resource, press Enter or click on another item in the tree view, and the name of the resource will change.

12

Deleting Resources

To delete a resource from the resource project, just click the resource name in the project tree to select it and then choose Delete from the context menu. You will be prompted to make certain you want to delete the item, after which it will be deleted. There is no undo for deleting a resource, so make sure a resource is no longer needed before you delete it.

Adding Resources from Other Resource Files

Unfortunately, there is no simple way to add a resource contained in a separate file to a resource project. What you can do, however, is open your project file and then open the individual bitmap, icon, or cursor file that contains the resource you want to add to the project. Go to the individual file and choose Edit | Select All from the main menu to select the resource; then choose Edit | Copy to copy the object to the Clipboard. Create the new resource in the resource project. When the resource editor window is displayed, choose Edit | Paste from the main menu to paste the resource into the new resource.

NOTE

> If the object you are adding to the resource project is a bitmap, be sure you check the bitmap attributes so that you know the width, height, and color depth of the bitmap. You will need those settings when you create the new bitmap in the resource project.

The Image Editor is not a high-end image editor, but it's good enough for many image-creation tasks. It's easy to use and is more than adequate for creating most icons and cursors.

WinSight: Spying on Windows

WinSight is a utility that enables you to spy on Windows. WinSight will show you every application running and every window running under that application. (Remember: Controls are windows, too.) WinSight shows you every message generated by Windows (every message sent to a window, that is). You can elect to view all messages or just messages sent to a specific window. To start WinSight, double-click the WinSight32 icon from the C++Builder folder (or double-click WS32.EXE from Windows Explorer). WinSight, like the Image Editor, is a standalone program that can be run outside the C++Builder IDE. Figure 12.8 shows WinSight spying on Windows Explorer.

As you can see from Figure 12.8, the WinSight window is split into two panes. The top pane lists the active windows, and the bottom pane shows the messages being sent to a particular window or to all windows. You can adjust the size of the panes by dragging the sizing bar between the two windows. The default is for the windows to be split horizontally, but you can opt to split the windows vertically. To change the window layout, choose either Split Horizontal or Split Vertical from the View menu.

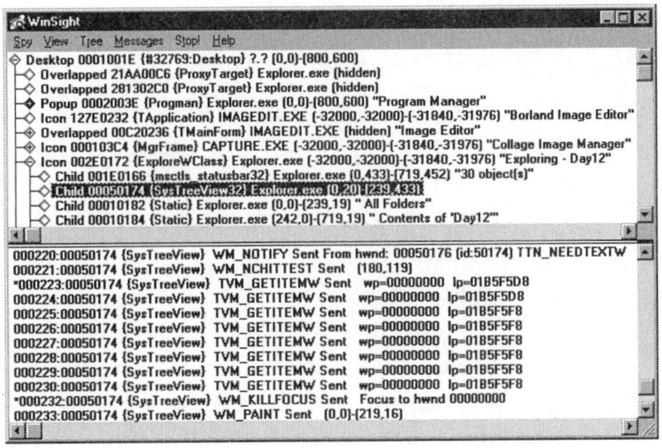

Figure 12.8.

WinSight in action.

You'll examine each of the two windows in more detail in just a bit, but first let me take a moment to talk about Windows messages.

The Windows Messaging System

Spying on Windows isn't helpful if you don't know what any of it means. (The thrill of being a legal Peeping Tom wears off quickly.) The truth is, you have to spend a fair amount of time at Windows programming before you can understand all the information presented by WinSight.

Programs like C++Builder and Delphi are great for enabling you to write true standalone Windows applications in the shortest time possible. If there is a disadvantage to this kind of programming environment, it is that you do not have the opportunity to learn what really makes a Windows program run.

What makes a Windows program run is messages. Lots and lots of messages. Windows sends a window message to instruct the window to do something or to notify the window that some event has taken place. When a window is in need of repainting, for instance, Windows sends it a WM_PAINT message. The WM_PAINT message instructs the window to repaint itself. When a window is resized, Windows sends a WM_WINDOWPOSCHANGING message to notify the window that its size and/or position is changing. This message is followed by WM_WINDOWPOSCHANGED and WM_SIZE messages after the window has been sized. This sort of thing happens dozens or even hundreds of times each second in an average Windows environment.

There are more than 100 messages that Windows can send to an application. I talked a little about that on Day 5, "C++ Class Frameworks and the Visual Component Model," when I discussed events in VCL. Many events that a C++Builder program responds to are Windows messages. The OnCreate event is generated in response to a WM_CREATE message, the OnSize event is generated in response to a WM_SIZE message, and the OnMouseDown event corresponds to both the WM_LBUTTONDOWN and WM_RBUTTONDOWN messages. The list goes on and on.

C++Builder enables you to deal with messages at a higher level, thus freeing you to write the more important parts of your application.

Eventually you will want to learn more about what makes Windows tick. The great thing about C++Builder, though, is that you can write Windows programs immediately and gradually learn about all the low-level stuff.

NOTE

> Some very good Windows programmers would argue that you should first learn to write Windows programs in C like in the good old days. The theory is that this kind of foundation is necessary for a Windows programmer to be effective in any programming environment. Although I would agree that that is the optimum scenario, I also recognize that few programmers these days have the time for that kind of learning curve.

With that primer on Windows messages behind us, let's get back to WinSight and how it works.

The Window Tree

The top pane of WinSight is called the Window Tree. The Window Tree shows you all windows currently open. It also tells you some details about the window class of a specific window. The detail looks like this (except that onscreen it all appears on one line):

```
Overlapped 00000D74 {ExploreWClass}
 EXPLORER.EXE (730,14)-(935,460) "Exploring - aTemplate"
```

The first item in this line shows the window style of the window. In this case it is an overlapped window (WS_OVERLAPPED for you old Windows hackers). Other possibilities include child and pop-up windows. (There are other window types, but overlapped, child, and pop-up are the most common.) The second column shows the window handle (HWND) of the window. This correlates to the Handle property of a VCL windowed component.

Next, you see the window class name in curly braces. This is the class name that the application used to register this particular window with Windows. Frequently, windows share a class name. The common button control, for instance, has a class name of Button. Dozens of buttons may exist in different applications at any given time, but they are all of the same window class. In the case of C++Builder applications, forms and components show the VCL class that represents that component. For a button component, the class name in WinSight shows TButton.

Following the class name is the module name of the process that created the window. Usually the module is an executable program. In this example, the module name is EXPLORER.EXE.

After the module name, you see the window's size and position. Finally, you see the window text of the window. For overlapped windows, this usually means the text appearing in the title bar. For other types of windows, it means different things, depending on the window type. For a button, for instance, it will show the text on the button.

NOTE

A common practice with commercial applications is to create hidden windows to accomplish a specific task in the application. Hidden windows just show (hidden) after the module name. Because the window is hidden, there is no size and position information, nor is there any window text.

The Window Tree is hierarchical. At the top of the tree is the Windows Desktop. Under that are any windows created as children of the desktop. An executable file, for instance, appears under the desktop node. A given window may have other child windows under it. Lines connect the parents, their children, and any siblings.

You will notice back in Figure 12.8 that a diamond appears to the left of each item in the Tree Window. If a window has children, the diamond contains either a plus sign or a minus sign. If the diamond has a plus sign, it means the node is contracted and can be expanded to reveal the child windows. If the node has a minus sign, the plus is already expanded. You can expand or contract a node by clicking anywhere to the left of the item. Blank diamonds indicate a window without children.

NOTE

If a particular window is enabled in the Window Tree, the diamond next to the item flashes whenever the window receives a message from Windows.

The Message Trace Window

The Message Trace window shows the individual messages as they are generated by Windows. A typical Message Trace item looks like this:

```
000684:00000854 {TMemo} WM_KEYDOWN Dispatched 48h 72d VK_H Scan 23h Down
```

It doesn't pay to analyze this in detail because the exact details vary so much from message to message. In this case, a memo component received a WM_KEYDOWN message with a parameter of VK_H. In other words, the user pressed the *h* key with the cursor in a memo component. As you can see, some of the information shown in a Message Trace item also appears in the Window Tree. For example, the window handle is displayed as well as the class name.

You begin the message trace by choosing the Start! item in the main menu. The messages will begin appearing in the Message Trace window as they are received by the window or windows you have selected. To stop the message trace, choose the Stop! item in the main menu.

NOTE

The Stop! and Start! items in the main menu occupy the same place on the menu bar. If the message trace is off, the menu item will say Start! If the trace is running, the menu item will say Stop!.

Messages scroll through the Message Trace window as they are received. You can always stop the message trace and scroll back through the list to view any messages that have scrolled out of view. Another option is to send the message output to a log file. WinSight options are discussed later, in the section "Message Trace Options."

Spying on a Window

WinSight enables you to view all messages sent to all windows or messages sent to a particular window. To view all messages, choose Messages | All Windows from the main menu. Although you can choose to view all messages sent to all windows, it isn't usually productive. There are so many messages flying around that it is hard to pick out the specific ones you are looking for.

A better method is to select a specific window and then watch the messages for just that window. That will keep the clutter in the Message Trace window at a manageable level. To view the messages for a specific window, locate the window in the Message Tree and click on it to select it. Now choose Messages | Selected Windows from the main menu. Choose Start!, and any messages sent to the selected window will show up in the Message Trace window.

TIP

It's best to have a specific idea of what you are looking for when you are using WinSight. Because there are so many messages sent to an individual window, the message you are looking for will probably scroll off the screen very quickly. To maximize the effectiveness of WinSight, select the window for which you want to see messages, start the message trace, manipulate the window any way you need to, and turn off the message trace again.

Message Trace Options

You can control the messages displayed in the Message Trace window via the Message Trace Options dialog box. (Refer to Figure 12.9.) You also can change the way the message is displayed. To view the Message Trace Options dialog box, choose Messages|Options from the main menu.

Figure 12.9.

The Message Trace Options dialog box.

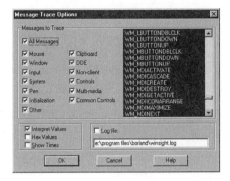

The section titled Messages to Trace comprises the bulk of this dialog box. This section shows several message groups on the left and a list box displaying all Windows messages on the right. As you select or deselect message groups, the corresponding messages will be selected or deselected in the list box.

NOTE

The list box messages that are all uppercase are the standard Windows messages. The lowercase messages are *undocumented* Windows messages. Undocumented messages are messages that are used by Windows, usually for internal use, but are not documented in the Windows API help files.

When the All Messages option is checked, WinSight will trace all Windows messages. To narrow things down and to reduce clutter in the Message Trace window, you can elect to view only certain groups of messages. If, for instance, you want to view only mouse messages, you can turn off the All Messages check box and turn on the Mouse check box. To further narrow it down, you can turn off all options and then choose a specific message from the list box on the right of the dialog box. For instance, if you want to see only the WM_LBUTTONDOWN message, you can turn off all options and then select just the WM_LBUTTONDOWN message from the list box. Only the WM_LBUTTONDOWN messages will be reported in the Message Trace window.

Another group of options on the Message Trace Options dialog box controls how the messages are displayed in the Message Trace window. The Interpret Values option tells WinSight to break down each message's parameters into a more readable format. For example, given a WM_KEYDOWN message, would you rather see

`0000309:00000474 {TMemo} WM_KEYDOWN Dispatched`

or

```
0000309:00000474 {TMemo} WM_KEYDOWN Dispatched 44h 68d VK_D Scan 20h Repeat
```

Most of the time I opt to see more detail, so I generally leave the Interpret Values option on.

The Hex Values option tells WinSight to display the values in the Message Trace window in hexadecimal format. This is useful in some situations but probably not until you've been programming for a while. The Show Times option is of limited use because it shows a system time that isn't generally meaningful.

The Log file option enables you to send the message trace output to a file on disk. When this option is on, the messages are still displayed in the Message Trace Window. This option is useful when you need a hard copy of the messages being generated.

TIP

Creating a log file has another advantage. After you have created a log file and loaded it into a text editor, you can use the text editor's Find function to search for specific messages or message parameters you want to review.

Other WinSight Features

WinSight has other features that make finding and examining windows easier.

Viewing Window Details

The Detail feature of WinSight shows you all the pertinent details of a particular window. To view a window's details, select the window in the Window Tree and then choose Spy|Open Detail from the main menu. You can also double-click the window in the Message Tree or press Enter on the keyboard. Figure 12.10 shows the details of Windows Explorer.

As you can see, the Detail window shows you a great deal about the window you are examining (probably more than you want to know!).

Follow Focus

This option enables you to select a window in an application and have that window become the active window in the Window Tree. The Window Tree usually contains dozens of windows. It is often difficult to find the window you are looking for, so the Follow Focus feature really comes in handy.

To use this feature, choose Spy|Follow Focus from the main menu. Next, switch to the application that contains the window for which you want to view messages and, if needed, click the specific control within that window that you want to spy on. WinSight automatically selects the window in the Window Tree. To begin spying on the window, choose Start! from the main menu.

Figure 12.10.

The WinSight Detail window.

Detail window showing:

```
WinSight - Detail 00050174
Window text:
Process Id:                  0000002C  Explorer.exe
Application instance:        01580000
Window handle:               00050174
Parent window:               002E0172
Window function:             FFFF043C
Window ID:                   00000000
Window rect in screen:       {-32000,-31980}-{-31761,-31567
Window rect in parent:       {0,20}-{239,433}
Client rectangle:            {0,0}-{219,409}
#Msgs processed:             2250
Window style:                5020000B
Child, Visible, VScroll ClientEdge, Left, LTRReading,
RightScrollBar HasButtons, HasLines, EditLabels


Class name:                  SysTreeView32
Executable module:           77BF0000  COMCTL32.dll
Class window function:       FFFF0476
Icon:                        00000000
Cursor:                      00010008
Background brush:            00000000
Window extra bytes:          00000004
Class extra bytes:           00000000
Class style:                 00004008
DblClks, GlobalClass
```

 TIP

> The Follow Focus option stays on until you turn it off. Unless you want to view other windows or controls in your application, you should turn off Follow Focus as soon as you locate the window you want to spy on.

Find Window

The Find Window feature of WinSight is the opposite of Follow Focus: In the Window Tree you locate the window you're searching for and then choose Spy|Find Window from the main menu. WinSight will place a thick frame around the window and will flash the frame. The frame stays around the window until you click the window or choose another window from the Window Tree. The thick frame is drawn on top of all windows so that you can find a window even if it's hidden under other windows. A window located with Find Window doesn't come to the top or gain input focus; it is merely identified for you.

NOTE

> Find Window cannot find hidden windows or windows that are minimized.

The Find Window mode shuts off as soon as focus leaves the Window Tree. If you click on another application or anywhere else in WinSight, the Find Window mode will turn off.

Switch To

The Switch To feature enables you to switch to a particular window in an application. To switch to a window, just find the window in the Window Tree and then choose

12

Spy|Switch To from the main menu. The window will come to the top and will have input focus. If the window is minimized, it will be restored to its previous location. Switch To has no effect on hidden windows.

It will take time working with WinSight before you understand each message and its significance. In time, though, you will pick it up.

The Resource Expert

The Resource Expert converts dialog and menu resources found in resource script files (.RC), menu files (.MNU), and dialog resource files (.DLG) into C++Builder forms and units. The Resource Expert is a wizard that is very easy to use. You provide the name of the resource file containing the resources you want to convert, and the Resource Expert does the rest. The Resource Expert converts most dialogs without any problems but can't convert every dialog perfectly. The purpose of the Resource Expert is to convert your dialog resources into VCL forms as quickly as possible. Some dialogs might contain controls (such as custom controls) that the Resource Expert can't deal with. In those cases the Resource Expert converts what it can and ignores the controls that it can't convert.

To start the Resource Expert, choose Tools|Resource Expert from the C++Builder main menu. The Resource Expert is a wizard with four pages. The first page gives you instructions on the conversion progress. The second page asks you to choose a resource file containing the resources you want to convert. The third page has a field called Include Path, where you enter the path to any files referenced by the resource script file being converted. For example, if you are converting dialogs from a Borland C++ OWL project, you might have references to the Borland C++ include directories in the resource script file. Enter those directories on this page of the Resource Expert. The last page contains a check box labeled Show all forms while converting. Clear this check box if you have a lot of dialogs to convert so that the conversion will go faster. To begin the conversion, click the Convert button on the last page of the Resource Expert.

The Resource Expert will begin to convert the menu and dialog resources in the resource file. If the Show all forms while converting option is set, the Resource Expert will stop after each resource is converted and display the finished form in test mode. To continue the conversion, close the form that was just converted. The Resource Expert will go on to the next item in the resource script file, convert it, and again show you the results. When the Show all forms while converting option is off, the Resource Expert doesn't show you each resource as it is converted.

If any errors are encountered during the conversion, the Resource Expert displays a log file called ErrorLog in the C++Builder Code Editor. This log file informs you of any problems the Resource Expert encountered while converting the resources. Most errors are due to included files that can't be found during the conversion.

Tip

> To find out which paths you need to add to the Include Path field on page three of the Resource Expert, run the expert and then examine the ErrorLog file to see which files are missing. Copy the path to the missing files to the Clipboard and rerun the Resource Expert. When you get to page three, paste the path in the Clipboard to the Include Path field.

After a successful conversion you will have forms for use in your C++Builder applications. In some cases the forms might have to be modified slightly to match the original dialogs. All in all, though, the Resource Expert is an excellent tool for quickly converting a lot of dialogs.

Command-Line Tools

In addition to GUI tools such as the Image Editor and WinSight, C++Builder ships with a number of command-line tools. Some of the tools are used by C++Builder itself when it compiles your project. Others are supplemental tools that you can use as needed. The following sections cover a few of the more commonly used tools. In some cases, the tools can be added to the Tools menu so that you can access them from the IDE rather than run them from an MS-DOS prompt.

Note

> All the command-line tools reside in the C++Builder bin directory. This directory is added to your system's PATH as part of the normal C++Builder installation. When running a given utility from an MS-DOS prompt, it should not be necessary to add the full path in addition to the filename. If, however, you get file not found errors, you may need to type the exact path to the bin directory when you run the utility.

12

GREP.EXE

GREP (Global Regular Expression Print) is a text-searching utility. You can use GREP to search for text in your source files (or any other text file for that matter). This is the standalone version of the Find in Files tool discussed on Day 10, "More on Projects." Although you will usually use Find in File instead of GREP, you might prefer to work from the command line. In that case, GREP is for you. I won't go into detail on how to use GREP; you can look it up in the C++Builder online help.

COFF2OMF.EXE

This utility will take a Microsoft import library file and convert it to a file that C++Builder can use. (Microsoft uses the COFF format for library files and Borland uses the OMF format. The two are not compatible.) This utility creates a new file rather than modify the existing import library file. For help on command-line syntax, run COFF2OMF from a command prompt (it's in your CBuilder/bin directory).

IMPLIB.EXE

You use this tool to create an import library file (.lib) for a dynamic link library (.dll). Before you can call functions in a DLL, the linker must be able to see the functions exported from the DLL. The linker reads an import library to determine which functions are contained in the DLL. Import libraries are discussed on Day 19, "Creating and Using DLLs."

IMPLIB is easy to use. Let's say that you have created a DLL named MyStuff.dll and you want to create an import library file for it. Open an MS-DOS box from Windows and switch to the directory where your DLL resides. From the MS-DOS prompt, type

```
implib MyStuff MyStuff.dll
```

An import library file called MyStuff.lib will be created, which you can then add to any C++Builder projects that reference this DLL.

NOTE

Microsoft and Borland use different name-mangling schemes for their compilers. If you buy a third-party control or library contained in DLLs, you may find that the import library file provided by the vendor doesn't work with your C++Builder project. If that happens, it is likely that the import library is in the Microsoft COFF format instead of the Borland OMF format. To produce an import library file that C++Builder can use, just run IMPLIB on the DLLs that came with the third-party library, or run COFF2OMF on the Microsoft library file.

IMPLIB has a few command-line options that you can use if needed. For a complete list, run implib -h (the -h option is for help) from an MS-DOS prompt.

TOUCH.EXE

You can use TOUCH to reset the time stamp on files. If you look at the files on the C++Builder CD-ROM, you will find that they all have the same file date and time. (The file time is sort of a code that identifies the version of C++Builder on the CD-ROM.) TOUCH is easy to use. Table 12.1 lists some TOUCH command-line options.

12

Table 12.1. Selected TOUCH command-line options.

Option	Description
-h	Prints a help screen. (Use -h2 for a more complete help screen.)
-s	Recurses through subdirectories.
-t*hh*:*mm*:*ss*	Sets the time of the files to the time specified. (The seconds parameter is optional.)
-d*mm*/*dd*/*yy*	Sets the date of the specified files to the date specified.

Let's say that you are releasing version 2.12 of your project and you want to set all file dates to the current date with a time of 2:12 a.m. Let's also assume that you have more than one directory and that you want to touch all the files in all directories. The command line would look like this:

```
touch -t02:12 -s *.*
```

Note that you don't have to provide the date. If you do not use the -d option, the current date is used. The same is true of the -t option.

TDUMP.EXE

TDUMP could probably be considered an advanced programming tool. TDUMP outputs the structure of an .exe, .dll, or .obj (and other file types as well). By default, the output from TDUMP goes to the console, but it can be redirected to a text file that you can later examine to obtain information about the program. TDUMP will tell you about the structure of the file, what DLLs the program uses, what functions in those DLLs the program calls, and other information. For example, here is a part of the file dump results on a program produced by C++Builder:

```
Portable Executable (PE) File

Header base: 00000200

CPU type          80386
Flags             818E [ executable 32bit ]
DLL flags         0000 [ ]
Linker Version      2.19
Time stamp        00000000
O/S Version        1.0
User Version       0.0
Subsystem Version   4.0
Subsystem         0002 [ Windows GUI ]
Object count         00000008
Symbols offset       00000000
Symbols count        00000000
Optional header size    00E0
Magic #           10B
```

12

```
Code size          0003C000
Init Data size       00009000
Uninit Data size     00001000

...(other information)...

Imports from OLEAUT32.dll
  SysAllocStringLen
  SysStringLen
  VariantChangeTypeEx
  VariantClear
  VariantCopyInd

Imports from MPR.dll
  WNetGetConnectionA

Imports from USER32.dll
  AdjustWindowRectEx
  BeginPaint
  CallNextHookEx
  CallWindowProcA
  CharLowerA

... (more DLL imports) ...
```

Typically you run TDUMP from the command line. Because the output from TDUMP is usually long, you are better off if you redirect the output to a text file. The following illustrates this:

```
tdump MyApp.e XE > dump.txt
```

Now you have an ASCII text file that you can browse with the C++Builder Code Editor or any other text editor. Although you may not use TDUMP often, it can be invaluable when you need it.

Configuring the C++Builder Tools Menu

The C++Builder Tools menu is configurable. By default, the C++Builder Tools menu has items for Database Desktop and Image Editor. You can add your own tools to the Tools menu, add other C++Builder tools, or add any other program you use frequently. You can also change the order of items on the Tools menu or even delete items.

The Configure Tools Dialog Box

Just about any application you use frequently can be added to the Tools menu. By adding items to the Tools menu, you can quickly load any program you frequently use during program development. Adding a tool to the Tools menu is a trivial task and takes only a few minutes. Adding, deleting, and moving items on the Tools menu is accomplished through the Tool Options dialog box. To display the Tool Options dialog box, choose Tools|Configure Tools from the main menu. (Refer to Figure 12.11.)

12

Figure 12.11.

The Tool Options dialog box.

The list box labeled Tools shows the tools that currently appear on the Tools menu. The tools are listed in the order in which they appear on the Tools menu. To reorder the list of tools, click the tool you want to move and click either the up or down arrow button. To remove a tool from the Tools menu, select the tool from the list box, and click the Delete button. The tool will be removed.

To add a tool to the Tools menu, click the Add button. The Tool Properties dialog box is displayed, and you can enter the properties for the tool you are adding. The Tool Properties dialog box is shown in Figure 12.12 with the properties for Windows Explorer displayed.

Figure 12.12.

The Tool Properties dialog box.

The Title field is where you type the tool's title as you want it to appear on the Tools menu. You may use an ampersand to indicate the shortcut key character. The Program field is where you enter the tool's path and filename. To ensure finding the program, you should enter the program's full path. If you don't know the exact path and filename, you can click the Browse button and go hunting for the file. The Working dir field is used to set the working directory for the tool. If you browse to find the tool, the working directory will be automatically set to the directory where the program resides.

The Parameters field requires some explanation. In its simplest form, this field is used to set the tool's command-line parameters. Type any parameters needed to run the tool. You can, however, use C++Builder's predefined macros in the Parameters field. If you click the Macros button in the Tool Properties dialog box, you will get a list of macros from which you can choose. To use a macro, you can type it in directly, or you can choose it from the list and click the Insert button. Figure 12.13 shows the Tool Properties dialog box with the list of macros displayed.

12

Figure 12.13.

The Tool Properties dialog box showing macros.

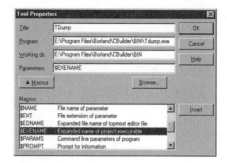

The $EXENAME macro will return the full path of the project's target executable. For example, if you had a project named MyApp in a directory called Projects, the $EXENAME parameter would pass the string c:\Projects\MyApp.e XE to the program. Some macros require parameters. To use only the path from your project's target without the filename, you would specify a parameters string of $PATH($EXENAME). Continuing with this example, that combination of parameters would yield c:\Projects\. For a complete list of the macros available, see the C++Builder online help.

Editing a tool on the Tools menu is as easy as clicking the Edit button on the Tool Options dialog box. The Tool Properties dialog box is displayed, and you can change any of the fields as necessary.

When you are done adding, editing, or rearranging your tools, click the Close button. The C++Builder Tools menu will reflect your changes.

Setting the Environment Options

The C++Builder Environment Options enable you to make changes to the C++Builder IDE at the global level. (The Project Options dialog box controls settings at the project level.) To display the Environment Options dialog box, choose Tools|Environment Options from the main menu. This is a tabbed dialog with eight pages. You learned about the Editor, Display, and Color pages when we looked at the Code Editor on Day 10. You learned about the Debugger page on Day 11 when we discussed debugger options. We will look at the Preferences, Palette, and Code Insight pages now.

The Preferences Page

The Preferences page of the Environment Options dialog box is where you set general C++Builder preferences: how the C++Builder IDE controls compiling, autosaving, and the appearance of the Form Designer. You can also set the Form Designer preferences on this page (see Figure 12.14).

Figure 12.14.

The Preferences page of the Environment Options dialog box.

The Compiling section has four options. The Show compiler progress option controls whether C++Builder displays the compiler progress dialog box when compiling projects. Most of the time you will leave this option on so that you can see what is happening with your project. Turning off this option does result in slightly faster compiles, but the difference is probably not dramatic. The Beep on completion option will beep the PC speaker when compiling is finished. This is handy if you have a long compile running in the background and you want to know when it has finished. The Cache headers on startup option tells C++Builder to load the pre-compiled headers as soon as C++Builder loads. If you have lots of system RAM, this option can speed up compilation time because the headers are already cached in memory before you start compiling. Without this option on, the pre-compiled headers are loaded from disk when needed. If you don't have an abundance of system RAM (probably 48MB or more), you might not want this option on. The Warn on package rebuild option displays warnings when packages are rebuilt during compile.

The Autosave options section enables you to specify that either the Editor files or the Desktop be saved automatically every time the program is run. Personally, I do not like to have my editor files saved automatically; I want the ability to abandon current edits if necessary. Still, I know others who really like this feature. For one thing, if your application misbehaves and crashes the C++Builder IDE or Windows itself, you know that your last edits have been saved. The Desktop option saves the current size and position of the Code Editor, all forms, the Alignment palette, the Object Inspector, and so on.

The Form designer section is self-explanatory. The Display grid option turns the visible grid in the Form Designer on and off. This affects only the grid's visible display, not whether objects snap to the grid. The Snap to grid option determines whether components placed and moved will snap to the grid points. The X and Y grid size fields enable you to set the size of the grid. By default, it is set at eight pixels. The Show component captions option pertains to nonvisual components placed on your forms. When this option is on, the Form Designer displays the Name property of nonvisual components below the icon representing the component.

The Running section controls how the IDE behaves when a program is run from the IDE. The Hide designers on run option hides the Form Designer, Object Inspector, and other Form Designer support windows when the program is run. The C++Builder main window and Code Editor are still visible, however. The Minimize on run option is similar. When this option is on, the entire C++Builder IDE minimizes whenever the target program is run from the IDE.

NOTE

> When the Minimize on run option is on, any action in the program that requires the debugger (exceptions, breakpoints, and so on) result in the C++Builder IDE being displayed again.

The Shared Repository section enables you to specify where the Object Repository information is saved to, by specifying the appropriate path in the Directory edit box. This can be very helpful in the case of repository items being used by a group of people working on the same project. You can set the Shared Repository's Directory to point to a place on the network, and all the items that you add to the Object Repository will be saved to the location on the network and can be inherited from by the other group members.

The Library Page

The Library page of the Environment Options dialog has just one field, called Library Path. Use this field to specify the path to the library files that C++Builder uses for the Component palette. Normally you don't have to change this path.

The Palette Page

The Palette page of the Environment Options dialog box enables you to customize the Component palette. The Palette page is shown in Figure 12.15.

This page enables you to change the order in which the pages appear in the Component palette. The Pages list box on the left side of the dialog box shows all the pages currently in the Component palette. At the bottom of the list you will see an item labeled [All]. This item shows all the installed components in all pages of the Component palette. The Components list box shows the components appearing in the page that is selected in the Pages list box.

To reorder the pages, drag a page within the Pages list box to the position you want it to occupy in the Component palette. If you wanted the Samples page to appear first on the Component palette, you could drag it to the top of the list in the Pages list box and drop it. You also can click on a page and use the Move Up or Move Down buttons to move the page to a new location.

Figure 12.15.

The Palette page of the Environment Options dialog box.

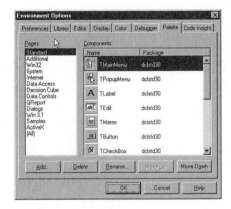

Pages can be added, deleted, or renamed, and those operations work exactly as you would expect. To add a page, click the Add button. You will be prompted for a name for the page. After you supply the page name, the new page will be created. You might add a page, for instance, if you have created your own components and want them on their own page in the Component palette. You could also take any of the VCL components that you use a lot and move them to a new page so that you can get to them quickly.

TIP

> You can move components from page to page, but you cannot copy components from one page to another. You can, however, add any installed component to any page on the Component palette. First, select [All] in the Pages list box. Then drag a component from the Components list box to any of the pages in the Pages list box.

Deleting and renaming pages is straightforward. As with the Object Repository, you delete a page only after it has been emptied of its components.

Components on a page can be rearranged just as pages can. To move a component, drag it to its new position in the Components list box or use the Move Up or Move Down buttons. To move a component to a new page, drag and drop it on the name of the page in the Pages list box where you want it to appear. To delete a component, first select the component and then click the Delete button.

The Code Insight Page

The Code Insight page is where you set the options for the specialized Code Editor features. This page contains a check box for enabling or disabling ToolTip expression evaluation. This page also enables you to add, edit, or delete code templates. Figure 12.16 shows the Code Insight page of the Environment Options dialog box.

12

Figure 12.16.

The Code Insight page of the Environment Options dialog box.

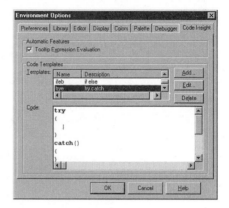

The Add button enables you to add a new code template. When you click the Add button, the Add Code Template dialog box is displayed. Type in a template name and a description and click OK. Now type the code for the template in the Code memo field. You also can paste code from the Clipboard. You can add as many templates as you want. When you click the OK button on the Environment Options dialog box, the new templates are added to the template file. To abandon changes to the code template file, click the Cancel button.

 TIP

You can edit the code template file with the C++Builder Code Editor if you find the Code Insight dialog box too small. The code template file is called `BCB.DCI` and is located in the `CBuilder\Bin` directory.

To delete a code template, first select the template in the Templates table and then click the Delete button. If you delete a template by mistake, just click the Cancel button on the Environment Options dialog box and your changes to the code template file will not be saved.

The Edit button enables you to change the name and description of a code template. When you click the Edit button, the Edit Code Template dialog box is displayed. This dialog box is identical to the Add Code Template dialog box. Type in a new name or description for the template and click OK. As with adding or deleting templates, the changes you make to the templates are not saved unless you click the OK button on the Environment Options dialog box. To edit the code for a template, modify the code in the Code memo field. Code templates are discussed in more detail on Day 10 in the section "Code Templates."

Summary

So now you know more about the tools included as part of the C++Builder suite. Some of these tools are easy to miss, so it helps to have an overview of what is available to you. Some tools you might not use right away, but in the future you can take another look at what's available to you. I ended the day by going over the Environment Options dialog box. For the most part, you can leave these settings on their defaults. When you begin customizing the IDE, you will have a better understanding of what the individual options do.

Workshop

The Workshop contains quiz questions to help you solidify your understanding of the material covered and exercises to provide you with experience in using what you have learned. You can find the answers to the quiz questions in Appendix A, "Answers to Quiz Questions."

Q&A

Q I'm creating an icon and trying to get an ellipse with a black border and a yellow fill. I set the foreground color to black and the background color to yellow, but all I get is a black circle. What do I have to do to get what I want?

A The Image Editor works differently than some bitmap editors in this regard. To accomplish what you're after, you have to first draw a black, hollow ellipse and then fill it with yellow.

Q How can I draw perfect circles or straight lines in the Image Editor?

A Hold down the Shift key as you draw the circle or line. The same is true for drawing perfect squares.

Q I created my own arrow cursor, but when I click with it, I can't seem to click with the point of the arrow. What's wrong?

A You need to set the hot spot for the cursor. By default, the hot spot is in the upper-left corner. Edit the cursor in the Image Editor and change the hot spot to the pixel at the tip of the arrow.

Q Am I required to create both a large version and a small version when I create an icon?

A Not necessarily. If you supply only a large icon, Windows will shrink it when needed. If, however, you don't like the way your icon looks when Windows reduces it, you could design a small icon as well as the large one. When a small icon exists, Windows uses it.

Q How can I copy part of one of my bitmaps to a new bitmap?

A In the Image Editor, open the original bitmap in one editor window and a new bitmap in another editor window. Drag a marquee around the section of the original bitmap and choose Edit | Copy from the Image Editor menu. Switch to the new bitmap and choose Edit | Paste. The bitmap in the Clipboard is pasted into the new bitmap you are creating.

12

Q WinSight seems slow on my system. Is that normal?

A It can be, yes. WinSight has to monitor everything that is going on in Windows, and that takes a lot of processing power. On slower systems it is more noticeable, of course. To reduce the effect as much as possible, make sure that only WinSight and the window you are spying on are open.

Q I am looking for a specific message in my program, but all the other messages are cluttering the Trace Window so that I can't find the message I'm looking for. What can I do about that?

A Two things. First, ensure that you are watching messages only for the specific window in which you are interested. Select the window in the Window Tree and then choose Messages | Selected Windows from the WinSight main menu. Second, go to the Trace Options dialog box and turn off all messages except the specific messages in which you are interested.

Q I want some components on the Component palette to appear not only in their original location but also in a new page that I create. Can I do that?

A Yes. Go to the Palette page of the Environment Options dialog. Click the [All] item in the Pages list box. Now drag a component from the Components list box to any page in the Pages list box.

Quiz

1. How is the transparent color used for icons and cursors?
2. How do you choose a color in the Image Editor?
3. How do you select an area on a bitmap to cut or copy?
4. What is the maximum number of colors allowed in an Image Editor bitmap?
5. What is a cursor's hot spot?
6. Can WinSight spy on hidden windows?
7. What's the fastest way to locate a window in the WinSight Window Tree?
8. How can you have your editor files automatically saved each time your program runs through the debugger?
9. Where do you go to rearrange the contents of the Component palette?
10. How can you add your own code templates?

Exercises

1. Using the Image Editor, create a bitmap that can be used as a splash screen for your company or for a specific application of yours.
2. Using the Image Editor, create an icon that has a transparent background and uses both the large and small icons.

12

3. Create a cursor resource in the Image Editor. Make certain you set its hot spot and test the cursor with the Cursor Tester.

4. Create a new resource file. Create two bitmaps and a cursor. Save the file.

5. Using the resource file you created in Exercise 4, create a new icon resource and copy the icon created in Exercise 2 to the new icon.

6. Create a new program in C++Builder. Change its Name property to Test and its Caption property to Test Window. Run the program. Now start WinSight. Locate the Test Window program and set message tracing to Selected Windows. Arrange WinSight and Test Window side by side. Choose Start! in the WinSight main menu. Move the Test Window, size it, click it, minimize it, and so on. Observe the messages in the Message Trace window.

7. Continuing with Exercise 6, go to WinSight, choose Messages | Options from the main menu, and turn off all messages except the Mouse message group. Again manipulate the Test Window program. Observe the output in the Message Trace window.

8. Open the Environment Options dialog box. Go to the Palette page. Create a new page in the Component palette. Name it MyStuff. Copy the Label, Image, and OpenDialog components to the new page. Close the Environment Options dialog box. Examine the new layout of the Component palette. Delete the MyStuff page when you are done with it.

9. Add a code template called File Open and enter the following code:

```
if (OpenDialog->Execute())
{

}
```

10. Load a program in C++Builder. Open the Environment Options dialog box. On the Preferences page, turn on the Minimize on Run option. Click Run to run the program. Notice the behavior of the C++Builder IDE.

12

Day 13

Beyond the Basics

Today you will learn ways to turn a good Windows application into a great Windows application. Specifically, I will discuss the following:

- ☐ Window decorations: toolbars and status bars
- ☐ Command enabling
- ☐ Printing in C++Builder applications
- ☐ Using cursors

Tomorrow we will continue this discussion as we look at implementing advanced Windows programming features in your C++Builder applications.

Window Decorations

No, I'm not talking about pretty lights a<ˇund the front window of your house. What I am talking about are things such as toolbars and status bars. These features are often called *window decorations*. This section deals with these types of decorations and how to implement them in your application.

Toolbars

A toolbar (also called a control bar or a speedbar) is almost standard equipment for Windows programs today. Users expect certain amenities, and a toolbar is one of them. A top quality toolbar should have the following features and capabilities:

☐ Buttons representing tasks that are also available on the application's menu.

☐ Enabling and disabling of buttons when appropriate.

☐ ToolTips describing a button's function. ToolTips pop up when the user places the cursor over a button and pauses.

☐ Additional hint text that is displayed in the application's status bar.

☐ Other controls such as combo boxes or drop-down menu buttons.

Some of these are optional features that not every toolbar needs to have. With C++Builder, creating much of this functionality is easy to accomplish. A little later in the chapter I will talk about command enabling in the section called, appropriately, "Command Enabling." I'll save discussion of command enabling for toolbar buttons for that time.

 NOTE

> It is considered good practice to place on the toolbar only buttons that have corresponding menu items. The toolbar is an alternative to using the menu. It should not contain items found nowhere else in the program.

Toolbar Review

On Day 9, "Creating Applications in C++Builder," I said that the easiest way to construct a toolbar is to use the Application Wizard. Even if you already have a partially written application, you can still use the Application Wizard to create a toolbar. Just generate an application with the Application Wizard, copy the panel with the toolbar to the Clipboard, reopen your original application (don't bother saving the Application Wizard application), and paste the toolbar into your application from the Clipboard. Slick and easy.

However, the Application Wizard doesn't give you everything you could possibly need in a toolbar. Most notably, the Application Wizard uses the old method of creating a toolbar—with a panel and speed buttons. The preferred way of creating a toolbar in a 32-bit program is to use the ToolBar and CoolBar components (found on the Win32 tab of the Component palette). Let's take a look at those components next.

NOTE

> The CoolBar and ToolBar components require version 4.70 or later of COMCTL32.DLL. If you don't have the latest version of this DLL, you can find it at Microsoft's Web site (http://www.microsoft.com). When you deploy your applications using these components, you should install COMCTL32.DLL, version 4.70 or later. Be sure you are using a good installation program so that you don't overwrite a new version of this DLL when you install your application.

The CoolBar Component

The CoolBar component is an encapsulation of the Win32 cool bar (sometimes called a rebar). This component is a specialized container control. Most of the time the CoolBar is used as a container for toolbars, but its use isn't limited strictly to toolbars.

Cool Bar Bands

A cool bar has bands that can be moved and resized at runtime. The bands show a sizing grip on the left side, giving the user a visual cue that the band can be moved or sized. Cool bar bands are represented by the TCoolBand class. A cool bar band can contain only one component. Usually that component is a toolbar, but it can be a combo box or any other component. Let's do an exercise to better understand how the CoolBar component works:

1. Start with a new application and drop a CoolBar component on the form.

2. Drop a ComboBox component on the cool bar. C++Builder creates a new band to hold the combo box. Notice that the combo box fills the width of the cool bar.

3. Drop another ComboBox component on the cool bar. Another band is created and is placed below the first band.

4. Place your mouse cursor between the sizing grip and the combo box on the second band. The cursor will change to a pointing hand, indicating that you can move the band (you can also use the sizing grip to drag the band). Drag the band up into the band above it. As you do, the first band will shrink to make room for the band you are dragging. Drop the band near the middle of the cool bar. You can now use the sizing grips to resize either band.

5. Place a Panel component on the cool bar. A new band is created to hold the panel.

6. Select the cool bar and change its AutoSize property to true.

7. Place a Memo component on the form below the cool bar. Set its Align property to alClient.

Now your form looks like Figure 13.1.

13

Figure 13.1.

The form with a cool bar and three bands.

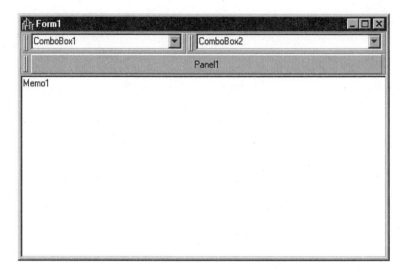

Now run the program. Experiment with the cool bar bands. Drag them up or down or resize them. Notice that as you drag the bands up or down, the cool bar resizes as needed and that the memo always fills the remaining client area.

Cool bar bands are accessed through the Bands property. This property is a TCoolBands, which is a list of TCoolBand components. If you wanted to hide the second band, you could do this:

```
CoolBar->Bands->Items[1]->Visible = false;
```

You can add bands in two ways. As you have already seen, you can create a band by dropping any component on the cool bar or by using the Bands Editor. To invoke the Bands Editor, double-click the cool bar, or click the ellipsis button next to the Bands property in the Object Inspector. You add bands by clicking the Add button; you delete bands by clicking the Delete button. The Move Up and Move Down buttons enable you to change the order of the bands.

NOTE 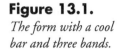 If the AutoSize property is set to true, you might have to turn it off temporarily if you want to add new bands by dropping components on the cool bar. Set the AutoSize property to false, make the cool bar higher, drop a component on the cool bar, and set the AutoSize property to true again.

When you select a band in the Bands Editor, the Object Inspector displays the band's properties. Figure 13.2 shows the Bands Editor and the Object Inspector when a band is selected.

Figure 13.2.

*The cool bar
Bands Editor.*

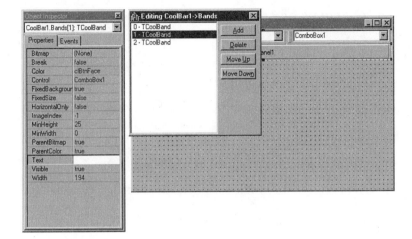

The Bitmap property enables you to set a background bitmap for a band. To select an image that will appear to the left of the band, you use ImageIndex. ImageIndex requires the ImageList property of the cool bar to be set to a valid TImageList. You can set a band's minimum height and width through the MinHeight and MinWidth properties. To make a band immovable, set the FixedSize property to true.

Other CoolBar Properties

A cool bar can be either vertical or horizontal. By default the Align property is set to alTop. To make a vertical cool bar, change the Align property to alRight or alLeft. When you place a component on the cool bar, it will automatically orient itself, based on whether the cool bar is vertical or horizontal. Another way to change the orientation of the cool bar is by setting the Vertical property.

The Bitmap property enables you to set a background bitmap for the cool bar. The bitmap you choose will be tiled to fill the cool bar's background. You use the ImageList property to set the image list that the bands will use to display an image to the left of any band that has its ImageIndex property set.

The AutoSize property determines whether the cool bar will resize itself when bands are moved. You saw the effect of the AutoSize property in the preceding exercise.

The ToolBar Component

The ToolBar component encapsulates the Win32 toolbar control. The toolbar will automatically arrange and size the controls placed on the toolbar so that they all have a consistent height. You can use the ToolBar component with or without a cool bar. If you have only a single toolbar, use the toolbar without a cool bar. If you have multiple toolbars that you want to allow the user to move, place two or more toolbars on a cool bar.

13

Creating a toolbar and adding buttons to it are very easy. If your toolbar buttons will have glyphs (and most do), you have to use an `ImageList` component for the glyphs. To illustrate how to build a toolbar with the `ToolBar` component, let's again go back to the `ScratchPad` program. You'll tear it apart and put it back together. First, you need to remove some components that you don't want anymore:

1. Click the `Memo` component and change its `Align` property to `alNone`. Drag down the top of the `Memo` to make room for the new toolbar.

2. Click the toolbar panel and delete it.

3. Click the `Bevel` component just under the main menu and delete it as well.

Now you can start adding components back again. The first thing to do is add a cool bar and a toolbar. You don't really need a cool bar at this stage because you have only one toolbar, but you may want to add another toolbar later, so we'll plan ahead. Perform these steps:

1. Drop a `CoolBar` component on the form. It automatically aligns itself to the top of the form. Change its `Name` property to `CoolBar`.

2. Drop a `ToolBar` component on the cool bar. Change its `Name` property to `MainToolBar`.

3. Double-click the `EdgeBorders` property in the Object Inspector to show all the edge border items. Change the `ebTop` style to `false` (all `EdgeBorders` styles should now be `false`).

4. Change the `Flat` property to `true`. This gives the toolbar buttons a flat appearance until the cursor passes over them.

5. Click the cool bar and change the `AutoSize` property to `true`. The cool bar sizes itself to the size of the toolbar.

6. Click the `Memo` component and change its `Align` property back to `alClient`.

Now you begin adding buttons to the toolbar; you will add several buttons and a few spacers. At first the buttons won't have glyphs on them, but you'll take care of that later. For now, follow these steps:

1. Right-click the toolbar and choose New Button. A button is placed on the toolbar. Change the button's `Name` property to `FileNewBtn`. Set the `Hint` property to `New¦Create A New File` and the `ShowHint` property to `true`.

2. Right-click on the toolbar and again choose New Button. A second button is placed on the toolbar, to the right of the first button. Change its `Name` property to `FileOpenBtn`. Set the `Hint` property to `Open¦Open An Existing File` and the `ShowHint` property to `true`.

3. Add another button. Change this button's `Name` property to `FileSaveBtn`. Set the `Hint` property to `Save¦Save A File` and the `ShowHint` property to `true`.

13

TIP

Buttons and spacers added to the toolbar always appear to the right of the toolbar's last control. You can't insert a button at a specific location in the toolbar, but after a button or spacer is added, you can drag it to a different location on the toolbar. The existing buttons will make room for the new button.

That finishes the first set of buttons (except for the glyphs). You are about to add a second set of buttons. Before you do, however, there needs to be a little separation between the first set of buttons and the second. Back to work:

1. Right-click on the toolbar again, but this time choose New Separator. A separator is added to the toolbar. Notice that the toolbar automatically aligns the buttons and makes them all the same height.

2. Add another button. This time change the `Name` property to `EditCutBtn` and the `Hint` property to `Cut¦Cut To Clipboard`.

3. Add buttons for Copy and Paste. Change their `Name` and `Hint` properties as appropriate.

4. Add another separator.

5. Add a button called `HelpAboutBtn`. Change its `Hint` property to `About¦About Scratch Pad`.

6. Select the Cut, Copy, Paste, and Help buttons (use Shift-Click to select each button). Change the `ShowHint` property to `true`. It will be changed for all buttons selected.

Your form now looks like the one in Figure 13.3.

Figure 13.3.

The `ScratchPad` *main form after adding a toolbar.*

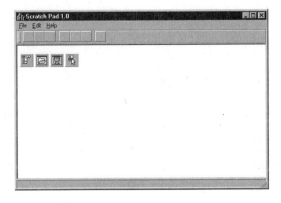

 13

You now have a good start on the toolbar. The toolbar buttons don't do anything because you haven't assigned any event handlers to their OnClick events. Let's do that next.

1. Click the FileNewBtn (the first button). Select the Events page in the Object Inspector. Click the drop-down arrow next to the OnClick event and choose FileNewClick. The button is now hooked up to the FileNewClick event handler.

2. Repeat Step 1 for each remaining button, being careful to select the appropriate OnClick handler for each button (FileOpenClick, FileSaveClick, EditCutClick, and so on).

3. If you haven't yet created an About Box for ScratchPad, create one. When you are done, create an event handler for the Help|About menu item. Hook the OnClick event of the HelpAboutBtn to the event handler for the Help|About menu item.

Obviously this toolbar is missing something. You need to add glyphs to the toolbar buttons. To do so, you must add an ImageList component to the form, following these steps:

1. Place an ImageList component on the form (you find it on the Win32 tab of the Component palette). In this case use the default name of ImageList1, so you don't have to change the Name property.

2. Right-click the ImageList component's icon on your form and choose ImageList Editor. The ImageList Editor is displayed (you can also double-click the ImageList icon on your form to display the ImageList Editor).

3. Click the Add button. Navigate to the Borland Shared Files\Images\Buttons directory. Select the FILENEW.BMP file and click Open.

   A message box appears and asks whether you want to separate the bitmap into two images. What is happening here is that the image list's Width and Height properties are both set to 16. The bitmap that you have selected is wider than 16 pixels, so it has to be split into two images or shrunk to fit. If you recall, the button bitmaps that come with C++Builder are a single bitmap with two images. The first image is the normal button bitmap and the second image is for the disabled button. You will have the ImageList Editor split the bitmap into two images, and then you will delete the second part of the image.

4. Click Yes to have the ImageList Editor split the bitmap into two images. The ImageList Editor now shows two images. You need only the first of these images, so click on the second image (the disabled button image) and click the Delete button.

5. Click the Add button again. This time choose the FILEOPEN.BMP file. Click Yes again when prompted to split the bitmap into two images. Click on the disabled image for this bitmap and delete it. Figure 13.4 shows the image editor as it looks just before deleting the second image.

13

6. Repeat Step 5 for each remaining button (File Save, Cut, Copy, Paste, and About). Use any bitmaps you like, but make certain you delete the extra bitmap each time you add an image to the list. When you are done, you will have seven images in the image list, numbering from 0 to 6.

7. Click OK to close the ImageList Editor.

Figure 13.4.

The ImageList Editor after adding two images.

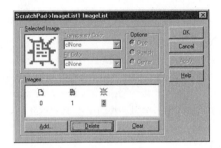

Now you are ready to hook the image list to the toolbar. Click on the toolbar. Locate the `Images` property in the Object Inspector and choose `ImageList1` from the drop-down list. If you did everything right, your buttons now have glyphs. You probably didn't notice, but each time you added a toolbar button, C++Builder automatically incremented the `ImageIndex` property for the button. Because you created the buttons and images in the same order, the glyphs on the buttons should be correct. If a button is wrong, you can either change the button's `ImageIndex` property or go back to the ImageList Editor and change the order of the images in the image list.

TIP

To rearrange the images in an image list, drag them to a new position in the ImageList Editor.

You aren't quite finished with the toolbar, but you are very close. Right now you have glyphs only for the buttons in the enabled state. You need to add glyphs that will be displayed when the buttons are disabled. You aren't disabling the toolbar buttons, but you will be before the day is done, so let's prepare. Just a few more minutes and you'll be done with the toolbar:

1. Add another `ImageList` component to the form. Leave the `Name` property set to `ImageList2`.

2. Right-click the second image list and choose ImageList Editor.

3. Click the Add button to add an image. Once again, start with the `FILENEW.BMP` file.

13

4. Click Yes when asked whether you want to split the bitmap into two images. This time, however, delete the *first* image in the image list. In this exercise you want to delete each image that represents the buttons in the enabled state and keep only the images that represent the button in the disabled state.

5. Repeat Steps 3 and 4 for the File Open, File Save, Cut, Copy, Paste, and About images. Then click OK to close the ImageList Editor.

6. Click the `ToolBar` component on your form. Set the `DisabledImages` property to `ImageList2`.

Poor old `ScratchPad` is back together again. This is a good time to save the project. After saving the project, click the Run button and give the program a workout. Click the buttons and see whether they do what they are supposed to do. If all went well, you have a working program again. If your program won't compile, review the steps and try to fix the problem. If all else fails, you can copy `ScratchPad` from the book's Web site at `http://www.mcp.com/info`.

Toolbar Tips and Hints

I covered nearly everything there is to be said about ToolTips and hints in the discussion of components on Day 8, "VCL Components;" again on Day 9, "Creating Applications in C++Builder," when adding hint text support for the `ScratchPad` program; and again today when rebuilding the toolbar.

There is one thing I didn't talk about, and that is changing the ToolTip properties. The `TApplication` class has four properties that control how the ToolTips behave. Table 13.1 lists these properties and their descriptions.

Table 13.1. `TApplication` **properties pertaining to ToolTips.**

Property	Description
HintColor	Sets the background color of the ToolTip window.
HintHidePause	Controls how long to wait (in milliseconds) before hiding the ToolTip if the mouse cursor remains stationary over the component.
HintPause	Controls the interval between the time the mouse cursor is paused over a component and the time the ToolTip appears (in milliseconds).
HintShortPause	Controls how long to wait before showing ToolTips after they have already been shown—for instance, when the user is roaming over a group of toolbar buttons.

13

The default values for these properties are sufficient for most applications. Still, if you need to change any hint properties, you have that option.

House Rules: Toolbars and Hints

☐ Don't use ToolTips on controls where they will be in the way when the user wants to read the text in the control. In particular, don't use ToolTips for edit controls and combo boxes. At a minimum, give the user the option to turn off ToolTips for those types of controls.

☐ Keep your ToolTip hint (the short hint) brief and to the point.

☐ Make your status bar hint (the long hint) more descriptive and meaningful.

☐ Consider giving your users the option of turning off hints altogether.

Adding Other Controls to Toolbars

Because the ToolBar component is so versatile, nothing special needs to be done to add other types of controls to your toolbar. The most common type of control to add to a toolbar is a combo box. You can use a toolbar combo box to select a font, a configuration option, a zoom setting…the possibilities are endless.

To add a component to the toolbar, select the component from the Component palette and drop it on the toolbar. The toolbar will take care of aligning the component. Add spaces as necessary to separate components visually. When the component is on the toolbar, you deal with it just as you would a component on a form. I could try to complicate this for you, but the truth is, it's just that simple. If you've never tried to implement a combo box on a toolbar by using the Windows API or even using OWL or MFC, you cannot appreciate how much work C++Builder saves you. Take my word for it—it's significant.

Toolbars come in many shapes and sizes. C++Builder makes creating and implementing toolbars very easy. With C++Builder you no longer have the excuse "That's too hard!" In fact, you may even enjoy creating toolbars with C++Builder.

Status Bars

A status bar is another feature that makes an application more marketable. Not all applications benefit from a status bar, but many can. The VCL StatusBar component, which encapsulates the Win32 status bar control, makes creating status bars a breeze. First, let's take a quick look at the major properties of the StatusBar component, listed in Table 13.2.

13

Table 13.2. StatusBar **properties.**

Property	Description
Panels	For status bars with multiple panels. This property defines the individual panels.
SimplePanel	Determines whether the status bar shows a simple panel or multiple panels.
SimpleText	The text for the status bar's simple panel.
SizeGrip	Determines whether the status bar displays the sizing grip in the lower-right corner. The sizing grip provides an area that the user can drag to size the window. The absence of the sizing grip doesn't prevent the window from being sized, but the presence of the size grip makes sizing a window easier.

As you can see from this table, a status bar can be a simple status bar or have multiple panels. Let's discuss this choice next.

Simple or Complex?

A status bar can be either a simple status bar or a complex status bar. A *simple status bar* has a single panel that occupies the entire status bar. If you want a simple status bar, set the SimplePanel property to true. The SimplePanel property acts as a toggle. You can switch between a simple and a complex status bar at runtime by setting SimplePanel to true or false, accordingly.

A *complex status bar* is one with multiple panels. If you elect to use a complex status bar, you can use the StatusBar Panels Editor to set up the panels you want to see on your status bar. To invoke the StatusBar Panels Editor, double-click on the Value column of the Panels property. To add a panel, click the Add button on the StatusBar Panels Editor. To delete a panel, click the Delete button. To edit a panel, select the panel and then make changes to the panel's properties in the Object Inspector. Figure 13.5 shows the StatusBar Panels Editor and Object Inspector when editing panels.

Figure 13.5.

The StatusBar Panels Editor.

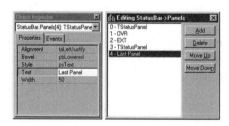

NOTE The individual panels in a complex status bar are instances of the `TStatusPanel` class.

Most of the properties are self-explanatory, but a couple require further note. The `Text` property contains the text that will be displayed in the panel. You can also use the `Text` property at runtime to change the text in the panel. Setting the status bar text is discussed a little later; you don't need to supply text for the panel at design time if you are going to change the text at runtime.

You can set the `Style` property to either `psText` or `psOwnerDraw`. If the `Style` is set to `psText`, the panel behaves as you would expect. The text is aligned in the panel according to the value of the `Alignment` property. If the `Style` is set to `psOwnerDraw`, it is up to you to draw any text or image that is displayed in the panel. Owner drawing of panel items is discussed later in the section titled "Owner-Drawn Status Bar Panels."

The `Width`, `Bevel`, and `Alignment` properties for the panel are straightforward. Experiment with these properties to see how they affect your status bar's appearance.

TIP In the Form Designer you immediately see the results of changes made to the status bar via the StatusBar Panels Editor. Position the StatusBar Panels Editor so that you can view the status bar as you work with the StatusBar Panels Editor. Each time you make a change, it will be reflected in the Form Designer.

The Web site accompanying the book has a program called `StatTest` that illustrates some of the things you can do with status bars. Run the program and examine its source for tips on implementing status bars in your applications.

When you are done adding panels to the status bar, close the StatusBar Panels Editor and return to the Form Designer.

NOTE When you modify the `Panels` property of a `StatusBar` component, the Form Designer automatically sets the `SimplePanel` property to `false`. The assumption is that if you are using multiple panels, you don't want to have a simple status bar.

13

Changing Text in the Status Bar

There are two ways to change text in a status bar:

☐ Manually modify the `SimpleText` property of the status bar (for simple status bars) or the `Text` property of an individual panel (for complex status bars).

☐ Respond to the `OnHint` event for the Application object.

Manually changing the text in the status bar is simple, particularly if you have a simple status bar. When the `SimplePanel` property is `true`, you can set the `SimpleText` property to the text you want displayed in the status bar:

```
StatusBar->SimpleText = "This shows up in the status bar.";
```

In the case of complex status bars, changing the text is only slightly more complicated. If you wanted to change the text for the first panel of a complex status bar, you would use something like this:

```
StatusBar->Panels->Items[0]->Text = "Status Bar Text";
```

Although this line seems a little strung out, it isn't too difficult to understand. The `Panels` property of the `StatusBar` component has a property called `Items` that is an array of panels in the status bar. Setting the `Text` property for an element in the array changes the text for that panel. As you can see, the array is 0-based. The first panel in the status bar is array element 0.

Changing the text via the `OnHint` event requires a little more effort but is simple after you've done it once. On Day 9 you added status bar hint support to the `ScratchPad` program. Let's review the steps you took:

1. Add a function declaration to the main form header for your own `OnHint` event:

   ```
   void __fastcall OnHint(TObject* Sender);
   ```

2. Add the function implementation to the main form source unit. In the function body, set the `Hint` property of the Application object to the status bar's `SimpleText` property:

   ```
   void __fastcall TMainForm::OnHint(TObject* Sender)
   {
     StatusBar->SimpleText = Application->Hint;
   }
   ```

3. In your `OnCreate` event handler for the main form, set the Application object's `OnHint` event handler to point to your own `OnHint()` function:

   ```
   void __fastcall TMainForm::FormCreate(TObject *Sender)
   {
     Application->OnHint = OnHint;
   }
   ```

4. Make certain that all components that should display hints have their ShowHint property set to true and that there is valid hint text in the Hint property.

As I said, it's not too terrible after you've done it a few times. This is easy enough for simple status bars, but if your application uses complex status bars, you need to modify your OnHint() function slightly:

```
void __fastcall TMainForm::OnHint(TObject* Sender)
{
  StatusBar->Panels->Items[0]->Text = Application->Hint;
}
```

To take it a step further, let's say your application switches between a simple status bar and a complex status bar, depending on the state of the program. In that case you need to check whether the status bar is currently set to a simple status bar or a complex status bar and set the text accordingly. This OnHint() function does it all:

```
void __fastcall TMainForm::OnHint(TObject* Sender)
{
  if (StatusBar->SimplePanel)
    StatusBar->SimpleText = Application->Hint;
  else
    StatusBar->Panels->Items[0]->Text = Application->Hint;
}
```

Now you're covered, no matter what type of status bar you are using. Of course, this code assumes that you are using the first panel in the status bar to display the hint text. If you are using some other panel to display the hint text, change the code accordingly.

NOTE

You can still modify the status bar's text manually even when using hints. There's nothing to stop you from changing the text manually, but remember that the text will be replaced the next time an OnHint event occurs.

Owner-Drawn Status Bar Panels

Earlier I said that a panel's Style property can be either psText or psOwnerDraw. When you set a panel's style to psOwnerDraw, you must take the responsibility of drawing anything in the panel that needs to be displayed there. It is unlikely that you are going to go to the trouble of using an owner-drawn panel just to display text, so usually it means you are going to display some sort of icon or bitmap in the status bar. Regardless of what is being drawn on the panel, the steps are the same:

1. Set the panel's Style property to psOwnerDraw (usually via the StatusBar Panels Editor).

2. Respond to the OnDrawPanel event.

13

Obviously the real work here is going to take place in the event handler for the `OnDrawPanel` event. The function signature for the `OnDrawPanel` event handler looks like this:

```
void __fastcall TMainForm::StatusBarDrawPanel(TStatusBar *StatusBar,
    TStatusPanel *Panel, const TRect &Rect)
{
}
```

In this function, the `StatusBar` parameter is a pointer to the status bar. Usually you have a pointer to the status bar anyway (the `Name` property of the `StatusBar` component), so this parameter is not all that useful. The `Panel` property is a pointer to the particular panel that currently needs drawing. You can use this parameter to determine which panel needs drawing if you have more than one owner-drawn panel in your status bar. The `Rect` parameter contains the panel's size and position. The `Rect` parameter is important because it tells you the exact dimensions of the drawing area.

The `OnDrawPanel` event handler is called once for each panel that has its `Style` property set to `psOwnerDraw`. If you have only one panel to draw, you don't have to worry about much except the `Rect` parameter. If you have multiple panels to draw, you must first determine which panel to draw and then do your drawing. An illustration might help to explain this. Earlier I mentioned the `StatTest` program. Figure 13.6 shows the `StatTest` program running.

Figure 13.6.

The StatTest *program with owner-drawn status bar panels.*

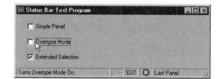

As you can see, the status bar in this program has multiple panels. The middle three panels are owner-drawn. The panels marked OVR and EXT simulate the status bar on a word processing program or code editor. In those types of programs, the Overtype or Extended Selection modes might be on or off. If the mode is on, the text in the status bar panel shows in black. If the mode is off, the text has a 3D disabled-text appearance. The third owner-drawn panel displays a stock Windows icon to illustrate the use of a graphic on a status bar. Run the program from the Web site and experiment with it to learn how it works.

Listing 13.1 shows the `OnDrawPanel` event handler from the `StatTest` program. Examine it and read the comments to understand what is going on in the code.

13

Listing 13.1. The `StatusBarDrawPanel()` function of the `StatTest` program.

```
1: void __fastcall TMainForm::StatusBarDrawPanel(TStatusBar *StatusBar,
2:       TStatusPanel *Panel, const TRect &Rect)
3: {
4:   //
5:   // Create a reference to the status bar Canvas so we
6:   // don't have to do so much typing.
7:   //
8:   TCanvas& c = *StatusBar->Canvas;
9:   //
10:  // Create a temporary TRect object. The Rect parameter
11:  // is const so we can't change it.
12:  //
13:  TRect temp = Rect;
14:  //
15:  // Check whether panel 3 is the panel that needs
16:  // to be drawn. If so, draw an icon in the panel.
17:  //
18:  if (Panel->Index == 3) {
19:    //
20:    // Load one of the stock Windows icons. This time
21:    // using the API is easier than using VCL.
22:    //
23:    HICON icon = LoadIcon(NULL, IDI_HAND);
24:    //
25:    // Draw the icon and shrink it down to 15 x 15 pixels.
26:    // Center it in the panel, too.
27:    //
28:    DrawIconEx(c.Handle, Rect.Left + 6, 3, icon,
29:      15, 15, NULL, NULL, DI_NORMAL);
30:    //
31:    // Nothing more to do.
32:    //
33:    return;
34:  }
35:  //
36:  // This rather lengthy if statement checks whether
37:  // either the Overtype Mode or Extended Selection
38:  // check box is checked. If so, then what we need
39:  // to do is to draw the text twice. First, we draw it
40:  // in white. Then we draw it again, offset by 1 pixel,
41:  // in gray. The effect is a 3D disabled-text look.
42:  //
43:  if ((Panel->Index == 1 && OvrMode->Checked == false) ||
44:    (Panel->Index == 2 && ExtendedSel->Checked == false)) {
45:    //
46:    // Move over and down one pixel for the offset.
47:    //
48:    temp.Left += 1;
49:    temp.Top += 2;
50:    //
51:    // Change the text color to white.
52:    //
53:    c.Font->Color = clWhite;
```

continues

13

Listing 13.1. continued

```
54:        //
55:        // Set the background mode to transparent so the
56:        // text appears hollow and so that the white
57:        // text can be seen under the gray.
58:        //
59:        c.Brush->Style = bsClear;
60:        //
61:        // Draw the text using the API function DrawText().
62:        // I use DrawText() because it allows me to center
63:        // the text both horizontally and vertically within
64:        // the given rectangle.
65:        //
66:        DrawText(c.Handle, Panel->Text.c_str(),
67:          -1, (RECT*)&temp, DT_CENTER | DT_VCENTER | DT_SINGLELINE);
68:        //
69:        // Set the color to gray because we're going to
70:        // draw the text in gray in a moment.
71:        //
72:        c.Font->Color = clGray;
73:        //
74:        // Set the rect back to the original size.
75:        //
76:        temp.Left -= 1;
77:        temp.Top -= 2;
78:    }
79:    //
80:    // Display the text. If the item is not disabled,
81:    // the default color (black) is used to draw the text.
82:    // If the item is disabled, the text color has
83:    // been set to gray by the code above.
84:    //
85:    DrawText(c.Handle, Panel->Text.c_str(),
86:      -1, (RECT*)&temp, DT_CENTER | DT_VCENTER | DT_SINGLELINE);
87: }
```

This code might seem intimidating, but most of it is comment lines. The code itself is simple. The comment lines explain what is happening at each step: The 3D appearance for the disabled text is accomplished by drawing the text once in white and then drawing it again in gray with a slight offset. The result is that the text looks recessed. The icon is displayed using the Windows API function DrawIconEx().

13

NOTE

Notice line 8 of Listing 13.1. Here I created a reference to the status bar's `Canvas` property to save some typing and to make the code less cluttered. After creating the reference, I can write code such as this:

```
c.Font->Color = clWhite;
```

instead of this:

```
StatusBar->Canvas->Font->Color = clWhite;
```

Granted, the use of `c` for the reference name is cryptic, but it illustrates how a reference can be used in a VCL application.

Owner drawing of status bar panels is daunting at first, but you'll soon find out that it's not all that bad. You may program for a long time and never need owner-drawn panels in your status bar, but if you ever need them, you'll know that's not impossible to accomplish.

Toolboxes

Toolboxes are not exactly window decorations, but they fit in this category, so I'll touch on them briefly. *Toolboxes* are secondary forms that contain speed buttons. You may have noticed that toolboxes such as the C++Builder Alignment window and Object Inspector have a smaller title bar than regular windows. You create this smaller title bar by setting the `BorderStyle` property to either `bsSizeToolWindow` (for sizable toolboxes) or `bsToolWindow` (for nonsizable toolboxes). Aside from that, a toolbox is just another form.

TIP

You might not be able to size your toolbox to the proper width at design time because of the standard buttons that appear on every form. For example, a toolbox with two buttons across should be approximately 54 pixels in width. The smallest the Form Designer lets you make the form is 112 pixels. The only thing you can do to get around this is to set the toolbox's `Width` property at runtime before the toolbox is displayed.

13

Command Enabling

Command enabling is the process of enabling or disabling buttons, depending on current conditions. For example, there's not much point of having the Cut or Copy button or menu item enabled for a text editor when no text is currently selected. Likewise, if there is no text in the Clipboard, the Paste button should be disabled.

Command enabling isn't difficult, but it takes time. It takes time because you have to pay attention to detail. (Sometimes it is attention to detail that separates the great applications from the mediocre applications.)

Comments on Command Enabling

You can handle command enabling whenever and however you like. All you have to do to enable a menu item or toolbar button is to set its Enabled property to true. To disable a component, set its Enabled property to false. The actual enabling or disabling of a component is as easy as that, but the real work is working out how and when to do the enabling or disabling. To put this into practice, let's go back to the ScratchPad program. What you will do is add command enablers for the menu items Cut, Copy, and Paste. (I say menu items, but I mean menu items, toolbar buttons, and pop-up menu items, collectively).

Before digging into the code that does the command enabling, let's lay the groundwork. First, let's assume that the Cut and Copy menu items should be enabled only when text is selected in the rich edit component. After all, if nothing is selected, there's nothing to cut or copy. In the case of pasting text, you want the Paste menu item to be enabled only if there is actually text in the Clipboard.

Okay—now you have laid the ground rules, so you can begin. Well, not quite. There's still something that you need to work out: When and where do you do the enabling?

You can do the enabling for Paste when the user selects either Cut or Copy from the menu. If you recall, you have event handlers for the Cut, Copy, and Paste menu items. So you can do some enabling there:

```
void __fastcall TScratchPad::EditCutClick(TObject *Sender)
{
  Memo->CutToClipboard();
  EditPaste->Enabled = true;
}
```

If the user chooses Edit | Cut, you know something is in the Clipboard, so you can enable Paste. Okay—so when do you *disable* Paste? And what happens if the user uses Ctrl+X to cut, instead of the menu? Further, what if the user copies text to the Clipboard in some other application and wants to paste it into dear old ScratchPad? Looks like you have some problems to work out. "Never do today what you can put off until tomorrow," I always say, so let's leave that problem on the back burner for now and see what you can do with Cut and Copy.

Cut and Copy should be enabled when text is selected. That's simple enough. If you dig through the VCL help files, you will discover that TMemo has a property called SelLength that tells you the length of the selected text in a rich edit component. So if SelLength is greater than 0, the user has selected some text. "Great! This will be easy." You think so? Bad news, I'm afraid. You have no way of knowing *when* the user selected the text. There is no event

13

called OnTextSelected, so you can't use events to tell you. You could use a system timer, but that's a messy solution. Besides, there are only so many system timers, and you can't be guaranteed that you'll get one when you want it. You could catch the mouse messages for the rich edit component. That might work. But what if the user selected text with the keyboard instead of the mouse? Then you'd have to catch all the mouse messages and all the keyboard messages and check whether SelLength is greater than 0. Yech. This is becoming complicated. And you still haven't solved the Paste problem simmering on the back burner. There *has* to be a better way. Fortunately, there is.

OnIdle **to the Rescue**

When your application runs out of messages to process, Windows sends it a WM_ENTERIDLE message. Windows, in effect, tells your program, "I don't have anything for you to do right now, so relax and take it easy for a while." When a C++Builder application receives a WM_ENTERIDLE message, it triggers the Application object's OnIdle event. You can provide an OnIdle event handler that you can attach to the Application object's OnIdle event. This event handler will be called whenever the OnIdle event occurs. You put this into practice exactly as you did when attaching an event handler to the Application object's OnHint event: Create a function in your main form's class and assign its address to the OnIdle event of the Application object.

So what's the benefit to you? The benefit is that you now have a function that will be called automatically at periodic intervals. You can use the function to check whether any text is selected in the rich edit component so that you can enable or disable the Cut and Copy menu items as needed. That takes care of that.

But it still doesn't fix your problem with Paste, does it? Take heart—the Paste problem has a reasonable solution, too. VCL has a class called TClipboard that encapsulates Clipboard operations. One of TClipboard's methods is HasFormat(). This method checks whether data of a particular format is currently in the Clipboard. If so, HasFormat() returns true. You can use this method to determine whether text is contained in the Clipboard with code like this:

```
if (Clipboard()->HasFormat(CF_TEXT))
  PasteBtn->Enabled = true;
```

If text is in the Clipboard, enable the Paste button and menu item. If no text is in the Clipboard, disable the Paste items. Another world problem solved.

The use of the OnIdle() function means that your command enablers will be called, regardless of whether the user selects text with the mouse, with the keyboard, or even from another application.

Okay, Let's Do It

As I said earlier, we have to create an event handler for the OnIdle event. That part is clearcut, so let's do it first:

13

1. Open the ScratchPad program and switch to the Code Editor.

2. Open the header for the main form unit (SPMain.h) and add the following at the end of the other includes near the top of the file:

```
#include <vcl\Clipbrd.hpp>
```

3. Add the following to the private section of the class declaration:

```
void __fastcall OnIdle(TObject* Sender, bool& Done);
```

4. Now switch to the SPMain.cpp file in the Code Editor. Add the following function to the end of the file:

```
void __fastcall
TScratchPad::OnIdle(TObject* Sender, bool& Done)
{
}
```

5. Locate the FormCreate() function and add this line to the function:

```
Application->OnIdle = OnIdle;
```

Now you have a function that will be called whenever your application enters its idle state. Obviously the function won't do any good without code in it, but you'll fix that in a minute. As long as you're at it, though, go ahead and add command enablers for the Save, Save As, Undo, and Select All menu items. Use OnIdle to do it all. Listing 13.2 shows the complete OnIdle() function.

Listing 13.2. The ScratchPad OnIdle() function.

```
 1: void __fastcall
 2: TScratchPad::OnIdle(TObject* Sender, bool& Done)
 3: {
 4:     //
 5:     // Command enablers for Cut and Copy. If no text is
 6:     // selected, disable these items on the main menu,
 7:     // on the toolbar, and on the popup menu.
 8:     //
 9:     bool textSelected = Memo->SelLength > 0;
10:     EditCut->Enabled = textSelected;
11:     EditCutBtn->Enabled = textSelected;
12:     PopupCut->Enabled = textSelected;
13:     EditCopy->Enabled = textSelected;
14:     EditCopyBtn->Enabled = textSelected;
15:     PopupCopy->Enabled = textSelected;
16:     //
17:     // Command enablers for Paste. Is there text in the
18:     // clipboard? If not, disable Paste.
19:     //
20:     bool cbHasText = Clipboard()->HasFormat(CF_TEXT);
21:     EditPaste->Enabled = cbHasText;
22:     EditPasteBtn->Enabled = cbHasText;
23:     PopupPaste->Enabled = cbHasText;
24:     //delete clipBrd;
```

13

```
25:     //
26:     // Command enabler for Select All.
27:     //
28:     bool hasText = Memo->Lines->Count > 0;
29:     EditSelectAll->Enabled = hasText;
30:     //
31:     // Command enabler for Save and Save As.
32:     //
33:     bool modified = Memo->Modified;
34:     FileSave->Enabled = modified && hasText;
35:     FileSaveBtn->Enabled = modified && hasText;
36:     FileSaveAs->Enabled = modified && hasText;
37:     //
38:     // Command enabler for Undo
39:     //
40:     EditUndo->Enabled = modified;
41: }
```

Some of this code might look a bit odd if you haven't encountered it before. Take a look at line 9, for instance. This line assigns the result of Memo->SelLength > 0 to the bool variable textSelected. If the SelLength property of the rich edit is greater than 0, the textSelected variable is assigned a value of true. If the SelLength property is less than or equal to 0 (meaning no text is selected), the variable is assigned a value of false. This value is then assigned to the Enabled property of the various Cut and Copy menu items and buttons. Other code in this function works in the same way. Examine Listing 13.2 and read the comment lines to learn how the function works. Enter the code into the OnIdle() function of the ScratchPad program to convince yourself that it works.

NOTE

Debugging code in the OnIdle event handler is tricky. The problem is that any breakpoints in the OnIdle event handler will arise as soon as you run the program. You will have to use debugging methods other than breakpoints when debugging code in the OnIdle event handler (using OutputDebugString() to send messages to the Event Lot, for instance).

13

NOTE

The OnIdle event handler might be called thousands of times per second. For that reason you must keep code in this function short and sweet.

An Alternative to Command Enabling with OnIdle

Using the OnIdle event is by no means the only way to handle command enablers in a C++Builder application. Another commonly used method is to create an event handler for the OnClick event of top-level menu items. For example, in the Menu Editor you could click on the File menu and then generate an OnClick handler that will be called every time the user clicks File on the main menu. This event will be generated before the menu is made visible, so you could do command enabling in this event handler for all items in the File menu. You could do the same thing for the Edit menu, the Window menu, or any other top-level menus you have. Although this solution makes command enabling easy for menus, it doesn't solve the problem of how or when to perform command enabling for toolbar buttons.

I happen to think that using OnIdle is an elegant solution to the problems that command enablers present. Every situation is different, so don't be afraid to adapt if this particular solution doesn't fit with the way your application works. In some cases you may want to do command enabling in direct response to some action by the user. No matter how you do it, command enabling is something that you should implement in your application when and where it's appropriate.

Printing in C++Builder Applications

Printing is an everyday necessity for most Windows users. Whereas there are plenty of programs without printing capability, the majority of Windows applications have some form of printing support. I'll cover the basics of printing in this section.

Providing printing capabilities in a DOS application used to be a real chore. A DOS program had to provide and install printer drivers for every type of printer that the program supported. That put a huge burden on software developers, especially on small companies or shareware developers. Windows changed all that. For the most part, Windows takes on the burden of dealing with different printers, printer drivers, and so on. All you have to do is send output to the printer just as you would send output to a window. I'll get to that soon.

Printing in C++Builder applications comes in several flavors. You'll probably be relieved to learn that in many cases printing is built into VCL and comes nearly automatically. In other cases, though, you have to do some specialized printing. Before you learn how to go about that, let's look at the common dialog boxes that pertain to printing. After that I'll discuss the different ways you can print from a C++Builder application.

The Common Printing Dialog Boxes

Windows provides the common Print and Print Setup dialog boxes for use in your applications. You use the Print dialog box just before printing begins and the Print Setup dialog box to configure the printer. First, though, you must add the components to your form.

The Print Dialog Box

As I've mentioned, the Print dialog box is displayed just before printing begins, usually when the user chooses File | Print from the main menu. If the user clicks OK, printing begins; if the user clicks Cancel, printing is aborted. Figure 13.7 shows the Windows Print dialog box in its most basic form.

Figure 13.7.

The Windows Print dialog box.

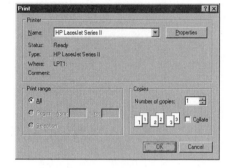

No doubt this is not the first time you have seen this particular dialog box. The combo box at the top of the dialog box enables you to choose the particular printer to which you want to print. The Properties button brings up a dialog box specific to the printer currently selected. The Properties dialog box enables you to set the orientation, resolution, and other properties specific to that printer. The Print range section enables the user to print all pages, a page range, or any objects or text currently selected in the application. The Copies section enables the user to specify the number of copies to print as well as whether to collate the copies.

The Print dialog box is encapsulated in VCL in the PrintDialog component. As with the other common dialog boxes, you display the Print dialog box by calling its Execute() method. It shouldn't disappoint you to learn that Windows accomplishes much of what the Print dialog box does. The printer selection, number of copies, and collating options are all handled by Windows, so you don't have to worry about them. Depending on your application, you might need to allow the user to print a specified range of pages or to print the current selection in the application. If you are providing that kind of support, you need to examine some of the PrintDialog properties before printing begins.

The PrintDialog component has the Execute() method only and no events. All the functionality of the PrintDialog component takes place through its properties, listed in Table 13.3.

13

Table 13.3. The `PrintDialog` **properties.**

Property	Description
Collate	Specifies collated copies. If this is set to `true`, Windows will print so that the copies are collated.
Copies	Specifies the number of copies to print. You can set this property before calling the Print dialog box if one of your application's options is the number of copies to print. Windows takes care of printing the correct number of copies.
FromPage	Specifies the starting page when the option of printing a range of pages is enabled. Applications that support page-range printing should read this property to determine which pages to print.
MaxPage	Specifies the maximum page number that can be specified in the `To` field when printing a range of pages. The Print dialog box takes care of validating entry in the From and To fields.
MinPage	Specifies the minimum page number that can be specified in the `From` field when printing a range of pages.
Options	Contains a set of options that control which features of the Print dialog box are enabled. You can elect to have a Help button, to display the Print to File option, or to enable the page-range or print selection options.
PrintRange	Controls which of the Print range radio buttons is selected when the Print dialog box is initially displayed.
PrintToFile	Indicates whether the user has chosen the Print to File option. It is up to the application to write the output to a file.
ToPage	Specifies the ending page number when printing a range of pages. Applications that support page-range printing should read this property to determine which pages to print.

The application doesn't have much to do in response to the Print dialog box closing unless the Print Range and Print to File options are enabled. For example, if your application enables printing a range of pages, you need to read the `FromPage` and `ToPage` properties to determine which pages to print. Other than that, you begin printing if the user chooses OK.

The Print Setup Dialog Box

The Print Setup dialog box, shown in Figure 13.8, is used when the user wants to change printers, page size, paper source, or orientation.

13

Figure 13.8.

The Print Setup dialog box.

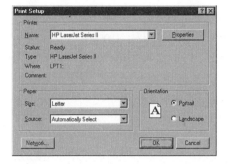

The Print Setup dialog box isn't necessary in most applications because the user can always press the Properties button on the Print dialog box to change the setup options (refer back to Figure 13.7). On the other hand, implementing the Print Setup dialog box is so easy that you might as well include it in your applications. How easy is it? Well, the PrinterSetup component has no properties, methods, or events specific to it. As with the PrintDialog component, the Execute() method is the only method in which you are interested. To further simplify things, Windows handles everything that the Print Setup dialog box does. In fact, the Execute() function doesn't even return a value. This is because Windows handles everything for you. If the user clicks Cancel, Windows does nothing. If the user clicks OK, Windows makes the appropriate changes in preparation for printing. All you have to do is display the Print Setup dialog box and forget about it. A typical event handler for the File | Printer Setup menu item would look like this:

```
void __fastcall TScratchPad::FilePrintSetupClick(TObject *Sender)
{
  PrinterSetupDialog->Execute();
}
```

That's all there is to it. As I said, implementing the Print Setup dialog box is so simple you might as well add it to your application.

Printing the Easy Way

Printing is an application-specific task. That may not sound profound, but it's true. Depending on what kind of application you have developed, printing can be as simple as one line or it can entail hundreds of lines of code. Let me first discuss the easiest forms of printing, and then I'll progress to the more difficult printing operations.

The Print() Method for Forms

The TForm class has a method called Print() that can be used to print the contents of a form. Only the client area of the form is printed; the form's frame and menu bar are not. Although this method works well for a simple screen dump, it is limited in its implementation. You can choose from three print options, which are controlled through the PrintScaled property. Table 13.4 lists the print scaling choices and their descriptions.

13

Table 13.4. The PrintScaled property options.

Option	Description
poNone	No special scaling is applied. The printed output of the form varies from printer to printer.
poProportional	This option attempts to print the form in roughly the same size as it appears on the screen.
poPrintToFit	This increases or reduces the size of the image to fit the current printer settings.

You can set the PrintScaled property at runtime or at design time. The Print() method's use is limited to simple screen dumps and isn't likely to be used for any serious printing.

The Print() Method for the RichEdit Component

The RichEdit component is powerful, primarily due to the amount of work done by the underlying Windows rich edit control. Printing in the RichEdit component is accomplished via a call to the Print() method. This function takes a single parameter called Caption that is used by the print manager when it displays the print job. Printing the contents of a RichEdit component is as simple as this:

```
RichEdit->Print("MyApp. e XE- readme.txt");
```

Everything is taken care of for you. Word wrapping and pagination are automatically implemented. If you are using a multiline edit control that requires printing, the RichEdit component is the way to go.

 TIP

You can use the Windows API function ShellExecute() to print a text file. ShellExecute() is used, among other things, to run a program based on a filename extension. For example, by default Windows registers the .txt extension as belonging to Windows Notepad. If you double-click on a file with a .txt extension in Explorer, Windows will look up the .txt extension in the Registry, see that Notepad.exe is registered to handle .txt files, and run Notepad. The file you double-clicked will be loaded automatically.

You can use this behavior to your advantage. Take this line of code, for instance:

```
ShellExecute(Handle, "print", "readme.txt", NULL, NULL, SW_HIDE);
```

13

> This code will load Notepad, print the file called `Readme.txt`, and then exit Notepad. In fact, you never see the Notepad program's main window because the `SW_HIDE` style is specified for the `Show` parameter. Using this technique assumes that the user has not modified the default registration of the `.txt` extension and has not deleted Notepad from his or her system.

Printing via `QuickReport`

Database programs can use `QuickReport` to print reports. I mention `QuickReport` here because it obviously pertains to printing. Because `QuickReport` is one of the database components, I will postpone a detailed discussion about its actual implementation until Day 18, "Building Database Applications."

Printing the Hard Way

Don't let the title of this section put you off. Printing isn't all that difficult; it just takes some time and organization. First, let's look at some things you need to know in order to implement printing in your applications. After that you will delve into the actual code.

What's a Device Context?

A *device context* (DC) is like a slate that Windows programs can draw on. A better word would be *canvas*. On this canvas you can draw text, lines, bitmaps, rectangles, ellipses, and so on. The type of line used when drawing on a device context depends on the current pen selected into the DC. The current fill color and fill pattern are taken from the brush that is currently selected into the device context. Device contexts must be carefully managed. There are a limited number of DCs available to Windows, and you have to be careful to release the device context as soon as you are finished with it. Also, if you don't properly delete the objects you select into the device context, your program will leak memory and perhaps even leave Windows itself in a precarious state. As you can imagine, working with DCs can be complicated.

The good news is that VCL shields you from having to know every detail of device contexts. VCL encapsulates Windows DCs in the `TCanvas` class. The `Canvas` property represents the canvas of each C++Builder form. Any time you need to draw directly on a form, you can do so by accessing the `Canvas` property. For instance, the following code will draw a line diagonally on a form from the top-left corner to the bottom-right corner:

```
Canvas->MoveTo(0, 0);
Canvas->LineTo(ClientRect.Right, ClientRect.Bottom);
```

The line will be drawn with the current pen for the canvas, as determined by the canvas's `Pen` property.

13

The nice thing about the Canvas property is that you don't have to worry about all the little details that can drive you nuts when dealing with Windows device contexts. VCL takes care of obtaining the DC, selecting the appropriate objects into the DC, and releasing the DC when it is no longer needed. All you have to do is draw on the canvas and let VCL worry about the rest.

So what does this have to do with printing? (Inquiring minds want to know.) Well, it's like this: Windows enables you to obtain a *printer device context* on which you can draw text, graphics, lines, and so on. In other words, you draw on a printer DC just as you draw on a screen DC. This concept represents quite a switch from the way printing was approached back in the good old days of DOS. In this case, it is Windows that comes to your rescue by enabling the use of a printer DC. VCL further aids you by encapsulating device contexts in the Canvas property. The bottom line is that printing is easier than it's ever been.

The TPrinter Class and the Printer() Function

VCL aids in printing operations by providing the TPrinter class. This class encapsulates the whole of printing in Windows. TPrinter has a Canvas property that you can use to output lines, text, graphics, and other drawing objects to the printer. I don't want to make it sound too easy, but all you have to do to print in your C++Builder programs is include Printers.hpp and then do something like the following:

```
Printer()->BeginDoc();
Printer()->Canvas->TextOut(20, 20, "Hello There!");
Printer()->EndDoc();
```

The Printer() function enables you access to a TPrinter object that is set up and ready to go. All you have to do is put it to work.

Now let's take a quick look at TPrinter's properties and methods. Table 13.5 lists the primary TPrinter properties, and Table 13.6 shows the primary TPrinter methods.

Table 13.5. TPrinter properties.

Property	Description
Aborted	This property is true if printing was started and then aborted before it was finished.
Canvas	The mechanism through which you can draw on the printer (the printer device context).
Capabilities	The current settings of a printer device driver.
Copies	The number of copies printed.
Fonts	A list of fonts supported by the current printer.
Handle	The handle to the printer device context (HDC). Use this property when you have to call a Windows API function that requires a handle to a device context.

Property	Description
Orientation	The printer orientation (poPortrait or poLandscape). This is automatically set when the user chooses a printer or modifies the printer setup, but you can also set it manually.
PageHeight	The height of the current printer page, in pixels. This value varies from printer to printer. In addition, this property can contain a different value based on the orientation of the printer. Some printers can use more than one resolution, which also causes this value to vary.
PageNumber	The page number of the page currently printing. This property is incremented each time you call NewPage() to begin printing a new page.
PageWidth	The width of the page, in pixels. As with the PageHeight property, this value varies, depending on the printer resolution, paper orientation, and paper size.
PrinterIndex	The index value of the currently selected printer in the list of available printers. Specify -1 to select the default printer.
Printers	A list of available printers on the system.
Printing	This property is true if the printer is currently printing.
Title	The text that identifies this printing job in the print manager window.

Table 13.6. TPrinter() **methods.**

Method	Description
Abort	Used to abort the printing before normal completion.
BeginDoc	Begins the printing process. Sets up the printer with Windows in preparation for printing.
EndDoc	Ends the printing process. Forces the current page to be printed and performs printing cleanup with Windows.
GetPrinter	Retrieves the current printer. Use the Printers property instead of this method. (The Printers property is the preferred method for accessing printers because you can use it for both retrieving and setting the current printer.)
NewPage	Used to force printing of the current page and start a new page. Increments the PageNumber property.
SetPrinter	Sets the current printer. Use the Printers property instead of this method.

13

The TPrinter class has no design-time interface. Everything is accomplished at runtime.

Putting It to Work

It's time to put your newly acquired knowledge to work. Once again we'll dust off the ScratchPad program and spruce it up a bit. After all, what good is a text editor that doesn't print?

First, you need to modify the main form slightly. You already have menu items set up for the Print and Print Setup menu items, but you need to enable them and add the Print and Printer Setup dialog boxes to the form. Here goes:

1. Double-click the MainMenu component to bring up the Menu Designer.
2. Choose File | Print from the ScratchPad menu in the Menu Designer. Change the Enabled property to true.
3. Do the same for the File | Print Setup menu item. Close the Menu Designer.
4. Place a PrintDialog component on the form. Change its Name property to PrintDialog.
5. Place a PrinterSetupDialog on the form and change its Name property to PrinterSetupDialog.

Okay, now that you've completed the form, it's time to go to work modifying the code. To start, you have to add a couple items to the SPMain.h header file by doing the following:

1. Switch to the Code Editor and open the SPMain.h file.
2. Add the following at the end of the other #includes near the top of the file:
   ```
   #include <stdlib.h>
   #include <vcl\Printers.hpp>
   ```
3. Add this line to the private section of the class declaration:
   ```
   void PrintFooter(TRect& rect, int lineHeight);
   ```
   This is the declaration for a function that will print the footer at the bottom of each page.

That takes care of the unit's header. Now you add code to the SPMain.cpp source code unit:

1. Switch back to the Form Designer and choose File | Print from the form's main menu. The FilePrintClick() function will be displayed. For now, leave the function empty.
2. Switch back to the Form Designer and choose File | Print Setup from the main menu. Enter one line at the cursor so that the entire FilePrintSetupClick() function looks like this:
   ```
   void __fastcall TScratchPad::FilePrintSetupClick(TObject *Sender)
   {
     PrinterSetupDialog->Execute();
   }
   ```

3. Still in the Code Editor, move to the end of the file and type the following:

```
void TScratchPad::PrintFooter(TRect& rect, int lineHeight)
{
}
```

Okay, now you're ready to fill in the `FilePrintClick()` and `PrintFooter()` functions. Listing 13.3 shows the entire `FilePrintClick()` function. You can enter the function by hand, or you can obtain the `ScratchPad` program from the Web site and examine it there. Listing 13.4 shows the `PrintFooter()` function. Enter the body of these functions in your `SPMain.cpp` file.

Listing 13.3. The `FilePrintClick()` function.

```
 1: void __fastcall TScratchPad::FilePrintClick(TObject *Sender)
 2: {
 3:   //
 4:   // Display the Print dialog.
 5:   //
 6:   if (PrintDialog->Execute()) {
 7:     //
 8:     // Set the title for the printer object.
 9:     //
10:     Printer()->Title =
11:       "ScratchPad - " + OpenDialog->FileName;
12:     //
13:     // Set the printer font to the same font as the rich edit.
14:     //
15:     Printer()->Canvas->Font = Memo->Font;
16:     //
17:     // Determine the line height. Take the Size of the
18:     // font and use the MulDiv() function to calculate
19:     // the line height, taking into account the current
20:     // printer resolution. Use the abs() function to get
21:     // the absolute value because the result could be a
22:     // negative number. After that add 40% for leading.
23:     //
24:     int lineHeight = abs(
25:       MulDiv(Printer()->Canvas->Font->Size,
26:       GetDeviceCaps(Printer()->Handle, LOGPIXELSY), 72));
27:     lineHeight *= 1.4;
28:     //
29:     // Determine how many lines will fit on a page. Trim
30:     // it back by three lines to leave some bottom margin.
31:     //
32:     int linesPerPage =
33:       (Printer()->PageHeight/lineHeight) - 4;
34:     //
35:     // Start printing on line 4 rather than line 0 to leave
36:     // room for the header and to allow for some top margin.
37:     //
38:     int lineCount = 4;
39:     //
40:     // Tell Windows we're starting and print the header.
```

13

continues

Listing 13.3. continued

```
41:        //
42:        Printer()->BeginDoc();
43:        TRect rect;
44:        rect.Top = lineHeight;
45:        rect.Left = 20;
46:        rect.Right =  Printer()->PageWidth;
47:        rect.Bottom = lineHeight * 2;
48:        DrawText(Printer()->Handle,
49:          OpenDialog->FileName.c_str(), -1, (RECT*)&rect, DT_CENTER);
50:        //
51:        // Loop through all the lines and print each one.
52:        //
53:        for (int i=0;i<Memo->Lines->Count;i++) {
54:          //
55:          // When we get to the bottom of the page, reset the
56:          // line counter, eject the page, and start a new page.
57:          //
58:          if (lineCount++ == linesPerPage) {
59:            PrintFooter(rect, lineHeight);
60:            lineCount = 4;
61:            Printer()->NewPage();
62:          }
63:          //
64:          // Get the next string and print it using TextOut()
65:          //
66:          String s = Memo->Lines->Strings[i];
67:          Printer()->Canvas->TextOut
68:            (0, lineCount * lineHeight, s);
69:        }
70:        //
71:        // All done.
72:        //
73:        PrintFooter(rect, lineHeight);
74:        Printer()->EndDoc();
75:      }
76: }
```

Listing 13.4. The PrintFooter() function.

```
1: void TScratchPad::PrintFooter(TRect& rect, int lineHeight)
2: {
3:   //
4:   // Build a string to display the page number. We'll use the
5:   // C++ char* method rather than a String object because
6:   // DrawText() will want a char* anyway.
7:   //
8:   char buff[10];
9:   wsprintf(buff, "Page %d", Printer()->PageNumber);
10:   //
11:   // Set up the rectangle where the footer will be drawn.
12:   // Find the bottom of the page and come up a couple
```

```
13:   // lines.
14:   //
15:   rect.Top = Printer()->PageHeight - (lineHeight * 2);
16:   rect.Bottom = rect.Top + lineHeight;
17:   //
18:   // Display the text using DrawText so we can center the
19:   // text with no fuss.
20:   //
21:   DrawText(Printer()->Handle, buff, -1, (RECT*)&rect, DT_CENTER);
22:   //
23:   // Draw a line across the page just above the Page x text.
24:   //
25:   Printer()->Canvas->MoveTo(0, rect.Top - 2);
26:   Printer()->Canvas->LineTo(rect.Right, rect.Top - 2);
27: }
```

This code illustrates how you can print directly through Windows rather than rely on the built-in printing that VCL provides. Although I always opt to do something the easy way when possible, there are times when the easy way isn't flexible enough. In those times it's good to have the knowledge to do the job without trouble.

Printing a Bitmap

Printing a bitmap is simple. All you need to do is create an instance of the TBitmap class, load a bitmap into the bitmap object, and send it to the printer, using the Draw() method of TCanvas. Here's the entire code:

```
Graphics::TBitmap* bitmap = new Graphics::TBitmap;
bitmap->LoadFromFile("c:\\winnt\\winnt.bmp");
Printer()->BeginDoc();
Printer()->Canvas->Draw(20, 20, bitmap);
Printer()->EndDoc();
delete bitmap;
```

When you print a bitmap, be aware that the bitmap might turn out very small, depending on the resolution of your printer. The bitmap may have to be stretched to look right. If you need to stretch the bitmap, use the StretchDraw() method instead of Draw().

Using Cursors

13

The use of cursors is not difficult, but I'll describe it here to give you a basic understanding of how it works. This section deals with cursors that you change at runtime. (To change a cursor at design time, select a new value for the component's Cursor property.) After a look at cursor basics, I will discuss how to load stock cursors and custom cursors.

Cursor Basics

First, you can change the cursor for a particular component or form or for the entire client area of your application. If you want to change the cursor for the entire application, you need to change the `Cursor` property of the `Screen` object. The `Screen` object represents your application's screen. By changing the `Cursor` property of the `Screen` object, you ensure that the cursor is the same, regardless of which component the cursor is over. Let's say, for instance, that you want to change the cursor to the hourglass cursor. If you change the `Cursor` property for the form only, the cursor will be an hourglass when over the form itself but will revert back to the default cursor when over any other components on the form. Changing the `Cursor` for the `Screen` object gives you the same cursor throughout.

Cursor management is the responsibility of the `Screen` object. All the cursors available for your use are contained in the `Cursors` property of the `Screen` object. Note that the name of this property is `Cursors` and is not the same as the `Cursor` property discussed in the previous paragraph. The `Cursors` property is an array that contains a list of available cursors for the application, and the `Cursor` property is the property that is used to display a particular cursor. Although this is confusing at first, you'll catch on quickly. All it takes is a little experience working with cursors.

Windows provides several built-in cursors for use in your applications. In addition to these built-in cursors, VCL adds a few cursors of its own. Together, these cursors are called the *stock cursors*. Each stock cursor has a named constant associated with it. For example, the arrow cursor is named `crArrow`, the hourglass cursor is named `crHourGlass`, and the drag cursor is named `crDrag`. All these cursors are held in the `Cursors` array and occupy positions -17 through 0 in the array; the default cursor is at array index 0 (`crDefault`), no cursor is -1 (`crNone`), the arrow cursor is -2 (`crArrow`), and so on. The online help for the `Cursors` property lists all the cursors and their constant names, so check C++Builder help for a complete list of the available cursors.

To use one of the cursors in the `Cursors` array, assign the name of the cursor you want to use to the `Cursor` property of the `Screen` object:

```
Screen->Cursor = crHourGlass;
```

At this point the VCL magic kicks in, and the correct cursor is loaded and displayed. The use of the `Cursors` property is transparent to you because you don't directly access the `Cursors` property when you use a cursor. Instead, you make an assignment to the `Cursor` property, and VCL takes care of looking up the proper cursor in the `Cursors` array and displaying it. The `Cursor` property of a component and the `Cursors` property of the `Screen` object work together to display different cursors in your application.

You will change cursors in your applications for any number of reasons— to display the wait cursor (the hourglass), to have a drawing program that uses special cursors, or to implement the help cursor in your application.

Now let's look at the two cursor types you can use in your applications.

Loading and Using Stock Cursors

Windows provides several built-in cursors for use in your applications. In addition to those, VCL adds a few more cursors from which you can choose. You can use these stock cursors anytime you like.

One of the most obvious times to change the cursor is when you have a lengthy process your application needs to perform. It is considered bad practice to tie up the program and give the user no indication that the program is busy doing something. Windows provides the hourglass cursor (Windows calls it the wait cursor) for exactly this purpose. Let's say, for instance, that you have a processing loop in your application that might take a long time. You would do something like this:

```
//
// save the old cursor
//
TCursor oldCursor = Cursor;
//
// change the cursor to the hourglass cursor
//
Screen->Cursor = crHourGlass;
//
// start the process
//
DoSomeReallyLongProcess();
//
// restore the oringinal cursor
//
Screen->Cursor = oldCursor;
```

Because you don't always know which cursor your application is using at any given time, it is a good idea to save the current cursor before changing the Cursor property. After you have finished with a particular cursor, you can restore the old cursor.

NOTE

> Sometimes you will change the Cursor property before a lengthy processing loop and nothing seems to happen. The reason is that Windows didn't get a chance to change your cursor before your program entered the loop. When in the loop, your application can't process any messages—including the message to change the cursor. The fix is to pump the Windows message loop for waiting messages while you are in your loop:
>
> ```
> Application->ProcessMessages();
> ```
>
> Now your application will enable messages to flow, and the cursor will change when your loop starts.

13

You can, of course, change the cursor for an individual component. For instance, a drawing program might change the client area cursor, depending on the current drawing tool. You don't want to change the cursor for the Screen object in that case because you want the arrow cursor to appear when the cursor is moved over the toolbar, status bar, or any other components that might be on the form. In that case you set the cursor only for the component that represents the client window of your application:

```
PaintBox->Cursor = crCross;
```

Now the cursor is changed for just this one component, and all other components use their own predefined cursor.

Loading and Using Custom Cursors

Loading custom cursors requires a little more work. As I mentioned earlier, the Cursors property of the TScreen class contains the list of cursors available to your application. To use a custom cursor requires several steps:

1. Create a cursor in the Image Editor or other resource editor.
2. Create an .rc file that references the cursor and add it to your project. (An alternative to this is to compile the resource and add the resulting .res file to your project.)
3. Load the cursor into the Cursors array, using the LoadCursor() function.
4. Implement the cursor by assigning the index number to the Cursor property for the form, the Cursor property for the Screen object, or the Cursor property for any other component.

The first two steps were covered on Day 12, "C++Builder Tools and Options," when I talked about the Image Editor and also about projects. After you have the cursor bound to the .exe, you can load it with the LoadCursor() function. Loading a cursor into the Cursors array is easy:

```
Screen->Cursors[1] = LoadCursor(HInstance, "MYCURSOR");
```

This code assumes that you have a cursor with a name of MYCURSOR and that you are assigning the cursor to position 1 in the cursors list (remember, positions -17 through 0 are used for the stock cursors). Loading the cursor has to be done only once, so you will probably do it in your main form's OnCreate event handler.

NOTE

All cursors are loaded into the Screen object's Cursors property, regardless of whether you use the cursor with the Screen object, with a form, or with a component. There is only one Cursors array, and it belongs to the Screen object.

To use the cursor, then, just assign it to the Cursor property of the Screen object or of any component:

```
PaintBox->Cursor = 1;
```

If you have several cursors, you might want to create global variables or #defines for each cursor so that you have meaningful names to use instead of integer values that are easy to mix up. Using that method, the preceding code would look like this:

```
#define myCursor 1
Screen->Cursors[myCursor] = LoadCursor(HInstance, "MYCURSOR");
// later on...
PaintBox->Cursor = myCursor;
```

As you can see, loading and implementing custom cursors isn't difficult when you know how to do it.

Summary

Today you learned about some features that make up a top-quality Windows application and how to implement them in your own programs. I should warn you that there does exist a temptation to overdo it with things such as control bars, status bars, and cursors. Implement whatever decorations your application needs, but don't overuse them. You also learned about printing today. In some cases printing support is built into a particular component, and in those cases printing is incredibly easy. In other cases you have to roll up your sleeves and go to work with the TPrinter class. Even at those times, though, printing is nothing to fear.

Workshop

The Workshop contains quiz questions to help you solidify your understanding of the material covered and exercises to provide you with experience in using what you have learned. Answers to the quiz questions are found in Appendix A, "Answers to Quiz Questions."

Q&A

Q Can I disable all the components on my toolbar at one time?

A Yes. Set the toolbar's Enabled property to false.

Q I want dockable toolbars like I see in other applications. Can I do that with C++Builder?

A You can do anything you want with C++Builder; it's just a matter of how much work is involved. C++Builder has no built-in support for dockable toolbars, so you have to create your own from scratch. You might want to investigate the various online sources to see what third-party or shareware dockable toolbar components are out there.

13

Q How do I put a bitmap on my status bar?

A Create a multipanel status bar. Change the style of the panel that will contain the bitmap to psOwnerDraw. Then, in your OnDrawPanel event handler, use the Draw() method of TCanvas to draw your bitmap on the panel.

Q I had a simple status bar that I later converted to a complex status bar. Now my hints don't show up any more. What's wrong?

A When you change to the complex status bar, you must change the code that displays hint text. Rather than use

```
StatusBar->SimpleText = Application->Hint;
```

you should use

```
StatusBar->Panels->Items[0]->Text = Application->Hint;
```

This ensures that the text is sent to the first panel of the status bar.

Q Why should I bother with command enabling for my menu items and toolbar buttons?

A Because users expect a consistent interface. When certain choices are not available (whether on menus or toolbars), they should be grayed out. This gives the user a visual cue that these commands are sometimes available but not currently applicable.

Q I just want basic output of a large, multiline edit control in my application. What's the easiest way?

A The easiest way is to use a RichEdit component and use its Print() method to print the contents of the component.

Q I see that there is a Handle property for the Printer object and also a Handle property for the Canvas property of the Printer object. What's the difference?

A In this case there is no difference. If you are calling a Windows API function that requires the printer device context handle, you can use either Printer()->Handle or Printer()->Canvas->Handle.

Q When I change the cursor for my main form, the cursor is correct when it's over the form but reverts back to the arrow cursor when it's over any of my buttons. Why?

A You need to change the cursor not only for the Screen object but also for the form. Changing the cursor for the Screen object ensures that the new cursor will be used whenever the cursor is over any part of your application.

Quiz

1. How do you attach an event handler to a toolbar button's OnClick event?
2. Can you put controls other than buttons on toolbars?

3. What component enables you to move and size multiple toolbars?

4. What does the SimplePanel property of the StatusBar component do?

5. How do you change the status bar text manually?

6. How do you enable and disable menu items and buttons?

7. How do you access the printer in a C++Builder application?

8. What method do you call to begin printing with the TPrinter class?

9. What method of TPrinter do you call when you want to start a new page when printing?

10. How do you change the cursor for a component at runtime?

Exercises

1. Write a program from scratch. Add a toolbar and place five buttons on it. Now add a status bar. Enable hints so that the toolbar buttons have both ToolTips and hint text in the status bar.

2. Change the status bar for the ScratchPad program and add a second panel. In this panel, display either Saved or Modified, based on the value of Memo->Modified.

3. Add Version Info to the ScratchPad program.

4. Change the About box of the ScratchPad program to read Version 1.05. Also, change the Title property in the Project Options dialog box and the Caption of the main form. After all, you added features, so you must let the users know!

5. Create a custom cursor with the Image Editor. Write a program that displays the cursor when a button on the main form is pressed.

6. **Extra Credit:** Modify the ScratchPad program from Exercise 3 to display different bitmaps on the status bar, depending on whether the current file is saved. (Hint: Look at the led1on.bmp and led1off.bmp bitmaps in the Borland Shared Files\Images\Buttons directory.)

7. **Extra Credit:** Modify the ScratchPad program so that the user can specify a top margin, bottom margin, right margin, and left margin for printed output.

13

Day 14

Advanced Programming

Today you will get into some of the more advanced aspects of Windows programming with C++Builder. Specifically, we will cover

- [ ] Implementing context-sensitive help
- [ ] Exception handling
- [ ] Using the Windows Registry
- [ ] Specialized message handling

We've got a lot to do today, so let's get right to it.

Implementing Context-Sensitive Help

Not too long ago you might have been able to get by with not providing context-sensitive help in your applications. In fact, for small applications you might have been able to get by without providing a help file at all. I wouldn't recommend that in today's market, though. Users are increasingly demanding when it comes to features. A help file is no longer an option but a required component of a full-featured application.

Context-sensitive help means that when the user presses the F1 key, a particular page of the application's help file is displayed, depending on the program's current context. Take the C++Builder IDE, for example. Let's say you have the Project Options dialog box open and have the Application page displayed. When you press F1 (or press the Help button on the dialog box), WinHelp will run and display the help topic for the Application page of the Project Options dialog box. Likewise, if you press F1 when the Object Repository Options dialog box is on the screen, you will get help for that particular dialog box. Context-sensitive help works with menu items as well. If you highlight a menu item and press F1, you will be taken to the help file page regarding that menu item.

To implement context-sensitive help in your application, you must perform the following steps:

1. Create a help file for your application. The help file should contain context identifiers.
2. Assign the name of your help file to the `HelpFile` property of the `Application` object.
3. Set the `HelpContext` property of any forms or components for which context-sensitive help is supported. The `HelpContext` property is set to the context identifier in the help file corresponding to that component.
4. Create menu items for the Help menu so your users can invoke help from the menu.

Let's examine these steps one at a time.

Writing the Help File

Writing help files is a chore. I don't exactly hate it, mind you, but it's not one of the things I look forward to. If you are fortunate, you have a documentation department that writes the help files for you.

NOTE

> Even some limited-budget programmers have documentation departments that write help files for them. Frequently they refer to the doc writers as "Honey" or "Dear." For instance, a programmer might say to her documentation writer, "Honey, when you get done with that help page, would you put the kids to bed?"

Regardless of who writes the help file, there must be some coordination between the help-file writer and the programmer. The context identifiers in the help file must match those specified for the components in the program itself. Although this is not exactly a difficult task, coordination is still required so that everyone is on the same page (pun intended).

A Windows help file might be constructed from several individual files. The source for a Windows help file is called the *topic file*. The topic file is a rich text format file (.RTF) with lots of special codes that the help compiler understands. If your help file includes graphics, you might have one or more *graphics files*. Graphics files used in creating a help file include bitmap (.BMP), Windows metafile (.WMF), and some other specialized graphics files. Finally, you have the help *project file* (.HPJ). The project file contains a description of how the help compiler should go about merging the topic file, the graphics files, and any other specialized files the target help file needs. It also includes a [MAP] section that maps context ID numbers to particular help topics. After the project file is created, it is compiled with a help compiler such as the Microsoft Help Workshop (you can find it in the \CBuilder\Help\Tools directory). The Help Workshop takes the help project file and compiles it to produce the final help file (.HLP).

Although you can write help files with any word processor that supports .RTF files, I would strongly recommend buying a help-authoring program. A good help-authoring package can take much of the frustration out of writing help files. Commercial help-authoring tools include ForeHelp by Fore Front, Inc. (http://www.ff.com), and RoboHelp by Blue Sky Software (http://www.blue-sky.com). I have used ForeHelp and I like the way it works. There are also some good shareware help-authoring tools out there. One such shareware help-authoring program is HelpScribble. You can check out HelpScribble at http://www.tornado.be/~johnfg/helpscr.html.

Context Identifiers and the HelpContext Property

Regardless of what method you use to create the help file, you need to have a context number associated with each major topic in the help file. The *context number* is used by the Windows help system, WinHelp32.exe, to display a particular page in the help file. For example, let's say you have an Options dialog box in your application. When the user presses F1 with the Options dialog box open, your program will pass the context ID for that dialog box to WinHelp. WinHelp will run and display the page in the help file that explains the application's Options dialog box. You don't need a context ID for every page in the help file, but you should have a help context ID for your main topic pages, dialog boxes, and other major components of your application.

Most components (forms, menu items, and controls) have a property called HelpContext. This property contains the context ID that will be passed to WinHelp if the user presses the F1 key when that component has focus. By default, the HelpContext property is set to 0. If the HelpContext property is 0 for a component, the component will inherit the HelpContext

14

value of its parent window. This allows you to set the `HelpContext` for a form and then, no matter which component on the form has input focus, the help context for the form will be used when F1 is pressed.

NOTE

You may have noticed that the `SpeedButton` component does not have a `HelpContext` property. Because a `SpeedButton` is a non-windowed control, it can never gain input focus. Therefore, the F1 key cannot be used with speed buttons.

At a minimum, you should provide context-sensitive help for each form in your application (a form being a dialog box or secondary window). Ultimately, it is up to you to decide which items to provide context-sensitive help for. If you are going to err, you should probably err on the side of providing too much context-sensitive help (if there is such a thing) rather than not enough.

Implementing Context-Sensitive Help

Implementing context-sensitive help in your C++Builder applications is relatively easy. As I said earlier, the real work in adding context-sensitive help to your C++Builder applications is in the writing of the help file. The rest is easy in comparison.

Setting the Help File

Regardless of how you implement context-sensitive help, you first have to tell Windows the name of the help file for your application. To do that, you assign the help file name to the `HelpFile` property of the `Application` class. You can do this in one of two ways. The easiesr way is at design time via the Project Options dialog box. On Day 10, "More on Projects," we looked at the project options. I discussed the fact that the Application page of the Project Options dialog box has a field called Help File that is used to specify the name of the help file for the application. Simply type the name of your help file in this field. VCL will assign the help file name to the `HelpFile` property, and then the application will use that filename each time help is requested.

You can also set the name of the help file at runtime. This might be necessary if you allow your users to place the help file in a directory of their own choosing. You could store the location of the help file in the Windows Registry (the Registry is discussed later, in the section titled "Using the Registry") and then assign the help file's path and filename to the `Application` object's `HelpFile` property. For instance, part of your `OnCreate` event handler might look like this:

```
String filename = GetHelpFileName(); // user-defined function
Application->HelpFile = filename;
```

Although it's not very common, you can change the HelpFile property at different points in your program if you want. You might do this to switch between different help files, for instance. After you have the help file name set up, you can go on to the actual implementation of the help system.

Adding F1 Key Support

To add F1 support for forms and components, all you have to do is set the HelpContext property to the matching context ID in the help file and VCL takes it from there. Be sure that you have assigned a help file name to the HelpFile property of the Application class and that the help file contains valid context identifiers. VCL will take it from there.

Adding Menu Support for the Help File

In addition to F1 key support, most applications have one or two menu items under the Help menu (where else?) that can be used to start WinHelp. There will usually be a menu item called Contents. Choosing this item will display the contents page for the help file. In addition to a Contents menu item, some applications have a Help menu item called Help Topics. Choosing this menu item displays the index for the help file (the index is created as part of the help file creation process).

To implement these and other help items, you will have to do some programming. (It's only one line of code in each case.) VCL provides a method called HelpCommand() that can be used to display WinHelp in one of several modes. If you were to implement the Help|Contents menu item, the code would look like this:

```
void __fastcall TMainForm::HelpContentsClick(TObject *Sender)
{
  Application->HelpCommand(HELP_FINDER, 0);
}
```

The HelpCommand() method calls WinHelp with the specified command. (See the Windows API help under WinHelp() for a complete list of available commands.) In this case, WinHelp is invoked with a command of HELP_FINDER. This command tells WinHelp to display the Contents page, as shown in Figure 14.1. The final parameter of the HelpCommand() method is used to pass additional data to WinHelp. This parameter is not used with the HELP_FINDER command, so it is set to 0.

NOTE

In order for WinHelp to show the Contents page, you must have a contents file for your help file. The contents file has an extension of .CNT and is a text file that describes how the Contents page should be displayed. You can read more about the contents file in the Microsoft Help Workshop help. You can find the Help Workshop and its help file in the \CBuilder\Help\Tools directory.

14

Figure 14.1.

The Scratch Pad help
Contents page.

NOTE

> A good index for your help file is invaluable. The quality of the help file—and the quality of the help file's index—are directly proportional to the amount of technical support you will have to provide. Don't overlook this fact.

Context-Sensitive Help on Demand

Most of the time, the two help implementations I just told you about are all you need for your application. At other times, however, you need to call WinHelp directly and with a specific context ID. For these times, VCL provides the `HelpContext()` method. This method takes, as its single parameter, the context ID of the page you want to see when WinHelp runs. For example, let's say you had a help page with a context ID of 99. To run WinHelp and display that specific page, you would do this:

```
Application->HelpContext(99);
```

By supplying a specific context ID, you can cause WinHelp to display any page of your help file on demand. This is what VCL does for you when you specify the `HelpContext` property for a particular component.

Using Help File Headers

Most of the time, setting the `HelpContext` properties for the forms or components for which you want to implement context-sensitive help is all you need to do. If, however, you need to call specific help pages in your application, you might consider defining symbols for your help identifiers. Using named symbols is much easier than trying to remember an integer value for a particular help context ID.

14

In the last section, I talked about using the `HelpContext()` method to call WinHelp with a particular context ID. I used the example of a help context ID of `99`. Rather than using the numerical value of the context identifier, you could use a constant like this:

```
Application->HelpContext(IDH_FILEOPEN);
```

Obviously, the string is easier to remember than its integer value equivalent. The context-sensitive help symbols can all be kept in a separate header file that is included in your application where needed (using the `#include` directive). Listing 14.1 shows a typical header containing context-sensitive help identifiers.

Listing 14.1. HELP.H.

```
 1: #define IDH_FILENEW         1
 2: #define IDH_FILEOPEN        2
 3: #define IDH_FILESAVE        3
 4: #define IDH_FILESAVEAS      4
 5: #define IDH_FILEPRINT       5
 6: #define IDH_FILEPRINTSETUP  6
 7: #define IDH_FILEEXIT        7
 8: #define IDH_EDITUNDO        8
 9: #define IDH_EDITCOPY        9
10: #define IDH_EDITCUT         10
11: #define IDH_EDITPASTE       11
12: #define IDH_EDITSELECTALL   12
13: #define IDH_EDITWORDWRAP    13
14: #define IDH_HELPABOUT       14
```

At the top of your source file, you can add a line that includes the help file header:

```
#include "help.h"
```

Now you can use the name of the context ID when needed rather than the actual integer value.

How the help file header is created depends on the tools you are using to write your help files. Most help-authoring software includes an option to generate a header of some description that contains the named constants. The specific implementation depends on whether the help file is being written by you or by a co-worker and what help-authoring software you are using. If you are not using help-authoring software, you can simply type the symbols in by hand.

Putting It to Work

It's time to put your newly acquired knowledge into practice. In this section, we'll add context-sensitive help to the `ScratchPad` program. (You knew we'd come back to old `ScratchPad`, didn't you?)

14

The Web site accompanying the book, `http://www.mcp.com/info`, contains a simple help file for the `ScratchPad` program. Copy the help file, `Scratch.hlp`, from the Web site to your working directory so C++Builder can find it when you build the `ScratchPad` application.

Context-sensitive help should take about 10 minutes to implement. Here we go:

1. Load the `ScratchPad` project. Go to the Application page of the Project Options dialog box and type `Scratch.hlp` in the Help File field. Click OK to close the dialog box. (Be sure you have moved the `Scratch.hlp` file into the project's directory.)

2. Display the `ScratchPad` main form in the Form Designer. Double-click the MainMenu icon to invoke the Menu Designer.

3. In the Menu Designer, select the File | New menu item from the `MainMenu` component (not the C++Builder main menu, of course). Locate the `HelpContext` property in the Object Inspector and change its value to `1`.

4. Repeat with the remaining menu items. Use the values from Listing 14.1 to set the `HelpContext` properties of each menu item.

5. Choose Help | Contents. Set its `Enabled` property to `true`. Close the Menu Designer.

6. In the Form Designer, choose Help | Contents from the Scratch Pad main menu. The Code Editor displays the `HelpContentsClick()` function. Type this line at the cursor:

   ```
   Application->HelpCommand(HELP_FINDER, 0);
   ```

7. Change the `HelpContext` property of the main form to `1000` (the context ID of the contents page).

Run the program and experiment with it. If you press F1 when the cursor is in the Memo window, the Contents page of the help file will be displayed. If you highlight a menu item and press F1, help for that menu item will be displayed. Also, check out the Contents item on the main menu to see if it works as expected.

If you compile and run the `ScratchPad` program on the Web site for Day 14, you will see that it has a feature not discussed here. The program has a help mode that can be used to get help on a specific speedbar button or menu item. To start the help mode press the Help button on the speedbar. The cursor changes to the help cursor. Now select any menu item or speedbar button. The help topic for the item selected will be displayed. The help mode turns off automatically after you choose an item. Browse the source code to see how the help mode is implemented. This feature also makes use of special message handling, as discussed later in the chapter.

Context-sensitive help is no longer a luxury. Whether your users are members of the general public or your co-workers, they are still your users. They demand certain features, and context-sensitive help is one of them. As easy as context-sensitive help is to implement in a C++Builder application, there is no reason for it to be missing from your applications.

Exception Handling

Even in the most well-designed program, things that are beyond the control of the program can go wrong. Users make mistakes. For instance, a user might input a bad value into a data field, or he could open a file of the wrong type for your application. Whatever the scenario, you should be prepared to handle these types of errors wherever and whenever possible. You can't anticipate your users' every move, but you can anticipate some of the more common blunders and handle them gracefully.

Exception handling is essentially a sophisticated form of error checking. While any program can implement and use them, exceptions are of primary benefit to users of components and other C++ classes. For instance, if you are using a component and something nasty happens within the component, you need to know about it. A well-written component will throw an exception when something goes wrong. You can catch that exception and handle it however you want—maybe by terminating the program or by allowing your user to correct the problem and try again.

NOTE

> There are two types of exception handling. First, there is true C++ exception handling, which is what we are discussing here. In addition, 32-bit Windows implements what it calls *structured* exceptions. These two types of exception handling are not exactly the same thing. I won't go into the differences, but I just want to point out that you might encounter two different discussions on exception handling as you get further into Windows programming. You are not likely to use structured exceptions because C++ has its own exception handling mechanism.

You might not write a lot of exception handling into your day-to-day code. Your primary use of exceptions will be in handling exceptions that VCL throws when things go wrong within a component. If you write components, you will almost certainly use exception handling more frequently.

14

NOTE

> The use of exceptions in your programs should be reserved for extreme error conditions. You should throw an exception if the error condition is serious enough to make continued use of the program difficult. Most runtime errors can be handled with parameter checking, validation of user input, and other more traditional error-checking techniques.

A full discussion of exception handling could easily take an entire chapter, so I will limit this discussion to how you can handle exceptions thrown by VCL components.

Exception-Handling Keywords: `try`, `catch`, **and** `throw`

Exception-handling syntax is not terribly complicated. The three exception-handling keywords are `try`, `catch`, and `throw`. The `try` and `catch` keywords are used when handling exceptions, and the `throw` keyword is used to initiate (throw) an exception. Let's look at these in more detail.

The try and catch keywords:

```
try {
    TryStatements
}
catch (TypeToCatch)
{
    CatchStatements
}
```

The `try` keyword marks the beginning of the try block. The statements in `TryStatements` are executed. If any exceptions of type `TypeToCatch` are thrown during the execution of `TryStatements`, `CatchStatements` are executed. If no exception is thrown, `CatchStatements` are ignored and program execution proceeds to the statement following the `catch` block. `TypeToCatch` can be one of the integral data types (`int`, `char`, `long`, and so on), an instance of a class, or an ellipsis (...). If `TypeToCatch` is an ellipsis, then all exceptions are caught regardless of the type of the exception thrown.

Before I attempt to explain the `try` and `catch` keywords, let's look at a simple example. Listing 14.2 contains a short code snippet that illustrates exception handling. This code attempts to load a picture file (`.bmp`, `.wmf`, or `.ico`). If the file chosen by the user is not a picture file, VCL will throw an exception. If that happens, we catch the exception and display a message box telling the user that the file was not a picture file.

Listing 14.2. An exception-handling example.

```
 1: try {
 2:    TImage* image = new TImage(0);
 3:    image->Picture->LoadFromFile(OpenDialog->FileName);
 4:    TChild* child = new TChild(this);
 5:    child->Parent = this;
 6:    child->Image->Picture = image->Picture;
 7:    child->ClientWidth = child->Image->Picture->Width;
 8:    child->ClientHeight = child->Image->Picture->Height;
 9: }
10: catch (...)
11: {
12:    Application->MessageBox(
13:      "This file is not a Windows image file.",
14:      "Picture Viewer Error", MB_ICONHAND | MB_OK);
15: }
```

In this code you see a try block and a catch block. The try block is used to define the code for which an exception might be thrown. The try statement tells the compiler, "Try this and see if it works." If the code works, the catch block is ignored and program execution continues. If any of the statements inside the try block throws an exception, the code within the catch block will be executed. The catch block must immediately follow the try block with no other code in between.

It is important to realize that as soon as an exception is thrown, program execution jumps immediately to the catch block. In this example, the code on line 3 is likely to be the line that throws an exception. If an exception is thrown on line 3, program execution will jump to line 12. In that case, lines 4–8 will never be executed.

Throwing Exceptions

As you can see, the catch statement catches an exception that was thrown somewhere in the program. Most of the time this will mean an exception thrown in VCL somewhere.

An exception is thrown by using the throw keyword. The code that throws the exception will throw an exception of a particular type. For example, a typical throw statement might look like this:

```
if (badParameter) throw("A bad parameter was passed");
```

The throw statement throws an object of the type passed as its parameter. In this case, a char* is thrown, but any type of object can be thrown. Let's say you had an error code 111 for a particular type of error. In that case, you could write the throw statement like this:

```
if (badParameter) throw(111);
```

14

Here an integer is being thrown. The compiler makes a copy of the object being thrown and passes it on to the `catch` statement immediately following the `try` block (we'll get back to that in a moment).

Most class libraries throw an instance of an exception-handling class. VCL defines several exception-handling classes for exactly this purpose. There are several reasons to throw an instance of a class. First of all, the class can contain data members and/or functions that describe everything you need to know to deal with the error. A basic exception-handling class might have data members called `Error` and `Msg` that would contain the error number and a text string describing the error. Then you could check the error number in order to properly handle the error or display the message string (or both).

More on `catch`

As I said, for starters your involvement with exceptions will likely be in catching VCL exceptions. If something goes wrong in a VCL component, VCL is going to throw an exception. If you do not handle the exception, VCL will handle it in the default manner. Usually this means that a message box will be displayed that describes the error that occurred. By catching these exceptions in your code, you can decide how they should be handled rather than accepting the default behavior.

Take a look at Listing 14.2 again. On line 10, you will see this:

```
catch (...)
```

This tells the compiler that you want to catch all exceptions of any type. If any type of exception is thrown in the `try` block, the `catch` block will be executed. This is convenient if you don't know what type of exception a particular piece of code will throw or if you want to catch any and all exceptions regardless of the type. In the real world, though, you will probably need to be more specific in what exceptions you catch.

Let's go back to Listing 14.2 again. The code on line 3 might throw an exception if the file the user is trying to open is not a graphics file. If that happens, VCL will throw an `EInvalidGraphic` exception. More specifically, VCL will throw an exception and will throw an instance of the `EInvalidGraphic` class. You can catch only that type of exception and let all others be handled in the default manner:

```
catch (EInvalidGraphic&)
{
  Application->MessageBox(
    "This file is not a Windows image file.",
    "Picture Viewer Error", MB_ICONHAND | MB_OK);
}
```

Notice that this is catching a reference to an `EInvalidGraphic` class. This is the preferred method of catching exceptions. Catching a class passed by reference is equivalent to passing a class by reference, as I discussed back on Day 4, "C++ Classes and Object-Oriented

14

Programming." Now any exceptions of this type will be caught by the catch block and all other exception types will be handled in the default manner.

NOTE

> VCL will handle many types of exceptions automatically, but cannot account for every possibility. An exception that is not handled is called an *unhandled exception*. If an unhandled exception occurs, Windows will generate an error message and your application will be terminated. Try to anticipate what exceptions might occur in your application and do your best to handle them.

You can have multiple catch blocks following a try statement. For example, let's say that you have written code that calls some VCL methods and also calls some functions in your program that might throw an exception. If a VCL EInvalidGraphic exception occurs, you want to handle it. In addition, your own code may throw an exception of type MyOwnException (a class you have written for handling exceptions). In that case, you would write the code like this:

```
try {
  OneOfMyFunctions();
  Form->Image->Picture->LoadFromFile(filename);
  AnotherOfMyFunctions();
}
catch (EInvalidGraphic&) {
  // do some stuff
}
catch (MyOwnException&) {
  // do some stuff
}
```

In this case, you are preparing to catch either a VCL exception or an exception of your own type. You want to handle each type of exception differently so you can catch each type of exception independently.

You can have as many catch statements as you want following a try statement. You must, however, have at least one catch statement, and it must immediately follow the try block. If you have multiple catch statements, they must follow each other, and there can be no other code between the catch statements. The compiler will issue a compiler error if you violate the try/catch syntax rules.

14

NOTE

This version of C++Builder adds the __finally keyword. __finally defines a section of code that will be called in all cases. In other words, the code in the __finally section will be called if an exception is thrown and will be called if no exception is thrown. If you use a __finally block, then you cannot use catch.

The primary reason to use __finally is to ensure that all dynamically created objects are properly deleted in the event an exception is thrown. For example:

```
TImage* image;
try
{
  image = new TImage(0);
  image->Picture->LoadFromFile(OpenDialog->FileName);
  // more code
}
__finally
{
  delete image;
}
```

Here the object called image will always be deleted properly, regardless of whether or not an exception is thrown. __finally is particularly useful when converting Delphi code to C++Builder.

Note that in the preceding examples we are catching a reference to a VCL exception class, but we aren't actually doing anything with the class instance passed to the catch block. In this case, we don't really care what information the EInvalidGraphic class contains because it is enough to simply know that the exception occurred. You should check the online help for the specific type of VCL exception-handling class you are interested in for more information about what properties and methods are available for that class.

TIP

The VCL exception classes all have a Message property that contains a textual description of the exception that occurred. You can use this property to display a message to the user:

```
catch (EInvalidGraphic& info)
{
  // do some necessary stuff since
  // an error occurred, and then...
  Application->MessageBox(
   info.Message.c_str(),
   "My Program - Error", MB_ICONHAND | MB_OK);
}
```

14

> Sometimes the VCL messages might not be descriptive enough for your liking. In those cases, you can create your own error message, but often the Message property is sufficient.

Catching Unhandled Exceptions at the Application Level

Your application can also handle exceptions at the application level. TApplication has an event called OnException that will occur any time an unhandled exception is thrown in your application. By responding to this event, you can catch any exceptions thrown by your applications.

NOTE

> This event occurs when an unhandled exception is thrown. Any exceptions you catch with try and catch are handled; therefore, the OnException event will not occur for those exceptions.

You hook the OnException event just like you do when hooking the OnHint or OnIdle events, as we did earlier:

1. Add a function declaration to the main form's header:

   ```
   void __fastcall OnException(TObject *Sender, Exception *E);
   ```

2. Add the function implementation to the main form's source unit:

   ```
   void __fastcall
   TMainForm::OnException(TObject *Sender, Exception *E)
   {
      // do whatever necessary to handle the exception here
   }
   ```

3. Assign your OnException() function to the OnException event of the Application object:

   ```
   Application->OnException = OnException;
   ```

Now your OnException function will be called when an unhandled exception occurs.

WARNING

> If you do not handle an exception properly, you could lock up your program and possibly even crash Windows. It is usually best to let VCL and Windows handle exceptions unless you know exactly how to handle them.

14

The ShowException() function can be used to display a message box that describes the error that occurred. This function is usually called by the default OnException handler, but you can use it in your applications as well. One of the parameters of the OnException event handler is a pointer to an Exception object (Exception is VCL's base exception-handling class). To display the error message box, pass the Exception object to the ShowException() function:

```
void __fastcall
TMainForm::OnException(TObject *Sender, Exception *E)
{
  // do whatever necessary to handle the exception here
  // then display the error message
  //
  Application->ShowException(E);
}
```

Now the error message box will be displayed just as it would if VCL were dealing with the unhandled exception.

As you can see, handling exceptions at the application level is an advanced exception-handling technique and is not something you should attempt unless you know exactly what you're doing.

Debugging and Exception Handling

Simply put, debugging when using exception handling can be a bit of a pain. Each time an exception is thrown, the debugger will pause program execution at the catch block just as if a breakpoint were set on that line. If the catch block is in your code, the execution point will be displayed as it would be if you had stopped at a breakpoint. You can restart the program again by clicking the Run button, or you can step through your code.

> **NOTE**
>
> You might not be able to continue execution of your program after an exception is thrown. Whether you can continue debugging depends on what went wrong in your program.

Sometimes the catch block is in the VCL code. This will be the case for VCL exceptions that you don't handle in your code. In this circumstance, the CPU view will show the execution point.

Another aspect of debugging with exceptions is that the VCL exception message box will be displayed even when you are handling the exception yourself. This can be confusing and somewhat annoying if you haven't encountered it before. To prevent the VCL message box from being displayed and the debugger from breaking on exceptions, go to the Debugger page of the Environment Options dialog box, click Delphi Exceptions in the Exception list box, and then select the User Program radio button in the Handled By field. Do the same for C++ Exceptions. With these exceptions set to User Program, the debugger will not pause program execution when a VCL exception is thrown.

As with many other aspects of C++Builder and VCL, learning exception handling takes some time. Remember to use exception handling where necessary, but use traditional error-handling techniques for the minor errors.

The Web site that accompanies the book, `http://www.mcp.com/info`, contains a program called `EHTest`. This program demonstrates throwing and catching several kinds of exceptions. For this program to function properly, you will want to be sure that VCL and C++ exceptions are being handled by the user program, as described earlier. Figure 14.2 shows the `EHTest` program running.

Figure 14.2.

The `EHTest` *program running.*

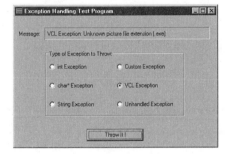

Using the Registry

Once upon a time Windows programs used configuration files (`.INI` files) to store application-specific information. The master configuration file, as you probably know, is called `WIN.INI`. Applications could store system-wide information in `WIN.INI` or application-specific configuration data in a private `.INI` file. This approach has several advantages, but also some disadvantages.

Somewhere along the line someone smarter (presumably) than I decided that the new way to do things would be to use the Registry to store application-specific configuration information. Throughout the land, knaves everywhere bowed to the king and said, "The Registry is good." Whether good or bad, conventional wisdom has it that the use of `.INI` files is out and the use of the Registry is in.

The term *Registry* is short for the Windows Registration Database. The Registry contains a wide variety of information about your Windows configuration. Just about every option and setting in your Windows setup is stored in the Registry. In addition to the system information stored in the Registry, you will find data specific to installed applications. The type of information stored for each application depends entirely on the application but can include things like the last size and position of the window, a list of most recently used documents

14

for the application, the last directory used when opening a file, and on and on. The possibilities are endless.

Windows 95 and NT come with a program called the Registry Editor (REGEDIT.EXE) that can be used to browse the Registry and to make changes to the entries in the Registry. Figure 14.3 shows the Registry Editor as it displays the C++Builder Form Designer options.

Figure 14.3.

The Windows Registry Editor.

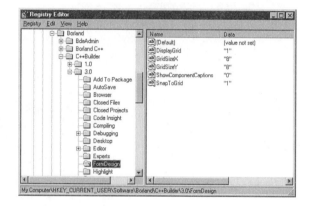

As you can see from Figure 14.3, the Registry is hierarchical. You can approach the Registry exactly as you approach files and directories on a hard drive.

Registry Keys

Each item in the Registry is called a *key*. A key can be likened to a directory on your hard drive. To access a particular key, you first have to open the key. After the key is opened, you can write to or read from it. Take a look at Figure 14.3. The key that is being displayed is

```
\HKEY_CURRENT_USER\Software\Borland\C++Builder\3.0\FormDesign
```

You can't see every branch of the Registry tree, but if you look at the status bar of the Registry Editor you can see the current key displayed. Also notice that the C++Builder\3.0 key has several *subkeys*. You can create as many keys and subkeys as you want for your application.

An individual key can store data in its *data items*. Every key has a data item called (Default). The default value is not normally used because you will almost always create your own data items for a particular key. By looking at Figure 14.3, you can see that the FormDesign key has the following data items:

```
DisplayGrid
GridSizeX
GridSizeY
ShowComponentCaptions
SnapToGrid
```

14

If you've been paying attention, you will recognize that these data items correspond to the Form Designer options on the Preferences page of the Environment Options dialog box. Each data item has an associated value. You can write to the Registry to change the data item or you can read the data item.

Registry Data Types

The Registry has the capability to store several different types of data in the data items. The primary types of data are the binary data, string, and integer data types. The *binary data type* can be used to store any kind of binary data. You could, for instance, store an array of integers in a binary data item. You probably won't directly use the binary data type very often, if ever.

For most of your purposes, you will probably only be concerned with reading and writing strings or integer values. As you can see from Figure 14.3, even numerical data can be stored as strings. It's really up to you to decide how to store data in the Registry.

Up to this point we have discussed what you can do with the Registry but not *how* you do it. Let's look at that next.

The TRegistry Class

The Windows API provides several functions for Registry manipulation. These functions include RegCreateKey(), RegOpenKey(), RegQueryValue(), RegSetValue(), RegDeleteKey(), and many more. Dealing with the Registry at the API level is a bit tedious. I am thankful (and you should be, too) that the folks at Borland thought to provide a VCL class called TRegistry that encapsulates Registry operations. This class provides everything you need to write to and read from the Registry. Before I get into how to use the TRegistry class, let's go over the properties and methods of this class.

TRegistry Properties

TRegistry has just four properties. The CurrentKey property contains the value of the current key. This value is an integer value that identifies the key. When you call a TRegistry method, that method acts on the current key. The CurrentKey property is set for you when you open a key. This property can be read, but reading it is of dubious value.

The RootKey and CurrentPath properties work together to build a text string to the current key. The CurrentPath property contains a text description of the current key's path, excluding the RootKey value. Take this key, for example:

```
\HKEY_CURRENT_USER\Software\Borland\C++Builder\3.0\FormDesign
```

In this case, the root key, \HKEY_CURRENT_USER, comes from the RootKey property, and the value, Software\Borland\C++Builder\3.0\FormDesign, comes from the CurrentPath property.

14

NOTE

> By default, the RootKey property has a value of \HKEY_CURRENT_USER. This is where you should store application-specific data, so it is not normally necessary to change the root key. If you need to change the root key, you can assign a new value to the RootKey property. Note that the root key types are not string values, but are special Windows-defined values. Other root key values include HKEY_CLASSES_ROOT, HKEY_LOCAL_MACHINE, HKEY_USERS, HKEY_CURRENT_CONFIG, and HKEY_DYN_DATA.

The LazyWrite property determines how the application writes the data to the specific key. If LazyWrite is true, control is immediately returned to the application when you close the key. In other words, the writing of the key begins and then your application goes on its way. If LazyWrite is false, control will not return to the application until the writing of the key is completed. By default, LazyWrite is true, and you should leave it set to true unless you have some critical data that needs to be written before your application resumes operation.

TRegistry **Methods**

The TRegistry class has several methods that you will use to read from and write to the Registry. Table 14.1 lists the primary methods and their descriptions.

Table 14.1. Primary methods of TRegistry.

Method	Description
CloseKey	Closes the key and writes the data to the key. You should close a key as soon as you are done with it, but you don't have to specifically call CloseKey() because the TRegistry destructor will close the key for you.
CreateKey	Creates a key but does not open it for use. Use the OpenKey() method rather than CreateKey() if you are going to create the key and begin writing data to it.
DeleteKey	Deletes the specified key. You can specify any key to delete. To delete the current key, pass an empty string to DeleteKey().
GetKeyNames	Returns all of the subkeys for the current key in a TStrings object. You can use this method if you need to iterate all the subkeys for a given key.
GetValueNames	Returns the names of all of the data items for the current key. Use this method if you need to iterate the data items of a given key.
KeyExists	Returns true if the key exists or false if it does not exist. You can use this method to check for the existence of a key before attempting to read the key.

14

Method	Description
LoadKey	Loads a key previously stored on disk. See the C++Builder online help for specific details.
OpenKey	Opens the specified key. If the key does not exist, the value of the CanCreate parameter determines whether the key will be automatically created. Use this method rather than CreateKey() if you are going to create the key and begin writing data to it because OpenKey() creates the key and then opens it whereas CreateKey() just creates the key but does not open it.
ReadBinaryData	Reads binary data from the specified data item.
ReadBool	Reads a Boolean value from the specified data item.
ReadDateTime	Reads a date and time value from the specified data item. The returned value is an instance of the TDateTime class. To retrieve just a date value, use ReadDate(); to retrieve just a time value, use ReadTime().
ReadFloat	Reads a floating-point value from the specified data item.
ReadInteger	Reads an integer value from the specified data item.
ReadString	Reads a string value from the specified data item.
SaveKey	Saves a key to disk so that it can be loaded later with LoadKey(). Generally speaking, you shouldn't store more than 2KB (2048 bytes) of data by using this method.
ValueExists	Returns true if the specified data item exists.
WriteBinaryData	Writes a binary data item to the specified key. Use this item to store arrays or other types of binary data.
WriteBool	Writes a Boolean value to the specified data item. The value is converted to an integer and then stored in the data item.
WriteDateTime	Writes a TDateTime object to the specified data item. To store just a date object, use WriteDate(). To store just a time object, use WriteTime(). The TDateTime object is converted to a binary data type before being stored.
WriteFloat	Writes a floating-point value to the specified data item after converting it to binary data.
WriteInteger	Writes an integer value to the specified data item.
WriteString	Writes a string to the specified data item.

14

Although there are a lot of methods listed here, many of them perform the same operations—they just use different data types. Once you know how to use one of these methods, you pretty much know how to use them all. Notice that several of these methods convert the value passed to binary data and then store it in the Registry.

Using TRegistry

Using TRegistry is really pretty easy. Most of your interaction with the Registry will require just these four steps:

1. Create an instance of the TRegistry class.
2. Create, if necessary, and open a key by using the OpenKey() method.
3. Read or write data, using one or more of the Read() or Write() functions.
4. Close the key by using CloseKey().

NOTE

> Before you can use TRegistry, you must first include the header for the Registry classes. Add the following line to your main form's header beneath the other headers listed there:
>
> #include <vcl\Registry.hpp>
>
> Failure to do this will result in a compiler error stating Typename expected or Undefined symbol.

The following code illustrates these steps:

```
TRegistry& regKey = *new TRegistry();
bool keyGood = regKey.OpenKey(
    "Software\\SAMS\\C++Builder in 21 Days", false);
if (keyGood) {
  int top = regKey.ReadInteger("Top");
  int left = regKey.ReadInteger("Left");
  int width = regKey.ReadInteger("Width");
  int height = regKey.ReadInteger("Height");
  SetBounds(left, top, width, height);
}
delete &regKey;
```

This code opens a key and reads values for the top and left coordinates and the width and height of a form. It then calls the SetBounds() function to move or size the window. I want you to notice a couple of things about the code. First, notice how I use a reference when I create the TRegistry instance. Doing so reduces clutter in the rest of the code (I don't particularly like the indirect member operator (->) so I avoid its use when I can).

Next, notice that the result of the OpenKey() method is assigned to a bool variable. OpenKey() returns true if the key was successfully opened and false if it was not. If the key was successfully opened, the individual data items are read. You should always check the return value of OpenKey() if there is any doubt that opening the key might fail.

NOTE

> VCL will throw exceptions if reading data from or writing data to a key fails. If you attempt to read data from an unopened key, you will get an exception. Either be prepared to handle the exception or be sure to check the return value from OpenKey() before reading or writing data items.

Finally, notice that the key is not specifically closed in the preceding code. If you fail to close the key, the TRegistry destructor will close the key for you. In that case the destructor will be called (and the key closed) as soon as the regKey object is deleted, so an explicit call to CloseKey() is not necessary.

NOTE

> The OpenKey() function automatically prepends the value of the RootKey property (HKEY_CURRENT_USER by default) to the front of the string passed to OpenKey(), so you don't have to include the root when opening a key.

We've got the cart just slightly before the horse here because we are talking about reading from the Registry when we haven't yet written to it. No matter—writing to the Registry is just as simple:

```
TRegistry& regKey = *new TRegistry();
regKey.OpenKey(
    "Software\\SAMS\\C++Builder in 21 Days", true);
regKey.WriteInteger("Top", Top);
regKey.WriteInteger("Left", Left);
regKey.WriteInteger("Width", Width);
regKey.WriteInteger("Height", Height);
delete &regKey;
```

This code simply opens a key and writes the form's Top, Left, Width, and Height properties to the key, by using the WriteInteger() method. Notice that the last parameter of the OpenKey() method is true. This specifies that the key should be created if it does not yet exist. If you use this construct, you should never need to call the CreateKey() method at all.

14

That's basically all there is to reading values from and writing values to the Registry. The other data reading and writing methods are just variations on the previous code snippet. Listings 14.3 and 14.4 contain a program that uses the Registry to store application-specific data. This program stores several items in the Registry: the last size and position of the window; the window state (normal, minimized, or maximized); the last directory, last file, and last filter index used when opening a file with the File Open dialog box; and the date and time the program was last run. To clear out the Registry key created by the RegTest program, you can click the Delete Key button on the main form (see Figure 14.4).

This program is also on the Web site that accompanies the book. Listings 14.3 and 14.4 show the Registry code so you can use it for reference. To actually run the program, you will also need the form file, which is not listed here. Load the complete project from the Web site to build the project.

Listing 14.3. RegMain.h.

```
 1: //-----------------------------------------------------------
 2: #ifndef RegMainH
 3: #define RegMainH
 4: //-----------------------------------------------------------
 5: #include <vcl\Classes.hpp>
 6: #include <vcl\Controls.hpp>
 7: #include <vcl\StdCtrls.hpp>
 8: #include <vcl\Forms.hpp>
 9: #include <vcl\Menus.hpp>
10: #include <vcl\Dialogs.hpp>
11: #include <vcl\Registry.hpp>
12: #include <vcl\ExtCtrls.hpp>
13: //-----------------------------------------------------------
14: class TMainForm : public TForm
15: {
16: __published:    // IDE-managed Components
17:     TMainMenu *MainMenu;
18:     TMenuItem *File1;
19:     TMenuItem *FileExit;
20:     TMenuItem *FileOpen;
21:     TOpenDialog *OpenDialog;
22:     TPanel *Panel1;
23:     TLabel *Label1;
24:     TButton *DeleteKey;
25:     TPanel *Panel2;
26:     TLabel *Label2;
27:     TLabel *Label3;
28:     TLabel *TimeLabel;
29:     TLabel *DateLabel;
30:     TLabel *Label4;
31:     void __fastcall FileOpenClick(TObject *Sender);
32:     void __fastcall FormCreate(TObject *Sender);
33:
34:     void __fastcall FormClose
35:         (TObject *Sender, TCloseAction &Action);
```

14

```
36:     void __fastcall FileExitClick(TObject *Sender);
37:     void __fastcall DeleteKeyClick(TObject *Sender);
38: private:            // User declarations
39:     void ParseFileName(String& path, String& fname);
40:     bool keyDeleted;
41: public:             // User declarations
42:     virtual __fastcall TMainForm(TComponent* Owner);
43: };
44: //-----------------------------------------------------------
45: extern PACKAGE TMainForm *MainForm;
46: //-----------------------------------------------------------
47: #endif
```

Listing 14.4. RegMain.cpp.

```
 1: //-----------------------------------------------------------
 2: #include <vcl\vcl.h>
 3: #pragma hdrstop
 4: #include "RegMain.h"
 5: //-----------------------------------------------------------
 6: #pragma package(smart_init)
 7: #pragma resource "*.dfm"
 8: TMainForm *MainForm;
 9: //-----------------------------------------------------------
10: __fastcall TMainForm::TMainForm(TComponent* Owner)
11:     : TForm(Owner)
12: {
13:     //
14:     // Initialize the keyDeleted variable to false. This
15:     // variable is used if the user deletes the key from
16:     // the program. See the MainFormClose() function.
17:     //
18:     keyDeleted = false;
19: }
20: //-----------------------------------------------------------
21: void __fastcall TMainForm::FormCreate(TObject *Sender)
22: {
23:     //
24:     // Create a TRegistry object to access the registry.
25:     //
26:     TRegistry& regKey = *new TRegistry();
27:     //
28:     // Open the key.
29:     //
30:     bool keyGood = regKey.OpenKey(
31:       "Software\\SAMS\\C++Builder in 21 Days", false);
32:     //
33:     // See if the key is open. If not, then this is the first
34:     // time the program has been run so there's nothing to do.
35:     // If the key is good then read all of the data items
36:     // pertinent to application startup.
37:     //
38:     if (!keyGood) return;
```

14

continues

Listing 14.4. continued

```
39:    int top = regKey.ReadInteger("Top");
40:    int left = regKey.ReadInteger("Left");
41:    int width = regKey.ReadInteger("Width");
42:    int height = regKey.ReadInteger("Height");
43:    SetBounds(left, top, width, height);
44:    WindowState =
45:      TWindowState(regKey.ReadInteger("WindowState"));
46:    //
47:    // The TDateTime class is a handy item to have around
48:    // if you are doing date and time operations.
49:    //
50:    TDateTime dt;
51:    dt = regKey.ReadDate("Date and Time");
52:    DateLabel->Caption = dt.DateString();
53:    TimeLabel->Caption = dt.TimeString();
54:    delete &regKey;
55: }
56: //-------------------------------------------------------
57: void __fastcall TMainForm::FileOpenClick(TObject *Sender)
58: {
59:    //
60:    // This function displays the File Open dialog but
61:    // doesn't actually open a file. The last path, filter,
62:    // and filename are written to the registry when the
63:    // user presses OK.
64:    //
65:    // Create a TRegistry object to access the registry.
66:    //
67:    TRegistry& regKey = *new TRegistry();
68:    //
69:    // Open the key.
70:    //
71:    regKey.OpenKey(
72:      "Software\\SAMS\\C++Builder in 21 Days", true);
73:    //
74:    // Read the values. If these items have not yet been
75:    // created then we will get an exception.
76:    //
77:    try {
78:      OpenDialog->InitialDir = regKey.ReadString("LastDir");
79:      OpenDialog->FileName = regKey.ReadString("LastFile");
80:      OpenDialog->FilterIndex =
81:        regKey.ReadInteger("FilterIndex");
82:    }
83:    //
84:    // We know what the exception is and it's no big deal
85:    // so we'll just catch it and ignore it.
86:    //
87:    catch (...) {}
88:    //
89:    // Display the File Open dialog. If the user presses OK
90:    // then save the path, filename, and filter to the
91:    // registry.
92:    if (OpenDialog->Execute()) {
```

14

```
 93:     String path;
 94:     String fname;
 95:     //
 96:     // A function to separate the path from the filename.
 97:     //
 98:     ParseFileName(path, fname);
 99:     regKey.WriteString("LastDir", path);
100:     regKey.WriteString("LastFile", fname);
101:     regKey.WriteInteger
102:       ("FilterIndex", OpenDialog->FilterIndex);
103:   }
104:   delete &regKey;
105: }
106:
107: void TMainForm::ParseFileName(String& path, String& fname)
108: {
109:   //
110:   // This function separates the path from the filename.
111:   //
112:   int pos = 0;
113:   String s = OpenDialog->FileName;
114:   int x = 1;
115:   while (x) {
116:     x = s.Pos("\\");
117:     s = s.SubString(x + 1, s.Length() - x);
118:     pos += x;
119:   }
120:   fname = s;
121:   path = OpenDialog->FileName.SubString(0, pos);
122: }
123: //------------------------------------------------------------
124: void __fastcall TMainForm::
125: FormClose(TObject *Sender, TCloseAction &Action)
126: {
127:   //
128:   // If the user pressed the button to delete the key
129:   // then we don't want to write out the information.
130:   //
131:   if (keyDeleted) return;
132:   //
133:   // Create a TRegistry object to access the registry.
134:   //
135:   TRegistry& regKey = *new TRegistry();
136:   //
137:   // Open the key.
138:   //
139:   regKey.OpenKey(
140:     "Software\\SAMS\\C++Builder in 21 Days", true);
141:   //
142:   // Write out the values.
143:   //
144:   regKey.WriteInteger("WindowState", WindowState);
145:   if (WindowState != wsMaximized) {
146:     regKey.WriteInteger("Top", Top);
147:     regKey.WriteInteger("Left", Left);
148:     regKey.WriteInteger("Width", Width);
```

14

continues

Listing 14.4. continued

```
149:     regKey.WriteInteger("Height", Height);
150:   }
151:   TDateTime dt;
152:   regKey.WriteDate("Date and Time", dt.CurrentDateTime());
153:   delete &regKey;
154: }
155: //-----------------------------------------------------------
156: void __fastcall TMainForm::FileExitClick(TObject *Sender)
157: {
158:   //
159:   // Bye!
160:   //
161:   Close();
162: }
163: //-----------------------------------------------------------
164: void __fastcall TMainForm::DeleteKeyClick(TObject *Sender)
165: {
166:   //
167:   // The user pressed the Delete Key button so delete the
168:   // key. Set a flag so that we don't re-create the key
169:   // when the program closes.
170:   //
171:   TRegistry& regKey = *new TRegistry();
172:   regKey.DeleteKey("Software\\SAMS");
173:   keyDeleted = true;
174:   delete &regKey;
175: }
```

By examining this listing and running the RegTest program, you can learn a lot about using the Registry in your applications. Figure 14.4 shows the RegTest program running; Figure 14.5 shows the Registry key that is created by the program.

Figure 14.4.

The RegTest *program running.*

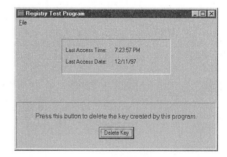

Figure 14.5.

The Registry Editor showing the RegTest *key.*

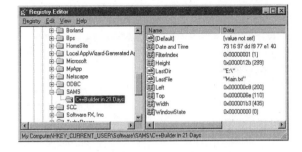

NOTE

The TRegIniFile class is a specialized Registry-manipulation class that can be used for applications that are moving from storing data in .INI files to storing data in the Registry. See the online help for TRegIniFile for complete information.

NOTE

Although conventional wisdom has it that the Registry is the place to store application-specific data, you still can use .INI files if you want. One advantage to .INI files is that less-sophisticated users can edit them with a text editor when necessary (which is also a disadvantage in some cases.) To make using .INI files easier, VCL includes the TIniFile class. Be sure to check out this class if you intend to use .INI files in your application.

Specialized Message Handling

On Day 11, "Using the Debugger," I talked about Windows messages as part of the discussion of the WinSight program. For the most part, C++Builder makes message handling easy through its use of events. As I have said, an event is usually generated in response to a Windows message being sent to an application. There are times, however, when you may want to handle messages yourself. There are two primary scenarios that require that you handle messages outside of the normal C++Builder messaging system:

☐ Windows messages that VCL does not handle

☐ User-defined messages

Handling messages on your own requires a few extra programming techniques; you'll learn about those techniques in this section.

14

More on Windows Messages

How do Windows messages get sent? Some messages are sent by Windows itself to instruct the window to do something or to notify the window that something has happened. At other times, messages are sent by the programmer or, in the case of VCL, OWL, or MFC, by the framework the programmer is using. Regardless of who is sending the messages, you can be guaranteed that a lot of messages are flying around at any given millisecond.

Message Types

Basically, messages fall into two categories:

☐ Command messages

☐ Notification messages

Command messages cause something to occur either in Windows or within a particular control. Notification messages are sent by Windows to notify you that something has happened. To illustrate the difference between these two types of messages, let's take a look at the standard edit control.

The standard Windows edit control has almost 80 command messages and nearly 20 notification messages. Surprised? It's true, and don't forget that the edit control is just one control out of dozens of Windows controls.

NOTE

> I lied to you back on Day 5, "C++ Class Frameworks and the Visual Component Model," when I talked about events. (Well, not exactly.) At that time I said that there are about 175 messages that Windows could send to an application, and that is essentially true. But when you consider messages specific to controls as well as messages that can be sent to main windows, the count goes to something like 700 messages. Wow! And that only includes command messages, not notification messages. You should have a new appreciation for VCL after reading this section.

A programmer writing a Windows program in C has to send a lot of messages to accomplish tasks. For example, to get the length of the currently selected text in an edit control requires the following code:

```
int start;
int end;
long result = SendMessage(hWndEdit, EM_GETSEL, 0, 0);
start = LOWORD(result);
end = HIWORD(result);
int length = end - start;
```

14

This is how C programmers (or C++ programmers not using frameworks) spend their days. Contrast that with the VCL way of doing things:

```
int length = Edit->SelLength;
```

Which do you prefer? Regardless of who is sending the message, command messages are used heavily both by programmers and by Windows itself.

Notification messages, on the other hand, are sent only by Windows itself. Notification messages tell Windows that something has happened within a control. For example, the EN_CHANGE message is sent when the contents of an edit control have changed. VCL has an event for the Edit, MaskEdit, and Memo components called OnChange that is triggered in response to the EN_CHANGE notification message (as well as some others). Programmers using traditional Windows programming tools have to intercept these messages and deal with them as needed. Which brings us to the next subject: Message Parameters.

NOTE

> Traditional C Windows programs have long switch statements that are used to determine which message was sent to the window.

WPARAM, LPARAM, and Message Cracking

Every Windows message has two parameters: the WPARAM (short for word parameter) and the LPARAM (short for long parameter).

NOTE

> In 32-bit Windows, WPARAM and LPARAM are both 32-bit values. In 16-bit Windows the WPARAM is a 16-bit value (a word), and the LPARAM is a 32-bit value (a double word, or a long). And that ends your history lesson on the names WPARAM and LPARAM. And now back to our program...

These two parameters could be likened to the parameters sent to a function. When a Windows message is received, the parameters are examined to obtain information specific to the message being sent. For example, the WM_LBUTTONDOWN message is a notification message that is sent when the left mouse button is clicked on a window. For a WM_LBUTTONDOWN message, the WPARAM contains a special code that tells which of the other mouse buttons was pressed and also what keys on the keyboard was pressed when the event occurred. The LPARAM contains the coordinates of the mouse cursor when the mouse button was clicked. The X position is contained in the low-order word, and the Y position is contained in the high-order word.

14

To get at this information, the message must be *cracked* to reveal what's inside. The code for cracking a WM_LBUTTONDOWN message might look like this:

```
int Shift = wParam;
int X = LOWORD(lParam);
int Y = HIWORD(lParam);
```

This is a fairly simple example, but it's indicative of what goes on each time a message is handled in a Windows application.

NOTE   HIWORD and LOWORD are Windows macros. HIWORD extracts the left-most 16 bits from a 4-byte variable (a long), and LOWORD extracts the right-most 16 bits.

You'll be relieved to know that VCL performs message cracking for you for all VCL events. For instance, if you set up a message handler for the OnMouseDown event, C++Builder will generate a function in your code that looks like this:

```
void __fastcall TScratchPad::FormMouseDown(TObject *Sender,
  TMouseButton Button, TShiftState Shift, Integer X, Integer Y)
{
  if (Button == mbLeft) {
    // put your code here
  }
}
```

As you can see, the event handler generated by C++Builder contains all the information you need. VCL will crack the WPARAM and LPARAM parameters for you and hand them to you in sensible pieces that you can deal with more easily. This same thing happens for every message for which VCL creates an event.

NOTE   VCL takes messaging and message cracking one step further in the case of the mouse button messages. Windows actually generates up to three different mouse down messages: one for the left button being pressed, one for the middle button (if one exists), and yet another when the right button is pressed. VCL handles all of these messages in a single event. The TMouseButton parameter of the OnMouseDown event tells you which of the three buttons was pressed.

With that primer on Windows messages under your belt, let's take a brief look at exactly how to send messages.

Sending Versus Posting

The Windows API provides two functions for sending messages: PostMessage() and SendMessage(). The PostMessage() function posts the message to the Windows message queue and immediately returns. This function simply hands the message to Windows and goes on its way. PostMessage() returns 1 if the function call succeeded or 0 if it did not. (About the only reason for PostMessage() to fail is if the message is sent to an invalid window.)

The SendMessage() function, on the other hand, sends the message to Windows and waits until the message is carried out before returning. The return value from SendMessage() depends on the message being sent. Sometimes the biggest reason to use SendMessage() over PostMessage() is because you need the return value from a particular message.

NOTE

The differences between situations when you use PostMessage() versus SendMessage() are subtle. For example, due to timing issues within Windows, there are times when sending a message will fail to have the effect you expected. In those cases, you'll have to use PostMessage(). The reverse is also true: Sometimes PostMessage() is wrong for a given set of circumstances, and you'll have to use SendMessage(). Although this is not something you really need to be concerned with right now, it is something to file away for future reference.

You can use both PostMessage() and SendMessage() in your C++Builder applications. For instance, to post yourself a message, you would do something like this:

```
PostMessage(Handle, WM_QUIT, 0, 0);
```

The first parameter of both PostMessage() and SendMessage() is the window handle of the window to which you want to send the message. In this case, we are sending the message to the main form (assuming this code was written in the main form's source code unit).

In addition to the Windows API functions, VCL provides a method called Perform() that you can use to send messages to any VCL window. Perform() bypasses the Windows messaging system and sends the message directly to the message-handling mechanism for a given window. The Perform() equivalent of the preceding example is:

```
Perform(WM_QUIT, 0, 0);
```

You can use any of these three functions to send messages to your application and to other windows within your application.

14

Handling Events

We've already discussed handling VCL events, but a short review can't hurt. When a particular component receives a Windows message, it looks up the message and checks to see if there is an event handler assigned for that particular message. If an event handler has been assigned for that event, VCL calls the event handler. If no event handler was assigned, the message is handled in the default manner. You can handle any messages you like and ignore the rest.

What happens in your event handlers depends on a variety of factors: the particular message being handled, what your program does in response to the message, and whether you are modifying the incoming message or just using the event handler as notification that the event occurred. As you get further into Windows programming, you will see that there are literally hundreds of things you might do in response to events.

Most of the time, you will be using the event handler for notification that a particular event occurred. Take the OnMouseDown event, for instance. If you handle the OnMouseDown event, you are simply asking to be notified when the user clicks the component with the mouse (remember that forms are components, too). You probably are not going to modify the message parameters in any way; you just want to know that the event occurred. A great number of your event handlers will be used for notification purposes.

Sometimes, however, you want to change one or more of the message parameters before sending the message on its way. Let's say, for instance, that you wanted to force the text in a particular edit control to uppercase. (You could set the CharCase property of the Edit component to ecUpperCase, of course, but we'll stick with this example for now.) To change all keystrokes to uppercase, you could do something like this in your OnKeyPress event handler:

```
void __fastcall TScratchPad::EditKeyPress(TObject *Sender, Char &Key)
{
  if (Key >= 'a') Key -= 32;
}
```

In this way you are actually modifying some aspect of the message before it gets sent on to VCL for processing. The parameters sent in the event handler are often passed by reference for exactly this reason.

NOTE

> C++Builder protects you a bit by passing message parameters that you should not change by value rather than by reference. This is also true of message parameters for which changing the value has no effect. Take the OnMouseDown event discussed earlier. This event is for notification only. There is no point in modifying the Button, Shift, X, or Y parameters, so all are passed by value.

14

Whether you change one or more of the parameters sent depends entirely on the message and what you intend to do with it. Over time, you will likely run into situations where modification of a particular message is required to cause Windows to behave in a particular way. At other times you will not modify the parameters at all, but will inspect them to determine what is happening with your application. Since the possibilities are so numerous, I'll have to leave further exploration of message parameters as an exercise for the reader.

Handling Other Windows Messages

There will undoubtedly be some point when you need to respond to a Windows message for which VCL provides no event. When that time comes, you are going to want to know how to handle those messages, and that is what this section is about.

VCL provides events for the most commonly used Windows messages. Obviously, with over 700 Windows messages, VCL does not provide events for them all. The 80/20 theory says, among other things, that 20 percent of the people do 80 percent of the work. The same is probably true of Windows messages. VCL might only provide events for 20 percent of Windows messages, but they are the messages you will use 80 percent of the time. Still, there are plenty of Windows messages that VCL does not provide events for, and you need to know how to handle those messages when the time comes.

You'll be glad to know that you can handle just about any Windows message once you know how. After you have the basics down, each message is just a variation on the same theme. The mechanism that C++Builder uses to handle messages not covered by VCL events is called the *message map table*. The message map table is used to associate a certain Windows message with a function in your code. When your window receives that message, the function is called. Hmmm…sounds like events, doesn't it? There are certainly some similarities.

Implementing message handling at this level is a three-step process:

1. Create the message map table in the class declaration and add the message you want to handle to the message map table.

2. Add the function declaration for the message handler to the class declaration.

3. Add the definition of the message handler to your form's source code unit.

First, let me show you the code to implement a message map for your class; then we'll look at the message-handling function.

The C++Builder Message Map Table

The message map table goes at the end of your class declaration. A message map table begins with BEGIN_MESSAGE_MAP and ends with END_MESSAGE_MAP. Between these two items are one or more MESSAGE_HANDLER declarations. You pass the name of the base class as the single parameter in END_MESSAGE_MAP. Even with today's inflation, a picture is still worth a thousand words, so let me show you an example message map table. It looks like this:

14

```
BEGIN_MESSAGE_MAP
  MESSAGE_HANDLER(WM_NCHITTEST, TWMNCHitTest, WMNCHitTest)
  MESSAGE_HANDLER(WM_ERASEBKGND, TWMEraseBkgnd, WMEraseBkgnd)
END_MESSAGE_MAP(TForm)
```

This message map table sets up the program to handle two Windows messages: WM_NCHITTEST and WM_ERASEBKGND.

NOTE

The WM_ERASEBKGND message is sent just prior to the WM_PAINT message (which is when Windows paints the window). In VCL programming, this means that WM_ERASEBKGND is received *before* the OnPaint event occurs. You can catch the WM_ERASEBKGND message to do any painting on the window that must be done independently of the OnPaint event handler. (When you respond to a Windows message, you are said to *catch* or *handle* the message.)

NOTE

You might be wondering, "So why all the caps?" The reason for the caps is that BEGIN_MESSAGE_MAP, END_MESSAGE_MAP, and MESSAGE_HANDLER are all macros, and macro names are traditionally written in all upper-case characters. Macros are text placeholders that expand to actual C++ code when the parser (part of the compiler) encounters them. The macro definitions for the message map table are tucked away somewhere in the VCL source code.

For those of you who can't live without knowing more, read on. All the message map table macros work together to create a function called Dispatch(). Because the message map table is contained in the class declaration, that automatically makes the function an inline function. For the preceding example, it would look something like this, once the macros were all expanded:

```
virtual void __fastcall Dispatch(void *Message)
{
  switch  (((PMessage)Message)->Msg)
  {
    case WM_NCHITTEST :
      OnNCHitTest((TWMNCHitTest&)*Message);
      break;
    case WM_ERASEBKGND :
      OnEraseBkgnd((TWMEraseBkgnd&)*Message);
      break;
    default:
```

14

```
        TForm::Dispatch(Message);
        break;
    }
}
```

It's not so mysterious once you break it down. If you want to see what the macros look like, take a look in \CBuilder\Include\Vcl\sysdefs.h.

Let's break down the MESSAGE_HANDLER handler macro and examine its pieces. Here I'll use one of those syntax lines I despise so much:

```
MESSAGE_HANDLER(<message>, <message structure>, <message handler>)
```

The message parameter is the Windows message you want to handle. Windows message names are always in uppercase (the documented messages, anyway).

The message struct parameter is used to pass the name of the message-cracking structure that will be used to pass the parameters once VCL has cracked the message. VCL has a message-cracking structure for most Windows messages. The structure name is the Windows message name, preceded by T and minus the underscore. For example, the Windows message WM_ERASEBKGND gets translated into the structure named TWMEraseBkgnd. You sort of have to guess at the capitalization, but for the most part it makes perfect sense. This structure gets passed along to the message handler (more on that in just a bit).

The message handler parameter is for the actual name of the message-handling function. You can use any name you like; however, there are two naming conventions that are used most widely. One naming convention has you remove the leading TWM from the structure name and add the word On. So, again using WM_ERASEBKGND as an example, the function name of the message handler would be OnEraseBkgnd(). The other naming convention is just using the name of the message minus the WM_ portion. Using this naming convention, the name of the message handler for the WM_ERASEBKGND message would be EraseBkgnd().

To put this in perspective, you need to see the entire class declaration for a class that implements a message map table. Listing 14.5 shows a typical main form class declaration for a class that uses a message map table.

Listing 14.5. Message.h.

```
1: //-------------------------------------------------------------
2: #ifndef MsgMainH
3: #define MsgMainH
4: //-------------------------------------------------------------
5: #include <vcl\Classes.hpp>
6: #include <vcl\Controls.hpp>
```

continues

14

Listing 14.5. continued

```
 7: #include <vcl\StdCtrls.hpp>
 8: #include <vcl\Forms.hpp>
 9: #include <vcl\ExtCtrls.hpp>
10:
11: #define MYMESSAGE WM_USER + 1
12:
13: //----------------------------------------------------------
14: class TMainForm : public TForm
15: {
16: __published:      // IDE-managed Components
17:    TButton *ShowTBar;
18:    TButton *Button1;
19:    TLabel *Label;
20:    TBevel *Bevel1;
21:    TCheckBox *Hatched;
22:    TCheckBox *LetVCLHandle;
23:    void __fastcall ShowTBarClick(TObject *Sender);
24:
25:    void __fastcall Button1Click(TObject *Sender);
26:    void __fastcall HatchedClick(TObject *Sender);
27:
28: private:          // User declarations
29:   void __fastcall OnNCHitTest(TWMNCHitTest& Message);
30:   void __fastcall OnEraseBkgnd(TWMEraseBkgnd& Message);
31:   void __fastcall OnGetMinMaxInfo(TWMGetMinMaxInfo& Message);
32:   void __fastcall OnMyMessage(TMessage& Message);
33: public:           // User declarations
34:    virtual __fastcall TMainForm(TComponent* Owner);
35: BEGIN_MESSAGE_MAP
36:   MESSAGE_HANDLER(MYMESSAGE, TMessage, OnMyMessage)
37:   MESSAGE_HANDLER(WM_NCHITTEST, TWMNCHitTest, OnNCHitTest)
38:   MESSAGE_HANDLER(
39:     WM_GETMINMAXINFO, TWMGetMinMaxInfo, OnGetMinMaxInfo)
40:   MESSAGE_HANDLER(WM_ERASEBKGND, TWMEraseBkgnd, OnEraseBkgnd)
41: END_MESSAGE_MAP(TForm)
42: };
43: //----------------------------------------------------------
44: extern PACKAGE TMainForm *MainForm;
45: //----------------------------------------------------------
46: #endif
```

Notice in particular the message map table at the end of the class declaration and the function declarations for the message-handling functions. (Don't let lines 11, 32, and 36 throw you. These lines implement a user-defined message that I'll talk about a little later.)

The Message-Handling Function

The *message-handling function* (or just *message handler*) is the function that will be called whenever the message you are responding to is received by your application. The message handler has a single parameter—the message-cracker structure I discussed earlier. The message handler for the WM_ERASEBKGND message would look like this:

14

```
void __fastcall
TMainForm::OnEraseBkgnd(TWMEraseBkgnd& Message)
{
  // your message handling code here
}
```

As I said, the message-cracker structure will contain all of the parameters necessary to handle the message. The message cracker structure for the WM_ERASEBKGND message is as follows:

```
struct TWMEraseBkgnd
{
  unsigned int Msg;
  HDC DC;
  long Unused;
  long Result;
};
```

All message-cracking structures have two data members in common: Msg and Result. The Msg member contains the message that is being sent. This parameter is used by VCL and is not something you will be concerned with.

The Result data member, however, is important. This is used to set the return value for the message you are handling. The return value varies from message to message. For instance, the return value from your message handler for WM_ERASEBKGND should return true if you erase the background prior to drawing, or false if you do not erase the background. (Check the Win32 API online help for the individual message you are processing to determine what to set the Result data member to.) Set the Result data member of the message-cracker structure as needed:

```
void __fastcall
TMainForm::OnEraseBkgnd(TWMEraseBkgnd& Message)
{
  // do some stuff
  Message.Result = false;
}
```

Any other data members of the message-cracking structure will vary from message to message.

Sometimes you will need to call the default message handler for a particular message in addition to performing your own handling. In that case, you can call DefaultHandler() or call the base class's Dispatch() method. Which one you use depends on the behavior you are after. For instance, you might want to paint on the background of your window in some circumstances but not in others. If you don't paint the background, you want VCL to paint the background in the default way. So, you would do this:

```
void __fastcall
TMainForm::OnEraseBkgnd(TWMEraseBkgnd& Message)
{
  if (LetVCLDoIt) {
    TForm::Dispatch(&Message); // pass it on to VCL
    return;
```

14

```
    }
    else {
      // do some painting stuff here
    }
    Message.Result = false;
  }
```

In other cases, you will use DefaultHandler() to perform some default processing for you. Whether you call DefaultHandler() before you do your processing or afterward depends, again, on what you are trying to accomplish.

User-Defined Messages

Besides the normal Windows messages, Windows allows you to create what is called a *user-defined message*. A user-defined message is nothing more than a private message that you can send to yourself or to one of the other windows in your application. There are a variety of reasons you might want to use user-defined messages in your application. Truthfully, VCL events reduce the need for user-defined messages, but there still might be times when you need to use them. For example, let's say you are performing a lengthy calculation that your application created in another thread. (We won't try to tackle threads today.) If something occurs in that thread that the application should know about, the thread can send a user-defined message back to the application to inform it that something noteworthy happened.

Implementing and catching a user-defined message are nearly identical to handling a regular Windows message. The one exception is that you need to first define the message. You define a user-defined message like this:

```
#define MYMESSAGE WM_USER + 1
```

This line sets up a user-defined message called MYMESSAGE.

NOTE

> The symbol WM_USER is a special symbol that marks the beginning of the range of numbers that can be used for user-defined messages. You can use anything up to WM_USER + 31,743 for user-defined messages. I usually just pick something in the WM_USER + 100 range. The exact number you use is not important; just be sure that you do not accidentally use the same value for two different messages.

If you look back to Listing 14.5, you will notice the declaration for the user-defined message on line 11. Once you have the message defined, you can add it to the message map table as follows:

```
MESSAGE_HANDLER(MYMESSAGE, TMessage, OnMyMessage)
```

14

Notice that the message-cracker structure passed is of the TMessage type. This is the generic message-cracker structure. It is defined as follows:

```
struct TMessage
{
  unsigned int Msg;
  long WParam;
  long LParam;
  long Result;
};
```

NOTE

> The actual declaration of TMessage looks slightly different, but the structure shown here is the end result.

When you send a user-defined message, you pass any parameters you want in the WParam and LParam members. For instance, let's say you were sending a user-defined message indicating that error code 124 occurred on iteration 1019 of a processing loop. The call to Perform() would look like this:

```
int result = MainForm->Perform(MYMESSAGE, 124, 1019);
```

You could use either PostMessage() or SendMessage() to send the message, too, of course. For user-defined messages you can probably use Perform() for most of your messaging.

Okay, so the message is defined and sent. Now you need to write code to handle it. The message handler for the MYMESSAGE message might look like this:

```
void __fastcall
TMainForm::OnMyMessage(TMessage& Message)
{
  char msg[100];
  sprintf(msg,
    "Error #%d occurred on iteration number %d.",
    Message.WParam, Message.LParam);
  Application->MessageBox(msg, "Error Message", MB_OK);
  Message.Result = true;
}
```

The return value from Perform() will be the value of the Result member of the TMessage structure. It's up to you whether you send parameters and whether your message handler returns a result.

The Web site that accompanies this book contains a program called Message that illustrates the use of handling Windows messages not covered by VCL events. It also illustrates the use of a user-defined message. This program illustrates the implementation of a Windows programming trick: The window can be dragged by clicking and dragging anywhere on the client area of the form.

14

Summary

You have covered a lot of ground today. You started with a look at context-sensitive help and how to put it to use for you. Remember, context-sensitive help is not necessarily easy, but it is something you should implement. After that, you looked at exception handling and how you can use it to trap VCL exceptions. You have also gotten some insights into the Windows Registry. The Registry is something that can and should be used to store application-specific data. Knowing how to use the Registry can help you to implement those little features that make users smile. Finally, we ended with a discussion on how to handle messages other than through the use of events. All in all, it was a long day but a rewarding one.

Workshop

The Workshop contains quiz questions to help you solidify your understanding of the material covered and exercises to provide you with experience in using what you have learned. You can find the answers to the quiz questions in Appendix A, "Answers to Quiz Questions."

Q&A

Q Writing help files with a word processor is kind of tedious. What do you suggest?

A Get a commercial help-authoring program. These programs take care of all of the little stuff that drives you crazy when trying to write help files "the hard way." Writing help files is not much fun for most of us, but using a good help-authoring program can really ease the pain.

Q Do I have to put context identifiers in my help file?

A Not necessarily. You can just have your users invoke help from the main menu. You won't be able to support context-sensitive help without help context IDs in the help file, though.

Q Why should I bother with exception handling?

A By using exception handling, you can more closely control what happens when errors occur in your program.

Q I've caught a VCL exception. How can I reproduce the error message box that VCL creates when it throws an exception?

A. Call `Application->ShowException()`, and VCL will display the error message.

Q Do I have to use the Registry to store my program's preferences and settings?

A No. You can use `.INI` files or any other type of configuration file. However, the Registry is the preferred location for application-specific data. The `TRegistry` class makes it easy to use the Registry, so you might as well put it to work for you.

Q **I get exceptions every time I try to create a key and then use `WriteString()` to write a data item to the key. What could be wrong?**

A You are probably using `CreateKey()` to create the key. `CreateKey()` creates the key but does not open it. Use `OpenKey()` to create and open your keys rather than `CreateKey()`.

Q **What is a user-defined message?**

A A user-defined message is a message defined by you, the user, for private use in your application. This is in contrast to Windows messages that are defined and used by Windows on a global level.

Q **What should I do to get the default message-handling behavior for a particular Windows message?**

A Call the base class's `Dispatch()` method:

```
TForm::Dispatch(&Message);
```

Quiz

1. How do you set the help file that your application will use?
2. How do you implement F1 key support for a particular form or dialog box?
3. What function do you call to display the index for your help file?
4. What types of objects can an exception throw?
5. Is it legal to have more than one `catch` statement following a `try` statement?
6. How do you throw an exception?
7. What is the default value of the `TRegistry` class' `RootKey` property?
8. Must you call `CloseKey()` when you are done with a key?
9. What is the difference between `SendMessage()` and `PostMessage()`?
10. What is the name of the VCL function that is used to send a message directly to a component?

Exercises

1. Research the availability of help-file authoring tools. Although this might seem like a strange exercise, it might be the most beneficial exercise you can do in regard to help files.
2. Create a new project. Add some components to the main form. Give each a different `HelpContext` number.
3. Attach a help file to the project (any help file will do). If you have help-authoring software, create a simple help file for the program to use. Run the program and press F1 when a component has focus.

14

4. Create a new project. Add a button to the main form. Place the following code in the OnClick handler for the button:

```
TImageList* list;
delete list;
```

Run the program and click the button. What happens?

5. Write a try/catch pair for the two lines of code in Exercise 4 to catch any exceptions. Display a message when the error occurs, but allow the program to continue to function.

6. Modify the ScratchPad program to use the Windows Registry. Save the filename and path of the last file opened.

7. Modify the ScratchPad program to use the filename and path retrieved from the Registry when the File Open and File Save dialog boxes are displayed.

8. Write a program that sends itself a user-defined message when a button is clicked. Display a message box when the message is received.

9. Add a message handler for the Windows WM_MOVE message to the program in Exercise 8. When the window is moved, beep the speaker and display the new coordinates on the form.

10. **Extra Credit:** Modify the PictureViewer program from Day 6, "The C++Builder IDE Explored," to catch an exception if the user attempts to open a file other than a graphics file.

14

WEEK 2

8
9
10
11
12
13
14

In Review

Wow, that was intense, wasn't it? But did you enjoy yourself? Are you starting to get the fever? By now I'll bet the wheels in your head are really turning. Likely, you have already envisioned an application or two of your own. Maybe you have even begun work on an application. I hope you have because, as I have said many times, that is where you really learn. If you haven't yet developed an idea for an application, don't worry about it. It will come to you in good time.

This week included a mixture of material. Early in the week you found out the basics of building a C++Builder application. You can drop components on a form all you want, but someday you have to write code. It can be daunting to branch out on your own. C++Builder has led you by the hand up to this point. But now it's time to leave the nest. You found out how to add your own functions and data members to your code. You found out how to add resources such as bitmaps and sounds to your programs. This is good stuff. Before long you'll be doing all these things on your own like a pro.

This week's less-than-exciting material dealt with more on C++Builder projects and how to use the debugger. These chapters might not be flashy, but they still contain vital information that you need when developing applications. It's all about maximizing your time. Learning how to use the debugger takes a few hours or even a few days, but it will save you weeks of work in the long run. Trust me. If you know how to use the debugger, you can really get in there and find out what is going wrong when you encounter a bug in your program. If you don't have a good handle on the debugger, I urge you to go back and review Day 11. As I said, the debugger is not the most thrilling thing you learn about in this book, but it certainly is one of the most valuable. Learning how to effectively use your projects falls into this same category. Proper project management will save you time in the long run, too.

Toward the end of the week you learned about some of the things that can take an average program and turn it into a great program. Let's face it, window decorations such as status bars and toolbars cannot take a weak programming idea and transform it into a great program. No amount of gadgetry can do that. But if you have a good program to start with, adding bells and whistles can make your program stand out from the competition. There's nothing stopping you from adding these kinds of goodies to your applications because C++Builder makes it easy.

You also had a chance to do some printing. Printing is, by nature, nonvisual. C++Builder's great visual programming tools can't help you here. Still, VCL makes printing much less frustrating than it would be with the straight API. When you begin printing, you will find that it is not all that difficult. Once again, experiment as much as you can. Playing around can be the best teacher. Don't worry about the boss—tell him or her that I said it was okay to play around. (That's *play around* not *play a round*. Don't blame me if you're caught playing golf on company time!)

Finally, you ended the week with some more in-depth programming techniques. Implementing context-sensitive help is something you will just have to do in today's competitive market. The good news is that C++Builder makes it easy. The bad news is that there is no shortcut to writing good help files. It can't be helped. Take my advice and get a good help authoring program. Such a program can take the frustration out of creating help files. If you write help files the hard way, you will probably get bogged down in the tedium and start skimping on the details. Using a good help authoring program helps you avoid that situation. Remember that the help file is as important as the program itself. After all, what good is a Maserati if you can't figure out how to get it out of first gear?

Using the Registry can put a real shine on your program, too. Oh, it won't make your program appear any different, but when you give the users options, you increase the value of your program. Storing these options in the Registry makes your job easier, too. There's no excuse for omitting features that users have come to expect. Sure, it takes a little time and you have to pay attention to detail, but there's no substitute for quality.

We ended the week with a discussion on message handling. This is a lower level of programming than you have encountered thus far. Handling messages is not something that you may have to do often, but when you must handle messages, knowing how will be more than half the battle. The section on message handling will benefit you down the road if not immediately.

At a Glance

This week you change gears a little. First, you have a little fun and tackle graphics programming. After that discussion you begin database programming. You learn about database architecture and how C++Builder and VCL implement database operations. You begin with the basics and work toward more advanced database programming techniques.

After our discussion of database programming, we will tackle the subject of dynamic link libraries (DLLs). DLLs are there for the taking. You can use them if you want, or not use them. But it is important that you make an informed decision on DLLs. To do that, you have to learn what DLLs are and how you can use them in your applications. Day 19 tells you all about it. After Day 19, you can decide whether DLLs are for you. No doubt you will find that you can use DLLs at some point in your programming journeys.

On Day 20 you take on a more advanced topic—writing components. Writing components is not for the faint of heart. It is real programming. You might love it…you never know (I know I do). On Day 20 you learn how to write a component. Creating a component requires a deeper understanding of properties, methods, and events than you presently have.

Finally, you learn how C++Builder and Delphi are similar and also how they are different. One of the great things about C++Builder forms is that you can use the same forms in Delphi and in C++Builder. C++Builder and Delphi are not competing products but rather complementary products.

So, one more week to go. Are you up for it? All right, then, let's go!

Day 15

Graphics Programming

Graphics programming represents the fun part of programming. In this chapter you will get an introduction to graphics programming with C++Builder. Most of that will come in the form of an examination of the TCanvas and TBitmap classes. We will start with a look at the easiest ways to display graphics in C++Builder. After that, you will learn about the Windows Graphics Device Interface and the components that make up that interface. Along the way we will talk about the various line and shape drawing routines and the different ways to display bitmaps. Later in the day we will look at offscreen bitmaps and how they can benefit you. So let's get started!

Graphics the Easy Way

Graphics programming does not have to be difficult. Sometimes all you need is to display a picture or a simple shape on a form. VCL provides ready-made components for those times. We'll take a brief look at some of these components before we move on to real graphics programming.

The Shape component can be used to add simple shapes to your forms. Using the Shape component is easy. Just drop one on a form and change the Brush, Pen, and Shape properties as desired. You can draw circles, ellipses, squares, rectangles, and rectangles with rounded edges. Change the Brush property to modify the background color of the shape. Change the Pen property to change the color or thickness of the border surrounding the shape.

An Image component can be used to display a bitmap on a form. This component is great for many graphics operations, including a bitmap background for a form. The Picture property of TImage is an instance of the TPicture class. You can select the picture at design time through the Object Inspector, or you can load a picture at runtime. For example, here's how you could change the image in the component at runtime:

```
Image1->Picture->Bitmap->LoadFromFile("bkgnd.bmp");
```

The Stretch property determines whether or not the image will be enlarged or compressed to fit the size of the component. The Center property determines whether or not the bitmap is centered in the component. The AutoSize property can be used to force the component to size itself according to the size of the image.

I'll also mention the PaintBox component here. This component provides a canvas on which you can draw if you want drawing confined to a certain area of a form. The only significant property of the PaintBox component is the Canvas property. This property is an instance of the TCanvas class. It is with this class that most drawing is done in a C++Builder application. Let's look at the TCanvas class now.

Device Contexts and TCanvas

Windows uses the term *device context* to describe a canvas on which you can draw. I talked about device contexts on Day 13, "Beyond the Basics," when I talked about printing. A device context can be used to draw on many different surfaces:

☐ To a window's client area or frame
☐ To the desktop
☐ To memory
☐ To a printer or other output device

These are just a few examples. There are other, more obscure device contexts (menus, for example), but these are the device contexts that you will be most interested in.

Dealing with device contexts at the API level can be a bit complex. First, you have to obtain a handle to a device context from Windows. Then you have to select various objects into the device context (pens, brushes, or fonts). After that, you can draw on the device context. When you are done drawing, you have to be sure that any objects you select into the device context

15

are removed before deleting the device context. If you forget to remove objects selected into the device context then your application will leak memory. It's a tedious process to say the least.

The good news is that VCL provides the TCanvas class to make dealing with device contexts easier. Let me give you a quick example. The following code uses the Windows API to draw a circle on the screen with a blue outline and red interior:

```
HDC hdc = GetDC(Handle);
HBRUSH hBrush = CreateSolidBrush(RGB(255, 0, 0));
HPEN hPen = CreatePen(PS_SOLID, 1, RGB(0, 0, 255));
HBRUSH oldBrush = SelectObject(hdc, hBrush);
HPEN oldPen = SelectObject(hdc, hPen);
Ellipse(hdc, 20, 20, 120, 120);
SelectObject(hdc, oldBrush);
SelectObject(hdc, oldPen);
ReleaseDC(Handle, hdc);
```

This code isn't so terribly bad, but it's easy to forget to restore objects when you are done with them. When that happens, your application will leak resources. Now look at the equivalent VCL code:

```
Canvas->Brush->Color = clRed;
Canvas->Pen->Color = clBlue;
Canvas->Ellipse(20, 20, 120, 120);
```

Not only is this code shorter and more readable, it is also much more robust. The TCanvas class takes care of freeing resources as needed so you don't have to worry about it. TCanvas is a simpler *and* more effective approach than using the API.

The TCanvas class has many properties and methods. We'll look at some of these properties and methods as we work through today's material. Table 15.1 lists the primary properties of TCanvas and Table 15.2 lists the primary methods.

Table 15.1. Primary TCanvas **properties.**

Property	Description
Brush	The brush color or pattern used for filling shapes.
ClipRect	The current clipping rectangle for the canvas. Any drawing will be confined to this rectangle. This property is read-only.
CopyMode	Determines how drawing will be performed (normal, inverse, xor, and so on).
Font	The font the canvas will use for drawing text.
Handle	The handle (HDC) of the canvas. Used when calling the Windows API directly.
Pen	Determines the style and color of lines drawn on the canvas.
PenPos	The current drawing position in X and Y coordinates.
Pixels	An array of the canvas' pixels.

Table 15.2. Primary TCanvas methods.

Method	Description
Arc	Draws an arc on the canvas using the current pen.
BrushCopy	Displays a bitmap with a transparent background.
CopyRect	Copies part of an image to the canvas.
Draw	Copies an image from memory to the canvas.
Ellipse	Using the current pen, draws an ellipse that is filled with the current brush on the canvas.
FloodFill	Fills an area of the canvas with the current brush.
LineTo	Draws a line from the current drawing position to the location specified in the X and Y parameters.
MoveTo	Sets the current drawing position.
Pie	Draws a pie shape on the canvas.
Polygon	Draws a polygon on the canvas from an array of points and fills it with the current brush.
Polyline	Using the current pen, draws a line on the canvas from an array of points. The points are not automatically closed.
Rectangle	Draws a rectangle on the canvas outlined by the current pen and filled with the current brush.
RoundRect	Draws a filled rectangle with rounded corners.
StretchDraw	Copies a bitmap from memory to the canvas. The bitmap will be stretched or reduced according to the size of the destination rectangle.
TextExtent	Returns the width and height, in pixels, of the string passed in the Text parameter. The width is calculated using the current font of the canvas.
TextHeight	Returns the height, in pixels, of the string passed in the Text parameter. The width is calculated using the current font of the canvas.
TextOut	Using the current font, draws text on the canvas at a specified location.
TextRect	Draws text within a clipping rectangle.

Believe it or not, these properties and methods represent just a small part of the functionality of a Windows device context. The good news is that these properties and methods cover 80 percent of the tasks you will need to perform when working with graphics. Before we can talk more about the TCanvas class in detail, we need to talk about graphics objects used in Windows programming.

GDI Objects

The Windows Graphics Device Interface (GDI) has many types of objects that define how a device context functions. The most commonly used GDI objects are pens, brushes, and fonts. Other GDI objects include palettes, bitmaps, and regions. Let's take a look at pens, brushes, and fonts first, and then move on to more complex objects.

Pens, Brushes, and Fonts

Pens, brushes, and fonts are fairly straightforward. Let's take a brief look at each of these GDI objects and how the TCanvas class uses them.

Pens

A pen defines the object that is being used to draw lines. A line might be a single line from one point to the next, or it might be the border drawn around rectangles, ellipses, and polygons. The pen is accessed through the Pen property of the TCanvas class. The Pen property is an instance of the TPen class. Table 15.3 lists the properties of TPen. There are no methods or events of TPen that are worthy of note.

Table 15.3. TPen **properties.**

Property	Description
Color	Sets the color of the line.
Handle	The handle to the pen (HPEN). Used when calling the GDI directly.
Mode	Determines how lines will be drawn (normal, inverse, xor, and so on).
Style	The pen's style. Styles can be solid, dotted, dashed, dash-dot, clear, and more.
Width	The width of the pen, in pixels.

For the most part these properties are used exactly as you would expect. The following example draws a red, dashed line:

```
Canvas->Pen->Color = clRed;
Canvas->Pen->Style = psDash;
Canvas->MoveTo(20, 20);
Canvas->LineTo(120, 20);
```

To test this code, drop a button on a form and type the code in the OnClick handler for the button. When you click the button the line will be drawn on the form.

NOTE

> The simple examples in this chapter can all be tested in this manner. Note, however, that if you cover the application and bring it to the top the drawing will be gone. This is because the drawing is temporary. If you want the drawing to be persistent, place the drawing code in the OnPaint event handler for the form. Any time a window needs to be repainted, its OnPaint event is generated and your drawing code will be executed.

The dashed and dotted pen styles can only be used with a pen width of 1. The psClear pen style can be used to eliminate the line that the Windows GDI draws around the outside of objects such as rectangles, ellipses, and filled polygons.

TIP

> You can experiment with the various properties of TPen by dropping a Shape component on a form and modifying the shape's Pen property. This is especially useful for seeing the effects of the Mode property of the TPen class.

Brushes

A brush represents the filled area of a graphical shape. When you draw an ellipse, rectangle, or polygon the shape will be filled with the current brush. When you think of a brush you probably think of a solid color. A lot of times this is the case, but a brush is more than just a color. A brush can also include a pattern or a bitmap. The TCanvas class has a property called Brush which can be used to control the appearance of the brush. The Brush property is an instance of the TBrush class. As with TPen, the TBrush class doesn't have any methods or events of note. The TBrush properties are listed in Table 15.4.

Table 15.4. TBrush **properties.**

Property	Description
Bitmap	The bitmap to be used as the brush's background. For Windows 95 the bitmap must be no larger than 8×8.
Color	Sets the color of the brush.
Handle	The handle to the brush (HBRUSH). Used when calling the GDI directly.
Style	The brush's style. Styles include solid, clear, or one of several patterns.

By default the Style property is set to bsSolid. If you want a pattern fill then you should set the Style property to one of the pattern styles (bsHorizontal, bsVertical, bsFDiagonal, bsBDiagonal, bsCross, or bsDiagCross). The following example draws a circle on the form using a 45 degree hatched pattern. Figure 15.1 shows the form when this code executes.

```
Canvas->Brush->Color = clBlue;
Canvas->Brush->Style = bsDiagCross;
Canvas->Ellipse(20, 20, 220, 220);
```

Figure 15.1.

A circle filled with a hatched brush.

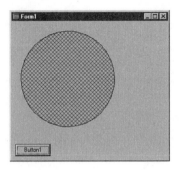

When using a pattern brush, the brush's Color property defines the color of the lines which make up the pattern. For some reason, VCL automatically forces the background mode to transparent when using a pattern fill. This means that the background color of the brush will be the same as the background color of the window on which the shape is drawn. Take another look at Figure 15.1 and you will see that the background color of the circle is the same color as the form (I know it's not easy to see in grayscale). If you want to specify a background color you need to circumvent VCL and go to the API. Here's how the code would look if you want to use a blue hatch on a white background:

```
Canvas->Brush->Color = clBlue;
Canvas->Brush->Style = bsDiagCross;
SetBkMode(Canvas->Handle, OPAQUE);
SetBkColor(Canvas->Handle, clWhite);
Canvas->Ellipse(20, 20, 220, 220);
```

Now the background color of the brush will be white. Figure 15.2 shows the circle with the new code applied.

Another interesting feature of brushes is the bitmap background option. First look at the code and then I'll tell you more about bitmap brushes. Here it is:

```
Canvas->Brush->Bitmap = new Graphics::TBitmap;
Canvas->Brush->Bitmap->LoadFromFile("bkgnd.bmp");
Canvas->Ellipse(20, 20, 220, 220);
delete Canvas->Brush->Bitmap;
```

Figure 15.2.

The hatched brush with a white background.

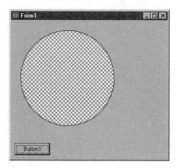

The first line in this code snippet creates a TBitmap object and assigns it to the Bitmap property of the brush. The Bitmap property is not assigned by default so you have to specifically create a TBitmap object and assign it to the Bitmap property. The second line loads a bitmap from a file. The bitmap must be 8 pixels by 8 pixels. You can use a larger bitmap, but it will be cropped to 8×8. The third line in this example draws the ellipse. After the ellipse has been drawn, the Brush property is deleted. It is necessary to delete the Brush property because VCL won't do it for you in this case. If you fail to delete the Brush property, your program will leak memory. Figure 15.3 shows the ellipse drawn with a bitmap background.

Figure 15.3.

An ellipse with a bitmap brush.

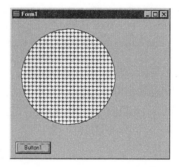

Sometimes you need a hollow brush. A hollow (or clear) brush allows the background to show through. To create a hollow brush, just set the brush's Style property to bsClear. Let's take the previous example and add a second circle inside the first using a hollow brush. Figure 15.4 shows the results. Here's the code:

```
Canvas->Pen->Width = 1;
Canvas->Brush->Bitmap = new Graphics::TBitmap;
Canvas->Brush->Bitmap->LoadFromFile("bkgnd.bmp");
Canvas->Ellipse(20, 20, 220, 220);
Canvas->Brush->Style = bsClear;
Canvas->Pen->Width = 5;
Canvas->Ellipse(70, 70, 170, 170);
delete Canvas->Brush->Bitmap;
```

15

Figure 15.4.

A circle with a hollow brush.

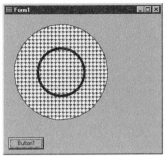

There are other things you can do with brushes if you go directly to the API. Most of the time, though, the VCL TBrush class does what you want.

Fonts

Fonts aren't anything new to you; you have been using fonts throughout the book. Fonts used with the TCanvas class are no different than those used with forms or other components. The Font property of TCanvas is the same as the Font property of any other component. To change the font for the canvas, just do this:

```
Canvas->Font->Name = "Courier New";
Canvas->Font->Size = 14;
Canvas->Font->Style = Canvas->Font->Style << fsBold;
Canvas->TextOut(20, 20, "Testing");
```

That's all there is to it. I'll talk more about what to do with fonts a little later in the section "Drawing Text."

Bitmaps and Palettes

Bitmaps and palettes go together most of the time. The TBitmap class encapsulates a bitmap object in C++Builder. Loading and displaying bitmaps is easy when using this class. You already saw TBitmap in action in the Jumping Jack program back on Day 9, "Creating Applications in C++Builder." The TBitmap class is used in a wide variety of situations. We'll look at some of those situations later today when we talk about drawing bitmaps and memory bitmaps. The TBitmap class is complex, so I won't go over every property and method here.

Palettes are one of the most confusing aspects of Windows programming. Most of the time the palette is maintained by the TBitmap object so you really don't have to worry about it. Rather than trying to explain the importance of palettes, let me show you an example. Start a new application and type the following code in the OnPaint event handler, or use a button click event if you want. You'll have to be sure to enter the correct path to the HANDSHAK.BMP file (you should find it in the Borland Shared Files/Images/Splash/256Color directory). Here's the code:

```
Graphics::TBitmap* bitmap = new Graphics::TBitmap;
//bitmap->IgnorePalette = true;
bitmap->LoadFromFile("handshak.bmp");
Canvas->Draw(0, 0, bitmap);
delete bitmap;
```

Notice that one line is commented out. Run the program and you will see a nice bitmap on the form. Now uncomment the line that is commented out. This line tells the VCL to ignore the palette information when displaying the bitmap. Run the program again. This time you should notice that the bitmap's colors are all wrong. This is because the palette is not being applied. The palette makes sure that the correct colors for this bitmap are mapped to the system palette.

Bitmap and palette objects play an important role in graphics operations. It takes a while to understand everything that is going on with bitmaps and palettes, so don't feel bad if you don't catch on to it right away.

Clipping Regions

Regions are areas of the screen that can be used to control the parts of the canvas which can be drawn on. The TCanvas class has a ClipRect property, but it is read only. To change the clipping region you have to use the Windows API. Let's take the previous example and modify it slightly to illustrate how clipping regions work. Here's the code:

```
Graphics::TBitmap* bitmap = new Graphics::TBitmap;
bitmap->LoadFromFile("handshak.bmp");
HRGN hRgn = CreateRectRgn(50, 50, 250, 250);
SelectClipRgn(Canvas->Handle, hRgn);
Canvas->Draw(0, 0, bitmap);
delete bitmap;
```

This time when you run the program you will see that only a portion of the bitmap is displayed. The SelectClipRgn() function sets the canvas' clipping region to the rectangle identified by the coordinates 50, 50, 250, 250. The bitmap is still being drawn in the same location it was before, it's just that only a portion of the bitmap (defined by the clipping region) can be seen. Everything outside the clipping region is ignored.

Regions don't have to be rectangular. Let's take the previous example and make it more interesting. Remove the line which creates the rectangular region and replace it with this line:

```
HRGN hRgn = CreateEllipticRgn(30, 30, 170, 170);
```

Now run the program again. This time, the bitmap will be limited to a circular region. Figure 15.5 shows the program with the elliptical region in place.

Let's try another type of region. Again remove the line which defines the region and replace it with these lines:

```
TPoint points[4] =
  { {80, 0}, {0, 80}, {80, 160}, {160, 80} };
HRGN hRgn = CreatePolygonRgn(points, 4, ALTERNATE);
```

15

Figure 15.5.

An elliptical clipping region.

This time we are using a polygon region. The `points` array defines the points that will be used to create the region. The `CreatePolygonRgn()` function creates a region from a series of points. You can use as many points as you want. You don't have to specify the closing point because the region is automatically closed between the first point and the last point. Run the program again and see what you get. Figure 15.6 shows the results of this exercise.

Figure 15.6.

A polygon clipping region.

Regions can be very useful when you are doing certain kinds of drawing operations. You may not need to use clipping regions a lot, but when you need them they are invaluable.

Basic Drawing Operations

You have already encountered some of the basic graphics routines as you have worked through the book up to this point. By now you know that the `Rectangle()` method is used to draw squares and rectangles, the `Ellipse()` method is used to draw circles and ovals, and the `MoveTo()` and `LineTo()` methods are used to draw lines. There is also the `Arc()` method for drawing arcs and the `Pie()` method for drawing pie-shaped objects. All in all, it's fairly basic. There's not much point in going into a lot of detail on those methods of `TCanvas`. Instead, we'll move on to the more interesting (and troublesome) graphics operations you are likely to encounter when writing C++Builder applications.

Drawing Text

Drawing text doesn't sound like it should be too difficult, does it? The truth is that there are several little things that if you aren't aware of them can make drawing text a difficult experience. In addition, there are several nice text-drawing features that you should know about.

TextOut() **and** TextRect()

The TextOut() method is the most basic way to draw text on a canvas. There really isn't too much to say about TextOut(). You just pass it the X position, the Y position, and the text to display. For example:

```
Canvas->TextOut(20, 20, "Mason P. Reisdorph");
```

This code displays the given string at position 20, 20 on the form. The X and Y coordinates specify the top-left corner of the text to be drawn, not the baseline. To illustrate what I mean, test this code:

```
Canvas->TextOut(20, 20, "This is a test.");
Canvas->MoveTo(20, 20);
Canvas->LineTo(100, 20);
```

This code displays some text at position 20, 20 and then draws a line from that same position to position 100, 20. Figure 15.7 shows the results of this code. Notice that the line is drawn across the top of the text.

Figure 15.7.

Text drawn with
TextOut().

Use TextOut() whenever you have text to display that doesn't need a lot of fine positioning.

The TextRect() method allows you to specify a clipping rectangle in addition to the text to be displayed. You would use this method if the text needs to be constrained within certain boundaries. Any of the text which falls outside of the boundary will be clipped. The following code snippet insures that no more than 100 pixels of the text will be displayed:

```
Canvas->TextRect(Rect(20, 50, 120, 70), 20, 50,
  "This is a very long line that might get clipped.");
```

Both TextOut() and TextRect() can only draw single lines of text. No wrapping of the text is performed.

TIP

To draw text with tab stops see the Windows API function TabbedTextOut().

Text Backgrounds

Refer back to Figure 15.7. Notice that the text has a white background—not very appealing on a gray form. The text background is obtained from the current brush (white by default). In order to remedy the unsightly results of Figure 15.7, you need to do one of two things: either change the color of the canvas' brush, or make the text's background transparent.

Changing the background color of the text is fairly easy. The question is, do you know what color to make the text's background? In this case, the text's background can be the same color as the form so you can do this:

```
Canvas->Brush->Color = Color;
```

This will work for most situations, but in some cases you need more control. It would be easier if you could just make the background of the text transparent. The good news is, you can. Here's how the code would look:

```
TBrushStyle oldStyle;
oldStyle = Canvas->Brush->Style;
Canvas->Brush->Style = bsClear;
Canvas->TextOut(20, 20, "This is a test.");
Canvas->Brush->Style = oldStyle;
```

First we save the current brush style. After that we set the brush style to transparent (bsClear). After we display the text we set the brush style back to what it was before. You should get into the habit of saving the previous style and resetting it when you are done drawing the text. It is unlikely that you want to leave the brush style set to transparent, so resetting the previous style is always a good idea.

Using a transparent background has other advantages as well. Let's say you wanted to display some text over a bitmap background. In that case you can't use a solid background. Here's a code snippet that illustrates the point (the FACTORY.BMP file can be found in your Borland Shared Files\Images\Splash\256Color directory):

```
Graphics::TBitmap* bitmap = new Graphics::TBitmap;
bitmap->LoadFromFile("factory.bmp");
Canvas->Draw(0, 0, bitmap);
Canvas->Font->Name = "Arial Bold";
Canvas->Font->Size = 13;
TBrushStyle oldStyle;
oldStyle = Canvas->Brush->Style;
Canvas->Brush->Style = bsClear;
Canvas->TextOut(20, 5, "Transparent Background");
Canvas->Brush->Style = oldStyle;
Canvas->TextOut(20, 30, "Solid Background");
delete bitmap;
```

This code first draws a bitmap on the form. Next, text is drawn on the form (over the bitmap) with a transparent background. After that, more text is drawn with the regular background. Figure 15.8 shows the results of this code. As you can see, making the background transparent makes for a much more appealing image.

Figure 15.8.

Text drawn over a bitmap with transparent and solid backgrounds.

Another reason for using transparent backgrounds for text was illustrated on Day 13, in the section "Owner-Drawn Status Panels." There we gave the status bar text a 3D look by drawing the text once in white and drawing it again, slightly offset, in black. The only way that code works is by using a transparent background. As you can see, sometimes a transparent background is the only thing that will achieve the effect you are looking for.

DrawText()

The Windows API `DrawText()` function gives you much greater control over text that is drawn on the canvas than does `TextOut()`. For some reason, the `TCanvas` class does not have a `DrawText()` method. To use `DrawText()`, then, means using the API directly. That's not so bad, but there are a couple of nuisances that you'll have to put up with. First, let's look at a basic `DrawText()` example and then I'll tell you more about the power of this function:

```
RECT rect = Rect(20, 20, 220, 80);
Canvas->Rectangle(20,20, 220, 80);
DrawText(Canvas->Handle, "An example of DrawText.",
  -1, &rect, DT_SINGLELINE | DT_VCENTER | DT_CENTER);
```

Figure 15.9 shows the results of this code as well as results from the following examples.

Figure 15.9.

Examples of the `DrawText()` function.

The first line in this example defines a `RECT` structure and initializes it with the Windows API `Rect()` function. After that, a regular rectangle is drawn on the canvas. This is just so that you can visualize the size of the rectangle that we are about to draw on. Finally, the `DrawText()` function is called to draw the text. Let's take a minute to discuss the various parameters of this function. The first parameter is used to specify the device context on which to draw. The `Handle` parameter of `TCanvas` is the `HDC` (handle to a device context) of the canvas, so we pass that for the first parameter. The second parameter is the string that will be displayed. The third parameter is used to specify the number of characters to draw. When this parameter is set to −1, all of the characters in the string will be drawn. The fourth parameter of DrawText() is a pointer to a RECT structure. This parameter is a pointer because some DrawText() operations modify the rectangle passed in.

The key to how DrawText() behaves is in the final parameter. This parameter is used to specify the flags that will be used when drawing the text. In this example we use the DT_SINGLELINE, DT_VCENTER, and DT_CENTER flags. These flags tell Windows that the text is a single line of text, and to draw the text centered both vertically and horizontally. All in all there are almost 20 different flags that you can specify for DrawText(). I'm not going to go over every flag, so for a complete list see the Win32 API online help.

The previous example illustrates one of the DrawText() function's most common uses: to center text either horizontally, vertically, or both. This is a great feature when doing owner-drawing of components. In particular, owner-drawn list boxes, combo boxes, and menus often need to center text. You may not realize the benefit of this function right now, but you will if you start doing owner-drawn components.

Another interesting flag of DrawText() is the DT_END_ELLIPSIS flag. If the text is too long to fit in the specified rectangle, then Windows adds an ellipsis to the end of the string. Take this code, for example:

```
RECT rect = Rect(20, 100, 120, 150);
DrawText(Canvas->Handle, "This text is too long to fit.",
  -1, &rect, DT_END_ELLIPSIS | DT_MODIFYSTRING);
```

When this code is executed it will result in this text being displayed:

```
This text is too long...
```

You can use this flag any time you anticipate text that could be too long for the rectangle in which the text is drawn.

DT_CALCRECT is another flag which is invaluable when you need it. This flag will calculate the height of the rectangle needed to hold the specified text. When you use this flag, Windows calculates the needed height and returns it but doesn't draw the text. You tell Windows how wide the rectangle should be, and Windows will tell you how high the rectangle needs to be to contain the text. In fact, Windows just modifies the bottom and left members of the RECT structure passed in so that it contains the needed values. This is particularly important when drawing multiple lines of text. The following example asks Windows how high the rectangle needs to be to contain all of the text. After that, a rectangle is drawn on the screen. Following that the text is drawn in the rectangle. Here's the code:

```
RECT rect = Rect(20, 150, 150, 200);
String S = "This is a very long string which will ";
S += "run into multiple lines of text.";
DrawText(Canvas->Handle, S.c_str(),
  -1, &rect, DT_CALCRECT | DT_WORDBREAK);
Canvas->Brush->Style = bsSolid;
```

```
Canvas->Rectangle(rect.left, rect.top, rect.right, rect.bottom);
Canvas->Brush->Style = bsClear;
DrawText(Canvas->Handle, S.c_str(), -1, &rect, DT_WORDBREAK);
```

I want you to notice something about this code; we have to use S.c_str() for the second parameter of DrawText(). This is necessary because DrawText() wants a pointer to a character array (a char*) for the text parameter. In this case I am using an AnsiString object to contain the text, so I have to use the c_str() method to convert contents of the AnsiString object into a char*.

Place this code in the OnPaint event handler for a form. Run the program several times, and modify the length of the text string that is displayed. Notice that no matter how much text you add to the string, the rectangle will always be drawn precisely around the text. Refer to Figure 15.9 for the results of this exercise as well as the results of the previous exercises on DrawText().

TIP

If you need even more text-drawing options you can use the DrawTextEx() function. See the Win32 API online help for full details.

NOTE

Drawing text with DrawText() is slightly slower than using TextOut(). If your drawing operations are speed sensitive you should use TextOut() rather than DrawText(). You'll have to do more work on your own, but the execution speed will likely be better. For most drawing, though, you won't notice any difference between TextOut() and DrawText().

DrawText() is a very useful and powerful function. When you start writing your own components you will no doubt use this function a great deal.

Drawing Bitmaps

Drawing bitmaps sounds like it should be difficult. As you have seen several times up to this point, drawing bitmaps is very easy. The TCanvas class has several methods for drawing bitmaps. The most often-used method is the Draw() method. This method simply draws a bitmap (represented by a descendant of the TGraphic class) onto the canvas at the specified location. You've seen several examples up to this point, but here's another short example:

```
Graphics::TBitmap* bitmap = new Graphics::TBitmap;
bitmap->LoadFromFile("c:\\winnt\\winnt256.bmp");
Canvas->Draw(0, 0, bitmap);
delete bitmap;
```

15

This code creates a TBitmap object, loads the file called WINNT256.BMP, and displays it in the upper-left corner of the form. Use Draw() when you want to display bitmaps without modification.

The StretchDraw() method is used when you want to alter a bitmap's size. You specify a rectangle for the location of the bitmap and an image to draw. If the supplied rectangle is larger than the original size of the bitmap, the bitmap will be stretched. If the rectangle is smaller than the bitmap's original size, the bitmap will be reduced to fit. Here's an example:

```
Graphics::TBitmap* bitmap = new Graphics::TBitmap;
bitmap->LoadFromFile("c:\\winnt\\winnt256.bmp");
TRect rect = Rect(0, 0, 100, 100);
Canvas->StretchDraw(rect, bitmap);
delete bitmap;
```

NOTE   No attempt is made by StretchDraw() to maintain the bitmap's original aspect ratio. It's up to you to be sure that the bitmap retains its original width-to-height ratio.

Another bitmap drawing method is CopyRect(). This method allows you to specify both a source rectangle and a destination rectangle. This allows you to split a bitmap into sections when displaying it. Take this code, for example:

```
Graphics::TBitmap* bitmap = new Graphics::TBitmap;
bitmap->LoadFromFile("e:\\factory.bmp");
const int strips = 6;
int stripSize = (bitmap->Height / strips);
HPALETTE oldPal =
  SelectPalette(Canvas->Handle, bitmap->Palette, true);
for (int i=0;i<strips;i++) {
  TRect src = Rect(0, i * stripSize,
    bitmap->Width, (i * stripSize) + stripSize);
  int x = random(Width - bitmap->Width);
  int y = random(Height - stripSize);
  TRect dst = Rect(x, y, x + bitmap->Width, y + stripSize);
  Canvas->CopyRect(dst, bitmap->Canvas, src);
}
SelectPalette(Canvas->Handle, oldPal, true);
delete bitmap;
```

This code loads a bitmap, dissects it into strips, and then displays the strips in random locations on the form. Figure 15.10 shows a sample run of this code. Enter this code in the OnPaint handler of your main form and run the program. Cover up the main form and then bring it to the top again. The images will be redrawn each time the form is repainted.

Figure 15.10.

Sections of a bitmap written randomly to the screen with
CopyRect().

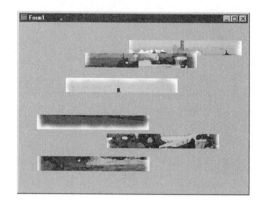

 NOTE

In the previous code example I used the SelectPalette() function to set the form's palette to the Palette property of the bitmap. For some strange reason the TCanvas class doesn't have a Palette property, so you have to go the to the API to set the palette for the form. If I didn't set the palette for the form then the colors would be wrong when the bitmap strips were displayed on the form. The CopyRect() method uses a different mechanism for displaying a bitmap on the canvas so taking this extra step is necessary when using this method.

There is one other bitmap drawing method I want to mention. The BrushCopy() method allows you to specify a source rectangle, a destination rectangle, an image, and a transparent color. The online help for BrushCopy() says to use the ImageList component rather than using this method. That's a bit extreme, in my opinion. There are times when BrushCopy() works nicely and it's a whole lot easier to use than the ImageList component. Don't overlook BrushCopy() if you are using bitmaps with transparent backgrounds.

Offscreen Bitmaps

Offscreen bitmaps, also called memory bitmaps, are used commonly in Windows programming. Offscreen bitmaps enable you to draw an image in memory and then display the image on-screen by using the Draw() method. Offscreen bitmaps help avoid the flicker that you see when you try to draw too much directly to the screen in a short period of time. Offscreen bitmaps are also good for complex drawing programs. You can prepare the image in memory and then display it when ready. Offscreen bitmaps are used in animation, although the most popular new technology for animation is Microsoft's DirectX SDK.

The principle behind offscreen bitmaps is a simple three-step process:

1. Create a memory bitmap.

2. Draw on the memory bitmap.

3. Copy the memory bitmap to the screen.

Creating a memory bitmap is easy. In fact, you've already done it several times in this chapter. Surprised? Each time you created a TBitmap object you were creating a memory bitmap. In those cases you were loading a file into the memory bitmap. In other cases you will create a memory bitmap, set its size, and then draw on it. For example:

```
Graphics::TBitmap* bitmap = new Graphics::TBitmap;
bitmap->Width = 500;
bitmap->Height = 500;
for (int i=0;i<20;i++) {
  int x = random(400);
  int y = random(400);
  int w = random(100) + 50;
  int h = random(100) + 50;
  int red = random(255);
  int green = random(255);
  int blue = random(255);
  bitmap->Canvas->Brush->Color = RGB(red, green, blue);
  bitmap->Canvas->Rectangle(x, y, w, h);
}
Canvas->Draw(0, 0, bitmap);
delete bitmap;
```

To try out this code, place a button on a form and type the code in the event handler for the button's OnClick event. Each time you click the button a new random set of rectangles is drawn on-screen. We are simply drawing on the memory bitmap and then copying the bitmap to the form's canvas. If you are using a 256-color video adapter, the colors will be dithered because we are not implementing a palette for this exercise.

NOTE   When you create a memory bitmap, the bitmap will have the same color depth as the current video display settings. In other words, if you have your video display set for 256 colors, the memory bitmap will be a 256-color bitmap. If you have your video display set for 24- or 32-bit video, your memory bitmap will contain 32KB, 64KB, or 16 million colors.

Saving a memory bitmap to a file is ridiculously easy. Here's all it takes:

```
bitmap->SaveToFile("test.bmp");
```

Yes, that's all there is to it. In fact, you can easily create your own screen capture program. All you have to do is copy the appropriate part of the desktop to a memory bitmap and then save it to file. It looks something like Listing 15.1.

Listing 15.1. Screen capture program.

```
 1: // Create a TCanvas object for the desktop DC.
 2: TCanvas* dtCanvas = new TCanvas;
 3: dtCanvas->Handle = GetDC(0);
 4:
 5: // Create a new TBitmap object and set its
 6: // size to the size of the form.
 7: Graphics::TBitmap* bitmap = new Graphics::TBitmap;
 8: bitmap->Width = Width;
 9: bitmap->Height = Height;
10:
11: // Create a palette from the form's Canvas
12: // and assign that palette to the bitmap's
13: // Palette property.
14: int nColors = GetDeviceCaps(Canvas->Handle, SIZEPALETTE);
15: LOGPALETTE* logPal = (LOGPALETTE*)new Byte[
16:    sizeof(LOGPALETTE) + (nColors - 1) * sizeof(PALETTEENTRY)];
17: logPal->palVersion  = 0x300;
18: logPal->palNumEntries = (Word)nColors;
19: GetSystemPaletteEntries(Canvas->Handle,
20:    0, nColors, logPal->palPalEntry);
21: bitmap->Palette = CreatePalette(logPal);
22: delete[] logPal;
23:
24: // Copy a section of the screen from the
25: // desktop canvas to the bitmap.
26: TRect src = BoundsRect;
27: TRect dest = Rect(0, 0, Width, Height);
28: bitmap->Canvas->CopyRect(dest, dtCanvas, src);
29:
30: // Save it to disk.
31: bitmap->SaveToFile("form.bmp");
32:
33: // Clean up and go home.
34: delete bitmap;
35: delete dtCanvas;
```

NOTE

This code goes the extra mile and implements a palette for the form in case the form is displaying graphics. This code was originally part of an article I wrote for The Cobb Group's *C++Builder Developer's Journal.* You can sign up for a free copy of the journal on The Cobb Group's Web site at http://www.cobb.com/cpb.

Listings 15.2 and 15.3 contain a program called MemBmp which illustrate use of memory bitmaps. This program scrolls a marquee across the screen when you click one of two buttons. The first button scrolls the text across the screen without using a memory bitmap (writing directly to the form's canvas). The second button uses a memory bitmap for smoother scrolling. A third button is used to stop the marquee. Figure 15.11 shows the MemBmp program running.

Figure 15.11.

The MemBmp *program running.*

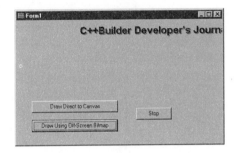

15

Listing 15.2. MemBmpU.h.

```
 1: //----------------------------------------------------------
 2: #ifndef MemBmpUH
 3: #define MemBmpUH
 4: //----------------------------------------------------------
 5: #include <vcl\Classes.hpp>
 6: #include <vcl\Controls.hpp>
 7: #include <vcl\StdCtrls.hpp>
 8: #include <vcl\Forms.hpp>
 9: //----------------------------------------------------------
10: class TForm1 : public TForm
11: {
12: __published:  // IDE-managed Components
13:    TButton *Button1;
14:    TButton *Button2;
15:    TButton *Button3;
16:    void __fastcall Button1Click(TObject *Sender);
17:    void __fastcall Button2Click(TObject *Sender);
18:    void __fastcall Button3Click(TObject *Sender);
19: private:  // User declarations
20:    bool done;
21: public:   // User declarations
22:    __fastcall TForm1(TComponent* Owner);
23: };
24: //----------------------------------------------------------
25: extern PACKAGE TForm1 *Form1;
26: //----------------------------------------------------------
27: #endif
```

Listing 15.3. MemBmpU.cpp.

```
 1: //----------------------------------------------------------
 2: #include <vcl.h>
 3: #pragma hdrstop
 4:
 5: #include "MemBmpU.h"
 6: //----------------------------------------------------------
 7: #pragma package(smart_init)
```

continues

Listing 15.3. continued

```
 8: #pragma resource "*.dfm"
 9: TForm1 *Form1;
10:
11: char* text = "C++Builder Developer's Journal";
12:
13: //----------------------------------------------------------
14: __fastcall TForm1::TForm1(TComponent* Owner)
15:   : TForm(Owner)
16: {
17: }
18: //----------------------------------------------------------
19: void __fastcall TForm1::Button1Click(TObject *Sender)
20: {
21:   Canvas->Font->Name = "Arial Bold";
22:   Canvas->Font->Size = 16;
23:   Canvas->Brush->Color = clSilver;
24:   done = false;
25:   while (!done) {
26:     for (int i=-Canvas->TextWidth(text);i<Width;i++) {
27:       Sleep(1);
28:       Application->ProcessMessages();
29:       if (done) break;
30:       Canvas->Font->Color = clGray;
31:       Canvas->Brush->Style = bsClear;
32:       Canvas->TextOut(i + 2, 12, text);
33:       Canvas->Font->Color = clBlack;
34:       Canvas->Brush->Style = bsClear;
35:       Canvas->TextOut(i, 10, text);
36:       Canvas->Font->Color = clSilver;
37:       Canvas->TextOut(i + 2, 12, text);
38:       Canvas->TextOut(i, 10, text);
39:     }
40:   }
41: }
42: //----------------------------------------------------------
43: void __fastcall TForm1::Button2Click(TObject *Sender)
44: {
45:   Graphics::TBitmap* bm = new Graphics::TBitmap;
46:   bm->Width = Width;
47:   bm->Height = 40;
48:   bm->Canvas->Font->Name = "Arial Bold";
49:   bm->Canvas->Font->Size = 16;
50:   bm->Canvas->Brush->Color = clSilver;
51:   bm->Canvas->FillRect(Rect(0, 0, Width, 40));
52:   done = false;
53:   while (!done) {
54:     for (int i=-bm->Canvas->TextWidth(text);i<Width;i++) {
55:       Application->ProcessMessages();
56:       if (done) break;
57:       Sleep(1);
58:       bm->Canvas->Font->Color = clGray;
59:       bm->Canvas->Brush->Style = bsClear;
60:       bm->Canvas->TextOut(2, 12, text);
61:       bm->Canvas->Font->Color = clBlack;
```

```
62:        bm->Canvas->Brush->Style = bsClear;
63:        bm->Canvas->TextOut(0, 10, text);
64:        Canvas->Draw(i, 0, bm);
65:    }
66:  }
67:  delete bm;
68: }
69: //--------------------------------------------------------
70: void __fastcall TForm1::Button3Click(TObject *Sender)
71: {
72:   done = true;
73: }
```

Summary

Graphics programming can be very interesting and very rewarding. It can also be very frustrating. VCL takes much of the frustration out of graphics programming by providing the TCanvas and TBitmap classes, along with their supporting classes such as TPen, TBrush, and TFont. These classes allow you to get on with the business of the visual aspects of graphics programming rather than worrying about how to load or save bitmap files. While I can't claim that this chapter is an in-depth look at graphics programming in C++Builder, I think that it's a good start and introduces you to some concepts that you can carry with you for a long time.

Workshop

The Workshop contains quiz questions to help you solidify your understanding of the material covered and exercises to provide you with experience in using what you have learned. You can find answers to the quiz questions in Appendix A, "Answers to Quiz Questions."

Q&A

Q Can the concepts discussed here be used when printing as well as drawing on the screen?

A Yes. As far as Windows is concerned, a device context is a device context. It doesn't matter whether that device context is for the display screen, a memory bitmap, or a printer.

Q I see the Ellipse() method, but I don't see a method for drawing perfect circles. How do I draw circles?

A Use the Ellipse() method. Just be sure that the rectangle used to draw the ellipse is perfectly square and you will get a perfect circle (if that makes any sense).

Q How do I change the color of the text that DrawText() produces?

A Change the Color property of the canvas' font.

Q Why should I bother with a memory bitmap?

A You may not need to. However, if you ever see noticeable flicker in your drawing routines, you should think about using a memory bitmap.

Quiz

1. What component can you use to draw graphics on a form?
2. Which TCanvas property controls the fill color of the canvas?
3. Which TCanvas property controls the color and appearance of lines drawn on the canvas?
4. What does a clipping region do?
5. What function do you use to draw multiple lines of text on a canvas?
6. What TCanvas method can be used to draw a bitmap with a transparent background?
7. Can clipping regions be irregularly shaped or must they be rectangular?
8. Which TCanvas method do you use to copy an entire bitmap to a canvas?
9. How do you save a memory bitmap to a file?
10. What determines the color depth of a memory bitmap?

Exercises

1. Write a program that displays a circle on the screen when a button is clicked.
2. Write a program that draws random lines on the screen each time the form is shown (including when the form is restored after being hidden).
3. Write a program that creates a memory bitmap, draws text and shapes on the bitmap, and then displays the bitmap on the form's canvas.
4. Modify the program you wrote in Exercise 3 to save the memory bitmap to disk.

Day 16

C++Builder Database Architecture

Today you will begin to learn about database programming in C++Builder. If you are new to database programming, at first glance it might appear overwhelming. Today I'll try to eliminate confusion by presenting a clear picture of the labyrinth known as database programming. First, I'll give you an overview of the C++Builder database architecture. After that I'll go over some of the data access components.

Make no mistake; database programming is complicated. I'll give you a high-level view of database programming in C++Builder, but I won't attempt to cover every detail.

NOTE

Not all the concepts and components discussed in this chapter pertain to every version of C++Builder. The Professional version of C++Builder has more database capability than the Standard version. The Client/Server version of C++Builder has much more database capability than either the Standard or Professional version.

Database Basics

Database programming comes with a whole gaggle of buzzwords: *BDE*, *client*, *server*, *ODBC*, *alias*, *SQL*, *query*, *stored procedure*, and so on. The good news is that it isn't all that bad after you learn some basics. First, let's take a moment to talk about databases. When you hear the word *database*, you probably imagine data stored in table format. The table probably contains fields such as FirstName, LastName, and PhoneNumber. These fields are filled in to create individual records in a database file. If that's what you envision when you think of a database, you're not too far off, but you aren't exactly correct, either. The term database is used to describe an all-encompassing data creation and maintenance system. It is true that a database can be as simple as one table. On the other hand, a real-world database can include dozens or even hundreds of tables with thousands or millions of records. These tables can contain one or more indexes. A complete client/server SQL database solution can also contain numerous queries and stored procedures. So as you can see, a database is more than just a table with data.

Speaking of tables, let's quickly cover some table basics. A table consists of at least two parts: fields and records. *Fields* are the individual categories of data in a table. For example, a table containing an address book would have a field called FirstName, a field called LastName, one called Address, PhoneNumber, and so on. Fields are also referred to as *columns*. A *record*, then, is one person's complete address: first name, last name, address, and so on. Records are also called *rows*.

A database is just a collection of data, of course, but database tables are often displayed in spreadsheet format. The column headers across the top indicate the field names. Each row in the table contains a complete record. Figure 16.1 shows just such a database table, displayed in grid (or table) format.

A database uses a pointer to the current record in the database.

NEW TERM The pointer to the current record within a database is called the *cursor*.

Figure 16.1.

A typical database table.

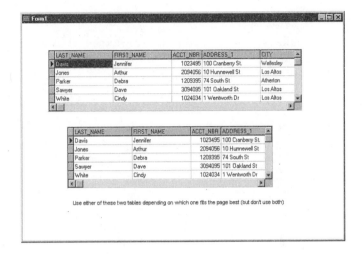

Use either of these two tables depending on which one fits the page best (but don't use both)

The cursor points to the record that will be read if data is requested and the record that will be updated if any edits are made. The cursor is moved when a user browses the database, inserts records, deletes records, and so on.

NOTE

When I say the cursor is a pointer, I don't mean it's a pointer in the C++ sense. I merely mean it is an indicator of the current record's position.

NEW TERM   A collection of data returned by a database is called a *dataset*.

A dataset can be more than just the data contained in a table. A dataset can be the result of a query containing data acquired from many tables. For example, let's say you have a database containing names and addresses of your customers, their orders, and the details of each order. This data might be contained in tables named Clients, Orders, and Order Details. Now let's say you request the details of the last 10 orders placed by Company X. You might receive a dataset containing information from the Clients table, the Orders table, and the Order Details table. Although the data comes from several different sources, it is presented to you as a single dataset.

Local Databases

The simplest type of database is the *local database*. A local database is a database that resides on a single machine. Imagine that you have a program that needs to store a list of names and addresses. You could create a local database to store the data. This database would probably consist of a single table. The table is only accessed by your program; no one else has access to it. Any edits made to the database are written directly to the database. Paradox, dBASE, and Access databases are usually local databases.

Client/Server Databases

The other way a database can be used is as a *client/server database*. The database is stored and maintained on a file server (the *server* part of the equation). One or more users (the *clients*) have access to the database. The users of this type of database are likely to be spread across a network. Because the users are oblivious to one another, more than one might attempt to access the database at the same time. This isn't a problem with client/server databases because the server knows how to handle all the problems of simultaneous database access.

The users of a client/server database almost never work with the database directly. Instead, they access the database through applications on their local computer. These applications, called *client applications*, ensure that the users are following the rules and not doing things to the database that they shouldn't. It's up to the client application to prevent the user from doing something that would damage the database.

As long as we are talking about client/server databases, let's take a moment to talk about database servers. Database servers come in several flavors. Some of the most popular database servers include offerings from InterBase (a Borland-owned company), Oracle, Sybase, Informix, and Microsoft. When a company purchases one of these database servers, it also purchases a license that allows a specific maximum number of users to access the database server. These licensed users are often referred to as *seats*. Let's say a company buys InterBase and purchases licenses for 50 seats. If that company grows to the point that 75 users require access to the database, that company will have to buy an additional 25 seats to be in compliance with the license. Another way that client/server databases are sold is on a *per connection* basis. A company can buy a license for 50 simultaneous connections. That company can have 1,000 users of the database, but only 50 can be connected to the database at any one time. The database server market is big business, no question about it.

Single-Tier, Two-Tier, and Multi-Tier Database Architecture

Local databases are often called single-tier databases. A single-tier database is a database in which any changes—such as editing the data, inserting records, or deleting records—happen immediately. The program has a more direct connection to the database.

16

In a two-tier database, the client application talks to the database server through database drivers. The database server takes the responsibility for managing connections. The client application is largely responsible for ensuring the correct information is being written to the database. A fair amount of burden is put on the client application to make sure the database's integrity is maintained.

In a multi-tier client/server architecture, the client application talks to one or more application servers that, in turn, talk to the database server. These middle-level programs are called application servers because they service the needs of the client applications. One application server might act as a data broker, responding to and handling data requests from the client and passing them on to the database. Another application server might only handle security issues.

Client applications run on local machines; the application server is typically on a server, and the database itself might be on yet another server. The idea behind the multi-tier architecture is that client applications can be very small because the application servers do most of the work. This enables you to write what are called *thin-client* applications.

Another reason to use a multi-tier architecture is management of programming resources. The client applications can be written by less experienced programmers because the client applications interact with the application server that controls access to the database itself. The application server can be written by more experienced programmers who know the rules by which the database must operate. Put another way, the application server is written by programmers whose job is to protect the data from possible corruption by errant client applications.

Although there are always exceptions, most local databases make use of the single-tier architecture. Client/server databases use either a two-tier or a multi-tier architecture.

So how does this affect you? Most applications you write with C++Builder for use with a client/server database will be client applications. Although you might be one of the few programmers given the task of writing server-side or middle-tier applications, it's a good bet that you will write primarily client applications. As an application developer, you can't talk directly to these database servers. Let's look next at how a C++Builder application talks to a database.

The Borland Database Engine

To enable access to local databases and to client/server databases, C++Builder provides the Borland Database Engine (BDE). The BDE is a collection of DLLs and utilities that enable access to a variety of databases.

To talk to client/server databases, you must have the Client/Server version of C++Builder. This version ships with SQL Links drivers used by the BDE to talk to client/server databases. Figure 16.2 shows the relationship between your application, the BDE, and the database.

Figure 16.2.

Your application, the BDE, and databases.

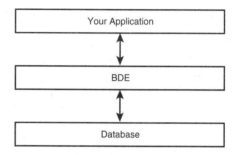

BDE Drivers

Naturally, database formats and APIs vary widely. For this reason, the BDE comes with a set of drivers that enables your application to talk to any type of database. These drivers translate high-level database commands (such as *open* or *post*) into commands specific to a particular database type. This enables your application to connect to any type of database without needing to know the specifics of how that database works.

The drivers that are on your system depend on the version of C++Builder you own. All versions of C++Builder come with a driver to enable you to connect to Paradox and dBASE databases. This driver, called STANDARD, provides everything you need to work with local databases.

The Client/Server version of C++Builder includes drivers to connect to databases by Sybase, Oracle, Informix, InterBase, and others.

BDE Aliases

The BDE uses an alias to access a particular database.

 A *BDE alias* is a set of parameters that describes a database connection.

This is one of those terms that might confuse you at first. The terms *alias* and *database* are often used interchangeably when talking about the BDE. When it comes right down to it, there isn't much to an alias. In its simplest form, an alias tells the BDE which type of driver to use and the location of the database files on disk. This is the case with aliases you will set up for a local database. In other cases, such as aliases for client/server databases, the alias contains other information as well, such as the maximum size of blob data, the maximum number of rows, the open mode, or the user's username. After you have created an alias for your database, you can use that alias to select the database in your C++Builder programs. Later today, in the section "Creating a BDE Alias," I'll tell you how to go about creating a BDE alias for your own databases.

As long as we're on the subject of aliases, let's take a quick look at the aliases already set up on your system. To view existing aliases, perform these steps:

1. Start C++Builder or create a new application if C++Builder is already running.

2. Switch to the Data Access tab of the Component palette, select a `Table` component, and place it on the form.

3. Click on the `DatabaseName` property in the Object Inspector and then click the drop-down arrow button to display a list of aliases.

After performing these steps, you'll see a list of available databases. At least one of these should be the `BCDEMOS` alias. This database alias is set up when C++Builder is installed. Select the `BCDEMOS` database from the list.

NOTE The list of databases you see depends on several factors. First, it depends on whether you have the Standard, Professional, or Client/Server version of C++Builder. It also depends on whether you elected to install Local InterBase. Finally, if you happen to have Delphi or another Borland product installed (such as Visual dBase or IntraBuilder), you might see additional databases.

As long as you are here, move to the `TableName` property and take a look at the available tables. The tables you see are the tables available for this database (this alias). Select another alias for the `DatabaseName` property. Now look at the table names again. You will see a different list of tables.

SQL Links

The Client/Server version of C++Builder comes with SQL Links in addition to the BDE. SQL Links is a collection of additional drivers for the BDE. These drivers enable C++Builder applications to connect to client/server databases such as those provided by Oracle, InterBase, Informix, Sybase, and Microsoft. Details regarding deployment of SQL Links drivers are also available in `DEPLOY.TXT`.

Local InterBase

The Standard and Professional versions of C++Builder come with a single-user copy of Local InterBase. Local InterBase is just what its name implies: a version of InterBase that operates on local databases. The client/server version of InterBase, on the other hand, is a full-featured client/server database. The main reason that C++Builder ships with Local InterBase is so that you can write an application that operates on local databases and then later change to a client/server database with no programming changes. This gives you an opportunity to hone your client/server programming skills without spending the money for a client/server database.

NOTE

> If you attempt to access a Local InterBase table, at either design time or runtime, you will be prompted for a username and password. The Local InterBase administrator is set up with a username of SYSDBA and a password of masterkey. You can use these for login, or you can go to the InterBase Server Manager utility and add yourself as a new user to the InterBase system.

C++Builder Database Components

Okay, so the proceeding section isn't exactly the type of reading that keeps you up all night turning pages. Still, it's important to understand how all the database pieces fit together. With that background we can now turn our attention to the database components provided by VCL and how those components work together to create a database application. First, I'll give you a quick overview of the VCL database components, and then we'll look at individual classes and components in more detail.

The VCL database components fall into two categories: non-visual data access components and visual data-aware components. Simply put, the data access components provide the mechanism that enables you to get at the data, and the visual data-aware components enable you to view and edit the data. The data access components are derived from the TDataSet class. They include TTable, TQuery, and TStoredProc. The visual data-aware components include TDBEdit, TDBListBox, TDBGrid, TDBNavigator, and more. These components work much like the standard edit, list box, or grid components except that they are tied to a particular table or field in a table. By editing one of the data-aware components, you are actually editing the underlying database as well.

NOTE

All the VCL database components can be termed data components. I use the term *data access components* for the non-visual database components on the Data Access tab of the Component palette and the term *data-aware components* for the visual database components from the Data Controls tab.

Interestingly, these two component groups cannot talk directly to each other. Instead, the TDataSource component acts as an intermediary between the TDataSet components and the visual data-aware components. This relationship is illustrated in Figure 16.3.

Figure 16.3.

Architecture of the VCL database components.

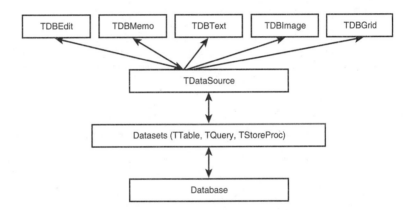

We'll look at these components in more detail, but first I'll walk you through a quick exercise to illustrate the relationship described in this section. Start C++Builder or create a new application. Now do this:

1. Place a Table component on the form.

2. Locate the DatabaseName property in the Object Inspector and choose the BCDEMOS database.

3. Locate the TableName property and choose the ANIMALS.DBF table.

4. Drop a DataSource component on the form and set its DataSet property to Table1 (choose Table1 from the drop-down list). The data source is now linked to the dataset (the Table).

5. Drop a DBGrid component on the form. Change its DataSource property to DataSource1. This connects the grid to the data source and, indirectly, to the dataset.

6. Now click the Table component on your form to select it. Change its Active property to true. You now have data in the table.

That was easy, but we're not done yet. Notice, by the way, that you can use the scrollbars on the grid even at design time. Okay, just a couple more steps:

1. Place a DBImage component on the form. Change its DataSource property to DataSource1 and its DataField property to BMP (BMP is a field name in the ANIMALS.DBF table that contains a picture of the animal). Hey, a fish! Size the DBImage as desired to fit the size of the image that is showing in the component.

2. Place a DBNavigator component on the form. Change its DataSource property to DataSource1.

Now run the program. Click any of the DBNavigator buttons. When you click the Next Record button, the record pointer changes in the DBTable and the picture changes in the DBImage component. All that without writing a line of code!

The data access components are used to connect to a database and to a particular table in a database. The Table component is used to access a database table. This is the simplest way of accessing the data in a table. The Query component is a way of accessing a database table using Structured Query Language (SQL) statements. SQL is a more powerful way of accessing tables but is also more complex. You will use either a Table or Query component to access a database, but not both. Another component is the StoredProc component that enables you to access a database via stored procedures. A *stored procedure* is a collection of database statements that performs one or more actions on a database. Stored procedures are usually used for a series of database commands that is often repeated.

The TDataSet Class

TDataSet is the ancestor class for TTable, TQuery, and TStoredProc. As such, most properties, methods, and events that these classes use are actually defined by TDataSet. Because so many characteristics of the derived classes come from TDataSet, I'll list the primary properties, methods, and events of TDataSet here, and later I'll list the properties, methods, and events particular to each derived class.

Table 16.1 lists the most commonly used properties of the TDataSet class, Table 16.2 lists the primary methods, and Table 16.3 lists the primary events.

Table 16.1. Primary TDataSet properties.

Property	Description
Active	Opens the dataset when set to true and closes it when set to false.
AutoCalcFields	Determines when calculated fields are calculated.
Bof	Returns true if the cursor is on the first record in the dataset and false if it isn't.

16

Property	Description
CachedUpdates	When true, updates are held in a cache on the client machine until an entire transaction is complete. When false, all changes to the database are made on a record-by-record basis.
CanModify	Determines whether the user can edit the data in the dataset.
DataSource	The DataSource component associated with this dataset.
DatabaseName	The name of the database that is currently being used.
Eof	Returns true if the cursor is at the end of the file and false if it isn't.
FieldCount	The number of fields in the dataset. Because a dataset might be dynamic (the results of a query, for example), the number of fields can vary from one dataset request to the next.
Fields	An array of TFields objects that contains information about the fields in the dataset.
FieldValues	Returns the value of the specified field for the current record. The value is represented as a Variant.
Filter	An expression that determines which records a dataset contains.
Filtered	When true, the dataset is filtered based on either the Filter property or the OnFilterRecord event. When false, the entire dataset is returned.
FilterOptions	Determines how filters are applied.
Found	Indicates whether a find operation is successful.
Handle	A BDE cursor handle to the dataset. This is only used when making direct calls to the BDE.
Modified	Indicates whether the current record has been modified.
RecNo	The current record number in the dataset.
RecordCount	Returns the number of records in the dataset.
State	Returns the current state of the dataset (dsEdit, dsBrowse, dsInsert, and so on).
UpdateObject	Specifies the TUpdateObject component to use for cached updates.
UpdatesPending	When true, the cached update buffer contains edits not yet applied to the dataset.

16

Table 16.2. Primary TDataSet methods.

Method	Description
Append()	Creates an empty record and adds it to the end of the dataset.
AppendRecord()	Appends a record to the end of the dataset with the given field data and posts the edit.
ApplyUpdates()	Instructs the database to apply any pending cached updates. Updates are not actually written until the CommitUpdates() method is called.
Cancel()	Cancels any edits to the current record if the edits have not yet been posted.
CancelUpdates()	Cancels any pending cached updates.
ClearFields()	Clears the contents of all fields in the current record.
CommitUpdates()	Instructs the database to apply updates and clear the cached updates buffer.
Close()	Closes the dataset.
Delete()	Deletes the current record.
DisableControls()	Disables input for all data controls associated with the dataset.
Edit()	Enables editing of the current record.
EnableControls()	Enables input for all data controls associated with the datset.
FetchAll()	Gets all records from the cursor to the end of the dataset and stores them locally.
FieldByName()	Returns the TField pointer for a field name.
FindFirst()	Finds the first record that matches the current filter criteria.
FindNext()	Finds the next record that matches the current filter criteria.
FindLast()	Finds the last record that matches the current filter criteria.
FindPrior()	Finds the previous record that matches the current filter criteria.
First()	Moves the cursor to the first record in the dataset.
FreeBookmark()	Erases a bookmark set previously with GetBookmark and frees the memory allocated for the bookmark.
GetBookmark()	Sets a bookmark at the current record.
GetFieldNames()	Retrieves a list of the field names in the dataset.
GotoBookmark()	Places the cursor at the record indicated by the specified bookmark.

Method	Description
Insert()	Inserts a record and puts the dataset in edit mode.
InsertRecord()	Inserts a record in the dataset with the given field data and posts the edit.
Last()	Positions the cursor on the last record in the dataset.
Locate()	Searches the dataset for a particular record.
Lookup()	Locates a record by the fastest possible means and returns the data contained in the record.
MoveBy()	Moves the cursor by the specified number of rows.
Next()	Moves the cursor to the next record.
Open()	Opens the dataset.
Post()	Writes the edited record data to the database or to the cached update buffer.
Prior()	Moves the cursor to the previous record.
Refresh()	Updates the data in the dataset from the database.
RevertRecord()	When cached updates are used, this method discards changes previously made to the record but not yet written to the database.
SetFields()	Sets the values for all fields in a record.
UpdateStatus()	Returns the current update status when cached updates are enabled.

Table 16.3. Primary TDataSet events.

Event	Description
AfterCancel	Generated after edits to a record are canceled
AfterClose	Generated when a dataset is closed
AfterDelete	Generated after a record is deleted from the dataset
AfterEdit	Generated after a record is edited
AfterInsert	Generated after a record is inserted
AfterOpen	Generated after the dataset is opened
AfterPost	Generated after the changes to a record are posted
BeforeCancel	Generated before edits are canceled

continues

Table 16.3. continued

Event	Description
BeforeClose	Generated before a dataset is closed
BeforeDelete	Generated before a record is deleted
BeforeEdit	Generated before the dataset goes into edit mode
BeforeInsert	Generated before a record is inserted
BeforeOpen	Generated just before a dataset is opened (between the time Active is set to true and the time the dataset is actually opened)
BeforePost	Generated before edits are posted to the database (or the update cache)
OnCalcFields	Generated when calculations are performed on calculated fields
OnDeleteError	Generated if some error occurs in deleting a record
OnEditError	Generated if an error occurs while editing a record
OnFilterRecord	Generated whenever a new row is accessed and Filter is set to true
OnNewRecord	Generated when a new record is added to the dataset
OnPostError	Generated if an error occurs while posting the edits to a record
OnUpdateError	Generated when an error occurs while cached updates are being written to the database
OnUpdateRecord	Generated when cached updates are applied to a record

The Fields Editor

Any TDataSet descendant (TTable, TQuery, or TStoredProc) gives access to the Fields Editor at design time. The Fields Editor enables you to select the fields that you want included in the dataset. To invoke the Fields Editor, right-click on a Table, Query, or StoredProc component on your form and choose Fields Editor from the context menu. The Fields Editor is displayed. At first the Fields Editor is blank, enabling all fields to be included in the dataset. You can add as many fields as you want to the dataset by selecting Add fields from the Fields Editor context menu. You can also create new fields for the table by choosing New field from the context menu. Figure 16.4 shows the Fields Editor as it appears after adding fields.

After you have added fields to the dataset, you can click on any field and modify its properties. The properties show up in the Object Inspector, enabling you to change the display format, constraints, display label, or other field characteristics.

16

Figure 16.4.

The Fields Editor.

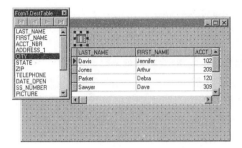

Cached Updates

Cached updates enable you to control when edits are applied to a database. Cached updates are controlled by the CachedUpdates property. When cached updates are allowed, changes to records aren't written directly to the database. Instead, the changes are written to an update cache on the local machine. Records are held in the cache until you call the ApplyUpdates() method. To abandon any changes in the update cache, you call the CancelUpdates() method. You cancel the edits made to the current record by calling the RevertRecord() method.

When cached edits are disabled (CachedUpdates is false), any changes made to a record are written to the database when the cursor leaves the record. This is fine for local databases but not a good solution for client/server databases for a variety of reasons. Most often you hear people talk about network traffic being the primary reason for using cached updates. Although it is certainly true that cached updates help reduce network traffic, the value of cached updates goes far beyond the issue of network traffic. Let me explain further.

Many client/server databases return a read-only result set as the result of a query. One advantage of cached updates is that the client can work with a local, read-only copy of a dataset, modify it as needed, and then write the edits to the database all at one time. This is possible because the database server handles updates, insertions, and deletions of records from a read-only dataset. A local database has to lock records when they are being actively edited. When a record is locked, other database users cannot access the record. Using cached updates reduces the time a record is locked to a very short period of time.

Another advantage to cached updates is that a user can make several changes to a dataset and then either *commit* (apply) all changes or *roll back* (cancel) all changes. This a two-edged sword, however, because if something happens to go wrong on the server when changes are being written to the database, all changes are lost.

One drawback to cached updates is that several users might be working with the same record at the same time. It becomes a race to see who gets the record updated first. In reality, this problem is reduced somewhat by implementing techniques in the client application that check whether multiple edits have taken place on a record. For example, if Joe tries to post an update to a record, the database and/or client application will notify Joe that Bob has changed the record since Joe initially retrieved it from the database. Joe will have to refresh his copy of the dataset to see whether he still needs to modify the record.

The `Table` Component

The `Table` component, represented by the `TTable` class, provides the quickest and simplest access to a table. Tables are more than adequate for most single-tier database applications. Usually you will use the `Table` component when dealing with local databases and the `Query` component when dealing with SQL database servers.

The `TTable` class has a lot of properties and methods in addition to those in its ancestor class, `TDataSet`. For the most part they are very intuitive. By that I mean that you can usually figure out what a property or method does by just looking at its name. It doesn't take a lot to figure out that the `LockTable()` method locks a table for an application's specific use and that the `UnlockTable()` method unlocks the table again. Likewise, you don't have to have an IQ of 150 to guess what the `CreateTable()`, `DeleteTable()`, and `RenameTable()` methods do. With that in mind, I'm not going to cover every aspect of every property and method listed here. Instead, let's get on to some of the more interesting aspects of the `Table` component.

NOTE

As you have already seen, the `DatabaseName` property is used to select a BDE alias. For local databases, rather than select an alias from the list, you can enter a directory where database files are located. The `TableName` property will then contain a list of database files in that directory.

Filters

A common need of a database application is to filter a table. Before I discuss filters in detail, I want to point out that filters are used primarily on local databases. Filters are rarely used with client/server databases; instead, a SQL query is used to achieve the same effect that filters have on local databases.

So why filter? Consider that you might have a table with thousands of records, but you are interested in displaying or working on only a small subset of the table. Let's say you have a database that contains names and addresses of computer users all over the world. Your company sells these names and addresses to other companies that want to do bulk mailings. I call up and want to order a mailing list from your company, but I want the list to contain only those computer users who live in Colorado. You could filter your table by postal code and generate a list of names with only Colorado addresses. Or, maybe Borland calls you and wants a list of computer users in Great Britain who are programmers by occupation. In that case, you could filter by occupation and country, thereby giving only the names and addresses the customer is interested in.

Filters in the `Table` component are handled one of two ways: through the `Filter` property or the `OnFilterRecord` event. Before I discuss these, let me talk about the `Filtered` property. This property determines whether the table is filtered. If `Filtered` is `true`, the table will apply the filter currently in force (either the contents of the `Filter` property or the results of the `OnFilterRecord` event). If `Filtered` is `false`, the contents of the `Filter` property are ignored and the `OnFilterRecord` event is never generated.

For the `Filter` property, you implement a field name, a logical operator, and a value. A filter might look like this:

```
FirstName = 'Bob'
```

This statement, in effect, says, "Show me all records in which the first name is Bob." Filters can also use the keywords `AND`, `OR`, or `NOT`:

```
CustNo = 1384 AND ShipDate < '1/1/94'
```

NOTE

The field name and logical operator (`AND`, `OR`, or `NOT`) are not case sensitive. The following two filter statements are identical:

```
CustName = 'TurboPower' and ShipDate < '1/1/94'
CUSTNAME = 'TurboPower' AND SHIPDATE < '1/1/94'
```

In the case of searching for text, the `FilterOptions` property determines whether the search string is interpreted as case-sensitive.

The following operators can be used in filter statements:

Operator	Use
<	Less than
>	Greater than
=	Equal to
<>	Not equal to
>=	Greater than or equal to
<=	Less than or equal to
()	Used to specify the evaluation order of compound expressions
[]	Used around field names containing spaces
AND, OR, NOT	Logical operators

Earlier I said there are two ways of filtering a table. One way is by using the `Filter` property. To use this property, all you have to do is type the filter statement directly into the `Filter` property in the Object Inspector at design time or assign a string value to this property at runtime. Naturally, you have to set the Filtered property to true as well. To see what I mean, perform the following exercise. First, we'll set up the core components:

1. Place a Table component, a DataSource component, and a DBGrid component on a form.

2. Click on the Table component and change its Database property to BCDEMOS, its TableName property to ORDERS.DB, and its Active property to true.

3. Click on the DataSource component and change its DataSet property to Table1.

4. Click on the DBGrid component and change its DataSource property to DataSource1. Size the DBGrid as desired.

At this point you should have a grid with data in it. Now we can get on with the business of filtering the table:

5. Enter the following in the Value column next to the Filter property:

   CustNo = 1384

6. Set the Filtered property to true.

Now the table should be showing only the orders for customer 1384. Spend some time experimenting with the filter statement and observe the changes to the table each time a different statement is used. Try the following:

```
CustNo = 1510
CustNo = 1384 and ShipDate < '1/1/94'
CustNo = 1384 and ShipDate > '1/1/94'
OrderNo > 1100 and OrderNo < 1125
```

NOTE
Note that the filter operators are different from the logical operators used in general C++ programming. The filter operator to test for inequality is <>, whereas the C++ operator for inequality is !=. Note also that any strings are enclosed in single quotes—not in double quotes as in C++ programming.

We are making changes to the filter at design time, but it's more likely that you will change the filter dynamically at runtime. In that case it's as simple as

```
Table1->Filter = "CustNo = 1510";
```

NOTE
If Filtered is set to true, but the Filter property is blank, the entire dataset is returned just as if the table were not filtered at all.

16

The other way you can filter a table is with the OnFilterRecord event. To generate an event handler for this event, double-click in the Value column next to the OnFilterRecord event in the Object Inspector. C++Builder will create an event handler. You can then write code to filter the table. Let's take the first filter example from earlier (CustNo = 1384) and filter using the OnFilterRecord event instead of the Filter property:

```
void __fastcall
TForm1::Table1FilterRecord(TDataSet *DataSet, bool &Accept)
{
  int Value = Table1->FieldByName("CustNo")->Value;
  Accept = (Value == 1384);
}
```

I've broken this down into two lines to make it more readable. The key element here is the Accept parameter. The OnFilterRecord event is called once for every row in the table. Set the Accept parameter to true for any rows that you want to show. The preceding code sets Accept to true for any rows in which the CustNo field contains a value of 1384. Earlier I gave you four sample filters to try. The first two filters would look like this if you were to use the OnFilterRecord event instead of the Filter property:

```
Accept = Table1->FieldByName("CustNo")->Value == 1510;
Accept = Table1->FieldByName("CustNo")->Value == 1384 &&
  Table1->FieldByName("ShipDate")->AsDateTime < TDateTime("1/1/94");
```

I'm sure you are thinking, "That's sort of messy." You are right. Using OnFilterRecord means more work, but it's also much more powerful than filtering with just the Filter property.

The FilterOptions property determines how the filter will be applied. This property is a set that can contain either or both foCaseInsensitive or foNoPartialCompare. By default this property is an empty set. This means that filters will be case sensitive and will enable partial comparisons. When partial comparisons are enabled, specifying a filter such as LastName = "M*" results in a dataset containing all records in which the LastName field begins with the letter *M*.

Finding Records

You can search a table for certain records by several different methods. In fact, this section applies to all TDataSet descendants, not just TTable.

NOTE

As with filters, finding records in a client/server database is almost always carried out via SQL queries. Finding records using the TTable methods is primarily a local database operation.

To search a filtered dataset, you can use the FindFirst(), FindNext(), FindPrior(), and FindLast() methods. These methods are the best way to search a filtered dataset because the filter is reapplied each time one of these methods is called. That means that if records that previously did not match the filter have been modified so that they now match the filter, they will be included in the dataset before the search is performed.

Another way to search a table is using the FindKey() and GotoKey() methods. These methods require an index. The FindKey() method searches the primary key field or fields for a particular value. If a secondary key is in place, the secondary key field is used to perform the search. The following example sets a secondary key and then searches for a customer number of 1384:

```
Table1->IndexName = "CustNo";
if (!Table1->FindKey(&TVarRec(1384), 0))
  MessageBox(Handle, "Record Not Found", "Message", MB_OK);
```

A third way of searching a table includes using the Locate() and Lookup() methods. One advantage to these is that they don't require a key. These methods differ in two ways. First, Locate() will use the fastest method available to search the table; if a table is indexed, Locate() will use the index. The second way these two methods differ is that the Lookup() method will also return the values of the fields you have specified in the ResultFields parameter before calling Lookup(). Both these methods enable you to specify a field or fields to search and the search value. The following example illustrates use of the Locate() method:

```
TLocateOptions Options;
Options << loPartialKey;
if (!Table1->Locate("CustNo", "1384", Options))
  MessageBox(Handle, "Record Not Found", "Message", MB_OK);
```

If the record is found, Locate returns true, and the cursor is updated to reflect the record where the match was found.

Master/Detail Tables

Setting up a master/detail relationship with the C++Builder Table component is easy. Let me explain a master/detail relationship and then I'll show you how to set up one. Let's say that you have a table called CUSTOMER that contains information on your customers. That table will likely be indexed on a field called CustNo. Let's further assume that you have a table called ORDERS that contains a list of all orders placed by your customers. Naturally, this table would also have a CustNo field. Now let's say you want to browse the table containing all your customers. Wouldn't it be nice if you could see each customer's orders while you browse? A master/detail table enables you to do that. Perform the following steps to get a good understanding of master/detail tables:

16

1. Start with a new application. Place a `Table` component on the form. Set its properties as follows:

   ```
   Name          Master
   DatabaseName  BCDEMOS
   TableName     customer.db
   ```

2. Place a `DataSource` component on the form and set its `DataSet` property to `Master`.

3. Now place a second `Table` component on the form and change its `Name` property to `Details`. We'll set the rest of this table's properties in just a minute.

4. Place a second `DataSource` component on the form. Change its `DataSource` property to `Details`.

5. Click on the `Details` `Table` component. Change its properties as follows:

   ```
   DatabaseName  BCDEMOS
   TableName     orders.db
   MasterSource  DataSource1
   ```

6. Click the ellipsis button next to the `MasterFields` property. The Field Link Designer dialog box is displayed.

7. At the top of the Field Link Designer dialog box is a combo box labeled Available Indexes. Select the CustNo index from this combo box.

8. Now both the Detail Fields list box and the Master Fields list box have a CustNo entry. Select CustNo in each of these list boxes and click the Add button to create the relationship. The Joined Fields list box shows that the two tables are joined by their CustNo fields.

9. Click OK to close the Field Link Designer dialog boxes.

10. Drop two `DBGrid` components on the form and link one to `DataSource1` and the other to `DataSource2`.

11. Change the `Active` property of both tables to `true`. The Master table will show all customers, and the Details table will show the orders for each customer.

What you just did was create a relationship between the master table and the detail table. This relationship joined these two tables through a common field: `CustNo`. To fully understand what this means, run the program and move from record to record in the master table. As you select a customer name in the master table, you will see only that customer's orders in the detail table.

The `Query` Component

The `Query` component is the preferred method of accessing data in client/server databases. The following sections describe the primary properties and methods of the `TQuery` class.

TIP

The `Query` component doesn't have a `TableName` property as the `Table` does. This means that at design time you can't immediately see a list of tables for the current database. To see a list of tables, you can do one of two things. First, you can temporarily drop a `Table` component on the form, set the `DatabaseName` property, and then view the list of tables in the `TableName` property. The other thing you can do is select the `Query` component on the form, right click on it, and then choose Explore from the context menu. This will take you to either the SQL Explorer (Client/Server version) or the BDE Administrator (Standard and Professional versions). You can use either tool to view the tables in a database.

The `SQL` Property

The `SQL` property is a `TStringList` that contains the SQL statements to execute. You can set the `SQL` property's value via the Object Inspector at design time or through code at runtime. To set the value at design time, click the ellipsis button next to the `SQL` property in the Object Inspector. The String List Editor dialog box is displayed, and you can type in one or more lines of SQL statements.

TIP

Remember that the String List Editor dialog box has a feature that enables you to edit string lists in the C++Builder code editor.

When adding lines to the `SQL` property at runtime, make sure that you clear the previous contents—for example,

```
Query1->SQL->Clear();
Query1->SQL->Add("select * from country");
```

It's easy to think of the `SQL` property as a string instead of a string list. If you don't clear the `SQL` property before adding a string, previous SQL statements will still be in the string list. Errors will almost certainly occur when you try to execute the SQL statement.

Executing SQL Statements

The statements in the `SQL` property will be executed when either the `Open()` method or the `ExecSQL()` method is called. If you are using SQL statements that include `SELECT`, use the `Open()` method to execute the SQL query. If you are using `INSERT`, `UPDATE`, or `DELETE` statements, you need to use the `ExecSQL()` method to execute the query. The following example sets the `SQL` property and then calls the `Open` method:

```
Query1->SQL->Clear();
Query1->SQL->Add("select * from country");
Query1->Open();
```

The SQL SELECT statement retrieves certain columns from a database. The asterisk tells the database server to return all the columns in a table. The preceding example, then, returns the entire table called country from the current database. To return specific columns, use code like the following:

```
Query1->SQL->Clear();
Query1->SQL->Add("select Name, Capital from country");
Query1->Open();
```

16

NOTE   Setting the Active property to true is the same as calling the Open() method.

The SQL DELETE statement deletes records from a dataset. To delete a record from a dataset, you can use code like this:

```
Query1->SQL->Clear();
Query1->SQL->Add("delete from country where name = 'Royland'");
Query1->ExecSQL();
```

Notice that the ExecSQL() method is used instead of the Open() method. As I said earlier, you need to use the ExecSQL() method to execute a query containing INSERT, UPDATE, or DELETE statements.

The INSERT command inserts a record into a dataset:

```
Query1->SQL->Add("insert into country");
Query1->SQL->Add("(Name, Capital)");
Query1->SQL->Add("values ('Royland', 'Royville')");
Query1->ExecSQL();
```

Updating a dataset using the UPDATE command looks like this:

```
Query1->SQL->Clear();
Query1->SQL->Add("update country");
Query1->SQL->Add("set Capital = 'Royburg'");
Query1->SQL->Add("where Name = 'Royland'");
Query1->ExecSQL();
```

Although it isn't my intention to teach SQL, I thought a few examples would help get you started.

Using Parameters in SQL Statements

SQL statements use parameters to add flexibility. A parameter in a SQL statement is much like a variable in C++ programming. A parameter in a SQL statement is preceded by a colon. Take the following SQL statement, for example:

```
select * from country where name = :Param1
```

The parameter in the preceding statement is named `Param1`. When this SQL statement is executed, the value of `Param1` in the `Params` property is substituted for the parameter name:

```
Query1->SQL->Add("select * from country where Name = :Param1");
Query1->ParamByName("Param1")->AsString = "Brazil";
Query1->Open();
```

You can set the parameter values of the `Params` property at design time via the Parameters dialog box, but most of the time you will be changing the parameters at runtime (which is the whole point of using parameters, of course). Notice in the preceding code that the `ParamByName()` method is used to set the value of `Param1`. This is probably the easiest way to set a parameter's value. There is another way, however:

```
Query1->Params->Items[0]->AsString = "Brazil";
```

Here the `Items` property of the `TParam` class is used to set the value of the parameter. Accessing a parameter by index is more error prone than accessing the parameter by name because you have to remember the orders of your parameters. Most of the time you will just use `ParamByName`.

NOTE

> Not all aspects of a SQL statement can be parameterized. For example, most SQL servers don't allow a parameter for the table name. Take the following SQL statement:
>
> ```
> select * from :TableName
> ```
>
> This statement results in a SQL error because you can't use a parameter for the table name.

The `StoredProc` Component

The `StoredProc` component represents a stored procedure on a database server. A stored procedure is a set of SQL statements that executes as a single program. Stored procedures are individual programs run against a database. Stored procedures can encapsulate particular often-performed database tasks. This makes it easier for programmers to do their work because they don't have to write line after line of code each time they want to perform a certain action. All they have to do is call the stored procedure on the server. This also results in smaller client applications because they don't have to contain unnecessary code. Another reason for stored procedures is to maintain data integrity. A stored procedure can validate data and either allow or disallow changes to the database based on whether the data validation passes.

As with SQL queries, some stored procedures make use of parameters, and some do not. For stored procedures that don't take parameters, all you have to do is set the procedure name and execute the procedure:

```
StoredProc1->StoredProcName = "DO_IT";
StoredProc1->Prepare();
StoredProc1->ExecProc();
```

Notice that the `Prepare()` method is called first to prepare the stored procedure. After that, the `ExecProc()` method is called to execute the stored procedure.

For stored procedures that take parameters, you will have to set the parameters before executing the stored procedure:

```
StoredProc1->StoredProcName = "ADD_EMP_PROJ";
StoredProc1->ParamByName("EMP_NO")->Value = 12;
StoredProc1->ParamByName("PROJ_ID")->Value = "VBASE";
StoredProc1->Prepare();
StoredProc1->ExecProc();
```

By the way, if you have C++Builder Professional or Client/Server, you can test the preceding code yourself. Do this:

1. Drop a `StoredProc` component on a form and set its `DatabaseName` property to `IBLOCAL`.

2. Place a button on the form and double-click it to create an `OnClick` event handler.

3. Type in the code from the preceding code snippet.

4. Place a `Table` component on the form. Set its `DatabaseName` to `IBLOCAL` and its `TableName` to `EMPLOYEE_PROJECT`. Place `DBGrid` and `DataSource` components on the form and hook them up to the table. Set the table's `Active` property to `true`. This enables you to see changes made to the table.

5. Add one line to the end of the code in Step 3:

   ```
   Table1->Refresh();
   ```

Now run the program. When you click the button, a new record will be added to the table with an employee ID number of 12 and a project ID of VBASE. Close the program. Now change the code so that the employee ID number is 10, and rerun the program. This time you will get an error message from the stored procedure, stating that the employee number is invalid.

NOTE

> You can view a stored procedure using the Explore feature found on the context menu. The stored procedure called ADD_EMP_PROJ looks like this:
>
> ```
> CREATE PROCEDURE ADD_EMP_PROJ (
>   EMP_NO SMALLINT,
>   PROJ_ID CHAR(5)
> )  AS
> BEGIN
>  BEGIN
>  INSERT INTO employee_project (emp_no, proj_id) VALUES
>  (:emp_no, :proj_id);
>  WHEN SQLCODE -530 DO
>   EXCEPTION unknown_emp_id;
>  END
>  SUSPEND;
> END
> ```
>
> Naturally, you shouldn't change a stored procedure unless you know what you are doing.

The UpdateSQL Component

The UpdateSQL component provides a way of applying edits to a read-only dataset when cached updates are enabled. Ordinarily, a read-only dataset is just that—read only. When cached updates are enabled, however, a read-only database can be modified and the results of those modifications written to the database. Most client/server databases have default actions that they perform when the changes in the update cache are applied. The UpdateSQL component enables you to provide your own SQL statements when a record in a read-only dataset needs to be updated, inserted, or deleted. For example, using an UpdateSQL component, you can specify default values for certain fields in a dataset.

The DeleteSQL property enables you to define a SQL query that will be executed when cached updates are applied and the update cache contains deleted records. Likewise, the InsertSQL property enables you to define a SQL query that will be executed when records have been inserted in a dataset and cached updates are applied. The ModifySQL property is used to define a SQL query that will be called when a record has been modified and cached updates are applied.

The DataSource Component

The DataSource component provides a mechanism to hook dataset components (Table, Query, or StoredProc) to the visual components that display the data (DBGrid, DBEdit, DBListBox, and so on). The primary purpose of DataSource is to enable making changes to your applications easier. All the data components on a form are hooked up to the DataSource, which is then hooked up to the dataset. Because the data components are not hooked directly

16

to the dataset, you can easily change datasets and not have to hook up each and every data component on the form each time you change the dataset. To change your dataset from a `Table` to a `Query`, for example, all you have to do is change the `DataSet` property of the `DataSource` component. There's no need to change anything at all in each of the data components.

`TDataSource` has very few properties. As you have already seen, the `DataSet` property is used to hook the `DataSource` to an underlying dataset. The `Enabled` property determines whether the data components hooked up to this data source display data. When `Enabled` is `true`, data is displayed. When `Enabled` is `false`, the data components are blank.

The methods of `TDataSource` are mostly insignificant, and I won't go over them here. The `OnDataChange` event is generated when the current record has been edited and the cursor moves to a different record. The `OnStateChange` event occurs when the state of the dataset changes (when the user moves from edit mode to browse mode, for instance).

The `Session` Component

The `Session` component manages a database session. Each time you start a database application, the BDE sets up a global `TSession` object, `Session`. You can use `Session` to access the current database session. You don't have to create your own `TSession` objects unless you are writing a multithreaded application. Most of the time this isn't the case, so the default `TSession` object is usually all you need.

`TSession` has a couple methods of particular interest. The `AddAlias()` and `AddStandardAlias()` methods can be used to create a BDE alias at runtime. You will probably need to create aliases at runtime when you deploy your applications. Creating a BDE alias is discussed later, in the "Creating a BDE Alias" section.

The `GetAliasNames()` and `GetDatabaseNames()` methods can be used to get a list of databases. This is handy if you want to allow your users to choose a database from a list. You could put the database names in a combo box, for example:

```
Session->GetDatabaseNames(DBNamesComboBox->Items);
```

In this case, the `Items` property of a combo box called `DBNamesComboBox` is filled with the list of database names. The `GetTableNames()` and `GetStoredProcNames()` methods can be used in a similar way.

The `Database` Component

The `Database` component enables you to access specific database operations. You don't need a `Database` component at all for some applications. There are certain operations, though, that require a `Database` component. These operations are discussed in the following sections.

Retaining Database Connections

The KeepConnections property is used to control how database connections are handled when a dataset is closed. If KeepConnections is false, when the last dataset is closed, the database connection will be dropped. This will require login the next time a dataset is opened. It's not so much that login is an annoyance (which it is), but more importantly login takes time. I don't mean that it takes time in the sense that you have to type a username and password in a login dialog box. I mean that it takes a lot of processing and network time to open a database connection and log in, even if that login process is automated. If you don't want to worry about login every time a dataset is opened, set KeepConnections to true.

Login Control

One reason to use a Database component is to control login operations. There are two ways you can control login. One is by setting the LoginPrompt property to false and explicitly setting the login parameters. You can do this before opening a dataset:

```
Database1->Params->Values["user name"] = "SYSDBA";
Database1->Params->Values["password"] = "masterkey";
```

The preceding code sets the username and password for a Local InterBase database connection.

NOTE

> You should be very careful about hard coding password information in your applications, for security reasons. Login prompts are used for a reason. Don't bypass login requirements unless you have a very good reason to do so.

Taking this example a little farther, let's assume that you have a form with a Database component and a Table component. Let's say you want to create a database connection and open a table without any login prompt. Here's the code:

```
Database1->AliasName = "IBLOCAL";
Database1->DatabaseName = "MyDatabase";
Database1->Params->Values["user name"] = "SYSDBA";
Database1->Params->Values["password"] = "masterkey";
Table1->DatabaseName = Database1->DatabaseName;
Table1->TableName = "CUSTOMER";
Table1->Open();
```

This code first sets the Database component's Alias property to IBLOCAL to connect to Local InterBase. Following that, the DatabaseName property is set to an arbitrary name. You can use any name you like for the database name. Next, the database connection parameters (username and password) are set. After that, the Table component's DatabaseName property is set to the value of the Database's DatabaseName property. This hooks the table to the database. Finally, the TableName property is set for the table, and the table is opened.

The other way to perform login is with the OnLogin event. This event is generated whenever login information is required. In order to generate this event, you need to make sure that you have the LoginPrompt property set to true. After that, you can provide an event handler for the OnLogin event. It will look like this:

```
void __fastcall TForm1::Database1Login(TDatabase *Database,
      TStrings *LoginParams)
{
  LoginParams->Values["user name"] = "SYSDBA";
  LoginParams->Values["password"] = "masterkey";
}
```

Does the code look familiar? It's essentially the same code used earlier when directly setting the connection parameters of the database. Usually you would not hard code the username and password (or at least not the password) but would probably pull that information from an outside source such as an edit component, a configuration file, or the Windows Registry.

Transaction Control

Another reason to use a Database component is transaction control. Normally, the BDE handles transaction control for you. There might be times, however, when you require complete control over transaction processing. In that case you can use the Database component's transaction control methods.

A *transaction* is a collection of updates to a dataset. Updates can include changes made to records, deleting records, inserting records, and more. You begin a transaction by calling the StartTransaction() method. Any changes made to the dataset are held until you call the Commit() method. When you call Commit(), all updates in the transaction are written to the database. If you want to abandon changes to all updates in the current transaction, you call the Rollback() method. The transaction isolation level is controlled by the TransIsolation property's value.

NOTE

All transaction updates are treated as a single unit. This means that when you call Commit, all updates are committed. When you call Rollback, all updates are canceled. It also means that if something goes wrong during a transaction commit, none of the updates in the current transaction are written to the database.

The BatchMove Component

The BatchMove component is used to copy records from one dataset to another. The Source property specifies the source dataset, and the Destination property specifies the destination dataset for the batch move operation.

The Mapping property is required if your source and destination datasets don't have identical columns. Mapping is a TStringList property. To specify mappings, edit the string list and add mappings like this:

```
FirstName = FName
LastName = LName
Notes = Comments
```

The column name left of the equal sign is the destination column, and the column name on the right of the equal sign is the source column. Setting the mappings like this tells TBatchMove, "These two datasets don't match, so copy the data from the FName column in the source dataset to the FirstName column in the destination dataset." If your source and destination datasets are not identical and you fail to set column mappings, the batch move will fail.

The Execute() method performs the batch move. To use TBatchMove, all you have to do is set the Source, Destination, and Mode properties and call the Execute() method. You can set the Source and Destination properties at design time or at runtime. The following code creates a copy of a table:

```
DestTable->TableName = "copy.db";
BatchMove1->Destination = DestTable;
BatchMove1->Source = SourceTable;
BatchMove1->Mode = batCopy;
BatchMove1->Execute();
```

The Mode property specifies how records are applied to the source dataset. Table 16.4 lists the possible values of the Mode property and their meanings.

Table 16.4. Mode property values.

Value	Description
batAppend	Appends records from source dataset to the end of the destination dataset.
batAppendUpdate	Combination of batAppend and batUpdate. If a matching record already exists, it is updated. If no matching record exists, a new record is added.
batCopy	Creates a new table and copies all records from the source table to the new table.
batDelete	Deletes records in the destination dataset that match the source dataset. The destination dataset must have an index.
batUpdate	Replaces records in the destination dataset with records from the source dataset that have the same key values.

16

WARNING

Be careful with the `batCopy` mode. Calling `Execute` in this mode will overwrite any existing tables and replace the contents with the contents of the source table.

TField

The `TField` class represents a field (column) in a database. Through the `TField` class you can set a field's attributes. These attributes include the data type (string, integer, float, and so on), the size of the field, the index, whether the field is a calculated field, whether it is required, and so on. You can also access or set a field's value through properties such as `AsString`, `AsVariant`, and `AsInteger`.

`TField` is a base class for more specific field classes. The descendants of `TField` include `TStringField`, `TIntegerField`, `TSmallIntField`, `TWordField`, `TFloatField`, `TCurrencyField`, `TBCDField`, `TBooleanField`, `TDateTimeField`, `TDateField`, `TTimeField`, `TBlobField`, `TBytesField`, `TVarBytesField`, `TMemoField`, and `TGraphicField`. These derived classes extend the base class in small ways to add functionality. For example, numerical field classes have a `DisplayFormat` property that determines how the number is displayed and an `EditFormat` property that determines how the value appears while being edited. Each `TField` descendant corresponds to a specific database field type. The `TIntegerField` class is used when the field type is integer, the `TTimeField` class is used when the field type is a date or time (or date/time), the `TBlobField` class is used when the field type is binary large object, and so on.

You can access the properties of `TField` at design time through the Fields Editor. After you have added fields, you can click on a field in the Fields Editor and the properties for that field will be displayed in the Object Inspector. Figure 16.5 shows the Fields Editor and Object Inspector while editing fields.

Figure 16.5.

The Fields Editor and Object Inspector.

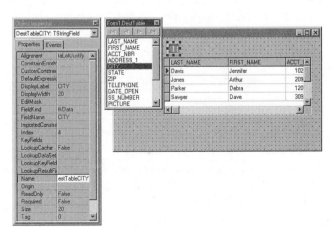

The TField properties and methods are so numerous that I'm not going to list them all here. Instead, I'll walk you through some ways you are most likely to use TField and its descendant classes.

Accessing Fields

Before you can get or set the field value, you need some way of locating a field. There are at least three ways to do this:

- [ ] By its pointer name
- [ ] By the Fields property of TDataSet
- [ ] By the FieldByName() method of TDataSet

Accessing a field by its pointer name is probably the least used method. It only works if you have previously added fields to your project using the Fields Editor. When you add fields via the Fields Editor, C++Builder creates a pointer for each field by combining the table name with the field name. If you had a table called Table1 and a string field called FirstName, C++Builder would create a TStringField pointer called Table1FirstName. You could use this pointer to access a field:

```
Table1FirstName->Value = "Per";
```

The problem with this approach is that you don't always need to add fields using the Field Editor.

The Fields property offers another way of accessing a field—by position. If you know that the LastName field is the first field in the table, you can use something like this:

```
Edit1->Text = Table1->Fields[0]->Value;
```

The problem with this approach, of course, is that you have to know the exact order of fields.

Of the three ways of accessing fields, the most commonly used and reliable is the FieldByName() method. Using FieldByName(), you only have to know the name of the field to access the field:

```
Table1->FieldByName("LastName")->AsString = Edit1->Text;
```

FieldByName returns a TField pointer. To make it more understandable, let me break down the preceding line of code:

```
TField* field;
field = Table1->FieldByName("LastName");
field->AsString = Edit1->Text;
```

In most cases FieldByName is the way to go. Oh, you might be wondering which record gets modified when you execute the preceding code. All these techniques retrieve the field from the current record.

Retrieving and Setting Field Values

After you have obtained a pointer to a particular field, you can change its value using the Value property or any of the As properties. By As properties I mean AsString, AsInteger, AsDateTime, AsBoolean, and so on. These properties perform conversions from one data type to another. Naturally, you can't always be assured that a conversion can be made. For example, if you try to convert a string field containing Smith to an integer, an exception will be thrown.

Setting a field's value is simple when you know the secret of FieldByName:

```
Table1->Edit();
Table1->FieldByName("LastName")->AsString = Edit1->Text;
Table1->Post();
```

First, the Edit() method is called to put the table in edit mode. If you fail to call Edit, you will get an exception when you try to modify a field's value. After the table is put in edit mode, the field's value is set. In this case I used AsString instead of the Value property. For a string field it's the same thing in either case. Finally, the Post() method is called to post the edit to the database (or the update cache if CachedUpdates is on). That's all there is to it. Retrieving a field's value is just as easy:

```
int AcctNo = Table1->FieldByName("ACCT_NBR")->Value;
```

TField Events

The TField events of note are OnChange and OnValidate. The OnChange event is generated each time a field's value changes. This occurs after the data has been posted. You can use this event if you need to be notified of changes to a field.

The OnValidate event, on the other hand, occurs just before data is posted. If you have a data control on a form associated with a field, that control can usually do validation of data. If, however, you are setting a field's value through code, you might want to do your own validation in the OnValidate event handler. This event is somewhat strange in that it doesn't pass you a parameter that you can use to reject an edit. Instead, you should throw an exception if the validation fails:

```
void __fastcall TForm1::Table1ACCT_NBRValidate(TField *Sender)
{
  if (Sender->AsInteger < 3000)
    throw (EDBEditError("Bad Account Number."));
}
```

When you throw an exception, the act of posting the data to the database is aborted.

To create an event handler at design time, you have to use the Fields Editor to add fields to the dataset. After you have done that, you can select a field in the Fields Editor and then double-click next to the event name in the Object Inspector, as you would for any other event.

Client/Server Database Components

The Client/Server version of C++Builder comes with three additional data access components that enable the creation of multi-tiered database systems. To recap, a multi-tiered database system is one in which client applications talk to one or more application servers (the middle tier) that in turn talk to the database server. The multi-tier database components are TRemoteServer, TProvider, and TClientDataset.

The TRemoteServer component is used in a client application to establish a connection to one or more application servers. The TProvider component, used in a middle-tier application server, acts as a conduit between the database server and the client application. The TClientDataSet component is used in a client application to gain access to the provider on an application server. A detailed account of the use of these components is beyond the scope of this book.

Creating a BDE Alias

You can go only so far in database programming without eventually creating a BDE alias. The sample databases are fine, but sooner or later you will need to create an alias for your own databases. When you deploy your C++Builder database application, you will also need to create one or more aliases on your users' machines as well. There are many ways to create an alias:

☐ Through the BDE Administrator utility from the C++Builder program group
☐ Through the Database Desktop program
☐ Through the SQL Explorer (Client/Server version only)
☐ Through code at runtime

To create an alias, either you must have your users run the BDE configuration utility or you must create any needed aliases through code. Obviously, creating the alias yourself through code is preferable (never underestimate the ability of your users to botch even the most simple tasks). First, I'll show you how to use the BDE Administrator to create an alias. Then, I'll show you how to create an alias through code.

Creating an Alias with the BDE Administrator

While you are developing your applications, you need to create one or more BDE aliases. This is most easily done using one of the BDE utility programs provided with C++Builder. The steps for creating an alias using the BDE Administrator and the SQL Explorer are identical, so for simplicity's sake I'll show you how to create an alias with the BDE Administrator.

Let's assume for a minute that you are going to create a mailing list application. The first thing you need to do is create an alias for your database. You can create an alias in several ways, but the easiest is probably with the BDE Administrator utility. Perform these steps:

1. Start the BDE Administrator (locate the C++Builder group from the Windows Start menu and choose the BDE Configuration icon). The BDE Administrator will start and will show a list of database aliases currently installed.

2. Choose Object|New from the BDE Administrator menu (make sure the Databases tab is selected). The New Database Alias dialog box comes up and asks which driver to use for the new alias.

3. You will be creating a database using the Standard driver, and because STANDARD is already selected, you can just click OK. Now the BDE Administrator looks like Figure 16.6.

Figure 16.6.

The BDE Adminis-trator creating a new database alias.

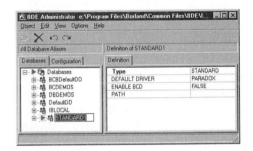

4. The BDE Administrator is waiting for you to type a name for your alias, so type MyDatabase and press Enter.

At this point, you need to provide a few items of information in the Definition window. The Type is already set to STANDARD, so there's nothing to be done there. The DEFAULT DRIVER field is set to PARADOX, which is the type we want, so there's nothing to be done there, either (other choices include DBASE, FOXPRO, and ASCIIDRV). You can also leave the default value for the ENABLE BCD field. The only thing you need to supply is the path on disk where the database files will be stored:

1. Click on the PATH field and either type a path or use the ellipsis button to browse to a path.

2. Close the BDE Administrator and say Yes when asked whether you want to save your edits. That's it. You have created a BDE alias.

Switch back to C++Builder and drop a Table component on a form. Check the DatabaseName property in the Object Inspector to see whether your database alias shows up. If you did everything right, you will see it listed there with the other database names. Your database doesn't yet have any tables, but that's okay. You can take care of that later.

Creating an Alias Through Code

To avoid confusion with your users, you will probably want to create any aliases your program needs the first time your program runs. Thankfully, creating an alias at runtime is simple. Here's the code to create a local Paradox alias called WayCool:

```
CreateDirectory("C:\\DATABASE", NULL);
Session->AddStandardAlias("WayCool", "C:\\DATABASE", "");
```

That's it? Yes, that's all there is to it. Naturally, you should perform some checks to ensure that the directory was created and that the alias was properly created, but that's about all there is to it.

NOTE   This example uses the AddStandardAlias() method to create a STANDARD type alias. To create aliases for database servers of other types, use the AddAlias() method.

Summary

That's a lot to absorb. The best way to solidify the material presented in this chapter is to spend a lot of time experimenting. Take some sample databases and perform filters on the tables, try out some SQL statements, and browse the databases with the BDE Administrator or the SQL Explorer. At this point you don't have to worry about writing complete database programs. Just spend some time with the various components and get a feel for how the BDE and the VCL database components work together.

Workshop

The Workshop contains quiz questions to help you solidify your understanding of the material covered and exercises to provide you with experience in using what you have learned. You can find answers to the quiz questions in Appendix A, "Answers to Quiz Questions."

Q&A

Q When I ship my C++Builder database application, can I just copy the appropriate BDE files to my users' machines?

A No. You must follow the guidelines outlined by Borland in the DEPLOY.TXT file. Generally speaking, this requires using an installation program certified by Borland to install any applications that use the BDE.

16

Q Why is it necessary to use a `DataSource` component? Why can't the data components and the data access components communicate directly?

A Using a `DataSource` component as an intermediary makes your job easier if you have to change datasets later on. Rather than change the `DataSet` property of numerous data components, you only have to change the `DataSet` property of the `DataSource`. For example, let's say you changed your dataset from a `TTable` to a `TQuery` (a major change). The change would be nearly transparent to your data components because the `DataSource` does all the work.

Q When do I use a `TTable` and when do I use a `TQuery`?

A Most of the time you will use a `TTable` when working with a local database (Paradox or dBASE) and a `TQuery` when working with a client/server database.

Q What's the point of Local InterBase?

A Local InterBase enables you to develop a local database application that can easily be converted to a client/server application later on.

Q Do I need to create a `TSession` for my application?

A Not normally. A default `TSession` is automatically created for every database application. You can use this object, called `Session`, any time you need access to the properties and methods of the `TSession` class. The only time you need to create your own `TSession` objects is when you are writing a multithreaded database application.

Q I am using a local database in my application. Do I need to worry about cached updates?

A Generally speaking, no. Cached updates are much more important for client/server databases.

Quiz

1. What is a local database?
2. What is the purpose of the BDE?
3. Are a dataset and a table the same thing?
4. Name one advantage of cached updates.
5. What is a stored procedure?
6. What is the purpose of the `SQL` property of the `TQuery` component?
7. Name one reason you might want to use your own `TDatabase` object instead of the default.
8. Why would you want to keep a connection to a remote database open even when you are not currently using the connection?

9. What does the `TBatchMove` component do?

10. What is a BDE alias?

Exercises

1. Describe how your application, the BDE, and a database work together.

2. Place a `DataSource`, a `Table`, and a `DBGrid` on a form. Hook up the components. Select a database and a table name for the `Table` component. Set the `Table`'s `Active` property to `true`. View the table contents in the grid.

3. Change the `Table`'s `TableName` property several times to view different tables. (Hint: You must set the `Active` property to `false` before changing the `TableName` property.)

4. Place a second `Table` component on the form created in Exercise 2. Select a database name and a table name. Set the `Active` property to `true`. Now change the `DataSet` property of the `DataSource` component to `Table2` (the second table). What happens to the `DBGrid`?

5. Create a new BDE alias on your system.

6. **Extra Credit:** Create a table under the BDE alias created in Exercise 5 and populate it with data.

Day 17

Building Database Forms

After a relatively unexciting look at C++Builder database architecture, we can move on to the more interesting task of building a database application. The first step in that task is to learn how to create database forms, so that's today's subject. You'll learn how to create database forms by using the C++Builder Database Form Wizard. You'll also learn how to build database forms from scratch. Towards the end of the day you will learn about the data components of C++Builder. These are the components that display the data from a database and enable you to edit that data (you can find them on the Data Controls tab of the Component palette). They are often referred to as *data-aware* components. I'll just call them data components in this chapter. So let's get to it.

The Database Form Wizard

The C++Builder Database Form Wizard provides a way of creating database forms quickly and easily. By using this wizard, you can create a database form from start to finish. You don't have to place any database components on the form. You just start the wizard and let the wizard take it from there.

 NOTE

> No automated process is good enough to be all things to all people. I won't pretend that the forms created by the Database Form Wizard will be everything you want or that it will do all your work for you. What the Database Form Wizard can do, though, is the initial work of setting up a database form. After the initial work is done, you can go to work customizing the form to make it look the way you want.

The Database Form Wizard enables you to create simple forms or master/detail forms. It enables you to choose whether your dataset will be a TTable or a TQuery. The wizard enables you to select a database table and to select the fields from that table that you want displayed on the form. It gives you a choice of layout options as well. After you have supplied the Database Form Wizard with all the information it needs, it creates the new form for you.

To start the Database Form Wizard, choose Database|Form Wizard from the C++Builder main menu. Alternatively, you can start the Database Form Wizard from the Business page of the Object Repository.

First, I'll show you how to create a simple form, and then I'll talk about master/detail forms.

Creating a Simple Form

When the Database Form Wizard starts, it displays the first page, as shown in Figure 17.1.

This page of the Database Form Wizard asks you to choose the type of database you are creating and the dataset type you would like to use. The Form Options section gives you the choice of creating a simple form (with a single dataset) or a master/detail form. We talked briefly about master/detail tables on Day 16, "C++Builder Database Architecture," in the section "Master/Detail Tables." I'll talk more about master/detail forms later today, in the section "Creating a Master/Detail Form." The first page of the Database Form Wizard also enables you to select from either a TTable-based dataset or a TQuery-based dataset. For this exercise, the default settings for creating a simple form using a TTable dataset are what you want, so you can click the Next button to move on to the next page.

Figure 17.1.

*Page 1 of the Data-
base Form Wizard.*

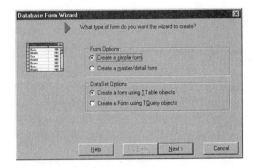

TIP

In some cases, you might want to implement data from more than one table on a single form but not use a master/detail relationship. The Database Form Wizard only enables you to choose from one table. What you can do, though, is run the Database Form Wizard and select the first table. Your form will be created. Change the names of the `Table` and `DataSource` components to something meaningful. Now run the Database Form Wizard again and choose the second table. When the form is displayed, select all the database components on the form and copy them to the Clipboard. Switch back to the first form, make some room on the form for the new components, and paste them from the Clipboard onto the form. Now remove the second form from the project, and you're all set.

The next page asks you to choose a table from which to obtain the data. The Driver or Alias name combo box enables you to choose a database name just as you do when setting the `DatabaseName` property for a dataset component at design time. It also enables you to choose a directory from which to select a table. For this example, choose the BCDEMOS alias. The tables available in the database will show up in the Table Name list box. Select the ANIMALS.DBF table. The Database Form Wizard now looks like the one in Figure 17.2. Click the Next button to go to the next page.

The third page of the Database Form Wizard asks you to choose the fields from the table that you want to include on the form. The Available Fields list box on the left shows the fields that are in the table you have selected. The Ordered Selected Fields list box on the right contains the fields that you want on your new form. Between the two list boxes are four buttons for adding or removing fields from the Ordered Selected Fields list box. To add a field, click the field name in the Available Fields list box and click the > button. Using this method, add any fields you want. You can select multiple fields and click the > button to add the selected fields. To add all fields in the table at one time, click the >> button.

Figure 17.2.

Selecting a table with the Database Form Wizard.

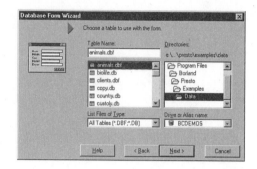

 TIP   You can double-click a field name to add that field to the Ordered Selected Fields list box or double-click it again to remove it from the list box.

After the fields have been added to the Ordered Selected Fields list box, you can change the order of the fields by drag and drop or by clicking the up and down arrow buttons below the list box. Figure 17.3 shows this page of the wizard when adding fields. For now, add all the fields to the Ordered Selected Fields list box and click the Next button to move to the next page.

Figure 17.3.

Page 3 of the Database Form Wizard, adding fields.

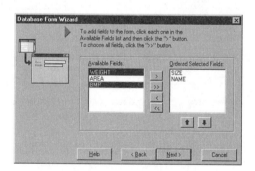

The next page of the Database Form Wizard dialog asks you how you want the components for each field laid out on the form. You have three layout choices. Click each of the three radio buttons and watch the image to the left of the wizard as you select different options. The image changes to show you the layout for each choice. Select the radio button labeled Vertically and click the Next button to continue. Figure 17.4 shows this page of the wizard.

17

Figure 17.4.

Selecting a layout style with the Database Form Wizard.

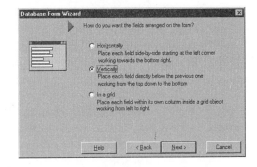

NOTE

When C++Builder creates the database form, it chooses the component type that most closely matches the data type of the field that component represents. For example, a regular text field is represented by a DBEdit component, a memo field by a DBMemo component, and a blob image field by a DBImage component. C++Builder makes a best guess as to the component type to place on the form for a given data type. You might have to edit the form to get exactly the component you want for a given field.

The next page asks you where you want to place the labels for the fields, relative to each data component. You can put the labels on top of the components or to the left. Notice that here, too, the image on the Database Form Wizard changes, depending on which of the two options is currently selected. For now, choose the second option in order to place the labels on top of the components. Figure 17.5 shows this page of the Database Form Wizard.

Figure 17.5.

This page enables you to place the labels.

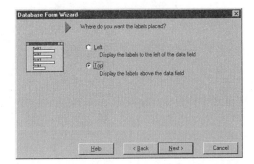

17

NOTE

The page shown in Figure 17.5 appears only if you select the option for vertical component layout on the previous page of the Database Form Wizard.

The final page of the Database Form Wizard asks you to make two choices. The first choice is in the form of a check box near the top of the page. Check this if the form is going to be the main form of the application. If it isn't the main form, clear the check box.

NOTE

If you choose to have C++Builder create the new database form as the main form of the application, be aware that the existing main form will still be part of the application's project. You need to remove the old main form from the project if you don't want it anymore.

The second choice asks you whether to create just the form or the form and a data module. If you choose the first option (Form Only), the form will contain all the data components, the `DataSet` component (`Table` or `Query`), and the `DataSource` component. If you choose the second option (`Form and DataModule`), the `DataSet` component and the `DataSource` component will be removed from the form and placed in a separate data module. I'll talk more about data modules tomorrow in the section "Working with Data Modules." For now, make certain that the Generate a main form check box is checked and that the Form Generation option is set to Form Only. Figure 17.6 shows the last page of the Database Form Wizard.

Figure 17.6.

The last page of the Database Form Wizard.

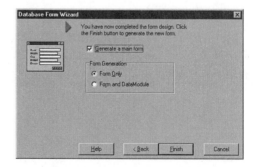

Click the Finish button and the form will be created. The finished form looks like the one in Figure 17.7.

Figure 17.7.

The finished form.

Notice in Figure 17.7 that the form contains a data component for each field that was selected and a label for each component. The label is capitalized because that's the way the field names are stored in this particular table. Notice that the top of the form contains a DBNavigator component, so you can browse the records of the table.

Now you are ready to click the Run button and see how the form works. When the application starts, the first record in the dataset is displayed. Use the buttons of the DBNavigator to move through the dataset. Keep in mind that you are working with live data at this point. You can edit a record by changing a value in one of the edit components. To save the changes to the database, click the Post button on the DBNavigator (the check mark). To cancel any changes to the record, click the Cancel button on the DBNavigator (the X button). When you post a record or move to another record, the changes are saved to the database.

Close the application and return to the C++Builder IDE. Spend some time examining the components on the form and the components' properties. Later I am going to go over some of the data components, but for now just experiment a little.

Creating a Master/Detail Form

Next, you'll create a master/detail form using the Database Form Wizard. When creating a master/detail form, the first few pages of the wizard are nearly the same as when creating a simple form. Only the labels that describe your options are different. First, perform the following steps. After that I'll explain the specifics of the Database Form Wizard that pertain to master/detail forms. Here goes:

1. Start the Database Form Wizard. On the first page, choose the option to create a master/detail form and the option to use TTable for the dataset components. Click the Next button.

2. Choose the table that will serve as the master. Select the BCDEMOS alias and then select the CUSTOMER.DB table. Click the Next button.

3. Select just the CustNo and Company fields and add them to the Ordered Selected Fields list box. Click the Next button.

4. Click on the Horizontally option to lay out the components horizontally. Click the Next button.

5. Now choose the table that will provide the details. Select the ORDERS.DB table and then click the Next button.

6. Select the CustNo, OrderNo, SaleDate, and AmountPaid fields and add them to the Ordered Selected Fields list box. Click the Next button.

7. Choose the option to arrange the components in a grid and click the Next button.

Now you are presented with a page you haven't seen before in the Database Form Wizard. This page asks you to select the fields that will join the two tables. First, click on the Available Indexes combo box at the top of the page and choose the CustNo field. The CustNo field is designated as a secondary index, so you'll use that field to join the two tables. Now, select CustNo in both the Detail Fields list box and in the Master Fields list box. After you select CustNo in both list boxes, the Add button between the two list boxes is enabled. Click the Add button to add the join to the Joined Fields list box at the bottom of the page.

 NOTE

> If you are paying attention, you might notice that this page of the Database Form Wizard looks almost identical to the Field Link Designer you saw yesterday, Day 16, when you set up a master/detail form by hand. Both perform the same task.

Figure 17.8 shows the Database Form Wizard after joining the two tables.

Figure 17.8.

The two tables joined on the CustNo field.

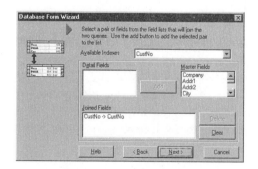

NOTE

The page illustrated in Figure 17.8 is slightly different if you are using TQuery, instead of TTable, components for the datasets. Specifically, the Available Indexes combo box isn't present when using TQuery components. The reason this combo box isn't displayed when using TQuery components is that the join is created using SQL statements, and indexes are not used in the same way they are with TTable components.

Click the Next button to move to the next page of the Database Form Wizard. Because this page already has the settings you need, just click the Finish button. C++Builder creates the form, and you are ready to try your new creation. Click the Run button to run the program. Use the DBNavigator to move from record to record. You will notice that the customer name is displayed in the top part of the form and that all the orders for that customer are displayed in the table in the bottom part of the form. Figure 17.9 shows the master/detail application running.

Figure 17.9.

Your new master/ detail form in action.

TIP

If you want to see the SQL statements for a master/detail relationship, run the Database Form Wizard again, but this time choose TQuery components for the datasets. After the form has been created, click on each Query component and examine its SQL properties.

Creating Database Forms by Hand

The Database Form Wizard is a good tool for quickly laying out a form. This wizard is particularly convenient for quick test programs. It will not be long, though, before you will need to custom design your database forms. After you gain experience creating database forms, you might actually prefer to create your forms by hand rather than use the Database Form Wizard.

There isn't a lot to know about creating database forms by hand. You drop one or more datasets (Tables or Queries) on the form and a DataSource component for each dataset, and then place a component on the form for each field in the dataset that you want to view. Sounds easy enough, and it is.

Let's build a new form that approximates the form you created earlier, in the section "Creating a Simple Form." First, you'll lay the groundwork and then start adding the data components. Perform these steps:

1. Start a new application. Place a Panel component on the form and set its Align property to alTop. Remove the caption.

2. Place a ScrollBox component on the form below the panel (you can find it on the Additional tab on the Component palette). Set the Align property to alClient.

3. Place a Table component on the form. You can place it anywhere you like, but the right side of the panel is probably the best place. Change the DatabaseName property to BCDEMOS and the TableName property to ANIMALS.DBF.

4. Place a DataSource component on the form next to the Table component. Change the DataSet property to Table1.

5. Place a DBNavigator on the panel at the top of the form. Change its DataSource property to DataSource1.

> **TIP**
> You can set the DataSource property quickly by double-clicking the Value column next to the property in the Object Inspector. C++Builder will cycle through the available DataSource components each time you double-click.

Your form now looks like Figure 17.10.

Now you need to add some data components to display the table's data. As you work through this exercise, you might want to refer back to Figure 17.7 to see the end result. Do the following:

1. Place a DBEdit component on the main part of the form, along the left side. Change the Name property to NameEdit. Change the DataSource property to DataSource1. Change the DataField property to NAME (choose NAME from the drop-down list).

Figure 17.10.

The form in the initial stages.

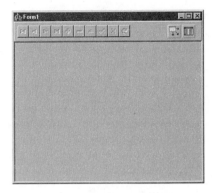

2. Place a Label component above the DBEdit you created in Step 1 (use a regular Label component from the Standard page of the Component palette, not a DBText component). Change its Caption property to Name.

3. Repeat Steps 1 and 2 and add DBEdits and Labels for the SIZE, WEIGHT, and AREA fields of the table. Make certain that you change the Name property and DataField property with respect to each field's name.

   In the next two steps we'll depart from Figure 17.7 and place the component for the BMP field to the right of the components you just placed. It makes more sense for it to be there rather than below the existing components.

4. Place a DBImage component on the form to the right of the edit components. Change the Name property to BMPImage. Change the DataSource property to DataSource1 and the DataField property to BMP.

5. Place a Label component above the DBImage and change its Caption property to Picture (the field name is BMP, but the word Picture is more descriptive).

Now your form looks like the one in Figure 17.11.

Figure 17.11.

The form with the data components in place.

Now you need to set the size of the DBImage component. Although you can't always be sure that each image will be the same size in every database, you can be certain in this case. You might guess at the size of the bitmap, but a better solution would be to set the size with a live image in the component. That's easy enough to fix. Click on the Table component and set its Active property to true. The image for the first record in the table is displayed. Now you can size the DBImage as needed to match the bitmap size.

You have nearly completed the form, but there's one more thing you should do. To imitate the form that the Database Form Wizard created, open the table when the form is created. First, set the Active property of the Table component to false (you just set it to true a minute ago). Now select the form itself in the Object Inspector. (Remember that, to select the form, you click on the panel and then press the Esc key on your keyboard. You can also select the form from the Component Selector at the top of the Object Inspector.) Switch to the Events page and create an event handler for the OnCreate event. Type this line of code in the event handler:

```
Table1->Open();
```

And that's it. Your new form is finished. Click the Run button to test your new creation. It will behave exactly like the first form you created with the Database Form Wizard.

A Closer Look at the Data Components

At this point, a quick look at the data components is in order. I'll give a brief overview of each component and highlight each component's key properties and methods. Most of the data components are derived from a standard component and have many of the properties associated with that type of component. I will discuss only the properties that are specific to the data version of each component.

Properties Common to Data Components

All the data components have properties in common. For example, all the components have a DataSource property. This property is used to link a data component with a data source, which is itself linked to a dataset. You have been using the DataSource property a lot in the past couple of days, so you should have a good idea of how it works.

Most data components also have a DataField property. You use this property to hook the data component to a particular field in the dataset. You saw how the DataField property is used when you built a database form from scratch. When you hook a data component to a field in the dataset, the contents of that field are directly displayed in the data component. In the case of Tables (and Queries if the RequestLive property is true), this means that editing the data control will result in changes to the data in the database.

Most data components also have a `Field` property. You use the `Field` property to gain access to a component's contents programmatically. For example, to change the contents of a `DBEdit` component, you could do this:

```
NameEdit->Field->AsString = "Clown Fish";
```

You can also change the field's display characteristics or other `TField` properties through the `Field` property.

You can use the `ReadOnly` property to prevent the user from editing the data in a data component that allows editing (`DBGrid` and `DBEdit`, for example).

The `DBGrid` **Component**

The `DBGrid` component displays a dataset in tabular, or spreadsheet, format. One of the most important properties of the `DBGrid` is the `Columns` property. This property enables you to change the number and order of the columns that appear in the grid. You can add, remove, or order columns using the Columns Editor. To invoke the Columns Editor, right-click on the grid and choose Columns Editor from the context menu. You can also click the ellipsis button next to the `Columns` property in the Object Inspector. By using the Columns Editor, you can add columns, remove columns, or arrange the order of columns. For example, a dataset might contain a dozen fields, but you might want to view only half those fields in the `DBGrid`. By using the Columns Editor, you can hide the fields you don't want to see.

NOTE

> Don't confuse the `DBGrid` `Columns` property (modified with the Columns Editor) with the `Table` component's `FieldDefs` property (modified with the Fields Editor). The `FieldDefs` property of the `Table` component controls which columns are actually contained in the dataset. The `Columns` property only affects which fields are *visible* in the grid.

The `DefaultDrawing` property indicates whether VCL draws the cells in the grid or the grid cells are owner drawn. If `DefaultDrawing` is `false`, you must respond to the `OnDrawColumnCell` and `OnDrawDataCell` events to provide drawing for the cells.

The `Options` property enables you to set the display and behavior options for the grid. Using this property, you can turn off column titles, allow or disallow column sizing, turn row and column lines on or off, and so on.

The `TitleFont` property enables you to set the font for the column titles. You use the `Font` property to set the font for the grid cells.

The DBGrid has only two public methods. When using an owner-drawn grid, you can call the DefaultDrawColumnCell() and DefaultDrawDataCell() methods to ask VCL to draw the cell for you. This is useful if you are owner-drawing particular columns but want default drawing behavior for the rest of the columns.

The DBGrid component has several events, most of which pertain to cell editing and data navigation. I won't list the events here because it is obvious from their names what functions they perform.

The DBNavigator Component

The DBNavigator component enables the user to browse a dataset record-by-record. The navigator provides buttons for first record, next record, previous record, last record, insert record, delete record, edit record, cancel edits, post edits, and refresh. This component is nearly automatic in that most of the time all you have to do is drop it on the form, hook it to a DataSource, and forget about it.

The ConfirmDelete property, when set to true, causes a dialog to be displayed whenever the user clicks the Delete button. You set the Hints property to true in order to enable fly-over hints for each button on the navigator. The VisibleButtons property is a set that enables you to control which buttons show up on the navigator. You can add or remove buttons at design time or runtime.

The DBNavigator has only one method of interest and one event. You can use the BtnClick() method to simulate a button click on the navigator. You can use the OnClick event to detect a click on the navigator. You rarely have to use OnClick, however, because the navigator already knows what to do when its buttons are clicked.

The DBText Component

The DBText component is the data-aware version of the standard Label component. It provides a way of displaying data from a field without allowing the user to modify the data. This component provides no database-specific properties, methods, or events, other than those common to all data components.

The DBEdit Component

The DBEdit component provides an edit control that is linked to a field in a dataset. You used a DBEdit earlier today when you created a database form from scratch. The DBEdit component, like the DBText component, doesn't have any database-specific properties, methods, or events, other than those common to all data components.

The DBMemo Component

The DBMemo is the data version of the standard Memo component. You can use this component to display data contained in database fields that contain large amounts of text. The

AutoDisplay property controls whether the data in the dataset field is automatically displayed when the cursor changes to a new record. When AutoDisplay is true, the data is automatically displayed. When AutoDisplay is false, the user must double-click the DBMemo to display the data (or press Enter when the control has focus). To force the memo to display its contents through code, you use a related method, LoadMemo(). This method is appropriate only when AutoDisplay is false.

The DBImage **Component**

The DBImage component is used to display binary large object (BLOB) data that is stored in image format. DBImage isn't necessarily a read-only component. You can change an image by pasting an image from the Clipboard or by using the Picture property to load a file from disk. The following code will change the image at runtime:

```
DBImage1->Picture->LoadFromFile("peregrine.bmp");
```

The main DBImage properties control how the image is displayed. The AutoDisplay property works exactly as described for the DBMemo component. The LoadPicture() method can be used to display the image when the AutoDisplay property is false. The Picture property enables access to the image itself and works the same as it does for components such as the standard Image component. The Center property determines whether the image is centered in the DBImage window. The Stretch property determines whether the image will be stretched to fit the current size of the DBImage window or whether it will be displayed in its original size. If Stretch is false, part of the image will be clipped if the image is too large for the DBImage window. The QuickDraw property determines whether to apply a palette to the image when displayed. When QuickDraw is true, no palette is used. When QuickDraw is false, a palette is used to display the image. This results in higher quality but slightly poorer performance when displaying images.

Methods of the DBImage component include CutToClipboard(), CopyToClipboard(), and PasteFromClipboard(). These methods do exactly what their names indicate.

The DBListBox **and** DBComboBox **Components**

The DBListBox component is, for the most part, a standard list box. What distinguishes it is that when the user selects an item in the list box, the selected item is written to the corresponding field in the dataset (set by the DataField property). To provide the strings the user can select from, you add strings to the Items property just as you do for a regular ListBox component. It is important to realize that the strings for the list box don't come from the database (that's what the DBLookupListBox is for).

The DBComboBox works in exactly the same way as the DBListBox except for the obvious differences between a list box and a combo box.

17

The DBCheckBox **Component**

You use the DBCheckBox primarily to display the contents of a database field containing logical data (true/false, yes/no, on/off). Set the ValueChecked property to a string that should be used to check for a match against the contents of the field—for example,

```
DBComboBox1->ValueChecked = "On";
```

In this case, if the associated field contains the value On, the DBCheckBox will be checked. If the field contains a value other than the one specified, the check box will not be checked. You can supply more than one value to check in the ValueChecked property—for example,

```
DBComboBox1->ValueChecked = "On;Yes;True";
```

If the value of the associated field contains any one of these values, the check box will be checked. The ValueUnchecked property works in exactly the same way except that any values matching the contents of ValueUnchecked will cause the check box to be cleared (unchecked). If you don't use both ValueChecked and ValueUnchecked, the check box state will be indeterminate (grayed check mark) for values that don't match.

The DBRadioGroup **Component**

The DBRadioGroup component works much like the DBListBox and DBComboBox components. You supply the items for the radio group and when an item is selected, the value (text) associated with that radio button is written to the associated field in the database.

The Values property holds the current value of the field in the database. You can use the Values property to substitute the display string in the radio group box with a different string. For example, you might have a radio group box with radio buttons labeled Yearly, Quarterly, and Monthly. Your database, however, might store codes such as Y, Q, and M instead of the full names. Given that scenario, you could set the Values property (a string list) like this:

```
Y
Q
M
```

Now, when a radio button is selected, the one-letter code will be written to the database field instead of the display string of the selected radio button. If the Values property is empty, the display string of the radio button will be written to the database when a radio button is clicked.

The DBLookupListBox **and** DBLookupComboBox **Components**

The DBLookupListBox component enables you to display a list of field values from a lookup field. Unlike the DBComboBox component, the list isn't provided by you; it is provided by a separate dataset. Set the DataSource and DataField properties to the dataset and field where the selection will be written. Set the `ListSource` and `ListField` properties to the lookup field from which the list should be populated.

The `DBLookupComboBox` works just like the `DBLookupListBox`. In addition, the `DropDownAlign`, `DropDownRows`, and `DropDownWidth` properties control how the drop-down list appears.

The `DBRichEdit` Component

The `DBRichEdit` component enables you to display and edit a rich text memo field in a dataset. The `AutoDisplay` property and `LoadMemo()` methods of this component work exactly as they do for the `DBMemo` component.

The `DBCtrlGrid` Component

`DBCtrlGrid` is a component that enables you to create custom scrollable grid components. You can place any data components you want on the first cell of the `DBCtrlGrid` (or any other components for that matter), and C++Builder will duplicate those components for each record in the dataset. An illustration would probably help this explanation make more sense. Figure 17.12 shows a form containing a `DBCtrlGrid` component that has been aligned so that it fills the form's client area. The `DBCtrlGrid` contains a `DBEdit`, a `DBMemo`, and a `DBImage`. All the data components are placed on the first cell of the grid. The second cell contains a hatch pattern to tell you that you can't place components on that cell. Figure 17.13 shows the same form when the application is running.

Figure 17.12.

A form at design time containing a DBGrid *component.*

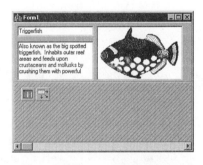

Figure 17.13.

The same form at runtime.

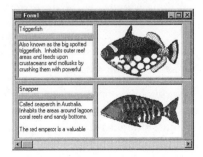

The DBCtrlGrid has a few properties worth mentioning. You use the Orientation property to determine where the scrollbar is to be placed and how the component is to act when the scroll bar is clicked (the DBCtrlGrid in Figures 17.12 and 17.13 has the Orientation set to goHorizontal). You use the PanelWidth and PanelHeight properties to set the width and height of a cell in the grid. The RowCount property determines how many records to show at one time.

The DBCtrlGrid component has one event, OnPaintPanel. This event is fired each time a grid cell needs painting. You can respond to this event in order to draw on the background of the panel. This pertains only to the panel's background. Any controls on the grid will be painted automatically, and you don't have to worry about them.

Other Data Components

DBChart is a charting component included with the Professional and Client/Server versions of C++Builder. This component is not only powerful but also complex. I can't begin to explain everything the DBChart component does, so you'll have to experiment with it to discover all that it is capable of.

The Client/Server version of C++Builder includes a tab named Decision Cube that contains six additional components. These components enable you to do complex data analysis such as cross tabulation of tables and graphs, drill down, pivot, and aggregation. A discussion of these components wouldn't be productive here, but I want you to be aware that these components exist in the Client/Server version of C++Builder.

Summary

Well, that about sums up the art of building database forms. Actually, I'm being facetious because I've just barely scratched the surface of database form creation and design. Use the Database Form Wizard for quick and easy database forms. Create database forms from scratch for more flexibility. Either way you go, building good database forms takes time and experience to master. It isn't something that you can be great at overnight. On the other hand, it isn't terribly difficult, either. Keep working at it and you'll be a database whiz in no time. The important thing is knowing the data components available to you as you craft your forms.

Workshop

The Workshop contains quiz questions to help you solidify your understanding of the material covered and exercises to provide you with experience in using what you have learned. Answers to the quiz questions are in Appendix A, "Answers to Quiz Questions."

Q&A

Q I like the way the Database Form Wizard saves me time, but I don't like the way the components are laid out on the form. What do you suggest?

A Run the Database Form Wizard to create components for any fields you want on your form. Then, manually rearrange the components to make the form look the way you want. The Database Form Wizard just gives you a head start. You can do anything you want with the form after the Database Form Wizard has done its job.

Q When using the Database Form Wizard, does it matter whether I create a form using `TTable` or `TQuery` objects?

A It all depends on the type of database you are talking to. If you are dealing with a local database such as Paradox or dBASE, you will probably use a `TTable`. If you are dealing with a client/server database, you will likely use a `TQuery`.

Q Is there any limit to the number of `DataSource`, `Table`, and `Query` components I can have on my form?

A There's no absolute limit, although there are practical limits to how many datasets you can work with at one time.

Q I noticed the `DBEdit` component doesn't have a `Text` property like the regular `Edit` component has. Why is that?

A The `DBEdit` component doesn't have a `Text` property because the component contents are obtained from a dataset. To access the contents of a `DBEdit` component, use the dataset's `GetFieldByName()` method and the `Value` property of `TField`.

Q Do I have to use a `DBNavigator` to enable my users to browse the database?

A No, you could provide your own buttons and then write code to move the cursor when the buttons are clicked. Using a `DBNavigator` is much easier, though.

Q My database contains a number of large images in BLOB fields, and it seems to take a long time to display the images. Is there something I can do to make the images draw faster?

A Make certain that you have the `QuickDraw` property set to `true`. Your images will draw faster, but they might not look as good.

Quiz

1. What's the fastest and easiest way to create a database form?
2. How do you control the order and number of columns that appear in a `DBGrid` component?
3. What component enables you to display a dataset in table format?
4. How can you add or remove buttons from a `DBNavigator`?

17

5. What component do you use to display BLOB image data?

6. What property is common to all data-aware components?

7. What property is used to select the field that a data component is linked to?

8. Can you rearrange the columns in a DBGrid component?

9. Which component is used to edit and display text fields in a database?

10. What does BLOB stand for?

Exercises

1. Create a new application that shows the contents of the VENDORS.DB table (BCDEMOS database).

2. Modify the application in Exercise 1 so that only the VendorName, City, State, and Phone fields are displayed.

3. Create a master/detail form from the IBLOCAL database (install Local InterBase from the C++Builder CD-ROM if necessary). Use the EMPLOYEE table as the master and the EMPLOYEE_PROJECT table as the detail table. (Hint: Use the EMP_NO field to link the tables.)

4. Create a database form that uses a DBCtrlGrid component to browse a table. Use any table and include any fields you like.

5. Create a database form by hand (not using the Database Form Wizard), using any table and any fields you like. Add a DBNavigator component to browse the table.

6. Remove all buttons from the DBNavigator used in Exercise 5 except the First, Next, Prior, and Last buttons.

17

Day 18

Building Database Applications

This chapter is about building database applications. The truth is, I cannot tell you everything there is to know about writing database applications in one short chapter. What I can do, however, is point out some things you are likely to encounter while writing database applications. Because you already know how to create database forms, you will spend most of this day dealing with lower-level aspects of database programming. You'll start with creating and populating a database entirely through code. Then you'll move on to data modules. Towards the end of the day you'll look at creating database reports with the QuickReport components. Finally, the day ends with a discussion on deploying database applications.

Non-Visual Database Programming

Until today you have examined mostly the visual aspects of database programming with C++Builder. That side of database programming is fun and easy, but sooner or later you have to do some real database programming. The kinds of programs that you have written so far have dealt primarily with simple viewing and editing of data. In this section you will learn how to perform certain database operations through code.

NOTE

I will mention only database operations that pertain to the TTable class. You could also use SQL to perform database operations in code, but I won't present that aspect of databases today.

Reading from a Database

This section is short because reading from an existing database isn't difficult. You will take the CUSTOMER.DB table and create a comma-delimited text file from the data. You won't write every field in the table to the file, but you'll write most of them.

The first step is to create a TTable object. After you have created the TTable object, you need to attach it to a database and to a particular table within the database. Here's how the code looks:

```
TTable* table = new TTable(this);
table->DatabaseName = "BCDEMOS";
table->TableName = "Customer.db";
```

This code emulates what C++Builder does when you set the DatabaseName and TableName properties at design time. The next step is to read each record of the database and write it out to a text file. First, I'll show you the basic structure without the actual code to write the fields to text file. After that I'll be more specific. The basic structure looks like this:

```
table->Active = true;
while (!table->Eof) {

  // Code here to read some fields from the
  // current record and write them to a text file.

  table->Next();
}
delete table;
```

This code is straightforward. First, the table is opened by setting the Active property to true (you could also have called the Open() method). Next, a while loop reads each record of the table. When a record is written to the text file, the Next() method is called to advance the database cursor to the next record. The while loop's condition statement checks the Eof property for the end of the table's data and stops the loop when the end of the table is reached. Finally, the TTable object is deleted when the records have been written to the text file.

NOTE

You don't specifically have to delete the TTable object. When you create a TTable object in code, you usually pass the form's this pointer as the owner of the object—for example,

```
TTable* table = new TTable(this);
```

This sets the form as the table's owner. When the form is deleted, VCL will automatically delete the TTable object. For a main form this happens when the application is closed. Although you are not required to delete the TTable object, it's always a good idea to delete the object when you are done with it.

Naturally, you need to extract the information out of each field in order to write it to the text file. To do that, you use the FieldByName() method and the AsString property of TField. I addressed this briefly on Day 16, "C++Builder Database Architecture," in the section "Accessing Fields." In the case of the CUSTOMER.DB table, the first field you want is the CustNo field. Extracting the value of this field would look like this:

```
String S = table->FieldByName("CustNo")->AsString + ",";
```

Notice that a comma is appended to the end of the string obtained so that this field's data is separated from the next. You will repeat this code for any fields for which you want to obtain data. The entire sequence is shown in Listings 18.1 and 18.2. These listings contain a program called MakeText. This short program takes the CUSTOMERS.DB table and creates a comma-delimited text file called CUSOMTERS.TXT. Listing 18.1 shows the header file for the main form's unit (MakeTxtU.h), and Listing 18.2 shows the unit itself (MakeTxtU.cpp). The form contains just a button and a memo. Look over these listings, and then we'll talk about how the program works.

18

Listing 18.1. MakeTxtU.h.

```
 1: //--------------------------------------------------------
 2: #ifndef MakeTxtUH
 3: #define MakeTxtUH
 4: //--------------------------------------------------------
 5: #include <vcl\Classes.hpp>
 6: #include <vcl\Controls.hpp>
 7: #include <vcl\StdCtrls.hpp>
 8: #include <vcl\Forms.hpp>
 9: //--------------------------------------------------------
10: class TForm1 : public TForm
11: {
12: __published:  // IDE-managed Components
```

continues

Listing 18.1. continued

```
13:    TButton *CreateBtn;
14:    TMemo *Memo;
15:    void __fastcall CreateBtnClick(TObject *Sender);
16: private:  // User declarations
17: public:   // User declarations
18:    __fastcall TForm1(TComponent* Owner);
19: };
20: //-----------------------------------------------------
21: extern PACKAGE TForm1 *Form1;
22: //-----------------------------------------------------
23: #endif
```

Listing 18.2. MakeTxtU.cpp.

```
1: //-----------------------------------------------------
2: #include <vcl\vcl.h>
3: #pragma hdrstop
4:
5: #include "MakeTxtU.h"
6: //-----------------------------------------------------
7: #pragma package(smart_init)
8: #pragma resource "*.dfm"
9: TForm1 *Form1;
10: //-----------------------------------------------------
11: __fastcall TForm1::TForm1(TComponent* Owner)
12:    : TForm(Owner)
13: {
14: }
15: //-----------------------------------------------------
16:
17: void __fastcall TForm1::CreateBtnClick(TObject *Sender)
18: {
19:    // Create the table and assign a database and table name.
20:    TTable* table = new TTable(this);
21:    table->DatabaseName = "BCDEMOS";
22:    table->TableName = "Customer.db";
23:
24:    // Change to the busy cursor.
25:    Screen->Cursor = crHourGlass;
26:
27:    // We can use a Memo to show the progress as well as to
28:    // save the file to disk. First clear the memo of any text.
29:    Memo->Lines->Clear();
30:
31:    // Open the table.
32:    table->Active = true;
33:    CreateBtn->Enabled = false;
34:
35:    // Loop through the records, writing each one to the memo.
36:    while (!table->Eof) {
37:
```

18

```
38:    // Get the first field and add it to the String S,
39:    // followed by the delimiter.
40:    String S = table->FieldByName("CustNo")->AsString + ",";
41:
42:    // Repeat for all the fields we want.
43:    S += table->FieldByName("Company")->AsString + ",";
44:    S += table->FieldByName("Addr1")->AsString + ",";
45:    S += table->FieldByName("Addr2")->AsString + ",";
46:    S += table->FieldByName("City")->AsString + ",";
47:    S += table->FieldByName("State")->AsString + ",";
48:    S += table->FieldByName("Zip")->AsString + ",";
49:    S += table->FieldByName("Phone")->AsString + ",";
50:    S += table->FieldByName("FAX")->AsString + ",";
51:
52:    // Add the string to the Memo.
53:    Memo->Lines->Add(S);
54:
55:    // Move to the next record.
56:    table->Next();
57:  }
58:
59:  // Write the file to disk.
60:  Memo->Lines->SaveToFile("customer.txt");
61:
62:  // Turn the button back on and reset the cursor.
63:  CreateBtn->Enabled = true;
64:  Screen->Cursor = crDefault;
65:  delete table;
66: }
67: //----------------------------------------------------------
```

All the action takes place in the `CreateBtnClick()` method. When you click the Create File button, the program extracts data from the database table and puts it into the Memo component. First, the value of the `CustNo` field is read and put into a string, followed by a comma. After that, each subsequent field's value is appended to the end of the string, again followed by a comma. After all the data has been extracted from a record, the string is added to the memo, using the `Add()` method. When the end of the table is reached, the memo contents are saved to disk.

I used a Memo component in this example for two reasons. First, by displaying the results in a memo, you can see what the program produces. Second, the memo component's Lines property (a TStringList) provides an easy way of saving a text file to disk. Figure 18.1 shows the MakeText program after the file has been written.

Creating a Database in Code

Most of what you read on database operations in C++Builder tells you how to create a database with utilities such as Database Desktop. That's fine if your application has pre-built tables. But if your application has to dynamically create tables, that approach doesn't work. You must have a way of creating tables through code. For example, if your application enables users to specify the fields of a table, you won't know what the fields are until the user has supplied them.

Figure 18.1.

The MakeText *program running.*

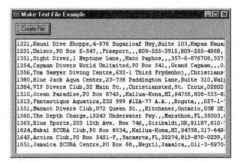

Creating a table in code requires these steps:

1. Create a BDE alias for the database.
2. Create a TTable object.
3. Add field definitions to the FieldDefs property.
4. Add index definitions to the IndexDefs property if your table contains indexes.
5. Create the actual table with the CreateTable() method.

Let's go over these steps individually so that you know what each step involves.

Create a BDE Alias and a TTable Object

You already performed Steps 1 and 2 on Day 16 when I talked about creating a BDE alias, and you created a TTable object in the preceding section. Here's a recap of those two steps:

```
CreateDirectory("c:\\mydata", 0);
Session->AddStandardAlias("MyDatabase", "c:\\mydata", "PARADOX");
Session->SaveConfigFile();

TTable* table = new TTable(this);
table->DatabaseName = "MyDatabase";
table->TableName = "MyTable.db";
```

This code first creates a BDE alias for a database called MyDatabase in the C:\MYDATA directory. After that a TTable object is created, and the DatabaseName property is set to the alias created in the first part of the code. Finally, the TableName property is set to the name of the new table you are about to create. At this point the TTable object has been created, but the table itself doesn't exist on disk.

Create the Field Definitions

The next step is to create the field definitions for the table's fields. As you might guess, the field definitions describe each field. A field definition contains the field name, its type, its size

18

(if applicable), and whether the field is a required field. The field's type can be one of the TFieldType values. Table 18.1 lists the TFieldType values.

Table 18.1. Database table field types.

Field type	Description
ftUnkown	Unknown or undetermined
ftString	Character or string field
ftSmallint	16-bit integer field
ftInteger	32-bit integer field
ftWord	16-bit unsigned integer field
ftBoolean	Boolean field
ftFloat	Floating-point numeric field
ftCurrency	Money field
ftBCD	Binary-Coded Decimal field
ftDate	Date field
ftTime	Time field
ftDateTime	Date and time field
ftBytes	Fixed number of bytes (binary storage)
ftVarBytes	Variable number of bytes (binary storage)
ftAutoInc	Auto-incrementing 32-bit integer counter field
ftBlob	Binary large object field
ftMemo	Text memo field
ftGraphic	Bitmap field
ftFmtMemo	Formatted text memo field
ftParadoxOle	Paradox OLE field
ftDBaseOle	dBASE OLE field
ftTypedBinary	Typed binary field

You create a field definition using the Add() method of the TFieldDefs class. The FieldDefs property of TTable is a TFieldDefs object. Putting all this together, then, adding a new string field to a database would look like this:

```
table->FieldDefs->Add("Customer", ftString, 30, false);
```

18

This code line adds a string field called Customer with a size of 30 characters. The field is not a required field because the last parameter of the Add() method is false. Add as many field definitions as you need, setting the appropriate data type and size for each field.

Create the Index Definitions

If your table will be indexed, you also need to add one or more index definitions. Adding index definitions is much the same as adding field definitions. The IndexDefs property of TTable contains the index definitions. To add a new index definition, call the Add() method of TIndexDefs:

```
table->IndexDefs->Add(
  "", "CustNo", TIndexOptions() << ixPrimary);
```

The first parameter of the Add() method is used to specify the index name. If you are creating a primary index (as in this example), you don't need to specify an index name. The second field is used to specify the field or fields on which to index. If you have more than one field in the index, you separate each field with a semi-colon—for example:

```
table->IndexDefs->Add(
  "", "Room;Time", TIndexOptions() << ixPrimary);
```

The last parameter of the Add() method is used to specify the index type. This parameter takes a TIndexOptions set. Different index options can be specified in combination. For example, an index might be a primary index that is sorted in descending order. In that case the call to Add() might look like this:

```
TIndexOptions options;
options << ixPrimary << ixDescending;
table->IndexDefs->Add("", "CustNo", options);
```

I used slightly different syntax in this example than that of the previous example, but the basic concept is the same.

Create the Table

After you have added all the field and index definitions to the table, you create the table. So far you have been setting up the table's layout but haven't actually created the table. Creating the table is the easiest step of all:

```
table->CreateTable();
```

The CreateTable() method performs the actual creation of the table on disk. CreateTable() takes the contents of the FieldDefs and IndexDefs properties and creates the table structure, based on those contents.

Now that the table is created, you can fill it with data, using any method required for your application. You can fill the table programmatically or allow your users to add or edit the data from a form.

18

The book's Web site, http://www.mcp.com/info, contains a program called MakeTabl. This
program first creates a table and then fills it with data. The program fills the table with data
from the CUSTOMER.TXT file created with the MakeText program earlier in the chapter. Listing
18.3 contains the header file for the main form (MakeTblU.h), and Listing 18.4 contains the
source file for the main form (MakeTblU.cpp).

Listing 18.3. MakeTblU.h.

```
 1: //-----------------------------------------------------------------
 2: #ifndef MakeTblUH
 3: #define MakeTblUH
 4: //-----------------------------------------------------------------
 5: #include <vcl\Classes.hpp>
 6: #include <vcl\Controls.hpp>
 7: #include <vcl\StdCtrls.hpp>
 8: #include <vcl\Forms.hpp>
 9: #include <vcl\DBGrids.hpp>
10: #include <vcl\Grids.hpp>
11: //-----------------------------------------------------------------
12: class TForm2 : public TForm
13: {
14: __published:  // IDE-managed Components
15:   TDBGrid *DBGrid;
16:   TButton *CreateBtn;
17:   TButton *FillBtn;
18:   void __fastcall CreateBtnClick(TObject *Sender);
19:   void __fastcall FillBtnClick(TObject *Sender);
20: private:  // User declarations
21: public:   // User declarations
22:   __fastcall TForm2(TComponent* Owner);
23: };
24: //-----------------------------------------------------------------
25: extern PACKAGE TForm2 *Form2;
26: //-----------------------------------------------------------------
27: #endif
```

Listing 18.4. MakeTblU.cpp.

```
 1: //-----------------------------------------------------------
 2: #include <vcl\vcl.h>
 3: #pragma hdrstop
 4:
 5: #include "MakeTblU.h"
 6: //-----------------------------------------------------------
 7: #pragma package(smart_init)
 8: #pragma resource "*.dfm"
 9: TForm2 *Form2;
```

continues

Listing 18.4. continued

```
10: //-----------------------------------------------------------
11: __fastcall TForm2::TForm2(TComponent* Owner)
12:    : TForm(Owner)
13: {
14: }
15: //-----------------------------------------------------------
16: void __fastcall TForm2::CreateBtnClick(TObject *Sender)
17: {
18:    // First create a BDE alias.
19:    const char* dir = "c:\\mydata";
20:    CreateDirectory(dir, 0);
21:    try {
22:      Session->AddStandardAlias("MyDatabase", dir, "PARADOX");
23:      Session->SaveConfigFile();
24:    }
25:    catch (...) {
26:      MessageBox(Handle, "Error Creating Alias", "Message", 0);
27:      return;
28:    }
29:
30:    Screen->Cursor = crHourGlass;
31:    // Now create the table.
32:    TTable* table;
33:    try {
34:      table = new TTable(this);
35:      table->DatabaseName = "MyDatabase";
36:      table->TableName = "MyTable.db";
37:
38:      // Add the field definitions for each field.
39:      table->FieldDefs->Add("CustNo", ftFloat, 0, true);
40:      table->FieldDefs->Add("Customer", ftString, 30, false);
41:      table->FieldDefs->Add("Addr1", ftString, 30, false);
42:      table->FieldDefs->Add("Addr2", ftString, 30, false);
43:      table->FieldDefs->Add("City", ftString, 15, false);
44:      table->FieldDefs->Add("State", ftString, 20, false);
45:      table->FieldDefs->Add("Zip", ftString, 10, false);
46:      table->FieldDefs->Add("Phone", ftString, 15, false);
47:      table->FieldDefs->Add("Fax", ftString, 15, false);
48:
49:      // Add an index definition for the primary key.
50:      table->IndexDefs->Add(
51:        "", "CustNo", TIndexOptions() << ixPrimary);
52:
53:      // Everything is set up, so create the table.
54:      table->CreateTable();
55:    }
56:    catch (...) {
57:      MessageBox(Handle, "Error Creating Table", "Message", 0);
58:      Screen->Cursor = crDefault;
59:      delete table;
60:      return;
61:    }
62:
63:    // All done. Let the user know.
```

18

```
64:    delete table;
65:    Screen->Cursor = crDefault;
66:    CreateBtn->Enabled = false;
67:    FillBtn->Enabled = true;
68:    MessageBox(Handle, "Table Created Successfully", "Message", 0);
69: }
70: //----------------------------------------------------------
71: void __fastcall TForm2::FillBtnClick(TObject *Sender)
72: {
73:    // Create a TTable.
74:    TTable* table = new TTable(this);
75:    table->DatabaseName = "MyDatabase";
76:    table->TableName = "MyTable.db";
77:
78:    // Create a data source and hook it up to the table.
79:    // Then hook the DBGrid to the datasource.
80:    TDataSource* datasource = new TDataSource(this);
81:    datasource->DataSet = table;
82:    DBGrid->DataSource = datasource;
83:
84:    // Open the table and the text file.
85:    table->Active = true;
86:    TStringList* lines = new TStringList;
87:    lines->LoadFromFile("customer.txt");
88:    String S;
89:
90:    // Put the table in edit mode.
91:    table->Edit();
92:
93:    // Process the lines.
94:    for (int i=0;i<lines->Count;i++) {
95:
96:      // Append a record to the end of the file.
97:      table->Append();
98:
99:      // Parse the string and get the first value.
100:     S = lines->Strings[i];
101:     int pos = S.Pos(",");
102:     String S2 = S.SubString(1, pos - 1);
103:     S.Delete(1, pos);
104:
105:     // Write the value to the CustNo field.
106:     table->FieldByName("CustNo")->Value = S2.ToInt();
107:
108:     // Continue for each of the fields.
109:     pos = S.Pos(",");
110:     S2 = S.SubString(1, pos - 1);
111:     S.Delete(1, pos);
112:     table->FieldByName("Customer")->Value = S2;
113:
114:     pos = S.Pos(",");
115:     S2 = S.SubString(1, pos - 1);
116:     S.Delete(1, pos);
117:     table->FieldByName("Addr1")->Value = S2;
118:
```

18

continues

Listing 18.4. continued

```
119:      pos = S.Pos(",");
120:      S2 = S.SubString(1, pos - 1);
121:      S.Delete(1, pos);
122:      table->FieldByName("Addr2")->Value = S2;
123:
124:      pos = S.Pos(",");
125:      S2 = S.SubString(1, pos - 1);
126:      S.Delete(1, pos);
127:      table->FieldByName("City")->Value = S2;
128:
129:      pos = S.Pos(",");
130:      S2 = S.SubString(1, pos - 1);
131:      S.Delete(1, pos);
132:      table->FieldByName("State")->Value = S2;
133:
134:      pos = S.Pos(",");
135:      S2 = S.SubString(1, pos - 1);
136:      S.Delete(1, pos);
137:      table->FieldByName("Zip")->Value = S2;
138:
139:      pos = S.Pos(",");
140:      S2 = S.SubString(1, pos - 1);
141:      S.Delete(1, pos);
142:      table->FieldByName("Phone")->Value = S2;
143:
144:      pos = S.Pos(",");
145:      S2 = S.SubString(1, pos - 1);
146:      S.Delete(1, pos);
147:      table->FieldByName("FAX")->Value = S2;
148:
149:      // We might get a key violation exception if we try to add a
150:      // record with a duplicate customer number. If that happens,
151:      // we need to inform the user, cancel the edits, put the
152:      // put the table back in edit mode, and continue processing.
153:      try {
154:        table->Post();
155:      }
156:      catch (EDBEngineError& E) {
157:        MessageBox(0, "Duplicate Customer Number", "Key Violation", 0);
158:        table->Cancel();
159:        table->Edit();
160:        continue;
161:      }
162:    }
163:
164:    // All done with the TStringList, so delete it.
165:    delete lines;
166:
167:    // We won't delete the table so that the table's data shows
168:    // in the DBGrid. VCL will delete the table and datasource
169:    // for us.
170:    //delete table;
171:    //delete datasource;
172: }
173: //-----------------------------------------------------------
```

Using Data Modules

As you know by now, setting up database components is easy in C++Builder. Still, there is some time involved, even for the simple examples you have been writing. You have to place a Table or Query component on the form and choose the database name. Then you have to set the table name (for a Table) or SQL property (for a Query). You may have to set other properties, depending on how you are using the database. You may also have several events to handle. Next, you have to place a DataSource component on the form and attach it to the table or query. If your application makes use of a Database component, you have to set that component's properties and events as well. None of this is hard, but it would be nice if you could do it all just once for all your programs. Data modules enable you to do exactly that.

At the base level, data modules are really just specialized forms. To create a data module, open the Object Repository and double-click the Data Module icon. C++Builder creates the data module and a corresponding source unit, just as it does when you create a new form. You can set the Name property of the data module and save it to disk, again, just like a form.

After you have created the data module, you place data access components on it. Then you set all the properties for the data access components, as needed. You can even create event handlers for any components on the data module. When you have set everything just the way you want it, you save the data module. Every form in your application can then access the data module. A simple exercise will help you understand this better. First, you'll set up the data module and then put it to work:

18

1. Create a new application. Change the main form's Name property to MainForm. Save the project. Save the main form as DSExMain.cpp and the project as DSExampl.bpr.

2. Choose File|New. When the Object Repository appears, double-click the Data Module icon to create a new data module. The Form Designer displays the data module. Change the Name property to BCDemos.

3. Click on the Data Access tab on the Component palette. Place a Table component on the data module. Change the DatabaseName property to BCDemos and the TableName to ANIMALS.DBF. Change the Name property to AnimalsTable.

4. Place a second Table component on the data module. Set the DatabaseName property to BCDemos and the TableName property to BIOLIFE.DB. Change the Name property to BiolifeTable.

5. Place a DataSource component on the data module. Change its Name property to Animals and its DataSet property to AnimalsTable.

6. Place another DataSource component on the data module. Change this data source's Name to Biolife and its DataSet property to BiolifeTable. Your data module now looks like Figure 18.2.

Figure 18.2.

The finished data module.

7. Double-click on the background of the data module. An `OnCreate` event handler will be created for the data module. Type this code in the event handler:

```
AnimalsTable->Open();
BiolifeTable->Open();
```

8. Save the project. When prompted, save the data module as `DataMod.cpp`.

Now let's put the new data module to use. You are going to create two buttons for the application's main form. One button will display a form that shows the `Animals` table, and the other will display the `Biolife` table. Here goes:

1. Create a new form. Change the form's `Caption` property to `Animals Form` and the `Name` property to `AnimalsForm`.

2. Choose File | Include Unit Hdr. Choose the `DataMod` unit from the Include Unit dialog box and click OK. The data module is now accessible from the main form.

3. Place a `DBGrid` component and a `DBNavigator` component on the form. Select both the `DBGrid` and `DBNavigator` components. Locate the `DataSource` property in the Object Inspector. Click the drop-down arrow next to the property. You will see the following displayed in the list of available data sources:

```
BCDemos->Animals
BCDemos->Biolife
```

Choose the `BCDemos->Animals` data source.

4. Save the unit as `DSExU2.cpp` (or a more meaningful name if you like).

5. Again, create a new form for the project. Repeat Steps 1 through 3, but this time choose `BCDemos->Biolife` for the data source and change the `Caption` to `BioLife Form`. Change the `Name` property to `BiolifeForm`. Save the form as `DSExU3.cpp`. Figure 18.3 shows the C++Builder IDE after completing this step.

These steps demonstrate that after you have created a data module, you can use the components on that data module from anywhere in your program. All you have to do is include the header for the data module, and then all data-aware components will be capable of detecting the data module. Let's finish this application so that you can try it out:

1. Place a button on the main form. Change its `Caption` property to `Show Animals`.

Figure 18.3.

The second form completed.

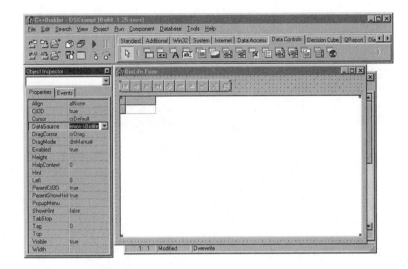

2. Double-click the button to generate an `OnClick` handler for the button. Type this code in the event handler:

```
AnimalsForm->Show();
```

3. Drop another button on the form. Change its `Caption` property to `Show Biolife`.

4. Create an OnClick event handler for this button and type the following code in the event handler:

```
BiolifeForm->Show();
```

5. Choose File | Include Unit Hdr. Choose the `DSExU2` header and click OK.

6. Repeat Step 5 to include the `DSExU3` unit's header.

Now you can run the program. When you click a button, the appropriate form will appear. Figure 18.4 shows the program running.

Data modules make it easy to set up your database components once and then reuse those components over and over. After you have created a data module, you can save it to the Object Repository, where it is always available for your use.

Creating Reports

A database program is not complete without some way of viewing and printing data, and that is where reports enter the picture. Up to this point you have been looking at ways to view individual records, or multiple records, with the `DBGrid` component. These methods might be perfect for some applications, but sooner or later you will need more control over the viewing of records. Besides viewing the data onscreen, you will almost certainly need to print the data. A database application that can't print is not much use. C++Builder's QuickReport components enable you to view and print your data with ease.

Figure 18.4.

The program running with both forms displayed.

QuickReport Overview

Before you can create a report, you need an overview of how the QuickReport components work.

The QuickRep Component

The base QuickReport component is the QuickRep component. This component acts as a canvas on which you place the elements that your report will display (I'll discuss the report elements soon). The QuickRep component has properties that affect the way the report will appear when printed. For example, the Page property is a class containing properties called TopMargin, BottomMargin, LeftMargin, RightMargin, Columns, Orientation, PaperSize, and so on. The PrinterSettings property is also a class. This property has its own properties, called Copies, Duplex, FirstPage, LastPage, and OutputBin. The ReportTitle property is used to display the print job description in the Windows Print Manager and in the title bar of the QuickReport preview window. The Units property controls whether margins are displayed in millimeters, inches, picas, and other choices. The DataSet property is used to set the dataset from which the report's data will be obtained.

NOTE   The DataSet property must be set, and the associated dataset must be active before anything will show up in the report.

Primary QuickRep methods include Preview() and Print(). The Print() method, as its name implies, prints the report. The Preview() method displays a modal preview window. The preview window includes buttons for viewing options, first page, last page, previous page, next page, print, print setup, save report, open report, and close preview. Figure 18.5 shows the QuickReport preview window at runtime.

Figure 18.5.

The QuickReport preview window.

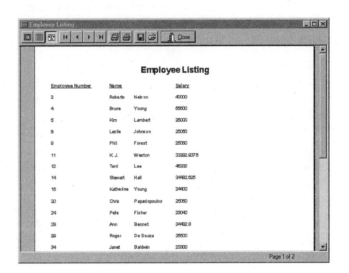

QuickRep events of note include OnPreview and OnNeedData. You can use the OnPreview event, instead of the default preview window, to provide a custom preview window. When using a data source other than a VCL database, you use the OnNeedData event. For example, you can create a report from a string list, an array, or a text file.

Report Bands

A QuickReport is composed of bands. Bands come in many different types. A basic report has at least three types of bands: a title band, a column header band, and a detail band. The title band contains the report title. The title is displayed only on the first page of the report. The column header band is used to display the column headers for the fields in the dataset. The column header appears at the top of every page. Some reports, such as a report used to generate mailing labels, do not have a column headers band.

The detail band is the band that does all the work. On the detail band you place any data that you want in the report. You define the contents of the detail band, and QuickReport will repeat the detail band for every record in the dataset. In a minute you'll do an exercise that illustrates how the bands work.

Other commonly used band types include page header, page footer, group header, group footer, and summary bands. The QRBand component defines a QuickReport band. The BandType property is used to specify the band type (title, detail, header, footer, and so on). The bands automatically arrange themselves on the QuickRep component, based on the band's type. For example, if you place a QRBand on the report and change its BandType to rbPageFooter, the band will be moved below all other bands. Likewise, a page header band will be placed above all other bands.

QuickReport Design Elements

QuickReport design elements come in three forms. The first form includes components for text labels, images, shapes, headers, footers, and so on. These components are primarily used to display static design elements. For example, the report title is usually set once and then doesn't change. Another example is a graphic used to display a company's logo on the report. The components in this group are very similar to the standard VCL components. The QRLabel component resembles a standard Label component, a QRImage is similar to the VCL Image component, the QRShape component is similar to the regular Shape component, and so on. Use these components to design the static portions of your reports.

The second category of elements is QuickReport versions of the standard VCL data-aware components. These components are placed on the detail band of a report. Components in this group include the QRDBText, QRDBRichEdit, and QRDBImage components. Data is pulled from the dataset and placed into these components to fill out the body of the report.

The third group of QuickReport components includes the QRSysData component and the QRExpr component. The QRSysData component is used to display page numbers, the report date, the report time, the report title, and so on. The QRExpr component is used to display calculated results. The Expression property defines the expression for the calculation. The Expression property has a property editor called the Expression builder, which is used to define simple expressions. An expression might be simple, such as multiplying two fields, or complex, complete with formulas such as AVERAGE, COUNT, or SUM.

Creating Reports by Hand

Certainly the best way to write truly custom reports is by hand. That might sound difficult, but fortunately the QuickReport components make it easy. The best way for me to explain how to create reports by hand is to take you through an exercise. This exercise creates a simple application that displays and prints a report in list form. I won't tell you to perform every single step in this exercise. For instance, I won't tell you to save the project or give you filenames to use—you can figure those out for yourself. Also, you're not to worry about making the report real pretty at this point. You can go back later and tidy up.

The first step is to create the main form of the application. After that you will create the basic outline of the report. Here goes:

1. Create a new application. Place two buttons on the main form. Change the caption of the first button to `Preview Report` and the caption of the second button to `Print Report`.

2. Choose File|New. Double-click the Report icon in the Object Repository. C++Builder creates a new QuickReport form.

3. Place a `Table` component on the QuickReport form. Change the `DatabaseName` property to `BCDEMOS` and the `TableName` property to `EMPLOYEE.DB`. Set the `Active` property to `true`.

4. Select the QuickReport form. Change the `DataSet` property to `Table1`. Change the `ReportTitle` property to `Employee Report`.

5. Switch back to the main form. Double-click the button labeled `Preview Report`. Type this code in the `OnClick` event handler:

```
QuickReport1->Preview();
```

6. Double-click the `Print Report` button and type the following in the `OnClick` event handler:

```
QuickReport1->Print();
```

7. Choose File|Include Unit Hdr and include the QuickReport form.

Now you have a blank report. What you need to do next is add a title band, a column header band, and a detail band. For the next few steps you may want to look ahead to Figure 18.6 to see the final result.

1. Select a `QRBand` component from the QReport tab of the Component palette and place it on the report. The band is a title band by default.

2. Select a `QRLabel` component and place it on the title band. Change the `Caption` property to `Employee Report`. Change the `Font` property to your preference (I used Arial, 18 point, bold). Align the component so that it is centered on the band.

3. Place another band on the report. Change the `BandType` property to `rbColumnHeader`. Change the `Font` to bold and underlined.

4. Place a `QRLabel` on the left side of the column header band. Change the `Caption` property to `Employee Number`. Place a second `QRLabel` on the band to the right of the first. Change the `Caption` property to `Name`. Place a third `QRLabel` on the band to the right of the last label. Change the `Caption` to `Salary`.

5. Place another band on the report. Change the `BandType` property to `rbDetail`. Notice that the band moves below the other bands after you change the band type.

18

6. Place a QRDBText component on the left edge of the detail band (align it with the Employee Number label on the column header band). Change the DataSet property to Table1 and the DataField property to EmpNo.

7. Place another QRDBText on the detail band, aligned with the Name component on the column header band. Change the DataSet property to Table1 and the DataField property to FirstName. Place another QRDBText just to the right of the last one (see Figure 18.6). Attach it to the LastName field of the database table.

8. Add a final QRDBText component on the form. Place it below the Salary component on the column header band, and attach it to the Salary field in the table. Your form now looks like Figure 18.6.

Figure 18.6.

Your QuickReport form.

You are probably wondering what the report will look like on paper. Guess what? You don't have to wait to find out. Just right-click on the QuickReport form and choose Preview from the context menu. The QuickReport preview window is displayed, and you can preview the report. To print the report, click the Print button. When you are done with the report preview, click the Close button. You can now run the program and try out the Preview Report and Print Report buttons.

NOTE   The report you just created is double spaced. To change the spacing, reduce the height of the detail band.

Before leaving this discussion of reports, let me show you one other nice feature of QuickReport. Right-click on the QuickReport form and choose Report settings from the context menu. The Report Settings dialog box will be displayed, as shown in Figure 18.7.

This dialog box enables you to set the primary properties of the `QuickRep` component visually rather than use the Object Inspector.

Figure 18.7.

The QuickReport Report Settings dialog box.

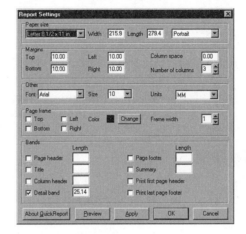

Creating Reports the Easy Way

C++Builder comes with three built-in QuickReport forms. These forms can be found on the Forms tab of the Object Repository. The forms are called Quick Report Labels, Quick Report List, and Quick Report Master/Detail. These forms give you a head start on creating reports. Generate one of the forms from the Object Repository and then modify the form as needed.

Deploying a C++Builder Database Application

As I said on Day 16, the Borland Database Engine (BDE) is a collection of DLLs and drivers that enable your C++Builder application to talk to various types of databases. When you ship an application that uses the BDE, you need to make sure that you ship the proper BDE files and that they are properly registered on your users' machines. The most sensible way to do this is with a Borland-approved installation program. Here at TurboPower Software, we use the Wise Install System from Great Lakes Business Solutions (http://www.glbs.com). Others include InstallShield and its little brother, InstallShield Express. Conveniently, InstallShield Express comes with C++Builder Professional and Client/Server, so if you have one of those versions of C++Builder, you don't have to rush right out and buy an installation program.

You might be wondering why Borland is involved in dictating how the BDE must be deployed. The reason is simple when you think about it. There are many BDE versions in use. Some folks might be writing and deploying applications that use the BDE from Delphi 1. Others might be using the BDE from C++Builder 1. Still others could be using the BDE that came with Borland C++ 4.5 in their applications. The important thing to realize is that the BDE is backwards compatible. Newer BDE versions are guaranteed to work with applications written for older BDE versions. This system will only work as long as everyone plays by the rules. Part of the rules say, "Thou shalt not arbitrarily overwrite existing BDE files." Certified installation programs check the version number of any BDE files they find. If the file being installed is older than the existing file, the installation program leaves the existing file in place. This ensures that the user will always have the latest BDE files on his or her system. Another thing that these certified installation programs do is to determine exactly which files you need to deploy for your application. You should read DEPLOY.TXT in the C++Builder root directory for more details on deploying applications that use the BDE.

Summary

There's no question that creating database applications requires a lot of work. The good news is that C++Builder makes the job much easier than other C++ development environments. Today you found out something about the non-visual aspects of database programming. You also found out about data modules and how to use them. You ended the day with a look at QuickReport. QuickReport makes creating reports for your database applications easy. I also talked about what is required to deploy a database application.

Workshop

The Workshop contains quiz questions to help you solidify your understanding of the material covered and exercises to provide you with experience in using what you have learned. You can find answers to the quiz questions in Appendix A, "Answers to Quiz Questions."

Q&A

Q **I am trying to create a database at runtime. I have created a BDE alias and have set all the field definitions, but the table is never created on my hard disk. What have I done wrong?**

A You have probably failed to call the CreateTable() method. You must call this method to physically create the table.

Q **When designing a report, can I set all my report's properties at one time?**

A Yes. Just right-click the QuickRep component and choose Report settings from the context menu. The Report Settings dialog box is displayed, and you can set most of the report properties visually.

Q Can a data module include code as well as components?

A Yes. A data module can contain any code necessary to carry out operation of the data module. The data module can contain event handlers or methods that you create. The methods you create can be public or private (for the data module's use only).

Q When I preview my report, it is blank. What is wrong?

A More than likely you have not set the Active property of the dataset to true. The dataset must be open before the report will function.

Q Can I use more than one detail band on a report?

A No. You can place more than one detail band on a report, but only the first one will be used when the report is generated.

Q Why do I need a Borland-approved installation program to install my database application?

A The BDE is complicated to install, and an approved installation program is guaranteed to do the installation correctly.

Quiz

1. What method do you call to create a database table at runtime?
2. What does the Edit() method of TTable do?
3. What method do you call when you want to apply the changes made to a record?
4. How do you create a new data module?
5. Is a data module a regular form?
6. What method do you call to print a QuickReport?
7. What type of QuickReport band displays the dataset's data?
8. What component is used to display the page number on a report?
9. How can you preview a report at design time?
10. What is the QRExpr component used for?

Exercises

1. Create a database (a BDE alias) and a table for the database, either through code or by using the C++Builder database tools.
2. Create a data module containing the database table from Exercise 1.
3. Generate a report that creates mailing labels. (Hint: Start with a QuickReport Labels object from the Forms page of the Object Repository.)

4. Modify the QuickReport you created in this chapter so that the employee's first and last names are displayed by a QRExpr component.

5. Read the DEPLOY.TXT file in your CBuilder directory to understand what is involved in deploying a C++Builder database application.

18

Day 19

Creating and Using DLLs

If you use Windows, you can't escape DLLs. Just take a look in your \Windows and \Windows\System directories. I run Windows NT 4, and I count more than 650 DLLs in the \Winnt directories on my system. So, let's not debate the facts. DLLs are part of everyday life in Windows.

The question, then, is whether *you* need to create and use DLLs. That's what you will find out today. Specifically, you will look at the following:

- ☐ What DLLs are and why you use them
- ☐ Calling functions and using classes in DLLs
- ☐ Writing DLLs
- ☐ Using forms in DLLs
- ☐ Using resource DLLs

By the end of today you will have a good idea of whether DLLs are for you. I suspect that DLLs will suit your development plan somewhere down the road.

DLL Overview

Simply put, DLLs are very useful. Today I will discuss the benefits of DLLs and how this translates for you, the C++Builder programmer. First, let's explore exactly what a DLL is.

What Is a Dynamic Link Library?

Simply put, a *DLL* (dynamic link library) is one or more pieces of code stored in a file with a .dll extension. The DLL code can be called from executable programs, but the DLL itself isn't a standalone program. You could consider the DLL a helper file for a main program.

There are two types of DLLs: code DLLs and resource DLLs. This is not an exclusive arrangement. You can have both code and resources in the same DLL, and there's no problem with that whatsoever. In some cases, though, it's convenient to store your code in one DLL and your resources in another. In a moment, in the section "Using Resources in DLLs," I'll talk about why you might want to do that.

Code contained in a DLL can be of two primary forms. The first form is a standalone function that you call from your main application. You have already done that several times in this book. Remember the code from Day 14, "Advanced Programming:"

```
Screen->Cursors[myCursor] = LoadCursor(HInstance, "MYCURSOR");
```

or this, also from Day 14:

```
DrawText(c.Handle, Panel->Text.c_str(),
  -1, (RECT*)&temp, DT_CENTER | DT_VCENTER | DT_SINGLELINE);
```

Both LoadCursor() and DrawText() are Windows API functions. You probably knew that. But did you know that these functions are called from DLLs? When you think about it, these functions have to be stored somewhere. But where? In this case, both LoadCursor() and DrawText() are contained in the Windows DLL called User32.dll.

And what about all those common dialog boxes you've been using, such as the File Open dialog box, the Print dialog box, and the Printer Setup dialog box? They have to come from somewhere. In this case these dialog boxes are stored as resources in the file called Comctl32.dll. So, without knowing it, you have been using DLLs all along.

The second form of code contained in a DLL consists of C++ classes. Rather than access individual standalone functions as I've discussed, you create an instance of a class and call member functions of that class, all of which are contained in the DLL. I will discuss this aspect of DLLs later in the section "Importing and Exporting Functions and Classes."

Using DLLs in this manner is one thing, but using and creating your own DLLs is another story entirely, right? Not really. After you've created a DLL, you can call functions from the DLL just as you do when calling Windows API functions. Creating DLLs is not tough, so there's nothing to stop you from putting DLLs to work for you.

19

Why Should I Use a DLL?

That's a good question. After all, what does a DLL give you, besides putting all that stuff in your executable file? DLLs offer these benefits:

- ☐ Effective code reuse
- ☐ Capability to easily share code among many applications
- ☐ Capability to compartmentalize code
- ☐ Internationalization of your application
- ☐ Effective use of Windows resources

Let's take a look at these points individually and see whether I can convince you what a good thing DLLs are.

Effective Code Reuse

Code reuse is a big part of object-oriented programming. After all, why reinvent the wheel? DLLs aid in code reuse in a big way. Let's say you had a set of classes that you wrote to handle multimedia in your programs. The classes might include a base class that handles basic multimedia operations and derived classes that include specialized handling of wave files, MIDI files, CD audio, and AVI video. Sounds like you've put a lot of work into this. Now that you've gone to all that trouble, it would be nice if you could reuse all that code in any of your applications that need it. DLLs enable you to do exactly that.

What you do is compile all your classes into a DLL. Then all you have to do, in order to use the class in any of your programs, is include the header file for the classes contained in the DLL and start creating class instances. What could be easier? (Actually, there are a couple other steps required, but they are simple and I don't want to get ahead of myself by explaining them now.)

Now you have these classes at your fingertips any time you need them. Better yet, you can give the DLL to your best programming pal, and he can use the classes, too. This is starting to sound good. Better yet, you can sell the DLL to other programmers. Hey, you put all that work into it, so you might as well get out of it what you can!

NOTE

> You can even create DLLs that can be called from applications written in Delphi, Borland C++, Visual Basic, Visual C++, or other programming environments. Of course, this depends on the code contained in the DLL and how that code is called, but it can be done.

19

So, do you see where this is heading? After writing a DLL, you can use it with ease whenever and wherever you want. Getting at all the goodies contained in your DLL is just a few mouse clicks away.

Sharing Code Among Applications

Sharing code ties in with code reuse but takes it a step farther. Let's say that you are a programmer for a large corporation. You might have hundreds of users, each with his or her own system (I'll ignore networking considerations for this example). Let's say that you've written five different applications for those users. Further, let's assume that each of those five applications uses your multimedia classes (discussed earlier) and that the multimedia classes compile to 100KB of code (a modest figure). If you don't use a DLL, you will have 100KB of code repeated five times (once for each of the five applications) for a total of 500KB of code. That's code waste, folks.

A better approach is to put the multimedia classes in a DLL. Each of the five programs can use the same DLL when the multimedia stuff kicks in. That's part of the beauty of DLLs: After the DLL is written, all your applications can share it. Each user will get an additional 100KB DLL on his or her machine, but each of the five applications will be reduced in size by 100KB. The bottom line is that each user saves 400KB of disk space. Saving 400KB might not sound like a lot, but if you multiply it times hundreds of users, it starts to add up, from a corporate perspective (bean counters tend to look at those types of things). This is just a simple example. In a real-world situation, you could easily save several megabytes per user by using DLLs.

What if three of the five programs are running simultaneously? No problem. Each program pulls code from the DLL as needed, and there are no conflicts. Windows keeps track of who's calling whom and that sort of thing. All you do is write the DLL and start using it. (If this discussion sounds familiar, it is probably because I used roughly this same argument when discussing runtime packages on Day 9, "Creating Applications in C++Builder.")

Compartmentalizing Code

By keeping your code compartmentalized, you can deal with it more easily when it comes time to update your code. I am not advocating a separate DLL for each aspect of your program, but when and where it is sensible to break up your program into related chunks of code, you should do so. There isn't much benefit in breaking an application into DLLs just for the sake of compartmentalizing the code. If you have libraries of classes that you have written, though, it does make sense to keep those libraries in separate DLLs. Again, this is most obvious when creating libraries that can be used by any of your programs.

NOTE

As you develop a class or component, you should always be thinking about how you might reuse that object in the future. In other words, plan ahead and design code for reuse from the beginning. Even if you

> feel that the code you are working on today will not likely be used again, you should still write it with reuse in mind. You never know when you will need that same type of code at a later date. When you are in the OOP mind-set, programming for reuse becomes second nature.

One advantage to this approach is that your applications can be more easily upgraded if necessary. Let's face it. Even the best of programs go to market with bugs. It's more a question of how many or how severe than a question of whether there are bugs at all. If you discover bugs in your DLL, you can fix the bug and ship a new DLL to your users rather than recompile and ship an entire executable file. At first this might not appear to benefit the types of applications you have written so far. However, you may eventually write programs several megabytes in size with dozens of source modules. In that case, compartmentalizing makes much more sense.

Internationalization

A few years ago you could write a program and not worry about the international market. You would write the program and create menu items, dialog boxes, hint text, error messages, and so forth in your native language, and that was that. You put the program on the market and didn't think about it again.

The world, however, is becoming smaller. With the explosion of the Internet and the World Wide Web, things are completely different than they were just a couple of years ago. You can create a demo of your program, or maybe a shareware version, and put it on the Net, and within hours, minutes even, people all around the world have access to your program. It's exciting and frightening at the same time. This phenomenon means that you must plan ahead and prepare for translating your program into different languages.

One way you can do that is to create resource DLLs that contain string resources in various languages. You can have a separate DLL for each language, or as an alternative you can have all the string resources in a single DLL and load the correct language version of each string at runtime. At runtime, you can use the Windows API function LoadString() to load the strings and assign them to various components as needed.

NOTE One disadvantage to the C++Builder programming model is that it doesn't use traditional resources as other programming environments do. Things such as menus are not loaded as resources but rather are contained within the form's resource. This makes internationalization more difficult and is one of the few times that this model works against you.

Again, planning ahead can save you a lot of work later. If you plan your application with internationalization in mind, it is much easier to translate your application into different languages when necessary.

Effective Use of Windows Resources

Today's systems are faster, have more RAM, and have more hard disk space. It's easy to fall into the mode of "Hey, I'm only using 2MB of system RAM, so what's the big deal?" The truth is, you should always be conscious of how much of your users' system resources you are consuming. Here again, DLLs can help.

This is really a continuation of the discussion on sharing code among different applications. Let's go back to the example I used earlier. (Remember, you have five applications using some common code.) If you don't use DLLs, when several of your programs are running at the same time, they will all load some of the same code into memory. You are wasting system resources because each program loads its own copy of the exact same code. Rather than have each program load the same code, you use a DLL and load the code once. All your applications can use the same code in memory and reduce the drain on the system.

Calling Functions and Using Classes in DLLs

In just a bit I'll talk about how to call functions contained in DLLs. But before you use a function in a DLL, you first have to load the DLL into memory. Let's take a quick look at how you go about loading a DLL.

Loading DLLs

Loading DLLs can be accomplished in two ways: static loading and dynamic loading. Both methods have their advantages and disadvantages. (Here again, this discussion resembles the section on packages on Day 9.)

Static loading means that your DLL is automatically loaded when the application that calls the DLL is executed. Your DLL will have functions that it exports. The description of these functions is contained in a special file called an *import library file*. The import library file has the same filename as the DLL it represents and has a filename extension of .lib.

To use static loading, you link the .lib file for the DLL with your project during the link phase. In a C++Builder application, that means adding the .lib file to the project via the Project Manager. The DLL is loaded when the application loads, and you call any functions exported from the DLL just as you would any other function. This is by far the easiest way to use code contained in a DLL. The disadvantage to this approach is that if a DLL that the program references is missing, the program will refuse to load.

Dynamic loading means that you specifically load the DLL when needed and unload it when you are done with it. This type of DLL loading has its advantages and disadvantages, too. One advantage is that the DLL is in memory only as long as you need it, so you are making more efficient use of memory. Another advantage is that your application will load more quickly when using dynamic loading because not all the code needed to run the program is loaded when the application initially loads.

The primary disadvantage to using the dynamic loading approach is that it is a lot more work for you. First, you need to load the DLL with the Windows API function LoadLibrary(). Then, when you are done with the DLL, you unload it with FreeLibrary(). Further (and this is where the work comes in), you need to use the GetProcAddress() function to obtain a pointer to the function you want to call. To say that this approach can be a tad confusing would be an understatement. To illustrate, let's look at calling functions from DLLs.

Calling Functions Located in DLLs

The method you use to call a function in a DLL depends on whether the DLL was statically or dynamically loaded. Calling functions from DLLs that are dynamically loaded isn't a lot of fun. It requires that you set up a pointer to the function in the DLL, and pointers to functions can be confusing. Let's say you had a function in a DLL called SayHello(). It would look like this in the DLL's source code:

```
void _export __stdcall SayHello(HWND hWnd)
{
  MessageBox(hWnd, "Hello There!!", "Message From a DLL", MB_OK);
}
```

To call this function from your program, you first have to declare the function pointer:

```
void (__stdcall *SayHello)(HWND);
```

Now that you've done that, load the DLL, use GetProcAddress() to get a pointer to the function, call the function, and, finally, unload the DLL. It goes like this:

```
// load the DLL
HINSTANCE dllInstance = LoadLibrary("mystuff.dll");
// get the address of the function
SayHello = (void(__stdcall*)(HWND))
    GetProcAddress(dllInstance, "_SayHello");
// call the function
SayHello(Application->Handle);
// unload the DLL
FreeLibrary(dllInstance);
```

Man, that's ugly, isn't it? Function pointers are one of the most confusing aspects of C++ from a syntax standpoint. Still, when you need to load a DLL at runtime, that's the way you have to do it. I should add that this code is pared down a bit. You would almost always add some error-checking code to ensure that the DLL loaded correctly and that GetProcAddress()

19

returned a good address. As you can see, you probably won't use dynamic loading of DLLs unless you absolutely have to.

Calling functions from DLLs that are statically loaded is simple. First you must have a function declaration for the function. After that, you call the function as you would any other function:

```
extern "C" __import void SayHello(HWND);
// later on...
SayHello(Application->Handle);
```

Unless you need the flexibility that dynamic loading provides, you should almost always opt for static loading.

NOTE

> Some third-party tools and libraries come in the form of DLLs. To use these tools or libraries, you place the DLL or DLLs that contain the libraries in your application's directory. Then in your source code you use the #include directive to include the headers that come with the library. Each library should come with complete instructions on how to implement it.

Creating a DLL

Creating a DLL is not difficult. There are a couple things to be aware of, but most of it is straight C++ programming. From the earlier discussion you know that static loading is probably the method you will use most often. For DLLs that are statically loaded, you will have four or more files:

- [ ] One or more source code files. These files do not need to be distributed with the DLL.

- [ ] One or more header files. This header will contain the declarations or classes that can be called from the DLL.

- [ ] The import library file. This file enables the linker to resolve calls in the application with addresses in the DLL.

- [ ] The DLL itself.

Of these files, the header (.h), import library (.lib), and final dynamic link library (.dll) must be shipped with the DLL.

NOTE

> You don't need an import library for DLLs that you load with `LoadLibrary()`.

Let's start with a discussion on the basics of creating DLLs. After that, you'll put together a DLL.

Importing and Exporting Functions and Classes

Functions in a DLL fall into three basic categories:

- ☐ Functions called from within the DLL
- ☐ Functions called from outside the DLL
- ☐ Functions that are members of a class contained in the DLL

Functions called within a DLL require no special handling. You declare this type of function just as you do any function. The function can be called by other functions within the DLL, but it can't be called from outside the DLL. In other words, a calling application will not have access to these functions. These functions could be considered private to the DLL, much as private class member functions are private to the class in which they reside. In effect, your application won't be able to "see" the functions to even know they exist.

NOTE

> Attempting to use a function in a DLL that is private to the DLL may or may not result in a compiler error, but will always result in a linker error. The linker error will say something like `Unresolved external 'MyFunction()' referenced from module unit1.cpp`. This is because the function has not been exported from the DLL. Exporting functions is discussed in the next section.

NOTE

> In addition to functions, a DLL may contain global data that all functions in the DLL can access. In 16-bit Windows, global data in a DLL is shared among all instances of the DLL. In other words, if one program changed the global variable x to 100, x would have the value 100 for all other applications calling the DLL as well. In 32-bit Windows, this is not the case. In Win32, a separate copy of a DLL's global data is created for each process that loads the DLL.

19

The __export **Modifier**

Another category of functions comprises those that can be called from outside the DLL. These are functions that are made public by *exporting* them from the DLL. They can be called by other functions in the DLL or by applications outside the DLL.

NOTE
Functions in a DLL can be called by executable applications and also by other DLLs. In other words, one DLL can call functions in another DLL.

After a function has been exported, you call it from your application. To export a function, you use the __export keyword when you build the DLL. The DLL source code for a simple function contained in a DLL might look like this:

```
void __export SayHello(HWND hWnd)
{
  MessageBox(hWnd, "Hello from a DLL!",
    "DLL Message Box", MB_OK | MB_ICONEXCLAMATION);
}
```

This function is now exported and can be called from any application.

Exporting a class works in essentially the same way, except that the __export modifier is placed in the class declaration. The class declaration for an exported class looks like this:

```
class __export MyClass {
  public:
    MyClass(HWND hwnd);
    void SaySomething(char* text);
    void Beep();
  private:
    HWND hWnd;
};
```

Notice that the __export modifier is placed between the class keyword and the classname.

TIP
If you are having trouble with exporting functions or classes, run the TDUMP utility on the DLL. TDUMP produces information containing a section on symbols exported from the DLL. Examining that section will give you a better idea of where the problem lies. To see just the exported symbols, run TDUMP with the -ee switch—for example,

```
tdump -ee mydll.dll
```

19

The __import Modifier

Exporting a function is only half the story. When you build the application that calls the function, you must *import* the functions you want to call from the DLL. As you might guess, importing a function is done with the __import modifier.

NOTE

> The __import and __export keywords both have double leading underscores preceding the keywords. This practice is commonly used by compiler vendors to distinguish a compiler-specific keyword from a C++ language keyword.

To import a function contained in a DLL, use the __import modifier in the function declaration. For example, given the SayHello() function shown earlier, part of the calling application would look like this:

```
extern "C" void __import SayHello(HWND hWnd);
//
// later on...
//
SayHello(Handle);
```

The __import modifier tells the compiler that the function being declared can be referenced in an import library file. The actual function call looks no different than any other function call.

NOTE

> This code marks the second time you have seen the extern "C" statement. extern "C" is used to prevent name mangling of the function name. Any time you use a standalone function in a DLL, use the extern "C" modifier. This enables the function to be imported by any calling application, including those compiled with compilers other than Borland compilers.

Importing classes works in exactly the same way. Before you use a class that lives in a DLL, you must first declare it with the __import modifier:

```
class __import MyClass {
  public:
    MyClass(HWND hwnd);
    void SaySomething(char* text);
    void Beep();
  private:
    HWND hWnd;
};
```

19

Now you can create an instance of this class and access any of its public functions or data members as needed:

```
MyClass Billy(Handle);
Billy.SaySomething("Hi, there!");
Billy.Beep();
```

The trick in writing and using DLLs, then, is in getting the imports and exports right. Otherwise, there's nothing to it.

The declspec() Keyword

Now, forget everything I just told you about __import and __export. Okay, so I'm being a little facetious. The __import and __export modifiers are a big part of writing and using DLLs, and you need to understand how they are used. However, C++Builder applications have a new method of importing and exporting classes and functions. Rather than use __import and __export in your C++Builder applications, it is better to use the __declspec() keyword.

This keyword gives you more flexibility in where you place the __import and __export modifiers. Previously you had to be sure that you placed the __import or __export modifier in exactly the correct place in the function definition, or compiler errors would result. Using the __declspec() keyword, you can place the modifier anywhere you like in the function declaration (within reason, of course). For instance, the following two lines are both legal:

```
__declspec(dllexport) void SaySomething(HWND hWnd);
void __declspec(dllexport) SaySomething(HWND hWnd);
```

If you were using __export, you would have to make sure that you placed the __export keyword between the return type and the function name. By using __declspec(), you don't have to worry about it.

TIP

The __declspec() keyword, as with __import and __export, has two underscores preceding it. Because __declspec() is a keyword, it will be highlighted in bold when typed correctly. This is a trait of the C++Builder Code Editor's syntax highlighting feature. If you use only a single underscore, the keyword will not be bold. Syntax highlighting confirms that you have typed a keyword correctly.

You will notice in the preceding example that __declspec() takes a single parameter. To export a function, use __declspec(dllexport); to import a function, use __declspec(dllimport). That's all there is to it. (Don't think that I led you down the wrong path earlier; understanding the __import and __export modifiers is a good thing to know because at some point in your

19

programming journey you may wind up programming with a compiler other than C++Builder and may have to use __import and __export with that compiler.)

The Secret of DLL Headers

You might have picked up on a potential problem in the previous section. If you are required to export a function or class when building the DLL and you must import the function or class when building the .exe, you will need two separate headers: one with all exported functions using the __export modifier and one with all imported functions using the __import modifier. Right? Actually, no. You can use macros so that you need only one header.

The header for just about every DLL will contain something like this:

```
#ifdef __DLL__
#  define DLL_EXP __declspec(dllexport)
#else
#  define DLL_EXP __declspec(dllimport)
#endif

extern "C" void DLL_EXP SayHello(HWND);

class DLL_EXP MyClass {
  public:
    MyClass(HWND hwnd);
    void SaySomething(char* text);
    void Beep();
  private:
    HWND hWnd;
};
```

NOTE The symbol name used in the preceding code is DLL_EXP. I borrowed this name from a sample program that ships with Borland C++. The symbol name can be anything you want. For instance, you might find the name BUILD_TYPE more descriptive. Use any name you are comfortable with.

The group of pre-processor directives at the top of the header works like this: If the symbol __DLL__ is defined, the DLL_EXP symbol will expand to the text __declspec(dllexport). If __DLL__ isn't defined, the DLL_EXP symbol will expand to __declspec(dllimport). The __DLL__ symbol is automatically defined by C++Builder when you create a DLL project and is not defined when you create an application project.

So what does that mean? It means that you can use a single header whether you are building the DLL or the calling application. When you build a DLL, all the classes and functions that use DLL_EXP will be exported because DLL_EXP expands to __declspec(dllexport). When you

19

build the calling application, the DLL_EXP symbol expands to __declspec(dllimport), and all
functions and classes that use the DLL_EXP symbol will be imported.

Creating a DLL with the Object Repository

Creating a DLL in C++Builder is accomplished through the Object Repository. Choose
File|New to display the Object Repository. Next, click the DLL icon to create a new DLL
and click OK. The Code Editor is displayed, and the file in the edit window looks like this:

```
 1: //---------------------------------------------------------
 2: #include <vcl.h>
 3: #pragma hdrstop
 4: //---------------------------------------------------------
 5: // Important note about DLL memory management:
 6: //
 7: // If your DLL exports any functions that pass String objects (or structs/
 8: // classes containing nested Strings) as parameter or function results,
 9: // you will need to add MEMMGR.LIB to both the DLL project and any
10: // EXE projects that use the DLL.  This will change the DLL and its calling
11: // EXE's to use the BCBMM.DLL as their memory manager. In these cases,
12: // the file BCBMM.DLL should be deployed along with your DLL.
13: //
14: // To avoid using BCBMM.DLL, pass string information using "char *" or
15: // ShortString parameters.
16: //---------------------------------------------------------
17: int WINAPI DllEntryPoint(HINSTANCE hinst, unsigned long reason, void*)
18: {
19:    return 1;
20: }
21: //---------------------------------------------------------
```

Let's talk about the comments on lines 5 through 15. This message is telling you that if your
DLL has exported functions that take an instance of the AnsiString class as a parameter, you
must do the following:

☐ Add a line to the source of both the DLL and the .exe that calls the DLL to
include the ShareMem.hpp header. Be sure that this include comes before other
includes in the file.

☐ Ship the Bcbmm.dll file with your DLL.

To avoid this requirement, just be sure that your DLL functions don't have any AnsiString
instances as parameters. For instance, rather than use

```
MyFunction(String& s)
{
}
```

use

```
MyFunction(char* buff)
{
}
```

This odd situation is easy enough to work around, so you should never have the need for Borlndmm.dll. You just need to be aware of the restrictions placed on using the AnsiString class in DLL functions. Note that you can use AnsiString objects within the DLL itself without the need for Borlndmm.dll. This applies only to exported functions that pass an AnsiString object, whether as a parameter or as the return value.

Now look at line 2. Notice that #include <vcl.h> is automatically added for you. This is for your convenience; it isn't a requirement. If your DLL contains only your own code (no VCL classes or forms), you should remove this include. This also applies to the code on line 15. If you are not using VCL forms in your DLL, you remove this line. (I'll talk about VCL forms in DLLs in just a bit).

NOTE

> At the time of this writing, the plan is to have two DLL projects in the Object Repository. One DLL project would be the same as described here. The other DLL project would not include any VCL headers or libraries. To build a non-VCL DLL, double-click the Console Wizard from the Object Repository.

Finally, notice the DllEntryPoint() function. This function is the entry point into the DLL. This function will be called when the DLL is initially loaded. It will also be called when another process (program or DLL) references the DLL. Further, it will be called whenever a process detaches itself from the DLL and, ultimately, when the DLL is unloaded. You might need to account for all that, but most of the time you don't have to worry about it. If you do need to keep track of those things, use the reason parameter to determine what is going on with your DLL. Most of the time you can leave the default DllEntryPoint() function as is.

19

NOTE

> The DllEntryPoint() function's first parameter is hinst. This is the instance handle (HINSTANCE) of the DLL. If you have any functions that require the instance handle of the DLL (such as LoadIcon() or LoadCursor()), use the hinst parameter to create a global variable. You can then access the global variable any time the instance handle to the DLL is required. (Using the instance handle is discussed later in the chapter, in the section "Using Resources in DLLs.")

Now that you have the Code Editor displaying the DLL's source code unit, all you have to do is start adding code. Be sure to use a header file for the DLL and follow the techniques I've mentioned for any exported functions or classes. Write any standalone functions or classes that you need in your DLL. When you are finished, choose Project|Build or Project|Make to compile and build the DLL.

Let's take this one step at a time so that it makes more sense:

1. Choose File|New. When the Object Repository is displayed, double-click the DLL icon to create a new DLL project. A new, blank DLL project is created for you.

2. In the Code Editor, change the line that reads #include <vcl.h> to read

   ```
   #include <condefs.h>
   #include <windows.h>
   ```

   (You won't be using VCL classes in this DLL, but you will need the Windows.h file.)

3. Delete all the comment lines about ShareMem.h and Borlndmm.dll.

4. Add this line just above the DllEntryPoint() function:

   ```
   #include "StaticLd.h"
   ```

5. Add the code following the DllEntryPoint() function until your code matches Listing 19.1. (The DllEntryPoint() function and the text above it will already be in the Code Editor window.)

6. Save the project with a filename of StaticLd.cpp.

7. Choose View|Project Manager. Right-click and choose Save Project Group to save the project group.

Listing 19.1. StaticLd.CPP.

```
 1: //------------------------------------------------------------
 2: #include <windows.h>
 3: #pragma hdrstop
 4:
 5: #include "StaticLd.h"
 6:
 7: int WINAPI DllEntryPoint(HINSTANCE, unsigned long, void*)
 8: {
 9:   return 1;
10: }
11: //------------------------------------------------------------
12: void DLL_EXP SayHello(HWND hWnd)
13: {
14:   MessageBox(hWnd, "Hello from a DLL!",
15:     "DLL Message Box", MB_OK | MB_ICONEXCLAMATION);
16: }
17:
18: MyClass::MyClass(HWND hwnd)
19: {
20:   hWnd = hwnd;
21: }
```

19

```
22:
23: void MyClass::SaySomething(char* text)
24: {
25:   MessageBox(hWnd, text,
26:     "A Text Message From a DLL Class", MB_OK);
27: }
28:
29: void
30: MyClass::Beep()
31: {
32:   MessageBeep(-1);
33: }
```

This file is called StaticLd.cpp because the DLL produced by this code will be loaded at runtime using static loading. The Web site accompanying this book, http://www.mcp.com/info, contains a sample program called CallDll.bpr that calls functions in a DLL, using static loading, and also calls functions in a different DLL, using dynamic loading. The filenames are meant to be as descriptive as possible while still complying with the standard eight-character rule. Remember that you can use long filenames with your own programs and DLLs, but I use the 8.3 convention in this book for reasons related to electronic publishing.

Now you have to create the header file for the DLL. Here goes:

1. Choose File|New. When the Object Repository appears, choose Text to create a new text file and click OK. The new text file is displayed in the Code Editor.

2. Choose File|Save. Save the file as StaticLd.h. (Save the file first so that the syntax highlighting works. Syntax highlighting does not work for a file with a .txt extension.)

3. Enter the code from Listing 19.2.

4. Choose File|Save All.

TYPE **Listing 19.2.** StaticLd.h.

```
1: #ifndef _STATICLD_H
2: #define _STATICLD_H
3:
4: #ifdef __DLL__
5: #  define DLL_EXP __declspec(dllexport)
6: #else
7: #  define DLL_EXP __declspec(dllimport)
8: #endif
9:
10: extern "C" void DLL_EXP SayHello(HWND);
11:
12: class DLL_EXP MyClass {
13:   public:
```

continues

19

Listing 19.2. continued

```
14:       MyClass(HWND hwnd);
15:       void SaySomething(char* text);
16:       void Beep();
17:    private:
18:       HWND hWnd;
19: };
20:
21: #endif
```

Now that you've entered the source code and the header, you build the project. Choose Project | Build StaticLd to build the project.

> **NOTE**
>
> A function in a DLL does not need a function declaration to compile successfully. If you find that a function doesn't appear to be exported, check whether you have forgotten to include it in the DLL's header file.

Creating an Import Library File

There isn't anything you need to do to have C++Builder create an import library file for your DLL. All that's necessary is that the Generate import library option is selected on the Linker page of the Project Options dialog box. This option is on by default for DLL projects, so you shouldn't have to change it. As long as this option is checked, C++Builder will automatically create an import library for the DLL each time the DLL is built.

Creating the Calling Application

Okay, you now have a working DLL. A DLL doesn't do much good without an application to call it, so let's get to work creating the application. Creating an application that uses a DLL requires only two steps in addition to what you normally do when creating an application (assuming dynamic loading):

☐ Add the include for the DLL's header file.

☐ Add the DLL's import library file to the project.

As I've said, after you have properly created the header, the rest is easy. To prove it, let's create a program that uses our DLL:

1. Select View | Project Manager to display the Project Manager. Click the New button and create a new application.

2. Place a button on the form and change the button's Caption property to Say Hello.

3. Double-click the button to display the OnClick handler for the button. Type the following code at the cursor:

```
SayHello(Handle);
```

4. Place another button on the form. Make the Caption of this button MyClass Test. Double-click the button and type the following code at the cursor:

```
MyClass mc(Application->Handle);
mc.SaySomething("Uh... Hello, there.");
mc.Beep();
```

This enables you to test the class that you exported from the DLL.

5. Save the unit as CallDllU.cpp and the project as CallDll.bpr.

Okay, now the calling application is nearly written. Before the file will compile, though, you need to add the include for the DLL's header.

Adding the Include for the DLL's Header

Adding the include for the DLL's header is simple:

1. Move to the top of the file and place the following line just below the line that reads #pragma hdrstop:

```
#include "StaticLd.h"
```

2. Save the project.

There. That was easy. That's all you have to do in the calling app. One more step and you'll be finished.

NOTE
> You might have several headers for a single DLL. For example, if your DLL exports five different classes, you might have five headers, one for each class. Just be sure that you add all the necessary headers. If you forget one, don't worry—the compiler will remind you.

You include the header in each unit that uses functions or classes from the DLL. Now let's add the import library file to the project.

Adding the Import Library File

You can add the import library for the DLL to the project in several ways. Without question, the easiest way is through the Project Manager:

1. Choose View | Project Manager.

2. Be sure that the CallDll project is the active project in the Project Manager. Right-click and choose Add from the Project Manager context menu.

19

3. When the Add to Project dialog box comes up, choose the `StaticLd.lib` file and click OK.

4. The library file will be displayed in the Project Manager window.

That wasn't difficult, either. As you can see, using DLLs is not complicated when you know the rules.

You can also add the library file directly to the project source file. If you view the project source after adding the `.lib` file (View | Project Source), you will see a line that looks like this:

```
USELIB("StaticLd.lib");
```

When you added the `.lib` file through the Project Manager, C++Builder automatically added this line to the project source. If you want, you can add a line similar to this on your own, rather than go through the Project Manager. Going through the Project Manager is easier than doing it yourself, though, plus it has the added benefit of allowing you to choose the file rather than depend on your memory to get the filename typed correctly.

Finally, you can add the `.lib` file directly into the project makefile. There isn't any reason for you to do this, but you certainly can if you want. If you look at the project makefile (View | Project Makefile), you will see a line like this:

```
LIBFILES =
```

Add the import library's name to the end of this line:

```
LIBFILES = StaticLd.lib
```

As I said, the easiest way is to add the `.lib` file through the Project Manager.

Now you are ready to compile and run the program. Click the Run button and test the program. When you click the buttons, the functions contained in the DLL will be executed.

Using Forms in DLLs

You place forms in a DLL just as you place code in one. There isn't much difference in the way the form is created, compared to the way a form in an application is created. To begin, you create a new DLL through the Object Repository, as you did before. When the project is displayed, create a new form by clicking the New Form button or by going through the Object Repository. Add components to the form and write code for the form's source unit, just as you would when creating a form in an application.

There are two types of applications from which you might call the form contained in the DLL:

☐ C++Builder applications

☐ Non-C++Builder applications

ROGUE COMMUNITY COLLEGE

REDWOOD CAMPUS BOOKSTORE HOURS
3345 Redwood Highway, Grants Pass, OR 97527
Regular hours are:
- Monday – Thursday   7:30 a.m. - 5:00 p.m.
- Friday   7:30 a.m. - 1:30 p.m.
- Saturday and Sunday   CLOSED

Hours for the first week of each term will be posted. Summer hours to be posted.

RIVERSIDE CAMPUS BOOKSTORE HOURS
227 E. 9TH Street, Medford, OR 97501
Regular hours are:
- Monday - Thursday 8:00 a.m.–12:00 and 12:30 p.m.– 4:00 p.m.
- Friday   8:00 am – 1:00pm
- Saturday and Sunday   CLOSED

Hours for the first week of each term will be posted. Summer hours will be posted.

1998-99
Where your Bookstore Dollars Go

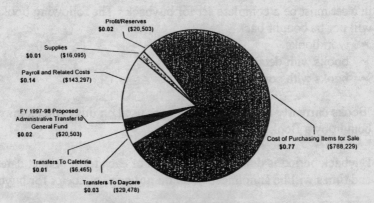

Profit/Reserves
$0.02 ($20,503)

Supplies
$0.01 ($16,095)

Payroll and Related Costs
$0.14 ($143,297)

FY 1997-98 Proposed
Administrative Transfer to
General Fund
$0.02 ($20,503)

Transfers To Cafeteria
$0.01 ($6,465)

Transfers To Daycare
$0.03 ($29,478)

Cost of Purchasing Items for Sale
$0.77 ($788,229)

The above chart identifies where every dollar you spend in the bookstore goes (based on fiscal year 1996-97 actual data) The majority, $ 77 of every dollar, is spent on the cost of goods sold (the bookstores cost of purchasing items for sale) Only $ 15 of every dollar is spent on necessary costs to operate the bookstore like staffing and supplies Three cents of every dollar is transferred to daycare to subsidize its operations, enabling RCC to offer affordable daycare to its students One cent is used to cover operating deficits of the cafeteria so that the RCC cafe may offer low cost and high quality meals to its students and staff A proposed $ 02 administrative transfer to the RCC general fund is for accounting, purchasing and plant services provided by the district The remaining $ 02 is the profit of the bookstore and is kept as a reserve against future operating losses for daycare and cafeteria operations

ROGUE COMMUNITY COLLEGE

REFUNDS
KEEP YOUR RECEIPT! No refunds are issued without it.

Do not write anything in your book unless you are prepared to keep it all term. A marked book will not receive a full refund.

To obtain a full refund, books must meet **ALL** of the following conditions:

- Returned during the first two weeks of the term for which it was purchased.
- Returned in exact condition purchased: i.e., no names or marks of any kind, no smudges, bent covers or pages. Software must be in original sealed packaging, etc. (We reserve the right to determine the acceptable condition of any returned book.)

Defective **NEW** books will be replaced. **USED** books are not guaranteed.

BUYBACK

The Bookstore **may** buy back current books *as needed*. Books sold in a set must be a complete set for buyback. The following books will not be bought back:
- ➤ workbooks
- ➤ books with detachable pages
- ➤ books with software.

Books currently in print, but no longer used on this campus **may** be bought by a Book Wholesaler.

Buyback period is during the **last** week of each term. Exact dates and times will be announced. You **do not** need a receipt for buyback.

Redwood Campus Phone 471-3500 ext. 227
Riverside Campus Phone 774-1004 ext. 1201

These two situations have to be handled differently. First, let's take a look at the easy route: calling a form in a DLL from a C++Builder application.

Calling a Form in a DLL from a C++Builder Application

If you want to call a form contained in a DLL, you need to ensure that the form's class is exported from the DLL. To do that, you implement the technique described earlier for exporting classes (it was in the section "The __export Modifier"). Specifically, you add macros that either export or import the form's class, based on whether you are building the DLL or the calling application. This means manually editing both the form's header and the form's source unit.

Writing the DLL and the DLL Header

First, you add the macros for importing or exporting the class. Open the header for the form and before the class declaration, add code similar to the following (I say *similar to* because you could use any identifier you want where I have used DLL_EXP):

```
#ifdef __DLL__
#  define DLL_EXP __declspec(dllexport)
#else
#  define DLL_EXP __declspec(dllimport)
#endif
```

Now you need to add the macro name to the form's class declaration. The class declaration begins with this line:

```
class TMyForm : public TForm
```

Place the macro name between the class keyword and the name of the form:

```
class DLL_EXP TMyForm : public TForm
```

You now have a form class that will be exported from the DLL. You can now build the DLL.

19

NOTE

You don't have to export the form's class if you don't want to. You could choose the technique used when calling a form from a non-C++Builder app (I'll discuss this in the section "Calling a Form from a Non-C++Builder Application"). In that case, though, you would pass the form's this pointer to the DLL function that creates and displays the form. That way the form in the DLL is properly parented to the main form in the calling application.

Writing the Calling Application

In your calling application, you perform the same two steps that you performed earlier, plus a third:

1. Add the include for the DLL's header file.
2. Add the DLL's import library file to the project.
3. Create the form before showing it.

The steps to include the form's header and add the .lib file to the project are identical to those outlined earlier.

On Day 10, "More on Projects," I discussed the auto-creation of forms. Because a form in a DLL isn't part of the calling application's project, the form can't be auto-created by the program when the program loads. You have to explicitly create the form before displaying it. I've discussed this already but not in this context, so let's review it. The code to display and execute the form is similar to this:

```
TMyForm* form = new TMyForm(this);
form->ShowModal();
delete form;   // optional
```

Aside from the fact that you need to create the form before displaying it, there is no difference between a form in the application's file and a form in a DLL, from the perspective of the calling application.

NOTE

> The preceding code snippet deletes the form's pointer after the form returns. This isn't required, but you can delete the form's pointer to free up memory. If you don't delete the form, the calling form will delete it when the calling form itself is deleted (usually when the application terminates). When you specified this in the form's constructor, you made the form a child of the main form, and VCL parent objects take care of deleting their child objects.

Calling an MDI Form in a DLL

The case of an MDI child form in a DLL is a special case. Let's say you have a C++Builder application and that the main form is an MDI form. If you try to use an MDI child form contained in a DLL, you will get an exception from VCL saying No MDI forms are currently active. "What? But I have an MDI form in my application!" Not according to VCL, you don't. Here's what happens.

When you attempt to show your MDI child form, VCL checks whether the Application object's MainForm property is valid. If the MainForm property is not valid, an exception is thrown. So what's the problem? The MainForm is valid, right? The problem is that the DLL also contains an Application object, and it is the DLL's MainForm that is checked, not the application's MainForm. Because a DLL doesn't have a main form, this check will always fail.

The fix for this problem is to assign the DLL's Application object to the Application object of the calling application. Naturally, this will only work if the calling application is a VCL application. That's not the whole story, though. Before the DLL unloads, you must also set the DLL's Application object back to its original state. This enables the VCL memory manager to clean up any memory allocated for the DLL. It means that you will have to store the DLL's Application object pointer in a global variable in the DLL so that it can be restored before the DLL unloads.

Let's back up for a moment and review the steps required to show an MDI child form in a DLL:

1. Create a global TApplication pointer in the DLL.
2. Save the DLL's Application object in the global TApplication pointer.
3. Assign the calling application's Application object to the DLL's Application object.
4. Create and show the MDI child form.
5. Reset the DLL's Application object before the DLL unloads.

The first step is easy. Just place the following code at the top of your DLL's source unit:

```
TApplication* DllApp = 0;
```

The pointer is set to 0 so that you can tell whether it has already been assigned. Next, create a function that will do the TApplication switch and create the child form. The function will look like this:

```
void ShowMDIChildForm(TApplication* mainApp)
{
  if (!DllApp) {
    DllApp = Application;
    Application = mainApp;
  }
  TChildForm* child =
    new TChildForm(Application->MainForm);
  child->Show();
}
```

Examine this code for a moment. When you call this function, you will pass the Application object of the calling app. If the DllApp pointer has not yet been assigned, you assign the DLL's Application object to the temporary pointer. Then you assign the Application object of the calling application to the DLL's `Application` object. This check ensures that the `Application` object is set only once. After that, the MDI child form is created, passing the calling application's `MainForm` as the owner. Finally, the form is shown.

All that remains is to reset the DLL's `Application` pointer before unloading the DLL. But when and where do you do this? Your first guess might be to perform this action in the `OnClose` event handler for the calling application's main form. This is a good guess, but the problem is that by the time the `OnClose` event is generated, it's too late because the DLL has already been unloaded. The next best thing is to perform the action in the `OnCloseQuery` event handler for the main form. First, you'll need a function in the DLL that resets the `Application` pointer:

```
void ResetDllApplication()
{
  if (DllApp)
    Application = DllApp;
}
```

Remember, you saved the DLL's `Application` pointer earlier, so now you just restore it. You call this function from your application's `OnCloseQuery` event handler, ensuring that the DLL will unload without incident. That's all there is to it.

As you can see, placing an MDI child form in a DLL requires extra work, but it is certainly possible. The book's Web site, `http//:www.mcp.com/info`, has an application project called `MdiApp` and a DLL project called `MdiDll` that illustrate using an MDI form in a DLL.

Calling a Form from a Non-C++Builder Application

If you want to call a form from a non-C++Builder application, you have to do a little more work. Because the calling app knows nothing about VCL, you can't import a VCL class and call its `ShowModal()` method, as you did when calling the form from a C++Builder application. What you have to do is create a standalone function in the DLL that is called by the calling application. This function can be called from any program if you specify `extern "C"` when declaring the function. Within the function body you then create and execute the form.

You create the form in the DLL as described earlier except that you don't have to export the form's class. Instead, in the main form's source unit, create a function that looks like this:

```
void ShowForm()
{
  TMyForm* form = new TMyForm(0);
  form->ShowModal();
  delete form;    // must do this
}
```

Notice that `NULL` is passed for the form's parent. This must be done because the non-C++Builder application doesn't have a VCL object that can be passed as the form's parent. You need to delete the `TMyForm` object in this case because the form isn't parented to a VCL object.

Next, you create a separate header for the DLL. Remember that the form's class is not going to be exported, so the form's header is meaningless to the calling application. All the calling application wants to see is a header that contains the ShowForm() function. Create a header that includes declaration for the ShowForm() function and then include it in the calling application's source file. (Be sure to write the macro to ensure proper importing and exporting of the function.) As before, you will have to link the .lib file for the DLL to the calling application when you build the calling application. You can also use runtime loading if you prefer. Which method you use depends on your preference and the language in which the calling application is written.

NOTE

> Borland and Microsoft use different object file formats. If you are writing a DLL for use in Microsoft development environments (Visual C++ or Visual Basic), you have to create an import library file compatible with those environments. See the Microsoft documentation for details on creating import library files using Microsoft tools.

Using Resources in DLLs

Sometimes it's convenient to have resources contained in a DLL. I've already mentioned internationalization and how a DLL can be used to make your program more easily ported to languages other than the one for which it was designed. Let's say you had an instructions screen for your application and that those instructions were contained in five strings in a DLL. The strings might be named IDS_INSTRUCTION1, IDS_INSTRUCTION2, and so on. You could load and display the strings like this:

```
char buff[256];
LoadString(dllInstance, IDS_INSTRUCTION1, buff, sizeof(buff));
InstructionLabel1->Caption = buff;
```

The first parameter of the LoadString() function contains the instance handle (HINSTANCE) of the module where the strings can be found. You could create DLLs in several different languages and just load the DLL in the appropriate language, based on a user selection. The code might look like the following:

```
String dllName;
switch (language) {
  case french : dllName = "french.dll"; break;
  case german : dllName = "german.dll"; break;
  case spanish : dllName = "spanish.dll"; break;
  case english : dllName = "english.dll"; break;
}
dllInstance = LoadLibrary(dllName.c_str());
```

19

You only have to load the correct DLL; the rest of the code remains the same. This is just one example of using resources contained in a DLL. You will find many uses for this technique.

Creating a Resource DLL

You can create a DLL that contains only resources, or you can mix code and resources in the same DLL. In this regard there are no restrictions on DLLs.

NOTE

> If your DLL contains only resources, you should remove the following lines from the default DLL project source unit:
>
> ```
> #include <vcl.h>
> #pragma hdrstop
> ```
>
> ```
> USERES("StaticLd.res");
> ```
>
> You also can delete the `DllEntryPoint()` function from the DLL, depending on whether you are loading statically or dynamically (more on that later). The easiest way to create a resource-only DLL is with the Object Repository's Console Wizard.

Placing resources in a DLL is much the same as adding resources to an application. From the Project Manager, click the Add Unit button and add the name of a resource script (.rc) or binary resource file (.res) where the resources can be found. When you build the DLL, the resources will be bound to the DLL.

You may have to perform one other step if you are loading a resource statically (at load time). As you can see from the preceding code snippet, you must have the DLL's instance handle before you can access resources contained in the DLL. When you load the DLL dynamically, this step is easy because `LoadLibrary()` returns the instance handle:

```
int dllInstance = LoadLibrary("resource.dll");
```

Now you can use the instance handle wherever required. In this case, using dynamic loading is actually easier. When using static loading, you need some way of obtaining the DLL's instance handle (remember, the DLL will be loaded when the application starts). To prepare for dynamic loading, you have to perform these steps when building the DLL:

1. Declare a global variable in the DLL that will hold the instance handle.
2. Assign the DLL's instance handle to the global variable in the `DllEntryPoint()` function.
3. Write a function to return the instance handle to the calling application.

Rather than walk you through this step by step, let me show you the complete source code for a DLL that uses this technique, in Listing 19.3.

Listing 19.3. Resource.cpp.

```
 1: #include <windows.h>
 2: #include <condefs.h>
 3: #pragma hdrstop
 4:
 5: #include "resource.h"
 6:
 7: HINSTANCE hInstance;
 8:
 9: //---------------------------------------------------------
10: int WINAPI DllEntryPoint(HINSTANCE hinst, unsigned long, void*)
11: {
12:   hInstance = hinst;
13:   return 1;
14: }
15: //---------------------------------------------------------
16:
17: HINSTANCE GetDllInstance()
18: {
19:    return hInstance;
20: }
```

As you see, I have removed much of what the default C++Builder DLL source code file initially contains when the DLL is created from the Object Repository. Notice that on line 5, I include the header file for the DLL. The header will only contain the declaration for one function in this case. Following that, line 7 declares a global variable called hInstance. Line 12 assigns the instance handle passed in the DllEntryPoint() function to the global variable.

NOTE

> The instance handle of the DLL is created by Windows and passed to the DllEntryPoint() function when the DLL is loaded.

Finally, lines 17 through 20 contain the function, called GetDllInstance(), that returns the DLL instance to the calling application. This function can be used in the calling application any time DLL instance handle is required:

```
LoadString(GetDllInstance(), IDS_TEXT, buff, sizeof(buff));
```

19

Implementing Resources in DLLs

Actually, there's not much left to say. I've pretty much covered how to use resources contained in a DLL, in the discussion on creating resource DLLs. To review, though, you know that you can load resource DLLs either statically or dynamically. If you load statically, you have to use an exported function to enable the instance handle of the DLL to get at the resources. If you load dynamically, you get the instance handle from the LoadLibrary() function. Don't forget to call FreeLibrary() when you are done with the DLL or before your application closes.

In the case of resource DLLs, dynamic loading is actually easier than static loading because you don't have to write any code in the DLL if you don't want to. It's also easier because you don't have to create an import library for the DLL. Just use LoadLibrary() and go to it.

NOTE

> Using dynamic loading has the added advantage of allowing your application to load faster. In many cases you load the resource DLL only when it's needed and unload it when it's no longer needed. This results in your application using less memory than when the resources are contained in the executable file. The downside to static loading is that your users might see a slight pause when the resource DLL loads. Try to anticipate as much as possible and load the resource DLL when it is least likely to be noticed.

When using static loading, remember to add the .lib file to the project of the calling application and also to include the header for the DLL. The advantage of static loading is that you don't have to worry about LoadLibrary() and FreeLibrary(). The disadvantage is that it's initially a little more work to set up. Also, your program takes longer to load and uses more memory when you use static loading.

Remember JumpingJack from Day 9, "Creating Applications in C++Builder"? The Web site accompanying this book, http://www.mcp.com/info, has a version of JumpingJack that loads the bitmap, sound, and string resources from a DLL. Check out that program for an example of using resources in a DLL.

Summary

Using dynamic link libraries isn't difficult, but it can be frustrating until you get the combination of export and import correct. This is made easier by using the _declspec() keyword, described in this chapter. Placing VCL forms in a DLL and then calling those forms from a non-C++Builder application is a powerful feature. This means that you can create forms that others can call from just about any type of Windows application, whether it be an application written in OWL, MFC, straight C, Visual Basic, or Delphi, and so forth. Using resources in DLLs is effective if you have a lot of resources in your application and you want to control when and where those resources are loaded.

Workshop

The Workshop contains quiz questions to help you solidify your understanding of the material covered and exercises to provide you with experience in using what you have learned. You can find answers to the quiz questions in Appendix A, "Answers to Quiz Questions."

Q&A

Q I have a relatively small program, and I don't see the need to use DLLs. Should I reevaluate my structure?

A Probably not. For small applications, DLLs often are not necessary. Any time you have classes that can be reused, you might as well use a DLL, but don't go out of your way to use DLLs in a small application.

Q I'm beginning work on what should be a large class. Should I plan on putting it in a DLL?

A Regardless of whether the class ends up in a DLL, you should always try to write the class with reuse in mind. If you do that from the start, putting the class in a DLL later will be a trivial undertaking.

Q That `GetProcAddress()` thing is a little weird. Do I have to use that to call functions in my DLL?

A No. Just use static loading and you won't have to worry about the `LoadLibrary()`, `GetProcAddress()`, and `FreeLibrary()` functions. Using static loading requires that you use an import library (`.lib`) for your DLL, but it's much easier in the long run.

Q My program compiles fine, but I keep getting a linker error that says `Undefined external MyFunction() in module MyUnit.cpp`. What's wrong?

A Either you have not exported the function from the DLL, or you are not properly importing the function from the DLL. This could be as simple as forgetting to add the `.lib` file for the DLL to the project, or it could be that you didn't properly set up your DLL's header and something is going wrong when you build either the DLL or the calling application.

19

Q **I have a form contained in a DLL, and my calling app is a C++Builder program. The size of the DLL is pretty large. Is there any way I can reduce that?**

A Unfortunately, no. This is where the power of programming in C++Builder works against you a little. Both the calling application and the DLL contain some of the same VCL code. In other words, the code is being duplicated in both the `.exe` and the `.dll`. You just have to live with the larger overall program size if you are using forms in DLLs.

Q **I have a lot of wave files for my application. Right now they are contained in separate files, but I would like to place them all in one file. Is a resource DLL a good idea here?**

A Absolutely. The only disadvantage is that if you just need one wave file, you must load the entire DLL. Still, by using dynamic loading, you can load and unload the DLL as required. The `PlaySound()` function makes it easy to play sounds from a DLL.

Q **I live in a French-speaking country. Why should I bother with internationalization of my program?**

A It depends entirely on your target audience. If you know that French is not the native language, you don't have to worry about internationalization at all. But if there is even the slightest possibility that your program could be marketed in other countries, you should plan from the beginning on international support. It's much easier to do it right the first time than to go back and fix it later.

Q **Will C++Builder automatically create an import library file for me when I create a DLL?**

A Yes, as long as the Generate import library option is selected on the Linker page of the Project Options dialog box (on by default for DLL projects).

Quiz

1. How do you load a DLL using static loading?
2. How do you load a DLL using dynamic loading?
3. How do you call a function from a DLL that has been loaded statically?
4. What steps do you have to take to ensure that a function in your DLL can be called from outside the DLL?
5. In the case of a DLL that has been dynamically loaded, can you unload the DLL at any time or only when the program closes?
6. What must you do to display a C++Builder form contained in a DLL from a non-C++Builder program?

7. What is the advantage of using import/export macros when building DLLs and the applications that call them?

8. How do you add resources to a DLL?

9. Does a resource DLL need to contain code as well as the resources?

10. Can a DLL containing resources be loaded statically (when the program loads)?

Exercises

1. Create a DLL that contains a function that displays a message box when called.

2. Create a calling application that will call the DLL in Exercise 1.

3. Create a DLL containing a form and a calling application that will display the form.

4. Create a DLL that has two bitmap resources.

5. Create a program that will display on demand either bitmap resource in your new DLL. (Hint: Use a TImage component and the `LoadFromResourceId()` method.)

6. **Extra Credit:** Write five DLLs, each of which contains the same strings but in different languages.

7. **Extra Credit:** Write a calling application that displays the strings you created in Exercise 6. Allow the user to choose the language to be used in the application. Display the strings in the language chosen.

19

Day 20

Creating Components

C++Builder provides a wide assortment of components to use in your applications. These components cover the basic Windows controls as well as provide some specialty components not inherent in Windows itself. Still, you might need to create a component in order to perform a task not provided by the pre-installed components. Writing a component requires these steps:

1. Use the New Component dialog box to begin the creation process.
2. Add properties, methods, and events to the component's class.
3. Test the component.
4. Add the component to the Component palette.

Today you will learn how to create components. As with most of C++Builder, it's not so bad after you've done it once or twice. You will learn by building a component called TFlashingLabel. TFlashingLabel is a regular Label component that flashes its text. By the time the day is done, you will know what you need in order to create basic components.

Creating a New Component

Writing components requires a higher level of programming expertise than you have used up to this point. First, you have to create a class for your new component. The class needs to be designed so that some of its properties will show up in the Object Inspector, whereas others will be used only at runtime. In addition, you will almost certainly have to write methods for your component. Some will be private to the component; others will be made public so that users of the component can access them. Finally, you may also have to write events for the component. Obviously, there is some work involved. As great as C++Builder's visual programming environment is, it won't help you here. Writing components is pure programming.

The New Component Dialog Box

The New Component dialog box gives you a head start on writing a component. To start the New Component dialog box, choose File | New to display the Object Repository, and then double-click the Component icon. Figure 20.1 shows the New Component dialog box when creating a new component.

Figure 20.1.

The New Component dialog box.

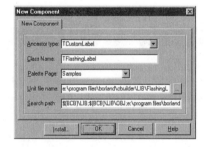

The Ancestor type field is used to choose an ancestor class for the new component. The classes of all installed components are listed in the Ancestor type combo box. When you create a new component, you should choose a base class that most closely matches the type of component you want to create. For example, the FlashingLabel component is just a label that flashes. In that case, the standard Label component has everything you need to get started, so you could use a TCustomLabel for the ancestor class. If, on the other hand, you wanted to create a label that creates Windows shortcuts, you would probably derive the component from TComponent (the base class for all components) because there is no other VCL component that gives you a base from which to work.

NOTE

C++Builder provides several classes that you can use as base classes for new components. The names of these classes all start with `TCustom`. For example, the base class for a `TLabel` is `TCustomLabel`. You can derive from one of these classes whenever you create a new component. The custom classes already provide the properties you are most likely to need for that component type, but the properties are not published (*published properties* are the properties shown in the Object Repository at design time). All you have to do to make the properties published is re-declare the base class's properties in the `__published` section of your component's class declaration. This is important because when a property is published, it can't be un-published. Starting with a custom class enables you to choose exactly the properties you want published.

When you derive a new component from an existing component, you are using the C++ feature called *inheritance*. It's been a while since I talked about inheritance, so refer back to Day 4, "C++ Classes and Object-Oriented Programming," if you need a refresher course. Inheriting from a component is, in effect, taking everything that component has and then adding some things of your own. The class you are inheriting from is the base class, and the new class is the derived class. In the previous example, `TCustomLabel` would be the base class, and `TFlashingLabel` would be the derived class.

After you have selected an ancestor class, type the name of your new component's class in the `Class Name` field. The classname should begin with a `T` and should describe the function the class performs. The component you build today will have the name `TFlashingLabel` (you'll begin creating the component soon). If you choose a classname that already exists in the component library, the New Component dialog box will tell you when you click the OK button. You will have to choose a unique classname before you can continue.

NOTE

There's no reason that you have to begin the classname with `T`; it just happens to be customary for Borland classes. (The use of `T` in Borland classes is a Borland tradition that goes back to the early days of Turbo Pascal. It is used in both OWL and VCL.) Some people use `T` when deriving from a Borland class but not when creating their own classes. It's entirely up to you.

20

NOTE

> Professional component writers learned long ago to be sure that their component classes have unique names. Imagine the problems if two component vendors both name a component TFancyLabel. At TurboPower, the Async Professional components start with TApd, the Orpheus components start with TOr, the Abbrevia components start with TAb, and so on. Although this doesn't guarantee that these component names won't clash with those of other vendors, it certainly goes a long way to prevent that from happening.

The Palette Page field enables you to specify the page on the Component palette where you want the component's icon to appear. (The component's icon won't actually appear on the Component palette until you install the design package containing the component.) You can choose an existing tab on the Component palette, or you can type the name of a new tab you want C++Builder to create for this component.

The Unit file name field is used to specify the name of the file that will contain the component's source. C++Builder automatically creates a unit filename based on the component's name, but you can change the supplied filename if you want. The Search path field is used to specify the search path that C++Builder should use when looking for component packages. You won't need to modify this field.

The Install button is used to install the new component directly into a package. You need not worry about that now, though, because you will create a package for your component when I discuss that later.

Creating the FlashingLabel Component

You are now ready to perform the first steps in creating the TFlashingLabel component. As I said earlier, this component is a regular Label component that flashes the label's text on the screen. With that in mind, let's get started creating the component:

1. Choose File|New to invoke the Object Repository.
2. Double-click the Component icon in the Object Repository. The New Component dialog box is displayed.
3. From the Ancestor type combo box, choose the TCustomLabel class as the base class.
4. Type TFlashingLabel in the Class Name field.
5. The Palette Page field contains Samples. Leave this field as is. The new component will be added to the Samples page of the Component palette when you install the component.

20

6. Click OK to close the New Component dialog box. The Code Editor appears and displays a new source code unit.

7. Save the unit as FlashingLabel.cpp.

NOTE

> You should save the unit generated by the New Component dialog box right away. When you save the unit, the reference to the unit's header is updated, as is the namespace name.

Listings 20.1 and 20.2 show the source unit and header as they appear now.

Listing 20.1. FlashingLabel.h.

```
 1: //------------------------------------------------------
 2: #ifndef FlashingLabelH
 3: #define FlashingLabelH
 4: //------------------------------------------------------
 5: #include <SysUtils.hpp>
 6: #include <Controls.hpp>
 7: #include <Classes.hpp>
 8: #include <Forms.hpp>
 9: #include <StdCtrls.hpp>
10: //------------------------------------------------------
11: class PACKAGE TFlashingLabel : public TCustomLabel
12: {
13: private:
14: protected:
15: public:
16:     __fastcall TFlashingLabel(TComponent* Owner);
17: __published:
18: };
19: //------------------------------------------------------
20: #endif
```

Listing 20.2. FlashingLabel.cpp.

```
 1: //------------------------------------------------------
 2: #include <vcl.h>
 3: #pragma hdrstop
 4:
 5: #include "FlashingLabel.h"
 6: #pragma package(smart_init)
 7: //------------------------------------------------------
 8: // ValidCtrCheck is used to ensure that the components created
 9: // do not have any pure virtual functions.
```

continues

20

Listing 20.2. continued

```
10: //
11:
12: static inline void ValidCtrCheck(TFlashingLabel *)
13: {
14:   new TFlashingLabel(NULL);
15: }
16: //----------------------------------------------------------
17: __fastcall TFlashingLabel::TFlashingLabel(TComponent* Owner)
18:    : TCustomLabel(Owner)
19: {
20: }
21: //----------------------------------------------------------
22: namespace Flashinglabel
23: {
24:   void __fastcall PACKAGE Register()
25:   {
26:     TComponentClass classes[1] = {__classid(TFlashingLabel)};
27:     RegisterComponents("Samples", classes, 0);
28:   }
29: }
30: //----------------------------------------------------------
```

In Listing 20.1, you see that the TFlashingLabel class is derived from TCustomLabel. The class declaration is empty except for the access keywords (private, public, protected, and __published). You'll fill in the blanks later, after I've had a chance to go over what comprises a component.

As you can see, the New Component dialog box gives you a head start by filling out some of the header and some of the source unit for you. You still have to do the hard stuff, but at least the Register() and ValidCtrCheck() functions are written and the class declaration is started. Let me sidetrack here and talk about these functions.

Register() and ValidCtrCheck()

Registering the component is necessary for C++Builder to know what components are in the component library and on what tab they should appear. A typical Register() function looks like this:

```
namespace Mycomponent
{
  void __fastcall PACKAGE Register()
  {
    TComponentClass classes[1] = {__classid(TMyComponent)};
    RegisterComponents("Samples", classes, 0);
  }
}
```

First, notice that the Register() function is wrapped in a *namespace.*

NEW TERM A namespace is a C++ feature that enables sections of code to be distinguished by name.

Namespaces are a C++ feature I haven't talked about yet. A namespace is used to keep this `Register()` function separate from the `Register()` functions of all the other components in the component library. The name of the namespace for a C++Builder component must follow a specific design. The namespace name must be the name of the file in which the component is contained, in all lowercase letters except for the leading character. Let's say you had a component called `TFancyEdit` and that it was contained in a file called `FancyEdit.cpp`. The namespace name for the `Register()` function in this case would be `Fancyedit`. If you use the New Component dialog box to create your component, you don't have to worry about the namespace name. The name will be set for you when you save the file and will be changed if you happen to change the filename, using File | Save As.

The first line in the `Register()` function creates an array of components to be registered and places this component in the array. If you were creating an entire library of components, you could register them all at one time by placing them all in the `TComponentClass` array. Most of the time, though, you will be dealing with one component at a time.

The second line in the `Register()` function tells C++Builder on which page of the Component palette the new component should be placed. After the component has been written and fully tested, you add the component to the component library. Adding the component to the component library is discussed in detail later in the section "Adding the Component to the Component Library."

C++Builder uses the `ValidCtrCheck()` function to insure that the component doesn't declare any pure virtual functions. The `ValidCtrCheck()` function looks like this:

```
static inline void ValidCtrCheck(TMyComponent *)
{
  new TMyComponent(NULL);
}
```

Here again, if you use the New Component dialog box to create the function, you don't need to worry about the `ValidCtrCheck()` function because C++Builder will create it for you.

At this point the component doesn't do anything special, but before you go on with the component's creation, I need to explain what makes up a component. After that, you'll write the rest of the `TFlashingLabel` component. Keep the component that you just created (such as it is) open in the IDE because you'll need it a little later.

20

Component Properties and Methods

A big part of writing components is writing the component's properties and methods. Events are also a big part of writing components, but let's talk first about properties, and then I'll discuss methods.

Properties

You have been using properties in your journey thus far; from a user's perspective you know what properties are. Now you need to understand properties from a component writer's perspective. Before you write components, you need to understand what properties are—and what they are not.

Specifically, properties are not data members. It is natural to think of properties as data members of the class to which they belong. After all, you treat properties just like data members when you do things like this:

```
int width = Width;
Height = width * .7;
```

But properties are not data members, and you must keep that in mind when writing components. Properties differ from data members in many ways but have at least one thing in common with regular data members: They have a specific data type. A property's type can be one of the integral data types (`int`, `long`, `double`, `enum`, and so on), a class (`AnsiString`, `TFont`, and so on), or a structure (`TRect`, for example).

What properties are, then, is a special type of object that meets the following criteria:

- [ ] Properties have an underlying data member that is used to store the property's value.
- [ ] Properties can implement a `write` method.
- [ ] Properties can implement a `read` method.
- [ ] Properties can use direct access instead of `read` and `write` methods.
- [ ] Properties can be read-only or write-only.
- [ ] Properties can have a default value.
- [ ] Properties can be published or non-published.

For this to make more sense, let's take a look at the features of properties, one at a time.

Properties Have Underlying Data Members

Each property has an underlying data member associated with it. It is this data member that holds the actual value associated with a property. Take a simple assignment—for example,

```
Label->Caption = "Pat McGarry";
```

20

This statement assigns a string to the Caption property of a Label component. What happens behind the scenes is more than just a simple assignment. Because a Caption property is of the AnsiString type, it has an AnsiString object as its underlying data member. When an assignment is made like this one, the underlying data member is given the value of the assigned string. Using an underlying data member is necessary because a property does not have the capability to store data.

You can name the underlying data member anything you want, but tradition dictates that the data member associated with a property have the same name as the property, with the addition of a leading F. For instance, the data member associated with the Caption property would be named FCaption.

NOTE

> This association between the property and its underlying data member can be the source of much confusion when you start writing components. It's not that it's difficult to understand; it's just that you might mix up the two when writing code for the component. For example, you might accidentally write
>
> ```
> Left = 20;
> ```
>
> when you meant to write
>
> ```
> FLeft = 20;
> ```
>
> This results in all sorts of interesting behavior in your component. You'll see why when I discuss write methods in the next section.

The underlying data member is almost always declared as a private data member. You want your users to modify the data member through the property or by calling a method, but never directly. This way you are in control of the data member as much as possible, which leads us to the next feature of properties.

Properties Have write Methods

When you make an assignment to a property, a lot of things can happen behind the scenes. Exactly what happens depends on the specific property. For instance, this code looks simple:

```
Left = 20;
```

But several things happen when this line is executed. First, the underlying data member, FLeft, is changed to the new value. Next, the form (assuming this code was executed from a form) is moved to the new left position, using the Windows API function MoveWindow(). Finally, the form is repainted by calling Invalidate() for the form. How does all that happen? It happens through the Left property's write method. The write method is a method that

20

is called any time the property is assigned a value. You can use the write method to do validation of the assigned value or to perform special processing.

You declare a property's write method when you declare the property. Here's an example of a typical property declaration:

```
__property int FlashRate = {read=FFlashRate, write=SetFlashRate};
```

This declaration contains syntax that you haven't seen before because it is syntax specific to properties and doesn't exist in standard C++. First of all, notice that the property is declared with the __property keyword and that an equal sign and additional code follow the declaration. The code following the declaration tells the compiler that the property's write method is called SetFlashRate(). You can name the write method anything you want, but tradition rules that you name the write method the same name as the property, prepended with the word Set. (Notice also that this declaration assigns a value to the read method. I'll get to the read method in just a bit.)

When the property is written to (assigned a value), the write method associated with the property will be called automatically. The write method must return void. The write method must have one parameter, and that parameter must be of the same type as the property itself. For example, the write method's declaration for the FlashRate property would be

```
void __fastcall SetFlashRate(int AFlashRate);
```

The value passed to the write method is the value that was assigned to the property. So, given this line,

```
FlashingLabel->FlashRate = 1000;
```

you end up with the value of 1000 passed to the SetFlashRate() function. What you do with the value within the write method depends on a wide variety of factors. At a minimum, you assign the value to the associated data member. In other words, the write method would look like this:

```
void __fastcall TFlashingLabel::SetFlashRate(int AFlashRate)
{
  FFlashRate = AFlashRate;    // FFlashRate now equals 1000
  // do some other stuff;
}
```

 NOTE

The use of the leading A for the parameter name in a write method is another tradition.

You will nearly always do something more than assign the value to the underlying data member. If you are only assigning the value to the data member associated with the property, you don't need a write method for the property. I'll explain that in just a moment. First, let's look at read methods.

NOTE

> The value passed to the write method can be passed by value or by reference. You should pass classes and structures by reference to reduce overhead. You can pass the integral data types by value.

Properties Have read Methods

The read method works exactly like the write method (aside from the obvious difference). When a property's value is read, the read method is executed and the value of the underlying data member is returned.

The name of the read method is the property name preceded by Get. The read method takes no parameters and returns the property type. For example, if you were to use a read method for the FlashRate property, it would be declared like this:

```
int __fastcall GetFlashRate();
```

The read method might perform some processing and then return the value of the underlying data member, FFlashRate in this case. The reading of a property happens in many different ways. Sometimes it's the result of an assignment to a variable:

```
int rate = FlashingLabel->FlashRate;
```

At other times it is used within a C++ statement:

```
switch (FlashingLabel->FlashRate) {
  case 1000 : SpeedUp(); break;
  // etc.
}
```

Regardless of how the property is read, the read method is called each time a read takes place.

Notice that I said *if* you are using a read method. Frequently you won't use a read method, but instead will use direct access to retrieve the value of the data member associated with a property. Let's take a look at direct access right now.

Properties Can Use Direct Access

You don't have to use read and write methods for your properties. If you are assigning a value to the underlying data member or reading the value of the underlying data member, you can use direct access. The declaration for a property using direct access looks like this:

```
__property int FlashRate = {read=FFlashRate, write=FFlashRate};
```

20

This code assigns the data member itself (FFlashRate) to both the read and the write specifiers rather than call a read method or a write method. When the property is written to, the data member is changed and nothing more takes place. When the property is read, the value of the underlying data member is returned. It's as simple as that.

NOTE

> It is common to use direct access when reading the property and to use a write method for writing to the property. Take a look at this earlier example of a property declaration:
>
> ```
> __property int FlashRate = {read=FFlashRate, write=SetFlashRate};
> ```
>
> The property uses direct access for reading, but a write method for writing. Writing to a property often produces side effects, as I explained in the previous section. In fact, the capability to spawn side effects is one of the big strengths of properties. To cause side effects when your property is written to, you use a write method. Reading a property, on the other hand, is usually just a matter of returning the value of the underlying data member. In that case, direct access makes the most sense.

Properties Can Be Read-Only or Write-Only

You can specify a property to be read-only or write-only. Making a property read-only is a useful feature. (VCL has many read-only properties). For instance, you may have a property that you want the user to be able to read but not modify. It could be that modifying the property directly would have adverse effects on the component, so you need to protect against that.

Making a property read-only is easy: You omit the write specifier in the property's declaration:

```
__property int FlashRate = {read=FFlashRate};
```

If the user attempts to write to a property that is declared as read-only, he or she will get a compiler error that says TFlashingLabel::FlashRate is not accessible. As you see, making a property read-only is very simple.

You can make a property write-only by omitting the read specifier from the property's declaration. It's difficult to imagine a use for a property that can be written to but not read, but you certainly can write such a property, if necessary.

Properties Can Have Default Values

A *default value* is another useful feature of properties. You will notice that when you place a component on a form, many properties that are displayed in the Object Inspector already contain values. These are the default values as defined by the component writer. Assigning default values makes things easier for the component user. All properties should have a default value, if possible. This enables the user to change only specific properties and leave the rest alone. Certain types of properties do not lend themselves to default values, but most do.

Like the read and write methods, the default value is set when the property is declared. Let's go back to the component's FlashRate property. Declaring the FlashRate property with a default value would look like this:

```
__property int FlashRate =
    {read=FFlashRate, write=SetFlashRate, default=800};
```

Now, when the FlashingLabel component is displayed in the Object Inspector, the value of 800 (milliseconds in this case) will already be displayed for the FlashRate property.

NOTE

Setting a default value for the property displays only the default value in the Object Inspector. It does *not* set the value of the underlying data member for the property. You must still assign the default value to the data member in the component's constructor. For example, the constructor for the FlashingLabel component would look like this:

```
__fastcall TFlashingLabel::TFlashingLabel(TComponent* AOwner)
    : TCustomLabel(AOwner)
{
    FFlashRate = 800;      // set the default value
    // other things here
}
```

Be sure to set the appropriate values for all data members that correspond to properties with default values.

If you don't want to use a default value for a property, omit the default specifier in the property's declaration.

Properties Can Be Published, Public, or Private

Some properties are available at design time. These properties can be modified at design time through the Object Inspector and can also be modified or read at runtime. These properties are said to be *published*. Simply put, a published property is one that shows up in the Object Inspector at design time. Any properties located in the __published section of the component's class declaration will be displayed in the Object Inspector at design time.

Other properties are runtime-only properties. These properties can't be accessed at design time (they don't show up in the Object Inspector). Properties of this type are declared in the public section of the component's class declaration.

20

Private properties are properties that are used internally by the component and are not available to the component users. Private properties are declared in the `protected` or `private` sections in the component's class declaration.

Writing Methods for Components

Writing methods for components is no different than writing methods for any C++ class. The one exception is that a component's public methods must use the `__fastcall` modifier. Other than that, your component's methods can be private, protected, or public. It pays to keep in mind access levels as you write components.

Determining what methods to make public is easy. A *public method* is one that users of your component can call to cause the component to perform a specific action. The use of private versus protected methods is more difficult to decide. After programming for a while, you will be better able to recognize the situations when protected access should be used instead of private access.

NOTE

read and `write` methods for properties are usually made protected. Thus, you allow classes derived from your component to modify the behavior of the `read` and `write` methods by overriding the method.

As I said earlier, methods of components are just methods and, for the most part, can be treated as regular class member functions.

NOTE

Keep the use of methods to a minimum in your components. Use a property to perform some action when possible. When that isn't possible, it's time to use a public method instead.

Adding Functionality to `TFlashingLabel`

A little later today I'll talk about events and how to write them, but for now you have enough information to write your first component. The `FlashingLabel` component will have the following features:

- [ ] A property called `FlashRate` that controls the blink rate
- [ ] A property called `FlashEnabled` that turns the flashing on or off
- [ ] `write` methods for the `FlashRate` and `FlashEnabled` properties

☐ Default values for the `FlashRate` and `FlashEnabled` properties

☐ A private class member (a `TTimer` class instance) to control the timing of the flash

☐ All the characteristics of a regular `Label` component

First, I'll show you the complete program listings for the header and the source unit. (Refer to Listings 20.3 and 20.4.) After that I'll go over what is happening with the code.

Listing 20.3. `FlashingLabel.h`.

```
 1: //-----------------------------------------------------
 2: #ifndef FlashingLabelH
 3: #define FlashingLabelH
 4: //-----------------------------------------------------
 5: #include <SysUtils.hpp>
 6: #include <Controls.hpp>
 7: #include <Classes.hpp>
 8: #include <Forms.hpp>
 9: #include <StdCtrls.hpp>
10: //-----------------------------------------------------
11: class PACKAGE TFlashingLabel : public TCustomLabel
12: {
13: private:
14:    //
15:    // Private data members.
16:    //
17:    bool  FFlashEnabled;
18:    int   FFlashRate;
19:    TTimer* Timer;
20: protected:
21:    //
22:    // Protected write methods for the properties.
23:    //
24:    void __fastcall SetFlashEnabled(bool AFlashEnabled);
25:    void __fastcall SetFlashRate(int AFlashRate);
26:    //
27:    // OnTimer event handler.
28:    //
29:    void __fastcall OnTimer(TObject* Sender);
30: public:
31:    __fastcall TFlashingLabel(TComponent* Owner);
32: __published:
33:    //
34:    // The component's properties.
35:    //
36:    __property bool FlashEnabled =
37:       {read=FFlashEnabled, write=SetFlashEnabled, default=true};
38:    __property int FlashRate =
39:       {read=FFlashRate, write=SetFlashRate, default=800};
40:    //
41:    // The properties of TCustomLabel redeclared.
42:    //
```

continues

20

Listing 20.3. continued

```
43:    __property Align ;
44:    __property Alignment ;
45:    __property AutoSize ;
46:    __property Caption ;
47:    __property Color ;
48:    __property DragCursor ;
49:    __property DragMode ;
50:    __property Enabled ;
51:    __property FocusControl ;
52:    __property Font ;
53:    __property ParentColor ;
54:    __property ParentFont ;
55:    __property ParentShowHint ;
56:    __property PopupMenu ;
57:    __property ShowAccelChar ;
58:    __property ShowHint ;
59:    __property Transparent ;
60:    __property Layout ;
61:    __property Visible ;
62:    __property WordWrap ;
63:    __property OnClick ;
64:    __property OnDblClick ;
65:    __property OnDragDrop ;
66:    __property OnDragOver ;
67:    __property OnEndDrag ;
68:    __property OnMouseDown ;
69:    __property OnMouseMove ;
70:    __property OnMouseUp ;
71:    __property OnStartDrag ;
72: };
73: //-----------------------------------------------------
74: #endif
```

Listing 20.4. FlashingLabel.cpp.

```
 1: #include <vcl.h>
 2: #pragma hdrstop
 3:
 4: #include "FlashingLabel.h"
 5: #pragma package(smart_init)
 6: //-----------------------------------------------------
 7: // ValidCtrCheck is used to ensure that the components created
 8: // do not have any pure virtual functions.
 9: //
10:
11: static inline void ValidCtrCheck(TFlashingLabel *)
12: {
13:    new TFlashingLabel(NULL);
14: }
15: //-----------------------------------------------------
16: __fastcall TFlashingLabel::TFlashingLabel(TComponent* Owner)
```

```
17:    : TCustomLabel(Owner)
18: {
19:    //
20:    // Set the data members to their default values.
21:    //
22:    FFlashEnabled = true;
23:    FFlashRate = 800;
24:    //
25:    // Initialize the timer object.
26:    //
27:    Timer = new TTimer(this);
28:    //
29:    // Set the timer interval using the flash rate.
30:    //
31:    Timer->Interval = FlashRate;
32:    //
33:    // Assign our own OnTimer event handler to the
34:    // TTimer OnTimer event.
35:    //
36:    Timer->OnTimer = OnTimer;
37: }
38:
39: void __fastcall
40: TFlashingLabel::SetFlashEnabled(bool AFlashEnabled)
41: {
42:    //
43:    // Set FFlashEnabled data member.
44:    //
45:    FFlashEnabled = AFlashEnabled;
46:    //
47:    // Don't start the timer if the component is on a form
48:    // in design mode. Instead, just return.
49:    //
50:    if (ComponentState.Contains(csDesigning)) return;
51:    //
52:    // Start the timer.
53:    //
54:    Timer->Enabled = FFlashEnabled;
55:    //
56:    // If flashing was turned off, be sure that the label
57:    // is visible.
58:    //
69:    if (!FFlashEnabled) Visible = true;
60: }
61: void __fastcall TFlashingLabel::SetFlashRate(int AFlashRate)
62: {
63:    //
64:    // Set the FFlashRate data member and the timer interval
65:    // both at the same time.
66:    //
67:    Timer->Interval = FFlashRate = AFlashRate;
68: }
69: void __fastcall TFlashingLabel::OnTimer(TObject* Sender)
70: {
```

continues

20

Listing 20.4. continued

```
71:   //
72:   // If the component is on a form in design mode,
73:   // stop the timer and return.
74:   //
75:   if (ComponentState.Contains(csDesigning)) {
76:     Timer->Enabled = false;
77:     return;
78:   }
79:   //
80:   // Toggle the Visible property each time the timer
81:   // event occurs.
82:   //
83:   Visible = !Visible;
84: }
85: //-----------------------------------------------------------
86: namespace Flashinglabel
87: {
88:   void __fastcall PACKAGE Register()
89:   {
90:     TComponentClass classes[1] = {__classid(TFlashingLabel)};
91:     RegisterComponents("Samples", classes, 0);
92:   }
93: }
```

ANALYSIS   First, let's take a look at the header (refer to Listing 20.3). Notice the private section, beginning on line 13. This section declares three data members. The first two, FFlashEnabled and FFlashRate, are the data members associated with the FlashEnabled and FlashRate properties. The last declaration, on line 19, looks like this:

```
TTimer* Timer;
```

This declares a pointer to a TTimer object. The TTimer object will be used to regulate the flash rate.

NOTE   I haven't discussed timers yet. A *timer* is set up to fire at a specified interval (in milliseconds). When a timer fires, a WM_TIMER message is sent to the window that owns the timer. As a result, the OnTimer event is triggered. For example, if you set the timer interval to 1,000 milliseconds, your OnTimer event will be called nearly every second. I should point out that the WM_TIMER message is a low-priority message and can be preempted if the system is busy. For this reason you can't use a regular timer for mission-critical operations. Still, for non-critical timings the TTimer does a good job. (For more information on timers, refer to the C++Builder online help under TTimer or the WM_TIMER message.)

The protected section of the class declaration, which begins on line 20, contains declarations for the write methods for the FlashRate and FlashEnabled properties. The protected section also declares the OnTimer() function. This function will be called each time a timer event occurs. It is protected and declared as virtual, so derived classes can override it to provide other special handling when a timer event occurs. For instance, a derived class might want to change the color of the text each time the label flashes. Making this method virtual enables overriding of the function to add additional behavior.

Finally, notice the __published section, beginning on line 32. Line 36 declares the FlashEnabled property. The read specifier uses direct access, the write specifier is assigned to the SetFlashEnabled() method, and the default value is set to true. The FlashRate property uses a similar construct. Beginning on line 43, I have declared all the properties of TCustomLabel that I want republished. If you don't perform this step, the usual properties of a label component won't be available to the class at runtime, nor later at design time (after you install the component to the Component palette).

Now, turn your attention to the component's source unit, shown in Listing 20.4. First, on lines 22 and 23 you see that the default values for the data members representing the FlashEnabled and FlashRate properties are assigned. Remember that you declared default values for these properties, but that only affects the way the property is displayed in the Object Inspector. So you must assign the actual values in the constructor.

Now, notice these three lines, which begin with line 27 (comments removed):

```
Timer = new TTimer(this);
Timer->Interval = FlashRate;
Timer->OnTimer = OnTimer;
```

The first line creates an instance of the TTimer object. The second line assigns the value of the FlashRate property to the Interval property of the Timer component. This sets the timer interval that will be used to flash the text on the label. Finally, the last line assigns the address of the OnTimer() function to the OnTimer event of the Timer object. This ensures that when a timer event occurs, you will receive notification.

The SetFlashEnabled() function (beginning on line 39) is the write method for the FlashEnabled property. On line 45, the FFlashEnabled data member is set to the value of AFlashEnabled. On line 54, the Enabled property of the Timer object is set according to the value of AFlashEnabled. By writing to the FlashEnabled property, the user of the component can turn the flashing on or off. This function also contains a code line that sets the Visible property to true when flashing is disabled. This eliminates the situation in which the flashing could be turned off in mid-flash and, as a result, keep the text hidden.

Beginning on line 61, you see the SetFlashRate() function. This is the write method for the FlashRate property. The user can assign a value to the FlashRate property to control how fast

20

the component flashes. (A rate of 1200 is slow, and a rate of 150 is very fast.) This function contains a single line:

```
Timer->Interval = FFlashRate = AFlashRate;
```

This line contains syntax that you may not have seen before. This is basic C++ syntax that assigns the value of AFlashRate first to the FFlashRate data member and then to the Interval property of the Timer object.

The OnTimer() function doesn't require much explanation. This function is called in response to an OnTimer event. All you do is toggle the component's visible state each time a timer event occurs. In other words, if the FlashRate were set to 1000, the timer events would occur nearly every second. When the first timer event occurs, the component is hidden. A second later, the next timer event occurs and the component is shown. This continues until the FlashEnabled property is set to false or until the application closes. Finally, lines 86 through 93 contain the component registration.

Enter the code from Listings 20.3 and 20.4 into the FlashingLabel.h and FlashingLabel.cpp files created earlier by the New Component dialog box. Don't worry about typing the comment lines if you don't want to. After you have typed in the code, test the component to see whether it works.

TIP

> The property redeclarations on lines 43 through 71 of Listing 20.3 can be copied directly from the VCL headers. Just open \CBuilder\Include\Vcl\StdCtrls.hpp, copy the properties list from the TLabel class declaration, and paste it into your class declaration.

The ComponentState Property

I'm getting a little ahead of myself here, but I want to point out some code that I didn't discuss in the analysis of Listing 20.4. There is one important line in the SetFlashEnabled() function that requires explanation. On line 50 you see this code:

```
if (ComponentState.Contains(csDesigning)) return;
```

This line checks whether the component is being used on a form at design time. If the form is being used at design time, you need to prevent the timer from starting. When a component is placed on a form in the Form Designer, it does not necessarily have full functionality—the Form Designer can't fully approximate a running program. In this case you don't want the timer to run while the component is being used in design mode.

> **NOTE**
>
> You could write the `TFlashingLabel` component so that the label flashes at design time as well as runtime. It is easier not dealing with that now, plus it gives me a chance to talk about the `ComponentState` property.

All components have a property called `ComponentState`. The `ComponentState` property is a set that indicates, among other things, whether the component is being used at design time. If the set includes `csDesigning`, you know that the component is being used on a form in the Form Designer. In this case, when you determine that the component is being used at design time, you can return from the `OnTimer()` function without starting the timer.

Lines 75 through 78 of Listing 20.4 check whether the component is being used on a form in the Form Designer. If the component is being used in the Form Designer, the timer is turned off and the function returns without performing the remaining code in the function. The timer, by default, will be started in the `TFlashingLabel` constructor, so it needs to be immediately turned off if the component is being used at design time.

Testing the Component

Ultimately, you will add your newly created component to the Component palette. First, though, you must test your component to be sure that it compiles and that it functions as you intended.

To test your component, write an application that will serve as a testing ground. Because you can't drop the component on a form from the Component palette, you have to create the component manually. In this case, because our `FlashingLabel` component has two properties, you want to make sure that each property works. For that reason, your test program will need to turn the flashing mode on and off. In addition, the test program should enable you to set several flashing rates to see whether the `FlashRate` property performs as designed. Figure 20.2 shows the test program running. This will give you an idea of what you'll be trying to accomplish.

Now that you've had a peek at the test program, let's create it. As always, start with a blank form. First, add the check box and radio group components as you see them in Figure 20.2:

1. Change the form's `Name` property to `MainForm` and the `Caption` property to `FlashingLabel Test Program`.

2. Using Figure 20.2 as a pattern, add a `CheckBox` component to the form. Change its `Name` property to `FlashBox`, its `Caption` property to `Flash`, and its `Checked` property to `true`.

20

Figure 20.2.

The test program running.

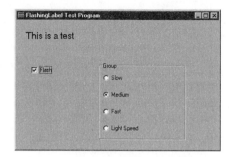

3. Double-click the check box to create an event handler for the `OnClick` event. When the Code Editor displays the `OnClick` handler, type this code at the cursor (the name of the `FlashingLabel` component will be `Flasher`):

```
Flasher->FlashEnabled = FlashBox->Checked;
```

This will enable or disable flashing, depending on the state of the check box.

4. Place a `RadioGroup` component on the form. Change its `Name` property to `Group` and its `Caption` property to `Flash Speed`.

5. Double-click on the Value column next to the `Items` property. When the String Editor is displayed, type these lines:

```
Slow
Medium
Fast
Light Speed
```

Click OK to close the String Editor. The strings you typed will be displayed as radio buttons in the group box.

6. Set the `ItemIndex` property to `1`. The Medium radio button will be selected.

7. Double-click the radio group component. The Code Editor will display the `OnClick` event handler for the group box. Type the following code at the cursor:

```
switch (Group->ItemIndex) {
  case 0 :  Flasher->FlashRate = 1200; break;
  case 1 :  Flasher->FlashRate = 800; break;
  case 2 :  Flasher->FlashRate = 400; break;
  case 3 :  Flasher->FlashRate = 150; break;
}
```

This will set the `FlashRate` value of the `FlashingLabel` component, based on the radio button selected.

8. Save the project in the same directory where your `TFlashingLabel` component resides. Save the main form's unit as `FTMain` and the project as `FlashTst`.

Okay, now you add the component itself. Because this component isn't yet visual (you can't add it from the Component palette), you add it manually.

20

1. Click the Add to Project button (from the toolbar, from the main menu, or from the Project Manager context menu). When the Add to Project dialog box is displayed, choose the `FlashingLabel.cpp` file and click OK.

2. Switch to the main form's header in the Code Editor and add the following line under the other VCL includes:

```
#include "FlashingLabel.h"
```

3. Add this declaration in the `private` section of the `TMainForm` class:

```
TFlashingLabel* Flasher;
```

4. Switch to the main form's source in the Code Editor and locate the main form's constructor. Type the following code in the constructor:

```
Flasher = new TFlashingLabel(this);
Flasher->Parent = this;
Flasher->SetBounds(20, 20, 200, 20);
Flasher->Font->Size = 16;
Flasher->Caption = "This is a test";
Flasher->FlashRate = 800;
```

You are ready to test the component. Click the Run button to compile and run the test program. If you encounter any compiler errors, carefully check your code and fix any errors the compiler points out.

When the program runs, click the Flash check box to turn the flashing on or off. Change the flash rate by choosing one of the radio buttons in the group box. Hey, it works. Congratulations, you've written your first component.

Adding the Component to the Component Palette

After the component is working properly and you are satisfied with it, add it to the Component palette. To add the `FlashingLabel` component to the Component palette, choose Component|Install Component. The Install Component dialog box will appear. This dialog box enables you to add a component to a package. Figure 20.3 shows the Install Component dialog box.

Okay, you're ready to add the `FlashingLabel` component to the Component palette. Perform the following steps:

1. Choose Component|Install Component from the main menu. The Install Component dialog box is displayed.

2. Click the Browse button to the right of the Unit file name field. When the Unit file name dialog box comes up, locate the `FlashingLabel.cpp` file and click Open.

20

Figure 20.3.

*The Install Compo-
nent dialog box.*

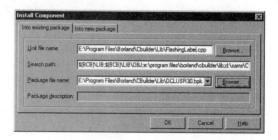

3. Now click the drop-down arrow in the Package file name field. You should see the DCLUSR30.BPK file listed there. If so, select it. If you don't see this package listed, click the Browse button and find the file (it is in the \CBuilder\Lib directory).

4. Click OK to close the Install Component dialog box. C++Builder displays a message telling you that it is about to build and install the package. Click Yes to continue.

5. C++Builder builds and installs the package. When the process is completed, C++Builder displays a message box telling you that the TFlashingLabel component has been registered.

Your component will appear on the Samples page of the Component palette. You will see a button that has the C++Builder default component icon. If you pause over the button, the ToolTip says FlashingLabel.

Start a new project and test the FlashingLabel component by dropping it on the form. Note that all the usual properties of a Label component are present in the Object Inspector, as well as the FlashRate and FlashEnabled properties. Note that the default values you specified for these properties are displayed in the Object Inspector.

I want to explain what you did in Step 3. C++Builder has a default package called DCLUSR30 that can be used to install individual components. I had you install the FlashingLabel component in this package primarily because TFlashingLabel is a single component (not part of an overall component library) and that's what this package is for. You could have created a new package rather than use the DCLUSR30 package, but it is easier to use the package provided.

Adding a Custom Bitmap to the Component's Button

You might have noticed a problem with your newly installed component; the button for the FlashingLabel component on the Component palette has the default C++Builder bitmap. We can't have that! Fortunately, you can specify a bitmap for your new component. You have to create a bitmap and place it in a resource file (a .res file or .dcr file).

20

NOTE

A `.res` file and a `.dcr` file are both binary resource files. The only difference is the filename extension. The `.res` extension is the customary extension for C++ programming environments. The `.dcr` extension has its roots in Delphi (*dcr* stands for *Delphi compiled resource*). You can use either for your C++Builder components.

TIP

Sometimes you might want to take the button for the base class and modify it slightly to represent your new component. In that case, start the Image Editor and open one of the `.dcr` files in the `\CBuilder\Lib\Obj` directory. You'll have to hunt to find the exact bitmap. For example, the bitmap for the `Label` component is in the file called `Stdreg.dcr`. Open that file, copy the `TLABEL` bitmap to the Clipboard, begin a new resource file, and paste the bitmap in the Clipboard to a new bitmap resource called `TFLASHINGLABEL`. Modify the bitmap as desired and then save the resource project.

The bitmap for the component's button must be 24×24 pixels. Most of the time a 16-color bitmap is sufficient. C++Builder uses the dark yellow color as the transparent color, so you should start with a dark yellow background when designing your bitmap.

When you have created the resource file, C++Builder automatically adds the component's bitmap to the Component palette when you install the component's package. For this to happen, you must follow a specific naming convention for the bitmap and for the component's resource file. First, the resource file must be named the same as the source file for the component and must reside in the same directory as the component. Next, the resource file must have a bitmap resource that exactly matches the classname of the component. For example, to create a bitmap for the `FlashingLabel` component's button, you would use Image Editor to create a file called `FlashingLabel.dcr` that contains a bitmap resource called `TFLASHINGLABEL`.

20

NOTE

As of this writing, C++Builder adds only `.dcr` files automatically. If you have a `.res` file, you add it manually to the package.

You manually add a resource file to a project in one of two ways. First, be sure that the component's resource file is in the directory where the component resides. Next, open the package file of the package that contains the component. After you have loaded the package source, the easiest way to add a resource file to a package is through the Project Manager. Open the Project Manager, right-click the package node, and choose Add from the context menu. The Add dialog box is displayed, and you can either type the path and name of the resource file or click the Browse button to browse for it. After you have selected the resource file, click Open on the Unit filename dialog box and then OK on the Add dialog box. Now rebuild or make the package and, if you've done everything correctly, the bitmap you created for the button will show up in the Component palette.

The second way to manually add a resource file to the package is by editing the package source. Just add a line like this near the top of the package source file:

```
USERES("Code\Day20\Flashing.res");
```

Be sure that you add enough path information so that C++Builder can find the resource file. Rebuild the package, and the bitmap will appear in the Component palette.

Writing Events for Components

Writing events requires some planning. When I speak of events, I am talking about two different possibilities. Sometimes an event occurs as the result of a Windows message, and sometimes an event occurs as a result of a change in the component. An event triggered by a Windows message is more or less out of your control. You can respond to this type of event, but you generally don't initiate the event. The second type of event is triggered by the component itself. In other words, as the component writer, you are in control of when this type of event occurs.

Working with events at this level can be confusing. I'll try to get past that and show you how events can be used on a practical level. To do this, let's add an event to the TFlashingLabel class. First, however, let's cover a few of the event basics.

Events Overview

To begin with, you should understand that events are properties. As such, they have all the features that a regular property has; for instance, you can assign a value to the read and write specifiers. Also, events use a private data member to store their values, as do other properties. In the case of an event, the underlying data member contains the address of a function that will be called when the specified event occurs. Like properties, events can be published or non-published. Published events show up in the Object Inspector, just as published properties do.

Secondly, events are *closures*. A closure is a special type of function pointer that contains the address of a function to call when an event occurs. Closures are like function super-pointers—they point not only to a function in a class instance but also to a function in an instance of an unrelated class. As long as the function declarations match (the same return type and the same function parameters), the closure happily calls the function, regardless of where it's located. For example, the OnClick event of a TLabel object can point to an event-handling function in a TEdit object, a TForm object, a TListBox object, and so on. Closures are more complicated than that, but I won't go into the gory details. (By the way, for those of you who are wondering, closures are not found in standard C++.)

NOTE

> Events always have a return type of void. An event might pass one or more parameters, depending on the type of the event, but it can't return a value. You can get information back from the event handler, though, by passing one or more parameters by reference and allowing the user to change those parameters to achieve a particular behavior.

You might deal with events on any one of several levels. For instance, you might want to override the base class event handler for a particular event to add some functionality. Let's say you want something special to happen if the user clicks on your component with the mouse. There's no use going to all the trouble of creating a new event for a mouse click because the event already exists in the form of the base class's OnClick event. You just tag onto that event rather than create a new event to catch the mouse click.

Another way you might deal with events is by creating an event that you trigger from within the component. I will describe this type of event first. As I said, you're going to add an event to the TFlashingLabel component that you created earlier. Adding this event requires that you also add a new property. The event will be called OnLimitReached, and the new property will be called FlashLimit. This event will be fired after the component flashes the number of times specified by FlashLimit. If FlashLimit is 0 (the default), the OnLimitReached event will never be fired. Okay, let's get to it.

Writing a user-defined event for a component can be divided into five basic tasks:

1. Determine the event type.
2. Declare the event.
3. Declare the underlying data member.
4. Create a virtual function that is called when the event is to be triggered.
5. Write code to trigger the event.

Let's walk through this so that you better understand what is involved.

20

Determining the Event Type

Earlier, when I discussed properties, I said that a property is of a specific type. The same is true of events. In the case of events, though, the type is a function pointer that includes a description of the event handler's parameters. Yesterday, Day 19, "Creating and Using DLLs," I talked a little about function pointers when I discussed DLLs (in the section "Calling Functions Located in DLLs").

As I have said several times, there are two basic types of events. One is the *notification event*. This event tells you that something happened; it doesn't give you any other details. The function declaration of the event handler for a notification event looks like this:

```
void __fastcall Clicked(TObject* Sender);
```

The only information you get in a notification event is the sender of the event. C++Builder provides the TNotifyEvent type for notification events. TNotifyEvent is actually a typedef that equates to a function pointer. Don't get hung up on that right now; just make a mental note that any events you create that are notification events should be of the TNotifyEvent type.

The other type of event is an event that has more than one parameter and actually passes information to the event handler. If you want to, you can create this type of event for your components, also. Let's say you wanted to use an event handler that is prototyped like this:

```
void __fastcall LimitReached(TObject* Sender, bool& Stop);
```

Using this type of event handler enables the user to modify the Stop parameter, thereby sending information back to the component. If you are going to create events that have parameters, you need to declare your own function type. Let's say you wanted to write an event type for the preceding function declaration and that the event type would be named TLimitReachedEvent. It would look like this:

```
typedef void __fastcall
  (__closure *TLimitReachedEvent)(System::TObject *Sender, bool& Stop);
```

Although that's kind of confusing, all you have to do is copy this pattern and then add or remove parameters as needed. Then you could declare an event to be of the type TLimitReachedEvent. (This won't make a lot of sense until you work through the whole process, so bear with me.)

 NOTE

> Place the declaration for a new event type just above the class declaration in the component's header file. Look ahead to Listing 20.5 if you want a peek at this.

Try to determine, to the best of your ability, what type of events (if any) you need for your component. If you need only notification events, you create your events to be of the TNotifyEvent type. If your events will pass parameters to the event handler, you need to define your own event type.

Declaring the Event

Now that you have determined the event type, you declare the event for the component. The declaration for an event looks almost identical to the declaration for any other property. Here's a typical declaration for an event:

```
__property TNotifyEvent OnSomeEvent =
    {read=FOnSomeEvent, write=FOnSomeEvent};
```

For the most part, this looks like the property declarations that you dealt with earlier. Notice that there is no default specifier. Notice also that the read and write specifiers both point to the FOnSomeEvent data member. This illustrates that events use direct access and do not use read and write methods. Finally, notice that in this example the event's type is TNotifyEvent. If your event passes parameters, you need to define your own type, as discussed earlier in the section "Determining the Event Type."

The OnLimitReached event will pass parameters, so you must define a special type and apply it to the event. Given that, our declaration for the OnLimitReached event looks like this:

```
__property TLimitReachedEvent OnLimitReached =
    {read=FOnLimitReached, write=FOnLimitReached};
```

Soon I'll show you the entire header so that you can see it in perspective. (If you want to look ahead, check out Listing 20.5.)

Declaring the Underlying Data Member

Declaring the underlying data member is the simple part. All you have to do is declare a private data member with the same type as your event. It looks like this:

```
TLimitReachedEvent FOnLimitReached;
```

As with properties, the data member's name is the same as the event name with the F on the front.

Creating a Virtual Function to Trigger the Event

Creating a virtual function to trigger the event requires explanation. You will trigger the event as a result of some change within the component. In this case you are going to trigger the event when the number of times the component has flashed reaches the value of the FlashLimit property. You trigger an event by calling the event:

```
bool stop = false;
OnLimitReached(this, stop);
```

20

You trigger the event from one of several places in the component, based on different factors. To centralize things, you create a virtual function that triggers the event. The virtual function will have the same name as the event, minus the On part.

 NOTE

> There is another popular naming convention for the names of functions that generate events. This naming convention removes the On prefix and replaces it with Do. In the case of the OnLimitReached event, the virtual method that generates the event would be called DoLimitReached. I've used both naming conventions and have a slight preference for this one.

First, declare the method in the class declaration:

```
virtual void __fastcall LimitReached();
```

Then, write the method that actually triggers the event. That method will look like this:

```
void __fastcall TFlashingLabel::LimitReached()
{
  bool stop = false;
  if (OnLimitReached) OnLimitReached(this, stop);
  FlashEnabled = !stop;
}
```

There are several things to note here. First, notice that you set up the default value of the Stop parameter. If the user doesn't modify the parameter, the value of Stop will be false. The Stop parameter is used to determine whether the flashing should stop when the FlashLimit value is reached. In the event handler for the event (in the application that uses the component), the user can set Stop to true to cause the flashing to stop or can leave the Stop parameter as is to allow the flashing to continue. Notice that this is passed in the first parameter, setting the Sender parameter to the component's pointer.

Now, notice the line that triggers the event:

```
if (OnLimitReached) OnLimitReached(this, stop);
```

If the component user has attached an event handler to the event, you call the event handler. If no event handler has been attached, you do the default handling for the event. (In this case, there is no default handling.) It is important to allow the user to ignore the event if he or she so chooses. This code enables that choice.

20

NOTE

One thing that is difficult to grasp when writing events is that the component itself does not provide the event handler. The application using the component provides the event handler; you merely provide the mechanism by which the event handler can be called when the event occurs.

As I mentioned earlier, this function is a virtual function. It is a virtual function because derived classes might want to redefine the event's default behavior. Because you were kind enough to make the function virtual, any components derived from your component only have to override the LimitReached() function to change the default event-handling behavior. This makes it easy to change the behavior of the event without having to hunt through the code and locate every place the event is triggered. The event is triggered only here in the LimitReached() function.

Writing Code That Triggers the Event

Somewhere in the component there must be code to call the LimitReached() function (which, in turn, triggers the event). In the case of the TFlashingLabel component, you call LimitReached() from the OnTimer() function. Here's how the function looks after being modified to trigger the event:

```cpp
void __fastcall TFlashingLabel::OnTimer(TObject* Sender)
{
  //
  // If the component is on a form in design mode,
  // stop the timer and return.
  //
  if (ComponentState.Contains(csDesigning)) {
    Timer->Enabled = false;
    return;
  }
  //
  // Toggle the Visible property each time the timer
  // event occurs.
  //
  Visible = !Visible;
  //
  // Trigger the event if needed. Only increment the counter
  // when the label is visible (on, if you prefer).
  //
  if (FFlashLimit && Visible)  {
    //
    // Increment the FlashCount data member.
    //
    FlashCount++;
    //
    // If the FlashCount is greater than or equal to the
    // value of the FlashLimit property, reset the
```

20

```
  // FlashCount value to 0 and trigger the event.
  //
  if (FlashCount >= FFlashLimit) {
    FlashCount = 0;
    LimitReached();
  }
 }
}
```

As you see, when the FlashLimit is reached, the LimitReached() function is called and the event is triggered. By the way, you count only every other OnTimer event. If you incremented the counter every time the OnTimer() function was called, you would get an inaccurate count because the OnTimer event is fired twice for every flash (on and off).

Overriding Base Class Events

The preceding discussion ties in with something else I want to mention briefly. If you want to override the default behavior of one of the events defined in the base class, all you have to do is override its event-triggering function, as I've described. Let's say you wanted to override the default OnClick event to make the speaker beep when the component is clicked. All you do is override the Click() function of the base class, like this:

```
void __fastcall TFlashingLabel::Click()
{
  //
  // Beep the speaker and then call the base class
  // Click() method for the default handling.
  //
  MessageBeep(-1);
  TCustomLabel::Click();
}
```

Because this function is declared as dynamic in the base class, it will be called automatically any time the component is clicked with the mouse. It will only work when the component is visible, so keep that in mind if you try to click the component while it is flashing. You make the speaker beep to prove that it works.

NOTE   A dynamic function is similar to a virtual function. Refer to Appendix B, "C++Builder Extensions to C++," for a description of dynamic functions. Appendix B can be found at the following Web site:

http://www.mcp.com/info

Putting It All Together

You took a peek at most of the new and improved TFlashingLabel component in the preceding pages, but let's look at the entire thing to put it all in perspective. Listing 20.5 shows the TFlashingLabel header, and Listing 20.6 shows the source file for the component. Study the implementation of the OnLimitReached event to gain an understanding of how events should be implemented in your components. Listing 20.7 shows the source unit for the FlashTst test program with the OnLimitReached event handler in use.

Listing 20.5. FlashingLabel.h (new and improved).

```
 1: //-------------------------------------------------------
 2: #ifndef FlashingH
 3: #define FlashingH
 4: //-------------------------------------------------------
 5: #include <SysUtils.hpp>
 6: #include <Controls.hpp>
 7: #include <Classes.hpp>
 8: #include <Forms.hpp>
 9: #include <StdCtrls.hpp>
10: //-------------------------------------------------------
11: //
12: // Define a new type for our event handler. This type takes
13: // a TObject* and a bool reference.
14: //
15: typedef void __fastcall
16:   (__closure *TMyEvent)(System::TObject *Sender, bool& Stop);
17:
18: class PACKAGE TFlashingLabel : public TCustomLabel
19: {
20: private:
21:   //
22:   // Private data members.
23:   //
24:   bool  FFlashEnabled;
25:   int   FFlashRate;
26:   int   FFlashLimit;
27:   int   FlashCount;
28:   TMyEvent FOnLimitReached;
29:   TTimer* Timer;
30: protected:
31:   //
32:   // Protected write methods for the properties.
33:   //
34:   void __fastcall SetFlashEnabled(bool AFlashEnabled);
35:   void __fastcall SetFlashRate(int AFlashRate);
36:   //
37:   // The LimitReached() function to trigger the event.
38:   //
39:   virtual void __fastcall LimitReached();
40:   //
41:   // An overridden Click() method just for an example
42:   // of overriding a base class event. This function will
43:   // be called whenever the component is clicked because
44:   // it is a dynamic function.
```

continues

Listing 20.5. continued

```
45:    //
46:    __declspec(dynamic) void __fastcall Click();
47:    //
48:    // OnTimer event handler.
49:    //
50:    virtual void __fastcall OnTimer(TObject* Sender);
51: public:
52:    __fastcall TFlashingLabel(TComponent* Owner);
53: __published:
54:    //
55:    // The component's properties.
56:    //
57:    __property bool FlashEnabled =
58:      {read=FFlashEnabled, write=SetFlashEnabled, default=true};
59:    __property int FlashRate =
60:      {read=FFlashRate, write=SetFlashRate, default=800};
61:    __property int FlashLimit =
62:      {read=FFlashLimit, write=FFlashLimit, default=0};
63:    //
64:    // The OnLimitReached event.
65:    //
66:    __property TMyEvent OnLimitReached =
67:      {read=FOnLimitReached, write=FOnLimitReached};
68:    //
69:    // The properties of TCustomLabel redeclared.
70:    //
71:    __property Align ;
72:    __property Alignment ;
73:    __property AutoSize ;
74:    __property Caption ;
75:    __property Color ;
76:    __property DragCursor ;
77:    __property DragMode ;
78:    __property Enabled ;
79:    __property FocusControl ;
80:    __property Font ;
81:    __property ParentColor ;
82:    __property ParentFont ;
83:    __property ParentShowHint ;
84:    __property PopupMenu ;
85:    __property ShowAccelChar ;
86:    __property ShowHint ;
87:    __property Transparent ;
88:    __property Layout ;
89:    __property Visible ;
90:    __property WordWrap ;
91:    __property OnClick ;
92:    __property OnDblClick ;
93:    __property OnDragDrop ;
94:    __property OnDragOver ;
95:    __property OnEndDrag ;
96:    __property OnMouseDown ;
97:    __property OnMouseMove ;
98:    __property OnMouseUp ;
```

```
 99:    __property OnStartDrag ;
100:  };
101:  //---------------------------------------------------------------
102:  #endif
```

Listing 20.6. `FlashingLabel.cpp` **(new and improved).**

```
 1: //----------------------------------------------------------------
 2: #include <vcl.h>
 3: #pragma hdrstop
 4:
 5: #include "FlashingLabel.h"
 6:
 7: #pragma package(smart_init)
 8: //----------------------------------------------------------------
 9: // ValidCtrCheck is used to ensure that the components created do not have
10: // any pure virtual functions.
11: //
12:
13: static inline void ValidCtrCheck(TFlashingLabel *)
14: {
15:    new TFlashingLabel(NULL);
16: }
17: //----------------------------------------------------------------
18: __fastcall TFlashingLabel::TFlashingLabel(TComponent* Owner)
19:    : TCustomLabel(Owner)
20: {
21:    //
22:    // Set the data members to their default values.
23:    //
24:    FFlashEnabled = true;
25:    FFlashRate = 800;
26:    FFlashLimit = 0;
27:    FlashCount = 0;
28:    //
29:    // Initialize the timer object.
30:    //
31:    Timer = new TTimer(this);
32:    //
33:    // Set the timer interval using the flash rate.
34:    //
35:    Timer->Interval = FlashRate;
36:    //
37:    // Assign our own OnTimer event handler to the
38:    // TTimer OnTimer event.
39:    //
40:    Timer->OnTimer = OnTimer;
41: }
42: //----------------------------------------------------------------
43:
```

continues

20

Listing 20.6. continued

```
44: void __fastcall TFlashingLabel::SetFlashEnabled(bool AFlashEnabled)
45: {
46:   //
47:   // Set FFlashEnabled data member.
48:   //
49:   FFlashEnabled = AFlashEnabled;
50:   //
51:   // Don't start the timer if the component is on a form
52:   // in design mode. Instead, just return.
53:   //
54:   if (ComponentState.Contains(csDesigning)) return;
55:   //
56:   // Start the timer.
57:   //
58:   Timer->Enabled = FFlashEnabled;
59:   //
60:   // If flashing was turned off, be sure that the label
61:   // is visible.
62:   //
63:   if (!FFlashEnabled) Visible = true;
64: }
65:
66: void __fastcall TFlashingLabel::SetFlashRate(int AFlashRate)
67: {
68:   //
69:   // Set the FFlashRate data member and the timer interval
70:   // both at the same time.
71:   //
72:   Timer->Interval = FFlashRate = AFlashRate;
73: }
74:
75: void __fastcall TFlashingLabel::OnTimer(TObject* Sender)
76: {
77:   //
78:   // If the component is on a form in design mode,
79:   // stop the timer and return.
80:   //
81:   if (ComponentState.Contains(csDesigning)) {
82:     Timer->Enabled = false;
83:     return;
84:   }
85:   //
86:   // Toggle the Visible property each time the timer
87:   // event occurs.
88:   //
89:   Visible = !Visible;
90:   //
91:   // Trigger the event if needed. Only increment the counter
92:   // when the label is visible (on, if you prefer).
93:   //
94:   if (FFlashLimit && Visible)  {
95:     //
96:     // Increment the FlashCount data member.
97:     //
98:     FlashCount++;
```

20

```
 99:     //
100:     // If the FlashCount is greater than or equal to the
101:     // value of the FlashLimit property, reset the
102:     // FlashCount value to 0 and trigger the event.
103:     //
104:     if (FlashCount >= FFlashLimit) {
105:       FlashCount = 0;
106:       LimitReached();
107:     }
108:   }
109: }
110:
111: void __fastcall TFlashingLabel::LimitReached()
112: {
113:   //
114:   // Set the default value for the Stop parameter. If the
115:   // user doesn't do anything to modify the parameter,
116:   // this value will be returned.
117:   //
118:   bool stop = false;
119:   //
120:   // If an event handler has been attached to this event,
121:   // then call it. (Event is triggered here.)
122:   //
123:   if (OnLimitReached) OnLimitReached(this, stop);
124:   //
125:   // Set the value of the FlashEnabled property based
126:   // on the value of the Stop parameter.
127:   //
128:   FlashEnabled = !stop;
129:   //
130:   // Beep just because.
131:   //
132:   MessageBeep(-1);
133: }
134:
135: void __fastcall TFlashingLabel::Click()
136: {
137:   //
138:   // Beep the speaker and then call the base class
139:   // Click() method for the default handling.
140:   //
141:   MessageBeep(-1);
142:   TCustomLabel::Click();
143: }
144:
145: namespace Flashing
146: {
147:   void __fastcall PACKAGE Register()
148:   {
149:     TComponentClass classes[1] = {__classid(TFlashingLabel)};
150:     RegisterComponents("Samples", classes, 0);
151:   }
152: }
153: //-----------------------------------------------------------
```

20

Listing 20.7. `FTMain.cpp.`

```cpp
 1: //----------------------------------------------------------
 2: #include <vcl.h>
 3: #pragma hdrstop
 4:
 5: #include "FTMain.h"
 6: //----------------------------------------------------------
 7: #pragma package(smart_init)
 8: #pragma resource "*.dfm"
 9: TMainForm *MainForm;
10: //----------------------------------------------------------
11: __fastcall TMainForm::TMainForm(TComponent* Owner)
12:    : TForm(Owner)
13: {
14:   Flasher = new TFlashingLabel(this);
15:   Flasher->Parent = this;
16:   Flasher->SetBounds(20, 20, 200, 20);
17:   Flasher->Font->Size = 16;
18:   Flasher->Caption = "This is a test";
19:   Flasher->FlashRate = 800;
20:   Flasher->FlashLimit = 5;
21:   Flasher->OnLimitReached = OnLimitReached;
22: }
23: //----------------------------------------------------------
24: void __fastcall TMainForm::OnLimitReached(TObject* Sender, bool& Stop)
25: {
26:   //
27:   // The OnLimitReached event handler. Set Stop to true to
28:   // stop flashing or leave as-is to continue flashing.
29:   //
30:   Stop = true;
31: }
32:
33: void __fastcall TMainForm::GroupClick(TObject *Sender)
34: {
35:   switch (Group->ItemIndex) {
36:     case 0 :  Flasher->FlashRate = 1200; break;
37:     case 1 :  Flasher->FlashRate = 800; break;
38:     case 2 :  Flasher->FlashRate = 400; break;
39:     case 3 :  Flasher->FlashRate = 150; break;
40:   }
41: }
42: //----------------------------------------------------------
43:
44: void __fastcall TMainForm::FlashBoxClick(TObject *Sender)
45: {
46:   Flasher->FlashEnabled = FlashBox->Checked;
47: }
48: //----------------------------------------------------------
```

This component and the `FlashTst` test program are included on the Web site that accompanies this book: `http://www.mcp.com/info`. However, the component's source is called `Flashing.cpp` and the header is `Flashing.h`.

Run the test program to see whether the event works as advertised. Experiment with the test program to get a better feeling for how the event and the event handler work. Notice that the speaker beeps when you click on the label (as long is it is visible). This is because of the overridden dynamic method called `Click()`. I added this function to illustrate overriding a base class event.

NOTE

> If you want to install the new and improved `FlashingLabel` component on the Component palette, open the `DCLUSR30` package and choose Project | Make DCLUSR30. The old version of `FlashingLabel` will be updated to the new version.

Writing events takes time to master. You must kiss a lot of frogs before being rewarded with the prince (or princess). In other words, there's no substitute for experience when it comes to writing events. You have to get in there and do it. You'll probably hit a few bumps along the way, but it will be good experience, and you'll find yourself a better programmer for it.

Summary

Well, you're in the big leagues now. Writing components isn't necessarily easy, but when you have a basic understanding of writing components, the world is at your fingertips. If you are anything like me, you will learn to enjoy your non-visual programming time as much as you enjoy the visual programming you do. If this chapter seems overwhelming, don't feel bad. You may have to let it soak in for a few days and then come back to it. You may have to read several different documents on writing components before it all comes together. Keep at it and it will eventually make sense.

Workshop

The Workshop contains quiz questions to help you solidify your understanding of the material covered and exercises to provide you with experience in using what you have learned. You can find answers to the quiz questions in Appendix A, "Answers to Quiz Questions."

20

Q&A

Q Is there any reason I must know how to write components?

A No. You can use the basic components that C++Builder gives you in your applications. You might never need to write components.

Q Can I buy components?

A Yes. A wide variety of sources exist for third-party component libraries. These libraries are sold by companies that specialize in VCL components. In addition, many freeware or shareware components are available from various online sources. Be sure to search the Internet for sources of VCL components.

Q Can I use my Delphi components with C++Builder?

A Yes. C++Builder has the capability to compile and install Delphi components. Install them just as you would a C++Builder component.

Q Do I have to use `read` and `write` methods to store my property's value?

A No. You can use direct access and store the property's value directly in the underlying data member associated with the property.

Q What's the advantage of using a `write` method for my properties?

A Using a `write` method enables you to perform other operations when a property is written to. Writing to a property often causes the component to perform specific tasks. Using a `write` method enables you to carry out those tasks.

Q Why would I want a property to be public but not published?

A A published property is displayed in the Object Inspector at design time. Some properties don't have a design-time interface. Those properties should be made public so that the user can modify or read them at runtime but not at design time.

Q How do I test my component to be sure it works correctly before I install it?

A Write a test program and add the component's source file to your project. In the constructor of the main form, create an instance of your component. Set any properties that you need to set, prior to the component being made visible. In the test program, manipulate your component's public properties to see whether everything works properly.

Q Do I have to write events for my components?

A Not necessarily. Some components make use of events; others do not. Don't go out of your way to write events for your components, but by the same token don't shy away from writing events when you need them.

Quiz

1. Must a property use a `write` method?
2. Must a property have an underlying data member?
3. Can you create a component by extending an existing component?
4. What happens if you don't specify a `write` specifier (either a `write` method or direct access) in a property's declaration?
5. What does *direct access* mean?

6. Must your properties have a default value?

7. Does the default value of the property set the underlying data member's value automatically?

8. How do you install a component on the Component palette?

9. How do you specify the button bitmap your component will use on the Component palette?

10. How do you trigger a user-defined event?

Exercises

1. Review the FlashingLabel component source in Listings 20.5 and 20.6. Study it to learn what is happening in the code.

2. Remove the FlashingLabel component from the component library. Reinstall the FlashingLabel component.

3. Write a test program that uses three FlashingLabel components, all with different flash rates.

4. Change the bitmap for the FlashingLabel button on the Component palette to one of your own design.

5. Write a write method for the FlashLimit property of the FlashingLabel component so that the user can't enter a number greater than 100.

6. Change the OnLimitReached event for the FlashingLabel component to a regular notification event (Hint: TNotifyEvent).

7. **Extra Credit:** Write a component of your own design.

8. **Extra Credit:** Test your new component and install it on the Component palette.

20

Day 21

C++Builder and Delphi

It's no secret that C++Builder is based on Delphi. Delphi was a huge success, so Borland decided to leverage that success by creating a RAD development environment for C++. Borland leveraged that success in more ways than one. One way was by reusing parts of Delphi in C++Builder. In this chapter you will learn about how C++Builder and Delphi are similar and how they are different. You will also learn how to exchange code between C++Builder and Delphi and how to convert code from Delphi to C++Builder.

Similarities Between C++Builder and Delphi

C++Builder and Delphi are more similar than they are different. We will look at those similarities in this section.

The IDE

If you have used both Delphi and C++Builder, you might have been struck by how similar their IDEs are. Those of you who haven't used both C++Builder and Delphi (and even those who have) should take a look at Figures 21.1 and 21.2.

One of these figures is a screen shot of Delphi 3 and the other is a screen shot of C++Builder 3. I have removed the icons and program name from the title bars so that it isn't immediately apparent which is which. Can you tell the difference?

Figure 21.1.

Delphi or C++Builder?

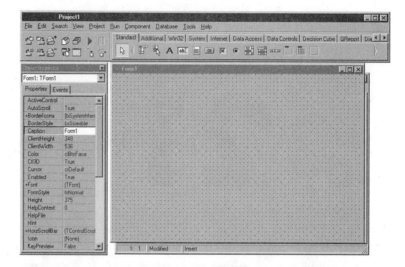

Figure 21.2.

Delphi or C++Builder?

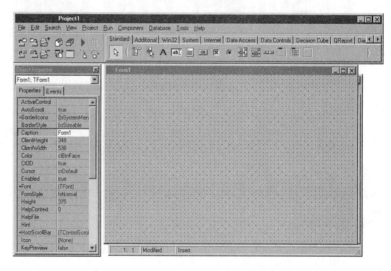

Do you give up? Figure 21.1 shows the Delphi IDE, and Figure 21.2 shows the C++Builder IDE. If you have used both C++Builder and Delphi, you might have recognized from the Object Inspector which figure shows the Delphi IDE and which shows the C++Builder IDE.

21

The Delphi Object Inspector shows properties with values of True and False, whereas the C++Builder Object Inspector shows true and false.

The point of this exercise is that the IDEs of C++Builder 3 and Delphi 3 are nearly identical. When you start examining the menus, you will naturally see some differences, but for the most part the IDEs are so similar that if you know how to use one of these development environments, you know how to use the other. This has obvious benefits. For example, let's say your company has been using Delphi and now wants to add C++ to its toolset. Using C++Builder as your C++ development tool saves you time and money because your programmers don't have to learn a new development environment. That leads us to another similarity between C++Builder and Delphi: the Visual Component Library.

The Visual Component Library

Not only are the IDEs of C++Builder and Delphi nearly identical, but also they share the exact same component library in the VCL. The VCL is written in Object Pascal, but both C++Builder and Delphi share the same code base.

NOTE

> There has been a fair amount of discussion on the Borland newsgroups among C++ programmers on the subject of a Pascal component library in a C++ development environment. Some C++ programmers can't get over the fact that the VCL is written in Object Pascal. Most programmers, though, take the sensible approach of not caring what language the VCL is written in. They just want to get their work done, on time and within budget. For these programmers the added productivity of C++Builder far outweighs the language issue.

The fact that both C++Builder and Delphi use the same framework is again a huge benefit if you use both C++Builder and Delphi. Other than the syntactical differences between C++ and Object Pascal, the VCL components are used identically in the two IDEs. Take the following C++Builder code:

```
if (OpenDialog1->Execute())
  Memo1->Lines->LoadFromFile(OpenDialog1->FileName);
```

Now look at the Delphi equivalent:

```
if OpenDialog1.Execute then
  Memo1.Lines.LoadFromFile(OpenDialog1.FileName);
```

As you can see, there is no difference in the actual code. The only differences are the differences between C++ syntax and Object Pascal syntax. This means that you don't have to learn a new framework if you want to switch between C++Builder and Delphi, or vice versa.

21

For a company with a large number of programmers, this means that you can leverage your programmers' knowledge to the maximum. Even if you are a single programmer, knowing both C++Builder and Delphi is very valuable.

Form Files

The form files used in C++Builder and Delphi are identical. You can create a form in Delphi and reuse that form in C++Builder. Later I will explain exactly how to do that, in the section "Reusing Forms." Although creating forms in C++Builder and Delphi is easy, it still takes time to design and create complex forms. By reusing your forms, you don't have to repeat work that has already been done.

Packages

Both Delphi 3 and C++Builder 3 use packages. In almost all cases, packages created for Delphi can be used in C++Builder. They will probably have to be recompiled in C++Builder, but that is a trivial task. The capability of C++Builder to use Delphi packages means that you have a wealth of commercial, shareware, and freeware VCL components available to you. These components are almost always written with Delphi, so they can be used in both C++Builder and Delphi. The ability to use Delphi components in C++Builder gives you a much wider range of choices than you would have if you were limited to components written specifically for C++Builder. At this time you cannot use packages written for C++Builder in Delphi, but that might change with the next version of Delphi.

Differences Between C++Builder and Delphi

Although C++Builder and Delphi have many similarities, they also have many dissimilarities. Most are a result of the variations in the C++ and Object Pascal languages.

Other differences are due to what I like to call the leapfrog effect. C++Builder 1 was patterned after Delphi 2 (which was released about a year before C++Builder 1). As such, C++Builder 1 acquired most of its features from Delphi 2. C++Builder 1 didn't add anything significant to what Delphi 2 offered. It was primarily a copycat. Shortly after C++Builder 1 was released, Borland released Delphi 3. C++Builder 3 is patterned after Delphi 3, just as C++Builder 1 was patterned after Delphi 2. However, C++Builder 3 adds several features not found in Delphi 3. The next version of Delphi (let's call it Delphi 4) will have those new features and will almost certainly add new features. C++Builder 4 will contain the new features of Delphi 4, will add more new features, and so on. This leapfrogging will likely continue for some time, with each release (whether it be Delphi or C++Builder) gaining the benefit of the previous release and adding new features of its own. Put another way, C++Builder is no longer just playing tag-along with Delphi.

21

Now let's look at the differences between C++Builder and Delphi. When appropriate, I will point out features that are new to C++Builder 3 and are not present in Delphi 3. It isn't hard to imagine that the next version of Delphi will inherit some of the new features in C++Builder 3.

Language

The most obvious difference between C++Builder and Delphi is that C++Builder generates C++ code and Delphi generates Object Pascal code. This leads to variations in the IDEs of the two products. For example, C++Builder has a menu item under the File menu called Include Unit Hdr. Object Pascal doesn't have header files, so the equivalent menu item in Delphi is called Use Unit. These types of differences abound throughout the two IDEs.

Filename Extensions

C++Builder and Delphi use different filename extensions for the files that build and maintain projects. This is partly a result of the language differences between the two products. The contrasting filename extensions enable you to easily distinguish a Delphi file from a C++Builder file. Table 21.1 lists the various project elements and their respective file extensions, for both C++Builder and Delphi.

Table 21.1. Delphi and C++Builder file extensions.

Element	Delphi	C++Builder
Project file	.DPR	.BPR
Source file	.PAS	.CPP
Header file	None	.H or .HPP
Form file	.DFM	.DFM
Compiled binary file	.DCU	.OBJ
Compiled resources	.RES	.RES
Saved desktop settings	.DSK	.DSK
Project options	.DOF	None
Package source files	.DPK	.BPK
Compiled package	.DPL	.BPL

Notice that in two cases—form files and compiled resource files—the extensions used by Delphi and C++Builder are the same. C++Builder uses other filename extensions in addition to the files listed in Table 21.1. I discussed those file types on Day 6, "The C++Builder IDE Explored."

21

Project Groups

C++Builder 3 added project groups to the IDE. This feature isn't in Delphi 3. Project groups enable you to group your C++Builder projects, primarily for convenience. A *project group* is a way of organizing related projects. You can compile all projects in a group, both from within the IDE and from the command line. Project groups make project management much easier than it was in previous versions of C++Builder and Delphi. Project groups were discussed in detail on Day 10, "More on Projects."

Project Manager

Although previous versions of C++Builder and Delphi had a Project Manager, the Project Manager in C++Builder 3 is brand new. Previously, the Project Manager was limited. The C++Builder 3 Project Manager is much more capable and is a welcome addition to the C++Builder IDE. The Project Manager was also discussed in detail on Day 10.

The Debugger

The C++Builder debugger is much more capable than the Delphi debugger. One feature found in C++Builder and not in Delphi is the Debug Inspector window. This is a great feature for examining class properties and data members. The CPU view is another feature that is much more capable in C++Builder than in Delphi. (The CPU view isn't even available from the Delphi IDE when Delphi is initially installed. You have to manually add a Registry entry to use the CPU view.) The Modules window is greatly enhanced in C++Builder, compared to what is available in Delphi. Also, the Event Log is available in C++Builder but not in the current version of Delphi.

Code Completion and Code Parameters

Delphi 3 has two editor features that are not in the C++Builder IDE: code completion and code parameters. Code completion works like this: When you type the name of a class object followed by the dot operator, Delphi pops up a list box containing all the properties and methods of that class. Just select a property or method from the list, and the Delphi Code Editor inserts it into your code.

The code parameters feature works in a similar way. If you enter a method name followed by an open parenthesis, the Delphi Code Editor displays the parameter list for that method in a ToolTip window. The parameter list includes the name and type of each parameter that the method requires. The parameter you need to type next is displayed in bold text. As you type a parameter, the next parameter in the list is displayed in bold text, and so on.

Why doesn't C++Builder have code completion and code parameters? In Delphi, the current unit is actually compiled each time the code completion or code parameters features are invoked. C++Builder doesn't have code completion and code parameters because of the length of time required to compile C++ code. There are alternative means of implementing

21

these features, so future versions of C++Builder will probably have code completion and code parameters.

C++Builder Can Compile Pascal Units

C++Builder can compile Pascal units just as easily as it can compile C++ units. This means that you can add a Pascal source file directly to your C++Builder project, and C++Builder will compile the unit and link that unit's code into the project's EXE. You can add a Delphi form and unit to a C++Builder project, and that form will be called just like a native C++Builder form. Whereas C++Builder has the capability to compile Pascal units, Delphi doesn't have the capability to compile C++Builder source files.

When you add a Pascal unit to your C++Builder project, you have to consider the order in which the units are built. For example, if you have a C++ unit that calls code in a Pascal unit, you must be sure that the Pascal unit is above the C++ unit in the Project Manager. This ensures that the header for the Pascal unit is created before the C++ unit that calls routines from the Pascal unit attempts to open the header.

Internet ActiveX Controls

The Internet ActiveX controls that come with C++Builder 3 are radically different from those that come with Delphi 3. The NetManage Internet controls in Delphi have been replaced with controls from NetMasters. The NetMasters controls also include several new controls.

ActiveX Support

Support for creating ActiveX controls is slightly different in C++Builder than in Delphi. Primarily, C++Builder ActiveX controls make use of the ActiveX Template Library (ATL), a C++ framework for ActiveX creation.

Delphi Compiles Faster and Produces Smaller EXEs

Delphi programs will always compile faster than C++Builder programs. Pascal compiles much faster than C++ because it isn't as complex. Pre-compiled headers and the incremental linker help reduce the effects by speeding up compile and link times, but Delphi programs still compile much faster than C++Builder programs.

Along the same lines, C++Builder programs are always slightly larger than Delphi programs. This is because of a number of factors but primarily because the VCL is written in Object Pascal. A C++Builder program has to include both the C++ runtime library and the Object Pascal runtime library. Both C++ and Pascal use different exception handling and runtime type information code, which results in extra code in a C++Builder application. This is probably the only significant disadvantage to an Object Pascal VCL (and I'm not sure it's that significant).

21

Converting from Delphi to C++Builder

At some point you might need to convert an application from Delphi to C++Builder or from C++Builder to Delphi. I have done dozens of such conversions and, although time consuming, they are not difficult. (By the way, when converting a project, I run C++Builder and Delphi simultaneously.) I am only going to discuss converting from Delphi to C++Builder. Converting the other way is simply a variation on the same concepts.

Converting a project from Delphi to C++Builder involves two basic steps. The first step is to copy the Delphi application's forms to the C++Builder project. The second step is to modify the Delphi code. Let's look at these two steps in more detail.

Copying the Delphi Forms

The first thing you need to do is to copy the Delphi forms to the C++Builder application. A C++Builder form and a Delphi form use the same basic format, but there is at least one significant difference that you should be aware of. It is obvious that a form file contains the size and position of the form itself and of every component on the form. What might not be obvious, however, is that the form file also contains information about events. Specifically, the form file includes a description of any event handlers that have been created for the form or for any components on the form. In a Delphi form file, the events contain references to event handlers that are Delphi methods. In a C++Builder form file, the events point to C++Builder event handlers. Naturally, you will have to remove the Pascal references in order to use the form in C++Builder. It isn't important that you understand this in detail, but it is a factor you will have to deal with when converting a Delphi form to C++Builder.

Here are the steps required to copy a Delphi main form:

1. Open the project in Delphi and make note of the main form's filename and its Name property.

2. Switch to C++Builder and select the main form. Change the Name property to the same name as the Delphi project's main form.

3. Save the C++Builder project. Save the main form's unit with the same filename the form had in Delphi (minus the .PAS extension, of course). Save the project with the same project name as the Delphi project.

4. Switch to Windows Explorer. Copy the main form's form file (the .DFM file) from the Delphi project's directory to the C++Builder project's directory. Make sure that you copy the file, not move the file. Explorer will warn you that a file with the same filename exists in the destination directory. Click Yes to overwrite the form file in the C++Builder directory. If you don't get this warning, you have done something wrong in saving the C++Builder unit.

5. Switch back to C++Builder. A dialog will be displayed that says `Module XXX.CPP's time/date has changed. Reload?`. Click Yes to reload the form. When the form reloads, it will contain the components found on the Delphi form.

6. Make sure that the form is selected and choose Edit|Select All from the C++Builder main menu to select all the form's components. Now choose Edit|Cut from the main menu, immediately followed by Edit|Paste. This step ensures that all the declarations for the individual components are placed in the main form's header file.

At this point you need to be certain that all references to the Delphi event handlers are removed from the C++Builder form file. Doing this is simple:

1. Choose File|Save from the C++Builder main menu or click the Save File button on the toolbar.

2. C++Builder will display a message box for each event handler, as shown in Figure 21.3. Click Yes each time the dialog is displayed, in order to remove all event handlers. Be aware that you might have to click Yes dozens of times to remove all the event handlers (I've had to remove as many as 100 event handlers for a single form!).

Figure 21.3.

Removing event handlers from the form.

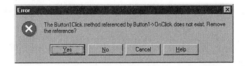

At this point you are done copying the form itself. Now you can move on to converting the code.

NOTE

You need to repeat this process for every form in the Delphi application.

Converting the Code

Converting the code from Delphi to C++Builder is much more difficult than copying the form. There are many ways to proceed, but I'll give you the method that I use. First, you look for any variables and methods that were created by the programmer and not by Delphi.

1. Locate the main form's class declaration in the Delphi unit.

2. Make note of any variables or methods declared in the `private` or `public` sections.

21

3. Copy any such declarations to the Clipboard. For example, part of the Delphi class declaration might look like this:

```
private
  { Private declarations }
  DrawColor : TColor;
  procedure DoDrawing;
  function  SetDrawColor : Integer;
```

In this case, you would copy the declarations for DrawColor, DoDrawing, and SetDrawColor.

4. Switch back to C++Builder. Display the main form's header in the Code Editor. Locate the private section and paste the code from the Clipboard.

5. Convert the declarations you pasted to C++ syntax. For example, the declarations in the example in Step 3 would look like this after being converted:

```
private:  // User declarations
  TColor DrawColor;
  void DoDrawing();
  int SetDrawColor();
```

6. Switch back to Delphi. In the implementation section of the Delphi unit, locate any methods declared in the class declaration (DoDrawing and SetDrawColor in this example). Copy the methods in the Delphi unit to the Clipboard.

7. Switch to C++Builder. Paste the methods copied from the Clipboard in Step 6 to the form's source unit. Convert the methods from Pascal syntax to C++ syntax. Don't worry about the function bodies or the begin and end statements. We'll fix that later.

The next step is to copy the code for the event handlers in the Delphi unit to the C++Builder unit. The best way I have found to do this is to start at the top of the implementation section in the Delphi unit and work down. Here are the steps to take when you encounter an event handler in the Delphi code:

1. Make note of the event handler's name. If the name is Button1Click, you know that the event handler is for the OnClick event of the component named Button1.

2. Copy the code inside the event handler to the Clipboard.

3. Switch to C++Builder. Generate an event handler that matches the event handler you copied the code from.

4. Paste the Delphi code from the Clipboard into the event handler.

Repeat Steps 1 through 4 for every event handler in the Delphi unit. When you are done, you will have several event handlers in your C++Builder project. The event handlers contain Pascal code, so you'll need to convert that code to C++. Fortunately you can do a lot of the conversion with C++Builder's Replace Text dialog. Table 21.2 lists the Pascal syntax you are searching for and the C++ syntax that is the replacement text. Spaces in the search or replace

21

text are denoted by a small dot. In most cases you will want to perform the Find and Replace operations in the order listed in Table 21.2.

Table 21.2. Find and Replace text when converting from Delphi to C++Builder.

Description	Find Text	Replace Text
Equality operator	•=•	•==•
Assignment operator	:=	=
Inequality operator	<>	!=
Membership operator	.	->
String quote	'	"
Begin comment	{	//
End comment	}	(Nothing)
Pascal True keyword	True	true
Pascal False keyword	False	false
if statement	if•	if•(
Start of block	begin	{
End of block	end;	}
End of block (form 2)	end	}
Pascal then statement	then	)•
Pascal do statement	•do•	(Nothing)
Pascal not statement	not•	!
Pascal nil keyword	nil	NULL
Pascal case statement	case•	switch•(
Pascal case statement	•of•	)•{
Pascal Self keyword	Self	this

When performing the Find and Replace, you should use the Replace All option, but you need to take care when doing so. For example, you don't want to replace all occurrences of a period with -> starting at the top of the file because the first several lines of every C++Builder source unit contain include statements with filenames. Make sure that if you replace Pascal comments (which begin with { and end with }) with C++ comments, you do so *before* replacing the begin and end statements. Also, when replacing words such as end, you should turn on the Whole words only option in the Replace Text dialog. This ensures that you don't accidentally replace individual characters within longer words. Be aware that some of your

21

Find and Replace operations could have undesirable side effects (such as replacing the period that separates a filename and its extension with ->).

After you have performed the Find and Replace operations, you will have a file that is a mixture of Pascal and C++. The easy part is finished, and now you must go to work converting the rest of the file by hand. You will have to know enough about each language to know how to convert Pascal syntax to C++ syntax. You're on your own from this point on, but I can point out a few things to be aware of as you convert the rest of the file.

First, there is no C++ equivalent to the Pascal with statement. Take this code, for instance:

```
with MyForm do begin
  Width   := 200;
  Height  := 500;
  Caption := 'Hello there';
end;
```

When you convert this code to C++Builder, you have to specifically reference each property:

```
MyForm->Width = 200;
MyForm->Height = 500;
MyForm->Caption = "Hello there";
```

Another Pascal statement that requires some work to convert is the as statement. You frequently see code like this in Delphi programs:

```
with Sender as TButton do
  Click;
```

In C++Builder this code would be translated as follows:

```
TButton* button = dynamic_cast<TButton*>(Sender);
if (button)
  button->Click();
```

Another area that will require special attention is that of string handling. Pascal has string manipulation functions that operate on the String data type. C++Builder, on the other hand, has the AnsiString class, which has its own string manipulation functions. Take, for example, this Pascal code:

```
X := StrToInt(Edit.Text);
```

This code will be translated to C++Builder code like this:

```
X = Edit->Text.ToInt();
```

Sets also present a challenge when translating code from Delphi to C++Builder. I talked about sets on Day 5, "C++ Class Frameworks and the Visual Component Model." Refer back to Day 5 for more information on how sets are handled in Pascal as opposed to C++Builder.

Reusing Forms

You don't have to convert Delphi forms to C++ at all if you don't want to. You can use Delphi forms in C++Builder just as they are. Simply add the .PAS file for the form directly to your C++Builder project. C++Builder will create a header for the Delphi unit that you can use in any C++Builder units that reference the Delphi form.

NOTE

> Although you can add a Delphi form to your C++Builder project, you cannot edit the form with the C++Builder Form Designer. Any modifications that you want to make to the form visually must be made from the Delphi IDE. You can, however, edit the form as text from within the C++Builder IDE. Choose the View As Text option from the C++Builder Form Designer's context menu to edit the form in text format.

Summary

Delphi and C++Builder are not so much competing products as they are complementary products. If you know how to program with C++Builder, learning Delphi is relatively easy. Moving from Delphi to C++Builder isn't quite as easy because of the complexity of the C++ language, but if you decide to move from Delphi to C++Builder, you can at least be assured that you won't have to learn a new framework all over again. Without question, being proficient in both C++Builder and Delphi makes you a more valuable programmer.

Workshop

The Workshop contains quiz questions to help you solidify your understanding of the material covered and exercises to provide you with experience in using what you have learned. You can find the answers in Appendix A, "Answers to Quiz Questions."

Q&A

Q Can I use Pascal units in my C++Builder projects?

A Yes. Add the Pascal unit to your project just as you would add a C++ unit. Be sure to put the Pascal units above any C++ units that reference code in the Pascal units in the Project Manager.

Q Can I use C++ units in my Delphi projects?

A No. You can use Pascal units in C++Builder but not the other way around.

21

Q As a programmer, I'm curious about something: Are the Delphi and C++Builder IDEs built from the same code base?

A Yes. Although C++Builder and Delphi have obvious differences, they have many similarities, so Borland uses a single code base for both IDEs.

Q Why do my Delphi projects compile so much faster than my C++Builder projects?

A Because Object Pascal is much less complex than C++ and thus compiles faster.

Q I have heard that if I know C++Builder, learning Delphi is simple. Is that true?

A Not exactly, no. Object Pascal is a very capable language and as such is relatively complex. Although going from C++Builder to Delphi is easier than the reverse, it is still not something that should be approached lightly.

Quiz

1. Do Delphi and C++Builder project files have the same filename extension?
2. Do Delphi and C++Builder form files have the same filename extension?
3. Can you use packages from third-party component vendors in both C++Builder and Delphi?
4. Can you open a Delphi form file in C++Builder?
5. Can you edit a Delphi form file using the C++Builder Form Designer?
6. Which is better, Delphi or C++Builder?

Exercises

1. If you have Delphi, take an example in the Demos directory and convert it to C++Builder.
2. Take a break, you've finished your 21st day!

21

Week 3

3

In Review

That was a pretty productive week, wasn't it? You probably had no idea that database operations could be so easy. Easy is a relative thing. I wouldn't go so far as to say that database programming is ever simple, but C++Builder certainly makes it easier than it would be in other C++ frameworks.

I told you that you would learn about DLLs and that you could then decide whether to use DLLs in your applications. Regardless of what you decide, you can now see the benefit of DLLs and can make an informed decision. If you plan on calling C++Builder forms from programs not written in C++Builder, you will have to use DLLs. DLLs can be frustrating to get working at first. As I said, the secret is to correctly design the headers. When you've accomplished that, the rest is just regular old C++ programming. DLLs are not difficult, but here again, a little experience goes a long way.

On Day 20 you learned about creating your own components. You either loved it or you were left scratching your head. If the latter, don't worry about it. You may never have to write your own components. There are plenty of sources for good, commercial-quality components. Plus, you can always go back and tackle Day 20 again after you've accumulated some time in your C++Builder log book. If you enjoyed learning about writing components, it was probably difficult for you to read the last chapter! I'd be willing to bet that at some time during Day 20 you could have been overheard saying, "Wow!" Writing your own components is rewarding, no question. We only had time to scratch the surface of writing components. There is a lot more to learn, and much of that can be learned by experience only. This chapter gives you enough to get you started.

Finally, you learned about C++Builder and Delphi and how they can work together. C++Builder and Delphi are two great products. If you know how to use one of these programming environments, then learning the other is very easy. The more you know, the more valuable you are as a programmer.

Day 22

Building Internet Applications

Are you one of those people who think the Internet is just a fad, something that will never last? If so, let me tell you something…you're wrong! The Internet is huge and it's getting bigger every day. In part, the Internet is about the Web and about people spending hour after hour browsing the Web. But the Internet is also about file transfers, email, and electronic commerce. The Internet is big business. It isn't going away anytime soon, so you might want to polish your Internet programming skills. Thankfully, C++Builder makes it easy to experiment with Internet programming and to do serious Internet programming as well.

Today we will look at some aspects of Internet programming with C++Builder. There's a whole world waiting out there on the Internet, so let's get to it.

Internet Controls Available in C++Builder

The Internet controls in C++Builder are located on the Internet page of the Component palette and fall into two categories. The first category is a group of ActiveX controls provided by NetMasters. Table 22.1 lists the controls in this group and provides a description of what each control is used for. The controls are listed in the order that they appear on the Component palette.

Table 22.1. NetMasters ActiveX Internet controls.

Control	Description
TNMDayTime	Obtains the date and time from Internet daytime servers.
TNMEcho	Sends text to and receives text from Internet echo servers.
TNMFinger	Obtains information about a user from an Internet finger server.
TNMFTP	Performs file transfers between networked machines using FTP (File Transfer Protocol).
TNMHTTP	Performs file transfers using HTTP (Hypertext Transport Protocol). Hypertext documents are normally viewed in a Web browser. You use THTTP to retrieve Web documents that don't need to be displayed in a Web browser.
TNMMsg	Sends simple ASCII text messages using TCP/IP.
TNMMsgServ	Receives messages sent with the TNMMsg control.
TNMNNTP	Sends messages to and receives messages from Internet news servers using NNTP (Networking News Transfer Protocol).
TNMPOP3	Retrieves email messages from mail servers using POP3 (Post Office Protocol).
TNMUUProcessor	Encodes or decodes MIME or uuencoded files.
TNMSMTP	Sends email through SMTP (Simple Mail Transfer Protocol) mail servers.
TNMStrm	Sends data streams to a network or Internet stream server.
TNMStrmServ	Receives streams sent by the TNMStrm control.
TNMTime	Obtains the date and time from Internet time servers.
TNMUDP	Transfers data across networks using UDP (User Datagram Protocol).
TPowersock	Encapsulates the Winsock API.
TNMGeneralServer	Used for general TCP/IP servers.

Control	Description
THTML	Displays HTML (Hypertext Markup Language) files. This is a Web browser component.
TNMURL	Converts URL data to a readable string and string data to URL format.

The second category of controls includes native VCL components. The TClientSocket and TServerSocket components come with both the Professional and Client/Server versions of C++Builder. The Web Broker components (TWebDispatcher, TPageProducer, TQueryTableProducer, and TDataSetTableProducer) come with only the Client/Server version. The VCL Internet components are listed in Table 22.2.

Table 22.2. Native VCL Internet components.

Component	Description
TClientSocket	Manages a TCP/IP client socket connection
TServerSocket	Manages a TCP/IP server socket connection
TWebDispatcher	Converts an ordinary data module to a Web module
TPageProducer	Enables building of dynamic HTML pages
TQueryTableProducer	Takes TQuery results and generates an HTML document from them
TDataSetTableProducer	Takes TDataSet records and generates an HTML document from them

These two groups of controls give you all the power you need to build high-quality Internet applications.

NOTE

As noted, the NetMasters Internet controls are ActiveX controls. If you want an all-VCL solution to Internet programming, try the IP*Works Internet controls from devSoft, Inc. You can read more at their Web site at http://www.dev-soft.com.

Building a Web Browser

One of the most visible Internet programming tasks is building a Web browser. Certainly it's the most glamorous. The good news is that it can also be the easiest.

Who Needs Yet Another Browser?

You might be wondering why anyone would want to build a Web browser. After all, the world already has Netscape Navigator and Internet Explorer, so who needs another browser? True enough, you probably aren't going to try to build a Web browser that competes with Netscape or Microsoft. On the other hand, consider a company that has hundreds or even thousands of employees who need access to the Web. It can be very costly to license thousands of copies of a commercial Web browser. On the other hand, you can write a quality Web application with C++Builder in just a few hours, thereby saving the company a lot of money.

Another reason a company might want a custom Web browser is to restrict access to the Web. For example, there might be sites on the Internet that employees have to visit from time to time. A custom Web browser allows access to authorized sites on the Web but not to any other (unauthorized) sites. In fact, a custom browser is perfect for your kids!

Finally, one of the most compelling reasons for a custom Web browser is an *intranet.* An intranet is a Web site that is local to a particular network. An intranet can contain a variety of information for a company's internal use—information on company benefits, company policies, an employee address book, meeting schedules, or even information on the company bowling league. A custom Web application can provide access to an intranet and prevent access to the Internet.

First Steps

The THTML control is a ready-to-use Web browser. All you have to do is place one of these controls on a form and call the RequestDoc() method. Well, that might be a little oversimplified, but you can display a Web document from anywhere on the Internet as easily as that. With that in mind, let me show you how quickly you can write a Web browser application. Here are the first steps:

1. Start with a new application. Change the form's Name property to WebMain and the Caption property to EZ Web Browser.

2. Place a Panel component on the form, change its Align property to alTop and its Height property to 60. Clear the Caption property.

3. Place a ComboBox component on the panel. Move it near the top of the panel and make it as wide as the panel itself. Change the Name property to URLComboBox. Change the Text property to an URL of your choice (try http://www.turbopower.com).

4. Place a StatusBar component on the form. It will automatically position itself at the bottom of the form. Change its Name property to StatusBar and its SimplePanel property to true.

5. Place an HTML control in the middle of the form. Change its Align property to alClient. The HTML control fills the screen. Change the Name property to HTML.

Now your form should look similar to the one in Figure 22.1. If your application doesn't look exactly like Figure 22.1, adjust as necessary or just leave it (a little individuality isn't a bad thing, after all).

Figure 22.1.

Your new Web browser after the first steps.

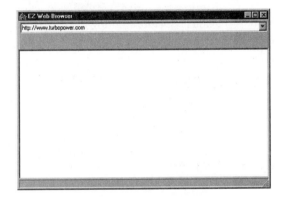

At this point you should save the project. Save the form as WebBrwsU.cpp and the project as WebBrows.cpp. Now you'll add just enough functionality to make the browser do something useful.

6. Click on the URL combo box. Generate an event handler for the OnClick event. Type the following code in the event handler:

```
if (URLComboBox->Text != "")
  HTML->RequestDoc(URLComboBox->Text);
```

7. Now generate an event handler for the OnKeyPress event. Type the following code in the event handler:

```
if (Key == VK_RETURN) {
  Key = 0;
  if (URLComboBox->Text == "") return;
  URLComboBox->Items->Insert(0, URLComboBox->Text);
  URLComboBoxClick(Sender);
}
```

8. Now compile and run the program. Type an URL in the combo box and hit Enter. If you typed in a valid URL, the page will load in the HTML control.

Wow! A Web browser in 15 minutes! You will notice that the browser acts like any other Web browser…well, sort of. We need to add a lot of functionality, but it's a start. Notice that each time you hit the Enter key, the URL you typed is added to the combo box's list.

NOTE

> If you are fortunate enough to have a full-time Internet connection, your new browser will work immediately. If you are using dial-up networking with auto dial enabled, the dialer will start automatically and connect to your Internet Service Provider (ISP). If you don't have dial-up networking installed, you will have to connect to the Internet manually before running the program.

Adding a Progress Indicator

You now have a good start on your Web browser. One of the things you are missing is some status information on each page as it loads. What you'll do is add a routine that updates the status bar as a page loads. You will make use of the THTML control's OnUpdateRetrieval and OnEndRetrieval events to obtain periodic status updates. You will use the GetBytesTotal() and GetBytesDone() methods to calculate a percentage and then display the percentage loaded in the status bar. Ready?

1. Click on the HTML control on your form. Generate an event handler for the OnUpdateRetrieval event. Type the following code in the event handler:

```
int total = HTML->RetrieveBytesTotal;
int done = HTML->RetrieveBytesDone;
int percent;
if (total == 0 || done == 0)
  percent = 0;
else
  percent = ((done * 100) / total);
char buff[80];
wsprintf(buff,
  "Getting Document: %d%% of %dK", percent, total/1024);
StatusBar->SimpleText = buff;
```

2. Now generate an event handler for the OnEndRetrieval event. Type this code in the event handler:

```
StatusBar->SimpleText = "Done";
```

Take a closer look at the code in Step 1. There isn't very much to it. The GetBytesTotal() method tells you how many bytes are in the document or the embedded object currently being loaded (objects include things like images). The GetBytesDone() method gives the number of bytes that have been retrieved for the page or object up to this point. From there it's a simple matter to calculate the percentage of the object that has been retrieved. Finally, you build a string with the information obtained from the HTML control and send it to the status bar. The code in the OnEndRetrieval event handler just updates the status bar after the entire document has been loaded.

Run the program again and watch what happens when you load a page. The status bar shows the percentage loaded for the page and for any embedded objects.

Some Finishing Touches

Now for some finishing touches. First, you'll add some buttons beneath the URL combo box. Look ahead to Figure 22.2 if you want a preview. Here goes:

1. Place a button on the panel beneath the URL combo box. Make its Name property GoBtn and change its Caption to Go!

2. Generate an event handler for the OnClick event for the new button. Enter the following code in the event handler:

   ```
   URLComboBoxClick(0);
   ```

3. Place another button on the panel, just to the right of the first button. Change the Name to StopBtn and the Caption to Stop.

4. Generate an event handler for the OnClick event for this button and type the following code in the event handler:

   ```
   HTML->Cancel(0);
   StatusBar->SimpleText = "Done";
   ```

5. Place a third button on the panel to the right of the other two buttons. Change the Name property to ReloadBtn. Change the Caption property to Reload.

6. Create an event handler for the OnClick event for this button and enter the same code as in Step 2:

   ```
   URLComboBoxClick(0);
   ```

7. Place a fourth (and final) button on the panel. Change the Name to SourceBtn and change the Caption to View Source.

8. Create an event handler for the OnClick event and enter this code:

   ```
   HTML->ViewSource = !HTML->ViewSource;
   if (HTML->ViewSource)
     SourceBtn->Caption = "View Document";
   else
     SourceBtn->Caption = "View Source";
   ```

Your form should now look like the one in Figure 22.2.

These steps introduce a couple new THTML elements. The Cancel() method stops the process of loading a document. The ViewSource property is used to toggle between viewing the document as HTML source or as a regular HTML document.

Figure 22.2.

The EZ Web Browser with buttons in place.

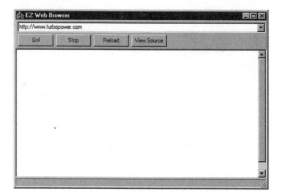

Now run the program again. Check out the new buttons and see what they do. In particular, give the View Source button a try.

Okay, you're almost done with your Web browser. Let's add a couple more features. We are going to respond to two more events of the THTML control in order to provide more status information.

1. Click on the HTML control on the form and select the Events tab in the Object Inspector.

2. Double-click next to the OnDoRequestDoc event. Type this code in the event handler:

   ```
   StatusBar->SimpleText = "Connecting to " + URL + "...";
   ```

3. Now double-click next to the OnBeginRetrieval event. When the event handler appears, type this code:

   ```
   StatusBar->SimpleText = "Connected...";
   URLComboBox->Items->Insert(0, URLComboBox->Text);
   ```

4. Locate the OnKeyPress event handler for the URL combo box you created earlier. This event handler, URLComboBoxKeyPress(), has the same line of code as the last code line in Step 3. Delete it. You don't need it anymore.

In this sequence, Steps 1 and 2 make use of the OnDoRequestDoc event. This event is generated when a document is requested. The URL parameter of the DoRequestDoc event handler is the URL of the site to which you are connected. As long as the URL is provided, you can use it to build a string to display in the status bar. Step 3 adds a little more status information when the document actually starts to load. Step 3 also takes the URL and adds it to the URL combo box's list. The reason you moved that code line to this event handler is simple: You need to make sure that you have connected to a site before adding the URL to the list of visited sites.

Congratulations, you have finished (or nearly finished) your first Internet application. Figure 22.3 shows the EZ Web Browser in operation.

22

Figure 22.3.

The finished EZ Web Browser displaying a page.

Hey, that's good work! Sure there are a lot of things that your Web browser doesn't do, but it does a lot, so you can be proud. Stand back and admire your work. You can take your new creation and add some new things of your own. One thing you might want to add is a list of URLs that can be used to implement back and next buttons. You could also replace the standard buttons with SpeedButtons and add glyphs to the buttons. If you really want to add the ultimate touch, provide an animation while the document is loading so that your users can tell when your browser is doing something. You can do that most easily with a TImageList component, although the TAnimate component would work, too.

The THTML control has lots of properties that I didn't cover. Most of these properties have to do with user preferences such as background color, the color of links, the color of visited links, the various fonts used for each heading size, and so on. I'm not going to explain those properties because they are easy to figure out. For the most part you can just accept the default values for these properties. If you want to customize your browser further, though, you can certainly spend some time reviewing the properties list for the THTML control.

Listing 22.1 lists the header for the main form of the browser program you have just written. Listing 22.2 contains the main form's source unit.

Listing 22.1. WebBrwsU.h.

```
 1: //----------------------------------------------------
 2: #ifndef WebBrwsUH
 3: #define WebBrwsUH
 4: //----------------------------------------------------
 5: #include <vcl\Classes.hpp>
 6: #include <vcl\Controls.hpp>
 7: #include <vcl\StdCtrls.hpp>
 8: #include <vcl\Forms.hpp>
 9: #include <vcl\ComCtrls.hpp>
10: #include <vcl\ExtCtrls.hpp>
```

continues

Listing 22.1. continued

```
11: #include <vcl\NMHTML.hpp>
12: #include <vcl\OleCtrls.hpp>
13: //----------------------------------------------------------
14: class TWebName : public TForm
15: {
16: __published: // IDE-managed Components
17:    TPanel *Panel1;
18:    TComboBox *URLComboBox;
19:    TStatusBar *StatusBar;
20:    THTML *HTML;
21:    TButton *GoBtn;
22:    TButton *StopBtn;
23:    TButton *ReloadBtn;
24:    TButton *SourceBtn;
25:    void __fastcall URLComboBoxClick(TObject *Sender);
26:    void __fastcall URLComboBoxKeyPress(TObject *Sender, char &Key);
27:    void __fastcall HTMLUpdateRetrieval(TObject *Sender);
28:    void __fastcall HTMLEndRetrieval(TObject *Sender);
29:    void __fastcall GoBtnClick(TObject *Sender);
30:    void __fastcall StopBtnClick(TObject *Sender);
31:    void __fastcall ReloadBtnClick(TObject *Sender);
32:    void __fastcall SourceBtnClick(TObject *Sender);
33:    void __fastcall HTMLDoRequestDoc(TObject *Sender, const WideString URL,
34:       const HTMLElement *Element, const DocInput *DocInput,
35:       WordBool &EnableDefault);
36:    void __fastcall HTMLBeginRetrieval(TObject *Sender);
37: private:  // User declarations
38: public:   // User declarations
39:    __fastcall TWebName(TComponent* Owner);
40: };
41: //----------------------------------------------------------
42: extern PACKAGE TWebName *WebName;
43: //----------------------------------------------------------
44: #endif
```

Listing 22.2. WebBrwsU.cpp.

```
1: //----------------------------------------------------------
2: #include <vcl\vcl.h>
3: #pragma hdrstop
4:
5: #include "WebBrwsU.h"
6: //----------------------------------------------------------
7: #pragma package(smart_init)
8: #pragma resource "*.dfm"
9: TWebName *WebName;
10: //----------------------------------------------------------
11: __fastcall TWebName::TWebName(TComponent* Owner)
12:    : TForm(Owner)
13: {
14: }
```

```
15: //------------------------------------------------------------
16: void __fastcall TWebName::URLComboBoxClick(TObject *Sender)
17: {
18:   if (URLComboBox->Text != "")
19:     HTML->RequestDoc(URLComboBox->Text);
20: }
21: //------------------------------------------------------------
22: void __fastcall TWebName::URLComboBoxKeyPress(TObject *Sender, char &Key)
23: {
24:   if (Key == VK_RETURN) {
25:     Key = 0;
26:     if (URLComboBox->Text == "") return;
27:     URLComboBoxClick(Sender);
28:   }
29: }
30: //------------------------------------------------------------
31: void __fastcall TWebName::HTMLUpdateRetrieval(TObject *Sender)
32: {
33:   int total = HTML->RetrieveBytesTotal;
34:   int done = HTML->RetrieveBytesDone;
35:   int percent;
36:   if (total == 0 || done == 0)
37:     percent = 0;
38:   else
39:     percent = ((done * 100) / total);
40:   char buff[80];
41:   wsprintf(buff,
42:     "Getting Document: %d%% of %dK", percent, total/1024);
43:   StatusBar->SimpleText = buff;
44: }
45: //------------------------------------------------------------
46: void __fastcall TWebName::HTMLEndRetrieval(TObject *Sender)
47: {
48:   StatusBar->SimpleText = "Done";
49: }
50: //------------------------------------------------------------
51: void __fastcall TWebName::GoBtnClick(TObject *Sender)
52: {
53:   URLComboBoxClick(0);
54: }
55: //------------------------------------------------------------
56: void __fastcall TWebName::StopBtnClick(TObject *Sender)
57: {
58:   HTML->Cancel(0);
59:   StatusBar->SimpleText = "Done";
60: }
61: //------------------------------------------------------------
62: void __fastcall TWebName::ReloadBtnClick(TObject *Sender)
63: {
64:   URLComboBoxClick(0);
65: }
66: //------------------------------------------------------------
```

continues

Listing 22.2. continued

```
67: void __fastcall TWebName::SourceBtnClick(TObject *Sender)
68: {
69:   HTML->ViewSource = !HTML->ViewSource;
70:   if (HTML->ViewSource)
71:     SourceBtn->Caption = "View Document";
72:   else
73:     SourceBtn->Caption = "View Source";
74: }
75: //----------------------------------------------------------
76: void __fastcall TWebName::HTMLDoRequestDoc(TObject *Sender,
77:       const WideString URL, const HTMLElement *Element,
78:       const DocInput *DocInput, WordBool &EnableDefault)
79: {
80:   StatusBar->SimpleText = "Connecting to " + URL + "...";
81: }
82: //----------------------------------------------------------
83: void __fastcall TWebName::HTMLBeginRetrieval(TObject *Sender)
84: {
85:   StatusBar->SimpleText = "Connected...";
86:   URLComboBox->Items->Insert(0, URLComboBox->Text);
87: }
88: //----------------------------------------------------------
```

Internet Explorer as an ActiveX Control

If you have Internet Explorer installed on your system, you can use it as an ActiveX control.
The first thing you need to do is import the control into C++Builder's Component palette.
After that, you can place it on a form just as you would for any control. First, let me show
you how to import Internet Explorer:

1. Choose Component|Import ActiveX Control from the main menu. The Import
   ActiveX dialog box is displayed.

2. Locate Microsoft Internet Controls (Version 1.0) in the list of ActiveX controls.
   (See Figure 22.4. Note that if you have Internet Explorer 4 installed, the control
   will be listed as version 1.1.) Notice that the Class names field shows TWebBrowser
   as the control contained in this file.

3. Click Install to install the control (the rest of the fields on this dialog box can be
   left on their default values).

4. The Install dialog box comes up, asking for a package name. Type IE3 in the File
   name field. (You can type a description if you want, but it's not necessary.) Click
   OK to create the package.

5. A confirmation dialog box appears, asking whether you want to build and install
   the package. Click Yes to create the package.

Figure 22.4.

*The Import ActiveX
dialog box.*

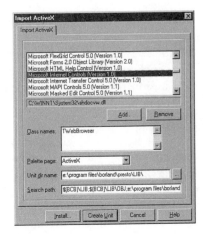

C++Builder builds the package and then displays a dialog box saying that the TWebBrowser control has been installed. Now you can try out the control:

1. First, choose File | Close All to close all windows, and then create a new application.

2. Click the ActiveX tab on the Component palette. Choose the WebBrowser control and drop it on your main form. Size the control as desired, but leave room on the form for a button.

3. Drop a Button component on the form. Double-click the button to generate an OnClick event handler. Type the following code in the event handler (use any URL you like):

```
wchar_t buff[100];
MultiByteToWideChar(CP_ACP, MB_PRECOMPOSED,
  "http://www.turbopower.com", -1,  buff, sizeof(buff));
WebBrowser1->Navigate(buff, 0, 0, 0, 0);
```

4. Click the Run button to run the program.

When the program runs, click the form's button. The Web page will load and be displayed in the WebBrowser control.

I'll comment briefly on the code you typed in Step 3. The Navigate() function of TWebBrowser requires the URL parameter to be in wide-character format. The MultiByteToWideChar() function converts a regular string into a wide-character array that the Navigate() function can understand. After the string is converted, it's a simple matter of calling the Navigate() function.

Unfortunately, there isn't any documentation for the TWebBrowser control (at least none that is immediately at your disposal—check Microsoft's Web site). When you install this control, C++Builder creates a header file called SHDocVw_TLB.h. You can look at this header to see what properties and methods are available for TWebBrowser.

Note that you can't necessarily redistribute the TWebBrowser control itself. However, if you know your users have Internet Explorer installed on their system, your application will work because the control is already installed. You still have to register the control on your user's machine for your application to run. See "Deploying Internet Applications" later in this chapter for more information on registering ActiveX controls.

Sending Mail

There are many reasons you might want to send mail from one of your applications. The good news is that sending email isn't difficult at all. Maybe you want your program users to be able to email you with any problems they encounter. In that case, your application could pop up a form containing a Memo component and a Send button. Your users could type text in the Memo component, hit the Send button, and the message would be emailed to you. You could even go so far as to attach a log file from your application to diagnose any problems the user is having.

The TNMSMTP control is used for sending mail through an SMTP server. SMTP is an odd protocol in that it doesn't require authenticated logon to the server (at least on most SMTP servers). You can simply connect to any mail server, send the email message, and disconnect. The Host property is used to specify the host name of the mail server to which you want to connect. Most of the time you can just use mail as the host name. Specifying mail tells the TNMSMTP control to connect to your local mail server, whether it's your ISP's mail server or your company's mail server. If you want, you can specifically set the mail server name (such as mail.mycompany.com), but it isn't usually necessary. The Port property is used to specify the port on which to connect. The default SMTP port is port 25. The Port property defaults to a value of 25, so you shouldn't have to change this property at all.

All the pertinent information for the mail message itself is contained in the PostMessage property. This property is a class that contains properties such as ToAddress, FromAddress, Subject, Body, and so on. You fill in the appropriate fields of the PostMessage property and then send the message.

Before you can send a mail message, you need to connect to the SMTP server. This is done with the Connect() method:

```
SMTP->Host = "mail";
SMTP->Connect();
```

When connected, you can send the email—for example,

```
SMTP->PostMessage->FromAddress = "bilbo@baggins.com";
SMTP->PostMessage->ToAddress->Add("gandolf@baggins.com");
SMTP->PostMessage->Subject = "Test";
SMTP->PostMessage->Body->Add("This is a test");
SMTP->SendMail();
```

This code sets up the FromAddress, ToAddress, Subject, and Body parameters of the PostMessage property and then sends the message with the SendMail() method. It's as simple as that. Note that the ToAddress and Body properties of PostMessage are TStringLists. The mail message body can contain several lines of text, so it's not surprising that the Body property is a TStringList. The ToAddress property is a TStringList, so you can specify several addresses for the message.

NOTE

> The OnConnect event is generated after you are connected to the SMTP server. Unfortunately, you can't send mail directly from the OnConnect event handler. If you want to automatically send mail when connected, you have to post a user-defined message to your form and then send the mail message from the message handler for the user-defined message. That's beyond the scope of this discussion, but I want to make you aware of that limitation.

NOTE

> The FromAddress and ToAddress fields are required fields. All other fields (even the message body) are optional.

After you know the message is successfully sent, you can disconnect from the SMTP server. The OnSuccess event is generated when the mail has been sent. Your OnSuccess event handler might be as simple as this:

```
void __fastcall TForm1::SMTPSuccess(TObject *Sender)
{
  SMTP->Disconnect();
}
```

You can send several messages per connection, of course. If you have several messages to send, you don't have to disconnect from the server and reconnect for each message. Just connect once, send all your messages, and then disconnect from the server.

Your mail message might go through without incident, or it might fail in one way or another. In either case, you must be prepared to disconnect from the server. The OnFailure event is generated if the mail message fails to go through, so you can use that event to disconnect from the server as well as the OnSuccess event.

Deploying Internet Applications

If your Internet application uses only the VCL Internet components, there is nothing special to do when you deploy your application unless you are using runtime packages. You need to ship INET30.BPL if you are using runtime packages, and INETDB30.BPL if you are using the page producer components.

Deploying an application that uses ActiveX controls, however, requires more work. ActiveX controls must be registered on the machine on which your application will run. The easiest way to register ActiveX controls is with a good installation program. InstallShield Express comes with C++Builder Professional and Client/Server versions, so you should try that program. Another good installation program is Wise Install from Great Lakes Business Solutions. The better installation programs register, as part of the installation process, the ActiveX controls that your application uses.

If you don't use a commercial installation program, you have to manually register any ActiveX controls your application uses. The REGSRVR.EXE utility is used to register and unregister ActiveX and OCX controls. This utility is in your CBuilder\Bin directory. For example, to install the EZ Web Browser application you created earlier today, you would ship the following files:

```
HTML.OCX
NMOCOD.DLL
NMSCKN.DLL
NWM3VWN.DLL
WEBBROWS.EXE
```

After you install all these files, you have to run REGSRVR.EXE on the HTML.OCX file to register it. From the command line you type:

```
REGSRVR HTML.OCX
```

The THTML control is now registered on your user's machine and your program will run as intended.

NOTE

> If you don't register your ActiveX controls properly, when your users attempt to run your program, they will see a message box that says, "Class not registered." Your application will then terminate, leaving your users wondering what went wrong.

To unregister a control, use the /u switch as follows:

```
REGSRVR /u HTML.OCX
```

22

Here again, a good installation program will have an uninstall option that takes care of this for you.

As you can see, ActiveX controls require a bit of work to install after your application is built. If you aren't aware of the fact that you need to register the ActiveX controls, it can lead to confusion for both you and your users. By the way, the files needed to deploy an application using the THTML control total about 900KB, so using ActiveX controls can be expensive in terms of disk space. I prefer to use native VCL controls whenever possible for exactly this reason.

Summary

Today you learned about the Internet components provided in C++Builder. You built a simple but usable Web browser with the THTML control, and you learned how to send mail using the TNMSMTP control. Internet programming is big business right now. It certainly can't hurt to have some Internet programming experience.

Workshop

The Workshop contains quiz questions to help you solidify your understanding of the material covered and exercises to provide you with experience in using what you have learned. You can find the answers to the quiz questions in Appendix A, "Answers to Quiz Questions."

Q&A

Q What components or controls should I use to create a TCP/IP client/server application?

A Use the TClientSocket and TServerSocket VCL components.

Q Can I create Web pages from my database tables?

A Yes. The TQueryTableProducer and TDataSetTableProducer VCL components create an HTML document from a database table.

Q The TNMSMTP control is for receiving mail, and the TNMPOP3 control is for retrieving mail. Why are there two controls for email operations?

A There are two controls because there are two separate protocols, one for sending mail (SMTP) and one for retrieving mail (POP3).

Q The Internet is relatively new. When were most of the protocols (SMTP, POP3, FTP, UDP, and so on) defined?

A You might be surprised to learn that many protocols used in Internet programming have been around for 20 years or more.

Quiz

1. What control do you use to display Web pages?
2. What control is used to connect to newsgroups?
3. What is the name of the method used to display an HTML document with the THTML control?
4. What event is generated when an HTML document has completed loading?
5. What control do you use to send email messages?
6. What control do you use to retrieve email messages?
7. What is the name of the method used to send mail with the TNMSMTP control?
8. What company provides the ActiveX Internet controls that come with C++Builder?

Exercises

1. Write an application for sending email. The application's main form should have fields for the *from* address, the *to* address, the mail subject, and the message text.
2. Add Forward and Back buttons to the EZ Web Browser application and make them operational.
3. **Extra Credit:** Add animation to the EZ Web Browser application so that the user can tell when the browser is loading a document.

APPENDIX A

Answers to Quiz Questions

Day 1, Getting Started with C++Builder

1. There is no main() function. Every program must have a main() function.
2. One. A function can have many parameters but can return only one value.
3. The strcpy() function copies the contents of one string to another.
4. You never know. A variable contains random data until it is initialized.
5. There is no limit to the number of functions a program can have.
6. Yes.
7. There is no function declaration for the doSomething() function.
8. One.
9. 19 characters plus the terminating null.
10. Zero.

Day 2, C++ Fundamentals

1. The statement immediately following the if statement. If a code block follows an if statement, the entire code block will be executed.
2. The first parameter is the starting value, the second parameter is the test expression, and the final parameter is the increment parameter.
3. A while loop checks the conditional expression at the beginning of the loop. A do-while loop checks the conditional expression at the end of the loop.
4. The break statement is used to break out of a loop. The statement following the body of the loop will be executed after a break statement. The continue statement forces program execution back to the top of the loop.
5. A global variable is one that is in scope anywhere in the program. It can be accessed by any functions in the program.
6. Yes. A structure can contain any number and type of data members.
7. With the direct member operator (.). Here's an example:
   ```
   record.LastName = "Noble";
   ```
8. Yes.

Day 3, Advanced C++

1. A pointer is a variable that holds the address of another variable or an object in memory.
2. To dereference a pointer means to get the value of the variable that the pointer points to and not the value of the pointer itself (which is just a memory location).

3. The memory address where the newly created object resides.

4. Usually classes and structures should be passed by reference to eliminate unnecessary overhead.

5. The const keyword prevents a variable from being modified.

6. No. Overloaded functions must vary by the type and number of parameters. These two functions vary only by return type.

7. It depends on the situation. No one situation is best every time. This is a trick question.

8. A class member function is a function that belongs to a class.

9. The compiler will place the entire contents of the inline function in the compiled code each time the inline function is encountered in the source code. In the case of a regular function, the function exists in the compiled code only once, and the compiler places a call to the function each time the function is encountered in the source code.

10. The function should use the delete[] form of operator delete:

```
delete[] buff;
```

Day 4, C++ Classes and Object-Oriented Programming

1. In C++, a structure is a class in which all data members and functions have public access by default, whereas classes have private access by default. Aside from that, there is no difference.

2. Private data members protect data from being modified directly by users of the class. Private data members can be modified through public member functions but not directly.

3. By using getters and setters, which are public member functions that can be called to change the value of a private data member.

4. The destructor is called when the object is destroyed. For local objects, this occurs when the object goes out of scope. For dynamically allocated objects, this occurs when the object is deleted.

5. To override a function means to replace a function in the base class with a function in your derived class. The new function must have the exact same name, parameters, and return type to override the base class function.

6. Call the base class function from within the overridden function:

```
void MyClass::DoIt()
{
  BaseClass::DoIt();
```

```
    // do some other stuff
}
```

7. An initializer list initializes a class's data members and calls any base class constructors prior to the body of the constructor being entered.

8. Yes. It's very common.

9. Multiple Inheritance. Derive the class from two separate base classes.

10. The `seekg()` function moves the stream position to a specific location.

Day 5, C++ Class Frameworks and the Visual Component Model

1. No. Only visual components can be seen at design time.

2. None is best. All have their own strengths and weaknesses.

3. No. VCL objects must be allocated dynamically (using operator new).

4. Yes and no. For the most part they are equivalent. Because VCL is written in
   Object Pascal, there are no overloaded VCL methods.

5. Yes.

6. `TOpenDialog`, `TSaveDialog`, `TRegistry`, `TColorDialog`, `TTimer`, `TImageList`,
   `TFontDialog`, and many more.

7. Yes. All components are ultimately derived from `Tcomponent`, so they all have the
   properties found in `Tcomponent`, such as `Name` and `Owner`.

8. `Top`, `Left`, `Owner`, `Parent`, `Width`, `Height`, and so on.

9. Yes.

10. A canvas. VCL encapsulates device contexts through the `TCanvas` class.

Day 6, The C++Builder IDE Explored

1. Right-click the toolbar and choose Properties from the toolbar context menu.

2. Drag them to the toolbar and drop them where you want them.

3. Drag unwanted buttons off the bottom of the toolbar and drop them.

4. Hold the Shift key when you click the component in the Component palette. Each
   time you click on the form, a new component will be placed.

5. Double-click the component's button in the Component palette.

6. `.bpr`, `.cpp`, `.h`, `.dfm`, and `.res`.

7. `Show()`.

8. `ShowModal()`.

9. In the Object Inspector, switch to the Events page. In the value column next to the event, click the drop-down arrow button. A list of compatible event handlers is displayed. Choose one.

10. Double-click the value column next to the property name in the Object Inspector.

Day 7, Working with the Form Designer and the Menu Designer

1. When selecting components that are children of another component (components on a panel, for example).

2. It is the anchor component. It retains its position, and all other components are aligned to it.

3. Drag a bounding rectangle around (or just touching) them.

4. Select all the components you want to modify. Then choose Edit | Size from the main menu and choose the Grow to Largest radio button.

5. The default event handler for that component is displayed in the Code Editor. In the case of many components, the OnClick event handler will be displayed. In some special cases (such as the Image component) a dialog box is displayed.

6. It forces the component to fill the entire client area of its parent, regardless of how the parent (usually a form) is sized.

7. Traditionally, it means that choosing that menu item will result in a dialog box being displayed.

8. In the Menu Designer you can drag the menu to a new location or you can use Cut and Paste.

9. When typing the caption for the menu item, add the ampersand (&) before the shortcut key you choose as the shortcut for that menu item. For instance, the Caption for the File | Exit menu item would read E&xit.

10. Set its Enabled property to False.

Day 8, VCL Components

1. Yes, but it's a very bad idea.

2. The Enabled property.

3. Its text is grayed out.

4. The long hint is used for the status bar text, and the short hint is used for the ToolTip text.

5. Invalidate(), Repaint(), Refresh(), and Update().

6. Three: simple, drop-down, and drop-down list.

7. When a button with a `ModalResult` property set to a whole number is clicked, the form will close. The value of the `ModalResult` property for the button clicked will be the return value from the `ShowModal()` method.

8. The `Panel` component. Several others qualify, too.

9. `true`.

10. Just change its `Title` property to `Save As`.

Day 9, Creating Applications in C++Builder

1. When you want all the features of the base object and you want the inherited object to change if the base object changes.

2. Choose Project|Add to Repository from the main menu or Add Project to Repository from the Project Manager context menu.

3. All the inherited forms alter to reflect the change made to the base form.

4. In the `private` or `public` sections. Never in the `__published` section (unless you know what you are doing).

5. In any source unit, but usually in the same unit as the rest of the code for that form.

6. If you switch to the Details view, the object's author is listed.

7. In the Object Repository configuration dialog box (which you get by selecting Tools|Repository from the main menu).

8. By using the Application Expert in almost all cases.

9. For small applications, static linking (no runtime packages) is almost always the best choice.

10. Yes, easily.

Day 10, More on Projects

1. F12.

2. No. It is only removed from the project.

3. On the Forms page of the Project Options dialog box.

4. You will have to take the responsibility of creating the forms before using them.

5. It's hard to say, but probably 32MB for Windows 95 and 40MB for Windows NT.

6. When debug information is generated, you will be able to step through your code during debugging sessions.

7. Find in Files is used to find text in files.

8. Ctrl+S.

9. Set a bookmark with Ctrl+K+0 through Ctrl+K+9. There are 10 bookmarks available.

10. Choose Read Only from the Code Editor context menu.

Day 11, Using the Debugger

1. Click in the gutter (the left margin) on that code line. You can also press F5 or choose Toggle Breakpoint from the Code Editor context menu.

2. A breakpoint that is inadvertently set on a source code line that generates no compiled code.

3. Set the breakpoint, choose View|Breakpoints from the main menu, click the breakpoint in the Breakpoint List window, and then choose Properties from the Breakpoint List context menu. Set the condition in the Condition field of the Edit Breakpoint dialog box.

4. Double-click the watch in the Watch List window. The Watch Properties dialog box is displayed. Modify the properties as needed.

5. Click the variable and type Ctrl+F5 (or choose Add Watch at Cursor from the Code Editor context menu).

6. The Debug Inspector.

7. F7.

8. Click the variable and then choose Evaluate/Modify from the Code Editor context menu. Change the value in the Evaluate/Modify dialog box.

9. By calling the Windows API function, OutputDebugString().

10. Choose Run|Inspect Local Variables from the main menu.

Day 12, C++Builder Tools and Options

1. The background shows through wherever the transparent color is used on the icon or cursor.

2. Click a color in the color palette.

3. Choose the Marquee tool and then drag a rectangle with the mouse. You could also use Edit|Select All to select the entire image or the Lasso tool.

4. 256.

5. The exact pixel in the cursor that is used to report the screen coordinates to Windows when the mouse is clicked.

6. Yes.

7. Choose Window | Follow to Focus from the main menu and then click on the window you wish to spy on.

8. Turn on the Editor files option on the Preferences page (Autosave options section) of the Environment Options dialog box.

9. Through the Palette page of the Environment Options dialog box.

10. Either through the Code Insight page of the Environment Options dialog box or by directly editing the BCB.DCI file.

Day 13, Beyond the Basics

1. In the Object Inspector, click the Event tab. Click the drop-down arrow next to the OnClick event. Choose an event handler from the list.

2. Yes.

3. A Notebook component works nicely.

4. Forces the status bar to have a single panel.

5. For a simple status bar:

```
StatusBar->SimpleText = "Text";
```

6. Set the component's Enabled property to true to enable the component and false to disable it.

7. Through the Printer() function.

8. BeginPrint()

9. NewPage()

10. Modify the component's Cursor property.

Day 14, Advanced Programming

1. Through the Project Options dialog box (Application page) or by setting the HelpFile property of the Application object at runtime.

2. Just assign a non-zero value to the HelpContext property. Make sure that there is a corresponding help context ID in the help file and that the help file has been set for the application.

3. HelpCommand()

4. Any type: integral data types, classes, or structures.

5. Yes. You can have as many as needed.

6. With the throw keyword.

7. \HKEY_CURRENT_USER

8. No. The TRegistry destructor will close the key for you. You shouldn't leave a key open indefinitely, though.

9. PostMessage() posts the message to the Windows message queue and returns immediately. SendMessage() sends the message and doesn't return until the message has been carried out.

10. Perform().

Day 15, Graphics Programming

1. Although you can draw directly on the form's canvas, the PaintBox component enables you to draw in a predefined area of a form (the area the PaintBox occupies).

2. The Brush property.

3. The Pen property.

4. The clipping region defines a canvas area within which drawing can take place, but outside which no drawing takes place. Any drawing outside the clipping region will not be displayed.

5. The DrawText() function with the DT_WORDBREAK

    BrushCopy() method.

7. Clipping regions can be rectangular, elliptical, or any shape defined by a series of points (a polygon region).

8. You can use several, but the easiest and fastest is the Draw() method. Others include BrushCopy(), StretchDraw(), and CopyRect().

9. With the SaveToFile() method.

10. The current settings of the video display.

Day 16, C++Builder Database Architecture

1. A local database is a database that resides on the user's machine rather than on a database server. This term usually refers to Paradox or dBASE tables.

2. The Borland Database Engine provides your C++Builder application access to databases.

3. No. A dataset might include an entire table's contents, or it might contain only a small subset of the table.

4. Cached updates reduce network traffic, enable you to modify a read-only dataset, and enable you to make several changes and then either commit or rollback all changes at once.

5. A stored procedure is an application that acts on a database and resides on a database server.

6. The `SQL` property contains the SQL statements to execute when the `Open()` or `Execute()` method is called.

7. To allow automatic login to a database.

8. To reduce the time required to log in to the database each time a connection is requested.

9. `TBatchMove` enables you to create or modify one dataset with the contents of another dataset.

10. A BDE alias is a set of parameters that describe a database connection.

Day 17, Building Database Forms

1. With the Database Form Wizard.

2. With the Columns Editor (right-click a `DBGrid` component and choose Columns Editor from the context menu).

3. The `DBGrid` component.

4. By modifying the `VisibleButtons` property.

5. The `DBImage` component.

6. The `DataSource` property (among others).

7. The `DataField` property.

8. Yes, through the Columns Editor at design time, or by drag and drop at runtime.

9. The `DBEdit` component.

10. Binary Large Object.

Day 18, Building Database Applications

1. `CreateTable()`.

2. The `Edit()` method puts the dataset in edit mode so that records can be modified.

3. The `Post()` method.

4. Through the Object Repository.

5. A data module is very similar to a regular form but not the same.

6. The `Print()` method.

7. A detail band.

8. The `QRSysData` component can display page numbers, the current date, the current time, and more.

9. Right-click the report and choose Preview from the context menu.

10. The QRExpr component is used to display the results of an expression (usually a calculated result).

Day 19, Creating and Using DLLs

1. Add the DLL's .lib file to the project. The DLL will load when the application starts.

2. Use the Windows API function LoadLibrary().

3. Call the function just as you would call a regular function.

4. The function has to be exported from the DLL and must use the extern "C" modifier.

5. You can unload the DLL any time you wish (with the FreeLibrary() function).

6. Create an exported function that the calling application can call. In this function, create the form and display it.

7. You can use a single header when building both the DLL and the calling application.

8. Add an .res or .rc file to the DLLs project via the Project Manager.

9. No. If the DLL uses static loading, it doesn't need any code.

10. Yes. Create a .lib file for the DLL just as you would for DLL containing code, and add the .lib file to the calling application's project.

Day 20, Creating Components

1. No. You can use direct access instead.

2. No, but they usually do. A property that does not store a value is unusual.

3. Absolutely. That's the easiest way to create a new component.

4. Then the property becomes read-only.

5. The underlying data member for the property is modified and/or read directly (no read method and no write method).

6. No. Default values are optional. Published properties should have a default value, though.

7. No. The default value only displays a value in the Object Inspector at design time. You must set the underlying data member to the default value in the component's constructor.

8. Choose Component | Install from the main menu.

9. Create a `.dcr` file with the same name as the component's source. The `.dcr` should contain a 24×24 bitmap with the same name as the component's classname. Be sure that the `.dcr` is in the same directory as the `.cpp` file for the component.

10. Just call the event after checking whether an event handler exists for the event:

```
if (OnMyEvent) OnMyEvent(this);
```

Day 21, C++Builder and Delphi

1. No. Delphi projects have a `.DPR` extension and C++Builder projects have a `.BPR` extension.

2. Yes. Both have `.DFM` extensions.

3. In most cases, yes. In some cases the packages will have to be rebuilt with C++Builder. Ask the component vendor for packages compatible with C++Builder.

4. Yes.

5. No. However, you *can* edit the Delphi form as text by choosing View As Text from the C++Builder context menu.

6. Neither is better. Both have their strengths. It depends largely on whether you prefer Pascal or C++.

Day 22, Building Internet Applications

1. The `THMTL` control.

2. The `TNMNNTP` control.

3. The `RequestDoc()` method.

4. The `OnEndRetrieval` event.

5. The `TNMSMTP` control.

6. The `TNMPOP3` control.

7. The `SendMail()` method.

8. NetMasters.

INDEX

A

Borland C++Builder How-To

John Miano, Tom Cabanski, & Harold Howe

Borland C++Builder is Borland's new object-oriented development tool that combines the power and control of the C++ programming language with the rapid application development productivity of Delphi. Using the award-winning question-and-answer format of the How-To series, this must-have guide provides programmers with everything they need to use this powerful tool to write professional programs and solve complex problems quickly.

Includes custom components programmers can use in their C++Builder applications.

Filled with over 100 real-world programming solutions.

Extensive coverage of multimedia, graphics, databases, and OLE.

$49.99 US $70.95 CDN   Waite Group Press
1-57169-109-X   750 pp.

Charlie Calvert's Borland C++Builder Unleashed

Charlie Calvert

Written by one of the foremost Borland C++ experts and part of the Borland Press collection, this all-in-one guide provides unparalleled technical accuracy and access to insider information.

C++Builder is the much-awaited programming tool of choice from Borland for developers.

Includes extensive coverage of the Windows 95 environment, object-oriented programming, serial communications, forms and ActiveX controls, SQL and Tquery, and handling messages.

CD-ROM includes electronic versions of two best-selling Sams Publishing titles, utilities, and source code from the book.

Covers Borland C++Builder.

$59.99 US $84.95 CAN   Programming   Accomplished—Expert
0-672-31022-8   1,300 pp.   Borland Press

Teach Yourself Borland JBuilder in 21 Days

Michelle M. Manning

Java is fast becoming the standard for Internet programming. This book teaches prospective programmers how to program Java applications for the World Wide Web using Borland's Latté.

Teaches readers how to use the Latté environment to do Java programming.

Includes a tutorial on using the latest Latté tools.

CD-ROM contains valuable source code.

$39.99 US $56.95 CDN
1-57521-104-1   *700 pp.*

Special Edition Using Borland C++ 5

Paul Kimmel

Following the tradition of the highly successful *Special Edition* series, this book delivers high-quality technical information in an understandable format that adds great value to the software documentation. The purpose of this book is to provide a one-volume, comprehensive guide for programmers as they move from learning the basics to becoming better, more productive programmers. Provides a wealth of information on how to get the most out of Borland C++ tools.

Covers advanced Windows programming topics and offers strategies and techniques for developing complex applications.

CD-ROM includes Patch 1 for Borland C++ 5 registered users and all the project files and source code from the book.

$49.99 US $67.99 CDN   *Que*
0-7897-0284-3   *912 pp.*

Tom Swan's Mastering Borland C++ 5, Third Edition

Tom Swan

The new release of Borland C++ 5.0 includes valuable tools developers are craving. Tools like new object-oriented scripting, a new C++ language environment that lets you control the IDE completely, and debugger control. With all those and many other new features, developers will turn to *Mastering Borland C++ 5, Third Edition* to receive the latest, most accurate information on how to exploit these new features in their programs.

CD-ROM includes source code from the book and powerful utilities.

Provides a complete introduction and thorough coverage of intermediate and advanced topics.

Includes hundreds of working examples.

Covers Borland C++ 5.0.

$59.99 US $81.95 CDN   *Programming*   *Casual—Accomplished—Expert*
0-672-30802-9   *1,088 pp.*

Database Developer's Guide with Borland C++ 5

Mike Cohn, Jay Rutten, Kristen Hill, Mark Gee, & James Moran

Database Developer's Guide with Borland C++ 5, 2E helps all programmers get the most from Borland's latest version of C++. They quickly learn, through the use of real-world applications and examples, the tricks and techniques necessary to efficiently enhance their programs. Exhaustive detail is given to every subject from Windows extensions like MAPI, TAPI, OLE 2, and NetDDE to cross platform programming. This is the most detailed book on developing programs with Borland C++.

Step-by-step instructions cover every detail.

Provides coverage of advanced C++ extensions like MAPI, TAPI, OLE2, and NetDDE.

Included CD-ROM contains source code from the book and sample applications.

Covers Borland C++ 5.

$59.99 US $81.99 CDN	*Internet Programming*	*Accomplished—Expert*
0-672-30800-2	*736 pp.*	

Teach Yourself Borland C++ 5 in 21 Days, Third Edition

Craig Arnush

Updated and revised, this book shows readers how to use the language and how to write beginning-level programs.

The author is a member of Team Borland and has access to the most frequently asked questions from the Borland help line.

Uses the successful *Teach Yourself* elements, including Workshop and Q&A sections, quizzes, and shaded syntax boxes.

Covers Version 5.

$39.99 US $53.99 CDN	*Programming*	*New—Casual*
0-672-30756-1	*864 pp.*	

Client/Server Developer's Guide with Delphi 3

Ken Henderson

With client/server gaining in popularity in the workplace today, the need for a comprehensive developer's guide is increasing. This indispensable resource shows users how to design sophisticated client/server applications using Delphi 3 that are safe, fast, and efficient.

Shows how to integrate the latest release of Delphi with major databases, including InterBase, Sybase, Oracle, and Microsoft.

CD-ROM contains all the source code and examples from the book as well as sample databases.

Covers Version 3.

$59.99 US $84.95 CAN	*Client/Server*	*Accomplished—Expert*
0-672-31024-4	*1,000 pp.*	*Sams Publishing/Borland Press*

Delphi 3 SuperBible

Paul B. Thurrott & Gary R. Brent

Delphi 3's enhanced ability to provide powerful object-oriented applications for Windows 95 is increasing the demand for the product and information on how to exploit its powerful 32-bit features. This book, written by expert Delphi and Windows 95 programmers, is the most complete resource for Delphi development.

Covers Internet/Web-programming enhancements to Delphi.

Includes an alphabetical jump table to give quick access to information by class, property, method, or event.

CD-ROM contains all the source code from the book, formatted reference files on the VCL, and demo versions of third-party software tools.

$54.99 US $77.95 CDN   Waite Group Press
1-57169-027-1   1,200 pp.

How to Program Delphi 3

Frank Engo

Delphi has become the fastest growing RAD tool in the industry and one of the fastest growing tools in the history of Borland. The latest version of Delphi will enable developers to create components that are compatible with ActiveX documents and ActiveX materials that can be reused in any application. It will also allow developers to create bridges between the Microsoft and Netscape worlds. Loaded with practical examples, this book helps users build a solid understanding of the language and take advantage of the tools it has to offer.

Covers the latest Internet aspects and interfaces of Borland's newest release of Delphi.

CD-ROM contains full source code of the Routine Library readers can pull and use, as well as a special version of Delphi.

$39.99 US $56.95 CDN   Ziff Davis Press
1-56276-526-4   416 pp.

Teach Yourself Delphi 3 in 14 Days

Dan Osier, Steve Grobman, & Stephen Batson

This resource is the ideal learning tool for beginning programmers who want to develop their own programming capabilities, as well as developers who want to make the transition to the latest version of Delphi. Written by best-selling authors and organized in a logical, easy-to-follow format, this step-by-step guide will help users master the ins and outs of this robust program from the ground up.

Outline was fully developed by Borland.

Workshops, Q&As, and Dos and Don'ts reinforce the information found in each chapter.

In-depth coverage of branching, looping, records, arrays, debugging, program flow control, structured programming, DLLs, data manipulation, and more.

Covers Delphi 3.

$29.99 USA $42.95 CAN   Programming   New—Casual
0-672-31114-3   650 pp.

Secrets of Delphi 2

Ray Lischner

Mastering the undocumented features of Delphi is essential for writing top quality Delphi components and applications. *Secrets of Delphi 2* provides the clear, in-depth information experienced Delphi programmers need.

Covers Delphi 2 in depth, without neglecting those still using Windows 3.X and Delphi 1. Reveals the secrets of easy porting between 16- and 32-bit versions of Delphi.

CD-ROM contains all the examples, code, resources, bitmaps, and complete working code examples.

$59.99 US $84.95 CDN   *Waite Group Press*
1-57169-026-3   *890 pp.*

Delphi 2 Developer's Guide, Second Edition

Steve Teixiera & Xavier Pacheco

This book empowers the reader with the ability to capitalize on the growing movement toward GUI (Graphic User Interface)-based applications. The reader will become adept at exploiting Delphi 32's tools and commands and will learn how to create object-oriented programs.

CD-ROM contains product demos and all of the source code from the book.

Demonstrates practical applications through the use of step-by step written procedures.

Details Delphi 2's tools for efficient OOP.

Covers latest version of Delphi 2.

$59.99 USA $81.95 CDN *Programming*   *Casual—Accomplished—Expert*
0-672-30914-9   *1,368 pp.*

Delphi 2 Unleashed, Second Edition

Charlie Calvert

This book helps every programmer get the most from the latest version of Delphi. It reveals all the latest information, including how to develop client/server applications, multimedia programs, and advanced Windows programming, in an easy-to-understand style.

CD-ROM contains source code from the book and sample applications.

Teaches the components of object-oriented programming.

Covers Windows 95 and multimedia programming.

Covers latest version of Delphi.

$59.99 USA $81.95 CDN *Programming*   *Accomplished—Expert*
0-672-30858-4   *1,440 pp.*

Add to Your Sams Library Today with the Best Books for Programming, Operating Systems, and New Technologies

The easiest way to order is to pick up the phone and call

1-800-428-5331

between 9:00 a.m. and 5:00 p.m. EST.
For faster service, please have your credit card available.

ISBN	Quantity	Description of Item	Unit Cost	Total Cost
1-57169-109-X		Borland C++Builder How-To	$49.99	
0-672-31022-8		Charlie Calvert's Borland C++Builder Unleashed	$59.99	
1-57521-104-1		Teach Yourself Borland JBuilder in 21 Days	$39.99	
0-7897-0284-3		Special Edition Using Borland C++ 5	$49.99	
0-672-30802-9		Tom Swan's Mastering Borland C++ 5, Third Edition	$59.99	
0-672-30800-2		Database Developer's Guide with Borland C++ 5	$59.99	
0-672-30756-1		Teach Yourself Borland C++ 5 in 21 Days, Third Edition	$39.99	
0-672-31024-4		Client/Server Developer's Guide with Delphi 3	$59.99	
1-57169-027-1		Delphi 3 SuperBible	$54.99	
1-56276-526-4		How To Program Delphi 3	$39.99	
0-672-31114-3		Teach Yourself Delphi 3 in in 14 Days	$29.99	
1-57169-026-3		Secrets of Delphi 2	$59.99	
0-672-30914-9		Delphi 2 Developer's Guide, 2E	$59.99	
0-672-30858-4		Delphi 2 Unleashed, 2E	$59.99	
❑ 3 ½" Disk		Shipping and Handling: See information below.		
❑ 5 ¼" Disk		TOTAL		

Shipping and Handling: $4.00 for the first book and $1.75 for each additional book. Floppy disk: add $1.75 for shipping and handling. If you need to have it NOW, we can ship product to you in 24 hours for an additional charge of approximately $18.00, and you will receive your item overnight or in two days. Overseas shipping and handling adds $2.00 per book and $8.00 for up to three disks. Prices subject to change. Call for availability and pricing information on latest editions.

201 W. 103rd Street, Indianapolis, Indiana 46290

1-800-428-5331 — Orders   1-800-835-3202 — FAX   1-800-858-7674 — Customer Service

Book ISBN 0-672-31266-2

MACMILLAN COMPUTER PUBLISHING USA

A VIACOM COMPANY

Technical ---- Support

If you need assistance with the information provided by Macmillan Computer Publishing, please access the information available on our web site at **http://www.mcp.com/feedback.** Our most Frequently Asked Questions are answered there. If you do not find the answers to your questions on our Web site, you may contact Macmillan User Services at **(317) 581-3833** or email us at **support@mcp.com.**